CW00457549

TUPOLEV
TU-128
'FIDDLER'

TUPOLEV TU-128 'FIDDLER'

ALAN DAWES
SERGEY BURDIN
NIKOLAI POPOV

FONTHILL

Fonthill Media Language Policy

Fonthill Media publishes in the international English language market. One language edition is published worldwide. As there are minor differences in spelling and presentation, especially with regard to American English and British English, a policy is necessary to define which form of English to use. The Fonthill Policy is to use the form of English native to the author. Alan Dawes was born and educated in Cumbria and now lives in St Ives, Cambridgeshire therefore British English has been adopted in this publication.

Fonthill Media Limited
Fonthill Media LLC
www.fonthillmedia.com
office@fonthillmedia.com

First published in the United Kingdom and the United States of America 2014

British Library Cataloguing in Publication Data:
A catalogue record for this book is available from the British Library

ISBN 978-1-78155-404-3

Typeset in Minion Pro 11/14
Printed and bound in England

Contents

Acknowledgements

Many people associated with the Tu-128 have helped in the creation of this book, but in the first instance I wish to acknowledge the assistance of the Tupolev Design Bureau (www.tupolev.ru) in the realisation of the project. Naturally, significant contributions were also made by those pilots who were the first to master this aircraft, namely former senior inspector-pilot and the head of the Department of Long-range Interception Systems in the Directorate of Combat Training for the General Staff of the PVO, Colonel Aleksandr Nyefyedov; former head of the First Department of the Directorate of Combat Training for the General Staff of the PVO, Colonel Elektron Yevglyevskiy; and former inspector-pilot of the Directorate of Combat Training for the General Staff of the PVO, Colonel Piotr Komyagin. Particular thanks also go to Major Yuri Korol'ko, Chief of Staff of the Airfield Technical Support Battalion at Savasleika airfield.

The authors are also grateful for comments and material from the personal archives submitted to us by the many PVO veterans who devoted the best part of their lives to this aircraft. These individuals occupied a variety of flying and ground positions, and still have great affection for the Tu-128 to the present day. Significant help in this regard was provided by veterans of the 64th Aviation Regiment (64 AP), among whom were former regiment commander, Colonel Mikhail Grechishkin; former Senior Regiment Navigator, Lieutenant Colonel Vladimir Yenyutin; former Deputy squadron commander, Major Leonid Rokin; former aircraft commander, Captain Khamit Ablyazin; former aircraft senior technician, Major Yevgyenniy Plyuta; and former aircraft equipment specialist, Vadim Bulgakov.

For their unstinting support I must also thank former squadron navigator on the 350th Aviation Regiment (350 AP), Major Aleksandr Mamet; and former Deputy regiment commander for engineering services, Lieutenant Colonel Vlad Kaplun; the 518th Aviation Regiment (518 AP) section commander, Major Aleksandr

Davidovskiy; 518 AP squadron navigator, Major Ivan Rodyukov; and 518 AP section navigator, Captain Sergey Vinokurov. The former 72nd Aviation Regiment (72 AP) Commander and later Head of Aviation of the 2nd Independent Army of the PVO, Major General Valeriy Yalyaev; and former Deputy Commander of 72 AP, Lieutenant Colonel Vyacheslav Moiseyev, helped considerably in our understanding of Tu-128 operations. I also wish to acknowledge the valuable contributions of 72 AP section navigator, Captain Valeriy Matyukin; 72 AP section commander, Major Oleg Vydryenok; 72 AP navigator, Lieutenant Colonel Aleksandr Zhabkin; and 72 AP senior navigator and Deputy Squadron Commander for Political Affairs and later Deputy Commander of the 144th Independent Aviation Regiment, Lieutenant Colonel Oleg Fedoseyenko.

I also acknowledge the valued contributions of the 356th Aviation Regiment (356 AP) veterans, namely Deputy regiment commander for Flight Training, Lieutenant Colonel Aleksandr Nikolayev; and squadron commander Lieutenant Colonel Grigoriy Zayats, and sons Dmitriy and Vladimir respectively. In addition, I extend my gratitude to the former Head of Flight Safety of the 14th Independent Army, Colonel Vitaliy Avdyeyev, for his involvement in this work. The authors have also benefited from the active assistance of the former commander of the 677th Independent Communications and Airfield Radar Support Battalion at Savvatiya, Lieutenant Colonel Aleksandr Yuzov, in providing the historical perspective on the 445th Aviation Regiment's conversion onto the Tu-128. Thanks also go to the Head of the Department of Combat Training for the 14th Independent Army of the PVO, Colonel Vasiliy Popov, for valuable additions to the book.

In the section dealing with the Tu-128's joint operations with the Tu-126 'Moss' airborne early warning aircraft, I received enormous help from a former Tu-126 second navigator on the 67th Independent Aviation Squadron, Major Mikhail Musatov, former crew guidance navigator (fighter controller) Major Oleg Makhar, and former combat control officer (fighter controller) Aleksandr Golubyev. I also wish to acknowledge the valuable contribution made by former Lieutenant Vyacheslav Gorshkov, commanding officer of one of the P-35 'Bar Lock' surveillance radar companies at Amderma airfield in the 1970s and today a professor of mathematics in Kiev.

Special thanks are also due to Irina Sadova—the daughter of Major Vladimir Nirodyenko, a section commander on the 72nd Aviation Regiment in the 1970s and a former inspector-pilot, for documents and photographs relating to her late father's service with the PVO. (Major Nirodyenko was the pilot of the Tu-128 famously captured on camera in 1972 by Captain 'Zot' Barazzotto, co-pilot of the USAF Boeing RC-135U intercepted by him in June 1972, this event being described separately in Appendix 1 to this book, 'That Tu-128 Photo!'

Of course, I must not forget to thank those personal friends who have helped me in my search for photography of the Tu-128, specifically aviation historians and photographers Andrei Zinchuk and Sergey Tsvetkov, as well as their colleagues Aleksandr Melikhov and Vladimir Pushkaryev. I also express my gratitude to Sergey Adamov, Aleksey Bashlyeyev, Yuri Kabernik, Aleksey Kalinovskii and Viktor Kudryavtsyev for the use of their own archive photographs of the Tu-128. Finally, but by no means least, the authors wish to acknowledge the contribution of all those who were involved in the design, creation, testing and operation of this unique aircraft, without whom there would be no story to tell.

Additionally, co-author and translator Alan Dawes wishes to express his appreciation of the help and advice given to him by Mrs Su Waymont of Huntingdon, Cambridgeshire, in the preparation and management of the manuscript.

Sergey Burdin
Minsk, Republic of Belarus
March 2014

Introduction

Throughout its seven decades of existence, the Soviet Union was a country enveloped in almost total secrecy where military affairs were concerned, leading Western defence analysts to indulge in imaginative speculation and unrestrained exaggeration of Russian military capabilities in order to justify NATO's own military posture. Even within the Soviet Union itself certain weapons were virtually unknown to the majority of its military personnel, the Tu-128 'Fiddler' being one such example of this phenomenon. In spite of the fact that around 200 examples of this huge fighter were operated by six regiments of the PVO, for almost a quarter of a century, from 1965 to 1988, it is still largely unknown to all but those who operated it.

This book describes the Tu-128 as experienced by the pilots and navigators who flew it, and the reputation it enjoyed among them and the ground crews who serviced and maintained it during its long career with the PVO. It is based on extensive research, using declassified documents released by the air force of the PVO, as well as the personal recollections of participants in the events described within its pages. We hope that these recollections will serve to put 'flesh on the bones' of the technical descriptions of the aircraft and provide a better understanding of its contribution to the air defence system of the USSR.

For the first time in English, readers are given details of the operational history of the Tu-128, including pilot training, the organisation of quick reaction alerts (QRA), automated ground-controlled intercepts (GCI) using the *Lazur'* data-link system and co-operation with the Tu-126 'Moss' airborne early warning (AEW) aircraft. Additionally, readers are given details of operations against Western reconnaissance balloons (its only recorded, albeit important, operational use) and participation in exercises, plus declassified accounts of many of the accidents suffered by the type during its service.

The book provides aviation enthusiasts and historians with an informed overview of this spectacular aircraft, which was without parallel in any of the world's air forces, its singular role being the air defence of the Arctic approaches to the Soviet Union. For this reason it was never offered for export, although at the time of the Falklands Conflict in 1982 it was rumoured that Argentina had expressed interest in acquiring a squadron of Tu-128s! Leaving aside the sheer improbability of being able to do this in the geopolitical climate of the 1980s, the 'Fiddler' was almost tailor-made for the air defence of Argentina's elongated landmass and extensive Atlantic seaboard.

Unique in being the largest 'fighter' ever to enter operational service, the Tu-128 was also unequalled in being the only jet-powered fighter to come out of a design bureau that had specialised in creating heavy bombers. Emerging like a phoenix from the ashes of the ill-fated Tu-98 'Backfin' tactical bomber project, the Tu-128 appeared at precisely the right time to serve the air defence needs of the Soviet Union at a crucial period in its history. Seemingly having 'neither a past nor a future', the aircraft disappeared virtually without trace at the end of its service and although now still fairly well remembered by knowledgeable enthusiasts and aviation historians in Russia, it is little known elsewhere.

However, we feel that the Tu-128 has earned a notable place in the history of post-war air power and hope that this book will provide readers with much interesting material from a hitherto unrecorded chapter of Soviet air operations in the Cold War period. We also hope that it will correct some long-standing misconceptions about this most enigmatic 'fighter'.

Sergey Burdin
Minsk, Republic of Belarus
March 2014

Nikolai Popov (former Tu-128 pilot)
Moscow, Russia
March 2014

Alan Dawes MRAeS
St Ives, Cambridgeshire, England
March 2014

1

Evolution of the Tu-128

In the years immediately following the Second World War, massive reductions were made in the Soviet armed forces from their high wartime levels. These reductions also affected the National Air Defence Forces (*Voyska Protivo-Vozdushnoi Oborony Territorii Strany*), as they were known at that time. Concurrently, relations between the USSR and its recent wartime allies were already deteriorating significantly, creating the atmosphere for the onset of the Cold War. Regular reconnaissance flights over Soviet territory by aircraft of the 'capitalist countries' had already begun, and aerial incursions by the former allies in subsequent years provided the main stimulus for post-war development of the air defence of the Soviet Union. In the search for an optimum air defence structure, four significant reorganisations of the Soviet air defence system (*Protivo-Vozdushnaya Oborona* or PVO) were implemented in the years 1948, 1949, 1951 and 1953. However, the systematic and unlawful violation of Soviet airspace by aircraft of the newly formed NATO alliance continued, with some reconnaissance routes even taking the aircraft directly towards Moscow. According to mass media reports, the USA and its allies conducted some 20,000 flights around the borders of the USSR and China between 1950 and 1970 and, in 1952 alone, thirty-four violations of Soviet airspace were recorded by the PVO. Of this number, three reconnaissance aircraft were shot down[1] and a further three were damaged, but the pivotal year in the post-war history of the PVO was probably 1954. On the night of 29 April that year, the eve of the annual 1 May national holiday, three Boeing RB-47 'Stratojet' reconnaissance aircraft violated the borders of the USSR from the direction of the Baltic Sea. The three aircraft followed a route that took them via Novgorod and Smolensk to Kiev in the then Ukrainian Soviet Socialist Republic, before departing Soviet airspace and heading back into the west. A similar violation occurred a week later, on 8 May (on the eve of Victory Day), leading to these pre-holiday incidents being discussed during a sitting of the Presidium of the Central Committee of the Communist Party of the Soviet Union.

Following this, on 27 May 1954, in response to the constant aerial incursions, the Council of Ministers of the USSR and the Central Committee of the Communist Party of the Soviet Union (KPSS) issued a special decree 'On unlawful flights by foreign aircraft over the territory of the USSR'.

Immediately after the issue of this decree, the fifth post-war structural reorganisation of the National Air Defences was initiated by order of the Soviet Ministry of Defence, which continued until 1957. This restructuring was more reasoned and well thought out than previous efforts and better suited the needs of the time—a period which saw burgeoning developments in the continental (home-based) and intercontinental strategic aviation capability of the USA. The leadership of the USSR considered that this threat to its 'strategic rear' and the entire economic potential of the country would come not only from the European but also from the polar and Asiatic directions, i.e. from the Kola Peninsula in the west to the Kurile Islands (Kuril'skiye Ostrova) in the Soviet Far East.

Apart from this, the increased scale of violations of the USSR's airspace by military aircraft of the NATO alliance needed to be challenged more immediately. Taking all of this into consideration, the country's leadership and the Ministry of Defence decided to transform one arm of service, the National Air Defence troops, into a separate branch of the armed forces. Practically all forces contributing to the air defence of the Soviet Union were included in this structure, and the boundaries of responsibility for the National Air Defence troops were drawn up along the state borders of the USSR. In the Military Districts (MD), which provided 'frontal' or tactical protection against air attack on a regional basis, there remained only small units of 'land forces air defence' at Soviet Army Corps and Division level, and only shipborne air defence assets for fleet air defence. The previous army structures known as *Ob'yedinyeniya* (District and Army level formations) and *Soyedinyeniya* (Corps and Division level formations), created in 1944 and abolished after the war, were reinstated for the National Air Defence troops, in place of air defence 'zones' and 'regions'. Moreover, Soviet Air Force (*Voyenno-Vozdushniye Sily* or VVS)[2] fighter aviation units of the military districts were operationally subordinate to these structures. Marshal of the Soviet Union (MSU) Leonid Govorov, a wartime commander of frontal land forces, was appointed Commander-in-Chief of the Troops of Air Defence, with former wartime frontal Chief of Staff Army General Sergey Biryuzov as his first deputy.

They were given the task of reorganising the air defence of the country (which had been well tested in wartime conditions) and establishing an all-arms basis for combating 'aerial adversaries'. Simultaneously in 1954, Col. Gen. Yevgeny Savitskiy, twice Hero of the Soviet Union (HSU), became the Commander of PVO Aviation (the interceptor arm of the PVO). Savitskiy was promoted Marshal of Aviation in 1961 and was to become the inspiration for the selection of the Tu-128 as the principal air defence fighter of the PVO.

Yevgeny Yakovlevich Savitskiy was born on 24 December 1910 into an ordinary working family in Novorossiysk (Krasnodar Kray), where his father was a welder in the local shipyard. After his father's death in 1922, 12-year-old Yevgeny left the family home to complete his schooling by means of a shipyard apprenticeship, but then took up work as a driver-mechanic in a local motor repair factory. In 1929, he volunteered for military service and enrolled in the 7th Stalingrad Military Aviation School as a trainee pilot, graduating in 1932 and then being 'creamed off' for two years as a flying instructor and deputy flight commander at the school. His regular service commenced in 1934 as a flight commander on a light ground attack squadron based near Kiev, followed by a short period in the same capacity on another ground attack squadron and then, between 1936 and 1938, command of an independent reconnaissance flight. From September 1938 to September 1940, he was initially deputy and then commander of a reconnaissance regiment, followed by an eight-month period as commander of a fighter regiment and later a fighter division, all on the Far Eastern Front. Unusually, he continued to fly combat missions even during his subsequent swift rise to the rank of general, serving in the armies of the Western, Voronezh, South-Western, Stalingrad, North Caucasus, Southern, 4th Ukrainian and the 1st and 3rd Byelorussian Fronts. Here, his intuitive skills as a tactician and commander ensured success in the later battles to liberate the Kuban, the Don Basin, Ukraine and the Crimea. Arguably, his most notable contribution to the Soviet war effort was command of the 3rd Fighter Corps from December 1942, helping to secure the liberation of the Crimea from the grip of the Wehrmacht. Thereafter, with further Russian victory in Byelorussia (present-day Belarus), the Baltic States and Poland, the way was now clear for the final Soviet push through Europe and on to Berlin.

Savitskiy flew a total of 216 combat sorties and personally shot down twenty-two enemy aircraft, plus a further two claimed jointly. What is remarkable is that all but three of his 'kills' were made in the rank of general, making him the highest scoring senior Russian fighter pilot of the war. He was twice awarded the title of Hero of the Soviet Union (in May 1944 and June 1945) and was also the holder of the Order of Lenin, the Order of the October Revolution and the Order of the Red Banner amongst a panoply of honours and awards. Promoted to colonel in July 1942 at the age of 32, he then quickly rose to the rank of major-general (March 1943) and lieutenant-general in May 1944. After the war he continued to command the 3rd Fighter Corps until October 1947, and from then until August 1948 he was head of fighter pilot training at Soviet Air Force HQ. (During this time he led the Soviet Union's first jet aerobatic team, on the Yak-15 'Feather', flying a fifteen-ship formation over Moscow in the 1948 Aviation Day celebrations.) As a colonel general, Savitskiy played a major role in the Russian response to Gary Powers' well-documented U-2 incursion into Soviet airspace in May 1960. In the 1960s, he had also entered politics as a candidate member of the CPSU and was a Deputy of the Supreme Soviet between 1962 and 1966. As the only PVO general officer to achieve the rank of Marshal of Aviation (from May 1961) he was appointed Deputy Commander in Chief of Air Defence Troops in July 1966 and remained in this post until April 1980. His last military appointment was as a military inspector and adviser to the corps of generals of the Inspectorate of the Ministry of Defence of the USSR. In retirement he wrote a number of articles and books on air defence theory and practice viewed from personal experience, the best known of which is probably his book *This is 'Dragon', I am attacking!* (*Ya 'Drakon'—Atakuyu!*), published in 1980. (Savitskiy was allowed to use the personal callsign 'Dragon' throughout his wartime service and into the final years of his flying career, although no details are available as to why this privilege was extended to him in the first instance.)

After the death of Govorov in 1955, his talented deputy (now Marshal of the Soviet Union) Sergey Biryuzov was appointed C-in-C of the Troops of Air Defence. Thanks to Biryuzov's authority and zeal, a sixth post-war reorganisation of the structure of the PVO was undertaken between 1957 and 1960. This included agreement on the size and limits of responsibility of PVO Districts, Armies, Corps and Divisions, not so much in relation to the boundaries of military districts but rather for the convenience of combating aerial aggressors. On the same day as the issue of the decrees 'On unlawful flights …' and 'On the improvement of the organisation of anti-aircraft defence of the country', another decree was issued by the Council of Ministers entitled 'On the provision of new equipment for the Troops of Air Defence of the Country'.

In the early 1950s, the resolution of all matters relating to the development of weapons and military equipment in the USSR was handled at both Party (KPSS) and State (Council of Ministers) level. The country's leadership demanded resolution of the problem of protecting the aerial borders of the USSR by two different routes, namely by the creation of separate fighter-interceptor and anti-aircraft missile 'complexes' capable of destroying targets at high altitude and long range. Among the design bureaux involved in these studies was OKB-301 (*Opytno-Konstruktorskoye Byuro 301*), led by Semyon Lavochkin, who during the Great Patriotic War had been responsible for the design of the famous La-5 and La-7 'Fin' series of piston-engined fighters.[3] In the post-war years, in addition to working on a variety of (largely unsuccessful) jet fighter projects, OKB-301 also became involved in missile design, playing a major part in the creation of the S-25 *Berkut* (Golden Eagle), Russia's first surface-to-air missile system, known by NATO as the SA-1 Guild. Concurrently, OKB-301 had also commenced development of the La-250K-15 'aviation missile complex', an integrated interception system employing the La-250 aircraft, equipped with eponymous K-15 fire control radar and armed with two air-to-air missiles. This was a new and fairly unusual theme for a Soviet aircraft design bureau—to design a loitering interceptor with 'supersonic dash' capability, able to destroy targets at altitudes up to 20,000 m (65,600 feet)

Marshal Yevgeny Savitskiy, the prime mover in the creation of the Tu-128, is seen on the far right of this group, with senior colleagues at an undisclosed formal gathering in Moscow in the 1950s. (*Piotr Komyagin Archive*)

and speeds of 1,250 kph (675 kts) at a distance of around 500 km (310 miles) from base. For the period, an innovative element of the fighter control procedure was the adoption of *Vozdukh-1* ground-based automated guidance equipment and *Lazur'* 'telemechanical' data reception apparatus (i.e. data-link) installed in the aircraft to receive the command data.[4] The relevant decree of the Council of Ministers supporting this development was signed in 1952—a timely decision as it happened, since the NATO countries (specifically the USA) were continuing to modernise their means of delivering nuclear weapons to targets on the territory of the USSR. Most worrying of all for the Soviet Union was the commencement of series production in 1954 of Boeing's eight-engined B-52 strategic bomber, an aircraft designed specifically to strike targets in the USSR.

The B-52 was capable of reaching the main naval bases of the Northern Fleet from the continental USA, as well as the central economic region of the USSR, using the shortest possible routes over the Arctic Ocean. The comparatively flat topography of northern Russia would allow USAF bomber crews to approach their targets in almost any flight profile and at any altitude without particular difficulty. Furthermore, it was assumed within Soviet military circles that the 'northern direction of attack' would largely determine an adversary's operational tactics in this theatre of military activity through, *inter alia*, exploitation of the sparse radar coverage and the paucity of Soviet military airfields in the area. In the first instance, an unhindered strike force could reach the launch boundary for the cruise missiles which were then just coming into service with the USAF,[5] without entering the lethal zone of surface-to-air missiles, or risking detection by Soviet fighters. Secondly, the enemy could overcome Soviet air defences with massed air strikes, establishing significant superiority over opposing forces wherever they achieved a break in the defensive line. The flight time required by USAF strategic bombers to reach major Soviet targets in the littoral regions of the Barents Sea and Kara Sea from an 'airborne alert' posture was around 2-3 hours, and 7-8 hours for the main strike force operating out of continental US bases.

Effective surveillance of the extensive area of the Barents Sea and Kara Sea regions posed acute problems for the PVO in the 1950s; defence of the northern maritime borders of the USSR against potential airborne intruders had become an urgent priority. This would have been an exceedingly demanding task at the time, requiring the establishment of a network of radar sites and the construction of new airfields in the harsh environment of the Soviet High Arctic. A less expensive option was to build a long-range fighter for the PVO, equipped with suitable missile armament, capable of intercepting incoming bombers at a considerable distance from the Russian coastline before they could wreak havoc on the mainland. However, the first prototype of the Lavochkin La-250 interceptor, designed specifically to fulfil this requirement, was completed only in 1956 and experienced major problems very early in its flight test programme. In essence, this was a consequence of 'over-stretch' by the Lavochkin team, whose engineers were involved in fundamental surface-to-air missile design whilst simultaneously trying to design both the new interceptor *and* its missile armament under the same roof. The La-250 was so closely linked to the circumstances leading to the PVO's eventual preference for the Tu-128 that its development and ultimate failure is briefly described here in order to give the reader a better understanding of the relationship between these two aircraft.

Lavochkin's OKB-301 had been the first design bureau to offer a fully integrated 'weapon system' (i.e. one incorporating aircraft, radar *and* missile armament) in response to a 1954 requirement for a long-range, high-altitude interceptor for the PVO. The resulting design, initially referred to as *Izdeliye 250*, and later designated La-250, was the central component of the K-15 (*Kompleks-15*) integrated weapons system that also included two Lavochkin-designed air-to-air missiles and the Tikhomirov K-15 *Uragan* (Hurricane) airborne interception (AI) radar. The aircraft itself, initially intended to be powered by all-new Klimov VK-9 engines but flown with the equally new and less powerful Lyul'ka AL-7F, employed an elegant tailed delta layout in a fuselage of exceptionally high fineness ratio. Planned to be a single-seater in operational form, all the prototypes were built as twin-seaters to accommodate a flight test observer. The first La-250 (no suffix) crashed while taking off on its maiden flight on 16 June 1956, when test pilot Andrei Kochetkov lost control following sudden pitching and rolling to the right just after lifting off the runway at Zhukovskiy. Kochetkov elected to make an immediate precautionary landing and his skilful handling of the situation saved both his life and that of his observer N. P. Zakharov, but the aircraft was destroyed by the ensuing fire. The accident investigators concluded that a lack of synchronisation between control column input and aileron movement (giving a perceptible delay between stick input and aileron deflection), compounded by a lack of feedback from the non-reversible actuators, made the aircraft uncontrollable. The prototype La-250's flight control system was extensively tested in a special electro-mechanical rig set up in OKB-301, which confirmed the findings of the accident commission, the resulting data being used to develop an improved flight control system that was installed in the second prototype (*Izdeliye 250A*). The main external difference between the 250 and the 250A was the former's continuous tear-drop cockpit canopy shape, shorter air intake ducts and the slightly different wing and tailplane geometry.

The 250A introduced a pure delta wing and tailplane, longer intake ducts, extending from just under the cockpit area, and a re-profiled cockpit canopy. The 250A-I made its first flight on 12 July 1957, but was written off on its sixth flight on 28 November in a landing accident. This was attributed to poor pilot visibility over the long nose, exacerbated by having to fly through drifting industrial haze on the approach to Zhukovskiy, causing test pilot Kochetkov to touch down in

The third La-250A, red 03, was the only prototype to be equipped with the Tikhomirov K-15M *Uragan* radar, although due to its unsatisfactory performance Lavochkin had taken the retrograde decision to install the earlier tried and tested *Sokol-2* (NATO 'Scan Three') in production aircraft. Evident in this view is the narrow track and long wheelbase of the undercarriage, which would have made crosswind landings rather 'sporty' for all but the most skilled pilots. (*Yefim Gordon Archive*)

the gravelled stopway ahead of the threshold. Undaunted, the design team set to work on yet another prototype, the 250A-II, improving pilot visibility by angling the aircraft's nose down by 6° from just ahead of the windscreen. As the aircraft was intended for stability and handling trials it was not equipped with radar, and made its first flight on 30 July 1958, powered by AL-7F engines albeit with non-functioning afterburners. A third 250A prototype, designated 250A-III, was eventually equipped with a functioning radar, which underwent ground trials in the aircraft in 1958, followed by the completion of the final, non-radar-equipped 250A-IV. Although all the components of the K-15 weapons system were available by then, the test programme had fallen well behind schedule and the aircraft's flight performance turned out to be demonstrably worse than calculated. Preoccupied with OKB-301's more successful missile projects and disappointed by the overall performance of the K-15 system, Semyon Lavochkin decided to abandon work on the project in mid-1959, and at virtually the same time the Council of Ministers issued a directive cancelling further work on the K-15 complex. Although the La-250A did not complete its test programme, the integrated approach adopted for its creation was applied in the design of the Tu-128, ensuring that the work was not entirely without purpose. However, the unexpectedly protracted and ultimately unsuccessful Lavochkin project, combined with the still urgent need to defend the northern borders of the USSR, forced the then C-in-C of PVO Aviation, Col. Gen. Savitskiy, to seek other means of achieving this objective.

Heavily retouched in the manner typical of 1950s Soviet military photography, the second La-250A, red 02, shows off the aircraft's long slim fuselage, sharply swept delta wing and tailplane and dummy rounds of the large Lavochkin-designed '275A' missile. The La-250A was somewhat ahead of its time, although the Lavochkin team committed the cardinal error of simultaneously employing too many untried innovations in the design. Attempting to integrate new engines, a new flight control system, new radar *and* new missiles into a radically new delta-winged airframe overburdened the capabilities of OKB-301 and doomed the project to failure. (*Yefim Gordon Archive*)

At this point it is opportune to digress briefly to say a little about the PVO leadership in order to understand better the decision-making psychology of Savitskiy and his deputy, Gen. Kadomtsyev, as recalled by Col. Yevglyevskiy:

Savitskiy was an 'ideas man'. He would come up with a dozen new ideas every day and the person who translated his ideas into actions was also a highly competent, intelligent and outstanding officer—General Anatoly Kadomtsyev—an equally legendary figure. As a young officer, Kadomtsyev had graduated from an engineering academy, but he very much wanted to be a pilot, so he virtually taught himself to fly and went solo (unauthorised) on a Yak-3 piston-engined fighter. Having completed a circuit of the airfield, he landed the aircraft without incident. The 'authorities' wanted to prosecute him, but the Minister of Defence, MSU Malinovskiy, in a statement presented to the subsequent court martial, wrote: '... teach him what he needs to know and let him fly'. Kadomtsyev spent several days in a detention cell at the time as a punishment, but was eventually allowed to undertake flight training as an 'external student'. That's how he became a pilot, and this unique individual eventually went on to become Deputy C-in-C of PVO Aviation to Savitskiy and assisted Savitskiy in realizing his innovative ideas.[6]

Here are just a few selected at random—he proposed the idea of employing the MiG-17 to shoot down enemy aircraft at night visually, using only moonlight to illuminate the target, as the early MiG-17s were not equipped with radar. On his initiative, the MiG-17 was modified to carry R-13 (NATO AA-2 'Atoll') infrared (IR)-guided air-to-air missiles. Industry had demanded two years of testing for this modification, but Gen. Savitskiy decided that the tests would be undertaken by the Combat Application Centre at Savasleika over a period of one week (!), the first test flight being conducted by Kadomtsyev. In the wake of the Cuban missile crisis in 1962, Savitskiy decided to use PVO MiG-17s for bombing and air-to-ground gunnery against ground and maritime surface targets. He then had the idea of attacking ground targets with Su-9 and MiG-19 interceptors, using their air-to-air weapons, even though ground attack was obviously not the 'natural province' of air defence fighters. Many other similar ideas were developed and eventually incorporated as amendments to the relevant KBP (*Kurs Boyevoy Podgotovki*) combat training manuals and adopted by PVO interceptor units. In the light of the foregoing, it is not surprising that Savitskiy came up with a truly original and innovative idea for the provision of a fighter cover in the isolated north of the Soviet Union. This was to take a large 'bomber-sized' aircraft with significant flight endurance and arm it with huge air-to-air missiles, thereby turning it into an ultra-long-range interceptor.

Such an aircraft would offer the real possibility of protecting the extreme northern boundary of the USSR against incursions by foreign (i.e. American) intruders coming in over the Arctic Ocean. The idea was not 'planted in barren soil'—in

The Tu-98 was an elegant design but proved to be less attractive to the Soviet Air Force hierarchy than its contemporary, the smaller and more promising Yak-28 'Brewer', as a 'light' supersonic bomber for frontal aviation. After being rebuilt as the '98-80' test-bed in 1958, it effectively became the systems prototype of the Tu-128 and flew in this capacity until the autumn of 1960, turning the failed bomber project into the forerunner of a successful air defence interceptor. (*OAO Tupolev*)

the summer of 1956 a new supersonic frontal (i.e. tactical) bomber, 'Aircraft 98' (*'Samolyot 98'*), designed under the leadership of Andrei Nikolayevich Tupolev at OKB-156, was undergoing trials at the Flight Test Institute (*Lyotno-Ispytatyel'nyi Institut* or LII) at Zhukovskiy. Unfortunately for Tupolev, by the end of 1956, the operational requirements for a new frontal bomber, originally expected to be fulfilled by 'Aircraft 98', had been redefined and could no longer be achieved by the Tupolev design. At this point, Savitskiy suggested to Andrei Tupolev that 'Aircraft 98', also known as the Tu-98 (NATO 'Backfin') in official documents, might well form the basis for a new long-range PVO interceptor.

Tupolev was very interested in Savitskiy's suggestion, since the creation of a new aircraft for the nation's air defence force could well save the '98' project and would mean that the design work already completed would not have been without purpose. The Tu-98 had also been designed to use two Lyul'ka AL-7F engines (as installed in the La-250), each producing 6,500 kg (14,330 lb) of thrust dry and 9,500 kg (20,945 lb) in reheat, and was to have had a maximum speed of 1,300-1,400 kph (700-755 kts), a range of 2,300 km (1,430 miles) with a bomb load of 3 tonnes (6,615 lb) and a ceiling of 13,000 m (42,650 feet). In spite of the lack of success with the Lavochkin La-250, the commanders of PVO Aviation still intended to acquire not only a new interceptor fighter but an entire 'interception complex'. This was to include the 'carrier aircraft', air-to-air missiles and ground-based and airborne systems to guide the aircraft onto its target. Industry was already producing the subsonic MiG-17P (NATO 'Fresco-B') and Yak-25M ('Flashlight-A'), as well as the supersonic MiG-19P ('Farmer-C'), and Sukhoi Su-9 ('Fishpot-B'), which were capable of intercepting targets at a distance of around 200-300 km (125-185 miles)

Andrei Tupolev in the company of the design team responsible for the Tu-128. On the extreme right of the picture is the future chief designer of the Tu-128, Iosif F. Nezval; on the extreme left is the lead designer of the Tu-98 project, Dmitriy S. Markov. (*OAO Tupolev*)

from base. Now, however, the PVO required an interceptor capable of destroying airborne targets at distances of up to 1,000 km (620 miles) from base.

Even before the Council of Ministers had decided on a new aircraft for the PVO, the projects department of Tupolev's OKB-156 led by Sergey Mikhailovich Yeger had submitted a preliminary layout for an interceptor based on the Tu-98. (This aircraft presumably evolved from the 'Aircraft 98A' project, a further iteration of the '98' theme, also known officially as the Tu-24. This was another attempt by Tupolev to create a light tactical/naval support bomber, albeit now armed with one internally carried P-15 missile or two on under-wing pylons).[7] Instead of the classic Soviet-style 'greenhouse glazing' over the navigator's station in the nose it was intended to install a powerful airborne interception radar under a large dielectric radome. The pilot's position was to remain the same as on the Tu-98, but the navigator's cockpit was now placed behind the pilot, with entry via a separate cockpit canopy. The diameter of the fuselage made it possible to install a large radar antenna in the nose, offering the possibility of significantly increasing the target detection range compared with other contemporary interceptors. (*This derives from the fact that a larger diameter antenna dish results in higher antenna gain, which in turn provides higher effective radiated power and increased receiver sensitivity. The aggregate of all of these features is increased detection range—A.D.)* In addition, the significant load-carrying capacity of the aircraft allowed the designers considerable freedom when selecting on-board equipment, without having to worry too much about exceeding size and weight limitations. Another factor that favoured the Tupolev project was the report by Marshal Konstantin Vershinin, C-in-C of the Soviet Air Force, highlighting the 'inexpediency' of further development of the La-250A, which was subsequently cancelled in July 1959.

Notwithstanding the complexity of developing the new interceptor, itself a notable innovation for this traditional heavy bomber design team, OKB-156, in consultation with the PVO, had also come up with the idea of developing a specialised airborne early warning aircraft like those operated by the US Air Force and Navy. Such an aircraft would enable radar cover to be extended to specific areas whenever required and provide radar guidance for interceptors in regions which were remote from GCI sites. In 1958, OKB-156 was given the task of designing the radar picket aircraft (*samolyot radiolokatsionnovo dozora* or SRLD), intended to operate within the nation's homeland air defence system, and was given the designation Tu-126. As described later in this book, the Tu-126 (assigned the reporting name 'Moss' in the NATO designation system) was based on the Tu-114 'Cleat' long-range four-turboprop airliner. Thus it was that this very sophisticated aircraft (for that period) was developed jointly with the Tu-28-80[8] 'long-range aviation-missile interception complex', both aircraft being ordered under one

This view of the Tu-98 illustrates very clearly a major shortcoming of the aircraft's layout – its extremely narrow undercarriage track, adopted to facilitate the use of an aerodynamically clean supersonic wing. Although this and other features of the aircraft would have made it very difficult for ordinary squadron pilots to master in routine operations, the Tu-98 turned out to be a useful 'development tool' for both the Tu-22 bomber and the Tu-128. (*OAO Tupolev*)

and the same decree of the Council of Ministers and the State Committee for Aviation Technology. Such a comprehensive joint military design and manufacturing project could only be realised within the almost unlimited framework of the Soviet 'command economy' system of the time, in which matters of national defence and security always took precedence over the 'domestic economy'.

The Tu-28 was conceived as the chief means of preventing an aerial attack on the Soviet Union over the Arctic Ocean, and was therefore planned to be operated from the outset in the High Arctic. It was designed to have a wide radius of action and to operate both autonomously and semi-autonomously, intercepting and destroying enemy strategic bombers before they reached the launch boundary of their missile armament. Furthermore, it was planned that these tasks would be carried out in concert with the Tu-126 airborne early warning aircraft. The required performance of the 'long-range aviation-missile interception complex' (*Aviatsionnyi Rakietnyi Kompleks Dal'nyevo Perekhvata* or ARKDP) was predicated on the assumption that its lower limit of operation would be not less than 8,000 m (26,250 feet). It was also assumed that interceptions would take place at considerable distance from the Soviet coastline and that enemy bombers would not fly below this level, since the cruising altitude of heavy jet aircraft of that era was above 8,000 m. For a long-range bomber to descend to medium or low level at the mid-course point would mean a reduction in range, making it impossible to reach its target, thereby negating the *raison d'être* of this category of aircraft. Apart from OKB-156, there were three other major design bureaux involved in the creation of the new Tupolev interceptor:

- OKB-45, under General Designer Arkhip Lyul'ka, responsible for improvements to the AL-7F powerplant selected for the Tu-128;
- OKB-15, led by General Designer Fyodor Volkov, responsible for the design of the aircraft's RP-S *Smerch* airborne intercept radar;[9]
- OKB-4, under the leadership of General Designer Matus Bisnovat, responsible for the design of the K-80 air-to-air missile (later designated R-4R and R-4T for the semi-active radar homing and infrared-guided variants respectively and known in the NATO system as AA-5 'Ash').

At the project definition phase for the new 'complex', the design team was faced with a unique situation. For the first time in the comparatively short history of Soviet jet fighter design, an aircraft chosen to be an air-to-air 'missile carrier' (*nosityel' rakiet*) was a non-manoeuvring fighter. This followed from selection of the prototype Tu-98 tactical bomber to serve as the 'aerodynamic prototype' for the Tu-28, with the latter aircraft then inheriting the bomber's operational manoeuvring limits, which were not to exceed 2.5 g. Thus, in order to destroy any potential target, the high manoeuvrability normally possessed by fighter aircraft had to be transferred to the K-80 missile itself, and OKB-4 designers set this level at 15 g. Another innovative aspect of the design of the new 'interception complex' was the fact that forward hemisphere interception was chosen to be the principal attack mode. Design of the new aircraft and its supporting infrastructure proceeded rapidly and testing of the weapons system commenced in 1959, using the Tu-98 as a flying test-bed (now designated Tu-98LL—*Lyetayushchaya Laboratoriya*—to reflect this). Later, it was decided that a converted Tu-104 'Camel' airliner would be more useful as a flying test-bed in the development programme, offering more on-board space for trials personnel and equipment and even allowing missile launches to be carried out. The 'mock-up commission' (*makietnaya komissiya*) for the Tu-28 ('Aircraft 128' in OKB-156's designation system) reviewed the design in early 1960, and it was given the designation of 'Article I' in the coding system used by the Soviet Ministry of Defence. (Inevitably, given the Russian penchant for nicknames, it was known colloquially by the air and ground crews as '*Ivan*'.) It had a two-man crew, comprising a pilot and navigator-operator (the latter having similar responsibilities to the weapons system officer/operator in Western air forces) housed in a common pressurised cockpit, albeit with separate access via tandem canopies. As with most aircraft of this type, the pilot was responsible for aircraft handling, whilst the navigator-operator looked after navigation, radio communications and radar operation. When carrying out an interception, the pilot would follow commands from the ground-based and on-board guidance systems and perform missile launch, whilst the navigator-operator monitored the *Smerch* AI radar system, observing, identifying, selecting and locking on to the most threatening target.

Within a year, the first prototype of the Tu-28, which had been assembled in OKB-156's experimental fabrication workshop in Moscow, was transferred to the

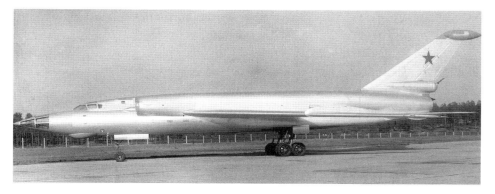

The only flying prototype of the Tu-98, in its incarnation as a tactical bomber, was rebuilt as the Tu-98LL flying test-bed, aka 'Aircraft 98-80', following discussions in June 1957 between Andrei Tupolev, Yevgeny Savitskiy and Sergey Yeger (Head of Tupolev's Technical Projects Department). (*OAO Tupolev*)

Design Bureau's Flight Test and Modification Base at Zhukovskiy on the out-skirts of the city. This aircraft made its maiden flight on 18 March 1961 in the hands of test pilot Mikhail Kozlov[10] and test navigator Konstantin Malkhasyan. It was equipped with a battery of flight test recorders that included an RTS-8 (*Radio-Telemetricheskaya Stantsiya*) telemetry unit[11] for the transmission of vital data to the test base, plus other equipment installed in a large under-fuselage pannier. The pannier was required because of lack of space on the aircraft for the bulky vibration and stress sensors used to monitor changing airframe parameters during flight. (The pannier remained on the prototype throughout the flight test programme, leading Western defence analysts to the erroneous conclusion that it was some kind of radar installation and that the aircraft was actually a new bomber design. This was not unreasonable, given Tupolev's history as a bomber designer.) The first stage of flight testing continued until 12 May 1961, with the prototype flown 'clean', without wing pylons, and comprised a total of eighteen flights. Speed was limited to Mach 1.2 because dry friction dampers and flexible undercarriage mountings had not yet been fitted, but high-speed flights continued after the appropriate modifications had been embodied. From 20 June to 9 July, the prototype was also involved in rehearsals for the annual flypast over Moscow, comprising a total of thirteen flights. Flight testing of the prototype then resumed, flying with two inner pylons and two dummy missiles, and from the end of July until the beginning of October stability and flight control checks were carried out. Additionally, abnormal flight attitudes were examined, along with a number of take-offs at maximum take-off weight (40 tonnes/88,185 lb), these flights lasting from 25 July to 9 October 1961, involving a total of twenty-five sorties. Following these flights, modifications were carried out to the communications interface units of the K-80 (prototype R-4) missiles and changes were made to the layout of the 'technical compartment' and the pilot's instrument panel.

At the same time, all four missile pylons were installed on the aircraft and on-board systems were checked out, after which a further eleven test flights were carried out between 21 December 1961 and 26 February 1962. These involved the carriage of missiles on the inner pylons, then on the outer pylons, and finally all four missiles simultaneously. Stability and control checks were conducted and wing surface (skin) distortions were measured, along with autonomous checks of elements of the *Smerch* fire-control and *Lazur'* data-link systems. Additionally, autonomous operation of *Smerch* was checked while operating against a Tu-16 'Badger' target. The results of these tests of the prototype Tu-28 were to be used to finalise the decision to lay down a batch of around five to ten pre-series aircraft at the production factory. These pre-production aircraft would be used to check actual flight performance against the calculated figures, as well as overall systems perfor-mance. However, as was often the case in OKB-156, the engineers were preparing production tooling for the new aircraft at the same time as they were rolling out the

In July 1961, the Tu-128 prototype took part in that year's Tushino Air Show, causing something of a furore among Western defence observers and analysts, who assumed that the large dark boat-shaped fairing covered the antenna of some unidentified radar system. Adding to their mystification was the fact that this bomber-sized aircraft was carrying two (dummy) missiles. A pair of ventral fins compensated for the adverse effect on lateral stability of the under-fuselage container. (*Aleksey Kalinovskii Archive*)

first prototype! The assembly plant chosen for series production of the new aircraft was Factory No. 64 at Voronezh, where the prototype Tu-98 had been converted into the test-bed for the Tu-28. The first series-production Tu-28 manufactured at Voronezh underwent factory flight tests in the summer of 1961, and in July of that year the prototype and the first production aircraft took part in the annual flypast over the centre of Moscow. Factory No. 64 completed an additional Tu-28 in 1961, but shortcomings noted in the first prototype led to continuous changes being incorporated in the initial production batches and the first 'series' actually consisted of only a single aircraft. Thereafter, from the 2nd to the 10th series-production batch there were only two aircraft per series (batch) and it was not until the 11th series that the production rate was established at five aircraft per batch, which continued until production ceased with the 46th series. It was not decided immediately to call this unusual aircraft an 'interceptor', and in the technical documentation of the period it was initially referred to, rather weightily, as an 'all-weather supersonic carrier of self-guiding air-to-air missiles' (*vsyepogodnyi svyerkhzvukovoy nosityel' samonavodyashchikhsya rakiet klassa 'vozdukh-vozdukh'*).

In due course, other OKB-156 pilots and navigators were assigned to the flight test programme, allowing the serious task of bringing the aircraft up to the requirements of the PVO to get under way. The work of eradicating systems failures and defects was supervised by leading production engineer A. Zalesskiy, and he

The first prototype of the Tu-128 (still referred to as the Tu-28 at this time), photographed during the test programme carrying early examples of the 'Ash' missile. The aircraft has a number of photo-reference markers on the forward fuselage and carries the prototype serial number '0' ('*Nolyevoy*' variant). Note also that the outer missile pylons of the prototype were not aligned with the wing fence. This aircraft is now displayed in the Central Museum of the Air Force at Monino near Moscow. (*Sergey Tsvetkov Archive*)

remained the 'permanent guardian' of the aircraft throughout its entire period of operation with the PVO. Joint State tests involving the 'customer' (*zakazchik*), i.e. the Soviet Ministry of Defence, commenced in 1962, with aircrew and engineers from OKB-156 and Technical Operations Department No. 2 of the Flight Test Institute being joined by military personnel from the State Red Banner Scientific Research Institute of the Air Force (GK NII VVS). The joint trials continued over a period of forty months, extending from the first flight on 18 March 1961 to 13 July 1964, and involved a total of 799 flights. (Up to March 1962, the prototype Tu-28 had completed sixty-seven flights, with a total flight time of 53 hours 7 minutes, during which time it was flown not only by the original crew [Kozlov/Malkhasyan] but also by another seven crews, including one from GK NII VVS and two crews from Factory No. 64 at Voronezh.)

It must be admitted that flight testing of the Tu-28 proceeded fairly smoothly, with only one alarming incident recorded, involving an aircraft flown by test pilot Maj. Yuri Rogachev and his navigator N. Mozgovoy. Their Tu-28 entered a deep spiral descent at an altitude of 11,800 m (38,700 feet) during an asymmetric missile-firing sortie, and it was only thanks to Rogachev's piloting skills that he was able to bring the aircraft back under control at an altitude of 2,000 m (6,560 feet) and land safely. Unfortunately, this incident was neither properly investigated nor written up fully at the time, and the Ministry of Defence and the PVO were not informed of the results

Another view of the Tu-128 prototype. Visible under the mid-fuselage is the conformal container for the KZA flight test data-recorder. The ventral fins fitted initially to compensate for the anticipated adverse handling effects of the container have already been removed, having been proved unnecessary after flight tests. (*Sergey Tsvetkov Archive*)

of the subsequent investigation. Consequently, ordinary line pilots were not given the opportunity to be shown how to avoid entering this dangerous flight regime, which probably led to the tragic loss of a Tu-128 in similar circumstances some nine years later. (This incident is described in Appendix 3.)

In terms of construction, the Tu-128 was designed to be simple to mass-produce and did not require the use of new materials or technological processes, except for the installation of integral fuel tanks in the comparatively thin wing. Airframe components were broken down into a large number of easily accessible units, with dimensions of component units sized so as to be easy to fabricate in a medium-sized assembly plant. Wide use was made of high-capacity processes such as hot stamping, chemical milling, impact riveting and the use of precision steel castings. The use of pressed panels and hot stamping reduced the number of butt joints and separate parts, permitting extensive use of mechanical assembly (*mekhano-sborka*) with a concomitant reduction in manpower requirements. Broadly speaking, the Tu-28 employed already tried and tested materials, including:

- V-95 and D-16 alloys for load-bearing panels, stringer sets, load-bearing frames and ribs;
- Magnesium alloy for moulded parts;
- 30KhGSNA steel for load-carrying assemblies, attachment bolts and control rods;
- Plastic material for honeycomb panels and bonded structures.

Of newer materials, the following were used:

- EI-643 steel for load-bearing elements of the undercarriage;
- V-93 alloy for undercarriage suspension components;
- SO-2-55 heat-resistant organic glass for the pilot's and navigator's cockpit canopies;
- U-30M increased heat-resistance sealants for joints and the seating of cockpit glazing, plus UT-32 sealant for the inner walls of the integral fuel tanks.

By command of the Soviet Ministry of Defence in December 1963 (Order No. 00134) the new 'long-range aviation-missile interception complex' was given the designation Tu-128S-4, comprising the Tu-128 missile carrier (as the Tu-28 was now to be called), plus two R-4T and two R-4R air-to-air missiles. The latter were Bisnovat K-80 missiles (redesignated as R-4), the suffix 'T' indicating *tyeplovaya golovka samonavyedyeniya* or infrared-homing head, and the letter 'R' *radiolokat-sionnaya golovka samonavyedyeniya* or radar-homing (i.e. semi-active radar homing) head. By this time, the Lyul'ka AL-7F-1 engine had been replaced by the more powerful AL-7F-2 variant (Article 41) and a significant amount of work had been carried out to improve the aircraft's structure, equipment layout and aerodynamics. Not surprisingly after all this, OKB-156 and the Soviet Ministry of Defence (and the PVO) were very keen to get the aircraft into service as soon as possible. The first stage of the State test programme was completed in the summer of 1964, after the investment of considerable effort on the part of the State Commission headed by Marshal of Aviation Savitskiy. This culminated in the award of a certificate of completion of joint State tests of the Tu-128S-4 'complex', albeit with several listed shortcomings, which had to be eradicated by the Tupolev design team, but in April 1965 the Tu-128S-4 was accepted for service with the PVO.

The Tu-128S-4 'complex' was designed for all-weather interception of long-range strategic bombers, cruise missile carriers and enemy reconnaissance aircraft flying at:

- altitudes from 10,000 m (32,800 feet) to 21,000 m (68,900 feet), at speeds up to 2,000 kph (1,080 kts) in a forward hemisphere attack;
- altitudes from 10,000 m to 21,000 m at speeds up to 1,100 kph (594 kts) and between 10,000 m and 17,000 m (55,775 feet) at speeds up to 1,250 kph (675 kts) in a rear hemisphere attack.

Combat performance of the 'complex' when intercepting targets flying at altitudes below 10,000 m remained to be established during the service acceptance trials phase.

The Tu-128S-4 'complex' consisted of the following elements:

The nozzle exit cross-section of the Lyul'ka AL-7F-2 engines had a two-position profile, changing in diameter by means of moving 'petals' or shutters. The 'petals' were made to open or close by the movement of a special ring operating in the direction of flight, driven by hydraulic jacks in response to engine power setting and flight regime. (*Nikolai Popov*)

- the Tu-128 'carrier aircraft' powered by two Lyul'ka AL-7F-2 turbojet engines;
- *Smerch* (Tornado) on-board 'radar-control' equipment (*apparatura radi-oupravlyeniya*), comprising an integral airborne intercept (AI) radar and the *Smerch-VM* computer. The AI radar itself was known as 'Big Nose' in the NATO code-name system assigned by the Air Standardization Coordination Committee;
- two Bisnovat R-4T infrared air-to-air guided missiles on the inboard pylons, and two R-4R semi-active radar homing missiles outboard;
- *Lazur'-M* radio-telemechanical (i.e. data-link) equipment designed to receive interception guidance commands from the *Vozdukh-1* fighter guidance system;
- *Vozdukh-1* ground-based automated guidance and control system installed in GCI stations equipped with *Kaskad-M* or *Vozdukh-1M* target data generation systems.

Compared with other Soviet interception 'complexes' in service at this time the Tu-128S-4 system exhibited the following main advantages:

A pair of 72 AP 'Fiddlers' photographed in the QRA dispersal at Amderma in the early 1980s. (*Nikolai Popov*)

- the possibility of destroying targets in a forward hemisphere attack with the target flying at 7,000-8,000 m (23,000-26,250 feet) above the interceptor;
- the possibility of destroying targets when attacking from large 'angles off the tail' (AOT);
- considerably greater interception boundaries (*rubyezha perekhvata*), i.e. interception range;
- increased resistance to jamming;
- greater lethality of missile armament, with a maximum launch range up to 20-25 km (12.4-15.5 miles) in a forward hemisphere intercept (FHI) and up to 10-12 km (6.20-7.45 miles) in the rear hemisphere (RHI);
- the possibility of autonomous operations, thanks to the system's greater detection and lock-on ranges, (up to 50 km [31 miles] and 35-40 km [21.75-25 miles] in FHI and RHI respectively), considerable flight endurance (up to 3 hours 20 minutes in subsonic cruise) and the fact that the aircraft was packed with up-to-date (for the mid-1960s) navigation-attack systems.

As mentioned earlier, the Tu-128 underwent its flight test programme at the same time as the Tu-126 airborne early-warning aircraft, the two having been designed to operate together as a system, compensating for the lack of GCI radar sites and airfields in the High Arctic. The Tu-126's main sensor was the *Liana* radio-technical complex (*radio-tekhnicheskii kompleks* or RTK),[12] based on the P-30 ground-based early warning radar. The radar's antenna was housed inside a discus-shaped radome mounted on top of the fuselage. The Tu-126 had a maximum speed at altitude of 805 kph (435 kts), indicated air speed of 530 kph (286 kts), a cruising speed of 650-700 kph (350-378 kts) and a range with one in-flight refuelling uplift of around 11,000 km (6,840 miles). Loiter time at 2,000 km (1,250 miles) from base was around 3 hours. The following performance requirements had been specified by the Soviet Ministry of Defence:

- endurance—10-12 hours;
- service ceiling—8,000-12,000 m (26,250-39,370 feet);
- detection range in the upper hemisphere against a MiG-17 'Fresco'-sized target—100 km (62 miles), Il-28 'Beagle' light bomber—200 km (124 miles) and a Myasishchev 3M 'Bison'-sized bomber—300 km (186 miles);
- an air-ground data transmission range of 2,000 km (1,250 miles).

Flight trials of the Tu-126 were undertaken between 1962 and 1965, and from 1965 the aircraft went into series production at Factory No. 18 at Kuibyshev (a large city on the eastern bank of the River Volga, known as Samara in pre-Soviet times). The Soviet Ministry of Defence referred to the aircraft as 'Article L', evidently in reference to the radar's code-name *Liana*. A total of nine Tu-126s were manufactured at Kuibyshev between 1961 and 1967, eight of which were assigned to the 67th Independent Aviation Squadron at Zokniai air base, near Shiauliai, in the then Lithuanian Soviet Socialist Republic. The prototype Tu-126 was completed in 1961 and given the construction number 61M601, also sometimes seen as 61801) indicating the year of manufacture and individual production serial number. The prototype did not enter service, but was retained for trials and equipment testing. The next two were completed in 1965, with production batch numbers 65M611 and 65M612, followed by three more in 1966 (66M613, 66M621 and 66M622) and then the final three in 1967 (67M623, 67M624 and 67M625). At the end of the 1960s the need arose to intercept targets at low altitude, which in turn required the Tu-126 itself to be able to fly below the target. Modifications and special training allowed the aircraft's loitering height to be reduced to around 600 m (around 2,000 feet), albeit detection range and flight endurance were substantially reduced. Nevertheless, these aircraft remained in service with the PVO until 1988, before being replaced by the more modern and capable Ilyushin-Beriev A-50 'Mainstay'.

The Tu-126 entered service in 1965 within the same timeframe as the Tu-128, and in recognition of their efforts in developing both aircraft a large number of engineers and industry 'specialists' were presented with government awards and prizes. Among these was test pilot Mikhail Kozlov, who was awarded the title of Hero of the Soviet Union for his part in the flight test programme.

After acceptance by the PVO, the main service trials (*voyskoviye ispytaniya*) of the Tu-128 were able to commence and were designed to determine:

- the most rational methods of operation and compatibility of the aircraft with the regiment and squadron structure of the PVO;
- operational performance;
- operational reliability;
- operational shortcomings;
- fitness for purpose and the required quantity of ground maintenance equipment;
- fitness for purpose of systems monitoring equipment;
- fitness for purpose of individual and group spares sets;
- the suitability of the aircraft's technical documentation;
- engineering manpower levels required at regimental level and below;
- the number of man-hours and overall time required for pre-flight checks and repair work, as well as the number of personnel and equipment required to support the aircraft during operational deployments.

Service trials of the Tu-128 were conducted by No. 8 State Red Banner Scientific Research Institute of the Air Force (8 GNIKI VVS) at Akhtubinsk in the Volgograd Region, this being the new title of the GK NII VVS with effect from 1965. This period is recalled by Col. Komyagin:

> The second stage of the State trials process concentrates on 'combat application' or operational use of the aircraft. These were carried out at Akhtubinsk. They were started by Colonel Nyefyedov and completed by me. We were assigned a number of aerial targets and we worked to a plan—'so many' targets had to be shot down in 'such and such' conditions and we shot them all down. For targets we had Tu-16s, Yak-25RVs, Il-28s and La-17s. I shot down Yak-25RV and La-17 targets. The flight regime was very strict and flights were only performed in reheat. You'd get up to maximum speed and maximum altitude and shoot …

The trials were conducted in the second half of 1967 and completed in 1968, during which it became clear that it was extremely difficult for the Tu-128 to intercept high-speed targets from a rear hemisphere engagement. If the aircraft had insufficient speed to catch up with a fast-moving target then it was necessary to perform a lag pursuit intercept, which required very precise timing and positioning in order to execute a successful attack.[13] Although it was an almost universal requirement of Soviet fighters at the time to be able to operate from unprepared, packed earth airfields, the Tu-128 did not undertake such operations formally during the service trials period. However, No. 8 GNIKI did evaluate the Tu-128's suitability for landing on earth runways, two flights being carried out from packed earth, but the results did not inspire confidence and the conclusion was that flights had to be performed from concrete runways. However, in an emergency separate take-offs and landings were permitted from or onto packed earth runways with a load-bearing strength of not less than 10 kg/cm² (142.25 lb/sq. in.) but a landing outside the airfield was forbidden.

In parallel with conducting service trials of the Tu-128, the Tupolev Design Bureau was already working on a modified version of the aircraft, although from the time of starting this work until its completion, almost ten years were to elapse. During this time, the operational use of air power in general and bomber aviation in particular had changed significantly and strike aircraft were now expected to perform low-altitude attacks to break through enemy air defences. However, the Tu-128 was practically useless in the low-level intercept role, so Tupolev suggested a modernisation programme to broaden the aircraft's operational capabilities. In 1968, a joint resolution was signed involving the Ministry of the Aviation Industry (formerly the State Committee for Aviation Technology), the Ministry of the Radio-electronic Industry (also a former State committee) and the Soviet Air Force (VVS). At this point it is perhaps expedient to remind the reader that the Soviet Air Force was the official 'customer' for *all* aviation-related equipment purchases for *all* branches of the armed forces in the USSR. At the end of 1968, the relevant decree was issued by the Council of Ministers concerning development of the improved Tu-128S-4M integrated interception system, by virtue of modifying the Tu-128 interceptor into the Tu-128M. In 1970, the PVO handed over two late-series Tu-128s from the 42nd production batch—Factory Nos 504201 (Bort[14] No. 74) and 504202 (Bort No. 75)—to serve as pattern aircraft for the new variant. (Incidentally, these two aircraft had not yet been assigned to a regiment, and it is believed that they had not even left the factory in Voronezh.) Also in this period, the design bureau had to start work on yet another project related to the Tu-128—the creation of a training variant of the aircraft, or '*sparka*', as trainers were known on the regiments.[15] Col. Komyagin notes:

> At first there were no Tu-128 '*sparki*', but no one had even thought that they were necessary. We operated the MiG-19 throughout its entire service in the PVO without having a training version. The MiG-15UTI was used as a trainer on MiG-19 regiments and when we started converting onto the Su-9 there were also no training variants of this aircraft. The MiG-15UTI was also used as a trainer for the Su-9.

Evidently, when the question arose about the need for a training version of the Tu-128, Savitskiy had agreed with the conclusions of the Tupolev design team (that a training variant was unnecessary). In fact, he was president of the State Commission overseeing the aircraft's flight tests, and in the document drawn up at the end of the test programme there was an entry that had to be completed regarding the need for a trainer. All the OKB-156 (i.e. Tupolev OKB) test pilots had made the comment that the Tu-128 was easy to fly and a training variant was therefore unnecessary, and the document was accepted in this form by the Soviet Ministry of Defence. It is easy to understand the design bureau's standpoint—creating a training variant would be a very complex procedure, and there was still a lot of work to do on refining the actual combat version itself. However, events turned out quite differently—the difficulties experienced by pilots converting onto the new interceptor forced the PVO to demand that the design bureau *should* create a training version of the Tu-128. Serendipity was evidently to play a part in accelerating work on this particular theme, as recounted by Col. Komyagin:

> I'd had to ferry a Tu-128 from Savasleika to Talagi. It was winter, but the weather was excellent as I approached the airfield at Talagi. An aircraft was landing ahead of us, so we were sent round again. Then I heard the controller on the radio shouting at the crew who had just landed, 'Brake! Brake! Where are you going!? Brake …' Then, I noticed that the aircraft had gone off the end of the runway at an angle to the centre-line and was stuck in the snow. I landed, taxied down the runway and had a look at what had happened.[16] The aircraft was a Tu-128 (Bort No. 45), a new aircraft with Factory No. 1405—that is, 14th series, 5th aircraft. The aircraft was resting with its nose pointing about 70° off the runway centreline. I climbed down from my aircraft and I could see that the AI radar antenna of the other aircraft was lying under the nose. The radome hadn't fallen off, but the antenna had punched through the bottom of it and dropped onto the ground. Later, the factory engineering representatives (*zavodskaya brigada*) came out to the aircraft. I said to them, 'Wouldn't it be better to make a "*sparka*" out of this one?!' and the reps replied, 'Of course not. You'd have to install another seat and there's no room.' We chatted about this and then I forgot all about it. Time passed and then in 1970 I received a phone call from the Tupolev OKB in Moscow. 'Don't you want to come and see your "*sparochka*"[17] at Zhukovskiy?!' I asked, 'What "*sparka*" and where's it from?' and was told, 'Yours. We made it out of that damaged Bort No. 45. Come over to Zhukovskiy and take a look at our "*pelikan*".'

Since there was no other way of quickly producing a Tu-128 trainer, the OKB had decided to install the instructor's cockpit in the space occupied by the *Smerch* AI radar. Thus, in order to retain the original view from the cockpit for the pilot under instruction, the instructor's cockpit had to be placed significantly below the fuselage waterline.[18] Consequently, the nose profile ended up resembling the deep characteristic beak of the pelican, and the Tu-128UT, as the trainer was to be designated, inevitably received the nickname '*pelikan*' in PVO service. As the aircraft lacked AI radar and most of the associated weapons systems, it was impossible to use the trainer to practise intercept techniques. The original contract with the Soviet Ministry of Defence envisaged the production of 198 combat variants, with no additional financing available for the purchase of a trainer, so it was decided to convert some of the existing Tu-128 interceptors into the Tu-128UT.

The first training (*uchebno-trenirovochniye* or UT) versions were converted from Tu-128 interceptors already built (up to the forty-second series), the characteristic external feature of these examples being the slanting fin tip. Four Tu-128UTs were converted from this original group—Bort Nos 99, 01, 11 and 15—the latter aircraft being the first '*sparka*', Factory No. 1405, described above. All four aircraft took part in the Tu-128UT flight test programme, completed in 1971, following which it was accepted into service by the PVO. Col. Yevglyevskiy adds:

> The decision to build the Tu-128UT was taken considerably later than the signing of the contract for the Tu-128 combat variant. There was no money available for building additional aircraft as trainers, so the Ministry for Aircraft Production set very strict conditions. Initially, Tu-128 combat variants were produced, which had been accepted by the 'customer' [i.e. the Soviet Ministry of Defence] and then the factory converted these aircraft into the Tu-128UT. Under this arrangement the Ministry of Defence paid an additional sum for converting the recently [newly] built Tu-128s into Tu-128UTs.

The 'new-build' Tu-128UT was completed in two series batches consisting of five aircraft each (the 45th and 46th series), these being the final series of Tu-128s manufactured by Factory No. 64 at Voronezh, and in 1971 production of all Tu-128s came to an end. (Thus, a total of fourteen Tu-128UTs were produced, comprising the original four mentioned above plus the ten converted 'new' off the production line. All ten of the 'new-build' trainers had the extended fin tip of the majority of the Tu-128Ms.)

However, development of the Tu-128 did not end here; the first upgraded Tu-128Ms modified in the factory at Voronezh were being prepared at the same time for joint military/industry trials. These were conducted in two separate stages by the Tupolev Design Bureau and No. 8 State Red Banner Scientific Research Institute of the Air Force (8 GNIKI VVS) at Akhtubinsk. Testing of the Tu-128M was completed only in the summer of 1974, although around another five years was required to eliminate defects and shortcomings revealed during the trials period. The design bureau attached to the manufacturing plant at Voronezh developed the methods and technologies required for the upgrade programme, whilst the location chosen as the re-fit base for aircraft of the 10th Independent Army (*10 Otdyel'naya Armiya*) of the PVO was Tolmachevo airfield, near Novosibirsk. Here, the 26th Aviation Repair Plant (*26 Aviatsionnyi Remontnyi Zavod* or ARZ), also known as Military Unit 13838 (*voyskovaya chast' 13838*), was already engaged in depot-level maintenance of the Tu-128. As the aircraft of the 10th Army were the oldest Tu-128s in service, with the highest airframe hours and the first to undergo major servicing in the ARZ at Novosibirsk, it was decided to combine major servicing with the upgrade and modification programme. Aircraft operated by the 14th Independent Army (*14 Otdyel'naya Armiya*), which still had a considerable number of operational hours left before major overhaul, underwent upgrade in a so-called 'fixed military aviation repair workshop' (*Statsionarnaya Voyskovaya Aviatsionnaya Remontnaya Mastyerskaya* or SVARM). These units, operated only by the PVO, were intended to provide repair, modernisation and upgrade of the service's interceptors. The 14th Army's SVARM, where the Tu-128s were converted into Tu-128Ms, was located on Zhana-Semey (Semipalatinsk) airfield, the SVARM's two inflatable hangars being situated between the 'divisional aviation repair workshop'[19] building and 356 AP's engineering support hangar.

The upgrade proceeded at a fairly leisurely pace and was still under way in 1984. Co-author Maj. Nikolai Popov adds:

> Externally it was very difficult to identify the upgraded aircraft. A few additional switches appeared in the cockpit, and the radar display looked a bit different. On the old indicator the targeting zone was engraved onto the screen surface, whereas on the new system it was electronic.

Flight at low level in the Tu-128M resulted in considerably higher temperatures in the aircraft's equipment bays and cockpit, so when carrying out the upgrade the radar cooling system was improved, along with improvements to the ventilation of equipment bays and the crew compartment. Simultaneous with the upgrade to Tu-128M standard, a range of essential modifications, dating back to when production ceased, were incorporated in the modernisation package.

The main external difference between the Tu-128M and the original Tu-128, apart from the colour of the radome, was the addition of a small retractable air intake for the upgraded air-conditioning system. This is just visible in its retracted position on the underside of the fuselage directly below the Bort number. (*Nikolai Popov*)

Service trials of the upgraded Tu-128S-4M weapons complex commenced in February 1978 at Sary-Shagan, using aircraft assigned to the 1st squadron of 356 AP at Zhana-Semey, the trials group remaining at Sary-Shagan for a week. This period is recalled by Col. Yevglyevskiy, who at the time was charged with the organisation of the tests in the capacity of head of the 1st Department Combat Training for PVO Aviation:

> We carried out the trials using ten aircraft and the work involved a large number of personnel. The State Commission included representatives from industry and No. 8 State Red Banner Scientific Research Institute of the Air Force, although only engineers from the latter were involved as the Institute probably didn't have any pilots who knew the aircraft sufficiently well by this late stage in its service life. There were engineers representing all specialisations from the 14th Independent Army. I personally selected the pilots who were to take part in the trials. The Commander of the 14th Army, General Abramov, authorised me to do this and checked everything personally, visited us frequently and took a great interest in what we were doing. At the end of the trials a list was drawn up on a sheet of A1-sized paper which included the signature of not only the C-in-C, but also a further 160 signatories concurring with the viability of low-altitude operation of the Tu-128M. The tests concluded with day and night live firing exercises using different intercept profiles. We were assigned five targets, including a MiG-17, Yak-25RV and Il-28, and all targets were destroyed.

The radio-controlled MiG-17M or M-17[20] was used as the target for forward hemisphere engagements in instrument meteorological conditions (IMC), usually flying at medium altitude, with the Tu-128M at 500 m (1,640 feet). The M-6 target was

The imposing 'bomber-like' dimensions of the Tu-128 can be appreciated in this view, with the wheeled access ladder and platform positioned in readiness for the arrival of the crew. (*Nikolai Popov*)

A Tu-128 of 356 AP parked in dispersal at Zhana-Semey. Visible on the lower fuselage, almost in line with the leading edge of the port air intake, is the blade antenna of the R-832 radio, which replaced the original RSIU-5V set. (*Nikolai Popov*)

used for group firing, with two interceptors flying as a pair in line abreast (*front paroi*), with a wing-tip to wing-tip separation (*interval*) of around 200-300 m (650-1,000 feet) between the aircraft. (Planned use of a Tu-16 target did not actually materialise, as the aircraft was not made ready in time at the re-fit base.) Four crews, led by regiment commander Col. Yevgyeniy Ivanovich Kostyenko, took part in these trials, which also included Lt Cols G. M. Zayats (CO of the 1st squadron) and N. N. Krushin (CO of the 3rd squadron). On 14 February 1978, Lt Col. Zayats carried out a rear hemisphere attack on an La-17 target from a height of 800 m (2,625 feet), and a forward hemisphere attack against another La-17 on the following day from a height of 1,300 m (4,265 feet). The targets were destroyed on both occasions. An armourer from the 356 AP second-line servicing unit (*Tekhniko-Ehksploatatsionnaya Chast'* or TEhCh), Vladimir Zayats, recalls the trials:

> The missile firings were carried out in dense cloud conditions. The task was made more difficult by the fact that the La-17 was flying at a speed close to the limiting interception speed for the Tu-128 at those heights. All of this forced the crew to exceed the operating g-limits of the aircraft while manoeuvring against the target and after the final missile firing detail it was towed immediately into the TEhCh hangar for close examination. I remember how everyone came to look around the aircraft, which was missing several inspection panels that had been torn off on the last flight.

After successful completion of the live missile firing phase, the Tu-128S-4M 'complex' was accepted for service and the planned upgrade programme was soon under way to bring all operational Tu-128s up to the Tu-128M standard.

With this, the first major modernisation of the Tu-128 conceived by the Commander of PVO Aviation, Gen. Anatolyi Kadomtsyev, finally reached fruition. The general had, however, wanted to carry out *two* upgrades of the PVO's 'long-range aviation-missile complex'—the first being the aforementioned achievement of low-level intercept capability with the Tu-128M. The second was to create an ultra-long-range interceptor similar in design and layout to the Tu-22M 'Backfire' variable-geometry bomber, which was under development in the mid-1960s for the Soviet Long-range Air Force (*Aviatsiya Dal'nyevo Dyeistviya*). An interceptor such as this would have had an endurance of more than 5 hours, a maximum speed close to Mach 2.0 and been able to carry six to eight missiles of better performance than the Bisnovat R-4/AA-5 used by the Tu-128. It was envisaged that the new interceptor would carry out combat air patrols of around 3-4 hours' duration before returning to its operating base. It was an extremely promising idea and was taken to the conceptual design stage in the form of a project designated 'Aircraft 148'.

Then, tragically, on 29 April 1969, Gen. Kadomtsyev was killed while testing a MiG-25P 'Foxbat' prototype at Akhtubinsk, robbing the project of its chief protagonist, although the Tupolev OKB nevertheless submitted the '148' design to the PVO High Command for evaluation. Col. Yevglyevskiy adds:

> We also had a department looking at new equipment at PVO Aviation HQ. This department was opposed to the new Tupolev aircraft and a 'stand-off' soon developed. The department was in favour of the MiG-25P and work on this aircraft was conducted in parallel with work on the new Tupolev design. I, of course, believed that that the Tupolev project would have been significantly better as an interceptor, although the MiG wasn't such a bad design. Nevertheless, 5 hours' flight duration [of the Tupolev design] was better than 3 hours' [for the MiG] and six to eight missiles were better than four! At that time the Commander-in Chief of the PVO, MSU Batitskiy, was not in Moscow, so the Tupolev design summary was reviewed by the deputy C-in-C, Col. Gen. Aleksandr Ivanovich Pokryshkin[21] and the commander of PVO Aviation, Col. Gen. Andrei Borovykh. They were both opposed to the new Tupolev interceptor.

With the tragic loss of Kadomtsyev the project was suddenly deprived of its main support inside the PVO High Command, the result being that within a very short time work on it ceased altogether. This, of course, also signalled the end of Kadomtsyev's dream of being able to provide defensive air cover for the whole of the northern region of the USSR with an ultra-long-endurance interceptor operating out of only three polar airfields. 'Aircraft 148' was the logical culmination of ideas arising out of the operation of the Tu-128 as a long-range air defence interceptor, but Tupolev designers had also examined a number of other Tu-128-based concepts throughout its lifetime, running parallel to its use by the PVO. These are described below.

TU-128 DEVELOPMENT PROJECTS

As with all Soviet military aircraft programmes, modified versions of the basic aircraft were being planned even as the aircraft was coming into service, and coincident with the introduction of the Tu-128 a three-stage study was initiated to examine its upgrade potential:

- Stage One examined the possibility of reducing the lower intercept altitude bracket from 8,000-10,000 m (26,250-32,800 feet) to 500-1,500 m (1,640-4,920 feet) in response to the newly emerging threat of low-level penetration of Soviet airspace by potential adversaries;
- Stage Two looked at the opposing need to be able to intercept targets flying at 23,000-25,000 m (75,460-82,020 feet) and to be able to deal with an increase in closing speed from 2,000 kph (1,800 kts) to 3,000 kph (1,620 kts);
- Stage Three focused on improvements to the aircraft in terms of maximum speed, acceleration characteristics, take-off and landing performance, and range.

Analysis of Stage One criteria convinced Tupolev designers that the basic Tu-128S-4 'complex' was capable of satisfying the low-altitude interception requirement, with appropriate modifications, resulting in the Tu-128M already described earlier and elsewhere in the book.

Apart from the 'Aircraft 148' project, a number of other developments had been considered during the lifetime of the Tu-128, differing from each other in terms of powerplant, avionics and weapons systems, although the majority never actually left the drawing board. One development project that did lead to the flight test stage involved the installation of the experimental Lyul'ka AL-7F-4 engine in the first series-production aircraft (0101) in early 1963. This engine developed 10,800 kg (23,810 lb) of thrust, but was a little heavier than the Tu-128's basic powerplant, weighing in at 2,180 kg (4,806 lb), and flight tests commenced at Zhukovskiy in February of that year. This was followed a little later by flight tests of a new spoiler system for improved lateral control in the supersonic regime and the installation of further-improved AL-7F-4G engines, with an ejector nozzle assembly. With the 'dash 4' engines the modified Tu-128 could reach Mach 1.6 with a full complement of missiles (Mach 1.96 according to some sources). Unfortunately, both the 'dash 4' and 'dash 4G' required extensive improvements to bring them up to production standard and this line of development was abandoned. However, OKB-156 continued to examine ways of improving the performance of the basic design and submitted a proposal for two new variants under the designations Tu-28A-80 and Tu-28A-100,[22] with either RP-SA *Smerch-A* (Tornado-A) or

Groza-100 (Thunderstorm-100) AI radar and Bisnovat K-80M or K-100 missiles respectively. Within the framework of the Tu-28A project, Tupolev designers offered the aircraft with the same Dobrynin VD-19 engines that had been proposed as the powerplant for the original 'Fiddler' at the initial design stage.

In broad outline, the Tu-28A resembled the original design (i.e. the original Tu-128), but as a consequence of using the more powerful VD-19 engines, with greater mass flow than the AL-7F, the shape and area of the air intakes was changed. Moreover, the intake semi-cones now operated not as fixed shock bodies (albeit still translating forwards to a fixed position after take-off) but moved continuously in flight, since the maximum speed of the aircraft with four missiles was calculated to be 2,000 kph (1,080 kts). Another consequence of the use of the VD-19 engines was an increase in the cross-sectional area of the rear fuselage, whilst the new AI radar necessitated a longer nose radome, with additional ventral fins à la prototype Tu-128, in order to restore directional control authority. The VD-19 engine underwent bench testing in February and March of 1964 in a special rig, using the Tu-28A air intake assembly, and in 1965 it was installed in the Tu-128LL flying test-bed and test flown at Zhukovskiy. The Tu-128LL was, in fact, intended to serve as the prototype for the Tu-28A, although in the absence of a working prototype radar a balance weight was installed in its place. The flight tests revealed that the maximum speed (without missiles) was only increased by around 110-120 kph (60-65 kts) and the anticipated 2,000 kph maximum speed turned out to be practically unachievable due to the extra drag resulting from the increased cross-sectional area of the mid-fuselage. Consequently, the use of the VD-19 was deemed to be inexpedient, which, along with considerable delays in developing the new radar, resulted in cancellation of both the Tu-28A-80 and the Tu-28A-100.

The remaining upgrade programmes were all largely conceptual, existing only as design sketches or wind tunnel models, but one project envisaged the installation of two Kolesov RD-36-41 engines in the existing basic Tu-128 airframe, along with the improved RP-SA *Smerch-A* AI radar (NATO 'Foxfire'). The RD-36-41 developed 16,000 kg (35,275 lb) of thrust in full reheat and offered a specific fuel consumption of 0.88 kg/hr/kg (1.94 lb/hr/lb) in maximum dry thrust and 1.9 kg/hr/kg (4.19 lb/hr/lb) in reheat. At a revised take-off weight of 52,140 kg (114,950 lb) the re-engined Tu-128 was expected to achieve a maximum speed of 2,650 kph (1,430 kts). Unfortunately, this engine also required considerable additional development work and, with flight tests in a Tu-16LL test-bed having only just commenced in 1968, would have led to a concomitant delay in the upgrade programme. Moreover, the PVO High Command had already declared itself satisfied with the preliminary performance of the *Smerch-A* radar and the new Tumansky RB-15 engines of the MiG-25 'Foxbat' prototype, thereby precipitating the cancellation of further upgrades of the Tu-128. As this effectively signalled the end of the line for development of the basic Tu-128, OKB-156 decided to offer two entirely new 'interception complexes' to meet the demands of Stage Two and Stage Three of the joint MoD/Design Bureau study for a future PVO interceptor. The first of these two 'complexes' was designated Tu-138-60, an interceptor equipped with *Smerch-A* radar and armed with K-60 air-to-air missiles, whilst the second was designated Tu-138-100, with *Groza-100* AI radar and K-100 missiles.

The Tu-138 retained the external appearance of the Tu-128, albeit with 'Foxbat'-style intakes and a new, thinner wing, plus an undercarriage that retracted partially into the wing and partially into the fuselage and was powered by the Dobrynin VD-19 engines proposed for the Tu-28A. The more powerful engines and the improved aerodynamics of the new wing promised a maximum speed of the order of 2,100-2,400 kph (1,135-1,295 kts) with four missiles. Subsonic interception radius was expected to be around 2,000 km (1,080 nm), while loiter time would be extended to 4.5 hours. It was also planned to use some of the original R-4 (AA-5 'Ash') missiles of the Tu-128S-4 as a reserve weapons pool. Work on the '138' project was taken to quite an advanced stage and a large number of wind-tunnel models were constructed, but tests carried out by TsAGI (*Tsentralniy Aerogidrodinamicheskiy Institut*—Central Hydroaerodynamic Institute) revealed that the desired subsonic lift/drag ratio could not be achieved. This, of course, meant that take-off and landing performance would be worse than predicted, high-speed performance was likely to be degraded by the increased form drag of the VD-19 installation, and the planned radius of action would be unattainable. A number of palliatives were suggested, including the installation of an in-flight refuelling system similar to that of the Tu-22 'Blinder' bomber and the use of blown flaps and slats, but these measures would have been heavy and complex, so the '138' programme was axed.

Still keen to come up with a replacement for the Tu-128, the Tupolev design team offered yet another 'interception complex' developed from the original theme of the 'Fiddler'. The first iteration of this project was to be known as the Tu-148-100, equipped with the *Smerch-100* fire-control system and armed with K-100 missiles, but unlike the earlier projects this aircraft was to be equipped with a variable-geometry wing and yet another new engine, the RD-19R-2. These engines were expected to develop 14,200 kg (31,305 lb) in reheat, offering a speed of 1,400 kph (756 kts) at heights from 50-100 m (165-328 feet) and 2,500 kph (1,350 kts) at 16,000-18,000 m (52,495-59,055 feet). Subsonic range was expected to be around 5,000 km (2,700 nm), dropping to 2,500 km (1,350 nm) in the supersonic regime. A particular feature of the Tu-148 was to have been the *Smerch-100* fire-control system, effectively an 'integrated infrared and radar guidance system for missile armament' (*teploradiatsionnaya sistyema upravlyeniya rakietnym vooruzheniem*) which would have given the aircraft an autonomous search capability. (Russia and the USA were pioneers in the use of infrared search and track [IRST] sensors on fighters, with the first IRST-equipped Russian interceptor being the MiG-23M 'Flogger-B', followed in turn by the MiG-25 'Foxbat' and MiG-29 'Fulcrum'.) An integrated system like *Smerch-100* would have been highly innovative on a Russian fighter in the late 1960s, placing this development of the 'Fiddler' many years ahead of several of its Western contemporaries.

In parallel with development of the Tu-148-100, the Tupolev design team continued to examine the requirement for a new 'long-range interception complex' and in the mid-1960s submitted their proposal for the Tu-148-33, a variant equipped with the *Zaslon* radar (NATO 'Flash Dance') and armed with R-33 (NATO AA-9 'Amos') long-range air-to-air missiles. (This radar and missile combination was to reach fruition, of course, on the later MiG-31 'Foxhound'.) A number of wing planforms were studied for this variant, including a variable-geometry layout similar to that of the Tu-22M 'Backfire' then in development, a fixed-sweep shoulder wing design with 'Foxbat'-style air intakes, a shoulder wing design of rhomboid planform and a double-delta with canard foreplanes. The preferred choice was the variable-geometry option, using Kolesov RD-36-41 engines.

The Tu-148-33 'complex' was designed to counter existing and future threats, operating under the control of GCI stations as well as with the Tu-126 'Moss' airborne early warning system. Its tasks were to be the interception of low-flying targets, over land and sea, particularly AGM-28 'Hound Dog', AGM-69 SRAM and AGM-86A cruise missiles, as well as having the capability to extend the closing speed in forward hemisphere interceptions to 3,500 kph (1,890 kts) and 2,400 kph (1,296 kts) in the rear hemisphere. Additionally, the target interception altitude was increased to 26,000-28,000 m (85,300-91,965 feet), while flight range was increased to 4,600 km (2,480 nm) and loiter time to 5 hours. Other improvements were increased electronic counter-measures (ECM) resistance, the ability for simultaneous engagement of two targets, and the potential for 'group operations'. Importantly, it was also planned to be able to operate the Tu-148 from the same airfields used by the Tu-128/Tu-128M. This was the Tupolev submission for an improved long-range interceptor which had so impressed Kadomtsyev before his tragic death in the aforementioned MiG-25 crash at Akhtubinsk in 1969, albeit regarded with much less enthusiasm by other members of the PVO High Command. Having thus lost such influential support within the PVO hierarchy, the Tu-148 effectively died along with Kadomtsyev.

Undaunted by setbacks experienced while attempting to maximise the development potential of the Tu-128 as a strategic air defence interceptor, Tupolev had continued to study its potential in the tactical arena, proposing a number of interesting variants for roles other than air defence. A multi-role variant was offered, armed with podded S-5K or S-5M 57 mm unguided rockets and two to four 240 mm S-24 rockets; a pair of AO-9 gun pods (with 200-250 rounds per gun); four 500 kg (1,100 lb) bombs and eight 250 kg (550 lb) bombs for ground attack. For weapons aiming, the pilot was to have been provided with an ASP-PF gunsight. Other options included arming the aircraft with two Kh-28 (AS-9 'Kyle') anti-radiation missiles, or modified K-80 missiles adapted for air-to-ground applications, as well as a variant modified to launch KSR-type cruise missiles.[23] Later, in 1969, OKB-156 offered the Tu-128B (*Bombardirovshchik*) tactical bomber, equipped with *Initsiativa-I* (NATO 'Shorthorn') navigation/bombing radar, linked to an OPB-16 optical bomb-sight. The Tu-128B was designed to operate at a speed of 1,770 kph (955 kts) at 11,000 m (36,090 feet) over a range of 2,345 km (1,266 nm) while carrying a bomb load of 1,500 kg (3,300 lb) in an internal bomb-bay. When carrying an additional 3,000 kg (6,600 lb) of bombs on external pylons, the maximum speed and range was reduced to 1,210 kph (653 kts) and 1,430 km (770 nm) respectively. However, within the same timeframe Yakovlev was developing the more viable Yak-28 'Brewer' series of light tactical bombers and these designs prevailed over Tupolev's late entry into this field. In an attempt to wring the last ounce of potential from the Tu-128 design, the Tupolev design team also offered the Soviet Defence Ministry specialised Tu-128PP (*Postanovshchik Pomyekh*) electronic jamming and Tu-128R (*Razvedchik/Razvedyvatyel'nyi*) reconnaissance variants, but again without success. These innovative, albeit failed, development projects notwithstanding, the basic (and later modestly upgraded) Tu-128 interceptor was to go on to serve the PVO in the defence of Soviet Russia for almost a quarter of a century, as described in succeeding chapters of this book. Here, readers can judge for themselves the success of this remarkable aircraft, which was and remains the largest fighter ever flown.

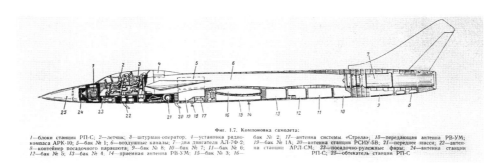

Фиг. 1.7. Компоновка самолета:

1—блоки станции РП-С; 2—летчик; 3—штурман-оператор; 4—установка радио-компаса АРК-10; 5—бак № 1; 6—воздушные каналы; 7—два двигателя АЛ-7Ф-2; 8—контейнер посадочного парашюта; 9—бак № 8; 10—бак № 7; 11—бак № 6; 12—бак № 5; 13—бак № 4; 14—приемная антенна РВ-УМ; 15—бак № 3; 16— бак № 2; 17—антенна системы «Стрела»; 18—передающая антенна РВ-УМ; 19—бак № 1А; 20—антенна станции РСИУ-5В; 21—передние шасси; 22—антенна станции АРЛ-СМ; 23—посадочно-рулежные фары; 24—антенна станции РП-С; 25—обтекатель станции РП-С

1 – Line replaceable units (LRUs) of RP-S (*Radiolokatsionnyi Pritsel-Smerch*) airborne interception (AI) radar; 2 – Pilot; 3 – Navigator/weapons system operator; 4 – ARK-10 automatic radio compass unit; 5 – Fuel tank No. 1; 6 – Air inlet ducts; 7 – Lyul'ka AL-7F-2 turbojet engines; 8 – Brake parachute housing; 9 – Fuel tank No. 8; 10 – Fuel tank No. 7; 11 – Fuel tank No. 6; 12 – Fuel tank No. 5; 13 – Fuel tank No. 4; 14 – Receiving antenna of RV-UM radio-altimeter; 15 – Fuel tank No. 3; 16 – Fuel tank No. 2; 17 – *Strela* Doppler navigation system antenna; 18 – Transmitting antenna of RV-UM radio altimeter; 19 – Fuel tank No. 1A; 20 – RSIU-5V VHF radio antenna; 21 – Nose landing gear; 22 – ARL-SM (*Lazur'*) data-link radio system antenna; 23 – Landing/taxi lights; 24 – RP-S AI radar antenna; 25 – Radome. (*Nikolai Popov*)

2

The Tu-128S-4 Weapon Complex

THE INTEGRATED LONG-RANGE AIRBORNE INTERCEPTION SYSTEM

The Tu-128 was the principal airborne component of the Tu-128S-4 'complex', and this chapter describes the interrelationship between the other components of this system and the manner in which the aircraft was used within the automated ground-controlled guidance system around which it was designed. As was customary at the time, all these components were known collectively as a '*kompleks*', meaning literally, of course, a 'complex', but more usually considered in the broader sense as an 'integrated system'. The Tu-128S-4 'complex' comprised the following:

- the Tu-128 long-range interceptor;
- the *Smerch* (Tornado) long-range AI radar and its associated *Smerch-VM* (*Smerch-Vychyslityel'naya Mashina*) computer;
- four Bisnovat R-4 (AA-5 'Ash') air-to-air missiles;
- the *Vozdukh-1* (literally 'Air-1') ground-based automated control and guidance system installed at GCI sites, supported by *Kaskad-M* ('Cascade-M') or *Vozdukh-1M* data generation equipment.

FLIGHT AND NAVIGATION SYSTEM, RADIOS AND THE KZA FLIGHT RECORDER OF THE TU-128

The Tu-128 had a variety of equipment designed to enable it to perform the tasks required of a fighter in the Soviet air defence forces (PVO) of the mid-twentieth century. This equipment could be divided into flight navigation systems, radio communications systems and a specialised KZA (*Kontrol'no-Zapisyvayushchaya Apparatura*) flight data recording system.

Flight and navigation equipment

The flight navigation equipment (*Pilotazhno-Navigatsionnoye Oborudovaniye* or PNO) of the Tu-128S-4 'complex' comprised the following principal systems and instruments:

- the *Put'-4P* (Route-4P) flight navigation system;
- the RSBN-2S *Svod-Struna* (*Radiotekhnicheskaya Sistyema Blizhnyei Navigatsii*) Short-range (Radio-technical) Navigation System, equivalent to the Western TACAN (Tactical Air Navigation) system;
- an NVU-B (*Navigatsionno-Vychislityel'noye Ustroistvo-Bortovoye*) navigation computer;
- a KS-6V (*Kursovaya Sistyema-6V*) course and heading system;
- an AP-7P (*Avtopilot-7P*) autopilot;
- a TsSV-1M-1V (*Tsentral' Skorosti i Vysoty-1M-1V*) airspeed/altitude reference unit;
- a DISS-2 *Strela* (Arrow) (*Doplerovskii Izmerityel' Skorosti i ugla Snosa*) Doppler ground speed and drift indicator;
- a ZVS (*Zadatchik Vysoty Stabilizatsii*) stabilized height selector;
- an ARK-10 (*Avtomaticheskii Radio-Kompass*) automatic radio compass;
- an RV-UM (*Radiovysotomyer Malykh Vysot*) low-altitude radio-altimeter;
- an MRP-56P (*Markyernyi Radio Priyomnik-56 Posadochnyi*) ILS marker receiver;
- a DA-200 combined indicator;
- an AGD-1 (*Aviagorizont Distantsionnyi-1*) remote-reading artificial horizon;
- a KUSI-2500 (*Kombinirovannyi Ukazatyel' Skorosti s Indeksom komand*) combined speed indicator, with command marker (later replaced by the UISMI [*Ukazatyel' Istinnoy Skorosti s Makhmetrom Integrirovannym*] and US-1600 [*Ukazatyel' Skorosti* reading to 1,600 kph] indicators showing true air speed and Mach number);
- a VDI-30 (*Dvukhstrelochnyi Vysotomyer s Dopolnityel'nym Indeksom komand-30*) twin-needle altimeter with supplementary command marker;
- an AUASP-1S-N (*Avtomat Uglov Ataki, Skol'zheniya i Peregruzki-1S-N*) automatic angle of attack and sideslip indicator with combined accelerometer.

The Put'-4P (Route-4P) Flight Navigation System

This provided semi-automatic control of the Tu-128, combining information from the main flight navigation sensors and converting this information into a form

The unequivocally 1950s 'black cockpit' of the Tu-128 is dominated by the large control yoke (complete with stylised Tupolev logo in the boss) more reminiscent of an airliner than a supersonic fighter. The large (black and yellow) striped handle on the left-hand side of the cockpit is the canopy emergency jettison lever. (*Yefim Gordon Archive*)

suitable for display to the pilot and navigator. The *Put-4P* system comprised the following units:

- a central computer (designated V-4P);
- two separate indicators—a PP-1PK flight instrument and an NKP-4K course deviation indicator;
- amplifiers and switching units;
- a TS-7 annunciator panel for the pilot, and a TS-8 annunciator panel for the navigator.

Navigation data were presented on combined instruments: on the PP-1PMK (*Pilotazhnyi Pribor*) pilot's flight instrument (flight director) and on the NKP-4K (*Navigatsionno-Kursovoi Pribor*) course deviation indicator. Director commands were shown on the PP-1PMK in the form of deviations of the command bar using the 'zero indicator' method. This meant that the vertically positioned command bar moved horizontally right to left and the horizontal command bar moved vertically up and down. The amount of deviation indicated the targeting (piloting) errors. The pilot had to fly the aircraft so that the command bars came together in the form of a cross in the middle of the PP-1PMK dial. The following parameters were displayed on the PP-1PMK and NKP-4K instruments:

- a lateral movement command;
- a vertical movement command;
- actual course—from the KS-6V;
- assigned course (from 0° to 360°)—from the *Lazur'-M* (Azure) data-link system, or inserted manually;
- current angle of bank from the TsGV-5 (*Tsentral'naya Girovertikal'-5*) master vertical gyro—(angle of bank was not allowed to exceed 60°);
- pitch angle from the TsGV-5;
- sideslip;
- targeting errors—horizontal and vertical, given by the *Smerch* radar;
- deviation from assigned height according to signals from the TsSV-1M-1V and the ZVS;
- deviation from the trajectory for penetration of cloud and glideslope from the SVOD (RSBN) system;
- angle for turning on to an assigned waypoint or target from the NVU-B computer;
- azimuth provided by RSBN;
- lateral deviation from an assigned route provided by RSBN.

The various stages of an intercept profile were displayed to the pilot and navigator on the TS-7 and TS-8 light panels (*Tablo Samolyotnoye*) as 'one-time' commands. The pilot received the following commands on his TS-7 display:

From the *Lazur'-M* equipment, during the ground-controlled stage of an intercept:

- turn commands—'Left', 'Straight Ahead', 'Right';
- 'Forward Hemisphere'—indicating that the intercept was to be a forward hemisphere engagement;
- range to target 36 km (22.4 miles);
- two meanings for the command 'End of Guidance': one meaning 'Re-targeting'; the other 'Guidance to the airfield'.

From the *Smerch* radar during the on-board guidance phase:

- 'Lock-on'—indicating lock-on to the target by the *Smerch* radar;
- 'Zoom Climb'—initiate a zoom climb towards the target;

At first glance this does not look like an air defence WSO's cockpit as there is no obvious sign of an AI radar screen – although he did have one, situated low down on the right-hand side of the of the main instrument group. The display simply provided visual confirmation of data-linked audio-visual target information in the terminal stage of the intercept. The three oblong panels on the upper canopy arch held frequency or callsign information cards. (*Yefim Gordon Archive*)

- 'End of Illumination'—target illumination by the *Smerch* radar had ceased;
- 'Break-off'—given to the pilot at the end of an attack and for setting up for the return to base.

The navigator received the following commands on his TS-8 display:

- Flight mode: 'Combined', 'Afterburner', 'Guidance to airfield';
- Range to target 100 km (62.1 miles);
- '*Nakal*'—indicating the start of the warm-up phase for the high-frequency units of the semi-active radar guidance heads of the R-4R (AA-5 'Ash') missiles. (The Russian word '*nakal*' has various meanings, but in the electronics context means 'heating' or 'warm-up'.)

The *Put'-4P* system provided semi-automatic control of the aircraft in the following flight regimes:

- in ground-controlled guidance mode, using signals from the *Vozdukh-1* system via the *Lazur'-M* data-link, the ZVS stabilized height selector and the TsSV-1M-1V airspeed/altitude reference unit;
- in on-board guidance mode (for missile targeting), using signals from the *Smerch* AI radar;
- in autonomous navigation mode (return to base, or flight to an assigned waypoint), using signals from the NVU-B navigation computer;
- in stabilized horizontal flight, using signals from the KS-6V course and heading system, giving an assigned heading to steer at an assigned altitude;
- in radio-navigation mode, guidance to own airfield or diversion airfield for landing, using signals from the RSBN-2SA *Svod-Struna* system.

The RSBN-2S Svod-Struna Short-range Navigation System

This system was (and, in upgraded form, still is) a Russia-wide short-range navigation and landing system and on the Tu-128 worked in conjunction with the NVU-B aircraft navigation system. ('*Svod*' can mean 'collection', 'canopy' or 'vault'; '*Struna*' means 'string' of a musical instrument or racquet.) The RSBN-2S provided en-route navigation and instrument approaches for landing in IFR (Instrument Flight Rules) conditions in daylight and at night. The *Svod-Struna* system, which in its current form is still the most widely used Russian tactical navigation system, consists of airborne processing and display equipment operating in conjunction with a network of ground transmitting stations. Its basic elements comprised a ground-based network of antennas and beacons transmitting encoded azimuth and distance-measuring data from RSBN-equipped airfields, providing course and glideslope information for aircraft flying within radio range of these airfields.

Brief parameters of the RSBN-2S system on the Tu-128
Number of channels—40
Operational range when flying at 10,000 m (32,800 feet)—360 km (224 miles)
Operational range when flying at 5,000 m (16,400 feet)—250 km (155 miles)
Operational range when flying at 250 m (820 feet)—70 km (44 miles)

The NVU-B navigational computer provided:

- continuous automatic computation and display of the coordinates of the aircraft's current position in the orthodromic (Great Circle) or conventional 'rectangular' system of coordinates using data from the DISS-2 *Strela* Doppler navigation unit (or from the TsSV-1M-1V airspeed/altitude reference unit), with periodic updates from RSBN *Svod*;
- continuous automatic computation of the polar coordinates (angles of turn and distance) to an assigned intermediate waypoint (PPM— *Promyezhutochnyi Punkt Marshruta*) to the target, or to the start of coordinates 'NK' (*Nachalo Koordinat* or Initial Course);
- continuous automatic computation and display of track angle;
- display of the distance to an RSBN navigation beacon in landing mode when using the *Svod* system, shown on the pilot's DME (range) indicator;
- programming of the rectangular coordinates of five previously assigned waypoints and input of a new waypoint;
- continuous and automatic computation of wind speeds using the DISS-2 *Strela* Doppler navigation system, and storage of this information when transferring to the TsSV-1M-1V airspeed/altitude reference unit;
- continuous calculation and indication of the aircraft's current position in the orthodromic system of coordinates, based on ground speed and drift from the *Strela* Doppler navigation system;
- correction of the aircraft's position using data from RSBN-2S;
- continuous computation of the polar coordinates of an assigned waypoint (PPM or aerodrome).

The computer processing units of the NVU-B were mounted on staging (i.e. racks) in the navigator's cockpit in the vicinity of Frame No. 10 on the right-hand side of the aircraft. The pilot had the range indicator and programme selector switch for the NVU-B on his instrument panel. The main control panel of the NVU-B, the grivation (*ugol karty*) selector,[1] coordinate display and selector and the navigator's range indicator were all mounted on the navigator's instrument panel.

> **Brief technical data for the NVU-B navigation computer**
> Range of equivalent air speeds—250-2,500 kph (135-1,350 kts)
> Altitude range—sea level up to 25,000 m (82,020 feet)
> Wind speed—up to 400 kph (215 kts)
> Drift angle—from −30° to +30°
> *Working range in the rectangular system of coordinates:*
> 2,900 km (1,800 miles) along each axis

> *Working range in the polar system of coordinates:*
> relative to 'NK' (Initial Course)—from 5 to 3,000 km (3 to 1,865 miles)
> relative to 'PPM' (Waypoint)—from 5 to 3,000 km (3 to 1,865 miles)
> relative to the target—from 5 to 1,000 km (3 to 621 miles)
> in indication of actual track angle ±2.5°

The KS-6V Course and Heading System

The KS-6V system was designed to resolve the following:

- determination and display of the aircraft's course;
- the aircraft's turning angle;
- transfer of course signals to user elements (the AP-7P autopilot, the NKP-4K navigation instrument of the *Put'-4P* system and the B-8 grivation selector of the NVU-B autonomous navigation unit).

The ID-2 induction sensor of the course and heading system was mounted in the starboard wing; other components of the system were mounted on racks on the right- and left-hand sides of the navigator's cockpit in the vicinity of Frame No. 8 and on the navigator's instrument panel, namely the UMK (*Ukazatyel' Magnitnovo Kursa*) magnetic course indicator.

> **Brief technical data for the KS-6V system**
> Error in determining magnetic course—±1.5°
> Error in transfer of course signals to users from the GA-1 (Giroagregat-1) selsyn (self-synchronising) gyro unit—±1.5°
> Working ambient temperature range from +50°C to –60°C
> Altitude range—up to 25,000 m (82,020 feet)
> Warm-up time—no more than 5 minutes

The AP-7P Autopilot

This was designed to stabilise the aircraft about the centre of gravity relative to the three principal axes, for manoeuvring control of the aircraft, and for automatic stabilisation of assigned altitude. The AP-7P (AP-7M) was capable of rapid damping of oscillations resulting from brief local disturbance of the airflow (gusts, missile launch, etc.) as well as longer-duration disturbances such as the failure of one of the engines, or an open hatch, etc.). The majority of the line replaceable units (LRUs) of the autopilot were located within the pressure cabin on special racks mounted in the vicinity of Frame Nos 7 and 8. The BDG (*Blok Dempfiruyushchikh Giroskopov*) gyroscope damping unit was mounted in the region of Frame No. 32, the elevator and rudder servo units were mounted in the rear of the fuselage, and the aileron servo was mounted on the main spar in the wing centre-section. The PV-2 autopilot control panel was situated on the right-hand side of the pilot's cockpit near Frame No. 6 and incorporated a small joystick. The navigator's PUSh (*Pul't Upravlyeniya Shturmana-operatora*) emergency control panel was mounted on the left-hand side of the navigator's cockpit.

The AP-7P (AP-7M) autopilot interfaced with the KS-6V course and heading system, the *Smerch* AI radar, the TsSV-1M-1V airspeed/altitude reference unit and the PP-1PK flight director of the *Put'-4P* system. However, on early-series Tu-128s, the AP-7P autopilot was not actually connected; on selection and deselection of the autopilot the operating lights would illuminate, but this *only* indicated that the electronic link from the switch to the lights was working. The actual linkage to the servo units themselves was inoperative, and servo units were not in fact installed in the autopilot circuit. The system only became fully functional following modifications carried out in 1969! The modification was undertaken on the regiments on an individual aircraft basis, the first modified aircraft being test flown by specially selected factory test pilots. However, it has to be admitted that even after the introduction of a functioning AP-7P, the autopilot was not used on the regiments to control the aircraft in automatic mode via the *Lazur'* data-link as had originally been planned for the 'Fiddler'.

The TsSV-1M-1V Airspeed/Altitude Reference Unit

The unit supplied the autopilot with true air speed, relative barometric altitude, relative air density, ambient (outside) air temperature and Mach number. Additionally, it was linked to the *Smerch* AI radar, the RSBN-2S navigation system and the NVU-B autonomous navigation system and provided data for the true air speed (TAS), relative barometric altitude and outside air temperature indicators, which were situated on the navigator's instrument panel. The Machmeter was located on the pilot's instrument panel. The TsSV-1M-1V LRUs were situated under the floor in the aircraft's pressure cabin in the vicinity of Frame Nos 9 and 10.

The DISS-2 Strela Doppler Ground Speed and Drift Indicator

This supplied automatic continuous calculation of the aircraft's ground speed and drift angle, displaying these parameters in the two cockpits and inputting the results into the NVU-B navigation computer. Ground speed and drift angles were shown on an analogue drift indicator on the navigator's instrument panel. This indicator incorporated a digital ground speed counter that allowed the navigator to know at any given moment during flight the current ground speed and drift, independent of outside visibility, in horizontal flight over featureless terrain along any flight route.

The ZVS Stabilized Altitude Selector

The ZVS height selector was designed for manual input of an assigned altitude into the *Put'-4P* navigation system during the combat phase of flight. The altitude was set within a height range of zero to 15,000 m (49,200 feet) by means of a selector knob. The assigned altitude could also be fed into the ZVS automatically from the ground via the *Lazur'-M* GCI data-link.

The ARK-10 System

The ARK-10 automatic radio compass aided:

- flight navigation using beacon and broadcast transmissions to establish the aircraft's position;
- calculation of the landing approach when in Instrument Landing System (ILS) mode;
- reception and monitoring of medium-wave (MW) radio stations.

Principal technical details of the ARK-10 system:

- range using a beacon from an altitude of 10,000 m (32,800 feet) when working with a PAR-3BM radio station—approximately 350 km (220 miles);
- rapid retuning in flight to any one of nine previously set frequencies within the working range, without excluding the possibility of continuous tuning;
- rod-type antenna designed to increase the reception range and reduce residual quadrantal error.

The RV-UM Low-altitude Altimeter

This was used for the measurement of the true height of the aircraft above the ground within the range 0-600 m, with the added capability of indicating an assigned height. 'Dangerous height signals' (*signaly opasnoi vysoty*) could be set to trigger at 50, 100, 150, 200, 250, 300 and 400 m above terrain height.

Radio equipment

The Tu-128's radio equipment comprised the following systems:

- a 1RSB-70-US-8 HF communications radio (transceiver);
- an RSIU-5V (R-802) command radio; (RSIU is the abbreviation for *Radio-Stantsiya Istrebityel'naya Ul'trakorotkovolnaya-5V*, i.e. Fighter Radio Station Ultra-short Wave [VHF]);
- an SPU-7 (*Samolyotnoye Peregovornoye Ustroistvo*) intercom system.

The 1RSB-70-US-8 Communications Radio

The transceiver was used to maintain two-way high-frequency (HF) contact with ground radio stations:

- The frequency spectrum of the 1RSB-70 (R807) *transmitter* covered 2-16.1 MHz;
- The frequency spectrum of the US-8 *receiver* covered 2.1-20 MHz and 230-500 KHz.

The radio operated in radio-telephone (RT), telegraph with undamped oscillations, and modulated telegraph (1,000 Hz) modes. The transmitter could be tuned to eleven fixed wavelengths, while the receiver was continuously tuneable, without fixed tuning, permitting reception of telegraph and telephone signals on four short wave- and one medium wave-length sub-range. The transmitter could operate continuously for 50 minutes, while longer-duration communications could be maintained by observing a cycle of 5 minutes of transmission and 10 minutes of reception. The radio's range in RT mode was 800-1,000 km (500-620 miles) and in WT mode 2,500-3,000 km (1,555-1,865 miles), while the air-to-air range between aircraft was 300-500 km (190-310 miles).

The 1RSB-70-US-8 radio was a very old piece of equipment, having been used initially on the Tu-4 'Bull' bomber derived from the Boeing B-29 'Stratofortress'. Therefore, from 42nd-series aircraft onwards (from c/n 504201), some Tu-128s began to receive the R-846OE *Prizma* HF radio, with its antenna mounted in a modified fin tip. With this modification, the folded dipole antenna array of the old radio, mounted on the starboard side of the fuselage in the area of the cockpit, was removed. (Although it has not been possible to confirm the meaning of the 'OE' suffix, it is believed to stand for '*Obshchii Ehmitter*' [Common Emitter], a type of receiver circuit designed to amplify weak signals, thereby improving the performance of the radio.)

An interesting perspective on a fully armed Tu-128. (*Irina Sadova*)

The RSIU-5V Command Radio

This provided two-way VHF RT communications with relevant ground stations and between aircraft in a formation. The working range of the RSIU-5V was 100-150 MHz on twenty pre-tuned frequencies, the time required to switch from one frequency to another being no more than 4 seconds. In an emergency situation the radio could be powered by the aircraft's on-board DC supply and with AC from the emergency PO-500 inverter.

The range of the RSIU-5V at altitude when working with ground-based RAS-UKV[2] airfield and GCI station installations was typically:

- at 1,000 m (3,280 feet)—not less than 120 km (75 miles);
- at 5,000 m (16,400 feet)—not less than 230 km (143 miles);
- at 10,000 m (32,800 feet)—not less than 350 km (220 miles).

RAS-UKV is the abbreviation for *Radiostantsiya Aviatsionnaya Svyaznaya-Ul'tra-Korotkie Volny*, meaning Aviation VHF Communications Radio Station. Later, the improved R-832 *Evkalipt* (Eucalyptus) radio was installed in place of the RSIU-5V.

The SPU-7 Intercom System

The system provided internal communications between the pilot and navigator, and acted as the interface between them and the aircraft radios (RSIU-5V, 1RSB-70), navigation equipment (ARK-10, RV-UM radio altimeter, RSBN-2S), the *Lazur'-M* GCI data-link and the *Smerch* AI radar. Each crew member could initiate an intercom call by pressing the 'SPU' button in the relevant cockpit, and an external radio call by pressing the 'Radio' button. Pressing this button initiated the 'Transmission' mode; releasing the button selected 'Reception' mode. The pilot received the following signals in his headphones:

- 'Dangerous height ('*Opasnaya Vysota*') indication from the RV-UM radio altimeter (a 400 Hz tone);
- 'Break-off' from intercept ('*Otboy*') from the *Smerch* AI radar computer;
- 'Co-operation' ('*Vzaimodyeystviye*') commands from the *Lazur'-M* data-link.

All these signals could be monitored independently of the position of the mode selector switches on the control panel. The fact that the 'Fiddler' was equipped with an HF radio enabled it to maintain contact with its base airfield and command posts (GCI stations) at distances exceeding the aircraft's operating radius, allowing it to be operated outside the normal range of GCI ground stations. The VHF radio equipment facilitated communications between the aircraft and the ground at distances up to 400 km (250 miles), not only in the medium latitudes but also in the northern latitudes, since the VHF frequency range was not adversely affected by ionospheric disturbances, although in certain situations the radios could be affected by snow clouds, snowflakes and ice.

KZA-B on-board flight recorder

The KZA-B on-board flight recorder was used to monitor the performance of the *Smerch* AI radar and its systems, the *Lazur'-M* data-link, the automatic systems of the R-4 (AA-5 'Ash') missiles and the *Put'-4P* flight navigation system, as well as a number of aircraft system and engine parameters. There were two variants of KZA-B:

- the standard KZA installation (*Shtatnyi Komplekt KZA*);
- the full KZA installation (*Polnyi Komplekt KZA*).

The standard KZA installation comprised the following:

- a PAU-476 camera system, used to photograph the pilot's instrument panel;
- a PAU-473 camera system, used to photograph the screen of the *Smerch* AI radar in the navigator's cockpit.

The film supply for each camera was sufficient for 40 minutes of filming.

The full KZA set was installed for the analysis of the operation of selected items of equipment during dedicated check flights and comprised the following units:

- a K10-51 oscillograph (for recording the parameters of the *Lazur'-M* data-link, 'one-time' commands, speed and flight altitude);
- a K12-21 oscillograph No. 1 (for recording parameters 1 and 3 of the R-4 (AA-5 'Ash') missile;
- a K12-21 oscillograph No. 2 (for recording parameters 2 and 4 of the R-4 (AA-5 'Ash') missile;[3]
- a K12-21 oscillograph No. 3 (for recording the operating parameters of the *Smerch* AI radar and its systems);
- a ZP-15 acceleration recorder.

The cameras were switched on (automatically) in response to the command 'Switch on HT' for the *Smerch* AI radar, or after placing the switch 'With Radar— Without Radar' on the navigator's control panel to the 'Without Radar' position. The K10-51 oscillograph was switched on following retraction of the nose-wheel leg (at this stage, film travel speed was 0.5 mm/sec). On the command 'Switch on HT for Smerch AI Radar' a relay operated to switch the film travel speed to 5 mm/sec and the ZP-15 acceleration recorder and oscillograph No. 3 (K12-21) commenced recording. Oscillographs K12-21 Nos 1 and 2 started recording on the command 'Lock-on' received from the *Smerch* AI radar.

The PAU-476 and PAU-473 cameras could both be switched on manually using the 'Event Marker' ('*Otmyetka yavlyeniya*') buttons in the pilot's and navigator's cockpits. Apart from the KZA-B flight recorder, the Tu-128 was also equipped with a K2-717 velocity-height recorder which produced a continuous height and equivalent airspeed print-out, using spring-balanced needles to scratch these variable parameters onto special film.

THE *SMERCH* AIRBORNE INTERCEPTION RADAR SYSTEM

The *Smerch* airborne radar guidance unit (AI radar) comprised the *Smerch* radar itself and the *Smerch-VM* associated computer system. The radar was known in the West by its NATO code-name 'Big Nose', the *VM* part of the Russian designation being an abbreviation of *vychislityel'naya mashina*, literally meaning calculating machine, i.e. computer.

The *Smerch* system performed the following tasks:

- searching for and detection of airborne targets in the aircraft's forward hemisphere;
- identification of airborne targets in conjunction with the SRZO-2M (*Samolyotnyi Radiolokatsionnyi Zaproschik-Otvyetchik*) IFF interrogator/transponder system;
- lock-on and automatic tracking of a selected target in range and elevation;
- calculation and display of data essential for the on-board guidance of the aircraft and missile targeting;
- provision of an interface (communication and information exchange) with the guidance heads of the R-4 (AA-5 'Ash') missiles;
- illumination of the target for the R-4R semi-active radar guided missiles during the autonomous flight phase after launch;
- provision of an interface with the *Put'-4P* flight navigation system;
- provision of an interface with the SOD-57M (*Samolyotnyi Otvyetchik Detsimetrovyi*) and SRZO-2M IFF systems;
- provision of an interface with the TsGV-5 master vertical gyro, the KS-6V course and heading system and the TsSV-1M-1V speed and altitude reference unit (receiving data on bank and pitch angles, speed, flight altitude and heading of the interceptor);
- hand-off commands to the weapons system for timely preparation of the missiles for launch during on-board guidance of the interceptor;
- calculation and display of commands indicating break-off from the attack.

The majority of units associated with the *Smerch* radar were mounted in the unpressurised nose section of the aircraft, in the pressure cabin and in the 'technical compartment'. A cooling system provided air at the appropriate temperature for normal operation of the *Smerch* radar and the on-board communications links for the automatic elements (*avtomatiki*) of the missiles, while the required level of constant pressure in the radar processing units was maintained by a pressurised air system. The navigator was responsible for the operation of the *Smerch* radar, the main radar screen and control panel being situated in his cockpit, enabling him to manage the process of detection, identification, selection and lock-on of targets. (A radar screen slaved to the navigator's screen was also situated on the lower right-hand side of the pilot's instrument panel.) When the *Smerch* radar was being used in conjunction with the *Lazur'-M* data-link system during an automatically controlled GCI intercept, the *Lazur'-M* system passed 'one-time' or 'on/off' ('*razoviye*') and continuous ('*plavniye*') commands to the radar.

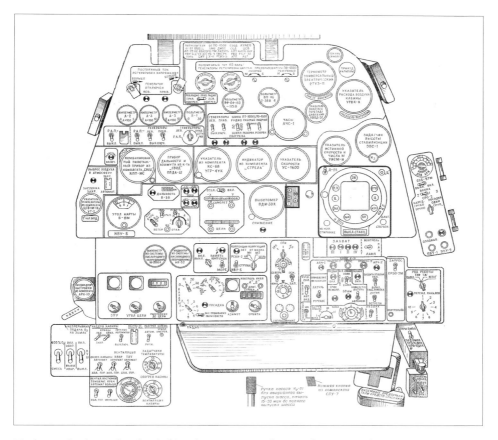

The larger display outlined in bold is the screen providing confirmatory information sent via the *Lazur'* data-link system, with associated light commands given on the navigator's small TS-8 light display, also outlined in red. Immediately below the radar screen are the missile lock-on lights, identified in Roman numerals. Controls for the SOD-57M ATC transponder are on the detached panel to the right of the radar screen. (*Nikolai Popov*)

The 'one-time' commands passed by the *Lazur'-M* data-link to the radar included the following:

- 'Forward Hemisphere', indicating that the ground-controlled intercept would be against a target in the interceptor's forward hemisphere. This command was displayed in the rear cockpit (for the navigator) by illumination of the relevant lamp around the frame of the radar screen and in the front cockpit (for the pilot) on the TS-7 indicator;
- '60 km', providing automatic switch-on of the radar transmitter HT supply and 'Search mode' for the radar antenna drive. This command was indicated by illumination of the relevant lamps on the radar control panel

and on the pilot's TS-7 annunciator panel of the *Put'-4M* flight navigation system, as well as being displayed on the radar screen;
- 'Re-targeting' and 'Beacon', indicating a change of task, with illumination of the relevant lamps on the navigator's radar screen.

Continuous target designation commands, used for the automatic displacement of the antenna search zone in azimuth and continuous displacement in elevation, contained azimuth and elevation information along the line between interceptor and target. Apart from that, continuous values for range and closing speed with the target were also passed.

Performance data of the Smerch AI radar	
Parameter	Value
Detection range against single Tu-16*-sized targets (with 60 per cent probability of detection)	Not less than 50 km (31 miles)
Lock-on range against Tu-16-sized target (with 90 per cent probability)	Not less than 35-45 km (22-28 miles)
Detection range against MiG-19*-sized target	30-45 km (19-28 miles)
Lock-on range against MiG-19-sized target	22-32 km (14-20 miles)
Search zone in azimuth	±30°
Displacement of axis of search zone in azimuth—manual or automatic: Left Right	−40° (tolerance of −2°) +40° (tolerance of −2°)
Search zone in elevation	14°
Displacement in elevation: Automatic Manual	+52° to 3.5° +34° to 10°
Auto-tracking zone in azimuth	±70°
Auto-tracking in elevation	+70° to −35°
Scan period	Not more than 3.5 seconds
Gyro-stabilisation of the search zone in bank	±70°
Gyro-stabilisation of the search zone in pitch	+70° to −35°
Size of 'dead zone'	0-2 km
Preparation time for the equipment after switching on	3-4 minutes

It has always been the Russian convention to use 'own aircraft' types when comparing target size relative to the interceptor, rather than using Western aircraft of similar dimensions that would have provided more realistic targeting parameters.

The *Smerch* radar conducted its search procedure within a defined area unsurprisingly called the 'search zone', although the design of the system permitted displacement of the axis of the search zone, thereby extending the search sector. Control of displacement of the search zone in the horizontal and vertical axes could be achieved either automatically from a GCI station or manually by the navigator. The search zone scan period was 3.5 seconds, and the *Smerch* radar operated in conjunction with the *Lazur'-M* radio-telemetry data-link and the SRZO-2M IFF system to locate and identify the target.

The SRZO-2M identification system

This is the airborne component of the national IFF system and is a radar interrogator/transponder. In transponder (*otvyetchik*) mode the SRZO-2M provided identification as a 'friendly' aircraft on the screens of the ground surveillance and GCI radar stations of the National Air Defence (PVO) network, as well as the radar screens of Soviet naval ships and other Soviet aircraft. In interrogation (*zaproschik*) mode it was used, in conjunction with the *Smerch* radar, to identify any aircraft that appeared on the navigator's radar screen. The equipment was fully automatic. The SRZO-2M control panel was in the navigator's cockpit and the antennas (eight in all) were mounted in cut-outs in the wing centre-section and fuselage, providing virtually 360° coverage around the aircraft. The range of the SRZO-2M was up to 300 km (186 miles) along an imaginary line from the ground (ship) to the aircraft, and up to 40 km (25 miles) along an imaginary line from aircraft to aircraft.

In target identification mode the *Smerch* radar and SRZO-2M radiated simultaneously on different frequencies during which time the responder components of SRZO-2M and SOD-57M were blocked from receiving signals, achieved using synchronisation commands passed to the receiving circuits from the *Smerch* radar. For extraction of the identification pulses, video signals from the interrogated aircraft were passed by the *Smerch* radar to the SRZO-2M system and, after processing and identification, were passed back to the *Smerch* radar for display on the navigator's screen, indicating whether the detected target was '*svoy*' (i.e. 'own side' or 'friend') or '*chuzhoy*' ('foe'). If the target return was a double bar marker (=) the target was 'friendly' but if there was no second marker then the target was 'foe'. When a Soviet aircraft was interrogated by other radars using the *Kremnii-2* (Silicon-2) national IFF system (airborne or ground-based), the SRZO-2M responded with signals confirming that it belonged to the armed forces of the USSR. Simultaneous with this, the 'target's' SOD-57M 'responder' provided the ground radar site with its range to that site, this simultaneous response being synchronised by a pulse sent to SOD-57M by SRZO-2M. Between 1982 and 1984, one of 356 AP's Tu-128s (Bort No. 24) was used for trials of the improved D-band

Parol' (Password) IFF system and SO-69 transponder. Although the trials proved the compatibility of this newer system with the older avionics of the 'Fiddler', the upgrade was not adopted for the entire fleet since the type was due to be replaced by the more advanced MiG-31 'Foxhound'.

Target interception and preparation to launch the Bisnovat R-4 (AA-5 'Ash') missiles

From the moment of lock-on by the *Smerch* radar, the *Smerch-VM* computer started to calculate the parameters essential for guiding the Tu-128 to the predicted point of impact of the missile with the target, carrying out the '*gorka*' zoom-climb manoeuvre and preparing the missiles for launch. The results were passed to the pilot's PP-1PK indicator in the form of targeting errors (deviation of the director arrows from the centre of the dial). The maximum permitted missile launch range was calculated by using the speed and altitude of the interceptor and the closing speed with the target. Before matching current range to target with maximum permitted launch range, the interceptor's targeting errors had to be corrected to permitted values and the missiles had to be ready for launch. In order to extend the potential missile launch zone, the Tu-128 could perform the zoom climb manoeuvre, the command

The forward antenna of the SOD-57M transponder was located on the centreline immediately behind the radome of the *Smerch* AI radar. The word stencilled on the radome support frame is 'НИ3' ('NIZ') meaning 'bottom'. This was a necessary instruction since the radome circumference was perfectly symmetrical but the mounting spigots had specific locations around the support frame and had to be correctly aligned. (*Viktor Kudryavtsev*)

to perform the climb being passed by the *Smerch-VM* computer. This command would only be given in the event that the calculated time for carrying out the zoom climb was equal to or greater than the calculated closing time of the interceptor with the target. The calculated closing time actually determined the time remaining for the achievement of maximum permitted launch range. The time for carrying out the zoom climb fell within the range: +25 seconds (i.e. up to the time of reaching a distance between interceptor and target equal to maximum permitted launch range) to –12 seconds (i.e. after reaching maximum permitted launch range). Dependent upon the value of the calculated closing time, the *Smerch-VM* computer calculated and passed to the 'communication and synchronisation unit' the 'one-time' and 'timing' commands (after a specific time interval) to prepare the missiles for launch. These comprised the following:

1. the command 'Switch over to Liter' ('*Pyerekhod na lityer*'),[4] sent to switch on and warm up the 'oscillator units' of the semi-active radar seeker heads of the R-4R missiles. Here the word '*lityer*' refers to the high-frequency oscillator in the missile seeker head and the corresponding unit of the *Smerch* radar. (The *lityer* unit determined the operating frequency [RF] of the radar transmitter and the seeker head receiving unit.) Switching from one *lityer* to another changed the operating frequency of the *Smerch* radar and the associated seeker head within a small tuning range. On the ground, the missile technicians could tune one missile to one frequency and the second missile to another, using interchangeable modules (*lityery*). The seeker heads of the R-4R missiles on other Tu-128s of the regiment would be tuned to other frequencies within the operating spectrum, the frequency difference allowing each missile to fly out to its target without suffering mutual interference from other Tu-128s in the group. Moreover, the peacetime frequencies used, for example, during live missile firing practice were different from the wartime settings, limiting the value of electronic intelligence gathering by NATO reconnaissance aircraft during these events;

2. the 'Readiness' ('*Podgotovka*') command, when the calculated closure time was not greater than 13 seconds (this command also triggering the preparation of other missile systems);

3. the 'Guidance' ('*Navyedyenie*') command, passed between 2.6 and 4 seconds after the 'Readiness' command. This command triggered the commencement of search for and lock-on to the target by the semi-active radar seeker heads of the R-4R missiles. Simultaneously the command 'Commencement of frequency stabilisation' ('*Nachalo stabilizatsii chastot*') of the 'high-frequency units' (oscillators) of the semi-active seeker heads was passed (when each of the two R-4R seeker heads would tune to the frequency of the signal reflected from the target);

4. the command 'Frequency stabilised' ('*Chastota stabilizirovana*') was passed 7 seconds after the 'Readiness' command. After a late lock-on by the *Smerch* radar this command was passed after 'Switch over to Liter' had been sent from the communication unit, but no sooner than 1 to ±0.5 seconds after the 'Guidance' command;

5. the 'Launch Permitted' ('*Pusk Razreshyon*') command was passed on reaching the maximum permitted launch range and with a calculated closure time of not more than 0.5 seconds. However, in order for the missiles to be able to leave the launch rails, each missile had to receive the command 'Ready for Launch' ('*K Pusku Gotov*');

6. generation of the general command 'Ready for Launch' occurred on fulfilment of the five following conditions:

   a. the calculated closure time was no greater than 0.5 seconds;
   b. the distance to target was no greater than the maximum permitted missile launch range;
   c. the *Smerch-VM* computer was continuously calculating targeting errors permissible for launch;
   d. the sighting angle to the target was no greater than 45°;
   e. the signals 'GG' ('*Golovka Gotova*')—'Seeker Head Ready'—and 'APR' (*Avtopilot Rakiety Gotov*)—'Missile Autopilot Ready'—were passed from the missile to the aircraft.

The command 'Ready for Launch' was indicated by the illumination of a red light on the pilot's instrument panel, with the appropriate number of the missile shown on the lamp cover. On illumination of this light, and the pilot pressing the 'Launch' button on the control wheel, the missile would then leave the launch rail.

7. the command 'End of Illumination' ('*Konyets Oblucheniya*') was passed by the *Smerch-VM* computer at a specific moment after launch of one or both R-4R missiles. It was passed if the distance to target was no greater than the break-off distance, or when the time of illumination was greater than 45 seconds;

8. the 'Break-off' command ('*Otvorot*') was passed after carrying out the above-mentioned commands, taking account of a safe exit from the attack.

The commands 'End of Illumination' and 'Break-off' were indicated on the pilot's TS-7 annunciator display and the navigator's radar display.

From those conditions necessary for creating the command 'Launch Permitted', it follows that missile launch was possible only within the spectrum from 'maximum' to 'minimum' permitted launch range, calculated by the *Smerch-VM* computer. The matching of these distances to the missile's potential launch zone in terms of range were the main criteria in the creation of the formula used to calculate the permitted launch distances. The potential launch zone (*Zona Vozmozhnovo Puska* or ZVP) was defined by the specific energy capabilities of the missile for various launch conditions. Generation of the command 'Launch Permitted' was not possible at a distance beyond which the missile would be incapable of destroying the target. Moreover, accurate calculation of ZVP was compromised by the (limited) processing capability of the computer, so for the majority of attack and missile launch conditions the potential launch zone calculated by *Smerch-VM* was smaller than that considered to be theoretically possible.

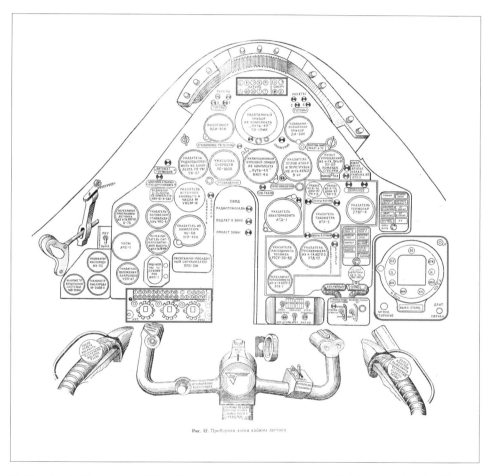

Рис. 12. Приборная доска кабины лётчика

Outlined in bold at the top of the pilot's instrument panel is the small oblong panel of the TS-7 interface with the data-link system, giving access to *Lazur'* (on the left of the panel) and *Smerch* radar status (on the right). This is flanked by eight missile status lights, four showing presence on pylon and four showing 'Readiness' ('ГОТОВЫ') respectively. On the lower left of the instrument panel are the *Lazur'* data-link control controls and confirmatory lights, with the *Smerch* ('Big Nose') screen on the far right of the panel. (*Nikolai Popov*)

THE R-4 (AA-5 'ASH') AIR-TO-AIR MISSILE

The standard armament of the Tu-128 was four Bisnovat R-4 air-to-air missiles, also known by the Soviet industry code as Article or Product 36 (*Izdeliye 36*). Two of these had semi-active radar seeker heads, developed under Tikhomirov in OKB-339; the other two had infrared seekers, developed under Nikolayev in TsKB-589 (Central Design Bureau-589), equipped respectively with RV-80 (*Radiolokatsionnyi Vzryvatyel'*) radar fuses and NOV-80N (*Opticheskii Vzryvatyel'*) optical fuses.[5] Later, design leadership on the semi-active seeker head passed to N. A.Viktorov in NII-648 (Scientific Research Institute-648) and on the infrared seeker, to D. M. Khorol. The RV-80 fuses had two antennas located close to the wing, with another two in the tail section of the missile. The NOV-80N optical fuses were aligned in three rows with two windows each, displaced around the body of the missile. The missiles were suspended on four specially configured APU-128 (*Aviatsionnoye Puskovoye Ustroistvo*) launch rails, mounted in pairs under each wing. The two semi-active radar-guided missiles, with PARG-10VV (*Polu-Avtomaticheskaya Radiolokatsionnaya Golovka*) seeker heads, were mounted on the outer pylons and the two IR-guided missiles, with T-80NB (*Tyeplovaya* [*Golovka*]) seeker heads, were mounted on the inner pylons. The APU-128, a load-bearing beam equipped with launch rails, attached to the load-bearing structure of the wing at the front and rear of the assembly, had the following functions:

- attachment of the missiles to the launch mechanism;
- provision of an emergency release mode, without fusing ('*nievzryv*', i.e. 'safe');
- provision of missile motor start-up and indication of missile status.

The missile pylons of the Tu-128 were equipped with detachable lifting gear to raise the missiles up to the launch rails. The lifting gear was in the form of a system of manually operated winches for each pylon, using DYa-SS drive mechanisms and was designed for loading container racks onto the Tu-16 'Badger' for some of its specialised roles. The winches were mounted on the sides of the APU-128 launch rail, while the missile itself had special attachment points; with the aid of the winches the missiles could be raised up to the launch rail and locked in position. The K-80 (R-4) 'automatic system' provided communication between the missile and the *Smerch* radar, as well as the electronic links necessary for preparing the missile for launch and the launch itself. The K-80 electronic units were mounted in the aircraft's main 'technical compartment' and on fuselage Frame No. 25. The pilot had a control panel with a sequence of four green lights to indicate the presence of a missile on each of the pylons, and another four red lights indicating missile launch readiness.

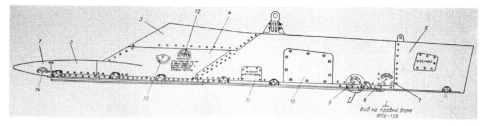

Diagram of APU-128 Missile Pylon: **1** – Nose fairing; **2** – Intermediate fairing; **3** – Upper fairing; **4** – Lower fairing; **5** – Rear fairing; **6** – Access to missile electrical power supply ('*Nakal*'); **7** – Main skin structure; **8** – Access to release lock after emergency missile jettison; **9** – Locking mechanism access; **10** – Access to firing mechanism; **11** – Access to warning light mechanism; **12** – Electro-pneumatic plug connection access; **13** – Electro-pneumatic plug arming selector; **14** – Arming/disarming of release mechanism. (*Nikolai Popov*)

The missiles were supplied with compressed air from the parent aircraft's own supply, the connection being made by means of special valves mounted on the launch pylons. On launch, or emergency jettisoning of the missiles, the valves shut off automatically and reverted to the closed position, preventing loss of air from the Tu-128's limited supply. The electrical connection linking the missile with the relevant equipment on board the aircraft was also made via a quickly detachable plug (albeit having eighty-two pins!) mounted on the launch pylon. The plug automatically disconnected from the missile on launch, or in the event of emergency jettisoning. The missiles could be jettisoned in an emergency by both the pilot and the navigator, the procedure involving simultaneous release of all four missiles, but only in 'safe' mode, without fusing. Emergency jettison was achieved with the aid of an explosive firing mechanism mounted on each launch pylon.

On switching on the HT power supply, the *Smerch* radar passed the 'one-time' command 'Warm-up' to the synchronisation unit. When being guided by ground-based data-link, the 'Warm-up' command was passed to the R-4 (AA-5 'Ash') missile control system via *Lazur'-M* encoded transmissions. This would normally occur around 4(±0.5) minutes before the end of data-link guidance. Independent of its source, the 'Warm-up' command was interlocked by the synchronisation unit and could only be cleared by switching off the HT for the *Smerch* radar, receipt of the 'Re-targeting' command, *or* by means of unlocking the original selection by briefly switching off the HT, then switching it on again, using the 'System' switch. Further preparation of the missile for launch, generation of the general command 'Ready for Launch' and radar illumination of the target occurred in the sequence calculated by the *Smerch-VM* computer.

Apart from the commands calculated in the pre-launch preparation phase, two particular commands were passed to the missile before launch, these being $V_0 > 600$ *m/sec* and $V_0 > 1,000$ *m/sec*, where V_0 was the average closing speed of

This view of an R-4RM variant of the 'Ash' missile shows how low the weapon was mounted on the aircraft. (*Nikolai Popov*)

the missile with the target. These signals produced changes in the coefficient of amplification of the control signal in the APR-80 missile autopilot and generation of an additional delay for operation. Missile launch occurred after fulfilling the previously mentioned five conditions. Selection of the relevant missile for launch depended upon these readiness conditions being met, and launch could either be performed singly or in salvo, with either two or all four missiles in the salvo. In this case the interval between missile release in salvo was between 0 and 0.2 seconds, the selector switch being on a special panel in the pilot's cockpit. Selection of a missile for launch was automatic, calculated in accordance with its readiness condition. Interrogation of the missile about readiness state took place in the following sequence: port inner, starboard inner, port outer, starboard outer.

Guidance of the missile onto the target employed the 'proportional closure rate' method, the essence of which was to guide the missile to a point where the missile and target would meet, determined by their current motion parameters. The targeting procedure consisted of the fact that the sight line between missile and target would not change its angular position relative to the axis of the missile body. After launching the semi-active radar-guided variant of the R-4 (AA-5 'Ash') missile, the Tu-128 had to continue to illuminate the target until it was destroyed, or the missile's own self-destruct mechanism triggered. In the case of firing an infra-red-guided variant, the 'Fiddler' could break away from the attack immediately.

If the missile passed within the permitted distance to trigger the fuse mechanisms (i.e. no greater than 15 m [50 feet] from the target) the fuse would command the warhead to detonate.

The control units for the missiles were located in the pilot's and navigator's cockpits. The pilot had a separate missile control panel on the starboard side of the cockpit, with indicator lamps showing the presence of missiles on the relevant launch rails and missile readiness lights mounted on the instrument panel. The missile launch button was located on the right-hand 'horn' of the control wheel. In the navigator's cockpit there was also a separate control panel, plus lamps indicating 'lock-on' by the semi-active radar-guided seeker heads of the relevant missiles and the missile emergency jettison switch. The missile control sub-panel was mounted on the left-hand side of the navigator's cockpit, with missile 'lock-on' and emergency jettison indicator lamps mounted on the instrument panel.

It is perhaps opportune at this point to mention the historical progression of the two missile types towards certification, 'factory tests' having been planned for the first quarter of 1961 and State trials for the end of the same year. The factory test programme was initiated only weeks after the first flight of the Tu-128 prototype on 18 March 1961, preceded by the first autonomous test launches of the K-80 (the prototype designation of the R-4 missile). This work involved four launches from a ground test rig and four from a Tu-104LL flying test-bed (SSSR-L5406).[6] The aircraft was one of the original pre-production batch, before the Tu-104 was assigned the CCCP-42xxx (SSSR-42xxx) series of registrations. It was also one of the few airliners (if not the only one) ever used to launch missiles! In 1962, further launches were made from the Tu-104LL and the Tu-128, nine of which were carried out using telemetry-equipped semi-active and IR-guided variants against PM-2 (*Parashutnaya Mishen'*)—i.e. 'parachute target' but also sometimes described as *Planiruyushchaya Mishen'* or 'gliding target'—and VUM (*Vysotnaya Upravlyayushchaya Mishen'*) high-altitude (radio)-controlled targets. After this, test firings of the IR-guided versions commenced, using radio-controlled converted Il-28 'Beagle' light bombers as targets, the first of which was shot down on 27 September 1962. A further two Il-28M (*Mishen'*—i.e. controlled target) targets were shot down before the end of the year, but forward hemisphere (semi-active seeker) engagements of the 'Beagle' targets were less successful: of fifteen launches against eight targets, only one was destroyed. However, after 'tweaking' the radar fuses, recognised to be the main cause of the failures, another Il-28M was shot down in a forward hemisphere engagement.

Availability of the third prototype (Bort No. 3), the first aircraft with a near production-standard avionics suite, including the *Smerch* AI radar, enabled full-scale testing of the semi-active variant of the 'Ash' missile to get under way. Thus, between August 1963 and May 1965, the missile armament of the Tu-128 was tested in conjunction with other elements of the aircraft's equipment as part of Stage 'B' of the State trials programme at Vladimirovka (Akhtubinsk).[7] Once again, the principal target used in the trials was the Il-28M, intercepted from both forward and rear hemisphere engagements. Following the trials, it was decided that the missile airframe needed to be 'beefed up' and the filter units of the radar fuses changed. Two successful launches had also been made against Yak-25RV Mandrake targets flying at 17,500 m (57,415 feet), with a height differential of 4,500 m (14,760 feet) above the launch aircraft. Successful conclusion of the State trials led to an official recommendation for acceptance of the Tu-128S-4 system into PVO service and for production to commence at Voronezh, with series production of the K-80 missile to be undertaken from 1963 by Factory No. 455 at Kaliningrad.[8]

Principal data for the R-4 (AA-5 'Ash') missile	
Parameter	Value
Operational altitude range	8, 000-21,000 m (*26,250-68,900 feet*)
Launch distance: – R-4R in forward hemisphere – R-4R in rear hemisphere – R-4T in rear hemisphere	up to 20-25 km (*12.5-15.5 miles*) up to 10-12 km (*6.2-7.5 miles*) up to 10-12 km (*6.2-7.5 miles*)
Firing angle: Semi-active radar-guided version IR-guided version	All-aspect 0-3/4 rear hemisphere
Range of initial launch velocities	250-500 m/sec (*820-1,640 feet/sec*)
Maximum height differential of target above the interceptor at launch	7,000 to 8,000 m (*22,965-26,250 feet*)
Range of closing speeds of missile on target	200-2,000 m/sec (*656-6,560 feet/sec*)
Length	5,360 mm (*11.817 feet*)
Diameter of missile body: Maximum In cylindrical section	343 mm (*1.125 feet*) 315 mm (*1.033 feet*)
Launch weight	483 kg (*1,065 lb*)
Warhead type	High-explosive fragmentation
Quantity and weight of fragments	2,400 x 0.006 kg (*0.013 lb*)
Warhead weight	53.5 kg (*118 lb*)
Operating time of the PRD-84 solid fuel rocket motor	5.8 ±1.2 seconds
Duration of control cycle	40 seconds
Lock-on distance of the semi-active radar seeker head against a Tu-16-sized target	20-25 km (*12.5-15.5 miles*)
Viewing angle of the radar seeker head	±5.5°
Field of view (width of polar diagram of the radar seeker head)	±7.5° ±0.5°

'Field of confirmation' of radar seeker head	±5.5°
Lock-on distance of the IR seeker head against a Tu-16-sized target with a 3/4-0/4 rear aspect	15-20 km (*9.3-12.5 miles*)
Viewing angle of the IR seeker head	±60°
Instantaneous field of view of IR seeker head	1°15'
'Field of confirmation' of the IR seeker head	±2.8°
Time of remote activation of the missile fuse after launch	4.6 ±0.8 seconds
Maximum g-loading	±21 g
G-limit in each control channel defined by structural strength	±15 g

The upgraded R-4M (AA-5 'Ash') air-to-air missile

After the Tu-128S-4M integrated 'long-range interception complex' had been accepted for service, the Tu-128M aircraft themselves were upgraded and equipped with the R-4M variant of the AA-5 'Ash' missile (also known as Article 36M). The area of the control surfaces of the R-4M (R-4MR and R-4MT) missiles was reduced and they were strengthened with steel wing tip anti-flutter plates, whilst the control servos were changed to a more powerful type with almost twice the power of the original units. Other control system changes were incorporated to enable the missiles to be launched at low altitude, including the addition of a 'compensating antenna' (*kompensatsionnaya antenna*) for the radar seeker head. The introduction of a 'compensatory contour' in the radar seeker circuitry allowed the system to filter out terrain reflections, which at low altitude interfered with guidance of the missile onto the target. New radar fuses were installed on the R-4MR semi-active radar homing variant, with four antennas mounted in front of the stub wings. Introduced in 1973, the improved R-4MT infrared-guided variant was equipped with LOMO-designed 'Sokol-M' twin-channel optical fuses (Article 123) incorporating three rows of three windows (two receiving and one transmitting window). They were displaced by an angle of 120° with respect to each other, to give 360° coverage around the body of the missile. Apart from this, a special unit was incorporated in the weapons control system of the Tu-128M, known as the BOP-36M (*Blok Ogranichenii Puska*) or launch limiter unit for Article 36M. This was designed to prevent simultaneous asymmetric launches of two missiles from one wing, as well as a salvo launch of all four missiles. The BOP-36M was always switched on, but depending upon height and the specific task, the pilot could override the limiter using the 'Cancel Limits' ('*Snyatie Ogranichenii*') switch on his instrument panel.

Data for the upgraded R-4M missile		Article 36MR		Article 36MT
Missile parameters		PPS	ZPS	ZPS
1.	Target destruction altitude (km)	2-21	0.5-21	
2.	Target altitude differential (m)	7,000-8,000		
3.	Target speed (kph)	Up to 2,500	1,250	
4.	Target aspect at launch	All-aspect		0/4-3/4
5.	Launch range against Tu-16-sized target	8-20/25 km		3-12 km
6.	Maximum manoeuvring g-load of selected target	1.5-2.0 at altitudes from 0.5 to 15 km 1.5-1.0 at altitudes from 15 to 21 km		

	Missile parameters	Article 36MR	Article 36MTI	Article 36R	Article 36T	Article 36TI
1.	Fuselage length (with tracking flare) (mm)	5538	5569	5530	5530	5652
2.	Fuselage diameter (mm)	315				
3.	Tail surface dimensions (mm)	1,060 x 1,060				
4.	Wingspan (mm)	1,500				
5.	Wing planform	Delta				
6.	Sweep angle	78° 30'				
7.	Type of control surface	Trapezoidal				
8.	Span (mm)/deflection angle	1,330/35°				
9.	Initial flight weight (kg)	500	492	483	489	485
10.	Terminal flight weight (kg)	370	362	361	367	363
11.	Weight of warhead (kg)	55	55	53	53	53
	Launch aircraft	Tu-128M		Tu-128M, Tu-128		

R-4R (MR)—missile with semi-active radar seeker head
R-4T (MT)—missile with infrared seeker head
PPS—*Peryednyaya Polusfyera* (Forward Hemisphere)
ZPS—*Zadnyaya Polusfyera* (Rear Hemisphere)

The letter 'I' in the missile designation indicates that it is equipped with an optical fuse; in this case the choice of letter is purely arbitrary and not an abbreviation.

The starboard side of the 'Ash' missile was devoid of any technical markings. (*Nikolai Popov*)

The requirement to upgrade the R-4 missile was driven by perceived changes in attack profiles by the potential enemy, involving anticipated low-level penetration of the Soviet mainland. This led to a decision in December 1968 to provide the Tu-128-80 (i.e. the Tu-128S-4) 'complex' with a commensurate capability, although trials did not get under way until the early 1970s. Trials of the modified aircraft and weapons duly commenced at Vladimirovka (Akhtubinsk) and ran from 10 March 1973 until 24 July 1974, leading to formal acceptance of the improved Tu-128-80M (Tu-128S-4M) system along with the upgraded R-4MR and R-4MT missiles. The 'MR' variant was equipped with a new seeker head, the PARG-15VV, while the infrared 'MT' version received the improved T-80NMD seeker and the aforementioned 'Sokol-M' optical fuse system. The missile motor was also upgraded to the PRD-84M (*Porokhovoy Reaktivnyi Dvigatyel'*) standard and ECM resistance was improved; target engagement with an IR-guided R-4MT could be achieved at heights down to 50 m (165 feet) in pursuit mode and from 2,000 m (6,560 feet) in forward hemisphere engagements, previously only possible with the semi-active variant.

Self-protection systems

In the late 1970s and early 1980s, a number of Tu-128s were modified to carry the SPO-3 (*Sistyema Preduprezhdyeniya ob Obluchenii*) radar homing and warning system, the antennas of which were mounted on the rear of the undercarriage nacelles and the leading edges of the wing. Also known as *Sirena* 3 (Siren 3),

SPO-3 was the only self-defensive system ever installed on the Tu-128, which, being designed as a pure defender of homeland airspace, was never expected to become a target itself.

MAIN DESIGN AND PERFORMANCE CHARACTERISTICS OF THE *VOZDUKH-1M* GROUND-CONTROLLED INTERCEPT (GCI) SYSTEM

In the 1960s and 1970s, GCI sites of the former USSR's PVO anti-aircraft air defence divisions and fighter corps incorporated *Vozdukh-1M* and *Vozdukh-1* ground-based control and guidance systems, linked with *Kaskad-M* data-encoding transmitters and *Lazur'-M* data-link airborne receivers. The automated *Vozdukh-1M* system was designed to provide air situation warning broadcasts and control of fighter assets in the relevant region, as required. *Vozdukh-1M* fulfilled the following tasks:

- collection of data on the air situation at GCI sites within a radius of 600 km (373 miles), or 1,000 km (621 miles) for the *Vozdukh-1M* system;
- data-link (i.e. automatic) guidance of air defence interceptors onto a target, or targets, with an accuracy of ±15° in angle of 'impact' and 3-5 km (1.9-3.1 miles) in distance to target;
- data-link homing guidance (i.e. automatic guidance) of the interceptor back to base to pick up the airfield's normal air traffic services for landing.

The *Vozdukh-1M* system comprised, *inter alia*, the following GCI, surveillance and height-finding radars:

- P-35 'Bar Lock', P-12M 'Spoon Rest', P-14 'Tall King', P-15 'Flat Face', P-80, PRV-9, PRV-10 or PRV-11 'Side Net', integrated with the following sub-systems:
- apparatus for the collection and transmission of data, providing auto-mated warning broadcasts to command posts concerning the air situation within a radius of 1,200 km (745 miles), the projection of these data onto electronic screens and plotting boards, and also control of radar units monitoring the activity of fighter assets within their jurisdiction;
- the *Kaskad-M* system, a specialised ground-based computer, designed to provide an automatic solution in terms of the guidance geometry neces-sary to direct the Tu-128 interceptor onto its target;
- ground and airborne elements of the *Lazur'-M* radio-telemetry data-link system used to send guidance and target designation commands processed by *Kaskad-M* to the Tu-128 for display on the pilot's navigation instru-ments and on the TS-7 indicator light panel;

- radios providing two-way communications for transmission and reception of air situation broadcasts, control of radar sites, communications with interceptors, other command posts and GCI sites, as well as internal communications within command posts. All elements of the *Vozdukh* system were road-mobile and mounted in specialised vehicles or trailers.

The ground-based *Kremnii-2* IFF and airborne SOD-57M transponder systems enabled GCI sites, command posts and base ATC facilities to track and monitor the 'Fiddler' during intercepts. The SOD-57M was an airborne transponder operating in the decimetric portion of the electro-magnetic spectrum (i.e. at a wavelength between 0.1 and 1 m, corresponding to frequencies between 300 and 3,000 MHz) and was designed to fulfil the following functions:

- to extend the effective range of centimetric wavelength ground radars (those operating on wavelengths around 0.01 m, i.e. frequencies of 3-30 GHz);
- individual identification and determination of the altitude of aircraft fitted with the system, displaying these parameters on the PPI (Plan Position Indicator) screens of radar sites monitoring given aircraft whenever the pilot pressed the 'Identification' ('*Opoznavaniye*') button on his control yoke;
- separation of the Tu-128's own radar return (blip) from background clutter from local fixed obstacles and heavy cloud;
- extension of guidance capability at short ranges from a radar site, when the aircraft could disappear in the 'dead zone' ('cone of silence').

The SOD-57M transponder worked, in general, with ground-based surveillance radars such as the P-20, P-25 and P-30 which operated in the 10-cm wavelength. Apart from this, it was also used in conjunction with *Globus-2* (Globe-2) ATC radars which provided regional, airfield and landing approach facilities at Soviet military airfields and enabled flights to be undertaken in IMC conditions.

Kaskad-M

This formed part of the *Vozdukh-1M* system and was used to generate an automatically calculated navigation and guidance solution (*pribornoye resheniye*) to direct the Tu-128 onto its airborne target or targets. The resolution of these tasks—navigation and guidance—could be achieved by using data from local radar stations or secondary data from broadcast systems (i.e. using data from other GCI stations). However, to increase the operational effectiveness of the earlier series *Vozdukh-1* installations, they were upgraded and *Kaskad-M* equipment could be integrated with the older system as a supplementary fit. *Kaskad-M* was not a computer as the term is understood today, calculations being performed using electro-mechanical devices which to some extent resembled the mechanical calculators used in bomb-sights of the 1950s and 1960s.

	Main technical performance characteristics of *Kaskad-M*			
	Parameter	Units	From	To
1	Rectangular coordinates	kilometres	−600	+600
2	Polar coordinates: Range to target (interceptor) Azimuth of target (interceptor)	kilometres degrees	20 0	350 360
3	Speed of target (interceptor)	Kph	500 (600)	3,600
4	Course of target (interceptor)	degrees	0	360
5	Altitude of target (interceptor)	metres	500	30,000
6	Monitored flight time of target (interceptor)	minutes	0	30
7	Maximum turning angle of the interceptor	degrees	0	315
8	Radius of turn	kilometres	10	80
9	Length of flight path segment after turn	kilometres	0	120
10	Distance from TKN (*Tochka Kontsa Navyedyeniya*—End of Guidance Point) to intercept boundary	kilometres	0	30
11	Angle of roll-out onto target	degrees	0	180
12	'Interceptor-Target' azimuth	degrees	0	360
13	'Interceptor-Target' elevation	degrees	-42	+42
14	Range 'Interceptor-Target'	kilometres	0	100
15	Closing speed 'Interceptor-Target'	Kph	0	+7,200
16	Vertical speed of interceptor	m/sec	0	±360

The Lazur'-M radio-telemetry data-link

Lazur'-M (*Radio-Telemetricheskaya Liniya* or RTL) was a major component of the *Vozdukh-1M* integrated fighter control system and was designed to provide automated GCI guidance of Soviet interceptors onto intruding enemy aircraft. *Lazur'-M* was itself an element of the Tu-128S-4 'interception complex', providing a 'speechless' link between GCI ground stations and the aircraft. It received data-linked guidance commands from the ground and displayed them on the pilot's flight instruments and the special light panels (TS-7 and TS-8) on the pilot's and navigator's instrument panels. Responding to these commands, the pilot would direct his aircraft onto the target right up to the moment when the *Smerch* radar achieved 'lock-on'. Additionally, special command signals were transmitted to the aircraft to accomplish the following:

- automatic switching on and off of the '*Nakal*' voltage required to warm-up the high-frequency units of the semi-active radar guidance heads of the R-4R variant of the AA-5 'Ash' missile;
- preliminary orientation of the antenna of the *Smerch* AI radar towards the target search zone.

Lazur'-M used 601 fixed frequencies in the VHF spectrum between 100 and 150 MHz, with eight discrete 'high-frequency channels' (*vysokochastotniye kanaly*) on each fixed frequency. Thus, on each 'high-frequency channel' the *Lazur'-M* data-link could simultaneously guide up to three interceptors (or three *groups* of interceptors) onto three targets (or three *groups* of targets). In order to separate the commands transmitted to aircraft of different groups, *Lazur'-M* incorporated a selection system using specifically assigned numerical codes, with signals transmitted in successive repeated cycles. The tempo of transmission of one set of commands to one interceptor was 1.5 seconds, to two interceptors 3 seconds, and to three interceptors 4.5 seconds. During its operating cycle, the *Lazur'-M* data-link became part of a so-called 'field of commands of tactical interconnection (*polye komand takticheskovo soyedinyeniya*)—a network of associated interlinking systems. This provided mutual co-operation with other guidance stations which were part of the *Vozdukh-1M* system, as well as with the command posts and interceptor units of the given tactical network. The range of *Lazur'-M* was limited to line-of-sight, as for other VHF radio transmissions.

Data relating to the approximate range of the *Lazur'-1M* data-link for various altitudes are given in the following table:

Altitude	1,000 m (3,280 feet)	2,000 m (6,560 feet)	5,000 m (16,400 feet)	10,000 m (32,800 feet)
Range	130 km (81 miles)	160 km (100 miles)	230 km (143 miles)	350 km (217 miles)

In practice, the operating range of *Lazur'-1M* could differ from theoretical values as a result of the influence of the earth's surface (i.e. local topography), atmospheric conditions, and the performance of the aircraft's receiving antennas. Typically these values could be around 10 to 15 per cent greater than the figures given in the table. The main function of the *Lazur'-M* radio-telemetry data-link was to receive continuous and 'one-time' commands generated by the *Kaskad-M* computing device and to pass them to the on-board processing equipment on PVO and Frontal Aviation (Tactical) interceptors.

	Continuous commands generated by *Kaskad*-M equipment and transmitted by the *Lazur'*-M data-link system		
	Parameter	Units of measurement	Limits of operation
1	Assigned course of interceptor	degrees	0-360
2	Altitude of target	metres	500-30,000
3	Speed of interceptor	kph	600-3,600
4	Range interceptor to target	kilometres	0-100
5	Closing speed of interceptor with target	kph	0-7,200
6	Elevation of target	degrees	±42
7	Azimuth interceptor to target	degrees	0-360
8	Vertical speed of interceptor	m/sec	±360

The 'one-time' commands were as follows:

- 'Left' ('*Vlevo*'), 'Right' ('*Vpravo*') and 'Straight ahead' ('*Pryamo*');
- 'Re-targeting' ('*Pyerenatselivaniye*');
- 'Homing' ('*Privod*');
- Range to target of 100 km, 60 km, 36 km and 'Break-off' ('*Otboy*');
- 'Forward Hemisphere' ('*Peryednyaya Polusfyera*') and 'Rear Hemisphere' ('*Zadnyaya Polusfyera*') attack;
- Eight values of command relating to the flight regime of the interceptor;
- The reheat commands 'Switched on' ('*Vklyucheno*') and 'Switched off' ('*Vyklyucheno*');
- The commands for switching the '*Nakal*' warm-up stage on and off for the semi-active radar seeker heads of the R-4R variant of the AA-5 'Ash' missile.

Apart from this, a 'Co-operation' ('*Vzaimodyeystviye*') command could be transmitted by the *Lazur'*-M link instead of a guidance command, enabling control of an interceptor to be handed off to *pre-selected* neighbouring GCI stations, since the receiving equipment of the *Lazur'*-M system allowed for twenty fixed frequencies to be pre-tuned. Switching of the on-board apparatus to new guidance data (i.e. new frequencies and selective codes) took place automatically on receipt of the 'Co-operation' command transmitted by the data-link.

Although comparatively advanced for the time, the *Lazur'*-M GCI data-link was similar to the Swedish Air Force's STRIL 60 (*Stridsledning*) air combat management system used by SAAB J-35 'Draken' fighters in the 1960s. It was also analogous in concept to the Ferranti OR946 data-link planned for but never operationally used on the English Electric Lightning.

3

Cockpit Pressurisation and Ventilation

The Tu-128 was equipped with a pressurisation and ventilation system designed to maintain a normal working environment for the two crew members at all operational altitudes. The pressurisation system was supplied with air tapped from the seventh compressor stage of each engine, although in the event of failure of one engine the pressurisation system could still function, the essential parameters being maintained by the ARD-54 (*Avtomaticheskii Regulyator Davlyeniya*) automatic pressure regulator. The regulator maintained atmospheric pressure in the cockpits up to an altitude of 2,000 m (6,560 feet) and a constant pressure equivalent to that at 2,000 m, from 2,000 m up to 7,000 m (22,965 feet). From 7,000 m it supplied a pressure equidistant to the external pressure (*davlyenie ehkvidistantnoye vnyeshniemu*), with a pressure differential of 0.4 kg/cm^2 (5.69 lb/sq. in.)—i.e. the relationship between cabin pressure and external pressure remained constant beyond 7,000 m.

Thus, at the Tu-128's service ceiling of 15,400 m (50,525 feet), the pressure in the pilot's and navigator's cockpit compartments was equivalent to that at 6,000 m (19,685 feet). In the event of failure of the ARD-54's automatic valve there was a safety valve in the cockpit which provided emergency venting of the pressurisation system to atmosphere to prevent excessive pressure building up. The necessary temperature regime in the cockpits was maintained within limits of 15-20°C by delivering cold air from the ventilation system and hot air from the heating system (at 60-70°C), with the actual mixing of the two air supplies taking place within the cockpits. Primary cooling of air tapped from the engine took place in ring air-to-air heat exchangers, which were part of the air intake channels of the engine. Part of the cooled air was fed to the ventilation system where secondary cooling occurred in a turbo-cooling unit via an air-to-air heat exchanger mounted in the technical compartment. Cockpit temperature regulation was provided by an ART-56-2 (*Avtomaticheskii Termoregulyator*) automatic thermo-regulator and an ART-56-1 temperature regulator in the ventilation system, but could also be adjusted manually.

Monitoring of cockpit pressurisation was provided by an altitude and pressure differential indicator, with monitoring of air fed into the cockpit in the ventilation circuit being shown on a separate indicator. These indicators and the heating and ventilation system control panel were mounted in the navigator's cockpit.

The ventilation system provided air for demisting the interior panels of the cockpit glazing in cold weather, but Tu-128 pilots often used to comment on the generally poor performance of the air-conditioning system in hot weather. Aircrew based at airfields in Siberia, with its distinctly continental climate characterised by bitterly cold winters and extremely hot summers, found it extremely uncomfortable sitting in the aircraft waiting to take off in the blazing heat of summer. Nikolai Popov recalls:

> There were, of course, ground air-conditioning units available, but throughout my entire service [flying the Tu-128] they were only used once or twice, and then only in winter. The airfield air-conditioning unit was plugged into the aircraft's own system using a special socket adjacent to the nose-wheel leg.

The introduction of the modified Tu-128M variant of the 'Fiddler' highlighted the ineffectiveness of the air-conditioning system at low level and the problem of providing adequate cooling at heights up to 2,000 m (6,560 feet). Therefore, on the modified aircraft a special shutter valve (*zaslonka*) was installed on the fuselage which could be lowered into the airstream when required, permitting the cockpits to be ventilated by an additional outflow of air, the increased rate of outflow resulting in a more active exchange of air in the two cockpits. The shutter closed automatically as the aircraft climbed above 2,000 m.

4

Crew Life Support Systems

OXYGEN SYSTEM

A comprehensive equipment assembly was provided for crews of the Tu-128 to enable them to operate comfortably in an unpressurised cockpit (if necessary) at altitudes up to the aircraft's dynamic ceiling of 19,000-20,000 m (62,335-65,616 feet). The KKO-3 (*Komplekt Kislorodnovo Oborudovaniya-3*) oxygen supply assembly was installed on aircraft up to and including the 40th production series. The KKO-3 comprised the following:

- VKK-4P high-altitude pressure suit with its associated GSh-4MP (or MS) pressure helmet;[1]
- RSD-3M pressure correlation regulator;
- KP-34 oxygen supply with DU-2 remote control panel;
- ORK-2M integrated switching assembly;
- KP-27M parachute oxygen supply.

Crews could also wear a VMSK-2M high-altitude sea survival (exposure) suit for protection in the event of having to eject over water. Oxygen was provided to the crew from two SKG-7M (*Samolyotnyi Kislorodnyi Gazifikator*) liquid oxygen units, delivered along two main supply lines. The oxygen system had a cross-feed facility so that in the event of one line being damaged, oxygen could still be supplied via the other. The oxygen bottles, mounted in the technical compartment, were charged on the ground via an on-board valve, and the oxygen instruments, shut-off valves and monitoring panels were located in the pilot's and navigator's cockpits. The KP-27M parachute oxygen bottles were mounted on the NAZ (*Nosimyi Avariinyi Zapas*) emergency survival pack in the seat pan of the ejection seat and were selected 'on', automatically, at the moment of ejection on operation of the ORK-2M integrated switching assembly.

Lt Col. G. Zayats, the CO of the 1st squadron of 356 AP, wearing a GSh-6A pressure helmet. This, along with the GSh-4MP (or GSh-4MS) pressure helmet, KKO-3 or KKO-5 oxygen supply assembly and VKK-3M pressure suit, formed part of the (high-altitude) exposure protection system for Tu-128 aircrew. However, as noted in the text, high-altitude clothing was not used as such by Tu-128 crews, but rather as an integral element of the VMSK exposure suit. (*G. Zayats*)

According to data supplied by OKB-918 (involved in ejection seat design), GK NII VVS (State Red Banner Scientific Research Institute of the Air Force) and NIAM (Scientific Research Institute of Aviation Medicine), the KKO-3 aircrew equipment assembly allowed the crew to survive in an unpressurised cockpit at an altitude of 19,000 m (62,335 feet) for 10 minutes, at an altitude of 16,000 m (52,495 feet) for 20 minutes, and at an altitude of 12,000 m (39,370 feet) for 10 hours. These times considerably exceeded the potential operating endurance of the Tu-128 at those altitudes, but the actual quantity of oxygen in the on-board supply was sufficient to permit the crew to remain in an unpressurised cockpit for only 5 hours, with a 20 per cent reserve. The oxygen system on aircraft from the 41st production series onwards (from c/n 4101) was changed to a gaseous oxygen supply with a working pressure of 150 kg/cm^2 (2,135 lb/sq. in.) replacing the liquid oxygen units. This work was undertaken as aircraft were cycled through maintenance at the Tu-128 re-fit plant, the upgraded system also including a new aircrew equipment assembly—the KKO-6, comprising:

- KP-52M (*Kislorodnyi Pribor*) oxygen supply and DU-2 (*Shchitok Distantsionnovo Upravlyeniya*) remote control panel;
- RPK-52 (*Regulyator Podachi Kisloroda*) oxygen supply regulator;

Lt Col. Zayats performs a pre-flight walk-round of his aircraft, wearing a ZSh-3M 'bone-dome' helmet and holding a KM-32 oxygen mask in his left hand. Although this is most likely a specially posed shot, Russian aircrew usually approached their aircraft already wearing their flying helmets, probably for added warmth in the low temperatures of winter. (*G. Zayats*)

- VUSh-6 (*Ventilyatsionnoye Ustroistvo Shlema*) helmet ventilation device;
- ORK-9A (*Ob'yedinyonyi Raz'yom Kommunikatsii*) integrated switching assembly;
- IK-52 (*Indikator Kisloroda*) oxygen flow indicator.

The following specialised aircrew equipment could also be used on the Tu-128:

- ZSh-3M (*Zashchitnyi Shlem*) protective helmet ('bone dome') with KM-32 (*Kislorodnaya Maska*) oxygen mask, or a ZSh-5 (ZSh-5A) helmet with a KM-34 oxygen mask;
- GSh-6A (GSh-6M) (*Germeticheskii Shlem*) pressure helmet (or the GSh-4MP [GSh-MS] pressure helmet if using the KKO-3 assembly);
- VKK-6M (*Vysotnyi Kompensiruyushchii Kostyum*) high-altitude pressure suit (see endnote 1 about use of the VKK suit);
- VMSK-2M (*Vysotnyi Morskoy Spasatyel'nyi Kostyum*) or VMSK-4 exposure suit (with the KKO-6 assembly);
- VK-3M (*Ventilyatsionnyi Kombinezon*) air ventilated suit;
- ASP-74 (*Aviatsionnyi Spasatyel'nyi Poyas*) life-saving belt;
- ASZh-58 or ASZh-58B (*Aviatsionnyi Spasatyel'nyi Zhilyet*) life-jacket.

It must be noted, however, that among pilots on the Tu-128 regiments a variety of different helmets were worn, including ZSh-3, ZSh-5 and even the later ZSh-7, with pilots making their own choice of helmet from the flight clothing stores.

In the raised position the sun visor on the ZSh-3 helmet was situated close to the face and on ejection dropped under its own weight to protect the face against the blast of air when entering the outside airstream. In spite of its old design, this helmet was very well liked among crews based in the polar regions, and in the severe winters of Russia's northern territories they preferred to wear the ZSh-3 helmet because it was warmer than any of the other designs. In winter, when dressing for flight, it was usual to don the cold weather helmet liner (*zimnii podshlemnik*) first, although its use was not actually authorised in the flight operations manual, then the fur-lined headset (*shlemofon*), and finally the ZSh-3 itself, making the whole assembly very warm and comfortable. Pilots commented that the modern plastic ZSh-7 helmet felt very cold on the head in a typical ambient air temperature of around –40°C, since they still had to walk out to the aircraft and it took some time to start the engines once they had climbed aboard.

Sadly, there was at least one tragic incident involving the ZSh-5 helmet in the history of Tu-128 operations, when during an in-flight emergency (described in Appendix 3) the crew had to eject from the aircraft. When the seat and its occupant (in this case the pilot) departed the stricken aircraft, air started to flow into the gap between the still retracted visor and the inner surface of the helmet. The ZSh-5 did not have an automatic visor-lowering facility on ejection and differed from the ZSh-3 in that the visor was positioned closer to the sincipital (i.e. top) part of the head and further from the face, preventing lowering by gravity action. Moreover, the ZSh-5 differed from the ZSh-3 and ZSh-7 in not having the row of ventilation (pressure relief) apertures across the upper surface provided on these helmets. As a consequence, a localised region of low pressure was created under the inner surface of the pilot's ZSh-5 helmet, which in turn created a lifting force on the visor of such intensity that it forced the pilot's head back violently, breaking his neck.

After this incident the helmets were modified and improved by fitting an automatic visor-lowering mechanism, the modified helmets receiving the designations ZSh-5A and ZSh-7A. However, since production of the ZSh-5 had only just begun and the number of available helmets was limited, an amendment to the flight operations manual was issued (Amendment No. 675/1063 dated 23 May 1986) permitting temporary use of ZSh-3M and ZSh-5 helmets by Tu-128 aircrew until 1 January 1988, although this was on the strict condition that pilots and navigators should be briefed specifically on the vital importance of lowering the visor manually before ejection.

As already mentioned, the other item of flight clothing available to Tu-128 crews was the VMSK-2M (and VMSK-4) sea survival (exposure) suit, designed

074. In 1982, 64 AP section navigator Capt. S. Shchelokov poses on the steps of his Tu-128 at Omsk-North, wearing a ZSh-5 protective helmet and holding a KM-34 oxygen mask. Note the 'Excellent Aircraft' symbol on the air intake and the stowage space on the steps for the air intake 'blanks'. (*S. Shchelokov*)

to provide pilots and navigators with a comfortable working micro-environment inside the aircraft at high altitude, but mainly intended to permit survival in water in the event of having to eject over the sea. These suits provided survival in the sea for a period of 12 hours at water temperatures of 0 to 10°C and at ambient air temperatures down to −15°C. The VMSK-2M survival kit comprised the following:

- a VKK pressure suit (see previous comments about pressure suits);
- a thermally protective suit;
- a water protective suit;
- a pressure helmet (or oxygen mask);
- boots;
- pressurised gloves;
- an inflatable collar.

The VMSK-4 differed from the VMSK-2M in that the water protective suit was replaced by a sea survival suit, made from a water protective membrane and a supporting membrane, with the ASP-74 life preserver replacing the inflatable collar.

Co-author Maj. Nikolai Popov recalls:

A 10th Air Army Tu-128 pilot in conversation with colleagues, wearing the later orange VMSK-4 exposure suit used by aircrew operating out of the northern bases, vital for their protection in the event of ejecting over and landing in Arctic waters. (*V. Yalyaev Archive*)

Up to the beginning of the 1980s we used to wear the grey-coloured VMSK-2M suits and then later converted to the orange VMSK-4. The older VMSK-2M suit was worse. It had an inflatable collar of very poor design and on entering the water it had a tendency to force the survivor's head under water! The VMSK-2M was uncomfortable for another reason. It had no provision for pockets where you could put your hands as you walked out to the aircraft in cold weather, it didn't have a comfortable neck seal and it was very cold to wear. You'd break into a sweat walking out to the aircraft, then you'd have to sit in the cold aircraft [during start-up] and freeze! However, there was also little pleasure in wearing the VMSK-4. As pilots didn't wear the VKK suits when flying the Tu-128 you'd first put on the thermal protection suit (*tyeplozashchytnyi kostyum*). This was a suit of thin quilted wadding [less than 1 mm thick], with integral socks and a circular fastening at the abdomen. The VMSK also had an aperture at the abdomen and you had to squeeze through this to get into the suit itself. The collar was made in two parts, one made out of knitted material and the other made of rubber. It was necessary to make sure that the rubber edge of the collar provided a good hermetic seal between it and the neck for full protection in an emergency [i.e. an ejection]. Then you'd have

The pilot and navigator of a Tu-128, dressed in two different variants of the VMSK exposure suit. On the left is navigator/WSO Aleksandr (Alexander) Zhabkin wearing the older grey VMSK-2M, with his pilot Capt. Syrovatkin on the right in the improved VMSK-4. (*Alexander Zhabkin*)

to connect the ORK-9 plug. The VMSK also incorporated socks, and all you'd have to do then was put on the boots and the life preserver. The instruction was that the life preserver should be laced on to the suit, but on our squadron only one pilot had his life preserver laced on—all the others simply put the ASP-74 on over the VMSK.

On the regiments, the ASP-74 was nicknamed 'the banana' because of its shape. Regular emergency egress (ejection) and survival training was carried out on all the Tu-128 regiments, and after the introduction of the ASP-74 into Soviet Air Force service, crews had an unpleasant surprise with this ostensibly life-preserving device—if the ASP-74 was worn in the manner recommended by the manufacturer, the pilot would be tipped face down on entering the water! Consequently, a quick-fix solution was soon developed which involved attaching the life preserver closer to the chest and the problem was solved. In spite of this initial shortcoming, pilots were unanimous in their opinion that the ASP-74 was considerably better than the ASZh-58 life-jacket, which was not particularly comfortable in the water when inflated and also irritated the neck in flight.

The VMSK-4 exposure suit is a variant of the standard Russian high-altitude pressure suit, comprising the KKO-5 or KKO-3 oxygen supply system and optimised for over-water use in climatically hostile regions, such as the Arctic. ASP-74 underarm life preservers were attached to the sides of the VMSK suit. (*S. Shchelokov*)

The following comments about the VMSK-2 exposure suit are also of interest. Although offering effective protection to the wearer, the early examples were very heavy, having been designed for use on large aircraft (i.e. bombers) which the PVO clearly did not possess. So, at the request of the PVO, industry developed a new, lighter model, designated VMSK-2OB ('OB' standing for *oblegchyonnyi* or lightened), differing from the initial design in that the number of insulating layers of the original suit was reduced. Col. Yevglyevskiy remembers the introduction of the new design:

> I was a member of the acceptance commission for this VMSK variant when it was delivered from the manufacturer. Consequently I had to try it on. It was rather comfortable and didn't hinder movement too much.

The use of a pre-flight air-conditioning system had originally been envisaged for the VMSK; this would have involved the use of suitcase-sized individual conditioning units which crews would have carried out to the aircraft themselves. Later, industry developed a special minibus for this purpose, mounted on a GAZ-66 chassis, designed to carry eight Tu-128 aircrew. The pilot and navigator would get into the minibus wearing their VMSK suits and plug themselves into the vehicle's air-conditioning system and the driver would take them out to their aircraft. However, because of incompatibilities between the individual conditioning packs and the minibus system, this was almost never used on the Tu-128 regiments. The early VMSK suits had another major design deficiency in that they had to be 'made to measure', each pilot and navigator having to be measured by a regiment medical specialist using measurement criteria developed for the cosmonaut fraternity. The measurements were then sent off to the factory in Moscow where the suits were made and since these first VMSK suits were individualised for each crew member, the manufacturing costs were commensurately high.

Consequently, the PVO Command decided that only 72 AP, the northernmost located operator of the Tu-128, tasked to conduct long-range patrol flights over the Arctic seas, would receive the VMSK suits in the early phase of operating the aircraft. However, over time, aircrew would be posted in and out of the regiments and some of the replacement pilots and navigators would not have a VMSK suit;

Amderma-based Tu-128 crews did not always have to wear VMSK immersion suits on QRA duty. During periods when most of the surface of the Arctic Ocean was frozen over, they were allowed instead to wear winter flying suits, flying jackets and boots. (*S. Fedoseenko*)

the new and improved VMSK-2OB suit was not ordered and, as a result, flights on which the VMSK was worn became less and less frequent. During exercises, the normal procedure was that all those aircrew who had a VMSK suit should wear it, and there was even a special exercise in the KBP training manual—'Flight in the VMSK' (clearly impossible for those without one!). However, the position improved when in the 1970s the PVO began to receive the standardised VMSK-4 suit described earlier, although many Tu-128 crews felt that an exposure suit itself would not necessarily save their lives:

> If you ejected over the tundra or the ice, there would be little chance of being found. There would only be a chance of surviving if you ejected and landed near habitation or alongside the airfield. Sometimes when you're flying over the sea you can see waves around 10-12 m [30-40 feet high]. If you ejected there, then who would find you around 1,000 km [620 miles] from base?

Tu-128 crews were psychologically well prepared by training and calmly faced the potential dangers of flying over such inhospitable terrain and seas with stoicism and grit. Additionally, it is important to recognise that not a single Tu-128 crew was lost after abandoning their aircraft over the frozen wastes of northern Russia.

The pilot and navigator of this 10th Air Army Tu-128 pose in front of their aircraft, wearing the VMSK-4 exposure suit and ZSh-3M flying helmets, with oxygen masks in their hands. Note that the aircraft is carrying a non-standard weapons fit, comprising only a single AA-5 missile. (*V. Yalyaev Archive*)

EJECTION SEATS

The Tu-128 prototype was equipped with K-22 ejection seats, but the first series-produced aircraft had TU-K21 ejection seats,[2] which along with the KSM-31-U (*Kombinirovannyi Strelyayushchiy Mekhanizm*) combined firing mechanism, three-stage parachute and SPS-4 unified attachment system permitted safe ejection throughout the normal flight regime of the aircraft, including during take-off and landing. A NAZ-5U (*Uluchshyonnyi*, i.e. 'improved') survival pack was located in the seat pan, the pan itself being adjustable to the height of the crew member. The actual height of the seat pan was adjusted using an MPS-5 (*Mekhanizm Pod'yoma Sidyen'ya*) electric 'seat-raising mechanism', with a range of travel of ±90 mm. The ability to adjust the height of the seat effectively removed any height restriction on aircrew selected to fly the Tu-128, and on the regiments there were pilots and navigators of widely differing stature. Pilots coming to the Tu-128 from the Su-15 'Flagon' found that the ejection seat of the large interceptor was quite remarkable. On the ground, seat height adjustment for a specific pilot normally involved switching on the MPS-5, used in conjunction with a collimating sight attached to the top of the pilot's instrument panel. When the focus of the pilot's eyes corresponded with the sighting line of the collimating device, the movement of the seat was stopped.

A 227-P-L pyrotechnic mechanism was used to blow the heavy canopies off in the event of having to eject from the aircraft, creating a clear aperture through which the pilot and navigator could leave the aircraft safely. The system of opening the canopy hoods employed a twin-drive mechanism, one pneumatic and the other mechanical. The pneumatic drive was set in motion using the 'Ready-Fire' ('*Izgotovka-Vystrel*') lever on the seats. On raising this lever to the upper stop position on either one of the seats, both canopies were jettisoned with a time delay to prevent them colliding with each other and with the seats when the crew ejected. (The navigator's canopy was jettisoned with a delay of between 0.3 and 0.5 seconds after the pilot's canopy had been blown off.) On moving the 'Ready-Fire' lever on the pilot's seat to the extreme upper position the control column and rudder pedals were also disconnected, hinging forwards under the instrument panel. This removed these two potentially hazardous obstacles to the safe departure of the pilot from the cockpit on ejection.

The mechanical drive was brought into play by using the emergency canopy jettison levers, located on the left-hand side of the pilot's and navigator's cockpits. This drive was a back-up system and was used only in the event of failure of the main jettison system. If the mechanical system *had* to be used, the pilot's control column and rudder pedals were disconnected using a separate handle on the left-hand side of the pilot's cockpit. The 227-P-L pyrotechnic charge was used to jettison the canopies regardless of which of the two drives was used. The canopies separated from the aircraft in a defined sequence, since their rear edges were connected to the airframe and released automatically only after each canopy had reached a specific angle after unlocking. For the pilot's canopy this was between 12 and 15°, and 5-6° for the navigator's canopy. The canopies had a cable interlock with the seat firing mechanism which obviated the possibility of ejection while the canopies were still locked. Protection of the head and face on ejection was provided by the GSh-4M pressure helmet, forming part of the VMSK-2 combined exposure suit, which was accepted as the standard item of flight clothing for the Tu-128 operating in the High Arctic. Alternatively, if crews were not wearing the VMSK, the ZSh-3 helmet also provided head and face protection on ejection.

An interlock system also operated in the seat firing sequence to avoid the likelihood of the pilot and navigator colliding with each other on ejection and prevent the hot gases of the KSM-312-U firing mechanism from affecting the navigator. The first crew member to leave the aircraft should have always been the navigator. In the event of the navigator not carrying out the command to leave the aircraft, the pilot could use a 'command ejection' facility to eject the navigator forcibly, which simultaneously unlocked the pilot's 'Ready-Fire' handle interlock on his seat. The handles were interlocked in the upper position until the moment the navigator ejected and could not be released until that time. This de-interlocking also occurred automatically after the ejection of the navigator if he carried out an ejection on the command of the pilot. Unfortunately, however, this de-interlocking procedure did not operate in the correct manner during one in-flight emergency involving the Tu-128 and the navigator's cockpit was scorched by the flames from the pilot's ejection seat firing mechanism. After this incident the engineering service of the IA-PVO issued an order decreeing that the pilot had to use the command ejection procedure to eject the navigator. An illuminated warning panel was placed in the navigator's cockpit, displaying the legend 'Prepare for Ejection' ('*Prigotovit'sya k katapul'tirovaniyu*'), switched on by the pilot from a panel in his cockpit, with the corresponding legend 'Ejection of Navigator' ('*Katapul'tirovaniye Shturmana*') illuminating in his own cockpit.

As previously mentioned, in the event of having to eject, the control column and rudder pedals were released by an emergency unlocking mechanism to prevent injury to the pilot on ejection. When unlocked, the control column and rudder pedals were automatically 'thrown' forward, away from the trajectory of the seat, with the aerodynamic control surfaces remaining in their original position at the time of initiating the ejection sequence. The control column and rudder unlocking mechanisms were operated by a pneumatic cylinder forming part of the ejection system and, in the event of failure of the pneumatic unit, by a handle mounted on the pilot's left-hand control console. On the right-hand side wall of the pilot's and navigator's cockpits there were two emergency axes of all-steel construction with a rubberised handle. Curiously, there were no particular instructions for the

In hot weather it was possible to open up the collar and inner lining of the VMSK-4 so that the wearer could walk around without overheating inside the suit. (*Alexander Zhabkin*)

crews regarding the intended function of these axes, but Tu-128 veterans recalled that they were originally intended to hack off the 'horns' of the control wheel. This would have allowed the pilot to eject safely even if the control column had not been hinged forward.

When preparing to eject from the Tu-128 the pilot and navigator had to place their feet on the footrests of the seat, the lower limbs being held in place by leg restrainers. Then, on ejection, as the seat rose above the fuselage into the airstream, another set of restrainers operated to restrict flailing of the arms. During service operation of the Tu-128 an unpleasant feature of the aircraft's ejection system became apparent, mainly affecting the pilots. The majority of Tu-128 pilots who had the misfortune to eject from the aircraft suffered compression fractures of the spine, but navigators seemed to be able to eject without suffering this problem. It was thought probable that this was because the navigators were usually 'command ejected' by the pilot and therefore did not have to bend to operate the ejection seat handle; they could, therefore, adopt the correct straight-backed pre-ejection posture in the seat.

It should be noted that in documents relating to the Tu-128 prototype and the first batch of series-produced examples used in trials, the aircraft was described as being equipped with the TU-K21 ejection seat, as already mentioned. However, in the aircraft's flight reference cards published in 1977, 'Instructions for the crew of the Tu-128 (Tu-128M) aircraft' ('*Instruktsii ehkipazhu samolyota Tu-128 [Tu-128M]*'), the seat was defined simply as the KT-1 (*Kreslo Tupoleva-1*). We have endeavoured to make sense of this confusion, and in fact the TU-K21 ejection seat recommended for installation on the Tu-128 was never actually used on the aircraft. For a number of reasons, the seat installed on series-production Tu-128s was a design close to that of the KT-1, built by OKB-156. This change was probably introduced from the first aircraft of the 4th series (0401). The main differences between this and previous units involved the use of the improved PS-T (*Spastyel'naya Parashutnaya Sistyema*) personnel parachute (later changed to the PS-T Series 2) and the NAZ-7 survival pack (NAZ-7M) in place of the NAZ-5. In normal use, the new PS-T Series 2 personnel parachute offered the following performance characteristics:

- survival of the pilot (navigator) after ejection in horizontal flight within a temperature range from −60°C to +50°C from sea level (zero height) up to the aircraft's service ceiling, at an EAS of 130-1,150 kph (70-620 kts);
- automatic operation of all components of the parachute system and the *Komar-2* (Mosquito-2) survival radio in the NAZ-7M survival pack;
- a g-loading arising from inflation of the primary and secondary stabilising parachutes of no more than 20 g and on inflation of the main chute no more than 16 g;
- the possibility of the pilot separating from the seat using only the main chute, in the event of abnormal operation of the stabilising chutes, or on leaving the aircraft without ejecting;
- operation of the *Komar-2M* survival radio in the NAZ-7M at altitudes no higher than 5,000 m (16,400 feet) and while descending under the inflated canopy of the main chute;
- manual operation of the MLAS-1-OB (*Malaya Lodka Aviatsionnaya Spastyel'naya-1-Oblegchyonnaya*) small lightweight life raft, at altitudes no higher than 1,500 m (4,920 feet), while descending under the inflated canopy of the main chute;
- a vertical rate of descent calculated for ISA and the weight of the 'pilot-parachute system' of 100 kg (220 lb) at a height of 30-35 m (100-115 feet) above the ground being no more than 6 m/sec (1,180 ft/min);
- weight of the PS-T with the PPK-U-165A parachute pack, KP-27M oxygen supply, NAZ-7 or NAZ-7M and the detached back-plate of the ejection seat—not more than 34 kg (75 lb).

The NAZ-7 differed from the NAZ-7M in the range of contents and particularly by the absence of the *Komar-2* survival radio. The range of contents of the NAZ was established by a joint decision of the Ministry for the Aviation Industry and the

Soviet Air Force, the packing of the NAZ-7 being defined by a directive issued on 15 February 1966, and the modified NAZ-7 by a directive dated 1 February 1974. As far as it is possible to understand, having studied the design of both seats, they exhibited a large degree of commonality, particularly after the installation of the NAZ-7M. It has to be admitted, however, that even with an element of commonality, the ejection seat installed on the Tu-128 exhibited substantial differences between it and the 'bomber version' of the KT-1, the most obvious of which were:

- the main parachute was housed in the seat head-rest;
- a NAZ-7 (NAZ-7M) was packed in the seat pan;
- the pilot separated from the ejection seat along with the seat back-plate.

This, however, did not prevent the Tupolev Design Bureau from unifying three ejection seats of very similar design under the single designation KT-1 or Tupolev Seat Series 1. Therefore, in the flight reference cards for the Tu-22 'Blinder' bomber and Tu-128 'Fiddler' interceptor, the ejection seats of both aircraft were described as KT-1, and in the 'Instructions for the crew of the Tu-22M aircraft' as KT-1M. The latter modification took account of the fact that the four-man crew of the 'tactico-strategic' Tu-22M2 'Backfire-B' bombers would have different survival requirements from the earlier 'Blinder' compared with the specialised role needs of the Tu-128 interceptor.

The rather utilitarian appearance of the flight clothing locker room for 72 AP aircrew at Amderma was typical of such facilities on other PVO bases. (*Valeriy Yalyaev*)

5

Initial Operational Experience

As already mentioned, the first prototype of the new interceptor, provisionally designated 'Aircraft 128' ('*Samolyot 128*'), was handed over in early 1961 to OKB-156's Flight Test and Modification Base at Zhukovskiy, the main operating airfield of the Soviet Union's Flight Test Institute (and later that of the Russian Federation). In spite of the fact that testing of the aircraft was only just getting under way, the decision had already been taken to accept the aircraft into service. Consequently, the senior command executive of the PVO had begun to prepare the way for the operation of the new fighter. This coincided with plans already in place at the time to re-equip many of the PVO air regiments with new aircraft, which in turn led to the important task of retraining air and ground crews to operate them. Already as far back as 20 February 1947, a special operational conversion unit had been set up for this purpose, based on the wartime 2nd Independent Aviation Training Regiment and designated the Red Banner Training and Methodology Centre for the Air Force of the PVO ([*Krasnoznamyonnyi*] *Uchebno-metodicheskii Tsentr Aviatsii PVO* or UMTs APVO]). The 2nd Training Regiment had, throughout the Great Patriotic War,[1] trained pilots and ground support personnel in preparation for deployment to their frontal operating bases. The location of the post-war UMTs was to be the rural settlement of Savasleika, situated in marshy woodland in the Gorky Region, some 260 km (160 miles) east of Moscow.

In 1961, the Training and Methodology Centre comprised three training regiments, in addition to the centre's own personnel; these were the 592nd Fighter Training Aviation Regiment (*592 Uchebnyi Istrebityel'nyi Aviatsionnyi Polk* or 592 UIAP) based at Klin, 69 km (43 miles) north-west of Moscow, and 594 UIAP and 615 UIAP, both based at Savasleika. These units were responsible for the retraining of aircrew from the line regiments, as well as carrying out various research and trials tasks set by the research department of UMTs and the PVO HQ staff. It was on the basis of their 'research and trials' experience that it was decided

A Tu-128 during service with the 1st squadron of 615 UIAP at Savasleika soon after the PVO started training crews on the new interceptor. (*Museum of 148 TsBP & PLS via Alexander Melihov*)

that the first group to be trained on the new interceptor would be drawn from the aircrew and engineering personnel of UMTs. The first cadre of officers selected for conversion onto the Tu-28 was quite small.[2] From PVO HQ the most senior officer selected was inspector-pilot Lt Col. Nyefyedov, who assumed a supervisory role for combat training with regard to the aircraft's introduction to service. The PVO Training and Methodology Centre nominated its own Head of the Flight Group of the centre's Scientific Research Department, Col. Yevglyevskiy, along with Maj. Vobrov, Chief of Flying, Air Combat and Tactical Training (*Nachal'nik Vozdushnoi, Ognyevoi i Takticheskoi Podgotovki* or VOTP)[3] of 615 UIAP, plus the squadron commander of the 1st squadron of 615 UIAP, Col. Komyagin, to undertake conversion training. Apart from these officers, a small number of navigators and engineers were also included in the first group of personnel to convert onto the new interceptor, the total number being around fifteen officers.

The early training lectures on the new aircraft were conducted in the Tupolev Design Bureau offices (OKB-156) and every day the students would assemble in the Tupolev building on Radio Street in Moscow. Here, engineers and designers from every department would meet their students to conduct lectures and discussions, covering such topics as the airframe, flight instruments and the weapons system, etc. Col. Yevglyevskiy recalls how these lectures were conducted at that time:

When we began to study the aircraft in the OKB the lectures were very interesting because all the information that we were given came straight from primary sources— from the Tupolev designers themselves. On one occasion a designer from the aircraft structures team visited our group and asked the senior member to assign not two but four hours for the study of the structure of the Tu-28. I wondered at the time how it was possible for anyone to devote so much time to the structure of one aircraft. This would not be necessary for us in the day-to-day operation of the aircraft. Moreover, it wasn't really interesting. We didn't have the education to be able to take it all in. However, he persisted in asking the question and the time was duly allocated for his lecture. Our instructor only had a fountain pen and a ruler in his hand and he didn't even use a blackboard, but we all sat for four hours without a break, 'open-mouthed and with ears pinned back' as he explained the basics of the Tu-28's structure to us in a very accessible, easy-to-understand manner. On another occasion Andrei Nikolayevich Tupolev himself called in to see us, and we had a useful and informative conversation with him about the aircraft and he replied frankly to all our questions.

After studying the airframe and aircraft systems, the group was sent to visit Factory No. 45, the engine manufacturing plant where the Tu-28's engines were made. This factory was also located in Moscow and manufactured a number of variants of the Lyul'ka AL-7F engine, which powered, *inter alia*, the Sukhoi Su-7 'Fitter' fighter-bomber and Su-9 'Fishpot' PVO interceptor respectively. Here, the group studied the AL-7F-2 variant of this engine which had been selected as the interim engine to power the Tu-28 pending the arrival of the Dobrynin VD-9M, which could not be brought up to operational readiness in time. Col. Komyagin recalls this period of training:

Studying the engine for the Tu-28 did not present any particular difficulties as all of us had flown the Su-9, powered by the AL-7F-1 version. The new engine was simply a significantly improved modification of the old one. It was, however, true to say that it was a much 'smokier' engine!

After their theoretical studies, the first group returned to their normal daily duties, since flight tests of the Tu-28 had only just begun and the test programme was destined to be a somewhat protracted affair.

At this critical time during the introduction to service of the Tu-128 the leading pilot for the programme was replaced in the PVO Department of Combat Training, as recalled by Col. Nyefyedov:

Kuz'minskii [the former incumbent] was quite an old man by this time and was, as they said at the time, 'on his way out'. This was at the beginning of the 1960s, so it was decided, after taking account of Kuz'minskii's age, to hand over responsibility for the new aircraft to a younger inspector-pilot. Thus, I became the leading pilot for the Tu-28 programme and I remained in this capacity until the end of my service [in 1974] as senior inspector-pilot and deputy head of the Department of Long-range Interception Complexes.

However, attempts to continue training in preparation for the reception of the new fighter were undertaken in 1962, as recalled by Col. Komyagin:

> I was commanding a squadron of Su-9s at Savasleika, subordinate to 615 UIAP. Then in 1962, I was called to HQ and informed that the squadron would be converting onto the new Tu-28 and I was designated to be responsible for the reception of the new aircraft. I was then further informed that there were only two examples of the Tu-28 undergoing tests at that time.

Although there were no series-production aircraft available, it was nevertheless decided to send Lt Col. Nyefyedov, Col. Komyagin and Maj. Vobrov to the Tupolev OKB to undertake flight training on the new interceptor. Apart from the pilots, a small group of navigators was also assigned to the training programme. As was the case with the theoretical studies phase, these aircrew were to perform their flight training under the auspices of the Tupolev OKB. Training was carried out in the spring of 1962 at OKB-156's Flight Test and Modification Base at Zhukovskiy. The instructor for the first group of PVO pilots was OKB-156's test pilot Mikhail Kozlov. It must be admitted, however, that it is not strictly correct to describe this procedure as 'training' in the normal sense, since the pilots carried out their conversion on one of the *prototypes* of the new aircraft. The test pilots themselves had a very tight schedule of flights planned for this still untested aircraft (!) and as a consequence there was little time for the luxury of a comprehensive briefing for the PVO trainees.

Col. Komyagin remembers his introduction to the Tu-28:

> We sat in the cockpit and test pilot Kozlov told us everything he knew about the aircraft up to that time. We tried taxiing the aircraft. Then we were allowed to carry out a solo flight [even though] the aircraft still hadn't been 'broken in'. When I carried out my first flight, I had as my navigator an officer called Obraztsov. Later, when we landed, he shouted out rather joyfully, 'The commander has landed!' I'd forgotten that he was there. The tension showed. After all, it was the first time both he and I had flown this aircraft [!].

Col. Nyefyedov had an equally memorable introduction to flying the Tu-128 since he was not in the first group and had not even been given a theoretical briefing on the aircraft, as he recounts here:

I arrived at the Tupolev Flight Test Centre at Zhukovskiy and I was told to go to the 'secret unit' (*sekretnaya chast'*), take the technical material with me and study it. When I came back there'd be an examination. So I did as I was told. My head was spinning for around a week, reading the technical manuals, then the engineers told me all about the aircraft from the engineering point of view. I flew a Tu-124 with the test pilots and then I was cleared to go solo on the Tu-28. I was teamed with a test navigator—on the Tu-28 the navigator assisted the pilot during the landing phase, whereas the pilot did everything himself in a traditional PVO fighter. You'd focus your attention on the runway, whereas on the Tu-28 the navigator dictated everything to you: distance to the runway, speed, height […] Although I had lots of experience on fighters it wasn't much use to me in flying the Tu-28. The design of the pilot's windscreen on the Tu-28 wasn't particularly good and there was major distortion when looking sideways through the two panels. You'd be on the approach and look to the left and everything would be normal—only a slight amount of bank. You'd correct it and fly straight and level without any sign of banking. You'd then look to the right—my God!! You're banking sharply! You correct this, looking to the right and then to the left—and again you're banking!! The diffraction index was different for each panel. The aircraft rocked a bit on landing. But that's all behind me now and the overall training was OK. By comparison with a normal fighter the handling was fairly simple—it wasn't necessary to perform rolls or any complex aerobatics. Take-off, climb, descend, level turns—that was it. I did my first two solo flights in the Tu-128 on October 7th and 8th 1964, signed by test pilot Agapov. After this, everyone considered that we, as military pilots, had converted [onto the new aircraft].

The following data have been extracted from the flying log book of Col. Nyefyedov for 1962, 1963 and 1964 and show the variety of types flown by the colonel during his conversion onto the Tu-128 in this period.

Year	Aircraft type	Period	Number of flights	Total time		Under 'blind flying hood'		In cloud		Above cloud		In limited visibility and at low altitude		In stratosphere	
				Hours	Minutes	Hours	Minutes	Hours	Minutes	Hours	Minutes	Hours	Minutes	Hours	Minutes
1962	MiG-17	Day	9	9	10	–	–	2	03	2	59	0	25	1	45
	MiG-17PF	–	2	1	40	–	–	0	04	1	28	0	04	–	–
	MiG-15UTI	–	6	4	54	1	27	1	05	1	53	0	11	–	–
	Il-14	–	21	31	19	2	25	5	34	–	–	–	–	–	–
	Tu-124	–	3	3	59	–	–	0	08	0	18	–	–	–	–
		Total day	41	51	02	3	52	8	54	6	38	0	40	1	45
	MiG-17	Night	9	6	34	–	–	3	07	2	34	0	52	–	–
	MiG-17PF	–	2	1	30	–	–	0	23	0	59	0	08	–	–
	MiG-15UTI	–	10	6	28	2	07	3	08	1	52	0	33	–	–
	Il-14	–	1	2	00	–	–	–	–	–	–	–	–	–	–
	Tu-124	–	2	2	15	–	–	–	–	–	–	–	–	–	–
		Total night	24	18	47	2	07	6	38	5	25	1	33	–	–
		Total flying	65	69	49	5	59	15	32	12	03	2	13	1	45

Year	Aircraft type	Period	Number of flights	Total time		Under 'blind flying hood'		In cloud		Above cloud		In limited visibility and at low altitude		In stratosphere	
				Hours	Minutes	Hours	Minutes	Hours	Minutes	Hours	Minutes	Hours	Minutes	Hours	Minutes
1963	MiG-17	Day	12	8	14	–	–	1	32	5	10	0	06	–	–
	Yak-25M	–	1	–	27	–	–	–	–	–	–	–	–	–	–
	MiG-17PF	–	2	1	40	–	–	0	38	0	40	0	02	–	–
	MiG-15UTI	–	19	10	51	2	21	3	59	2	05	0	27	–	–
		Total day	34	21	12	2	21	6	09	7	55	0	35	–	–

Aircraft type	Period	Number of flights	Hours	Minutes	Hours	Minutes	Hours	Minutes	Hours	Minutes	Hours	Minutes	Hours	Minutes
MiG-17	Night	16	10	55	–	–	2	53	1	31	0	21	–	–
Yak-25M	–	2	1	11	–	–	–	–	–	–	–	–	–	–
MiG-17PF	–	1	0	30	–	–	0	28	–	–	0	02	–	–
MiG-15UTI	–	47	23	24	0	05	11	16	1	49	0	18	–	–
Total night		66	35	50	0	05	14	37	3	20	0	41	–	–
Total flying		100	57	02	2	26	20	46	11	15	1	16	–	–

Year	Aircraft type	Period	Number of flights	Total time		Under 'blind flying hood'		In cloud		Above cloud		In limited visibility and at low altitude		In stratosphere	
				Hours	Minutes	Hours	Minutes	Hours	Minutes	Hours	Minutes	Hours	Minutes	Hours	Minutes
1964	MiG-15UTI	Day	13	8	23	0	40	3	03	2	20	0	47	–	–
	MiG-17	–	12	8	35	–	–	2	36	4	05	0	13	–	–
	MiG-19P	–	3	2	41	–	–	2	23	–	–	0	06	–	–
	Yak-25M	–	6	4	48	–	–	3	48	0	10	–	–	0	10
	Yak-25R	–	3	2	10	–	–	0	50	0	15	–	–	–	–
	Il-14	–	6	5	00	–	–	3	30	–	–	0	22	–	–
	Tu-124	–	5	2	54	–	–	0	35	1	05	–	–	–	–
	Tu-104	–	2	1	15	–	–	–	–	–	–	–	–	–	–
	Tu-16	–	11	5	54	–	–	–	–	–	–	–	–	–	–
	Tu-128	–	7	5	13	–	–	0	55	1	08	0	18	0	25
	MiG-15UTI	Night	4	2	25	–	–	0	52	–	–	–	–	–	–
	MiG-17	–	10	6	02	–	–	1	40	0	32	0	09	–	–
	Yak-25M	–	3	1	18	–	–	1	22	0	33	0	03	–	–
	Il-14	–	15	5	19	0	10	1	00	–	–	0	30	–	–
	Total flying		100	61	47	0	50	22	34	10	08	2	28	0	35

Even at this early stage it became clear that the Tu-28 was a very unusual aircraft for pilots used to flying a traditional fighter. First of all, it had a control wheel (*shturval*) instead of the conventional joystick (control column) of a normal fighter; secondly, the aircraft had toe brakes on the rudder pedals, whereas all Russian fighters had a brake lever on the control column. The motor reflexes developed after hundreds of hours spent in the cockpit of a standard fighter aircraft therefore had to be 'unlearned' on this new aircraft. There had never been a comparable aircraft in the PVO fighter force, so there had never been any requirement to develop relevant training procedures for pilots converting onto it. (A training variant of the Tu-28 had not been envisaged as a design requirement at this stage, the first example only appearing in 1970, around ten years after the combat variant had entered service.) Col. Nyefyedov recalls, 'Suddenly the question arose—how do we train the pilots?!'

The absence of a dedicated trainer was a major problem for the PVO, since the Tu-28 (as it was still called) was essentially a bomber design with distinctly non-fighter handling qualities. In these circumstances, everyone tried to find the most rational way to train pilots selected to fly the aircraft. The highly innovative Commander-in-Chief of the PVO, Lt Gen. Yevgeny Savitskiy, ordered that a ground training rig be constructed to simulate the motion of the new interceptor during the take-off run, including the moment of raising the nose-wheel at the point of rotation. The engineering staff of 615 UIAP undertook this rather complex task, the result being extremely original, if not a little bizarre, at least for a jet-age training aid!

What they came up with was a metal framework on wheels with an open cockpit, recalling that of the Wright Flyer! As a powerplant they used a time-expired RD-45 engine taken from one of the MiG-15UTI 'Midget' trainers used by the regiment as pre-flight weather reconnaissance aircraft.[4] Apart from the jet engine, the training rig also had rudder pedals, a 'Tu-28-type' control wheel, plus limited hydraulics and a brake system. The rig was designed so that the nose would lift when the control wheel was pulled back, as on the real aircraft. Externally, of course, it bore no resemblance to an aircraft at all, nor did it really reproduce the motion of an aircraft during taxiing. Former commander of the 1st training squadron of 615 UIAP, Col. Komyagin recalls his early experiences with this unusual ground training rig':

> Our engineers built this contraption and we started taxiing it around the airfield at Savasleika. We taxied around and the entire airfield laughed at us. I pulled the stick back and the nose went up, exactly as the designers had planned. The speed was not particularly high, of course, but if you turned too sharply the whole thing would tilt over to one side. This was what Savitskiy had designed. He was a great inventor.

Dissatisfied with the poor performance of the training rig as an instructional tool, Gen. Savitskiy then adopted a different solution. This time he suggested using the twin piston-engined Ilyushin Il-14 'Crate' transport aircraft as a basic trainer for pilots selected to fly the new aircraft. This was actually a wise choice. The dimensions of the Il-14 were similar to those of the Tu-128 and, more importantly, it had a control wheel and brakes operated via the rudder pedals, as on the new interceptor.[5] Moreover, using a transport aircraft as a vehicle for converting single-seat fighter pilots onto the new PVO fighter allowed each trainee pilot to get used to the idea of working with another crew member, as well as flying the aircraft via a control wheel and controlling the aircraft on the ground using the toe brakes. In 1964, the first batch of 615 UIAP pilots selected to undergo conversion onto the 'Fiddler' were sent to Klin airfield, the base of the 978th Independent Transport Air Regiment (*978 Otdyel'nyi Transportnyi Aviatsionnyi Polk* or 978 OTAP) equipped with Il-14 'Crates', serving the day-to-day and VIP transport needs of PVO HQ. Among this first group of pilots were Capt. Kol'tsov, Maj. Dudkin and Capt. Yekimov, led by the commander of the 1st squadron of 615 UIAP, Col. Komyagin.

Two Il-14s were assigned for training the first batch of pilots, one of them, Bort No. 14, being the personal aircraft of the Commander of the Air Force of the PVO (*Komanduyushchiy Aviatsii PVO*, i.e. the commander of all the manned aircraft assets of the PVO, as distinct from the organisation's AAA and missile units). The aircraft commander of this Il-14 and the first instructor for the Tu-128 group was Lt Col. Gamayurov, the CO of the 1st squadron of 978 OTAP. Training on the Il-14 went very well, which was not too surprising since all the trainees were

The piston-engined Ilyushin Il-14 'Crate' must have seemed a rather retrograde step in pilot training terms for the first Tu-128 crews, coming as they did from the PVO 'fast jet' community. However, it served a useful purpose as a transitional trainer and was not altogether unusual in this regard, since many RAF jet pilots of the same period acquired their initial multi-engine experience in the similarly configured piston-engined Vickers 'Varsity'. (*Yuri Kabernik*)

Pilots First Class with extensive flying experience gained on a variety of different aircraft types. Here, on their introduction to the Il-14, the fighter pilots were soon to be convinced of the benefits of having an additional person in the crew. After take-off the aircraft commander would hand over control to the second pilot, and throughout the flight a navigator would pass heading changes and monitor the aircraft's position while a radio operator would maintain communications with base and regional ATC authorities etc. The Tu-128 trainees who successfully completed an accelerated training programme on the Il-14 had each accumulated around 30 hours on the piston-engined transport and were now authorised to undertake 'solo' flights in the capacity of aircraft commander in day and night visual meteorological conditions (VMC).

However, there was still no sign of the Tu-128 being issued to the PVO regiments, and in order to maintain flying 'currency' on their 'own' aircraft, the 615 UIAP pilots continued to fly from their home bases. Savasleika received its first Tu-128 only at the beginning of 1965, this aircraft being ferried from Zhukovskiy by OKB-156's own test pilot Mikhail Kozlov. On 26 January 1965, the commander of the 1st squadron of 615 UIAP, Col. Komyagin, made his first flight in this aircraft at Savasleika. Thereafter, the 1st squadron began to get to grips with mastering the new aircraft, a task made slightly easier after Col. Nyefyedov, the type-specialist inspector-pilot from PVO HQ, ferried the second Tu-128 to Savasleika. By the end of the first half of 1965, the document signalling the end of the initial phase of State flight tests had been signed and the Decree of the Council of Ministers of the USSR and the relevant Order of the Ministry of Defence were issued. Once this had occurred, the aircraft which had been used in the flight test programme conducted by the State Scientific Research Institute of the Air Force (*Gosudarstvyennyi Nauchno-Ispytatyel'nyi Institut Voyenno-Vozdushnykh Sil* or GNII VVS) were released for service in the summer of 1965. As a result of the efforts made by Factory No. 64 (Voronezh Aircraft Manufacturing Plant), OKB-156 and the GNII VVS, seven Tu-128s were handed over to the PVO in October 1965 to enable the so-called 'troop trials' (*voyskoviye ispytaniya*) of the aircraft to begin. It was these aircraft which began to equip the 1st squadron of 615 UIAP at the end of 1965, and according to the recollections of regimental veterans, there was a total of four Tu-128s on strength by that time.

Again, Col. Komyagin recalls this period:

Before the Tu-128, many of us had flown the Su-9, a classic fighter with a normal joystick and integral brake lever and then we were confronted with the Tu-128, with its bomber-type cockpit—wide and comfortable—with an [airliner-style] control wheel and toe-operated brakes. However, the main thing that puzzled us about the new interceptor was its low limiting load factor. We'd grown accustomed to the fact that on the Su-9 the limiting load factor could reach a value of 9.5 g and there were cases when the airframe had become distorted during hard manoeuvring but the aircraft had still landed safely. One Su-9 pilot, by the name of Fursyenko, when pulling out of a dive (perhaps a little over-enthusiastically) during a range firing programme at Astrakhan', had the pitot tube torn off by the g-force. He landed safely even though the aircraft's aluminium panels were all wrinkled and buckled. However, we discovered that the Tu-128 had a limiting load factor of only 2.5 g. How could you fly such an aircraft supersonically and intercept targets successfully?! After all, during an intercept pilots can always make mistakes and there can be delays in receiving data-link or voice commands during GCI sorties. In this case you can correct the mistake by use of energetic manoeuvring, i.e. you can reduce the radius of the turn and increase the load factor. However, if you overloaded the Tu-128, the AUASP (combined angle of attack indicator and g-meter) would start ringing out its warning chimes in the cockpit. The AUASP was designed 'specially for idiots'—a red light would start flashing and the bell would ring, warning the pilot that he had reached the maximum manoeuvring g-limit. You'd then have to do a 360-degree turn [to regain the intercept heading]. This was inconvenient for the crew. It was necessary to adapt to these new procedures, but eventually we got used to it and started to fly the aircraft as it was supposed to be flown.

This transition onto the Tu-128 was complicated not only for the Savasleika regiment—the entire central executive apparatus of the PVO HQ was also preparing for the introduction of the new aircraft, resulting in a particularly heavy workload for personnel in the 'combat training and flight safety area'. Among the duties of the inspector-pilots of this department was the flight-checking (known as 'trapping' in the RAF) of the flying skills and 'airmanship' of all pilots assigned to the PVO air regiments. Every flyer in the PVO, as in all other air forces, from ordinary line pilots up to the commander of the PVO air force had to undergo these periodic checks on the aircraft on which they were currently qualified. (Squadron pilots were checked by the squadron commander, the squadron commander was checked by the deputy regimental commander, etc.) However, there was no one to check the commander of an Air Army, or the head of an Air Army's flying personnel, so for this task they had to call upon the inspector-pilots from PVO HQ. Additionally, the Combat Training Department of PVO HQ assisted the regiments in the assimilation of new aircraft and equipment, plus new tactical methods, as well as discussing the question of upgrading aircraft that were already in service etc. Simultaneous with the introduction of the new aircraft, 'temporary instructions for the crew' (*vremyennaya instruktsiya ehkipazhu*) and the first edition of the KBP combat training manual had to be drawn up for the Tu-128. This work was undertaken by PVO inspector-pilots Col. Nyefyedov, Col. Yevglyevskiy and Col. Komyagin, now promoted to commander of the 1st squadron of 615 UIAP. At the request of the C-in-C of the PVO air force, Lt Gen. Savitskiy, it was written into the Tu-128 KBP that candidates for conversion onto the aircraft should have a minimum of 500 flying hours and a flying category of Pilot First Class.

Even before large-scale conversion onto the 'Fiddler' had started, the PVO HQ directorate had decided to change the aircraft used for the initial training of candidates selected to fly the new fighter. Consequently, Col. Nyefyedov continued to search for a suitable type and recalls that even the Tu-16 bomber was considered as one of the possible candidates for this role:

> Following my training on the Il-14 at Klin, I flew to Sary-Shagan with a pilot from PVO HQ. Based there on the airfield alongside Lake Balkhash was an Independent Composite Instructional-Research Regiment which had a number of Tu-16s on its strength that were used for releasing parachute-retarded targets over the range at Sary-Shagan. I performed around ten flights in the Tu-16; it was a large and heavy machine, with a take-off weight of around 70 tonnes [154,000 lb]. Of course, there was no comparison with a fighter … After returning to Moscow I also did a couple of flights in a Tu-104 at Zhukovskiy.[6]

By this time, the Il-14s of 978 OTAP were being replaced by the new twin-turbofan Tu-124 'Cookpot' short-haul airliner, which had already been selected to replace the piston-engined Ilyushin transport in both civil and military service. The Tu-124 was better suited to the task of converting single-seat fighter pilots onto the big new interceptor than the piston-engined Il-14. Its overall dimensions and all-up weight were very close to those of the Tu-128 and, importantly, it was a jet and flown via a control wheel similar to that of the new fighter, albeit without hydraulically boosted flying controls. With the Tu-124 it was possible to demonstrate the difference between the handling of a large jet compared with that of a lightweight fighter. After all, it was one thing to fly a small aircraft with a wingspan of 8-10 m (26-33 feet) but quite another for a single-seat fighter pilot to find himself at the controls of an aircraft over 30 m (98 feet) long with a wingspan of more than 17 m (55 feet). The trainees learned how to taxi the Tu-124 around the airfield, getting used to the narrowness of the taxiways when turning, as well as the large size of the aircraft, making the transition onto the Tu-128 less of a culture shock.

The technique of piloting the Tu-128 differed so much from other types that it demanded particular attention from a pilot flying this aircraft and another fighter during the same flying 'shift', as recalled here by Col. Nyefyedov:

> I was visiting Savasleika with my boss to do some refresher training, but the flights were organised so that only I flew the Tu-128. [However], after landing from my '128' sortie I was told, 'Hurry up! Your boss is waiting for you in a MiG-19.' I had to fly an interception sortie in a MiG-19P [Farmer-B], with the target flying in cloud. The

The Tu-124 'Cookpot' earned an unexpected place in the history of 'Fiddler' operations with the PVO when it was selected as an interim 'lead-in' trainer pending the arrival of the Tu-128UT. The two roof-mounted sensors located above the rear cabin area of this Tu-124Sh2 were BTs-63A star-tracking units used by trainee navigators for the LRAF bomber fleet. This aircraft was last operated by 64 AP at Omsk-North. (*Yefim Gordon Archive*)

MiG-19 was an aircraft which was very light on the controls. You only had to touch the control column with your fingertips and the aircraft would respond instantly. For some reason I got into the cockpit of the MiG-19 without paying too much attention to the layout of the instruments and switches. I got airborne quickly because I was being hurried, retracted the flaps and undercarriage and entered the climb. Cloud-base was around 1,000 m [3,280 feet], with tops above 9,000 m (29,530 feet). I entered cloud and began to study the cockpit [!]. I needed to find the ARK [automatic radio compass] and check how it was tuned and retuned since in the event of Savasleika airfield being closed for any reason, I'd have to fly to the designated alternate. I held the control column with my left hand and felt my way around the instrument panel with my right hand. By looking around, I'd understand where everything was. I looked at the instruments, but couldn't understand a thing. According to the instruments, I was flying vertically, but the speed was zero! The engines were operating normally, but I knew that the aircraft could not fly with zero air speed. Then it dawned on me that while I was sorting out the ARK I had pulled back on the stick a little and the aircraft had gone into a vertical climb. It was only thanks to experience and a good margin of height that I was able to recover the aircraft from this attitude. All this, because I'd switched rather too quickly to the MiG-19 from the Tu-128, where the controls were extremely heavy compared with an 'ordinary' fighter.

Two Tu-124 'Cookpot' transports parked alongside an Antonov An-14 'Clod' piston-engined light transport at Zhana-Semey. (*G. Chergezov*)

Apart from passenger variants of the Tu-124, the PVO also acquired the Tu-124Sh (*Shturmanskii*—literally 'Navigator' as an adjective), a specialised variant originally designed to train navigators for the Long-range Air Force (LRAF). The main difference between the Tu-124Sh and other versions of the aircraft was the provision of work stations in the passenger cabin for the trainee navigators, equipped to resemble the plotting desks of Tu-16 'Badger', Tu-95 'Bear' and Myasishchev 3M 'Bison' bombers. A trainee navigator could pass plotting data from any one of these positions to the pilots during flight, and some twenty trainees could simultaneously undergo navigation training in the course of a single flight, with obvious benefits in terms of curriculum planning and training costs.[7] Since a navigator-operator (*shturman-operator*) was to be included in the crew complement of the Tu-128, a specialised training aircraft also had to be considered for these personnel, and the Tu-124Sh was the perfect aircraft for the task. The Tu-124 was duly assimilated into the inventory of 978 OTAP at Klin and, as planned, the first group of pilots to convert onto it were Tu-128 candidates from 615 UIAP. This time, the instructors were more senior in rank, with the conversion training programme being led by the commanding officer of 978 OTAP, Col. Sokolov. Col. Yevglyevskiy recalls:

> A short instructional programme was devised for us, covering about 5-6 hours of flying. Then General Savitskiy told us that there was no point in 'ironing the sky' around Klin—we should fly the civil air routes. So we started to fly all over the Soviet Union on airways, training for around a month in this way, which was actually quite sufficient.

Conversion of the line regiments involved both theoretical and flight training, with the theoretical phase for both aircrew and engineering personnel being undertaken in the Training and Methodology Department of the 148th Combat Training and Aircrew Conversion Centre (*148 TsBP i PLS*) at Savasleika. (This was now the newly granted title for the Red Banner Training and Methodology Centre for the Air Force of the PVO.) Flight training was to be carried out by 978 OTAP at Klin using the Tu-124 and by the 1st squadron of 615 UIAP at Savasleika on the Tu-128 itself.

Since the trainer variant of the Tu-128 was yet to fly, it was decided to equip each regiment with a single Tu-124Sh, the first few examples of which had actually been delivered to the Stavropol' branch of the Armavir flying school. Here at the airport serving Stavropol', the 63rd Independent Aviation Squadron (63 OAE) were already using the aircraft to train student navigators for the LRAF bomber force. The PVO HQ flight safety department staff had to prepare a flying programme urgently so that the fighter pilots could perform the interim conversion training on the Tu-124 before moving on to the Tu-128. However, the qualification period defined in the Military Transport Aviation (KBP VTA) Combat Training Course, allowing aircraft commanders to be authorised as instructors in day and night conditions and defined weather minima, was around 4 to 5 years' experience on type. Clearly, a pilot had first of all to gain his qualification as an aircraft commander and build up his flying hours on type; only then could he train to be an instructor. For pilots who would eventually convert onto the Tu-128 and only use the Tu-124 as an 'interim trainer' for the big new fighter this was completely unacceptable. Consequently, Col. Yevglyevskiy was given the task of writing a special training programme for pilots nominated to fly the Tu-128, and describes the situation thus:

> It was impossible to train our pilots according to the KBP VTA criteria, so I had to devise a programme comprising around [only] 30 hours of instruction. I confirmed this programme with the commander of the PVO air force and went off to 'our' [i.e. the PVO] military college at Stavropol' and reported that I had to be trained up as an instructor on the Tu-124 on the basis of this programme. This would also include day and night flying in reduced weather minima, all of which had to be achieved within a 30-hour period.
>
> I began my flight training and I obtained all my clearances within that time, spread over about a month and a half. I'd flown the aircraft in day and night VMC conditions, from both the left-hand seat and in the co-pilot's position, and completed my training with some route flying, using the USSR's civil airways system. The squadron commander set various routes for me all over the Caucasus region and I performed this task successfully, only being sworn at once by ATC [!]. During these flights I forbade my radio operator to use the radio. I flew the aircraft and made all the radio calls myself in order to simulate as near as possible the experience of flying the Tu-128, although the navigator was allowed to prompt me about whom to call. After

this training I returned to PVO HQ. When 'our' transport pilots saw my log book they held their head in their hands and said, 'This is impossible! You don't have the right to do this! What about the KBP VTA?' I simply said, 'Excuse me. Here are the signatures in my log book. I'm ready to fly. You're welcome to come and check me out.'

So this was how we gained the right to train our pilots on the new interceptor, using the Tu-124 as an interim trainer.

The PVO HQ directorate decided that the first regiment to convert onto the Tu-128 would be 518 'Berlinskiy' Order of Suvorov III Degree Fighter Air Regiment (*518 Berlinskiy Ordyena Suvorova III Stepeni Istrebityel'nyi Aviatsionnyi Polk* or 518 IAP).[8] This regiment had a long and distinguished history, including participation in the Korean War, with three of its pilots being awarded the title of Hero of the Soviet Union (HSU). After the Korean War the regiment was based at Vas'kovo, south-west of Arkhangel'sk (Archangel), and by the early 1960s was equipped with the MiG-17 'Fresco'. However, before converting onto the Tu-128, the regiment was assigned a new status (*shtat*) and was relocated to a new airfield at Talagi, around 5-6 km (3-3.75 miles) north of Arkhangel'sk. On transfer to the new operational status, all regiments which were to re-equip with the 'Fiddler' dropped the word '*istrebityel'nyi*' (fighter) from their title. Thus, 518 IAP (Fighter Aviation Regiment) became the 518th Aviation Regiment (518 AP), albeit retaining all of its previous honorific titles. The first group of pilots, led by Lt Col. Korotyeyev, the regiment commander, started their conversion training in early 1966, by which time the first full training programme had been drawn up.

This was a rather demanding time for the instructors on 615 UIAP, who were only just marginally ahead of their students in their 'mastery' of the Tu-128. However, PVO HQ, keen to get the new fighter into service as quickly as possible, wanted to 'move things on'. Having completed their theoretical studies, the 518 IAP pilots immediately progressed to the flying phase. Two familiarisation flights on the MiG-15UTI 'Midget' had been programmed into the course to allow the students to get used to the area around Savasleika airfield. The 'Midget' was very well known to all the trainees, and after this short introduction they moved on to the Tu-124, as well as receiving ground instruction and cockpit familiarisation on the Tu-128 itself. They conducted basic taxiing exercises and fast-taxi runs on the main runway and gradually, dependent upon the level of readiness of individual pilots, received authorisation to carry out their first solo flight on the Tu-128.

All the pilots in the first group selected had the requisite number of qualifying flying hours and held the category of Pilot First Class. However, in spite of their experience levels and an excellent flying category, a range of difficulties soon presented themselves. As already mentioned, these pilots had previously flown the MiG-17, an aircraft that was essentially subsonic and very easy to fly. After the small 5-tonne MiG-17, the pilots were expected to fly a supersonic aircraft twice

Cadet technicians at Nikulino, one of the special schools established to train national service conscripts, undertook courses dealing with the construction of the Tu-128 and its systems. Here, an instructor explains the operation of the aircraft's air intake shock cones. (*Viktor Kudryavtsev*)

the length of the MiG fighter and weighing more than 34 tonnes! It was not only the huge size of the aircraft that made an impression on the MiG-17 pilots—the cockpit of the Tu-128 was about the same height as the second floor of a domestic dwelling and reached via a long ladder. More broadly, the former MiG pilots had no idea how the new interceptor would behave in flight; seen from the ground, on first acquaintance, it simply took their breath away and sent a cold shiver down their spines! So, in addition to providing normal flying instruction for the 518 IAP trainees, the 615 UIAP instructors also had to introduce an element of 'psychological conditioning' to help them adapt to the demands of flying this big new fighter. Col. Komyagin recalls how he had to exhort the trainees:

> 'Don't forget! When you've taxied onto the main runway, align the aircraft exactly on the centreline. Put the parking brake on. On the take-off run, when you select the afterburners, you'll be forced back in your seat. At that moment the brakes [pedals] have to be released sharply and simultaneously, otherwise you'll shoot off to one side of the runway ...'

Nevertheless, the 518 IAP regiment commander Lt Col. Korotyeyev and his deputy Lt Col. Megyera made their first solo flights on the Tu-128 on 10 February 1966, followed in due course by the remainder of the regiment's pilots. The training programme was quite comprehensive, embracing day and night flights in VMC and IMC conditions and also introduced the crews to 'combat application' (i.e. operational use), learning how to use the Tu-128 as an integrated weapons system. This involved interception of targets using different pursuit profiles, with particular emphasis on forward hemisphere attacks—the principal intercept profile for the Tu-128.

The following data show the day flying programme at Savasleika for the first group of 518 AP aircrew converting onto the Tu-128:

Period within 24 hours	Weather Conditions		Aircraft type	Number of flying days	Maximum altitude (km)	Flight time (minutes)	Flying task
DAY	VMC [PMU] Visual Meteorological Conditions		MiG-15UTI	6	16	35	Flight at service ceiling
				7	18	35	Flight at service ceiling
			Tu-124	1	4-8	45	Flight into handling zone
				2	0.5	14	Circuit flying
						14	Circuit flying
				2	0.5	14	Circuit flying
						14	Circuit flying
				2	0.5	14	Circuit flying
						14	Circuit flying
				2	0.5	14	Circuit flying
				3	2-8	45	Flight into handling zone
			Tu-128	4	3-0.5	45	Circuit flying
				5	1-0.5	45	Take-off to conduct landing from box-pattern approach
				6	5-8	45	Flight into handling zone
					9	45	Flight into handling zone
				7	13	45	Flight at service ceiling
					13	45	Flight at service ceiling
				8	Ceiling	45	Flight at service ceiling
			Tu-124	9	7-8 (4-8)	45	Flight into handling zone (under hood)
			Tu-128	10	7	45	Flight into handling zone
					10	45	Flight into handling zone
	Raised Meteorological Minima		Tu-124	11	2-8	45	Flight into handling zone (in cloud)
				12	0.5	45	Box-pattern in cloud
			Tu-128	13	2-8	45 (50)	Flight into handling zone (in cloud)
				14	1-0.5	45	Box-pattern in cloud
	Meteorological Minima		Tu-124	15	0.5	45	Box-pattern approaches
			Tu-128	16	1-0.5/0.5-1.5	45	Box-pattern approaches
	IMC	Aircraft handling	Tu-124	17	8-11	120	Cross-country route flying
			Tu-128	18	8-11	120	Cross-country route flying
	VMC & IMC	Combat Application (Operating technique)	Tu-128	20	8-10	50	Interception familiarisation flight
				21	9-13/8-10	60	Forward and rear hemisphere interception practice
				22	13	60	Forward hemisphere interception practice with target 'on the nose'—i.e. aspect angle 4/4
				23	15-18	60	Forward hemisphere interception practice with target 'on the nose'—i.e. aspect angle 4/4

Night flying programme for the first group of 518 AP aircrew at Savasleika:

Period within 24 hours	Weather Conditions		Aircraft type	Number of flying nights	Maximum altitude (km)	Flight time (minutes)	Flying task
NIGHT	VMC [PMU] Visual Meteorological Conditions			25	8-10/7-8	50	Flight into handling zone
			Tu-124	26	0.5	14	Circuit flying
					0.5	14	Circuit flying
					0.5	14	Circuit flying
					0.5	Cdr's decision	Circuit flying
					0.5		Circuit flying
		Task for pilot	Tu-128	27	1.5-2/3-0.5	30	Circuit flying
			Tu-124	28	Cdr's decision	50	Flight into handling zone (in cloud)
			Tu-128	29	8-9	50	Flight into handling zone
				30	13	45	Flight into handling zone
		Aircraft Handling	Tu-124	36	8-10	120	Cross-country route flying
			Tu-128	37	9.5-11/8-11	120	Cross-country route flying
		Combat Application (Operating technique)	Tu-128	39	9.5-13/8-10	60	Forward and rear hemisphere interception practice
				40	9.5-13	60	Forward hemisphere interception practice with target 'on the nose'—i.e. aspect angle 4/4
					13-15	60	Forward hemisphere interception practice with target 'on the nose'—i.e. aspect angle 4/4

In 1967, a total of seventeen pilots and sixteen navigator/WSOs (weapons systems officers) from 518 AP underwent flight training with 148 Combat Training and Aircrew Conversion Centre at Savasleika. Pilots carried out 218 flights, completing forty-seven airborne interceptions (nineteen at night) and accumulating a total of 250 hours 45 minutes of flight time; the navigators completed 206 flights, including seventy-three airborne interceptions (nineteen at night), accumulating 233 hours 29 minutes of flight time. There is no recorded explanation for the discrepancy between the pilots' and navigators' flight time totals and the daytime airborne interception totals.

At this particular time, Tu-128s were still being delivered to Savasleika directly from the factory, but whereas the first aircraft were ferried from Factory No. 64 at Voronezh by the plant's senior test pilot Aleksandr (Alexander) Voblikov, this task was now undertaken by 615 UIAP's own pilots. The procedure was that the military representatives based at the factory would report to PVO HQ that the next batch of aircraft was ready for delivery and the HQ staff would then issue the

The pilot of Tu-128 (Bort No. 47) signing the engineering log at the end of his flight, with his navigator waiting to climb out onto the small platform on the access ladder. (*S. Shchelokov*)

relevant instruction to 615 UIAP, who in turn would send the appropriate number of crews to Voronezh. On arrival at the factory airfield the aircraft commanders would present their temporary detachment instructions, signed by the regiment commander, and then accept the aircraft for delivery. By this time, Factory No. 64 was increasing the tempo of production of the Tu-128, and in the spring of 1966 they had managed to equip the 1st squadron of 615 UIAP with twelve aircraft. These were aircraft from Series 4 to 9, delivered in small batches of only two aircraft per batch, with each Tu-128 exhibiting a number of manufacturing defects, typical of any new aircraft. Consequently, a team (*brigada*) of factory engineers and technicians was permanently attached to Savasleika for the duration of the assimilation period in order to iron out any snags.

During their conversion training on the Tu-128 at Savasleika, the 518 IAP pilots were 'introduced' to an unexpected manufacturing defect (*konstruktivno-proiz-vodstvyennyi defekt*) on the aircraft. Two aircraft experienced a main undercarriage leg fracture during the ground roll on landing, the first incident involving Maj. Shein, the Head of Flying, Air Combat and Tactical Training (*Nachal'nik VOTP*) on 518 IAP. Not long after this, the deputy regiment commander, Lt Col. Megyera, experienced the same problem, and it was only thanks to the great skill of both pilots that the consequences were not worse than they were. Both aircraft were damaged, but they were repairable, the work being undertaken at Savasleika by the attached factory team from Voronezh, using the engineering facilities of 615 UIAP. The work was fairly complicated and it took several months to restore the aircraft to flying condition, although it had not been possible to establish the cause of the two accidents. The subsequent accident commission simply concluded that the pilots were to blame, but because they had only just converted on to a rather complicated aircraft, no formal punishment was handed out! (The true cause of these failures is, however, discussed later in Appendix 3.)

There was another incident at Savasleika during this period, which although very serious, fortunately did not end disastrously, this time involving the head of 148 Combat Training and Aircrew Conversion Centre, Maj.-Gen. Vlasenko. After his first take-off in the Tu-128, and when somewhat preoccupied with handling the aircraft, he became distracted and failed to monitor the air speed. During the climb he allowed the speed to build up to 700 kph (378 kts) (the maximum permitted climb speed being 550 kph [297 kts]), at which point both sets of flaps were torn off. Fortunately, the flaps were torn from each wing simultaneously, otherwise the ensuing banking moment arising from asymmetric flap operation would have almost certainly led to disaster as the aircraft had not yet gained sufficient height from which to recover. Having burned off fuel, Maj.-Gen. Vlasenko set up for the landing approach, with the truly 'flapless' landing having to be made at a higher than normal speed, since the highly swept wing of the big fighter provided little lift in this condition. Thanks to his skill, the ensuing high-speed landing was made successfully, without further drama, although the incident did demonstrate the need to respect the 'slippery' performance characteristics of the 'Fiddler'.

Since not all pilots on 518 IAP had the requisite flying category or hours necessary to convert onto the Tu-128, a number of changes had to be made to the personnel structure of this regiment when it received its new aircraft. Pilots who did not fulfil the selection criteria, or had failed the special medical board (the medical criteria for flying the MiG-17 were not quite as demanding) were posted to other units. In turn, suitably qualified pilots were posted in to 518 IAP from other PVO units in order to top up the numbers, one of the 'donor' units being 265 IAP, based at Poduzhem'ye and, like 518 IAP, subordinate to the 10th Independent Army of the PVO. In the spring of 1966, an order was issued to 265 IAP requesting that they select a group of eight Pilots First Class, with not less than 700 qualifying hours in their log books. These pilots would be transferred to 518 IAP and then attached to 148 Combat Training and Aircrew Conversion Centre for the theoretical phase of their conversion training, becoming the second group of 518 IAP pilots to undergo Tu-128 training at Savasleika. Having completed the now fairly well-tried training programme, this second group was attached to Klin to undertake interim training on the Tu-124. On completion of this phase they returned to their original regiment at Poduzhem'ye, where they were given time to organise the 'final' move to their new base at Talagi along with their families.

On 10 January 1981, a group of 72 AP pilots and navigators from Amderma pose for a commemorative photograph while deployed to Talagi during an exercise. (*Irina Sadova Archive*)

Here, they would carry out their first flights on the Tu-128 under the tutelage of their own instructors at their 'home' base.

When preparing to re-equip with the Tu-128 the PVO HQ executive staff identified a serious problem quite early in the programme concerning the two-man crew of the new interceptor. Specifically, the problem arose because the first regiments selected to re-equip with this large *twin-seat* fighter were all operating the *single-seat* MiG-17 'Fresco' and Su-9 'Fishpot' at the time. There were only two other fighter aircraft operated by the PVO in this period which had two-man crews—the Yak-25 'Flashlight-A' with a (radar) operator (*operator* or *shturman-operator*) in the rear seat, and the Yak-28P 'Firebar', which was itself just entering service and had a pilot-operator (*lyotchik-operator*) as the second crewman in the rear seat. So, in the early stage of crewing the Tu-128, the PVO had to select navigators from either the Yak-25 or the Yak-28P community or 'poach' them from the Soviet Air Force (VVS). (It is important to remember that PVO Aviation and the VVS were separate and independent organisations until 1998.) Within this timeframe, the VVS was undergoing manpower cuts, releasing personnel who could perhaps be retrained as specialist air defence navigators.

Col. Komyagin recalls this period:

I had a navigator on my squadron by the name of Nagib, who had previously flown as a navigator on the Il-28 ['Beagle'] light frontal bomber, but his regiment had been disbanded. He ended up in a surface-to-air missile unit, where he became an antenna specialist. He'd somehow found out that they were looking for navigators for a new 'aircraft' [*novaya aviatsionnaya tekhnika*]. He submitted a request to be considered for one of these posts and managed to come to see us. He did his first flight with me. When we climbed down from the aircraft after the flight he was crying. I asked him what was the matter. He replied, 'I never thought that I'd ever get to fly again …' These were the kind of people with whom we had to start operating the Tu-128, but all the navigators were well trained and knew their stuff.

Subsequently, the first Tu-128 navigators from 615 UIAP were transferred to the line regiments as senior regimental navigators (*starshii shturman polka*), where they could pass on their valuable experience to subordinates. However, the presence of a second crew member created yet another fairly significant problem—that of co-operation between pilot and navigator. The pilots were all very experienced and self-assured in their flying skills, having come from single-seat fighters, but now they had to listen to 'some navigator' sitting behind them. It was essential to break the stereotype and prove that the navigator was not just a 'map bag' (*meshok s kartami*) but a valued member of the crew. However, as they gradually began to master the aircraft, the pilots also began to understand that it was very useful to have the assistance of a navigator/weapons system operator who could plan flight routes, monitor the aircraft's position and pass heading information when necessary. More importantly, it would have been impossible to fire the missiles without a navigator because all the relevant controls and switches were in his cockpit. He also assisted the pilot to a large extent during the landing phase, witnessed by the creation of a separate check-list as part of the crew's flight briefing material for the Tu-128, entitled 'Navigators' Duties on the Approach'. These included:

- checking the operation of the DPRM (outer marker beacon) and BPRM (inner marker beacon) and reporting their serviceability;
- providing the pilot with height read-outs, speeds and times to commence turns during box-pattern approaches;
- reporting deviations from the runway centreline on approach, giving corrective headings to fly and approach and touchdown speed;
- reporting a steady roll-out along the runway centreline after touchdown, as well as reaching the 600 m (2,000 feet) point from the end of the runway.

By August 1966, some of the first group from 518 IAP had completed their training programme and six crews from this group delivered their Tu-128s from Savasleika to Talagi on the 6th of the month. These were aircraft which had previously been operated by 615 UIAP and had now become the first aircraft for 518 IAP. The next seven crews from the first group for 518 IAP duly completed their training and flew to their home base at Talagi on 12 October 1966, in 615 UIAP aircraft. Finally, on 15 November of that year, the last four crews departed Savasleika for Talagi. The personnel involved in this transfer are listed in the following table, which also shows the typical 'split' of training hours between the MiG-15UTI, Tu-124 and the Tu-128 for crews converting onto the 'Fiddler'. (Note that the Russian designation of the 'Midget' trainer was often given as UTI MiG-15, as shown in the table, or MiG-15UTI. UTI stands for *Uchebno-Trenirovochnyi Istrebityel'* and translates as 'instructional-training fighter').

	Rank	Name	Date of arrival on Rgt.	Total		of which on the following aircraft					
						UTI MiG-15		Tu-124		Tu-128	
				Flying time: Hours & Minutes	No. of Flights	Hours & minutes	No. of flights&	Hours & minutes	No. of flights	Hours & minutes	No. of flights
1	Lt Colonel	Korotyeev	6.8.66	32.35	44	–	–	12.35	20	20.00	24
2	Lt Colonel	Megyera	6.8.66	33.45	46	1.10	2	12.35	20	20.00	24
3	Major	Volkov	6.8.66	33.45	46	1.10	2	12.35	20	20.00	24
4	Major	Galanov	6.8.66	33.45	46	1.10	2	12.35	20	20.00	24
5	Major	Nikiforov	6.8.66	33.45	46	1.10	2	12.35	20	20.00	24
6	Captain	Altunin	6.8.66	33.45	46	1.10	2	12.35	20	20.00	24
7	Major	Shein	12.10.66	33.45	46	1.10	2	12.35	20	20.00	24
8	Lt Colonel	Strokun	12.10.66	33.45	46	1.10	2	12.35	20	20.00	24
9	Major	Tyurmenko	12.10.66	33.45	46	1.10	2	12.35	20	20.00	24
10	Captain	Granitskii	12.10.66	33.45	46	1.10	2	12.35	20	20.00	24
11	Captain	Kravchenko	12.10.66	33.45	46	1.10	2	12.35	20	20.00	24
12	Captain	Trukhin	12.10.66	33.45	46	1.10	2	12.35	20	20.00	24
13	Captain	Krupin	12.10.66	33.45	46	1.10	2	12.35	20	20.00	24
14	Major	Ivlyev	15.11.66	33.45	46	1.10	2	12.35	20	20.00	24
15	Captain	Lyenyushkin	15.11.66	33.45	46	1.10	2	12.35	20	20.00	24
16	Captain	Smertin	15.11.66	33.45	46	1.10	2	12.35	20	20.00	24
17	Captain	Koldomov	15.11.66	33.45	46	1.10	2	12.35	20	20.00	24

In sum, the results of the training programme for 518 IAP in 1966 were considered to have been 'good'. The majority of personnel had completed the theoretical phase, aircrew of two squadrons had undergone flight training on the Tu-124, and the 1st squadron and 'regiment executive' had converted onto the Tu-128. However, since there was still no dedicated training variant of the aircraft, the PVO leadership decided to provide each Tu-128 regiment with a Tu-124Sh to fulfil day-to-day training requirements, although the winter period of 1966/67 proved to be a challenging time for the regiment. 'Troop trials' of the Tu-128 had got under way at regimental level, but the aircraft was still exhibiting a large number of design and production defects that required the constant remedial attention of the factory specialists attached to the regiment. As a consequence, the aircraft stood idle for months on end, but surprisingly there were no other aircraft available for the pilots to fly, the majority of the regiment's older equipment (MiG-17s and MiG-15UTIs) having been passed on to other units. Only two or three MiG-15UTI 'Midget' trainers remained on strength for pre-flight weather reconnaissance and maintenance of flight proficiency of instructor-pilots from divisional and Air Army HQ. Those who had already converted onto the Tu-128 only rarely had the chance to fly the sole Tu-124, while some occasionally had the opportunity to fly the MiG-15UTI. The other crews continued their theoretical studies, by reading flight briefing material and 'practising' their flying techniques, mainly by use of the uniquely Russian technique known as *Pyeshiy po-lyotnomu*. This will be familiar to anyone who has watched light aircraft aerobatic pilots preparing for competition by 'walking through' the entire sequence of the display, simulating every control input with exaggerated movement of hands and feet. (*Whilst entirely satisfactory for the sport of competition aerobatics, with a finite sequence of planned manoeuvres to fly, it was less appropriate, if perhaps no less effective, for the simulation of flight in a large jet interceptor—A.D.*)

The situation became quite paradoxical when the onset of better weather conditions in the spring and summer ought to have led to an increased tempo of flight training. However, the majority of pilots had experienced such a long break in flying that their airmanship skills had been degraded substantially. At this point the PVO Command intervened, realising that it was essential to restore these skills by returning to flying the older familiar aircraft types and only after this continue with the conversion programme. As a result, 518 IAP received yet another Tu-124Sh and a small batch of MiG-15UTIs and MiG-17s to enable this 'retro-training' to get under way, this procedure being organised and monitored on the regiment by PVO HQ inspector-pilot Col. Yevglyevskiy. Attempts to restore the regiment's flying skills and the particular attention shown by PVO HQ officers at all levels played a very positive role. This was also aided by the fact that the regiment was staffed by Pilots First Class, with an already high level of flying ability.

However, the negative effects of the break in the planned training programme did have significant consequences. During one of the early flights on the 'Fiddler' a pilot made a particularly hard landing and although the two crew members were unharmed, the aircraft was damaged beyond repair (this incident is described in Appendix 3). This was a harsh lesson for everyone and in particular for the crews who had to fly this big new fighter for the first time. The incident was just another graphic reminder that the Tu-128 was a very 'serious' aircraft requiring an altogether different approach to its handling. Finally, in the spring of 1967, the time came for the pilots who had been posted in to 518 IAP from Poduzhem'ye to perform their first solo flights. After dual-control introductory flights (*vyvozniye polyoty*) on the Tu-124, comprehensive ground instruction under the guidance of the instructors, taxiing and high-speed runs down the main runway in the Tu-128, the pilots were authorised to perform their first solo flights on the new Tupolev fighter. This is how the future CO of 518 IAP, Col. Skok, remembers this experience:

> We climbed into the cockpit. Captain Popov, the navigator, started to read the pre-flight checks and we received permission to start the engines, then to taxi out and turn on to the main runway. After a short take-off run, we entered the climb with a high angle of attack [compared with the MiG-15UTI and MiG-17], retracted the flaps and undercarriage and shut down the afterburner. At an altitude of 3,000 m [9,840 feet] I levelled the aircraft off and finally managed to breathe more calmly. We entered the circuit pattern and flew back over the take-off point; here it suddenly occurred to me that 'so far everything was normal'—the tension had lifted and it all seemed to have become surprisingly easy. However, the tension soon returned when the time came to set up for the landing approach, since everything on the Tu-128 was different from any other aircraft that I'd previously flown. The circuit speed, the reaction of the aircraft to control inputs, even the view of landmarks on the ground through the different style of cockpit glazing, were all quite unusual. Nevertheless, the landing itself was 'within the norm' …

Pilot training for the Tu-128 went rather well, and within a month and a half to two months of their first solo flights the pilots were entrusted with the task of conducting ferry flights of new aircraft from Factory No. 64 at Voronezh. Capt. Skok (his rank at the time) and his navigator, Capt. Popov, were even entrusted with the ferrying of Bort No. 02 from Savasleika to Talagi following major repairs after a training accident at Savasleika. This was probably the aircraft that had earlier suffered an undercarriage collapse when flown by Lt Col. Megyera during his initial conversion training. By the end of 1967, 518 IAP continued to build up its inventory of aircraft and had expanded its pool of pilots and navigators. However, the critical problem of selecting navigator-operators for the Tu-128, resolved in the early phase of re-equipping the regiment, was considered likely to arise in the near future, and for other regiments programmed to re-equip with the Tu-128 the problem of navigator training had still not been resolved. Consequently, this time, the PVO leadership decided to adopt a timely and proactive approach by starting to train navigator-operators under the auspices of the Armavir Higher Military College for Pilots (*Armavirskoye Vysshyeye Voyennoye Aviatsionnoye Uchilishche Lyotchikov* or AVVAUL). Since October 1945, the college had been involved in the training of PVO fighter pilots as AVAUL (*Armavirskoye Voyennoye Aviatsionnoye Uchilishche Lyotchikov*) and was upgraded to a Higher Military College in 1960, becoming AVVAUL in the process.[9] In the mid-1960s it was decided to set up an affiliate branch of AVVAUL, using the facilities of Stavropol' Military Radar College, to train navigator-operators for the Tu-128. The Radar College itself was relocated to Vilnius in the Lithuanian Soviet Socialist Republic (now the independent Republic of Lithuania).

All military institutions training pilots and navigators at this period in Soviet Air Force history were designated 'Higher' (colleges), meaning that their graduates received a degree-level diploma of State education along with the granting of officer rank. However, it required four years of study to train a navigator who would graduate with the higher diploma, and the PVO Command did not have this time available in their training system. Consequently, the first navigator candidates from the Stavropol' affiliate of AVVAUL finished their training with only a secondary level of specialist education. Creation of the affiliate branch in 1965 had enabled selection of cadet navigators (*kursanty shturmany*) to be made from the recruitment centre in Armavir. At that time only students from the Aviation Training Centres (*Uchebniye Aviatsionniye Tsentry* or UATs) of DOSAAF (*Dobrovol'noye Obshchestvo Sodyeistviya Armii, Aviatsii i Flotu*)[10] who had completed the first year and 40 hours of flight training could enrol in military flying colleges. Weather played a part in the timing of courses in order to be able to plan a full flight training programme, so new entrants would start arriving at Armavir from the end of July, with a cut-off date on 20 August. The first arrivals would be seen by an acceptance commission and sit examinations, and if their results were acceptable they would be enrolled in the college. For those candidates arriving towards the end of the recruitment period the entry criteria were more demanding and the competition was stiffer, as a consequence of the reduced number of remaining places. Moreover, selection of pilot candidates had been completed by this time and late candidates were usually only offered entry to train as navigators.

As a result of this procedure, 105 personnel were selected to form Company[11] No. 9 (*Rota N°. 9*) of the affiliate branch of AVVAUL at Stavropol' and after their personal credentials had been checked the company was dispatched to Stavropol'. This company became the first course to be held at the affiliate branch of AVVAUL, but at the time the students of the Stavropol' Radar College were sitting their State examinations and for a period of around one month there were effectively two colleges at Stavropol'. Unfortunately, setting up the course at Stavropol' could still not even partially satisfy the PVO's urgent need for navigators. Consequently, an intermediate solution was devised—to provide accelerated training for a single intake of navigators for the Tu-128. What was different about this solution was the fact that candidates for this course would not be selected straight from secondary school, but instead from existing students at the Daugavpils Military Aviation Technical College (*Daugavpilskiye Voyennoye Aviatsionnoye Tekhnicheskiye Uchilishche* or DVATU) in the Latvian Soviet Socialist Republic (now the independent Republic of Latvia). This institution trained specialist technicians, with an intermediate level of technical education, to operate ground-based equipment used by the PVO. The Aviation Technical Colleges were organised on a battalion basis and a routine intake had been recruited in the summer of 1964, with the first course being commanded by a Maj. Spitsyn. His battalion comprised five companies: two comprising future technicians with the specialisation 'Aircraft and Engines', one for 'Avionics', one for 'Aircraft Equipment' and another for 'Aircraft Weapons'.

The students had completed the first course and gone on summer leave in 1965, but when they returned to the college a medical board (*vrachebno-lyotnaya komissiya*) had been set up for them. This had been established on the orders of Savitskiy, C-in-C of PVO Aviation in September 1965. The task of this board was to select candidates who could meet the aircrew medical standards and who were no taller than 184 cm (6 feet). This selection procedure was unique in Soviet Air Force practice, and it is possible that the idea was originated by Gen. Kadomtsyev himself, who had become a pilot after first gaining an engineering qualification. Former navigator Lt Col. Zakharchenko recalls his experience of this procedure:

The technician training school at Nikulino had two time-expired Tu-128s on its inventory, seen here in the dispersal, with apartment blocks of nearby suburban Moscow in the background. (*Viktor Kudryavtsev*)

> I had enrolled in DVATU in 1964 and then at the beginning of October 1965 some
> of the command staff of AVVAUL and an aero-medical board arrived at the college.
> First of all they checked everyone from Company No. 10 for their suitability for flying
> duties. Few were selected initially, so they had to test the remaining companies of
> the second course [second year students].

Eventually, however, a total of around 114-120 candidates were selected from the second year course of the Daugavpils syllabus, the selected candidates travelling to Stavropol' by train on the morning of 25 October 1965. Thus, Company Nos 9 and 10 formed the cadet battalion of the Stavropol' affiliate branch of AVVAUL, commanded by Lt Col. Dianok, formerly of the Stavropol' Military Radar College, both groups then commencing their training as navigators for the Tu-128 fleet.

This first course was of abbreviated duration as the students had already studied for a year at a military college, covering, for example, physics, maths and electronics. Consequently, they were not starting from 'zero', although the course for these future navigators was to last another two years and three months, as they were to become a vital part of the crew of the PVO's latest and most important aircraft. In order to inculcate a greater sense of respect for this new fighter, the students were told that each aircraft cost 3.5 million roubles, an enormous sum of money at that time.[12]

The lecturing and instructional staff of the Stavropol' branch of AVVAUL made huge efforts to set up the training programme of ground and flying instruction for these future navigators. Their efforts culminated in 1967 in a joint production, with PVO HQ, of the document 'Flight Training Course for Fighter Aviation Navigators (*Kurs Uchebno-lyotnoy Podgotovki Shturmanov—Istrebityel'noy Aviatsii—KULPSh-IA-67*). The actual flight training was carried out on two types of aircraft: the Lisunov Li-2Sh 'Cab' piston-engined transport (licence-built version of the venerable Douglas DC-3/C-47) and the twin-turbofan Tu-124Sh 'Cookpot'. Both of these aircraft were configured as dedicated navigational trainers, hence the 'Sh' suffix, the flights being conducted at Shpakovskoye, the airfield serving Stavropol'.

During their training the student navigators accumulated around 60-80 hours on the Li-2Sh and a further 90 hours on the Tu-124Sh, of which approximately one-third was 'solo' experience, with a further third of training time devoted to night flying. The first graduation of navigators from AVVAUL (at Stavropol') took place in 1967, differing from the norm in that these young officers had received only a secondary education qualification as a consequence of following an 'accelerated course' which did not give them time to gain the higher qualification. Nevertheless, on leaving Stavropol' these newly qualified navigators were authorised for route training flights on the Tu-124Sh. Altogether, the first three courses for navigator-operators (in 1967, 1968 and 1969) graduated with a secondary education qualification, whereas students on all subsequent courses followed the standard four-year training programme, graduating with a higher education diploma (degree). Apart from this,

The two Tu-124Sh aircraft operated by 356 AP at Zhana-Semey were unofficially given girls' names sometime after 1978. Bort No. 25 (here poorly retouched) acquired the name *Matilda*, while Bort No. 15 was named *Lyusya*. Following the regiment's conversion onto the MiG-31 'Foxhound', *Lyusya* was transferred to 350 AP at Bratsk, while *Matilda* went to 64 AP at Omsk-North. (*Alexander Mamet*)

Stavropol' had started training GCI controllers (*shturmany-navyedyeniya*), with the first course graduating in 1970, these officers being posted to regimental and divisional GCI stations and command posts. Aircrew students knew from the first day in college which aircraft they would be assigned to fly, and those intended for the 'Fiddler' would study this aircraft and its equipment in great detail. Consequently, no other training was given other than that directly aimed at successful completion of 'stage examinations'. On completion of training they would go straight onto the Tu-128 itself, although there were occasional exceptions. From the first class of navigators from AVVAKUL (Stavropol') either eighteen or nineteen were posted to 518 IAP at Talagi and sixteen and eighteen were posted to 445 IAP and 64 IAP respectively. The navigators assigned to 518 IAP arrived at Talagi between 5 and 12 December 1967, after their end-of-course leave period. The difference in dates was because 'travelling time' had been added to their leave to cater for the fact that many of the young officers lived some distance from their new base in the north of Russia. The new navigators were accommodated in relative comfort, on the second floor of the Officers' Mess at Talagi, but were surprised by the outside temperature of around –40ºC, the normal winter temperature for this region!

The regiment was still being formed, and even the 1st and 2nd squadrons did not have a full inventory of aircraft, whilst the 3rd squadron had only older MiG-15UTIs and MiG-17s on strength. Meanwhile, there was also continuous movement of personnel, and new pilots who were posted in to the regiment on an individual basis were detached immediately to 148 Combat Training and Aircrew Conversion Centre at Savasleika. These officers were then attached to the intake of aircrew from the next regiment to convert onto the Tu-128 and underwent their theoretical training with them. Navigators posted to the regiment in the same manner were given a theoretical studies course on the 'Fiddler' and had to pass an examination covering the aircraft and its equipment set by the regiment's specialist engineers. The level of training achieved up to this stage still did not give the new crews the immediate authority to fly the new interceptor, and the young navigators had a long way to go before they could be allowed to fly the Tu-128. However, by the beginning of January 1968, after a further month of theoretical study, they were authorised for flights on the Tu-124Sh, which by then was on the regiment's strength. From this time, they started to follow the programme laid down in the training document KBP-VAS-67, which had been specially drawn up and confirmed in 1967.

The 518th Aviation Regiment entered the new year of 1968 having achieved satisfactory training results. Pilots had mastered various routine day flying tasks and were just about to move on to night-flying training, but then certain leadership issues suddenly arose. The dedicated training variant of the Tu-128 was still another two years away, so the pilots had to carry out their dual checks on the Tu-124, but it was now essential for the regiment commander to take a decision regarding the organisation of night flying on the Tu-128. However, because of what he regarded as an excessive burden of responsibility, the 518 AP commander, Col. Korotyeyev, delayed implementation of a night-flying programme on a variety of pretexts. The year 1968 came and went, and the regiment was supposed to have already assumed combat alert status (*boyevoye dezhurstvo*), but it was not combat-ready and crews were not fully and adequately trained. The PVO HQ executive once again had to intervene in the life of the regiment, in March 1968, when one of its Tu-128s was involved in an accident. (This event, involving aircraft commander Capt. Krupin and his navigator Capt. Karoyev is described in detail in Appendix 3.) The situation on the regiment was complicated. The majority of pilots were all over 35 years of age and the lack of relevant combat training, plus an accident probably attributable to lack of training, could have generated a certain psychological distrust of the Tu-128. Squadron navigator Maj. Ivan Rodyukov remembers this period:

> When we started to have accidents [with the Tu-128] we also started to have special lectures on how to deal with in-flight emergencies. During one of these lectures a section commander (*komandir otryada*), with the rank of major, was asked how he would act in 'this' or 'that' situation. He replied, 'I wouldn't eject [*katapul'tirovat'sya*]. If something happened, I wouldn't jump [*prygat*].' He was struck with fear at the thought that a flight could end this way.

The position was really quite serious. In the period from August 1966 to April 1968, 518 IAP suffered the loss of three Tu-128s, two of which were attributed to 'human factors'. Immediately after Capt. Krupin's accident the PVO HQ inspector-pilot, Col. Komyagin, flew into Talagi to investigate the incident. Here are the impressions made on Col. Komyagin when he arrived on the regiment:

> I saw that everything was going badly. The Commander of 518 IAP was not coping with the task. He flew in a rather timorous way, managed the regiment badly and held back the development of the regiment. To the question 'Why are you carrying out the training plan so badly?' he replied that the weather was not normal up there [i.e. at Arkhangel'sk]. We got the synoptic charts out. 'Is this really bad weather?! Neighbouring units are flying, but you are not!' So I said to the regiment CO, 'You are at fault.' Just then, the deputy commander of the 10th PVO Air Army called me on the telephone and asked, 'Who is to blame for the accident?' I replied that the regiment commander (*kompolka*) was fully to blame; supervising the flights with inexpert actions had allowed the accident to happen. The commander should be removed from his post.

The 10th Air Army leadership acted immediately and took the decision to dismiss Korotyeyev and install in his place Lt Col. Megyera (by now an inspector-pilot) as the commander of 518 IAP. With the arrival of a new regimental commander, the unit commenced an intensive day- and night-flying programme and from that moment the regiment's combat training was placed on a more business-like level.

Following the departure from 148 Combat Training and Aircrew Conversion Centre of the final group of trainees from 518 IAP at the end of 1966, it was now time for the next regiment to convert onto the Tu-128. This was to be 445 'Lenin Komsomol' IAP (*445 imyeni Leninskovo Komsomola IAP*), which was based at Khotilovo and subordinate to the Moscow District (*Moskovskiy Okrug*) of the PVO. Two interceptor regiments were based here: 445 IAP, equipped with the Yak-25M 'Flashlight-A', and 790 IAP with the Su-11 'Fishpot-C'. The first group of 445 IAP aircrew, led by regiment commander Col. Saninyn, commenced their conversion onto the Tu-128 at the beginning of 1967. At about the same time, an order was given to 148 Combat Training and Aircrew Conversion Centre to train 445 IAP pilots and navigators to participate in the air show planned to celebrate fifty years of Soviet power. The air parade was planned for 9 July 1967, with flypasts being made over Moscow and centred on Domodiedovo airport. This order to participate in the air show significantly complicated 445 IAP's conversion programme since now, in addition to the normal training programme, the pilots had to be taught how to fly the 'Fiddler' in close formation before they had really mastered the aircraft.

A line-up of pristine Tu-128s at Amderma in the early years of operation, with profiled covers over the cockpit, air intakes and the environmentally vulnerable engineering break on the rear fuselage. (*Aleksey Kalinovski*)

Obviously, in a flypast such as this, aircraft had to maintain the closest possible formation as they overflew the spectators at Domodiedovo, but the Tu-128 pilots had not yet been trained to do this. The aerodynamics of the aircraft were such that it accelerated rapidly; even at low power settings it exhibited high inertia and, not being equipped with air brakes, was reluctant to decelerate. However, with expert training and leadership from the regiment commander, the pilots of 445 IAP successfully demonstrated the new fighter to an admiring Moscow public as well as to intensely curious Western observers. After the flypast, the crews returned to their home base, although this was no longer Khotilovo, since while converting onto the Tu-128 at Savasleika the regiment had been redeployed to a new airfield at Savvatiya, a few kilometres south of Kotlas. The decision to build a new airfield for 445 IAP had been taken some time earlier and construction of the airfield and the military township (*voyennyi gorodok*) around it had actually started in 1963.[13] The location was selected because of the proximity of the railway linking the towns of Kotlas and Kirov, whilst the distance from Kotlas meant that the take-off and landing paths would not take aircraft directly over the town. (Surprisingly, many older military airfields had been built quite close to the boundaries of nearby towns, such as Rzhev, Smolensk, Morshansk, Kursk and Pravdinsk.) The runway and infrastructure were designed from the outset for the operation of the Tu-128, construction of the airfield and living accommodation being supervised personally by Gen. Batitskiy, the commander of the PVO's Moscow District.

By the spring of 1967, the main buildings at Savvatiya had been completed, with support units for the new airfield being set up from scratch. On 15 March, the 677th Independent Communication and Airfield Landing Aids Division (ODSRSP) began to form at Tunoshna airfield near Yaroslavl' and in parallel with this unit, an Independent Airfield Support Battalion (OBATO) was formed at Bezhetsk airfield. A radio-technical (i.e. radar) battalion (*radiotekhnicheskiy batal'on* or RTB) was attached to 677 ODSRSP which itself had been created from the radar battalion billeted in Vologda. Then 677 ODSRSP was renamed the 677th Independent Communications and Airfield Radar Support Battalion (OBSRTO). From 27 April 1967, when 677 OBSRTO arrived at Savvatiya, until August, the unit completed the deployment of communications facilities and airfield radar installations at the new base. Thus, the military airfield construction brigades had completed the work in time for the regiment to move into its new base in that year, complete with garrison and married quarters. Industry had also started to roll out new Tu-128s more regularly, allowing 445 IAP to build up its inventory, and mastery of the big new Tupolev interceptor proceeded very successfully. Nevertheless, some Yak-25M 'Flashlight-A' and Yak-25U aircraft had been relocated to the new airfield, which was a wise decision as it allowed crews who had not yet converted onto the Tu-128 to maintain their flight currency. *(The Yak-25U was never separately identified by NATO as a training variant of the 'Flashlight' and did not receive a NATO code-name in the 'miscellaneous' category like other trainers. Similarly, nothing has been written about the Yak-25U in Russian studies of the Yak-25/26/27/28 family and it is likely that the small number of Yak-25Us used for conversion and proficiency training were modified from obsolescent or obsolete interceptor variants –A.D.)*

The initial period of training on the 'Fiddler' was seen as a time for bold experimentation, and the idea cropped up within the PVO fighter community that Tu-128 aircraft commanders could be recruited from the bomber force. After all, the cockpit and overall size of the new interceptor were similar to that of a medium bomber such as the Tu-16 'Badger'. (It will be recalled that the Tu-16 had earlier been evaluated as a possible interim conversion trainer for the Tu-128.) The opportunity to consider this idea more closely arose quite unexpectedly. For quite some time a Tu-16 based at Savasleika had been used during exercise periods as a realistic target for PVO interceptors. The pilot of this Tu-16 was one Capt. Nyeklyudov, who, having seen the new Tu-128, had shown great interest in the aircraft.

Col. Komyagin takes up the discussion about this particular development in the history of Tu-128 operations:

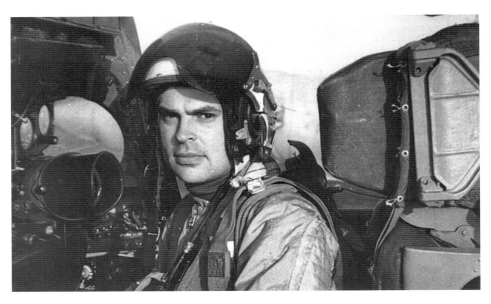

In spite of the large size of the Tu-128, the cockpits seemed to be quite compact. Note the light-excluding visor of the radar scope on the left. (*S. Fedoseenko*)

Nyeklyudov looked at the cockpit of the Tu-128 and came to the conclusion that it was very similar to the cockpit of the Tu-16. He said, 'What about flying it here and now? I could get in and fly off!' The deputy head of 148 Combat Training and Aircrew Conversion Centre eventually heard about our conversation and suggested that we should see if we could retrain Nyeklyudov on the Tu-128. The Tu-16 pilot agreed. Another thing that pleased him was that the job of section commander carried with it the rank of major [the equivalent in a Western air force would be flight commander]. It was duly decided that by way of experiment we would attempt to retrain him on the Tu-128. We obviously already had a training programme set up for 'our' [the Tu-128] aircraft. Firstly, however, I accompanied him on a [check] flight in the Tu-124 and I was greatly impressed; he was a skilful pilot, with an excellent feel for the aircraft. He flew very calmly, chatting to me throughout the flight. He held the controls in a relaxed manner, holding the control wheel with arms slightly bent, flying the aircraft so smoothly that I was prompted to ask if he had flown the Tu-124 before. He replied, 'Of course not! But it's 'our' aircraft … [Probably meaning it was a Tupolev and therefore similar to his own regular mount.]

He took off like a bird and landed beautifully; I couldn't even hear the usual squeal of the tyres as we touched down. I decided that there was no need to go through the entire dual-control phase with him—there was no point in wasting time needlessly. So I told him, 'You fly splendidly; I'll brief you on the details and then you can fly the Tu-128 tomorrow.' However, he said that he still needed a little more time and

I could see that something was troubling him. I'd carried out several flights with Nyeklyudov in accordance with our standard conversion programme and decided that I had to send him off on the 'combat version' [the Tu-128]. At about the same time, I had to go off on leave in a couple of days and I personally wanted to send him on his first solo on the Tu-128 before that. I was on the point of authorising his first solo on the aircraft, but he was very nervous and although he put on a brave face, his body language showed that he was very uneasy about it. I then realised that he was psychologically afraid of the speed with which everything happened on this aircraft and the fact that it didn't have a second pilot. I tried to reassure him by saying that the main thing was not to exceed the speeds for retraction of flaps, as they were not particularly robust in design. The Tu-128 gained height rapidly, with unstick occurring at 320 kph [173 kts], while the landing speed was 310 kph [167 kts]. By contrast, the Tu-124 took off and landed at 240-250 kph [130-135 kts], quite a major difference in speeds. I reminded him, 'You don't have a second pilot and the navigator can't help you because he can't see anything. All his hopes will rest on you. You must bring him back alive!' Nyeklyudov confirmed to me that he understood everything and he sat for a long time in the cockpit, going over everything time and again.

The flight controller [*Rukovodityel' Polyotov* or RP] for that day was our regiment commander Colonel Zakharov and he handed over control of Nyeklyudov's flight to me, saying, 'I don't fly this aircraft. You control him yourself.' Finally, 'my' pilot took off and I saw the aircraft lurch upwards and then lurch downwards, producing two strong phugoid manoeuvres. I called to him on the radio, 'Steady, steady. Hold it steady. Retract the undercarriage. Retract the flaps ...' He made two passes over the airfield and I asked him, 'Are you ready for the landing?' He said he was and commenced his approach, touching down a little short, just before the 'piano keys', but this was fairly normal for a first flight on the Tu-128. I met him after he had taxied in and watched as he climbed out, quite drained by the experience. I asked him, 'How was it?' He was full of praise for the aircraft, but declined to make a second flight that day. I reported to the regiment commander that Nyeklyudov did not want to fly and then I went off on leave the following day. When I returned I was told that he hadn't flown the Tu-128 since that first occasion. I had a chat with him and he explained that he wanted to go back onto the Tu-16, so we had achieved nothing from our little experiment. He had not been able to cross the psychological barrier caused by the absence of a second pilot on such a heavy aircraft.

Although that experiment had concluded rather negatively, the next regiment selected to re-equip with the 'Fiddler' had already arrived at Savasleika. This was 64 IAP which was based at Omsk-Severnyi (Omsk-North), operating the Su-9 'Fishpot'. This was the first PVO line regiment to convert onto the Tu-128 directly from the Su-9 and the conversion did not present the 64 IAP pilots with any particular difficulties. (As a general rule, pilots coming onto the Tu-128 from the much smaller and lighter MiG-17 found the transition particularly hard.) The regiment had several pilots holding the flying category of Pilot First Class and a minimum of not less than 500 flying hours' experience; only a small number of 64 IAP's younger pilots did not satisfy this stringent requirement and were transferred to 350 IAP. (This regiment was located together with a Long-range Air Force unit at Belaya in Irkutsk Oblast [province] until 1984, after which it was relocated to Bratsk, further to the east in the Irkutsk Oblast.) In their place, four pilots with the requisite flying category and experience were posted in to 64 IAP. The regiment's aircrew included pilots with the ranks of captain, major and lieutenant colonel and were all over 35 years of age, except for senior lieutenants Lyebyedyev and Grishin, both of whom were only 26 years old. In spite of their relative youth, both pilots had the necessary flying category and the qualifying flying hours to undergo conversion onto the Tu-128. Even the regiment commander, Col. Sinyukaev, who had formed 64 IAP, had not passed the medical board to allow him to fly the Tu-128. However, this was not the only unusual thing about 64 IAP—there were only two pilots on the regiment who had a higher (degree-level) education qualification, namely the two lieutenants, the older pilots having only graduated from 'secondary' military colleges. The 64 IAP pilots found the transition from the rugged little Sukhoi fighter onto the big Tupolev interceptor comparatively easy, helped by the fact that the Su-9 had a similar landing speed to that of the Tu-128. They were also impressed by the fact that the 'Fiddler' made the transition to supersonic flight much more easily than the Su-9. They were also comforted by the fact that the Tu-128 had two engines (virtually identical to those on the Su-9), so if one failed the outcome would not be as disastrous as an engine failure on the Sukhoi fighter. Moreover, if they took off in the Su-9 and used afterburner continuously in the climb they would run out of fuel after around 17-20 minutes, particularly when flying without drop tanks. By contrast, the 'Fiddler' with a full fuel load could fly for around an hour to an hour and a half without requiring the pilot to monitor the fuel state constantly.

However, 64 AP was still faced with the problem of recruiting navigators for the Tu-128 and had initially taken 'back-seaters' from the Yak-25 'Flashlight' and Yak-28P 'Firebar' communities. One of these officers was Maj. Spirin who had previously flown as navigator for Marshal Vladimir Sudyets, a Hero of the Soviet Union and former commander of the LRAF, former C-in-C of the PVO and Deputy Defence Minister. Then, in December 1967, the first class of navigators graduated from AVVAUL's sister branch at Stavropol', swelling the pool of navigators available for service on the Tu-128, and this group immediately commenced flight training on the new interceptor. It was not only newly trained navigators who arrived on the regiment at the end of 1967, but also new engineering officers, who, like the navigators, had enrolled in the Daugavpils college (DVATU) in 1964.

Bleak QRA dispersal scenes such as this at Omsk-North in April 1981 epitomised the normal operating environment of the Tu-128. (*Aleksey Bashlyeyev via Yuri Kabernik*)

On the first course the young lieutenants had initially studied the Su-9, then later the Yak-28P, with more than sixty completing their studies in a variety of specialisms. After an initial posting to 64 AP they were then sent off to Savasleika to study the Tu-128 under the auspices of 148 Combat Training and Aircrew Conversion Centre. In this period the final group of 64 IAP pilots and navigators were converting onto the 'Fiddler', along with the remaining technicians and engineering officers who had not yet completed their training on the new aircraft, including a particularly large group from the 3rd (training) squadron. One of the students in this group was Col. Yolkin who had just been appointed aviation commander of the 14th Independent Army of the PVO, after graduating from the Military Academy of the General Staff (*Voyennaya Akademiya General'nogo Shtaba*), completing both the theoretical and the flight training programme for the Tu-128 at Savasleika.

Initial conversion of a regiment onto the new aircraft involved a group that included the regiment executive (i.e. the commander and his deputy), the squadron commanders of all three squadrons, and some of the pilots of the 1st squadron. All other pilots who were not included in the first group received only theoretical training at Savasleika whilst the flying phase was carried out on their home airfield. Here, the instructors would be pilots from the first group to convert, while the ground engineering personnel would have their first real contact with the 'Fiddler' only on their return to home base, since all they had been able to study at Savasleika were 'manuals, placards and notes'. The study phase for ground crew lasted about two months, but as the group of twenty-seven engineers had arrived in the middle of the training period (in early September) they had to study on their own all the material that they had missed. The final group of 64 AP personnel successfully completed their theoretical training and returned to Omsk on 28 October 1967. At that time the 1st squadron was fully equipped with the Tu-128, the 2nd squadron was partially equipped, and the 3rd squadron was involved in the preparation for storage and transfer of Su-9s formerly operated by all three squadrons of the regiment. Engineers and pilots from other Su-9 regiments were sent to Omsk to ferry these aircraft to their appointed storage base, leaving two or three MiG-15UTIs for weather reconnaissance flights. There was also a single Yak-12 'Creek' light aircraft at Omsk which was flown occasionally by Lt Col. Dyervanov, the regiment's Chief of Flying, Air Combat and Tactical Training.

By the spring of 1968, the 2nd squadron of 64 IAP had been completely re-equipped with the Tu-128 and the re-equipping of the 3rd squadron had already started, newly delivered aircraft being from the 24th and 25th production batches. Although the 3rd squadron was still converting onto the Tu-128, the regiment commander, Lt Col. Semikai, had already started preparing the regiment for deployment to the High Arctic. The considerable experience of the aircrew and bold leadership from the regiment commander contributed greatly to the successful conversion of 64 IAP onto the 'Fiddler'.

With 64 IAP having completed the theoretical phase of Tu-128 conversion training at Savasleika's 148 Combat Training and Aircrew Conversion Centre in the autumn of 1967, the next regiment to undertake this phase at the centre was 356 IAP, in 1968. This regiment was based at Zhana-Semey (Semipalatinsk-1) and subordinate to the 14th Independent Army of the PVO. In the late 1950s/early 1960s, 356 IAP comprised two squadrons of MiG-17s, and in 1960 a squadron of Yak-25Ms from 611 IAP at Bezhetsk was transferred to 356 IAP, becoming the regiment's 3rd squadron. Shortly afterwards, the 1st and 2nd squadrons converted onto the Su-9 and, in December 1963, the 3rd squadron began converting onto the Yak-28P (at Zhana-Semey). Thus, from the winter of 1964, 356 IAP was operating both the Su-9 and the Yak-28P. Conversion onto the Tu-128 was also carried out on a squadron-by-squadron basis, the Su-9 squadrons converting first, in 1968, followed by the Yak-28P squadron in 1969.

Starting with 356 IAP, only the theoretical phase would be taught at Savasleika, with all flying training to be performed at the regimental airfield. On their return to Zhana-Semey the pilots flew the Yak-28P only to regain flight currency, after which all flying was carried out in the Tu-128, albeit with weather reconnaissance flights often still being performed in the Yak-28P. The following table of data has been extracted from the flying log book of Lt Col. Zayats and shows his first month of conversion training at Zhana-Semey to qualify on the Tu-128 with 356 AP. Noteworthy is the fact that there is a considerable break in the programme for 'academic study' at Savasleika, with no flying in August and one night sortie each on the Tu-124 and the Tu-128 on resumption of flying training back at base.

Period within 24 hrs	Aircraft type	Date of flight	Flight task
DAY	Tu-124	26.05.69	Wide box-pattern introductory flight
	Tu-124	27.05.69	Wide box-pattern introductory flight
	Tu-124	03.06.69	Flight into the general handling zone
	Tu-128	06.06.69	First solo wide box-pattern flight
	Tu-124	11.06.69	Wide box-pattern check flight
	Tu-128	12.06.69	Wide box-pattern flight
	Tu-128	12.06.69	Wide box-pattern flight
	Tu-128	13.06.69	Flight into the general handling zone
	Tu-124	16.06.69	Cross-country flight Semipalatinsk–Omsk
	Tu-124	19.06.69	Wide box-pattern check flight
	Tu-128	23.06.69	Supersonic handling flight
	Tu-128	24.06.69	Training flight with climb to service ceiling
	Tu-128	24.06.69	Cross-country training flight
	Tu-128	24.06.69	Flight to handling zone to practise flying with hydraulic boosters switched off and shutdown and relight of a (selected) engine
	Tu-124	24.06.69	Check flight 'under the hood' (instrument practice)
	Tu-124	30.06.69	Check flight 'under the hood' (instrument practice)
	Then further activity in accordance with the programme		
	Tu-128	12.07.69	First airborne interception sortie
NIGHT	Tu-124	08.09.69	First check flight into the handling zone
	Tu-128	19.09.69	First flight performing wide box-pattern approach

Under this procedure (i.e. conversion at home base) the flying instructors would come from PVO HQ and from a pool of instructor pilots from Division and Air Army HQ, who by this time had already had experience of flying the Tu-128 in this capacity with 64 IAP. After type conversion, the regiment commander and his deputies would also receive additional training to allow them to instruct the remaining members of the regiment, the pace of conversion of 356 IAP being determined by delivery of aircraft from the factory at Voronezh and graduation of crews from the theory phase at Savasleika. The final group of 356 IAP pilots to complete the theoretical phase left Savasleika in 1971, having graduated as pilots from Armavir (AVVAUL) in 1970 and been posted initially to 22 IAP at Bezrechnaya.

A similar programme was followed in 1969, when the fifth regiment to receive the Tu-128 began training on the new aircraft. This was 350 IAP (350 AP), based at Belaya, near Irkutsk in Siberia, also subordinate to the 14th Independent Army of the PVO and equipped with the Su-9. The deputy commander of 350 AP for engineering services recalls the decision to re-equip the regiment:

The entire regiment greeted the news of our impending re-equipment with great joy. The fact was that everyone was rather bored with the Su-9. In particular, the engineering personnel did not like it very much because it was difficult to maintain. I remember how the engineers and technicians would joke, 'The designer is "dry", but the aircraft is "wet".' [*Konstruktor Sukhoi, a tekhnika mokryi!*][14] The pilots also had good reason not to like the aircraft and, frankly, everyone saw re-equipment as offering great benefits in terms of promotion prospects and rates of pay, which were better on those regiments equipped with the Tu-128.

The process of conversion was a 'grandiose event'—we had to study the design, construction and operating characteristics of an aircraft which was totally new to us, and set up the facilities for servicing and repairing it. The aircraft's dimensions were so great that we had problems in parking it on hardstandings and in the hangars, as well as on the engine run-up pans. A huge problem arose with the location of the [KTS-128] flight simulator, which was a very expensive item of equipment almost as large as the aircraft itself. The only place big enough to house it and its supporting electronic equipment was the regiment's sports hall [gymnasium], which had only recently been built using the regiment's own personnel and resources. It was our pride and joy. The gym was where everyone assembled during their free time, to play volleyball or use the gymnastic apparatus when it was so cold that even skiing could not tempt people to go outside. Now, this building, erected with our own 'sweat and tears' for our recreation, had to be given up. Quite understandably, this caused much dissatisfaction among the officers and men. Unfortunately, there was no alternative and eventually everyone just came to accept it.

Adapting the airfield facilities was not easy and rather slow. We prepared areas for parking the aircraft in the squadron dispersal zones and equipped them with new platforms for gas replenishment cylinders [oxygen, nitrogen, etc.], as well as the storage of large items of ground equipment. We erected masts to support powerful searchlights to illuminate the extensive squadron parking area. At the same time, we received new ground equipment delivered by rail to the airfield, as well as taking some material out of storage. We also received new tractors for towing the aircraft, plus other specialised ground equipment. The ground engineering personnel studied the aircraft and its systems at the factories where they were produced. My own personal retraining took place in one such group where we spent several weeks in Moscow, studying the AL-7F-2 engine at Factory No. 45. Having thus studied the airframe and engines in detail, we returned to the regiment to begin the process of mastering the new aircraft in its operational environment. Apart from this, steps were taken to refurbish old classrooms where we could study and consolidate the information we had received from the factories, using a variety of training aids.

In all, there were five regiments which had already converted onto the 'Fiddler', but there was to be one other regiment slated to operate this aircraft. This was the 72nd Guards 'Polotskiy' Order of Suvorov III Degree Fighter Aviation Regiment (*72 Gvardyeyskiy Polotskiy Ordyena Suvorova III Stepeni IAP*) based at Amderma in the extreme north of the Soviet Union. This regiment had a unique historical operational structure and a long-established combat tradition, having made its name during the Second World War. In the post-war years 72 GvIAP (Guards Fighter Aviation Regiment) was effectively formed from a rotating pool of fighters drawn from other regiments, which would deploy periodically to Amderma in squadron strength to stand QRA duty for the air defence of the northern USSR. From 1956 and through the early 1960s, squadrons were deployed to Amderma from the Moscow region and Gromovo, Khaapsalu and Petrozavodsk in the north, to provide standby cover under the 'umbrella structure' of 72 GvIAP, with Yak-25P, MiG-19 and MiG-17 fighters. In the summer of 1965, even the 3rd squadron of 61 IAP, equipped with the Yak-25M, was deployed to Amderma from its base at Baranovichi in the Byelorussian ASSR (today the independent Republic of Belarus) to stand QRA duty. (It will be recalled that the 3rd squadron of any PVO combat regiment was a training squadron, manned by young pilots 'building hours' and accumulating operational experience after gaining their wings.)

An armed Tu-128 in 72 AP's QRA dispersal at Amderma. Unlike other PVO interceptors, the Tu-128 had only one weapon 'fit' throughout its service – two IR-guided versions of the AA-5 'Ash' mounted inboard and two semi-active radar-guided variants outboard. (*S. Shchelokov*)

With the introduction of the Tu-128 into PVO service, it was decided in 1968 to try to set up a combat alert system with this aircraft at Amderma under the auspices of 72 GvIAP. As the experience of performing combat alerts (QRA) using 72 GvIAP's facilities had been considered positive in the past, it was initially decided to equip one squadron of the regiment with the Tu-128. The regiment's executive group and its commander, Lt Col. Aleksandrov, underwent theoretical training on the Tu-128, but the latter failed the medical board and was passed unfit to fly the new fighter. Shortly afterwards, in 1969, the first Tu-128 crews arrived for QRA duty at Amderma, these being Maj. Karabanov and personnel from 64 AP based at Omsk. However, failure to be allowed to fly the new aircraft had had an adverse psychological effect on Lt Col. Aleksandrov and he chose deliberately to thwart planned operations by the deployed Tu-128 squadron from Omsk. The command authorities of 10th Air Army HQ were forced to intervene and appointed Lt Col. Zdatchenko as 72 GvAP commander in place of Lt Col. Aleksandrov in 1969. (It should be noted here that it was only 64 IAP's air and ground crews who deployed initially to Amderma, the regiment's Tu-128s remaining at Omsk. The first Tu-128s actually to operate from Amderma were transferred from 445 AP at Savvatiya.) At the same time it had been decided to equip the entire regiment with the Tu-128, this being facilitated by taking trained aircrew from other regiments. The regiment's personnel strength reached its established total by the end of 1973, when eight pilots were posted in to Amderma, comprising two pilots each from 445 AP, 64 AP, 356 AP and 350 AP. In order that re-equipment of 72 GvAP could be achieved more rapidly, it is likely that some aircraft were transferred from the factory at Voronezh and others from 518 AP.

The Amderma dispersal of 72 AP, with the regiment's Tu-124 'Cookpot' trainers on the left of the picture and engineering support buildings visible behind the three Tu-128s. (*S. Shchelokov*)

PVO Fighter Regiment Structure

The re-equipment of PVO regiments with the Tu-128 involved the adoption of a range of measures designed to facilitate its early introduction into service. The scale of the work depended upon the equipment needs of the new regiment, since along with the introduction of new aircraft certain items of ground equipment had to be replaced or added to the inventory. A large amount of airfield reconstruction work had to be undertaken, because the overall dimensions of the Tu-128 were significantly greater than any other PVO fighter, requiring the widening of taxiways, enlargement of hardstanding parking areas and the installation of new 'centralised refuelling pans' (*Tsentral'niye Zapravochniye Toplivom* or TsZT). The TsZT was a large concrete pan, usually located near the main taxiway (*Magistral'naya Rulyozhnaya Dorozhka* or MRD), which itself was parallel to the main runway. The TsZT got its name from the fact that it was equipped with centralised refuelling and electrical power points. The TsZT power points were low structures, around 1.5-2 m high (5-6.5 feet), most often made of brick, covering an area of around 5-6 m^2 (55-65 sq. ft) and fed from the airfield's fuel storage tanks through a network of pipes, plus electrical cables connected to the base electricity supply. These made it possible to reduce the need for TZ (*Toplivo-Zapravshchik*) refuelling bowsers and APA (*Aehrodromnyi Podvizhnyi Agregat*) mobile generator sets, or even dispense with them altogether, although where necessary the aerodrome technical battalion motor pool received additional specialised vehicles. It was also necessary to enlarge the fuel storage facilities to take account of the greater fuel capacity of the new Tupolev fighter.

The standard manning levels and aircraft inventory of Tu-128 regiments differed from those of an ordinary PVO regiment, although like the latter they also had a three-squadron structure and a standard regimental executive team. However, the Tu-128 regiments differed in that each squadron comprised three sections (flights) of three aircraft, giving a total of nine aircraft per squadron (i.e. twenty-seven

A Tu-128 of the 3rd squadron of 356 AP undergoing maintenance at Zhana-Semey. (*Vyacheslav Moiseev*)

aircraft per regiment), plus an additional aircraft used exclusively by the regiment commander. For this number of aircraft there was a total of forty-two crews per regiment. Each regiment also had a second-line servicing unit (TEhCh) and a 'preliminary missile preparation position' (*Pozitsiya Predvarityel'noy Podgotovki Rakiet* or PPPR), the latter being an area of the airfield where missile handling could be carried out safely. In addition, a Tu-128 regiment also had one Tu-124Sh 'Cookpot' turbofan transport on strength for navigator and pilot training, later supplemented by two Tu-128UT 'Fiddler-C' trainers. The Tu-124Sh used by the PVO regiments did not differ in any way from the Tu-124Sh used in the flying training colleges. However, since there was no requirement for weapons (i.e. bombing) training, the PVO Tu-124Sh was not fitted with the bomb racks that were a standard feature of Soviet Air Force and Naval Air Force 'Cookpots'.

Lt Col. Yenyutin describes the Tu-124Sh used by the PVO:

When the Tu-124Sh first arrived in the flying training colleges and we commenced our training on it, there was an OPB-15 [*Opticheskii Pritsel' Bombomyetaniya*] optical bomb-sight (if I'm not mistaken) in workplace No. 1. This 'bandura'1 occupied half of the most important area of the cockpit, up in the glazed nose, and since we weren't taught bombing it simply got in the way. When the aircraft arrived on the regiments the first thing that we did was to remove the bomb-sights. Everything else about the aircraft was standard for the navigation trainer variant—nine work stations in the main cabin and the one already mentioned up at the front. Each of the nine work stations was equipped with the same kind of navigation aids [RSBN-2, ARK-10, etc.], as well as air speed indicators and altimeters. It was thus possible to instruct ten student navigators at a time, although not all of the equipment was used during our training. Since we were being trained specifically to operate the Tu-128, we were only taught about equipment which was also fitted to the fighter. This was, essentially, the DAK-DB astro-compass [*Distantsionnyi Astrokompass*—'DB' probably refers to its original application on Long-range Air Force bombers—Dal'nii Bombardirovshchik], the RSDN long-range navigation system [*Radiotekhnicheskaya Sistyema Dal'niei Navigatsii*], the SPI-1 ILS instrument and the astro-sextant. The Tu-124Sh was not used by PVO regiments for continuation training (CT) of already qualified navigators, since it was not necessary and there was insufficient spare airframe life on the aircraft. As a rule, the Tu-124Sh on a PVO Tu-128 regiment was crewed by an established pilot and navigator (i.e. a *shtatnyi ehkipazh*), who never flew the Tu-128. Later, pilots who had been medically downgraded from the 'supersonic fraternity' would often transfer to the Tu-124Sh. Navigation and inter-airfield flights were only ever flown with an established crew, but regiment training flights were flown with an instructor in the right-hand seat and a trainee pilot on the left. The instructor could be a deputy squadron commander or a squadron commander who had already converted onto the Tu-124, whilst the navigator would be an established staff navigator.

The aircrew strength of a Tu-128 squadron comprised three section (flight) commanders, six pilots (*komandiry korablyey*—i.e. aircraft commanders), the squadron commander, deputy squadron commander and the deputy squadron commander for political affairs (the 'political' officer). Additionally, of course, there were the navigators, assigned the title of 'aircraft navigator' (*shturman korablya*), 'section navigator' (*shturman otryada*) and 'squadron navigator' (*shturman ehskadril'yi*) in accordance with their specific duty. The regiment executive group included the regiment commander and the head of the political department/deputy regiment commander for political affairs (usually referred to as the *zampolit*)[2] who could be either a pilot or a non-flying officer. There was also the first deputy regiment commander, the deputy regiment commander with responsibility for flying matters, the Chief of Flying, Air Combat and Tactical Training, the senior regiment navigator and his deputy.

From the historical viewpoint, two important name changes took place when the PVO received the 'Fiddler'. Firstly, since the new aircraft was considered to be a *vozdushnyi korabl'*, literally an 'air ship', (perhaps more poetically a 'ship of the air'), a term used in the Soviet and Russian air forces to denote a large, multi-engined and multi-crewed aircraft, Tu-128 pilots were given the title of 'ship commander'.

The use of this title was more widespread in the bomber and transport community and would have been quite a novelty in the PVO when the term was first applied. By extension, Tu-128 navigators were also designated 'ship navigator'. The use of the word 'ship' when referring to military aircraft will be familiar to anyone with an interest in USAF operations, where the term is often interchangeable with 'airplane'. The term is now also widely used by most Western air forces when describing multi-aircraft groups, e.g. in the expressions 'two-ship' and 'four-ship' formations. The second name change involved the designation of fighter regiments that had converted onto the 'Fiddler', the word *'istrebityel'nyi'* (fighter) being dropped to reflect the fact that the new aircraft was a heavy, long-range missile carrier and not a nimble dog-fighting interceptor. All Tu-128 regiments were thereafter referred to as plain *Aviatsionnyie Polki* or AP (aviation regiments), although sometimes in official documents they were given the title of Long-range Interceptor Regiment (*Aviatsionnyi Polk Dal'nyevo Perekhvata* or APDP). Unlike the procedure used in most Western air forces, the standard abbreviations of most Russian military units are written in lower case letters, although capital letters are used in this book to aid clarity.

With the introduction of the Tu-128 other 'non-fighter' characteristics were adopted by the regiments, affecting in particular the composition of the aircraft's ground servicing crews. These now comprised four-man teams, led by the aircraft's senior technician (*starshii tekhnik samolyota*), an aircraft technician (*tekhnik samolyota*), a senior aviation mechanic (*starshii aviatsionnyi mekhanik*) and an aviation mechanic (*aviatsionnyi mekhanik*). The technicians were all officers, trained at military engineering colleges, whereas the mechanics were usually of senior non-commissioned or warrant officer rank who received their training in so-called 'schools for young aviation specialists' (*Shkoly Mladshikh Aviatsionnykh Spetsialistov* or ShMAS). The composition of these teams remained static until around 1982/83 and they were typical for heavy multi-engined aircraft at the time and widely used in the long-range bomber force and in Frontal Aviation bomber units. However, in 1984, as an economy measure, one of the ground crew posts was disbanded, the move being justified on the grounds that the aircraft was by now considered well established in service and its equipment easy to maintain.

Tu-128 regiments had the same ground crew maintenance teams that were traditionally established for other air regiments of the PVO and Soviet Air Force. These were the 'aircraft and engines' group—(*samolyot i dvigatyel'*—SD), the 'armaments' group—(*aviatsionnoye vooruzhenie*—AV), the 'aircraft equipment' group—(*aviatsionnoye oborudovaniye*—AO) and the avionics group (*radioehlektronnoye oborudovaniye*—REO). However, with the transfer to new manning levels for this more complex aircraft, a new servicing group was introduced to the ground crew establishment—the 'radar group'—(*radiolokatsionnaya stantsiya*—RLS). The

Nikulino, near Moscow, which specialised in the training of mechanics to work on the Tu-128. (*Viktor Kudryavtsev*)

standard manning of a single Tu-128 was established as pilot, navigator and the ground servicing crew; pilots most often flew with their own navigators, whereas a 'section', 'squadron' or 'regiment' navigator could fly with any pilot. Similarly, a 'section commander' and other senior pilots could fly with any navigator. Crews could sometimes be changed if personnel were detached on duty or on leave, and on most regiments there was always a 'navigator without a pilot' and 'a pilot without a navigator'. Not all personnel went on leave 'as a crew'; very often individuals would go on leave separately. Attempts to introduce the concept of 'everyone on leave as a crew' did not catch on in the units because of the difficulty of integrating the flying roster with the leave roster.

In the early stages of re-equipping with the 'Fiddler', when all pilots on a regiment were Pilots First Class, all the squadrons were notionally equal in terms of the level of pilot training and experience. However, gradually the level of pilot classification (*klassnost'*) began to change as personnel moved on, and it became necessary to designate the 3rd squadron as a dedicated training squadron. This, of course, was not in itself unusual, since this had been an established procedure in the Soviet air forces for some years, but the more rigorous criteria for selection to fly the Tu-128 meant that there were no inexperienced pilots in the original intakes. There was, however, an exception in that the 2nd squadron of 64 AP was designated as the training squadron. This evidently arose because the 1st and 3rd

An instructor explains the tyre-change procedure to two cadets studying the 'aircraft and engines' discipline at Nikulino. The information board in the background provides guidance for the 'Maintenance of the Hydraulic System'. (*Viktor Kudryavtsev*)

squadrons were located on the edge of the airfield at Omsk-North, whereas the 2nd squadron was located more centrally. This meant that it was more convenient to use this squadron's aircraft for training flights, since it did not involve towing the aircraft far for pre-flight preparation and fuelling. Eventually, however, younger pilots did start coming onto the Tu-128 units and, as in other regiments, they were placed initially in the 3rd squadron, where they would be trained up to Pilot Third Class (if they were 'unclassed' graduates of a flying school) or Pilot Second Class standard. They would then be transferred to the 2nd or 1st squadrons as and when vacancies occurred. It should be remembered that only the 1st and 2nd squadrons were entitled to stand combat alerts with fully armed aircraft.

In spite of the established manpower needs of a Tu-128 regiment, the number of aircraft on the inventory during the period of its operation changed for a number of reasons. Firstly, of course, there would be losses due to accidents, and then the number of Tu-128UT and Tu-124Sh trainers on strength would vary when they were transferred to other regiments as necessary. Typical regimental holdings of Tu-128 and Tu-128UT are given in the following table for two regiments of the 14th Independent Air Army of the PVO at the beginning of the 1980s:

Regiment	Squadron	Bort Number of Tu-128 (Tu-128M)	Bort Number of Tu-128UT
350 AP Belaya	1st Aviation Squadron	*04, 11, 15, 17, 31, 34, 36, 41, 71, 85*	
	2nd Aviation Squadron	*18, 24, 25, 27, 43, 93, 95*	
	3rd Aviation Squadron	*01, 14, 19, 23, 29, 35, 45, 63, 65, 81*	*03, 15, 45, 49*
356 AP Semipalatinsk-1	1st Aviation Squadron	**01, 05, 22, 23, 35, 61, 85, 93, 94, 95**	
	2nd Aviation Squadron	**02, 12, 21, 24, 44, 82, 91**	
	3rd Aviation Squadron	**03, 04, 19, 33, 34, 41, 75**	**11, 15**

It should be noted that there was no unified system for the creation of Bort numbers at manufacturing plants, although in general they were formed from elements of the construction number of the aircraft. When 64 AP at Omsk-North first started operating the Tu-128 the following system was in use: as on most Soviet military aircraft the Bort number consisted of two digits, the first of which was taken from the series number and the second from the number of the aircraft in the series. For example, if the factory construction number (c/n) was 1307, then the Bort number would be 37, although in 64 AP there were exceptions. A Tu-128 with Factory No. 2103 was not given the universally disliked Bort No. 13, as would be expected from the general principle outlined above, but was instead numbered 21. There were, however, regiments where Bort No. 13 could be found on the Tu-128. There was an aircraft on 64 AP with this number, which was flown most often by the regiment commander, Col. Starovyerov, but when he was promoted and posted away from the regiment the Bort number was changed. When Col. Komyagin, who was not a superstitious person, commanded the training squadron of 615 UIAP there was a Tu-128 and a Tu-128UT on strength, both of which carried the 'ominous' number 13.

The majority of regiments equipped with the Tu-128 were based at joint-user airfields, i.e. airfields which usually also served as the local civil airport. For example, Talagi was the civil airport for the town of Arkhangel'sk, and Zhana-Semey served as the airport for Semipalatinsk, whilst Amderma airfield was also the airport for the nearby town of the same name. From 1984, the civil airport at Bratsk became host to 350 AP after it was transferred from Belaya. Prior to that, 350 AP had shared the airfield at Belaya with an LRAF bomber regiment operating the Tu-16 'Badger', this airfield being the only Tu-128 base exclusively 'owned' and operated by the military. The airfield at Omsk-North was shared with the local aircraft manufacturing plant, Factory No. 166, which in the late 1940s had produced the Tu-2N 'Bat' light piston-engined bomber, and then in the 1950s the Il-28 'Beagle' twin-jet tactical bomber, followed by the Tu-104 'Camel' twin-jet passenger liner. After switching to the manufacture of ballistic missiles and space vehicles, the plant returned to aircraft manufacturing in the 1970s, eventually adopting the title Federal State Unitary Enterprise 'Polyot'. The factory had an aviation section (*otryad*) comprising four Lisunov Li-2 'Cab' and two An-12 'Cub' transports, occupying a separate small parking area on the airfield. In the main, these were old and established airfields, Talagi, for example, having been used during the Great Patriotic War. In order to provide year-round operations at that time the main runway and taxiways had been covered with metal planking (a form of pierced steel planking, or PSP, similar to that used by Western air forces). In the 1950s it was decided to create a civil airport within the territory of the military airfield at Talagi, capable of taking the Il-14 'Crate' passenger transport, at that time the Soviet Union's principal modern short-haul airliner. As a result, Talagi was provided with a well-equipped concrete runway capable of handling the most modern aircraft of the day.

The most favourably located Tu-128 airfield was Savvatiya, near Kotlas in Arkhangel'sk Oblast, built from scratch specifically to meet the requirements of the new interceptor. The only shortcoming of the new airfield from a pilot's perspective was the slightly narrow main runway, which at a width of 47 m (154 feet) was a little tricky for the 22 m (72 feet) turning radius of the Tu-128's outer bogies. The radar and instrument landing aids at all airfields where the 'Fiddler' was based were located at one end of the runway, which was not a limiting factor since nine out of ten take-offs would be in that direction and the prevailing wind direction rarely changed. The only exception was at Omsk, where the landing aids were situated at both ends of the runway, although later one system was removed and re-installed at the diversion airfield at Khatanga. If a landing had to be made on the runway not served by ILS and radar then pilots could make the approach using information from the automatic radio compass (ARK).

Even after the introduction of the Tu-128 there was still a need for a certain amount of airfield construction work on some of the bases, as recalled by Maj. Plyuta, a former aircraft technician on 64 AP:

> When we came to Omsk in 1967 we didn't even have a TsZT [central refuelling point] on the airfield. During flight operations the first departure of aircraft would be made from the squadron area and the next from one of the taxiways. [After the sortie] the aircraft would then land, taxi along the main taxiway and park at an angle to the centreline. The next aircraft would park behind it, at an angle to the main taxiway and parallel to the first aircraft. They were parked so that servicing vehicles could approach the aircraft, but only from the earth surrounding the taxiway itself.

In these circumstances it was impossible to carry out a safe engine start while parked directly on the main taxiway. The flight crews would therefore carry out

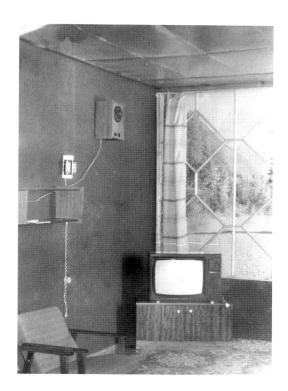

Local artists, using 'photo-wallpaper' panels, created 'false' scenic views, like those visible from the crew room, depicting the surrounding countryside. Aircrew 'relaxation rooms' such as this one at Amderma were designed solely for that purpose, hence the absence of instructional posters or military photographs on the walls. (*Valeriy Yalyaev*)

the pre-flight inspection and external checks of the aircraft and then climb into the cockpit, after which a tractor would tow them out to the main runway. Here there would be a pre-positioned APA vehicle to provide ground power, and the crew would start engines, taxi onto the runway and take off.

The technician who had seen off his aircraft would drive the tractor to the end of the runway and meet the incoming aircraft after completing its sortie. It was only some time later that 64 AP would be provided with a sufficiently wide TsZT to meet the needs of the Tu-128. Thereafter, the regiment's aircraft could taxi in and out of dispersal and park parallel to each other between the refuelling points (*kolonki*), as was the practice at Soviet Air Force (VVS) bases. Although 64 AP occupied virtually all of the airfield area, Factory No. 166 had a separate taxiway and a parking area adjoining the regiment's combat alert dispersal, and there were a number of single-storey buildings in the squadron dispersal area for the ground crew and maintenance equipment. Up until 1968, each squadron had its own 'squadron zone', although the aircraft were not housed in shelters but simply parked side by side in the open. It was only in the spring and summer of 1969 that mounded earth-type shelters (*obvalovanie* in the singular) were created for each Tu-128 and its servicing vehicles, a decision taken by the Soviet Ministry of Defence, drawing on the experience of the Arab–Israeli Six-Day War in 1967.

In that conflict, Egypt suffered huge losses to Israeli air strikes that destroyed scores of unprotected aircraft lined up alongside each other on open taxiways and parking areas. The work of creating the earth shelters turned out to be something of an epic, with all units and personnel on the base co-opted onto the project, working without breaks or free time, piling up the earth and covering it with turf, creating up to twelve shelters per squadron. On 445 AP, a TsZT centralised refuelling pan was built at the same time as the shelters were being created, the work being carried out by an engineering battalion from Vyshniy Volochek, although for various reasons the work dragged on from 1971 to 1974.

As well as handling problems associated with the assimilation of new equipment, most of the regiments also had to deal with the additional problem of accommodating the officers, since the number of technical personnel and aircrew had effectively doubled for the Tu-128. This problem was particularly acute in the major towns adjoining the air bases, and at Omsk-North, for example, the aircrew had to live in a 'garrison town' (*sluzhebnyi gorodok*) within the city itself. In the early period of 64 AP's Tu-128 operations the situation as far as officers' accommodation was concerned was simply lamentable. The pilots and navigators lived in what was really an airmen's club, situated on the military garrison. A large hall in the building was partitioned off with movable panels, dividing the area into several small 'cells'. Here the crews lived with their families!

Soon, however, on the advice of Col. Komyagin, now a PVO inspector-pilot, the regiment's senior officers approached the city authorities with a request to allocate one building to accommodate the families of service personnel. But everyone knew that there would be little point in putting this request to them directly as it would be refused, so the regiment resorted to a little bit of military subterfuge. The regiment commander invited the chairman of the Omsk city executive committee and the First Secretary of the Omsk Communist Party committee to visit the base as guests of the regiment. The pretext for this visit was to see at first hand the regiment's new aircraft, and the VIPs and their entourage duly arrived at the base on the appointed day, where the Tu-128 was demonstrated to them in the air and on the ground. Then, after a celebratory meal, the civic dignitaries were taken to see how the crews lived in their off-duty time. The regiment did not have to wait long for a result—presumably suitably shamed by what they had seen of the officers' accommodation, the city's administration handed over an entire residential block for the exclusive use of 64 AP!

It was quite some distance from the military garrison and barrack accommodation in Omsk to the airfield at Omsk-North, so as a rule, if there was no urgent military activity or flying taking place, personnel would work on the airfield until lunchtime and then would be involved in working in and around the garrison area. Transport between the garrison and the town was provided by Ural-375 three-axle trucks, primarily used for towing the aircraft on the airfield, each Tu-128 squadron having two of these vehicles at its disposal for this purpose.

The most southerly located Tu-128 unit was 356 AP based at Zhana-Semey (Semipalatinsk), a major railway town, with the airfield located adjacent to it. The airfield has a long and interesting history, serving as the airhead for the Semipalatinsk nuclear test range, although by the middle of the 1960s the airfield had lost much of its previous importance and began serving the civil air transport needs of the local population. In the 1960s, the civil airport and 356 AP were situated on the same side of the main runway, but later the airport facilities were moved to the opposite side of the airfield. Towards the end of the 1970s, the name Semipalatinsk-1 came to be used to describe the military side of the airfield, the garrison itself being about half an hour's walk from the airfield. Flight operations by 356 AP were conducted from three dispersal zones (*zony rassredotocheniya*) where almost all the aircraft were parked in protected hardstandings; only the Tu-128UTs and one Tu-128 of the 3rd (training) squadron were parked out in the open.

Semipalatinsk airfield was equipped with a 3,000 m (9,850 feet) main runway, a legacy from the previous occupants of the base, although it did have an interesting feature in that one end was considerably lower than the other. If the flight was being conducted in the 'uphill' direction then the pilot did not really have to take this into consideration, and in any case the ILS facility was available on this runway. However, if it was 'downhill' then the landing was a little more difficult and the pilot had to push the control column forward just before touchdown rather than pulling it back and allowing the aircraft to sink onto the runway. If the point of touchdown was outside the ideal area, some 150-200 m (490-660 feet) from the threshold, then the aircraft had to be 'forced' down onto the runway, otherwise it could balloon upwards because of the downward curvature of the surface and significantly overshoot the touchdown point. This, in turn, could result in a 'critical write-up' in the Controller of Flying log book, or worse, it could lead to an accident. The main runway underwent repairs between 1980 and 1982, receiving cosmetic refurbishment work in 1980/81 and then a programme of major repairs in the summer of 1982. While this work was being carried out, 356 AP was deployed to Omsk-North for several months. In the spring and autumn period the ground adjacent to the runway at Semipalatinsk used to become very waterlogged and could remain so for up to a week. If during this time a heavy aircraft such as an Ilyushin Il-76 was to land there, water would be squeezed out from the concrete panels and spread over the runway surface for several metres.

Perhaps the most difficult basing challenge, however, was faced by 350 AP, which up to 1984 was located at the old military airfield of Belaya in Irkutsk Oblast, some 85 km (52 miles) north-west of Irkutsk city. This was a well-established military airfield with all necessary infrastructure to support the operations of a Tu-128 regiment, both in terms of personnel accommodation and technical support facilities. However, in July-August of 1984, the regiment was relocated to the airport serving the city of Bratsk, further east in Irkutsk Oblast. The regiment

Starting from the 42nd series of Tu-128s, the long stub antenna array for the 1RSB-70-US-8 HF communications radio so characteristic of the aircraft was removed, giving the forward fuselage a cleaner appearance. This aircraft was operated by 356 AP at Zhana-Semey. (*Nikolai Popov*)

Another view of the same aircraft at Zhana-Semey, showing the modified fin tip, incorporating the antenna for the R-846OE HF radio, which replaced the Second World War-era 1RSB-70-US-8. (*Nikolai Popov*)

occupied an area on the opposite side of the runway to the airport, and it has to be admitted that the facilities were not really suitable to sustain a large military unit, its aircraft, personnel and ground support equipment. Only one dispersal area for the Tu-128 had been made available and the aircraft of the 3rd squadron had to be parked in a row out in the open, on a separate hardstanding. The second-line servicing unit (TEhCh) had not been made ready, and instead of a hangar and associated support buildings for aircraft maintenance and repair there was simply a large concrete pan. The only 'technical accommodation' was a small building around which were ranged the vehicles of the *ad hoc* 'field TEhCh'. When it is remembered that the ground crews had to work on the aircraft in the winter, when the outside air temperature plummeted to –40ºC, then the arduous nature of Siberian operations can be fully appreciated. It was only in 1987 that a normal infrastructure was established at Bratsk, by which time the 'Fiddler' was coming to the end of its service, to be replaced by the MiG-31 'Foxhound'.

The airfield was located around 20 km (12.5 miles) from the town, personnel travelling from their living accommodation to the base by vehicle, usually in one of the Ural or Zil trucks from the motor pool. For the first few months after relocating to Bratsk the garrison HQ serving 350 AP was actually on the airfield, but later it was decided to move it about 2-3 km (around 1.25-1.85 miles) beyond the airfield perimeter. As on most joint-user airfields operating the Tu-128, there was only one ATC control tower and even 350 AP's assistant flight controller occupied a runway caravan belonging to the airport. There was a similar arrangement in the 1980s for 72 AP at Amderma, the most northerly situated Tu-128 base, in the permafrost region of the Soviet Union. Here, the harsh climatic conditions had a significant impact on all aspects of life in the area. Paradoxically, the foundations of the regimental TEhCh and its hangar were connected to a powerful sub-surface refrigeration network which was kept switched on round-the-clock during the summer months to prevent the ground underneath the buildings from thawing out. If this was not done they would sink beneath the surface within a year!

As already mentioned, the only airfield constructed specifically from the outset to operate the Tu-128 was Savvatiya, a special garrison base remote from any towns. It was only possible to get to the nearest town, Kotlas, by train, which ran only once a day, and television was only provided in the garrison as late as 1975. In spite of the northern location and remoteness of the base, the conscripts and officers did not receive any pay supplements during their service there and it was only in September 1981 that pay supplements were introduced for time served in the region. From then on, one year of service at Savvatiya was regarded as a year and a half of service elsewhere and personnel were awarded one and a half times rate of pay (*polutornyi oklad*) while stationed there.

7

The Tu-128UT Training Variant

As mentioned elsewhere in the book, the Tu-128 regiments had to operate for quite some time without having a dedicated training variant of the aircraft, relying instead on the Tu-124Sh navigation trainer for this purpose. On each Tu-128 regiment there was a single example of this twin-engined transport—incidentally, the world's first turbofan airliner—designed originally as a replacement for the piston-engined Il-14 'Crate' on Aeroflot's short-haul routes. Apart from the Tu-124Sh, the Tu-128 regiments also had small numbers of MiG-15UTI 'Midget' twin-seat trainers on their inventory, mostly used for pre-flight weather reconnaissance. The sole exception was 445 AP, which used the Yak-25U for weather reconnaissance, these aircraft having been part of its original inventory. In most cases the Tu-124Sh, MiG-15UTI and Yak-25U were on the strength of the 3rd squadron of a regiment. The aircrew used to refer to the 'big trainer' (*sparka bol'shaya*) when talking about the Tu-124Sh, and 'little trainer' (*sparka malyen'kaya*) for the MiG-15UTI. (The word '*sparka*' is the traditional Russian military term usually reserved for a two-seat training variant of a single-seat fighter and derives from the word '*para*', meaning a pair. '*Sparka*' means literally 'with a pair', or 'paired' [of seats], but over time it has come to mean any trainer, without specific reference to the number of seats.)

The decision to develop a dedicated training variant of the Tu-128 was formalised in a joint statement by the Soviet Air Force (VVS), PVO and the Ministry of Aircraft Production (MAP) in September 1966.[1] The draft project for the Tu-128UT was then drawn up in the Voronezh affiliate of OKB-156 under the design leadership of A. I. Putilov. On completion of this phase and by a joint VVS/PVO/MAP decision taken on 4 August 1970, four series-production Tu-128s were earmarked for conversion into the Tu-128UT training variant. Two were to be available for flight testing in the first quarter of 1971 and the remaining two in the second quarter. Then, after conversion and completion of the test programme, the Tu-128UT was accepted for service under MAP order No. 0160 dated 14 September 1971. In that same year, Factory No. 64 at Voronezh built ten brand-new Tu-128UTs (also known by the factory's manufacturing code as 'Article I-UT'). These aircraft differed externally from the four 'prototypes' in having an extended fin tip which was parallel to the fuselage waterline, rather than the cut-back tip of the original Tu-128, this extension housing the antenna for the new R-846 *Prizma-M* HF radio. (*The majority of sources mention a production total of 188 Tu-128 combat variants, including prototypes, plus ten Tu-128UT trainers, manufactured between 1962 and 1971. However, these sources invariably fail to include the four converted 'UT' prototypes, even though the above-mentioned figures clearly indicate that a total of fourteen Tu-128UT airframes* must *have been produced—A.D.*)

The ten new-build Tu-128UTs comprised five aircraft each from the 45th and 46th production batches respectively (4501-4505 and 4601-4605), marking the end of the Tu-128's nine-year production run. Somewhat surprisingly, it was only in the late 1970s that NATO intelligence analysts first became aware of the three-seat Tu-128UT and it was assumed, not unreasonably, that the new version was perhaps intended to perform a specialised combat role, such as ECM or airborne command and control. Available information reveals that the first Tu-128UT was probably delivered to 615 UIAP at Savasleika (in 1971?) by Lt Col. Voblikov, the Voronezh factory chief test pilot. This was almost a decade after the first flight of the combat variant and around six years after the Tu-128S-4 'interception complex' had been accepted for service.

As the drooped nose of the instructor's cockpit on the Tu-128U 'Fiddler-C' resembled that of a pelican, the trainer variant soon acquired the nickname '*pelikan*' in regiment use. (*Aleksey Bashlyeyev via Yuri Kabernik*)

Before PVO pilots could start operating the new '*sparka*' in its intended role, they had to be given formal authorisation to fly it, which meant that at first they were unable themselves to collect new Tu-128UTs from the factory. As none of the line regiment pilots had yet been given such authority, this led to stalemate; moreover, it was impossible to undertake the necessary training flights at the Voronezh factory airfield as this was forbidden by local regulations. The Combat Training Department of PVO Aviation HQ then submitted a request to No. 8 State Scientific Research Institute of the Air Force (8 GNII VVS) at Akhtubinsk to authorise one pilot to fly the Tu-128UT. In due course, Col. Komyagin, the PVO inspector-pilot with responsibility for the Tu-128, was sent to Akhtubinsk with an official letter requesting this permission. This is how he remembers the visit:

I arrived at Akhtubinsk, with 'our' [i.e. the IA PVO's] letter requesting help to qualify on the Tu-128UT. The request did not inspire much enthusiasm from the personnel at Akhtubinsk. This was because some months earlier [on 26 April 1969] the then C-in-C of PVO Aviation, General Kadomtsyev, had been killed at Akhtubinsk while performing a test flight in a MiG-25P prototype [the E155P11]. After this tragedy the senior personnel of 8 GNII VVS were unwilling to assume personal responsibility for such flights. I was directed to seek permission from the Head of GNII. He was a difficult man, but luckily he had already planned to go off on an official visit somewhere. His deputy was Stepan Anastasovich Mikoyan, [nephew of the famous MiG designer Artem Mikoyan and son of Anastas Mikoyan, a prominent member of the Soviet political hierarchy for over fifty years]. I knew Stepan Mikoyan very well [...] Having waited until the Head of the GNII had departed in his aircraft, I went off to see him. I explained to a surprised Mikoyan that I needed authorisation to fly the Tu-128UT. His reply was a simple wave of the hand. 'No, not after the experience with your Kadomtsyev ...'. However, I insisted on having my own way and continued to press him with my request.

In the end he telephoned someone and explained how he was expected to help: '... yes, OK! I know him. Let him have two or three flights and that's it.' He put the phone down and sent me off to see Col. Manucharov, Head of the First Department of GNII VVS [i.e. the fighter department]. It turned out that at that time they only had one Tu-128UT at Akhtubinsk and there was only sufficient time-between-overhaul remaining on the engines for the 40 already planned test flights and it would be impossible to use it for training flights. Nevertheless, after some 'serious' discussions, a decision was taken to combine some test flights with training flights and I was taken off to see the crew [...] The flights were not complex. We performed multi-step climbs to various altitudes and measured fuel consumption rates after stabilising at those heights. I carried out the landing 'under the hood'. Altogether I carried out nine flights on the Tu-128UT with one of the Akhtubinsk test pilots. Having received the required authorisation I went to the factory at Voronezh and picked up our first Tu-128UT.

Col. Komyagin ferried the Tu-128UT (Bort No. 01) from Voronezh to Zhana-Semey and authorised 356 AP's Head of Flying, Air Combat and Tactical Training to undertake training flights on the aircraft. After familiarising himself with the aircraft, he trained up the other pilots on the regiment and in due course the aircraft was introduced into all the other Tu-128 regiments. (By way of example, the following Tu-128UT trainers had been delivered from Voronezh by the autumn of 1971: Capt. Moiseyev had ferried Bort No. 91 to 356 AP at Zhana-Semey, while another '*sparka*' [Bort number not recorded] was delivered to 356 AP by Maj. Shul'gin and navigator-operator Sr Lt Osipenko. Bort No. 62 was ferried to 64 AP at Omsk-North by Lt Col. Zayats and Sr Lt Golynskiy. Another [Bort No. 46] was delivered to 350 AP at Belaya by Maj. Vrublyevskiy and his navigator Sr Lt Korolyov, whilst Bort No. 03 was delivered to 350 AP by Capt. Konovalov and Lt Kusik.)

Some unexpected problems were encountered with the introduction of the Tu-128UT, the first of which mainly affected the instructors. The problem was that the instructor's cockpit was subjected to vibrations of such intensity when taxiing that they felt their 'teeth would fall out'. It seemed at first that the culprit was the nose-wheel leg. The Tupolev OKB came up with the suggestion that the nose-leg suspension (shock absorber) was insufficiently firm [*sic*] and after lengthy work on the problem the nose-wheel leg was replaced. However, this did not produce the desired result and the vibrations continued. The pilots had to put specially made cushions on the ejector seat in an attempt to 'damp' the vibrations. However, the instructors noted that the front cockpit continued to vibrate even after lift-off, up to a height of around 500 m (1,640 feet). There were many arguments on the subject between the line units and the General Staff HQ of the PVO and between the latter and the Tupolev OKB. At General Staff HQ the vibration problem became the responsibility of Col. Yevglyevskiy, the senior Tu-128 inspector-pilot:

I was carrying out flight checks at Belaya, near Irkutsk. We were conducting our flying programme when an aircraft landed, carrying General Fyodor Ivanovich Smetanin, Deputy Commander of PVO Aviation. Having heard about my report on the vibration problem he asked, 'Can we go for a flight in the Tu-128?' I replied, 'Fyodor Ivanovich! Your wish is my command.' I sat General Smetanin in the instructor's cockpit [the engines could not be started from this position and some other equipment on the combat variant were not installed in the trainer] and strapped myself into the pilot's seat.

The take-off was normal and once we were airborne he asked me to let him have control. After about one and a half to two minutes General Smetanin suddenly said, 'You have control!' Without practice it was difficult to maintain straight and level flight, made all the more difficult when it was a little turbulent as it was that day. This was not an ordinary fighter […] and the General clearly did not feel too happy being at the controls. After a short flight we commenced the approach. I had given the General two cushions so that he was not shaken too violently while taxiing and in the circuit. Apart from this I made the landing particularly soft, touching down gently, rolled out quite slowly and taxied into dispersal. I asked him for his impressions of the flight and he retorted, 'You're just a bunch of panic-mongers! There was hardly any vibration in your front cockpit!' I was annoyed that I'd put two cushions on the General's seat to make it softer. Nevertheless, under pressure from PVO Aviation HQ the Tupolev OKB eventually 'capitulated' [and agreed that there was a vibration problem].

The design bureau leadership assigned responsibility for resolving the cockpit vibration problem to Deputy Chief Designer Zalesskiy, whose task it was to oversee Tu-128 flight operations throughout its service with the air defence forces. Col. Yevglyevskiy continues:

Zalesskiy telephoned me and asked if I could take him for a spin around the airfield in the '*sparka*', so that he could experience the vibrations for himself. There would be no need to take off, just simply taxi around the airfield. I, of course, agreed and we arranged to meet up with the personnel of 64 AP at Omsk-North, where I was due to carry out a programme of 'inspection flights'. Zalesskiy came up to the regiment dispersal area and after preparing one of the Tu-128UTs I sat him in the instructor's cockpit and strapped him in, making sure not to give him any cushions, remembering my experience with the General! I decided that the seat had to be firm, as per the Pilots' Notes.

I taxied around the perimeter track, accelerating and braking in turn and then did a fast run down the main runway, raising the nose-wheel, then chopping power and lowering the nose again and braking as I would after landing. After that I taxied around the entire perimeter of the airfield at quite high speed and wanted to give him another 'tour' of the airfield. However, he did not respond to my calls on the intercom and I wondered if he had lost consciousness for some reason, so I stopped the aircraft and called for a vehicle to approach. When the ground crew opened the canopy we found Zalesskiy with his straps undone. Realising that everything was OK, I explained to him why he couldn't hear me—the intercom lead had become disconnected, but because of the vibration Zalesskiy couldn't find it. I asked him if he wanted to do another circuit of the airfield, but he declined the offer, saying, 'Everything is now obvious to me.'

The Tupolev Design Bureau immediately addressed the problem and fairly soon came up with an explanation for the vibration. Evidently it was due to flexing of the less rigid instructor's cockpit with respect to the main fuselage structure, inducing resonance between the two sections. All Tu-128UTs were put through a modification programme and the vibration problem disappeared. Having dealt with this successfully another problem arose, this time relating to the forward (instructor's) cockpit glazing. The two front fixed panels followed the sloping nose profile of the aircraft and were therefore set at a very shallow angle. During take-off or landing the pilot viewed the ground through either the right-hand or left-hand panel, with the angle between his line of sight and the glazing being of the order of 164°. No other aircraft, Russian or otherwise, has ever incorporated such a design, either before the introduction of the 'Fiddler' or since. With the delivery of the first Tu-128UT to Savasleika the rather unfortunate properties of the glazing became evident during the landing approach on a training flight. When looking through each panel in turn there seemed to be a discrepancy of around five metres in the perceived view of the terrain below. Col. Yevglyevskiy recalls his first encounter with this phenomenon:

> I was landing at Savasleika on the first flight, with Col. Nyefyedov in the front seat and me carrying out the landing. After landing I asked him for his impressions. Col. Nyefyedov's response was, 'If I'd landed the aircraft from the front seat then we would have probably crashed. There was no way that I could judge the height for beginning the flare through those panels.' Then we changed places and carried out another flight. The visual sensations were the same for me.

Col. Yevglyevskiy then got in touch with the manufacturers of the canopy glass, the Scientific Research Institute for Technical Glass Products (*Nauchno-issledovatyel'skii Institut Tekhnicheskovo Stekla* or NIITS) which was based in Moscow. It turned out that in accordance with the State Standard (*Gosudarstvyennyi Standart*) for aviation-quality glass in force at that time, the zone ten centimetres from the edge of the frame seal was not regarded as a 'working surface'. If a pilot viewed the ground through the glass at a more or less direct angle (i.e. looking straight through) then the working surface was sufficient for him to see the ground normally. However, on the Tu-128UT the instructors had to look through the glazing at an angle where the field of view of the greater part of it fell within the 'non-working zone'. In order to eradicate the problem the State Standard had to be changed and the 'non-working' zone had to be reduced to 1.5-2 centimetres from the edge of the frame seal. Then it was discovered that during manufacture the layers of glass making up each panel were not parallel to each other. If, for example, the glazing of the left panel was 'inclined' in one direction and the right-hand panel in the other direction then they would have different refractive properties, which exacerbated the problem for the pilot in seeing the ground through the canopy. This problem led to the selection of canopy panels according to their 'inclination', but the quality standards of glass manufacture at the time meant that only one pair of canopy panels in five could be passed as suitable for installation on the Tu-128UT.

Yet another problem with the front canopy glazing manifested itself after the new panels had been fitted. During night-flying operations, reflections from the forward projecting runway lights could be seen around the canopy; the lights on the right-hand side of the runway were reflected in the left-hand canopy panel and the left-hand lights were reflected in the right-hand panel. The instructors were thus subjected to a sea of coloured lines on the canopy during such operations, as recalled here by Col. Yevglyevskiy:

> We arranged a meeting at Voronezh, to which several representatives of NIITS had been invited. The factory engineers towed a Tu-128UT onto the main runway at night, switched on the airfield lighting and then demonstrated the 'illuminations'. I said to them, 'The aircraft isn't moving, but imagine what it's like when we're flying [...] we've got coloured reflections flashing and jumping all over the canopy ...'

The Tupolev designers struggled with the problem for months, but it was never satisfactorily resolved, although a 'half and half' expedient was reasonably successful. Factory engineers installed an *ad hoc* screen down between the two forward panels and later also fitted an anti-glare shield, the instructors eventually learning to put up with the limited visibility from the front cockpit. It was difficult to do anything more effective than this with an aircraft converted from a two-seat interceptor having the fuselage configuration of the Tu-128UT. It is worth noting here that differing refractive indices were also detected later in the pilot's canopy glazing on the 'UT', (i.e. on the canopy of the pilot under instruction), and in specific instances even on the Tu-128 itself.

In addition to its designed function as a 'dual-control' procedural trainer for PVO 'Fiddler' pilots, the Tu-128UT was also the only Soviet fighter aircraft in which it was possible to fly ground crew members between bases when required. Although written records of how often this was done are sparse, aircraft technicians were flown in the aircraft on at least two known occasions in the course of their duty. Lt Col. Moiseyev recalls one of these occasions in the autumn of 1976 when 356 AP had to return to base at Zhana-Semey from Omsk-North (where the regiment was deployed during major runway repairs at home base). This required the head of 33 Division (Col. Yevgyeniy Ivanovich Kostyenko) to be present at Zhana-Semey to 'accept' the runway after its refurbishment and, in addition, to carry out weather reconnaissance there for the returning crews. He therefore took the unique decision (particularly for those times!) of making the transit from Omsk to Zhana-Semey on his own authorisation, flying his senior technician Sr Lt Yuri Ivanov in the instructor's cockpit. So, the following morning, he was able to resolve all his problems in one fell swoop, having his own technician on hand to perform post-flight checks when they landed back at base, then prepare to accept the main body of personnel when they arrived back themselves. Maj. Mamet of 350 AP recalls another similar situation:

In a scene from the early 1980s, Lt Col. Yalyaev and his crew prepare to climb aboard their Tu-128UT to carry out a check flight at Amderma. (*Valeriy Yalyaev*)

A senior aircraft technician and crew from the 350th Aviation Regiment had picked up an aircraft from the Novosibirsk re-fit base after it had been refurbished. The aircraft had to be ferried back to base at Belaya and so as to avoid sending the technician back by train, the crew decided to fly senior technician Vladimir Shurygin back in the empty instructor's seat.

These events, clearly unremarkable in themselves, were commonplace in Western and NATO air forces but quite rare under the more strict protocols of the Soviet military system.

THE TU-128UT AND KTS-128 FLIGHT SIMULATOR

Although the Tu-128UT offered inexperienced pilots the opportunity of honing their flying skills under the tutelage of an experienced instructor, the Soviet Defence Ministry had also ordered a dedicated Tu-128 flight simulator for pilot training. Flight simulators had been in use in the Soviet air forces (i.e. in Frontal Aviation, Long-range Air Force, etc.) for some time and the air force of the PVO already used flight simulators to train pilots on the MiG-17, MiG-19 and the

Su-9. The Tu-128 flight simulator only started to appear on the regiments when the majority of units had already converted onto the aircraft, although it had been ordered considerably earlier. There was nothing unusual about this at that time because the simulators of the day were analogue devices, requiring a huge body of accumulated mathematical data in order to model flight behaviour, usually obtained from extensive testing and operational flying. Such data took a long time to collect and then required hours of programming time to produce an analogue simulation of the aircraft's flight profiles. The KTS-128 (*Kompleksnyi Trenazhor Samolyota-128*) simulator for the Tu-128 was developed in a separate design bureau under the leadership of an engineer named Yefimov (about whom little else is known) and built in 1968 in Leningrad (renamed Saint Petersburg in September 1991). The word '*kompleksnyi*' in the designation, although meaning a 'complex' in general, also indicates an 'integrated system of systems' linking, in this case, a number of electro-mechanical computers simulating the aircraft's flight dynamics. The KTS-128 was quite a complicated device with fairly advanced capabilities for the time, being able to simulate take-off, interception, zonal flights (i.e. general handling flights), landing approach and the landing itself.

A useful feature of the KTS-128 was that navigators (vital crew members on the Tu-128) could also 'fly' missions with their pilots. Simulator 'flights' were carried out regularly by Tu-128 aircrews on the regiments, with simulator 'sorties' taking up about 12-20 hours of training time per month. The officer responsible for accepting the simulator from the manufacturer was Col. Stepan Mikoyan, deputy head of 8 GNII VVS, although he had never flown the Tu-128 and invited Col. Komyagin to perform this task on his behalf. This is how Col. Komyagin recalls this assignment:

> Mikoyan told me why he'd called me: 'I've never flown this aircraft, so it's better if you fly the simulator and I shall sign the appropriate documents.' So I 'took off', performed a simulated flight and reported that everything was normal. Then he got into the simulator and carried out a brief 'flight'. Afterwards he said, 'I don't understand anything about your aircraft,' but Mikoyan signed the acceptance documents and the simulator eventually began to appear on the regiments.

As the KTS-128 was very expensive it was not supplied to every regiment at first. The first simulator was delivered to 445 AP at Savvatiya, the second went to 72 AP at Amderma, with the third unit going to 518 AP at Talagi in 1971. Gradually, the KTS-128 featured on the inventories of every Tu-128 regiment and one was also supplied to the Armavir flying college (AVVAUL) affiliate branch at Stavropol'. It was upgraded several times during the course of operation, but it must be admitted that it was a temperamental device and required special attention from the maintenance personnel. In those regiments where servicing standards were high the KTS-128 worked successfully and reliably right up to the end of its operational use. According to Tu-128 pilots, the simulator operated by 356 AP at Zhana-Semey (Semipalatinsk-1) at the end of the 1970s/early 1980s was the best among all the regiments, possibly because the regiment's executive command insisted on its regular use. By contrast, 350 AP's simulator was used only at Belaya airfield and was not particularly reliable; when the regiment relocated to Bratsk it was dismantled and the engineers never managed to reassemble it. Initially this was because of the lack of a suitable place to accommodate it, but later as a result of the loss of essential parts.[2] Gradually, over time, the KTS-128 began to be used mainly to simulate in-flight emergencies that could not be safely practised in the Tu-128UT, the combination of simulated flight and actual flights in the trainer enhancing the quality of pilot training until withdrawal of the Tu-128 in 1988.

In addition to the capabilities of the KTS-128, realistic simulation of certain in-flight emergencies in the Tu-128UT was possible using the SIO-128 (*Sistyema Imitatsii Otkazov*) 'malfunction simulation system for the [Tu-]128'. This enabled the instructor to 'insert' a number of simulated critical malfunctions into the central warning system and then monitor the student's response in terms of reaction time and subsequent corrective action. This type of malfunction simulation system was used on the majority of Soviet combat trainers and had the great advantage that the aircraft's flight dynamics did *not* require simulation, leaving only comparatively 'simple' systems malfunctions to be displayed to the student. Until the advent of full-motion, fixed-base simulators, the use of an actual aircraft equipped with an on-board malfunction simulator created a highly realistic training tool for Russian aircrews.

Nevertheless, although the Tu-128UT was very useful for the teaching of general aircraft handling, the absence of radar meant that it was virtually useless for demonstrating operational missions (*boyevoye primyenyenie*). However, the radar- and missile-related switches and controls of the combat variant were replaced on the Tu-128UT by dummy switches to preserve the standard cockpit layout and 'switchology' of the Tu-128. 'Fiddler' regiments were able to compensate for the combat training limitations of the Tu-128UT by placing an experienced navigator-operator with a younger pilot for his first missile firing practice on the Tu-128 combat variant. As the six 'Fiddler' regiments received their normal complement of Tu-128UTs, the two or three 'stopgap' Tu-124Sh trainers on each regiment were gradually withdrawn, some being passed on to the training branch at Stavropol' and others going to 978 OTAP (Independent Air Transport Regiment) at Klin. However, this was eventually proved to be a flawed decision, since although each regiment had at least one Tu-128UT on strength they were flown so intensely that they soon ran out of available flying hours before requiring overhaul.

The situation became so critical in 1977 that additional training aircraft had to be sought. Fortunately, this coincided with 63 OAE, subordinate to Saratov Higher

Military Aviation Flying College, converting onto the Antonov An-26Sh 'Curl' twin-turboprop navigation trainer, freeing up a number of Tu-124s which could be passed on to the 'Fiddler' regiments. Maj. Aleksandr Mamet recalls the period:

> In 1977, two pilots and two navigators from each regiment were selected [to fly the Tu-124] and a permanent crew was established, comprising a flight technician, flight mechanic and a radio operator. The whole group came to Stavropol' where they followed a theoretical conversion course on the Tu-124 under the auspices of the flying college there before going on to Klin in January 1978 to undertake the flying phase. Within a couple of months we were trained to fly the Tu-124 in day and night conditions within specified weather minima of 150 m [490 feet] cloud-base and 1,500 m [4,920 feet] horizontal visibility. Later, we were authorised for route flying after a further course of training at Novosibirsk.

However, as regular Tu-128 crews were still not permitted at the time to conduct 'self-authorised' route flying (navigation exercises) on the 'Cookpot', the 'new' Tu-124Sh aircraft were delivered to recipient regiments by crews from Saratov. Thus, in 1978, the following Tu-124s were transferred from the Saratov flight training college:

- Tu-124Sh Bort Nos 15 and 25 to 356 AP at Zhana-Semey;[3]
- Tu-124Sh Bort No. 65 to 350 AP at Bratsk;
- Tu-124Sh Bort Nos 35 and 45 to 72 AP at Amderma.

Apart from this, Tu-124 Bort No. 02 was transferred from 978 OTAP at Klin to 518 AP at Talagi. Thus, the Tu-124Sh was able to play an important role in the maintenance of flying skills of crews flying its more combative stablemate right up until the time that the Tu-128 was withdrawn from PVO service.

8

Aircrew Training in the 1970s and 1980s

As we have seen, the early problem of training navigators for the Tu-128 fleet was resolved in 1964 by introducing a navigation 'stream' to courses held at the Stavropol' branch of the Armavir Higher Military Aviation College for Pilots. The first navigator trainees at Stavropol' graduated in 1967, completing their operational training 'on the regiment'. Thus, 518 AP at Arkhangel'sk-Talagi, the first regiment to convert onto the new interceptor, provided intensive tuition for newly qualified navigators on the Tu-124Sh navigation trainer before letting them loose on the Tu-128 combat variant. This procedure continued until the spring of 1970.

The intensity of flight training for Tu-128 navigator-operators can be seen from this table:

Year	Average Number of Training Flights Per Year	Night Flights in Hours (Average)	Total Number of Flights
1968	150-160	50-60	400-450
1969	220-250	65-75	500-570
1970	100-120	40-50	300-310

During this time, newly qualified navigators were trained up to the level of Military Navigator Third Class, the lowest qualification category in the Soviet military flying system, although by early 1971 they were able to undertake flights in daylight IFR conditions on the Tu-124Sh. By the beginning of March 1971, they were authorised for 'solo' navigation sorties on the Tu-128 in VMC weather minima. Regimental training on the Tu-128 was based on the second edition of the combat training manual for the type, issued in 1969—i.e. 'KBP-Tu-128-69'. Postgraduate navigator training was very thorough, and by the autumn of 1971 they were authorised to undertake IMC sorties on the Tu-128. The basic minima for these flights included a cloud-base of 600 m (1,970 feet) and horizontal visibility of 6,000 m (3.75 miles), but by the end of 1971 they were already authorised to undertake flights in established minima of 350 m (1,150 feet) cloud-base and horizontal visibility of 4,000 m (2.5 miles). By this stage new entrant navigators had accumulated an average of 70-90 hours on the Tu-128.

Within a year, such training allowed these navigators to reach the standard of Navigator Second Class, with the Tu-124Sh still employed intensively by all regiments, as recalled here by Lt Col. Yuzov, commander of the communications company of the 677th Independent Communications and Airfield Radar Support Battalion (677 OBSRTO) in the early 1970s:

> At that time the Tu-128UT did not yet exist and all training flights were carried out on the Tu-124Sh. For us this was a form of 'hard labour'. The entire complement of students would clamber aboard, taking turns at aircraft handling and for the next 4-5 hours they would carry out a training detail, often with the weather right 'on limits'. They would take off into the standard box-pattern circuit—then land, roll-out, taxi back to the take-off point and get airborne again, repeatedly, without shutting down the engines. For night flying they were provided with searchlights to illuminate the runway [a common Russian practice where the touchdown end of the runway and the area on either side was lit by two powerful searchlights, rather than using edge and centreline lights. The searchlights pointed down the runway and were angled so as to avoid blinding the pilots]. During a typical night-flying 'shift' the carbon-arc searchlights would use up three or four sets of carbon rods.

Intakes of trainee navigators had been recruited to the Stavropol' branch of AVVAUL as early as 1966, and simultaneous with this a separate platoon (*vzvod*) was selected to train 'combat control officers' (*ofitsery boyevovo upravlyeniya*), i.e. GCI controllers. Graduation of both specialisations took place in 1970, but not all the graduates of the college went on to the Tu-128. For example, some of the graduates of Company No. 9 (around thirty officers) who had completed their training at Stavropol' in 1968, remained there as flying instructors. Although they had all entered the Armavir college as navigator trainees, having undergone basic training in DOSAAF Aviation Training Centres, it was decided to train them as pilots, in spite of their initial 'navigator streaming'. These young lieutenant navigators then underwent a year of conversion training to become flying instructors on the L-29 'Delfin', after which they successfully taught future pilots to fly! Apart from this group, some of the graduates from Company No. 9 were posted onto the Yak-28P 'Firebar-A' as pilot-operators, the specialised weapons system officers for this twin-seat, twin-jet PVO fighter, while others ended up on PVO transport units. However, a large number of the college's graduates were assigned to four of the PVO Aviation regiments operating the Tu-128—at Kotlas, Talagi, Omsk and

Semipalatinsk. This was a unique graduation procedure, involving both navigators and pilots, although only the navigators were assigned to the Tu-128. There was an individual case of one navigator cadet, by the name of Sergunin, who, having entered the Stavropol' branch in 1967, decided that he wanted to become a pilot. After a year of study, during which he made excellent progress, he submitted his application and was eventually placed on the first course (first year) at Armavir. Then after completing the full pilot's course at AVVAUL, he was posted to 518 AP at Talagi to fly the Tu-128.

The PVO High Command understood that apart from the initial manning deficit concerning navigator-operators, the Tu-128 fleet would soon face problems with a deficit in pilot numbers and had decided to create a separate flying college based on the AVVAUL affiliate at Stavropol'. So, on 15 September 1969, in accordance with a decision taken by the government of the USSR, the Soviet Defence Ministry signed a directive on the formation of the Stavropol' Higher Military Aviation College for Pilots and Navigators of the Air Defence Forces. Formation of the new college was completed by 1 November and on 8 April 1970 it was awarded military banner status (*Boyevoye Znamya*). Then, on 24 July 1970, the Soviet Defence Minister declared that 6 November would be the designated day for celebrating the foundation of the college. From that date, two colleges, AVVAUL at Armavir and SVVAULSh at Stavropol', would train aircrew for the aviation units of the PVO. As mentioned above, Stavropol' also trained 'combat control officers' who, on completion of their training, were posted to GCI sites as controllers for the PVO interceptor fleet. Like their aircrew colleagues, they also studied for four years and graduated with a degree-level qualification. By the early 1970s, the Tu-128 regiments had reached a high level of combat readiness and every aircraft had a fully trained crew, capable of carrying out their military tasks in all weather conditions, by day or night.

A serious manning problem began to manifest itself at around the same time, due to a comparatively sudden and large-scale departure of pilots for a variety of reasons. The reasons leading to these departures were numerous: many pilots had reached pensionable age and decided to retire from military service; others, lacking a higher education, saw no further prospects for them in their military career; many simply wanted to leave because the major part of their careers had been spent flying aircraft which were considerably easier to fly and had now been replaced by more complex types. However, it is probably fair to say that the major factor was that all pilots fell into approximately the same (older) age category. After all, the selection criteria for the initial intake of pilots were that they should be Pilots First Class, an experience level which by implication meant that they had probably been flying for many years, which in turn equated to being in an older age group.

In an attempt to resolve this impending manning problem, the PVO Aviation Command decided to modify the criteria relating to pilot category and number of flying hours achieved by pilots wishing to fly the Tu-128. Belief in the correctness of this decision was reinforced by the presence of the KTS-128 flight simulator and the Tu-128UT '*sparka*' on the regiments. As vacancies occurred in the Tu-128 fleet, PVO Aviation Command replaced departing personnel with an influx of young pilots holding Pilot Second Class and Pilot Third Class categories who had previously qualified on other fighters. Naturally, not all pilots agreed to serve on the Tu-128 and there were cases where pilots who had already converted onto the aircraft later requested a posting back to their old unit. One such case occurred on 64 AP at Omsk-North, involving a pilot from 174 IAP at Monchegorsk in the northern USSR. He was a former flight commander with 320 hours on the Yak-28P 'Firebar-A' and had already secured accommodation at his new base, even though this was never easy in the large garrison towns like Omsk. He had completed virtually twice the requisite pre-solo training time on the Tu-128, a situation which had actually occurred more by chance than design. In fact, he had already completed the basic programme and was due to go solo on the Tu-128, but because of adverse weather conditions on the day, the flight was postponed. On the next planned flying day he was given a preliminary check flight on the Tu-128UT, but before the solo flight on the Tu-128 the weather deteriorated again.

This sequence of events occurred several times, so that in terms of flights completed he had eventually accumulated twice the planned number of hours necessary. Col. Yevglyevskiy takes up the story when this pilot was finally able to go solo:

> I sent him off on his first solo flight. On take-off he over-rotated slightly and then retracted the undercarriage only after prompting by the flight controller [RP], starting to climb and then correcting. He carried out a circuit of the airfield and then lined up for the landing approach. The RP talked him down as if the trainee was 'sucking on the teat' (*na soskie*), in other words by prompting every action he made. After landing, the pilot wrote out a report stating his refusal to fly the Tu-128 again and requesting his return to flying the Yak-28P at Monchegorsk. I decided to have a brief chat with him and we had a one-to-one conversation in the regiment commander's office. In the conversation he told me frankly that whenever he had flown in the '*sparka*' it was actually the instructor who had had control of the aircraft. It seems that the instructor had 'protected' him to such an extent that he was unable to impart any flying skills to his student. Consequently, the student was unable to overcome his psychological fear of the Tu-128 and he had to return to Monchegorsk and the Yak-28P, which, ironically, was itself not an easy aircraft to fly.

A similar case occurred on 356 AP in the 1970s at Zhana-Semey (Semipalatinsk-1), involving an officer who was an experienced second pilot (*pomoshchnik komandira korablya*) on one of the regiment's Tu-124Sh navigation trainers. Although he had always been in the 'transport world' and had accumulated 1,200 hours on the Tu-124, he was very keen to retrain as a 'fighter pilot' on the Tu-128. He was a persistent person and had submitted his request to every senior officer, right up to the commander of the 14th Independent Army of the PVO and the PVO inspector-pilot cadre. He had pestered everyone with his request for so long that in the end the head of the PVO Aviation Combat Training Department, Col. Yevglyevskiy, with the permission of the C-in-C, authorised him to attend the medical board, followed by training on the Tu-128. Col. Yevglyevskiy recalls the circumstances:

I told the regiment commander [of 356 AP] to train the pilot—Captain Galkin— and when he was ready, to invite me along. The regiment devised a well-planned programme for him and in due course they told me he was ready. I flew down to Zhana-Semey and decided to give Captain Galkin two flights in the '*sparka*' and then send him off on his first solo in the Tu-128. However, on the first flight he could not even line up on the approach to the main runway and the aircraft was wandering to the left and right, with the navigator having to prompt him all the time—'Go right one degree, left two degrees' etc. The pilot followed the navigator's instructions but could not line the aircraft up, even though the visibility was excellent. Somehow or other we landed. Before the second flight I said to the navigator, 'As soon as we turn onto the landing course you remain silent; don't say anything else to him.' I warned Galkin that he was to do the approach and landing himself—without any prompts. As soon as the navigator stopped 'pestering' him with heading corrections he settled down on the approach and landed the aircraft without drama. He flared a little too high but it was not that bad and when the RP told him about this Galkin immediately corrected his mistake. I was pleased that he had responded appropriately to the RP's instructions and I decided that I could send him off on his first solo. I made a call on the radio telling the ground crew to prepare a '*boyevoy samolyot*' (i.e. the normal 'combat variant' of the Tu-128) for Captain Galkin. I made the radio call specifically to gauge his reaction there and then, while we were airborne. After landing we climbed out of the '*sparka*' and he looked a little flustered. I asked him if he was ready to go solo on the '*boyevoy*' and he replied that he was ready, although I felt that he was a bit stressed and nervous. We walked over to the crew rest room, drank some tea and had a smoke and chatted about the flight. After this short break I sat him in the cockpit of the Tu-128, checking that everything was as it should be and then said, 'OK, I'm driving over to the flare point at the runway threshold and I'll have a radio with me. If necessary, I'll give you prompts. Listen out for my commands.' We often used this procedure with new pilots, mounting a radio in one of the vehicles and going out to the runway to monitor their first touchdowns. Captain Galkin carried out his first solo circuit and commenced his approach. I had to prompt him with frequent commands to reduce height and he landed, taxied in and said to me, 'That's it! I can't fly this aircraft. Send me back to transport flying.'

To be truthful, such cases were fairly unusual and the majority of pilots who converted onto the Tu-128 and flew the aircraft on the regiments did so with great enthusiasm. Unsurprisingly, in view of the size of the aircraft, it handled more like a bomber than a fighter and required very smooth control inputs from the pilot. The Pilots' Notes for the Tu-128 instructed:

> … in handling the aircraft it is essential to produce continuous, co-ordinated and proportionate movements of the control column, without pulling too hard and allowing the aircraft to reach an angle of attack beyond which the visual and audio signals of the AUASP indicator [the combined angle of attack and g-meter] are triggered.

However, the problem with the dwindling numbers of Tu-128 pilots in the early 1970s was so acute that the PVO General Staff had to try and resolve it fairly urgently, albeit this time using a much more conventional approach. It was decided to recruit pilots from the reserve officer pool, pilots who had completed courses at the Aviation Training Centres (UATs) of DOSAAF.1 Within the DOSAAF training structure there was an extensive network of UATs flying schools whose task it was to train the mobilised reserve for the aviation branches of the Soviet armed forces that would be called up in the event of war. In peacetime, young men would be detached for flight training at designated UATs airfields, whilst retaining their civilian jobs and salaries. There were two 'streams' in the UATs organisation—a fixed-wing aircraft course and a helicopter course—with each stream divided into centres offering first and second years of training. The fixed-wing UATs for the first year of training provided instruction on the Czech-built L-29 'Delfin', involving several months' tuition on the aircraft. The first year programme included both ground instruction and flying, providing around 50 hours of flying training. After the first year, graduates of these courses received the rank of sergeant in the reserve (*Serzhant zapasa*). The second year UATs taught pilots to fly the MiG-17 'Fresco' fighter, using the MiG-15UTI 'Midget' as the relevant trainer, and pilots usually amassed around 40 hours on the MiG-17 by the end of the course. On completion of the full two-year UATs programme graduates received the rank of junior lieutenant in the reserve (*Mladshiy Lyeitenant zapasa*) and continued to work in their civilian specialisation, often unconnected with aviation. These UATs centres existed unchanged right up to the middle of the 1980s. One of the UATs airfields was Kupino in the Novosibirsk district of Siberia and was specifically involved in training reserve pilots for the PVO. In 1970, it was decided to accept some of the pilots graduating from the DOSAAF UATs courses to enter full-time service in Soviet military units, thereby helping to resolve the major problem of temporary pilot shortages. A significant number of such pilots were absorbed into PVO fighter units. A former navigator on 518 AP at Talagi, Maj. Vinokurov, recalls that pilots coming into the PVO via the DOSAAF route were known on the regiments as 'khunveibiny' ('*khunveibin*' in the singular), a transliteration of the Chinese Hóng Wèi Bīng, or Red Guards. (The Red Guards formed a mass movement of civilians, mainly students, mobilised in the name of Mao Tse-tung between 1966 and 1968, during the Cultural Revolution in China.) The word '*khunveibin*' gradually assumed a rather pejorative meaning to the Russians, describing someone who was not particularly bright but prepared to work without questioning authority. By loose analogy, the DOSAAF pilots were seen as weak on theoretical training but very good at flying an aircraft!

In early 1971, pilots who had come through the DOSAAF training system could be found on all three Tu-128 regiments within the 14th Independent Army of the PVO. These pilots were awarded the rank of lieutenant and put through a training programme on the Tu-128UT, amassing around 60 hours of instructional flying 'on the regiment'. Thus, with 40 hours of flying time on the MiG-17, the overall total of military flying experience for these pilots was around 100 hours, the 50 hours on the L-29 not counting as true 'military' flying experience. This was a far cry from the 500 hours' flying experience and Pilot First Class qualification initially required of candidates wishing to convert onto the Tu-128! There was thus an enormous responsibility on the shoulders of those instructors who had to send these pilots off on their first 'solo' on the Tu-128. This task fell, essentially, to the inspector-pilots assigned to the PVO General Staff. Col. Komyagin remembers this period in the history of operating the Tu-128:

When we sent off the DOSAAF pilots for their first Tu-128 flight it was frightening. When I flew in [to Zhana-Semey (Semipalatinsk-1)] to authorise the first batch of pilots, I was acting on the instructions of the C-in-C of PVO Aviation, General Borovykh, who had told me quite bluntly, 'If anything happens, I'll have your head on a plate. And they'll probably have my head too.' The first pilot to be sent solo was from 356 AP at Semipalatinsk. I decided to begin with the best pilot of the group. I flew with him on the Tu-128UT—the weather wasn't bad, although horizontal visibility was poor, with slight haze. I gently warned the pilot, 'Do everything yourself—I won't do a thing. Just fly the aircraft as if I wasn't on board.' We took off and it turned out that the visibility aloft was excellent, which was often the case at Semipalatinsk. The flight went very well and I decided to let him do his first solo on the '*boyevoy*' Tu-128. The regiment commander, Lt Col. Kostyenich and the Head of Aviation for the 14th Independent Army of the PVO, General Starovyerov, were not so keen, because of poor weather on the appointed day, but I insisted. I picked up the pilot, drove him out to the aircraft and gave him a few words of encouragement while he was doing his pre-flight checks. He took off and did the regulation one short box-pattern circuit of the airfield, then a 'big box' circuit and then the landing approach, completing the flight with an excellent landing. This pilot was one of three DOSAAF 'uncategorised pilots' (*lyotchiki byez klassa*) who we successfully sent solo on the Tu-128 after the *ad hoc* training programme.

Among the DOSAAF 'reinforcements' there was an interesting pilot by the name of Antonyenko, a lieutenant. He served on 64 AP at Omsk-North and not only had he not been a regular officer, he had had no previous connection with aviation! Before coming to 64 AP he was the personal driver of Vladimir Dolgikh, who was later to become a member of the Politburo of the Central Committee of the Soviet Communist Party. In his capacity as a chauffeur, Antonyenko worked in Noril'sk when Dolgikh was the director of the Noril'sk Mining and Metallurgical Combine, and in Krasnoyarsk after Dolgikh had been appointed president of the Communist Party Committee for the Krasnoyarsk administrative region. This was at the time when posts for military pilots were being offered to suitably qualified personnel from the DOSAAF training system, as described above, and Antonyenko, using the influence of his highly placed boss, managed to complete the relevant courses to become a pilot on 64 AP. He served on the regiment successfully as a Tu-128 pilot, although his commanders noted a certain lack of discipline in his behaviour, a trait manifest in several of the DOSAAF contingent. Unfortunately, Antonyenko was killed in a flying accident a few years later during a training flight in a MiG-15UTI, indiscipline of the two pilots involved in this accident being cited as the main cause of the crash. Whether the accident was the reason for removing the MiG-15UTI from service or not is difficult to say, but the start of a phased withdrawal of the '*little sparka*' coincided with the publication of the accident report on Antonyenko's fatal crash in 1973. The last MiG-15UTI trainer was withdrawn from PVO service on 72 AP at Amderma in July 1976.

The recruitment of pilots via the DOSAAF training route meant that the temporary aircrew deficit could be overcome, pending the arrival of the first batch of pilots to graduate from the Stavropol' Higher Military Aviation College for Pilots and Navigators. As noted elsewhere, the course at this flying college lasted for four years, with students beginning to fly the L-29 'Delfin' trainer in the first year (*pyervyi kurs* or first course) of their studies. (However, it should be noted that cadets on the first course at Stavropol', i.e. the group who graduated in 1976, only started to fly the L-29 jet trainer from 1973. Before this graduation, cadets did not go near an aircraft in their first year, except for parachute training, and aerodynamics and aircraft design and construction were only studied from the third semester.) Flight training, as in all military flying schools, always took place in the summer months. The Stavropol' Higher Military Aviation College 'controlled' four subordinate airfields housing its associated training regiments. Before 1975/76, when construction of the airfield at Kholodnogorsk was completed, training regiments were based at Sal'sk, Tikhoretsk and Khankala near the (Cossack) village of Sleptsovskaya—today the airport of Ingushetia. The 1st and 2nd squadrons of the Sal'sk regiment were equipped with the Su-15, while the 3rd and 4th squadrons flew the MiG-17 (training regiments usually had four squadrons, instead of the three of an operational regiment). The 3rd and 4th squadrons of this regiment converted onto the MiG-23M in the 1980s. The regiment at Tikhoretsk operated the MiG-17, but converted later onto the MiG-23. Khankala airfield was located not far from Grozny and operated the L-29 'Delfin', before re-equipping with the L-39 'Albatros', as did the regiment at Kholodnogorsk. Apart from this, there were three satellite airfields for use in the summer, these being:

- near the village of Korenovskaya (later redesignated as a town, with the slightly amended name of Korenovsk), used by the 3rd and 4th squadrons of the Sleptsovskaya regiment;
- Zimovniki, used by the 3rd and 4th squadrons of the Khankala regiment and the 4th squadron of the Sal'sk regiment;
- near the town of Svetlograd, used by two squadrons of the Tikhoretsk regiment.

From the late 1970s/early 1980s, the airfield at Mirinovka, 42 km (26 miles) south-west of Volgograd, was added to the 'network' of training airfields. Cadet pilots flew the MiG-17P 'Fresco-C' and Su-15T 'Flagon-D' in the third year of their training, perfecting their skills in the final year on the Su-15TM 'Flagon-F'. Pilots graduating from Stavropol' Higher Aviation College were spilt into two groups, based on ability, with some pilots going on to the MiG-17P and others going to Su-15TM regiments.

Whereas pilots were previously selected from those with Pilot First Class status, then later Pilot Second Class, and with not less than 400 hours on jets (and ideally members of the Communist Party), selected Stavropol' graduates in the period 1975-77 were posted directly to the Tu-128 regiments. It was a fairly bold experiment, with ten pilots each going to 518 AP at Talagi and 64 AP at Omsk-North, with a lesser number posted to 356 AP at Zhana-Semey, the justification being that it was considered that the aircraft had been 'sufficiently mastered' (*dostatochno osvoyen*) by that time. Consequently, for these well-trained pilots it was unlikely to present the sort of difficulties envisaged when the aircraft first entered service a decade earlier.

Throughout the Tu-128's early service the typical handling errors committed by pilots had been noted by instructors and categorised according to the stage of flight. During take-off the most common errors were:

- failure to keep the aircraft straight during the ground roll as a result of 'poor distribution of attention' when accelerating, allowing the aircraft to drift off the centreline and depart from the runway because of the high inertia of the aircraft;
- insufficient raising of the nose-wheel, attributed to handling error, or incorrect adjustment of the height of the pilot's seat, resulting in a shallow

First year cadets at the Saratov flight training college parade in front of a MiG-15UTI, a MiG-17 and a Tu-128 in this 1970s photograph, taken during the ceremony of accepting the Oath of Allegiance to the Soviet Union. (*E. Chergezov*)

climb, allowing the aircraft to exceed the permitted speed with undercarriage and flaps down;

- raising the nose too high at the 'unstick' point, for the same reasons as above, leading to a climb at a high angle of attack, loss of forward speed and stalling.

Handling errors in flight fell mainly into two categories:

- failure to remain in the designated airfield training zone, leading to loss of orientation or potentially dangerous approaches to nearby civilian aircraft;
- errors when turning, leading to stalling and entry into a steep spiral descent.

Most piloting errors were, of course, noted in the final stage of flight up to and including the landing, the final approach and touchdown being the most difficult and demanding phase of flight in any aircraft. For this reason, piloting errors could be encountered among the younger pilots as well as the older, more experienced group. The most widely noted error was landing with one wing down, i.e. with an angle of bank (*posadka s krenom*). Errors committed by Tu-128 pilots on take-off, approach and landing were the most difficult to eliminate and then instil appro-priate corrective procedures, although the instructors nevertheless managed to inculcate good flying practice in the cadre of younger pilots assigned to the big Tupolev interceptor. However, following a fatal accident at Zhana-Semey involving a young pilot from the 1976 graduation (described in Appendix 3), PVO Aviation Command decided to stop taking pilots straight from the flying colleges to fly the Tu-128. Even after it was felt that the Tu-128 had been sufficiently mastered, the aircraft clearly remained something of a 'handful' for the younger, inexperienced pilot. The experiment was suspended for this reason, and before going on to the Tu-128, newly qualified pilots had to gain at least one year's experience on another PVO fighter type.

The problem in meeting the required manning levels for pilots on Tu-128 regiments was partially resolved in 1978 when certain PVO regiments started to convert from the Su-9 onto the MiG-23. The Su-9 regiments received a tele-gram from Gen. Moskivityelev (the commander of PVO Aviation) on the subject of 'making up [pilot] deficiencies on Tu-128 regiments by taking Pilots Second Class from Su-9 regiments designated to convert onto the MiG-23'. Following this 'request', some Su-9 pilots were reassigned to the Tu-128, instead of converting onto the MiG. (It will be recalled that pilots converting from the Su-9 onto the Tu-128 found the transition much easier than pilots converting from 'lightweight' fighters.) Pilots assigned to the 14th Independent Army of the PVO after graduat-ing on the Su-15TM from Stavropol' (SVVAULSh) in 1978 were posted to 712 IAP at Kansk in the Krasnoyarsk region of Siberia, and those qualifying on the MiG-17 were posted to 22 IAP at Bezrechnaya (aka Khada Bulak North and Mirnaya) in the Chita Oblast of Siberia. After a year flying these two fighters, pilots who had been accepted for retraining on the Tu-128 were transferred to the relevant regiment. The change-over of personnel coincided with the beginning of the new training year, which in the Soviet armed forces at that time commenced on 1 December. Assignment to the Tu-128 was considered to be a good move, since the commander of a 'Fiddler' crew received a salary increment of 190 roubles, whereas other PVO pilots at the time received a monthly increment of only 160 roubles.[2]

Special *ad hoc* courses were organised for these newly arrived pilots, and regi-ment engineers of all specialisations were co-opted as instructors to teach aircraft systems. The Tu-128 regiments had used so-called 'methodological training aids' for some time to help aircrews to study the aircraft, these being based on a two-part manual that was both well illustrated and clearly written. The first part of the manual was intended to familiarise students with the aircraft and its systems, whereas the second part was devoted to a brief overview of the operational use of the Tu-128. The theoretical phase lasted for one month, with simultaneous study of the aircraft's cockpit interspersed with simulator training sorties on the KTS-128. This was followed by an orientation flight in an Antonov An-14 'Clod' twin-piston-engined light transport to familiarise the new pilots with the airfield area, after which dual-instruction flights on the Tu-128UT were programmed. However, it should be mentioned that extremely strict training methods were also employed on the regiments, giving rise to the expression 'methodological banditry' ('*metodicheskiy banditizm*') among aircrew. Older pilots who had graduated from flying schools in the 1950s and '60s were particularly guilty of this approach.

Maj. Nikolai Popov recalls here his own knowledge of this practice:

> There was a deputy commander of the 3rd squadron of 356 AP at Zhana-Semey, by the name of Major Burzak, who even used to force his pilots to take off 'under the hood' [the blind-flying screens used for instrument flying practice]. You'd have to taxi onto the main runway at night [flying the aircraft from the normal pilot's seat], and this instructor would close the forward blinds and you'd take off. You'd gauge your position on the runway during take-off using peripheral vision.

Because of his unbending authoritarianism the commander of the 3rd squadron, Lt Col. Moiseyev, was known on the regiment by the nickname of 'the Führer', an allusion to the German dictator Adolf Hitler. Nevertheless, it has to be said that harsh methods were successful in turning out good pilots, capable of flying and landing safely in the changeable weather conditions of this base. Maj. Popov continues:

> The blind flying screens on the Tu-128UT consisted of three elements: one on each of the windscreen panels and one on the upper canopy window, above the pilot's head. The latter was rarely if ever closed. On one occasion I even *landed* under the hood (*pod shtorkoi*).[3] The regiment commander, who was flying with me as my instructor, forgot to open the hood on the landing approach. [On the Tu-128, the normal practice was for the blind flying screen to be closed and opened at a height of around 75-100 m (245-330 feet).] I landed the aircraft, but it was quite difficult taxiing around the airfield with the hood closed. I couldn't see anything in front of me; I could only see through the side panels of the canopy. I was scared to ask for the hood to be opened—after all, the regiment commander was there to give me a 'check ride'. However, when it became too difficult to continue taxiing, I tentatively asked over the intercom, 'Is it OK to open the hood?' The instructor opened the hood and I taxied in to dispersal. We climbed out and I went up to him for my post-flight briefing. He simply said to me, 'Idiot!' and walked off. Overhearing this, the squadron commander, Lt Col. Moiseyev, asked me what had happened. I explained that I had landed with the blind flying hood in the closed position and that the regiment commander had called me an 'idiot'. Moiseyev listened to me attentively and then said, 'He was right!' and he also walked away. No one mentioned the incident again and I carried on flying the Tu-128.

'Methodological' training aids, like this poster at Amderma explaining low-level flight procedures, were displayed on all aviation regiments as *aides-mémoire* for aircrew. (*Nikolai Popov*)

For pilots under instruction, or those being checked by an instructor-pilot, there was a specific manner in which radio calls had to be made, which required the final syllable of operative words to be pronounced clearly and without variation. For example, in the phrases '*777, shassi vypusti*' (This is callsign 777, I have lowered the undercarriage') and '*777, shassi, zakrylki vypushcheno*' ('This is callsign 777, undercarriage and flaps lowered') the underlined syllables had to be clearly emphasised and stressed. Punishments were meted out for those who transgressed and usually involved writing out the entire sequence of radio calls by that pilot on a given flight ten times in an exercise book (!).[4] Even the touchdown point on the runway was checked to see which pilots had landed before reaching the 'piano keys' (or the 'zebra' in Russian, for obvious reasons). The tyre marks were then recorded and dated and the lowest total of 'undershoots' for the week's flying programme could earn a young pilot a pass for an extra day off. These procedures were in force not only on 356 AP but to a greater or lesser extent were employed by all Tu-128 regiments. A favourite practice of the Head of Flight Safety of 10th PVO Air Army, Col. Lenyushkin, when flying as an instructor, was to select one engine to 'Flight Idle' without warning his student, thereby 'encouraging' his pilots to react with lightning quick responses in an emergency! The need for such methods was rather contentious and many pilots considered them to be dubious at best, since they could have had serious consequences. However, it has to be admitted that in all the known accidents examined, no single incident could be attributed to this practice. Moreover, the level of flying discipline and responsiveness was heightened as a result.

Former commander of 356 AP, Col. Vasiliy Popov, recalls his experience of the training system:

> I was struck by the level of diligence on 356 AP when I arrived at Zhana-Semey from Yelizovo (Petropavlovsk-Kamchatsky). After the 'nepotism' of Kamchatka, where almost every other person was someone's son or nephew,[5] everything here worked efficiently and in harmony, like clockwork.

Conversion training for young pilots lasted three to four weeks, involving around fifteen dual-control flights and a total of about 5 hours on the Tu-128UT. After successful completion of this programme, the new pilots were authorised to go solo, although in the harsh conditions of the High Arctic rather more flights would be required, spread over five or six months. Initially at this stage in the Tu-128's operation, all conversion flights for new pilots were carried out on the Tu-128UT and only after a few months did they start to use the Tu-124Sh again as a trainer. This approach had been adopted because, not unreasonably, the younger pilots found it difficult to master two new types at the same time, particularly as one was a large 'slippery' supersonic interceptor and the other a rather 'pedestrian' passenger aircraft. They were allowed to use the Tu-124Sh only for continuation training when they had acquired sound piloting skills on the interceptor, although, of course, they did not 'convert' onto the Tu-124 in the strict sense of the term. Trainees would study the Pilots' Notes, the cockpit layout and undergo '*trenazh*' (literally 'training' in the sense of repetitive exercises in the cockpit), after which they could get airborne in the actual aircraft. Exploiting the passenger-carrying capability of the Tu-124Sh, a group of around eight to ten students would get into the aircraft, with the instructor performing the first flight. Then the first pilot from the group would occupy the left-hand seat in the capacity of 'aircraft commander', take off and perform a box-pattern circuit and then land. Without shutting down the engines, the second student would then move into the left-hand seat and repeat the exercise, followed by all the others in turn until they had all demonstrated a take-off, circuit and landing to the instructor's satisfaction. The Tu-124Sh could not, of course, replicate the flight dynamics of the Tu-128, since both aircraft had different touchdown speeds and trim requirements etc., but the aircraft was invaluable as a procedural training tool since it helped to reduce wear and tear on the Tu-128UT.

Pilots on the 3rd squadron of 356 AP accumulated around 130 flying hours per year, a figure probably typical for the training squadrons of the other Tu-128 regiments. The 'flying shifts' (*lyotniye smyeny*) for pilots on the 3rd squadron of all the regiments differed in the way they were organised, and on 356 AP for example, the 3rd squadron conducted its flying programme as an entirely separate 'shift'. If the regiment had a night-flying programme, then the 3rd squadron would fly during the day; if the regiment's programme was 'day-night' then the 3rd squadron would take the morning 'slot'. The function of the 3rd squadron (in any PVO regiment) was to take 'unclassed' pilots to the Pilot Third Class level, after which they would move up to the 2nd squadron. With sufficiently intensive combat training on the regiments, a young pilot could reach Pilot First Class level within two years by carrying out the relevant exercises and flying tasks set out in the combat training manual. Pilots with the First and Second Class rating usually accumulated an annual total of around 80-100 flying hours, which by way of an example compared well with the annual norms set by PVO Aviation Command for the 1983 training year. For the combat and training variants of aircraft assigned to fighter aviation these 'norms' were as follows:

- MiG-23P, MiG-23M, MiG-23ML, Su-15TM, Tu-128 and Yak-28—Pilots First Class 65 hours, Pilots Second Class 75 hours, Pilots Third Class 90 hours, Unclassed Pilots 100 hours;
- MiG-31, MiG-25PD, MiG-25PDS—Pilots First Class 70 hours, Pilots Second Class 85 hours.

For transport aircraft crews and crews assigned to special purpose units:

- An-12, An-24, An-26, Tu-124, Tu-134—100 to 250 hours;
- Tu-16, Tu-126—80 to 110 hours;
- An-2, An-14—100 to 110 hours;
- Mi-8 helicopters—100 to 150 hours.

Overall total time in flight simulators had to be not less than:

- 10 hours for Pilots First Class;
- 20 hours for Pilots Second Class;
- 30 hours for Pilots Third Class and Unclassed Pilots.

Additionally, the 'norms' for instrument flight practice 'under the hood' of the relevant training aircraft were:

- 3 hours for Pilots First Class;

- 5 hours for Pilots Second Class;
- 10 hours for other pilots.

The training of navigators was no less demanding, as former 518 AP navigator Capt. Sergey Vinokurov recalls:

When we came to the regiment we were trained by section navigators—the first graduates of the navigator faculty of AVVAKUL (Armavir) in 1967/68. All without exception were specialists with outstanding expert knowledge. In order to pass any examination set by them we had to find any switch in the cockpit with our eyes closed, explain which switch it was and describe its function. These navigators were very good 'methodological-style' teachers. Of course, after they retired, the demand for their skills declined. Everything became much simpler.

9

Flying the Tu-128

PREPARATION FOR FLIGHT

Each regiment had its own specific flying days within the week, dependent upon the number of regiments based at a particular airfield. Of the two training regiments at Savasleika, for example, one flew on Mondays, Wednesdays and Fridays, whilst the second regiment flew on Tuesdays, Thursdays and Saturdays. If flying was not possible due to adverse weather conditions, then the programme was simply shifted to another day, with all other units rescheduling their programmes in turn. The 356th Aviation Regiment at Zhana-Semey (Semipalatinsk-1) usually also flew on three days of the week, with Mondays being dedicated to preparatory work on the aircraft and ground training, Tuesdays and Wednesdays were flying days, Thursday was another preparation day and Friday was the last flying day of the week. Sometimes Friday's programme would be carried forward to the following Monday. As a rule, the three squadrons of 64 AP at Omsk-North used to fly on Tuesdays and Thursdays, although the programme could be changed in response to prevailing weather conditions. With each regiment having only two Tu-128UTs available for dual-control training in the early years of operation, the workload on these aircraft was very high, being used for continuation training by squadron pilots and QFIs and for check flights on pilots returning from leave etc. Intensive operation of the 'UT' placed particular demands on engineering resources, and if a trainer went into the maintenance shed (TEhCh) on a Friday, it had to be returned to the regiment on the Monday morning, work continuing throughout the weekend without a break.

A normal flying day was generally organised around two separate shifts (*smyeny*), with both shifts generally using the same group of aircraft. Since each aircraft was always supposed to have its own designated technicians, the maintenance effort was shared between two teams. If the aircraft senior technician of

The 72 AP QRA dispersal pan at Amderma, with a Tu-128 already plugged into the ground power unit and a pilot about to enter the cockpit. (*S. Shchelokov*)

a given aircraft worked on the first shift, then the aircraft technician would work on the second shift. Additionally, in order to provide a full team of maintenance personnel to support flying operations, a technician would be co-opted from the maintenance team whose aircraft was not actually flying that day. Flights were always supported by a four-man maintenance crew, comprising two officer-rank technicians and two NCO mechanics. The first personnel to arrive at the aircraft before flight were the ground crew, as on all other PVO and VVS flying units. They would go out to the aircraft around 3-4 hours before the start of the flying programme, during which they would carry out all their pre-flight checks and preparation. Former aircraft senior technician Maj. Plyuta recalls his experience of working on the Tu-128:

> Access to the various components and equipment modules was perfectly adequate. Even in winter you could climb into most equipment compartments wearing a winter anorak. The engine compartment panels were large and it was quite easy to reach the engine accessory units and to change the engines. You didn't need to have 'six joints on your hands'.

The aircraft were towed onto the TsZT (central refuelling point) hardstanding if it was not planned to start the engines directly in the parking area; Tu-128s were

Four of 72 AP's Tu-128s lined up ready for the day's flying programme at Amderma. (*S. Shchelokov*)

usually lined up on the TsZT side by side in two columns. This was done primarily to reduce the amount of space taken up by the aircraft on the hardstanding. It has to be said that when compared with the aircraft previously operated by the Tu-128 regiments the Tupolev interceptor was simply enormous and did take up a lot of room in the dispersal area. As already mentioned, the Tu-128 was not equipped with centralised refuelling and it was no easy task for the ground crew to refuel the aircraft with the 19,200 litre (4,225 imp. gals) maximum capacity of the fuel tanks. The most difficult part of the process was filling the last tank, which could only be monitored from the fuel gauge in the cockpit or the gauge mounted on the bowser. The normal procedure was for one technician to sit in the aircraft and open the canopy side panel on the left-hand side of the cockpit, the panel opening out and upwards. The technician sitting in the cockpit had to have a loud voice in order to warn the other technician monitoring the fuel flow at the neck of the tank that refuelling was complete. In fact, it required not only a powerful voice but also a great deal of experience since there was an obvious element of delay in using this method of communication. If the technician in the cockpit shouted too early, the tank would not be filled completely and if he left it too late then fuel could spill out of the tank over the aircraft and drench the technician with kerosene. This was not a pleasant experience for the ground crew, particularly in the winter when a special additive (Liquid 'I') was put into the fuel to prevent the formation of ice crystals, but caused severe burning if it came into contact with the skin. The fuelling options (*varianty*) were given in a special table, shown in this extract from the 'Aide-memoire for crews preparing Article I [Tu-128] for turn-round'.

Fuel Load Variant	Number of fuel tank and fuel load		Fuel uplift (indicated by fuel quantity gauge in summing mode 'Σ') for various fuel densities (specific gravity), in kg				Engine	Flow meter setting
			Specific Gravity 0.77	Specific Gravity 0.79	Specific Gravity 0.80	Specific Gravity 0.81		
I	Full fuel		14,850	15,250	15,450	15,650	L	7700
							R	7450
II A [A]	*1, 1A, 2-4, 5-7, 8—Full; Tank No. 9 (in wings) refuelled in litres:*	3,000	13,950	14,350	14,480	14,650	L	7250
							R	7000
Б [B]		2,000	12,350	12,700	12,900	13,050	L	6450
							R	6200
В [V]		1,000	10,350	11,150	11,260	11,400	L	5650
							R	5400
Г [G]		0	9,350	9,550	9,680	9,800	L	4850
							R	4600
III	1, 1A—Full; 9L, 9R—Empty; 2-4, 5-7—refuelled in kilograms	3,300				8,200	L	4100
							R	3850
		2,500				6,600	L	3300
							R	3050
		1,700						

After checking the quality of the fuel from the bowser, using a portable test kit, the aircraft would be refuelled via the throat nozzles of tank Nos 1, 5 and 8 and the wing tanks. In the words of the technicians, tank Nos 1 and 5 were always filled 'to the brim' (*pod obrez gorloviny*), an experienced technician or mechanic being able to check by ear for the tell-tale gurgle when the tank was almost full. Tank No. 8 was never filled with more than 570 litres (125 imp. gals) of fuel. After refuelling, the gauge readings were checked in the pilot's cockpit and the fuel flow meter (counter) set for the corresponding 'fuel state variant'. During given flying programmes the 'variants' could change, dependent upon the task, but at the end of flying the wing tanks of the aircraft of the 1st and 2nd squadrons were always topped up by 3,600 litres (792 imp. gals). This was done just in case the aircraft were needed for an actual combat task. The aircraft of the 3rd squadrons

Since the hose was rather heavy it had to be supported by another person during the refuelling process, as seen here, with a mechanic holding the hose for his colleague replenishing the wing tanks. (*S. Shchelokov*)

were permitted to fly without fuel in the wing tanks, so if the regiment was placed on a general alert all the TZ-22 (*Toplivo Zapravshchik*—capacity 22,000 litres/4,849 imp. gals) refuelling bowsers would be tasked immediately with refuelling these aircraft. During the time that the 3rd squadron was preparing and arming its aircraft with R-4 missiles, the maintenance personnel would attend to the refuelling. This was usually carried out by the aircraft mechanics, one of them refuelling the group of tanks for the port engine and another for the starboard engine group.

If a six-hour flying programme had been planned, this would usually commence at 09.00 hours, the weather reconnaissance crew arriving at the airfield 3 hours before flying started. The crews designated to fly on a given day would be picked up 2 hours before flight and the aircrew would be given a pre-flight medical check by one of the base doctors. During this time the weather reconnaissance aircraft would get airborne, around 2 hours before the first planned sortie for the day. Pre-flight weather reconnaissance flights were organised to finish an hour before flying started so that the regiment's meteorologists had the most recent information with which to prepare their synopsis. Until the middle of the 1970s, weather reconnaissance was carried out in the MiG-15UTI, although later the task was given to the regiments' Tu-124 crews and, less frequently, to pilots flying the Tu-128UT. After the weather reconnaissance crew had landed and crews had been given their

The absence of single-point refuelling on the Tu-128 meant that conscripts had to be employed to refuel the aircraft 'by hand'. Here, a 64 AP aircraft mechanic prepares to refuel a Tu-128 using a hose equipped with a petrol filling station-style of nozzle. (*S. Shchelokov*)

pre-flight briefing, the pilots and navigators would walk out to the aircraft assigned to them in the 'flight planning table' (*planovaya tablitsa*). This document, having the same function as a flight-planning board in Western squadrons, was confirmed as accurate and signed by the regiment commander before flying commenced. It listed the flights, flight duration, exercise number in the KBP combat training manual and the identity (i.e. the Bort number) of the aircraft to be flown by a given crew. As in all military flying units in the USSR, the aircraft commander would then receive a verbal report from the 'aircraft technician', concerning the aircraft's readiness for flight, the fuel state and the serviceability of the aircraft's systems and its weapons. The pilot would also tell the technician to adjust the rudder pedals and the seat straps for his height (informing him which adjustment numbers to use for his girth and leg length).

Co-author Maj. Nikolai Popov recalls an incident arising from this practice during his time flying the Tu-128:

This almost led to a nasty experience for me on one occasion because of the carelessness of one of the technicians. It happened on 28 December 1987 when I had to test fly a Tu-128UT '*sparka*' at the repair base at Novosibirsk. It had rained during the previous evening, a completely unexpected event at Novosibirsk in the winter, with the temperature then plunging to minus 30°C the following day. This resulted in a crust of ice around 3-5 cm [1-2 inches] thick forming over most of the airfield area, although the airfield maintenance party managed to clear a strip around 30 m [100 feet] wide on the main runway. Everywhere else there was just ice. I arrived at the aircraft and said to the technician, 'Set the pedals "one notch back"' [*odnu na syebya*—literally 'one to self', i.e. move the pedals one fixed position *closer* to the pilot]. Unknown to me at the time he'd actually set them 'one notch forward' [*odnu ot syebya*—literally 'one from self']. I got into the seat and strapped in, but could hardly reach the pedals. So there I was, in these cataclysmic weather conditions, having to turn the aircraft round on the runway, with the added complication of a limited turning radius on the narrow strip of runway. Turning the Tu-128 on the ground required the pilot to actively 'work' the pedals, but I could reach them only with difficulty. If I hadn't been wearing a 'bone-dome' I could have bent forward and perhaps, with the agility of a gymnast, move the pedals myself, to release the locking catch. However, this was impossible wearing a 'bone-dome'—it just kept hitting the instrument panel, and my arms weren't long enough to reach the release mechanism. So I was left with the sole option of using the 'tips of my toes' to operate the brake pedals in order to turn the aircraft within the required radius …

A 64 AP aircraft mechanic responsible for the maintenance of the KZA flight-data recorder signs the 'ZhPS' engineering log for his aircraft during pre-flight checks at Omsk-North in 1982. Note the triangular badge on his sleeve denoting that he is from the 2nd squadron of the regiment, and another badge showing that he is on the KZA maintenance team. (*S. Shchelokov*)

(It is surprising that the Novosibirsk technician did not have a ground intercom facility by which he could communicate with visiting pilots such as Maj. Popov, and also that Maj. Popov did not call for assistance on the radio!—A.D.)

After giving this order to the technician, the pilot would do his walk-round checks in the following sequence: nose and forward fuselage, starboard wing, tail section and, finally, port wing. The pilot and navigator would then climb aboard. Access to both cockpits was facilitated by a combined ladder and platform, pushed into place on its own four wheels by the ground crew. After settling into their cockpits and checking around for loose objects, they would strap in, either with the help of the ground crew or on their own, and then commence equipment checks, as well as confirming full and free movement of the controls before engine start. During this procedure, the navigator, as on all heavy aircraft in the Soviet air forces, would read the check-list, often referred to on the regiments as 'the prayers' (*molitva*), acknowledged by the pilot's corresponding actions. In the early years of operating the Tu-128, the Voronezh factory personnel and the Tupolev OKB worked jointly on improving the aircraft's cockpit ergonomics, taking note of the wishes expressed by test pilots and the first batch of squadron pilots. Consequently, the cockpits of the early aircraft (up to and including Series 12 aircraft) differed from each other in the position of switches and levers etc., so before carrying out his cockpit checks, the pilot would have to spend around three or four minutes acquainting himself with the cockpit layout of his particular aircraft. This was essential since pilots usually develop specific motor skills in order to interact rapidly with the cockpit environment, particularly in emergency situations. These reflex motor skills would, without question, be compromised by the need to adjust to the different cockpit layouts of the early Tu-128s, although from Series 13 onwards all Tu-128 cockpits were identical, only a few universally applied changes being incorporated when the aircraft was upgraded to Tu-128M standard. Former 518 AP navigator Maj. Ivan Rodyukov recalls that younger, inexperienced pilots were not allowed to fly the early-series aircraft as there was a considerable amount of refraction from the canopy glazing, giving pilots a distorted view of the runway.

In the opinion of most Tu-128 pilots, the cockpit was fairly well laid out ergonomically. Even when strapped tightly in the ejection seat the pilot could easily operate the throttle levers, whereas on the more modern MiG-31 'Foxhound' this could be a problem. If a MiG-31 pilot had his head right up against the head-rest, then on selecting reheat he would not be able to reach the throttles and so had to fly slightly hunched forward (!). Compared with the MiG-31, the Tu-128 canopy did not produce a glare effect on the cockpit glazing and had a large anti-glare coaming above the instrument panel. Cockpit lighting on the Tu-128 was rather effective, the only noticeable shortcoming being the light used to illuminate the instrument panel, mounted on the back of the control wheel boss. The beam from this light illuminated the instruments and sometimes produced a glare effect, although it could be switched off if necessary, of course; in this event, the instruments were still clearly visible. A curious feature of the Tu-128 cockpit was that the pilot and navigator were each provided with a small axe, evidently a relic of tradition, since axes were provided for the pilot on the PVO's Su-9 'Fishpot' interceptor. On earlier fighters like the MiG-17 and MiG-19 the pilot could eject directly through the canopy, whereas the canopy of the Su-9 incorporated a framework that prevented the pilot from ejecting straight through it in the event of it failing to separate from the aircraft. However, it was possible to break the fairly thick canopy glazing with the axe and parachute free from the aircraft, the same philosophy being applied to the Tu-128, keeping an axe as part of the cockpit fittings.

After completion of the cockpit checks, the aircraft technician would remove the intake blanks from the engines on the command of the pilot and also close the upward-opening side panel of the pilot's canopy, along with the main canopies over the pilot and the navigator. Great attention was paid to this last operation throughout the operating life of the 'Fiddler', although in spite of this, incidents still occurred. The designers' decision to use a pneumatic system to open and close the canopies was always a contentious point in the Tu-128 community. Even with the slightest misalignment of the canopy support struts, the canopy would not lock properly and could be sucked open in flight. Such incidents occurred regularly right up to the retirement of the Tu-128 from service, the last noted occurrence being on 24 June 1987 at Zhana-Semey (Semipalatinsk-1), when the navigator's canopy flipped open during the landing roll.

Engine start commenced after the aircraft technician had removed the steps, the pilot then carrying out further equipment and control checks with the engines running. If aircraft were parked on the TsZT central refuelling area side by side, the engines would be started on the first aircraft, with the intake blanks of all the other aircraft remaining in place, followed thereafter by other aircraft in the given flying programme. The engines were usually started on airfield electrical power and, in case of necessity, a simultaneous start of both engines could be carried out, observing an interval of 3-4 seconds between each selection. In specific cases it was permitted to start the engines on aircraft battery power. The engine start sequence was automatic and within less than one minute the engine would stabilise at 47.5 per cent rpm—the ground idle setting. After checking engine performance, the pilot would switch on the hydraulic servos of the ailerons, rudder and horizontal stabilizer, first on one hydraulic circuit, then on the other. The handles of the hydraulic servo valves had two positions—a 'mid position' (switching on the primary hydraulic system) and fully 'forward' (*ot syebya*), which selected the secondary hydraulic system. At the moment of switching on the hydraulic servos the pilot would check the smoothness of travel and full and free deflection of the relevant control surfaces, initially on one system and then on the other. Then he would check the operation of the trimming mechanisms, dry friction dampers and

A 64 AP technician places an intake 'blank' on his Tu-128 after performing engine checks, before declaring the aircraft for QRA duty at Omsk-North in 1983. (*S. Shchelokov*)

the emergency cross-feed of the rudder and ailerons. Here, it is worth mentioning a positive feature of the AL-7F-2 engine, as pointed out by Lt Col. Moiseyev:

> Since the components of any jet engine are made from different alloys, they each have a different coefficient of expansion when hot. Engines therefore required a preliminary warm-up period in order to prevent misalignment of the rotating elements and had a so-called 'cold position' (*kholodnaya pozitsiya*) and a 'hot position' (*goryachaya pozitsiya*). The virtue of the AL-7F-2 was that the transition from 'cold position' to 'hot position' and back was automatic, occurring within three minutes of closure (or opening) of the 4th-stage compressor bleed valve, when the aircraft was airborne. In both positions there was a maximum temperature limitation at maximum rpm [665° at 'cold position' and 680° at 'hot position']. When increasing rpm from idle setting ('*Malyi gaz*') to maximum dry thrust ('*Maksimal*'), the engine's 'automatics' (*avtomat*) maintained this temperature-limiting regime, obviating the need for preliminary warm-up prior to take-off, regardless of outside air temperature on the airfield.

TAKE-OFF

After all the pre-flight checks had been completed, and when authorised by ATC, the pilot would commence taxiing. For this he had to increase engine power to 60-70 per cent and release the parking brake, requiring a firm push on the rudder pedals before releasing them with smooth toe action. When the aircraft was moving, the pilot then selected nose-wheel steering, maintaining the pedals in the neutral position, and pressed the taxi mode selector button to switch over to the 'maximum manoeuvrability setting' of 35°(±1°). This was necessary since after lowering flaps to the take-off setting, nose-wheel steering automatically switched to the 'take-off and landing mode' with a turning limit of only 8°, under the control of the MRK (*Mekhanizm Razvorota Kolyos*) 'wheel turning mechanism'. The 8° turning limit was insufficient for taxiing, but a curious feature of the Tu-128 was that if the nose-wheel lifted off the ground during taxiing (i.e. if the nose leg became 'unloaded' for any reason), the MRK would immediately revert to the 8° 'take-off and landing mode'. In order to return to the normal taxiing mode, with 35° turning capability, the pilot had to brake the aircraft sharply to fully compress the nose leg and then reselect the MRK. In spite of the considerable length of the aircraft's fuselage and long wheelbase, the Tu-128 could easily enter a type of phugoid state during taxiing, sufficient to unload the nose undercarriage and reset the MRK. At Zhana-Semey, for example, there was a curved section of taxiway near the 3rd squadron dispersal area. In order to taxi along it accurately, pilots had to brake carefully when negotiating the bend, squeezing the brakes cautiously to avoid letting the nose nod up and down, which could initiate inadvertent 'selection' of the 8° turning limit.

Another interesting feature of the Tu-128 was that the front windscreens of the aircraft were each of a different size, the left-hand panel being larger than the right-hand section. This gave the pilot good forward visibility but he could not see the wings, and it was always necessary to take account of the wingspan when taxiing close to potential obstacles, reporting 'visibility to the left and right is normal' to ATC to confirm that he was happy to proceed. The aircraft had a minimum turn radius on the inner bogie of around 15 m (50 feet) and about 22 m (72 feet) on the outer bogie. Added to this limitation it was forbidden to turn the aircraft on the ground with one bogie braked, which was the normal procedure on smaller fighters, but potentially damaging on a multi-wheeled bogie like that of the Tu-128. There were, of course, problems arising from this, and pilots recall that aircraft at Nar'yan-Mar deployment airfield would occasionally run off the edge of the runway with one bogie when turning. In fact, because of this airfield's unsuitability for receiving the Tu-128 (having been designed for smaller fighters), the latter could *only* turn around directly on the runway. The runway at Nar'yan-Mar was only around 40 m (131 feet) wide, so simple arithmetic tells us that turning

Омск. 1983 год

The Tu-128 had massive main undercarriage bogies for a fighter, determined by the significant weight of the aircraft. Here, in a photograph from 1983, a 64 AP aircraft senior technician inspects the starboard undercarriage leg of his Tu-128 at Omsk-North. (*S. Shchelokov*)

the aircraft on the runway in accordance with the Pilots' Notes would lead to it coming off the edge of the concrete. So, in spite of the prohibition on turning with a braked bogie, Tu-128 pilots operating from this airfield would use the brakes judiciously to turn the aircraft on the runway, taking care not to go over the edge. Fortunately, the big Tupolev interceptor was very forgiving of such 'experiments'!

At the holding point (*predvarityel'nyi start*) the flaps would be lowered to 30° and the engine supplementary air intake doors (*stvorki podpitki dvigatyelyei*) would open. The procedure for lowering the flaps on the Tu-128 is worthy of detailed explanation. There was a safety catch on the flap selection panel, below which there were two rubber buttons (one red and one green). On pressing the green button, the flaps would travel to the 30° setting, shown by the UZP-47 (*Ukazatyel' Polozheniya Zakrylok*) flap position indicator needle, rather like the hand of a clock. (The word order in the expansion of the abbreviation differs from the abbreviation itself, avoiding ambiguity with systems such as UPS—see below.) As soon as the flaps reached the 30° position the safety catch had to be pulled and the retraction button pressed. If the flap setting for take-off was incorrect (less than 29°) at the moment of applying full power on both engines, a siren mounted on the right-hand side of the pilot's cockpit would sound automatically, warning the pilot that take-off was not allowed. The audio system was not triggered if the inner flaps were set between 29° and 32°

192

and the electrical circuitry of the audio warning system was interlocked for landing. The audio warning system would also trigger if engine power was reduced and the undercarriage had not been lowered, reminding the pilot to lower the wheels. In order to lighten the control force on the control wheel during take-off, the pilot would set the horizontal stabilizer to the position of '–9° back' (*–9° na syebya*) according to the UPS (*Ukazatyel' Polozheniya Stabilizatora*) stabilizer position indicator and then trim the aircraft at this setting. Having taxied onto the main runway and rolled about 20-30 m (65-100 feet) along the centreline, he would stop the aircraft, holding it on the parking brake. As previously mentioned, the parking brake was a toe-operated device, and it occasionally caused serious problems. There was a return spring under the brake pedals (i.e. rudder pedals) that released the wheel brakes by lifting the pedals. Quite often towards the end of the Tu-128's service there were cases of this spring breaking, which led to the aircraft landing with the brakes on, causing the tyres to burst. In order to avoid this happening, pilots would change the position of their feet during braking. Under the pedals there was a platform structure on the cockpit floor and they would usually place their feet on it, forcing their heels against the platform, holding the brakes on and pushing the pedals to the stops. Pilots claimed that the take-off was not difficult, but it required 'focused attention and careful actions'. Particular attention had to be paid to positioning the aircraft accurately on the runway centreline during line-up (*ispolnityel'nyi start*).

A Tu-128M of the 3rd squadron of 356 AP taxies out for a range firing sortie, carrying training rounds of the R-4T and R-4R missiles. (*Nikolai Popov*)

The afterburners were engaged with the aircraft held on the parking brake, but if the runway was slippery and the aircraft started to slide even under maximum dry thrust, then reheat could be selected whilst moving.[1] This is recalled by 356 AP's deputy regiment commander and former squadron commander, Lt Col. Moiseyev:

This method was called '*forsazhi vdogon*' [literally, 'afterburners in pursuit', i.e. afterburners selected while accelerating]. On the Su-9 it was standard operating procedure, but on the Tu-128 it was generally only employed on icy runways. Steering the aircraft in these conditions was achieved through unequal [asymmetric] selection of reheat and not by use of the brakes, which were ineffective on an icy runway. We only used the '*forsazhi vdogon*' procedure during transits and flights to another airfield, but definitely not for routine flights. Anyone deciding to perform a routine flight in icy conditions, after assessing the situation for himself, was [regarded as] a 'criminal'!

Former section commander Maj. Vydryenok adds:

At Talagi, I myself saw a '*sparka*' [i.e. the weather reconnaissance aircraft for that day] turn through 180° on the runway after selecting reheat with the brakes on and I tried to imagine the look on the faces of the crew in the cockpit at that time! The '*sparka*' taxied back to dispersal, where the commander of the OBATO (Independent Airfield Support Battalion) received a dressing down [because of the condition of the runway surface]. The weather reconnaissance flight was put back by one hour, while the take-off end of the runway was cleared with a 'snow-blower' vehicle.[2] Eventually, the '*sparka*' was able to take off on its weather recce flight, but when it returned it almost ran off the end of the 2,500 m [8,200 feet] runway in spite of using its brake chute. The reason for this was that during the take-off roll, the Tu-128UT had worsened the situation, with hot exhaust gases condensing onto concrete slabs that had a temperature significantly lower than the ambient air. This resulted in the formation of a thin film of ice on the runway surface, turning it into a skating rink. Civil aircraft with reverse thrust could still brake fairly safely, but the Tu-128UT almost overran the end of the runway. Knowing all of this, when flying out of Nar'yan-Mar in icy conditions on an unprepared runway, I always selected afterburners 'on the move' ('*vdogon*') once I had established steady forward movement.

Apart from this, there were also a few recorded instances of pilots attempting to take off in normal conditions with the brakes still applied, which usually resulted in the aircraft skidding and bursting the tyres.

The afterburners were selected on each engine separately, with an interval of 3-5 seconds between each selection. Unlike the majority of MiG and Sukhoi fighters, the Tu-128 did not have a locking catch on the throttle lever but was simply held at the selected setting by internal friction at the axis of rotation (adjustable on the ground by the maintenance personnel). This was a relic from its 'bomber genealogy'; on the Tu-16 and also the Tu-124 the throttle levers were held in place by the second pilot during the take-off. However, during the entire period of operation of the Tu-128 there was never a single case of the throttle lever moving from the setting made by the pilot. This could not be said for the afterburners, which were selected by a simple upward action of a special trigger mounted on the throttle lever. Locking of the triggers was achieved in the same manner as for the throttle—by friction—and although the throttle control was never a problem, there were a number of unpleasant incidents regarding afterburner selection on some aircraft. These included switching off the afterburner simply by touching the trigger quite gently or when the pilot, with his hand on the undercarriage lever during take-off, would snag the afterburner triggers with the sleeve of his flying jacket. The triggers would 'unlock' and the afterburners would switch off, although in most cases this occurred at a safe height after unstick and was more of an irritating distraction than the precursor to an accident. It was difficult for pilots to monitor the actual moment of afterburner ignition; on the Tu-128 this was achieved by noting a slight rise in exhaust gas temperature (EGT) after an initial drop, and, of course, by the characteristic 'jolt' of ignition. Additionally, at the rear of the right-hand console in the pilot's cockpit there were two afterburner fuel pressure gauges, which allowed him to monitor automatic fuel delivery to the igniters while still on the ground.

The aircraft always took off in reheat, although during operation there were several cases where take-off was performed (inadvertently) without afterburners or with only one engine in reheat. One such incident occurred in 1970, involving an aircraft belonging to 64 AP at Omsk-North. Lt Col. Nikolayev recalls the circumstances:

We had received orders to deploy ten aircraft and crews from Omsk to Arkhangel'sk [Talagi] to reinforce 518 AP during Exercise '*Okean*' [Ocean], with Col. Starovyerov being appointed senior officer in charge of the group.[3] We flew a route taking us from Omsk to Kotlas [Savvatiya] then on to Talagi. After refuelling at Kotlas, the crews departed singly en route to Talagi. The first aircraft had already departed and I took off with my navigator for the flight, Captain Bel'skii. We taxied out and requested permission to take off. One of the regiment's aircraft was on the approach, so we had to make a swift departure. I selected afterburner as I started to roll; I felt the first 'jolt' as the port afterburner ignited, but not the second, because of the distraction of the heavy background noise on the radio, and started my take-off run. At the mid-point along the runway, I felt that the aircraft was not accelerating normally. There wasn't sufficient runway length remaining to abort the take-off, so I decided to continue. I ordered the navigator to prepare to eject if we couldn't unstick in time: 'Feet on the footrests and get ready.' During the take-off run I didn't raise the nose, in order to accelerate quicker to unstick speed. At the very end of the runway I pulled the control column back sharply and the aircraft lifted to about 100 m [330 feet]. I retracted the undercarriage but left the flaps down since our speed was still low [around 320-340 kph/173-183 kts]. It seemed to 'hang' in the air, at a high angle of attack, at the limits of control; it should also be mentioned that we had a full fuel load and were carrying four missiles.

At a height of 100 m, I continued in horizontal flight; the speed was still not increasing and I again warned the navigator about the possibility of ejecting. The aircraft was in 'second regime', i.e. on pulling the control column back it started to sink and the only way out was to increase speed.[4] So, at the expense of losing a little height, I decided to lower the nose and very, very slowly, at around 40-50 m [130-165 feet], the speed had increased to 400 kph [216 kts]. We couldn't go any lower since the tops of trees were flashing by underneath, but gradually I was able to climb away at around 5 m/sec [around 1,000 ft/min]. The entire take-off process from lift-off to transition into the climb had taken about 10 minutes! During the climb, the speed increased to 420 kph [227 kts], with the engines operating at take-off power in reheat [*or so he thought—A.D.*]. So I climbed to 4,000 m [13,125 feet], where I shut down the afterburners and retracted the flaps. Thereafter, the speed began to increase rapidly. I reported that everything was OK on board and set course for Arkhangel'sk. On arrival at Talagi, it became clear that after replenishing the oxygen bottles, one of the valves [closed as standard procedure for replenishment] had not been re-opened. The oxygen reserve in the system after closing this valve was sufficient only for engine start and ignition of the port afterburner. Before my arrival at Talagi, a group of officers from the military security service had already come to the base to establish the reason for the 'precursor to a flying accident' (*predposylka k lyotnomu proisshestviyu*), [i.e. the protracted take-off run]. In this case, I was given a verbal reprimand by the senior officer of the group for taking off with the starboard afterburner deselected, although it should be noted that there were no instruments on the Tu-128 to monitor selection of reheat. Afterburner selection was monitored through the physical jolt of ignition, although this was less perceptible during reheat selection when moving forward on the runway. Moreover, exhaust gas temperature varied only insignificantly [580° without afterburner and 600° with afterburner]. If monitoring instruments *had* existed, then in similar circumstances it would have been possible to shut down the afterburner of the affected engine in order to increase thrust.[5] Thereafter, during my briefings I always reminded pilots of the correct action to be taken in such situations.

With afterburner selected, the pilot would smoothly and synchronously release the parking brakes and commence the take-off run. The aircraft accelerated smoothly but 'energetically', without any tendency to yaw. In order to eliminate any slight deviation from the centreline in the first half of the take-off run (i.e. with all three undercarriage units still on the ground) it was sufficient just to deflect the pedals in the appropriate direction. However, if the deviation from the centreline in the first half of the take-off run was fairly large then it was considerably more difficult to correct, due to the aircraft's high inertia. The thrust of each engine in reheat at sea level, against the brakes, was 10,050 kg (22,156 lb), giving a thrust-to-weight ratio at maximum take-off weight of 43,000 kg (94,800 lb) of only 0.468 kg thrust/kg mass, whilst the wing loading on take-off was 443 kg/m² (90.73 lb/sq. ft). Pilots recall that the take-off performance of the Tu-128 was not spectacular, given its thrust-to-weight ratio of only 0.47 (for the Su-15 and Su-15TM this was 0.7 to 0.8). Thus, take-off was not at all like on the Su-15, where the pilot held the stick fully back during acceleration and unstick. The Tu-128 left the ground quite sedately and smoothly, but after unstick the horizontal stabilizer was set to the zero position in order to reduce drag. This was particularly necessary in the heat of summer when taking off with missiles on all four pylons; in these conditions the control column was normally pushed forward slightly after unstick to build up speed for the climb. Here is how the take-off stage was described in the Pilots' Notes 'Instructions for the crew of the Tu-128 (Tu-128M) aircraft':

At a speed of 260-270 kph [140-145 kts], pulling the control column back smoothly, raise the nose so that on reaching a speed of 290-300 kph [156-162 kts] the aircraft assumes the normal take-off angle (with the line of the natural horizon passing approximately 2 cm [about 0.75 inches] below the upper curvature of the centre of the instrument panel).

The force on the control column to raise the nose-wheel off the ground is around 15-20 kg [33-44 lb] and the amount of movement of the stabilizer is –17° to –18° on the UPS stabilizer position indicator. With the nose-wheel raised off the ground, and accelerating on the main undercarriage bogies, there is no tendency to develop a longitudinal 'swing' or phugoid motion.

At a speed of 320-340 kph [173-183 kts], [depending upon pitch angle and take-off weight] the aircraft will smoothly leave the ground. After rotation, even at maximum take-off weight of 43,000 kg [94,800 lb], the aircraft is stable in the climb and shows no tendency to develop an undemanded turn or bank. After lift-off, and without introducing an angle of bank or sideslip, allow the aircraft to accelerate into a smooth climb, maintaining pitch angle approximately equal to the angle at unstick.

During early operation of the Tu-128 (i.e. during conversion training), pilots would commit handling errors by allowing the aircraft to develop an angle of bank during the initial climb phase, without detecting this immediately and taking corrective action.

In spite of the fact that the engines of the Tu-128 were mounted in the fuselage, the thrust line was located above the centre of gravity. Therefore, with power on, the aircraft experienced a nose-down pitching moment, the magnitude of which depended upon engine thrust and flight speed. At the beginning of the take-off run, when the engines were operating in afterburner mode and forward momentum was low, the pitch-down moment due to thrust was at its highest value. As speed increased during the take-off run, along with increasing dynamic pressure, the pitch-down moment reduced in strength, but was still quite high. In order to raise the aircraft's nose prior to rotation it was necessary to pull the control column back firmly to deflect the horizontal stabilizer. It was also important to consider that the proximity of the runway surface (ground effect) during take-off influenced the pitching characteristics of the aircraft in the direction of increasing the negative pitching momentum. This in turn required additional deflection of the stabilizer on the take-off run. The tailplane travel required to balance the pitching moments due to thrust and those due to ground effect decreased substantially as a function of the increase of flight speed and release from ground effect. However, tests conducted in the early period of operation of the first series of Tu-128s led to the rather depressing conclusion that the aircraft had very poor take-off performance. Thus, armed with four AA-5 'Ash' missiles, at a take-off weight of 43,000 kg (94,800 lb) in ISA (international standard atmosphere) conditions, with afterburners engaged, supplementary air intake doors open and inner and outer flaps set to 30°, the aircraft had a coefficient of lift (C_L) of 0.8 at the moment of rotation. Therefore, the Tupolev OKB suggested providing the aircraft with 'differentially deflecting flaps', where the inner flaps would travel to 30° and the outer section to 15°. This allowed rotation at fairly high angles of attack, giving a figure of 10.6°, where the permissible angle of attack was 15°. In this case, the take-off performance figures were $C_{L\ ROTATE}$ 0.92, V_{ROTATE} 316 kph (170 kts) and take-off run 1,350 m (4,430 feet). After this modification, all Tu-128s were brought up to the same standard to incorporate the 'differentially deflecting flaps', earlier-series aircraft undergoing modification in service during routine overhauls.

Maj. Nikolai Popov describes here a typical take-off in the Tu-128 during the very hot summer months:

> There was an occasion when I was taking off from Kansk air base in Siberia in the summer with an outside air temperature of +35°C. The main runway at this airfield was 2,500 m [8,200 feet] long and to be honest, it wasn't so much a case of 'rotating' in these conditions, more a case of the aircraft 'jumping' off the last slab of concrete. It got into the air more as a result of the curvature of the earth and the will of the pilot [than the aerodynamics and power of the aircraft]!

After lift-off, at a height of 10-15 m (30-50 feet), the pilot would start to retract the undercarriage and flaps. With undercarriage and flaps down, it was not permitted to exceed 500 kph (270 kts) and the pilot had to adjust speed by changing the pitch angle in the climb. Exceeding this speed by 150-200 kph (81-108 kts) would lead to the flaps being ripped off the wing. (Such an incident involving a Tu-128 of 615 UIAP occurred at Savasleika during conversion training, and there was a similar occurrence on 518 AP at Talagi.) Pilots were also advised not to be too hasty in placing the undercarriage selection lever in the neutral position. The process of retracting the undercarriage took around 8 seconds, whereas the flap retraction took around 24 seconds. Simultaneous with undercarriage and flap retraction, the intake cones translated forward, along with the closure of the supplementary air intake doors on the side of the fuselage. The afterburners were shut down at a height of 600 m (1,970 feet). The climb trajectory was flat, around 10-12°, practically the same as the angle of attack at unstick. A feature of the Tu-128 was that there was a noticeable increase in drag on retracting the undercarriage when the doors opened into the airflow. Therefore, in the event of an engine failure on take-off, the undercarriage was not retracted in order to allow the aircraft to accelerate as quickly as possible and climb away from the ground. The pilot also had to remember that retraction of the undercarriage and flaps combined with switching off the afterburners produced a pitch-up moment which had to be countered with an appropriate forward movement of the control column.

With a shallow angle of attack on take-off, the aircraft accelerated quite rapidly and could quickly reach the undercarriage limiting speed for climb-out, so in order to guarantee safe retraction of the undercarriage the pitch angle had to be increased by about 2-3°. During the next stage of the climb-out the pilot could vary the pitch angle as a function of aircraft weight, flight speed and the limit imposed by flap retraction time. Apart from the parameters mentioned above, the pitch angle limits on the 'Fiddler' depended to a large extent on atmospheric conditions and could reach 16-18° in negative temperature conditions. During the course of Tu-128 operations, PVO specialists established that for every 10° rise in air temperature, taking off from a concrete runway in ISA conditions, the take-off run increased by 13 per cent, and for every 10° reduction in air temperature this was reduced by 10 per cent. The aircraft had only one weapons 'fit', comprising four R-4 (AA-5 'Ash') air-to-air missiles, although a 'half-variant' (*polovinnyi variant*) comprising only two missiles was used solely for training flights. Therefore, the difference on take-off at maximum and minimum weights was characterised purely by a longer take-off run at the heavier weight and the more sluggish behaviour of the aircraft in the climb. The time of the normal take-off run without missiles was around 35-40 seconds.

Take-off was permitted with a 90° crosswind of up to 12 m/sec (23 kts), a crosswind of 6 m/sec (12 kts) presenting little difficulty for pilots, so in the early stages of training the regiment QFIs tried to inculcate good practice by first demonstrating the procedure in the less demanding conditions. These involved take-offs with a crosswind component of 4-6 m/sec (8-12 kts), and only after demonstration of

The 'Fiddler' carried only two missiles for live firing against parachute-retarded targets, as demonstrated by this 518 AP aircraft on its way to the Northern Fleet firing range. (*Alexander Melihov*)

sound aircraft handling ability would pilots be permitted to conduct take-offs with a crosswind of around 10-12 m/sec (19-23 kts). In a crosswind take-off the aircraft had a tendency to 'weathercock' into wind on the take-off run, but after rotation exhibited a tendency to bank 'with the wind'. In order to prevent the angle of bank developing and departure from the take-off heading, the pilot had to use the ailerons, but in this flight regime the ailerons were not very effective. By contrast, the rudder was very effective during the take-off run, so to counter the banking tendency after unstick in a limiting crosswind, the pilot had to use an appropriate amount of 'into wind' rudder. The speed at which the nose-wheel had to be raised was the same as that when taking off into wind, but the pilot had to rotate at a slightly reduced pitch angle (by around 1-1.5°), trying not to exceed the undercarriage limiting speed of 350 kph (189 kts). A concluding series of tests to establish the Tu-128's take-off performance were carried out in 1973 by Tupolev OKB test pilot Mikhail Kozlov, but his tragic death in the Tu-144 crash at Le Bourget on 3 June of that year meant that the final test could not be completed. As there were no other Tupolev test pilots with currency on the Tu-128, Col. Yevglyevskiy was invited by the OKB to conduct this important test:

This required me to demonstrate a maximum weight take-off with a simulated engine failure half-way down the runway. The test was conducted at the Flight Test Institute airfield at Zhukovskiy, which had a 5,000 m [16,400 feet] runway, making things easier than using a normal runway. Calculations had shown that such a take-off could be achieved in standard atmospheric conditions; I performed the flight without incident and thereby completed the final test phase of the aircraft.

During flight testing, the maximum times to climb to various heights were established for a take-off weight of 32,000 kg (70,550 lb) and are given in the following table:

Altitude in metres	Max reheat			Max dry		
	Rate of climb (m/sec)	Time to climb (mins)	Climb speed (kph)	Rate of climb (m/sec)	Time to climb (mins)	Climb speed (kph)
0	76.5	–	800	45.5	–	750
2,000	79.5	0.4	853	37.5	0.8	793
4,000	78.5	0.8	905	30.0	1.8	828
6,000	71.5	1.3	960	23.5	3.1	855
8,000	59.5	1.8	995	16.5	4.7	887
10,000	46.0	2.4	968	12.0	7.0	927
11,000	38.5	2.8	955	8.5	8.75	955
12,000	30.5	3.3	955	4.5	11.6	955
13,000	22.0	4.0	955	–	–	–
14,000	13.5	5.0	955	–	–	–
15,000	4.5	6.8	955	–	–	–
Service ceiling	15,400 m	15,400 m	15,400 m	12,300 m	12,300 m	12,300 m

However, even in the early stage of operation, it became clear that the tables were not that easy to use, so the Tupolev OKB came up with a simpler set of recommendations. The pilot had to set up a climb speed of 750 kph (405 kts) after retraction of the undercarriage and flaps, independent of take-off weight and missile load, in order to reach the altitude specified by the given task. This speed had to be established by the time the aircraft reached 1,000 m (3,280 feet). The aircraft would then accelerate to a true air speed of 870 kph (470 kts) while climbing in maximum dry thrust, or to 950 kph (513 kts) in full afterburner. Further climbing would be carried out at these true air speeds. Pilots recall that the Tu-128 would enter the supersonic regime quite easily, normally achieved at 11,000 m (36,000 feet)—they would simply select reheat and the aircraft would accelerate smoothly. By contrast, the Su-9 would 'rear up' immediately on selection of reheat, requiring the pilot to push forward on the control column, with the reverse happening during deceleration from supersonic speed. It was the same with the Yak-28P. The actual moment of going through the 'sound barrier' was barely discernible on the Tu-128 and was marked only by a slight 'jump' of the needles of the aneroid-barometric instruments and a slight rocking of the wings. Altitude and speed indications would increase sharply and then return to their real values; altimeter readings could jump by 300-400 m (985-1,312 feet). During deceleration, the readings would show a downwards 'blip'. The Tu-128 also flew very well without afterburners up to an altitude of 11,000 m (36,000 feet), whereas its successor, the MiG-31 'Foxhound', exhibited poor performance without reheat at altitudes close to 10,000 m (32,800 feet). A characteristic feature of the Tu-128 compared with its successor was that even with a fuel remainder of 7,000-8,000 kg (15,430-17,640 lb) and in maximum dry thrust (*maksimal*) the Tu-128 would easily go supersonic at altitudes above 9,000 m (29,530 feet), where the Mach number would be around 1.05.

However, beyond this speed the aircraft would accelerate slowly in reheat, particularly after reaching Mach 1.3 to 1.35, while at speeds around 1,500 kph (809 kts) it exhibited poor roll (banking) performance. There were no special zones for supersonic flight in the Tu-128 over the Soviet Union, but the remote location of the majority of bases meant that there was no real need for them anyway. In peacetime the aircraft was allowed to go supersonic at altitudes above 11,000 m (36,000 feet), although on cross-country flights over the uninhabited territories of Siberia and the 'Soviet North' it was permitted to go supersonic from an altitude around 10,500-10,600 m (34,450-34,775 feet). The highest speeds in horizontal flight were achieved at an altitude of 11,000 m (36,000 feet) in reheat mode (engines operating at 8,500 rpm). For an established weight of 32,000 kg (70,550 lb) and in the reheat regime used for the zoom climb manoeuvre of a typical intercept profile, the achievable maximum speed was 1,665 kph (898 kts) or approximately Mach 1.57.

The table below shows the maximum horizontal flight speeds depending on altitude at maximum dry thrust and in maximum reheat for a weight of 32,000 kg (70,550 lb) with missiles:

Altitude	Max Speed in Max Dry Thrust	Max Speed in Max Reheat
0	870	870
4,000	990	990
6,000	1,050	1,050
8,000	1,083	1,120
10,000	1,053	1,250–1,622
11,000	1,030	1,665
12,000	1,010	1,605
13,000	–	1,485
14,000	–	1,320
15,000	–	1,050

For any interceptor an important stage of flight is the deceleration phase after breaking away from the attack, and the Tu-128 was no exception. The pilot would switch off the afterburners and reduce engine rpm smoothly to end the pursuit, setting power at not less than 90 per cent (at a speed of more than Mach 1.4). After reducing speed below Mach 1.4 the engines were set to 'Flight Idle' and the aircraft was decelerated in horizontal flight to subsonic speed. In the event of further speed reductions, one of the limiting flight regimes could arise: on reaching a speed of around 350-360 kph (190-195 kts) during deceleration, the AUASP warning system could be triggered, indicating that the angle of attack had exceeded the permitted limit. In this speed range a warning buffeting could be felt, which would continue down to a speed of around 320-330 kph (173-178 kts), followed by slight wing rocking. In spite of the reduced effectiveness of the ailerons in these conditions, they had sufficient authority to counter any bank angle generated in this way. Any further reduction in speed could lead to 'speed instability', this manifesting itself in the fact that on reducing speed it required more and more forward deflection of the control column in order to maintain straight and level flight. In this flight regime an increase in speed was only possible after putting the aircraft into a descent. In the process of descending, the aircraft reluctantly gained speed even with the engines at maximum thrust. The loss of height as a result of accelerating the aircraft from these regimes and making the transition to horizontal flight was around 1,000-1,500 m (3,280-4,920 feet).

MANOEUVRING CAPABILITY

In spite of the aircraft's 'bomber lineage', the Tu-128 was able to perform simple 'aerobatic' manoeuvres such as (steep) turns, the chandelle (*boyevoy razvorot*),[6] zoom climb, dives and spiral descents. The carriage of the full complement of four AA-5 'Ash' missiles did not substantially affect handling while carrying out any of these manoeuvres, pilots noting only that the aircraft was more sluggish in this condition. Steep turns could be performed with an angle of bank up to 60° at any power setting, with or without reheat, dependent upon altitude and flight speed. The aircraft was stable in the turn throughout the full operational range of g-loading, speed and altitude limitations and did not exhibit any difference in handling when turning to the right or left. Turns were easiest to perform at an angle of bank of 45-60° at altitudes between 2,000 and 6,000 m (6,560-19,685 feet), within the speed range 600-700 kph (378 kts). At a speed of 800-850 kph (432-459 kts) a 60° banked turn was slightly more demanding to execute because of increased control effectiveness, requiring only very small control movements to initiate the manoeuvre. A bank angle of more than 60° was not permitted, particularly when descending. Co-author Nikolai Popov, who was qualified on both the Tu-128 and the MiG-31, makes the following comparative observation:

The MiG-31 could not perform a 60° banked turn at around 5,000 m [16,400 feet] with a fuel load of 7,000-8,000 kg [15,430-17,640 lb] and at 8,000 m [26,250 feet] would even lose speed in the turn at a bank angle of greater than 30°. By contrast, the Tu-128 would perform banked turns at any altitude completely without drama. Even at 9,000 m [29,530 ft] the Tu-128 could perform banked turns at such angles [i.e. greater than 30°], although without missiles, of course.

In the PVO Aviation combat training manual great attention was paid to the correct execution of banked turns, with some justification, since they were a vital component of the GCI intercept profile of the Tu-128. The aircraft was cleared only for basic 'aerobatic' manoeuvres (*prostoy pilotazh*), although as mentioned in the preceding paragraph, these were nowhere near the true aerobatic capabilities of smaller, more agile fighters. However, pilots (including test pilots) *were* known to have performed barrel rolls in the aircraft, although squadron pilots are only likely to have attempted this before 1972. Before then, no one ever looked at the KZA flight recorder data if the pilot had entered 'No reported defects' ('*Zamyechanii nyet*') in the aircraft's engineering log (*zhurnal podgotovki samolyota k polyotu*), so unauthorised manoeuvres would have gone unnoticed. Col. Yevglyevskiy recalls:

I'd heard that someone had tried to perform a '*bochka*' [barrel roll] in the Tu-128 and once, when I was visiting 445 AP at Savvatiya with Tupolev OKB test pilot Mikhail Kozlov, I asked him to show me a barrel roll in the Tu-128UT. He tried to deny that anyone had ever rolled the aircraft, but I just kept saying, 'I know that they do it!' Finally he agreed to show me. We took off in the Tu-128UT and Kozlov demonstrated the barrel roll. Naturally, it wasn't difficult for him to do, but there was nothing pleasant about it. In the first place the entry speed had to be quite high—the higher the speed, the easier it was to do. So if the indicated air speed was 900 kph [486 kts] then everything would go swimmingly. Secondly, the pitch angle had to be around 10° and the roll was executed quite slowly because of the aircraft's poor lateral stability, rotating for quite a long time. It was not at all like a fighter aircraft manoeuvre. And you don't experience any pleasure when the aircraft goes past the 90° bank angle. You hang in the straps, although the nose continues to drop. If you don't hang in the straps then the roll is worse. The exit from this 'roll' is achieved rather like 'getting out of a pit'. The nose is already lowered. Finally, you recover and the aircraft begins to level out. If you did this at low level then you'd probably just fly into the ground, and if it was at 600-700 kph [324-378 kts] then all of the foregoing sensations would be doubled or even trebled.

Pilots used to say that it was really not so much a '*bochka*', more a '*kadushka*' (a tub, as used in Russian bath houses, whose height was considerably less than its width), an allusion to the manoeuvre described by the aircraft in the roll.

A typical post-flight scene, with a Tu-128 pilot signing off the aircraft's engineering log or 'Aircraft Flight Preparation Log Book' (*'Zhurnal podgotovki samolyota k polyotu'*). (*Ivan Rodyukov*)

Of course, carrying out a barrel roll was really nothing more than sheer bravado and had no practical combat application. On one occasion, however, performing such a manoeuvre helped to save a 64 AP aircraft (a Tu-128UT) and the life of its crew. After take-off, at a height of 350 m (1,150 feet) and flying at 600 kph (324 kts), the pilot discovered that the control column had jammed and it was impossible to push it forward to reduce the pitch angle and the steepness of the climb. Stabilizer pitch setting at the time was –6°. It transpired that the emergency manual undercarriage extension handle had jammed against one of the control columns, having fallen out of its normal stowage location and struck the control column. To avoid reducing speed and risking a stall, the pilots put the aircraft into a steep turn with almost 90° of bank. One of the pilots pulled back on the stick while the other put the emergency undercarriage lever back into its normal housing, after which the aircraft was returned to normal flight. This occurred at 1,300 m (4,265 feet) and the incident was handled very professionally by both pilots, without allowing the aircraft to enter a critical flight regime.

GCI intercepts were normally carried out as a forward hemisphere engagement, although in the event of overshooting the target this could be converted into a rear hemisphere attack. In this case, it was necessary to perform an 'energetic' steep turn immediately after passing abeam the target, turning back onto a pursuit heading, or pulling up into a chandelle (i.e. a combat turn). A combat turn was carried out in full afterburner, with manoeuvre entry speeds from 650 kph (350 kts) up to the maximum permitted speed. To perform a combat turn the pilot would set up an initial bank angle of 10-15°, establishing and maintaining a g-load of 2.3-2.5 g, taking care not to exceed an angle of 60° when banking. The height gain in a combat turn, with the manoeuvre initiated in the height range 500-1,000 m (1,640-3,280 feet) and at a speed of 650-850 kph (351-459 kts), was from 3,000-4,000 m (9,840-13,125 feet) with a full complement of AA-5 'Ash' missiles and 4,000-5,000 m (13,125-16,400 feet) 'clean'. Naturally, pilots who had come to the Tu-128 from the Su-9, for example, immediately noticed the difference when comparing the turning performance of these two fighters.

> On the Su-9 you could pull as hard as you were able to in the turn. You would begin to experience 'grey out' from the g-loading. You wanted to turn as quickly as possible. But on the Tu-128, the slightest bit of 'over-pulling' on the control column would immediately trigger the alarm bells and flashing lights of the AUASP combined angle of attack and g-meter warning system and the navigator would be shouting, 'Commander, the bells are ringing back here!' It was somehow more scary to fly the manoeuvre at bank angles greater than 45°. It felt like there wasn't enough power to maintain the aircraft at the same height.

Apart from steep turns and chandelles, dives and zoom climbs also formed part of the Tu-128's repertoire of combat manoeuvres. The aircraft could perform a zoom climb throughout the entire range of operating altitudes in full afterburner. At low and medium altitudes this manoeuvre was performed at pitch angles up to 40° and at high altitude this was reduced to angles up to 25°. It was essential that entry to a zoom climb at these defined limiting angles, at low and medium altitude, should be carried out at a speed of not less than 700 kph (378 kts), and at high altitude this had to be at a speed equivalent to not less than Mach 1.2. The height gained in a zoom climb carrying four AA-5 'Ash' missiles using an entry speed of 700-850 kph (378-459 kts) at an altitude of 500-1,000 m (1,640-3,280 feet), with a pitch angle of 40° was of the order of 3,000-4,000 m (9,840-13,125 feet), whilst this was increased to 6,000-7,000 m (19,685-22,965 feet) using an angle of 20°. Dives could be performed at an angle of up to 30°, with the engines set at 'Flight Idle', the aircraft being stable and handling well in this condition. Diving when carrying missiles, or without them, was stable and fully controllable. When pulling out of a 30° dive at a height of 2,000 m (6,560 feet) at 800 kph (432 kts), and sustaining 2.3-2.5 g, the height loss was of the order of 1,400-1,600 m (4,590-5,250 feet). A controlled spiral descent could be carried out with a bank angle of not greater than 60° at 500-700 kph (270-378 kts), but during initial training it was recommended to perform this type of descent with a bank angle not greater than 45° at a speed of 500-550 kph (270-297 kts), with engines set at 'Flight Idle'. The height when pulling out of a spiral descent had to be not less than 2,000 m (6,560 feet).

FEATURES OF FLIGHT FOR MAXIMUM CEILING AND MAXIMUM RANGE

The Tu-128 had a curious feature with regard to performance that was not immediately obvious—it had a higher ceiling at subsonic speed than it did in the supersonic regime. This is perhaps best illustrated in the following table:

Climbing Regime	Ceiling	Weight at Ceiling
Max without reheat	10,500 m	40,000 kg
Max reheat (and true air speed in climb of 950 kph)	14,250 m	38,800 kg
Max reheat (Mach 1.3)	12,750 m	36,000 kg

The ceiling values given in this table are for an aircraft carrying four AA-5 'Ash' missiles in standard outside air temperature of –56.66°C, a rate of climb of 3 m/sec (590 ft/min) and 100 per cent engine rpm. Using the above data as a point of reference it should be noted that an increase in *weight* of 1,000 kg (2,204 lb) at the ceiling altitude would reduce that altitude by 200 m (656 feet). A *temperature* increase would have an analogous effect on ceiling altitude; an increase of 10°C would reduce the achievable ceiling (climbing at Mach 1.3) by 1,200 m (3,937 feet), whilst this would be reduced by 350 m (1,150 feet) for a true (climbing) air speed of 950 kph (512 kts). This anomaly was the result of the aircraft's aerodynamic layout. It has to be said that thanks to its aerodynamic efficiency the 'initial height' (i.e. the height at which it was necessary to accelerate in order to achieve the dynamic ceiling) was not less than 9,000 m (29,530 feet). By contrast, its successor, the MiG-31, had an 'initial height' of 7,300 m (23,950 feet) with a full complement of missiles. Pilots recall that 'at ceiling the Tu-128 handled normally but exhibited very poor control when banking, and turning performance was slow'.

FLIGHT AT LOW ALTITUDE

After the upgraded Tu-128M began arriving on the regiments, PVO Aviation Command was faced with the problem of training its crews in low-level flying, a capability added to this variant but not part of the aircraft's original specification. This was in fact quite a serious problem for a number of reasons, including:

- the 'morale-psychological effect' (*moral'no-psikhologicheskoye vozdyeist-viye*)[7] on the pilot of flying in close proximity to the ground;
- the stability and aircraft handling characteristics in this flight regime;
- the good acceleration performance of the aircraft;
- the difficulty of maintaining a good visual look-out;
- the range reduction of radar and radio equipment.

The Tu-128's speed at low level was limited by static and dynamic stability considerations and the possibility of the onset of aileron reversal and flutter. The maximum indicated air speed was 850 kph (459 kts) or Mach 0.95 at these levels. Moreover, at low level and high speed, pilots had to remember that the required amount of travel and force on the control column (for a 1 g load) was less than the values experienced in supersonic flight at an altitude of 10,000 m (32,800 feet). So manoeuvring at low level at 750 kph (405 kts) pulling a constant 2 g was difficult; in fact, in these conditions, the pitch damper actuators were at the limit of their travel and pitch damping was virtually non-existent. This substantially reduced the stability margin in terms of g-loading. The above-mentioned handling features demanded from the pilot precise and carefully measured movements of the control column in order to avoid exceeding the aircraft's g-load limits. The condition of 'auto-instability in pitch' (*avtoraskachka po tangazhu*) was possible when flying at indicated air speeds of 830-850 kph (448-459 kts) at heights of 500-1,000 m (1,640-3,280 feet), a consequence of the effectiveness of the control surfaces and the characteristics of the actuators. Consequently, pilots were recommended not to strive to be too accurate in trying to maintain pitch attitude. These particularities were not noticeable in the bank channel.

The handling behaviour of the aircraft at low level had to be studied when the regiments began to convert onto a modified variant. When the Tu-128M was delivered to 356 AP at Zhana-Semey the first personnel to undergo training were engineers from the regiment's technical-engineering group (*inzhenyerno-tekhnich-eskiy sostav*) and the senior management group (*upravlyenie polka*). They then introduced the upgraded systems and capabilities of the Tu-128M to the remaining aircrew and ground maintenance personnel, with strong emphasis being placed on flight training at low level and the modified combat techniques required in this hitherto unfamiliar regime. First and foremost, of course, it was vital to develop the requisite piloting techniques, particularly for the less experienced pilots, for whom low-level flying in the PVO context was perhaps a totally unexpected skill to be mastered. The head of the PVO Aviation's flight safety department, Col. Yevglyevskiy, developed the Tu-128M training programme, with 'dual' flight training being carried out on the Tu-128UT. Col. Yevglyevskiy remembers one of his early students from 356 AP:

The programme required us to carry out a series of integrated exercises, involving setting out on a cross-country sector at low level, entering the manoeuvring zone and performing some basic handling. At the time there had been heavy snowfalls and the surrounding terrain was white, making visual estimation of height quite difficult. I'd only flown with this pilot for about a minute and he was already requesting permission to enter 'the zone'. About 40 seconds later he again requested permission to enter 'the zone'. I responded by telling him that we had to fly the low-level segment right up to the end of the exercise, which was supposed to be about 5 minutes' flying time in all for that part of the programme. However, he found it so demanding that it seemed to him that we'd been flying for about an hour. He asked me three times on this segment to depart for 'the zone', i.e. to climb away from low level. There is no question that low-level flight in the Tu-128M certainly proved to be very difficult.

However, a training programme was drawn up and finalised by Col. Yevglyevskiy, approved and assimilated by the PVO, and gradually all Tu-128 pilots successfully mastered the 'new' variant.

When teaching low-level flying techniques in the Tu-128, great attention was paid to the fact that the size and shape of landmarks could be distorted in perspective, and for the control and monitoring of flights a radio-relay aircraft was sometimes used to provide route clearance. Another method was to perform a 'pop-up' (*podskok*) manoeuvre on specified sections of the route to gain height, in order to obtain better radio and radar performance. Low-level flights were usually carried out at around 500-1,000 m (1,640-3,280 feet), heights for which the aircraft was clearly not designed, its primary task being to carry out combat air patrols and

An elegant study of the Tu-128 (here a Tu-128M) which emphasises the long wheelbase of this huge fighter. (*Nikolai Popov*)

intercepts as far away as possible from base. The 'Fiddler' had, without question, a very long range for an aircraft not equipped with in-flight refuelling. Maximum range was obtained in cruising flight at speeds corresponding to Mach 0.855, calculated to take account of 400 kg (880 lb) fuel used for engine checks on the ground and the figure of not less than 1,850 kg (4,080 lb) required for landing. The optimum cruising altitude varied as a function of aircraft weight, from 9,300 m (30,500 feet) at the beginning of a flight to 11,600 m (38,220 feet) at the end of the sortie. Unfortunately, although the Tu-128's successor, the MiG-31, represented a significant advance in terms of avionics and weapons system performance, it did not possess such a long-range capability (2,150 km/1,160 nm) without in-flight refuelling. This was because on the one hand the Tu-128 carried almost a tonne of extra fuel compared with the MiG-31 and, secondly, because the specific fuel consumption of the Tupolev fighter was 4.7 kg/kg*t, whilst that of the MiG-31 was 5.5 kg/kg*t.

Former Tu-128 pilot Capt. Vinokurov comments:

> Not one of the PVO's other interceptors could perform as many approaches in the same flight if conditions required it. In the harsh conditions of the north and extremely unstable weather, the Tu-128 easily allowed a diversion to be made to practically any diversion airfield. On one occasion I was returning from a navigation exercise (navex) with my section commander Major Kuz'minnyi, making a standard approach to enter the circuit. On the radio I heard two other aircraft on the approach, with both the airfield ATC and the 'near zone' controller constantly directing them where to turn, climb or descend. The voices of both the aircrew and the ground controllers sounded tense. I said to Kuz'minnyi, 'Have we run into a bit of a problem?!' He just replied in a very calm voice, 'What are you concerned about? Don't worry! If we don't get in the first time, we'll go round again. If we don't get in off the second, then we'll definitely get in off the third!' We *did* land off the first approach, but I have to say that I was a bit taken aback at first by his calm, philosophical assessment of the situation. Probably because of my youth! With a fuel remainder for landing of 8-9 tonnes [17,640-19,840 lb] and fairly economical engines [*for that time—A.D.*], the Tu-128 was reassuring to fly if the weather suddenly worsened on the approach. In such circumstances, it was possible to carry out several approaches at base, or divert to a reserve airfield. This was very important when flying in the north, where the weather was unpredictable and regiment weather forecasters were the most respected people on the base—poor devils!

This was one of the reasons why many pilots had an almost exaggerated belief in the flight endurance of the Tu-128. In the final months of its service there was a particular episode that did indeed testify to the aircraft's range performance. In 1987, eight Tu-128s were being ferried from Omsk-North to the storage base at

Rzhev in the Tver Oblast of southern Russia, with four aircraft scheduled to make an interim landing at Perm' and the other four at Yoshkar-Ola in what is now the Mari El Republic. Maj. Nikolai Popov was one of the pilots involved in this flight:

> It was Friday, September 1st and the day was drawing to a close. I landed at Perm' and taxied into the parking area designated for us, which was covered in gravel […] Fortunately, for the Tu-128 this was not a problem, as the air intakes were mounted quite high. Here, they told us that we had to do a turn-round within the hour and then continue on to Rzhev. If we couldn't do this within that time then we'd have to stay for the weekend and continue the ferry flight on the Monday. However, we all had various plans for the weekend. If we'd all refuelled completely then this would have taken quite some time. So the first two aircraft were topped up with 1,200 litres each in the centre-section tanks, another two with 600 litres in the centre tanks and one of the aircraft which landed at Yoshkar-Ola was not refuelled at all. It turned out that both 'four-ship' groups arrived at Rzhev at the same time and since it was necessary to separate the aircraft by extending the circuit pattern some of them landed with minimum fuel remainders. One aircraft landed with only 250 kg [550 lb] of fuel remaining and suffered a flame-out of the starboard engine during the landing run, but managed to taxi in on the remaining engine [the straight-line distance between Omsk and Rzhev is just over 2,430 km or around 1,510 statute miles].

LANDING THE TU-128

The landing highlighted a number of features which set the Tu-128 apart from all previous and subsequent Soviet fighters. One of these features was the fact that the aircraft had an emergency fuel dumping system, although a similar facility was incorporated into the design of the more advanced MiG-31. However, the principle of operation differed significantly between the two aircraft—on the MiG-31 fuel was jettisoned via a high-capacity augmenter pump, whereas the Tu-128 employed a much simpler system. The integral wing tanks were fitted with special retractable sleeves which could be lowered directly into the airstream, thereby providing an outlet to atmosphere for the jettisoned fuel. Since the fuel was jettisoned purely by gravity flow, only the contents of the integral wing tanks could be dumped by this method. The normal landing weight of the Tu-128 was 31,000 kg (68,340 lb), including a fuel weight of 2,850 kg (6,280 lb) and the 1,900 kg (4,190 lb) weight of four 'Ash' missiles. If no missiles were carried, then the fuel weight could be increased to 4,750 kg (10,470 lb) and the maximum permitted landing weight to include a series of roller landings at the end of a sortie, in good VFR (Visual Flight Rules) conditions, was 34,000 kg (74,955 lb). The aircraft could land with a fuel remainder of 7,000 kg (15,430 lb), which in fuel fraction terms was considerably higher than for all other PVO interceptors. There were specific instances of Tu-128s landing with a fuel remainder of 9,000 kg (19,840 lb) without drama, thanks to the ruggedness of the aircraft's structure. The Tu-128's emergency fuel jettison system did, of course, have its failings. Often, after deploying the sleeves, they would not retract fully into the wing tanks, which was possibly the result of partial or local deformation of the wing surface after a long period in service. The problem was usually resolved on the ground by the aircraft's maintenance team resorting to the universal practice of 'percussion engineering'—using a hammer to drive the projecting sleeve back into its normal housing! The aircraft did, however, have one other fuel jettison technique. The pilot could open the engine exhaust nozzles manually and then increase engine rpm, after which fuel would start to be burned off by both engines. In this non-rated engine operating regime the fuel was consumed very rapidly and was normally held for around 6 minutes, burning off a substantial quantity of fuel in the process. In normal flight, of course, the nozzles were controlled automatically, but manual reversion was an option in case of need. It has not been possible to establish why the Tupolev designers envisaged a need for such a system, but the authors know of no other aircraft which use it.

Since the Tu-128 had a very good lift-to-drag ratio, the technique required for landing differed substantially from that of other Soviet interceptors. The Pilots' Notes recommended carrying out an approach at 500-600 m (1,640-1,970 feet) using the 'large' and 'small' box (*bol'shaya* and *malaya korobochka*) procedure to simplify handling when entering the course and glideslope zones of the landing beacon system. However, the circuit height for the Tu-128 on all the regiments had been set at 800 m (2,625 feet) and 400 m (1,312 feet) for all other fighters. When making an approach using the box-pattern procedure, (i.e. completion of four turns to line up on final approach), the initial speed was established at 500 kph (270 kts) and flaps were lowered when passing abeam (*na travyerzye*) the runway threshold. The undercarriage was lowered after the second turn, at a speed of 450 kph (245 kts), and the pilot would then complete the third turn, setting flaps to the landing position (a process which took 28 seconds, producing a slight pitch-up moment that was easily countered by forward movement of the control column). After this he would proceed to the fourth turn, following which he would stabilise the aircraft on the landing heading. Roll-out onto the landing heading was performed at a distance of 18 km (9.7 nm) and at a speed of around 450 kph (245 kts). A set of notes was developed on the Tu-128 regiments, known by the collective title of 'Methodological procedures for landing the aircraft' and authorised by the squadron commanders. These notes included 'Factors affecting landing performance', 'Overshoots and go-arounds', 'The go-around with one inoperative engine', 'Cross-wind landings', 'Landing errors', 'Safety measures' and the actual 'Method of carrying out the landing' itself.

The 'Method' incorporated the following points:

1. Pass over the outer marker (DPRM) at a height of 230 m (755 feet) and a speed of 420-400 kph (226-216 kts) on landing course;
2. Report passing over the DPRM to ATC (RP), lower undercarriage and flaps and report ready for landing;
3. Set engine rpm 78-76 per cent;
4. Note pitch angle and angle of descent;
5. Check speed, height, engine rpm (permitted deviation of no more than 3-5 per cent);
6. Check passing the middle marker (BPRM) at a speed of 370-360 kph (200-195 kts), level off in alignment with the runway axis at a height of 60-70 m (196-230 feet);
7. Increase engine rpm by 1-2 per cent to give a speed of 330-320 kph (178-173 kts) at commencement of the flare;
8. At a height of 20 m (65 feet) transfer your view from the cockpit to the ground, to the left and right, at an angle of about 10-15°;
9. Commence the flare at a height of 8-10 m (26-33 feet), which should be completed before passing over the runway at a height of around 1 m (3 feet);
10. After passing over the edge (lip) of the runway pull back on the control column, set the aircraft in the landing attitude and select 'Flight Idle';
11. Before touchdown confirm that the feet are correctly positioned on the pedals and not touching the brake pedals;
12. After touchdown, hold the control column steady and at a speed of 320 kph (173 kts) release the brake chute, select spoilers and hold the nose up;
13. Transfer your view from the cockpit to directly ahead and maintain landing heading;
14. Lower the nose, place the pedals in the neutral position;
15. Commence braking, fully depressing both sets of brake pedals and begin to retract the flaps;
16. Clear the runway and release the brake chute.

Here are some impressions of landing the Tu-128, as recalled by co-author Nikolai Popov:

I consider the landing procedure to have been well thought out and it didn't have the typical stepped glideslope of the smaller PVO fighters. The most frequently used landing pattern was an approach from 'the boundary' ('*s rubyezha*'), where the aircraft was lined up with the runway at a distance of 40 km [22 nm] and a height of 2,000 m (5,560 feet). Then the pilot would select the ILS to capture the localizer and glideslope beams [the latter being set at 2°40' for the Tu-128], while maintaining

The doors of the brake parachute compartment remained open on deployment of the two chutes, as seen in this view, which also emphasises the height of the Tu-128 on the runway. (*Grigoriy Zayats*)

an indicated air speed of 450 kph [245 kts] and a vertical rate of descent of 7 m/sec [1,380 ft/min]. The aircraft would maintain this rate of descent until touchdown, the only parameter needing to be changed being to lower the flaps to the landing setting at 1,000 m [3,280 feet].[8]

Flaring the Tu-128 was slightly unusual in that the pilot had to hold the control wheel with one hand while working the throttles with the other. Some pilots chose to employ a different method, holding the wheel with both hands and then rapidly changing the power setting with one hand before placing both hands back onto the wheel. The main thing was to avoid inducing an angle of bank in this critical phase of flight. Many experienced pilots are, unfortunately, prepared to admit that the 'genial simplicity' of the Tu-128's landing method was not carried over to the MiG-31, although some of these 'old hands' did nevertheless try to teach their subordinates using the 'old methods'. The younger pilots mastered them quite well, but they were not widely applied after the 'Fiddler' was withdrawn from service. The Tu-128 could perform an overshoot, if it had sufficient speed reserve, from any height down to the commencement of flare (8-10 m/26-33 feet); consequently, pilots tried to hold some speed in reserve. There was little point in engaging reheat, since this required around 19 seconds for both burners to cut in and indeed resulted in a brief loss of thrust due to the opening of the nozzles, before both systems were fully operative. Pilots were briefed to commence an overshoot on both engines at a height of not less than 50 m (165 feet) and with only one operative engine, from a height of not less than 70 m (230 feet). Pilots on 356 AP at Zhana-Semey recall that their regiment commander recommended passing over the middle marker beacon at a speed of 475 kph (202 kts), leading to pilots starting to land with an excess of speed. This in turn led to some very heavy landings, and there were at least two cases where aircraft had to be withdrawn from service following a number of hard landings after hairline cracks had been detected in the airframe. Since the cracks were detected during inspection checks at a repair and maintenance unit, the subsequent striking off charge was not classed as an accident and a direct cause could not be attributed.

A similar incident occurred on 64 AP at Omsk-North, involving an aircraft with the construction number 2103. As explained in Chapter 6, the Bort number of this aircraft ought to have been '13', but as the majority of the aviation fraternity were superstitious, the numbering system was modified to give the aircraft Bort No. 21 instead. Nevertheless, this particular Tu-128 had always been an unlucky aircraft.

Having signed the 'ZhPS' post-flight engineering log, the pilot receives the film cassette from the 'objective control' flight-data monitoring unit. The 35-mm film recorded all flight parameters exceeding accepted values and was used in long-term engineering analysis of individual aircraft operation. The pilot, with his back to the camera, is holding the cassette in his right hand. (*S. Shchelokov*)

At the very beginning of its service life, in 1968, the then commander of 64 AP, Col. Rostenbyergskiy, had made a very hard landing at Kadala (Chita) during a deployment exercise. He had touched down right on the lip of the main runway, where the surrounding earth meets the edge of the concrete, bursting all the tyres on the main undercarriage and damaging the horizontal stabilizer. The skin of the rear fuselage was also extensively buckled, but none of the rigging reference datum marks had been compromised and were all still in place when the aircraft was inspected later; the external geometry of the aircraft had not been affected. Consequently, it was decided to replace the damaged horizontal stabilizer, the buckled skin of the rear fuselage and the tyres and brake drums, and the aircraft was ferried back to Omsk-North. After a complete check on the ground, it was flown once or twice a month so that it could be considered 'airworthy'.

A former technician on this aircraft, Maj. Plyuta, recalls another incident involving this 'unfortunate' aircraft:

It was a little more than six months after the hard landing of 'my' aircraft at Kadala— the New Year, 1969, was approaching and we had just completed our last flying day of 1968. 'Our' Bort No. 21 had just landed safely, signalling the end of the squadron's flying programme. It had been a night-flying detail and we had –40°C of frost on the ground. We met the aircraft on the squadron dispersal area and a bus was waiting for the aircrew. After climbing down from the aircraft they reported that there were no equipment malfunctions to report (*zamyechanii nyet*) and then they were driven off to debrief. We attached the tractor's tow bar to the aircraft and started to push it back into the shelter in reverse gear. The aircraft senior technician was sitting in the cockpit and I was behind the tractor driver, using a torch to illuminate the painted guideline leading into the shelter. We weren't quite lined up on the first attempt, so we had to brake and then pull the aircraft back a little to try and line it up more accurately. As I was looking down from the tractor I saw a fresh patch of reddish-coloured liquid on the concrete where one of the main undercarriage bogies had been. I immediately gave the command 'Stop!' to the tug driver. When I shone the torch on the patch it turned out to be a large pool of AMG-18 hydraulic fuel from the brakes. Then I shone the light onto the undercarriage leg and could scarcely believe my eyes! The main oleo was split open as if by a knife and the shock strut piston was sticking through the bogie between the wheels. All the rods were broken. When the squadron engineer saw the damage he was also horrified. How had the aircraft landed safely? How had it taxied back into dispersal?! The aircraft went in for repair the following day and it was eventually restored to flying condition. Only two years later this unfortunate aircraft was sent off for planned maintenance at the Tu-128 re-fit base (Novosibirsk-Tolmachevo). After undergoing a very thorough flaw detection (*defektoskopiya*) programme it was decided to scrap the aircraft …

Hard landings could usually be attributed to the practice employed by many pilots of maintaining an excessively high approach speed. The PVO Aviation General Staff therefore decided to conduct a series of 'demonstrative lectures' on the regiments, with the participation of Tupolev test pilots, aimed at discouraging the practice. Col. Yevglyevskiy was involved in setting up these lectures:

In the early years of operating the Tu-128 it became the rule for pilots to land at higher speeds than recommended in the Pilots' Notes. We tried to convince them that it was necessary to maintain the recommended speed on landing, i.e. establish the minimal speed with sufficient engine rpm and a high angle of attack. This should have resulted in the ideal landing profile. However, we could not manage to convince them in any way. I thought long and hard about the problem and decided to call Mikhail Kozlov, the Tupolev OKB test pilot responsible for the Tu-128 at the time, to see whether he could demonstrate the technique of landing at 'minimal speed'. He agreed and we organised a series of demonstration flights which were held at Savvatiya, the base of 445 AP. Everyone was very impressed and found the demonstrations very useful. However, after the 'high-speed landing' syndrome and these demonstrations another 'malaise' took its place—everyone started to land at minimum speed. I even began to regret that we'd organised the low-speed demonstration flights at all. Eventually, the pilots had to go back to their original practice.

As noted in the text, some pilots used to practise landing approaches at comparatively low speed (contrary to that recommended in the Pilots' Notes for the Tu-128), with the nose held fairly high, requiring higher engine power in order to avoid stalling. Viewed from the side, a landing by such a large aircraft with its nose held high was quite impressive. Although not of spectacular quality, this view of an aircraft from 518 AP at Talagi reveals the low-speed landing attitude of the 'Fiddler'. (*Ivan Rodyukov*)

Some pilots, however, tried to justify the use of the low-speed landing technique, one of whom was Capt. Khamit Ablyazin:

> I often landed using the 'second regime' method [low speed, high angle of attack, increased engine rpm]. This allowed me to land on 3,100 m (10,170 feet) runways without using the brake parachute.

Most pilots commented that the Tu-128 was quite a 'lively' aircraft which would glide or plane for quite a long distance on landing and therefore touch down more softly and smoothly than, for example, the Su-15. This allowed the 'Fiddler' to easily remain airborne and even perform a landing approach on one engine, without using afterburner. Pilots always cited the example of the MiG-31 by way of emphasising the Tu-128's aerodynamic qualities, as the 'Foxhound' would have to engage reheat if it had to make a single-engined approach with a fuel remainder of more than 2,000 kg (4,410 lb). In this condition the MiG-31 could not remain airborne without use of afterburner. The only flight regime that the Tu-128 did not like was flight in the low-speed corner of the envelope. This was the main reason why pilots liked to maintain a slightly higher speed than recommended, particularly when weather conditions were 'on limits':

> When landing you'd hold the speed around 10-20 kph [5-10 kts] above the figure in the Pilots' Notes, overfly the BPRM [inner marker] at 380 kph [205 kts] and when you had the runway in sight, you'd chop the power. If you hadn't seen the runway at that stage you'd simply increase power and overshoot into the circuit pattern. I don't even know anyone who landed at the speed set out in the 'Notes'. If you were landing at 300-310 kph [162-167 kts] you could pull the speed back to 290-280 kph [156-151 kts], but everyone landed at 310-320 kph [167-173 kts].

The Tu-128 had yet another foible—it was very stable but was a very difficult aircraft to control. Because of its inertia on the pre-landing 'glide' approach it was recommended not to correct any deviations from the landing course with large bank angle inputs. The fact was that it was very difficult for the pilot to determine the moment of commencement of, and the rate of exit from, a banked condition. A consequence of this was that the aircraft could quickly depart from the runway centreline, leading eventually to the pilot 'hunting' the course and glideslope. Even in the 'State Acceptance' document signed on conclusion of the flight test stage it was noted that 'on the pre-landing glide, the aircraft exhibits poor control qualities'. Consequently, if at the 8 km (4 nm) point on the approach the aircraft was not established on course and on the glideslope, it was recommended that the pilot should initiate an overshoot and set up another approach. Pilots recall:

In spite of the many thousands of flights carried out by the Tu-128 during its service with the PVO, this is one of only a handful of photographs of an operational aircraft in landing configuration. Here, a 72 AP Tu-128M is seen crossing the threshold at Amderma, emphasising the aircraft's characteristically flat approach and the downward-angled main undercarriage bogies typical of all Tupolev 'big jets'. (*Valeriy Yalyaev*)

> You couldn't experiment with turns [on the landing approach]. The Tu-128 handled very badly when banking, unlike the MiG-31, which [in the words of Nikolai Popov] responded 'like a pygmy on a log'. [This is a slightly oblique reference to the fact that the MiG-31 was very easy to control in the 'roll channel', rotating about its own axis very rapidly, rather like someone spinning on a floating log.]

Considering the ineffectiveness of the ailerons at speeds close to the touchdown speed, the pilot had to be very cautious on the landing approach when using the rudder since with undercarriage and flaps down for landing, rudder deflection produced an increased banking reaction. The maximum deflection of the rudder at an indicated air speed of 340 kph (183 kts), where aileron effectiveness was still sufficient, was 12°, corresponding to half the travel of the pedals. When approaching the flare, the pilot had to reduce engine rpm with one hand on the throttles and with the other hand simultaneously pull back on the control column to maintain the correct landing attitude. As this was rather difficult for one person to do, these actions had to be carried out sequentially; reducing engine rpm and pulling back on the stick alternately until touchdown, but all the same there was still a risk of landing with some bank on. All in all, however, it can be said that the most characteristic landing incidents with the Tu-128 were touching down in the undershoot area and running off the side of the runway on take-off or landing.

The approach and departure flight path at Amderma passed directly over the local town, which overlooked the airfield and was situated close to sea level. (*Valeriy Yalyaev*)

The undercarriage acquitted itself well on landing and the tyres lasted twice as long as those on the MiG-31, while higher landing speeds did not adversely affect the use of the brake chute. The limiting speed of the early strip-type chute, used up until the mid-1980s, was 320 kph (173 kts), whereas the operating instructions for the later cruciform chute gave a limiting speed of 370 kph (200 kts). The feeling among Tu-128 crews was that the old strip-type chute was very effective; they could actually feel the jolt when it deployed, but they were scarcely aware of the release of the later cruciform chute. Pilots discovered that a good technique for releasing the chute was to push the control column forward slightly before selecting it, deployment then being more stable, otherwise the nose-wheel could slam down hard onto the runway, causing the KZA flight recorder to register an excessively large g-loading. (By contrast, on the Su-15 the technique was precisely the opposite and the pilot would pull the stick right back into his groin after selecting the brake chute.) Without the brake chute the Tu-128's landing run was increased by around 300-400 m (985-1,300 feet). The majority of flights were of between 40 minutes and 2 hours' duration, dependent upon the nature of the task. However, this was somewhat different for the Tu-128UT, which flew a virtual 'conveyor-belt' cycle (*konveyer*) of up to fifteen sorties during one flying shift (*smena*). After a standard training detail the '*sparka*' would land and roll out from the runway onto the taxiway where the pilot would stop and shut down the port engine, to enable the next student to climb aboard. The instructor and navigator would usually stay on board during the hand-over, the aircraft technicians would replace the brake chute canister, and the trainer would set off for another sortie, reducing 'downtime' to a minimum.

The Tu-128 regiments used the following performance table to assess the pilots' abilities in various stages of flight:

Assessed Flight Condition	Excellent Rating	Good Rating	Satisfactory Rating
Take-off	Aircraft aligned with axis of runway. Nose-wheel raised normally.	Aircraft aligned with axis of runway. Nose-wheel raised with slight deviation from normal position, but without compromising flight safety.	Performed in straight line, with slight deviation from axis of runway, but within safety limits. Raising of nose-wheel accompanied by slight pitching.
Level flight: Holding heading: Holding speed: Holding height in horizontal flight: At low level in VMC: At medium and high level up to 9,000 m: At altitudes above 9,000 m:	Permitted deviation ±2° ±20 kph ±30 m (but no lower than safety height) ±50 m ±100 m	Permitted deviation ±4° ±30 kph ±40 m (but no lower than safety height) ±100 m ±150 m	Permitted deviation ±6° ±40 kph ±50 m (but no lower than safety height) ±150 m ±200 m
Turning: Holding speed: Holding altitude: At low level: At medium and high level, but not higher than 9,000 m: Bank angle less than 60°: Bank angle more than 60°:	Permitted deviation ±20 kph ±30 m ±40 m ±100 m ±5°	Permitted deviation ±30 kph ±50 m ±60 m ±150 m ±10°	Permitted deviation ±50 kph ±70 m ±100 m ±200 m ±15°
Spiral: defined by height: by angle of bank:	Permitted deviation ±20 kph No deviation	Permitted deviation ±30 kph ±5°	Permitted deviation ±50 kph ±10°
Landing	Performed with established flare profile and 'hold-off', with gentle touchdown at the established angle of attack, within the touchdown zone.	Performed with slight deviation from established point of flare and 'hold-off', with subsequent gentle touchdown at the established angle of attack for landing, within the touchdown zone.	Performed with allowable deviation from the established flare profile, with subsequent touchdown within the limits of the touchdown zone, on the main bogies.

All landings required the use of brake chutes to reduce the landing distance and stabilise the aircraft in the roll-out. (*S. Shchelokov*)

DANGEROUS FLIGHT REGIMES

Like all aircraft, the Tu-128 was susceptible to certain flight conditions potentially inimical to flight safety. The aircraft's behaviour in these conditions was defined essentially by its aerodynamic layout, airframe design, the flight control system and the rigidity of the relationship between the fuselage and the wing structure. Quite early in the Tu-128's State flight test programme it became apparent that the aircraft possessed the following inherent design characteristics:

1. Pitch instability, manifest in the form of low-speed (pre-stall) buffeting (*sryvnoy podkhvat*);
2. Speed instability and the potential for resultant high-speed buffeting (*skorostnoy podkhvat*);
3. Pitching in the longitudinal plane (*prodol'naya raskachka*);
4. Loss of aileron effectiveness and aileron reversal in certain flight regimes;
5. The phenomenon of 'reverse banking reaction to the deflection of the rudder'.

The most serious consequence of the above-mentioned flight regimes was for the aircraft to enter a deep spiral dive (*glubokiy spiral'*). A spin (*shtopor*), as distinct from a spiral dive, was considered to be an unlikely consequence, but in the unfortunate event that a spin did occur, it was considered pointless attempting recovery as there would probably be insufficient height to pull out safely.[9] The Tu-128 test pilots and the flight trials group also inclined to this view, and unlike other Soviet fighters, the aircraft did not even undergo spin trials during the flight test phase.[10] If the aircraft did enter this dangerous flight regime, the crew were recommended to eject. The KT-1 ejection seat operating minima when descending in a spin or deep spiral dive were 1,980 m (6,200 feet) for the navigator and 1,060 m (3,480 feet) for the pilot.

Buffeting could occur if the pilot pulled the control column back rather 'energetically' when manoeuvring hard at high indicated air speeds and at altitudes up to 8,000 m (26,250 feet). On reaching specific angles of attack the aerodynamic centre would migrate forward of the centre of gravity, simultaneously increasing the effectiveness of the horizontal stabilizer as it came under the influence of the wing's downwash. This could then lead to a spontaneous pitch-up moment, even with the control column held steady. At Mach numbers less than 0.75, pitch-up would occur without any preliminary buffeting, but at higher Mach numbers it would be preceded by detectable airframe 'burbling'. Buffeting could also occur at speeds less than 320-330 kph (173-178 kts) but in this case it was not accompanied by undemanded bank (wing drop) or nose lowering and it was sufficient simply to push the control column forward quite firmly to return to a normal angle of attack. Delayed detection of buffeting could result in short-period excursions beyond the aircraft's g-limits (2.5 g), or going into a spin.

Apart from instability in g-loading, the Tu-128 also exhibited a tendency towards speed instability. Evidence of slight speed instability could occur at speeds less than 270 kph (146 kts), when the undercarriage and flaps were down for landing, attributed to the movement of the stabilizer out of the wing's downwash and its subsequent loss of effectiveness. This could be countered by pushing the control column forward, with attendant lowering of the nose, followed by acceleration out of the 'minimal speed range'. A more significant manifestation of speed instability could occur at all altitudes, in the speed range of Mach 0.95 to Mach 1.1 (i.e. the transonic region) when accelerating in horizontal flight, in the descent or when climbing. At these speeds the aerodynamic centre would move back, due to the intrinsic properties of the aerodynamics of the wing and of the aircraft as a whole, as a result of which an additional nose-down moment would arise. The aircraft would start to lower its nose smoothly, with a concomitant increase in speed. This phenomenon would continue up to speeds equivalent to Mach 1.1, and as height increased, the degree of instability would also increase. In the transonic speed range and at Mach numbers greater than 1.4 it was necessary to counter speed instability by pulling back on the control column. Pilots were also recommended to accelerate the aircraft in the descent. In this case, the aircraft would rapidly pass through the transonic speed range, whereas acceleration in horizontal flight took place slowly, particularly from Mach 1.08 to Mach 1.15.

Speed instability also occurred in another flight regime—decelerating from supersonic speed within the range Mach 1.08 to Mach 1.0 whilst executing turns with bank angles of up to 60°. This could lead to the phenomenon of high-speed buffeting, manifest in a spontaneous increase in the angle of attack, even with the control column held in a fixed position. The reason for this centred on localised aerodynamic effects intrinsic to the airframe: when decelerating within this Mach range the aerodynamic centre moved forward, restoring the effectiveness of the horizontal stabilizer. Since the stabilizer was deflected to a large angle for pitch control at high speeds, on reaching these speeds the aircraft's nose would begin to rise spontaneously, increasing the angle of attack. If the pilot did not manage to push the control column forward in time, then the aircraft could enter a stall. At speeds less than Mach 1.0 this flight regime 'normalised' because the AU-128 auto-stabilizer and DT-128 pitch damper cut in, producing a nose-down (diving) moment. Decelerating in the turn with an angle of bank up to 45° and a g-loading of 1.5 was achieved without the occurrence of this phenomenon, leading to the adoption of a 45° bank angle as the maximum permissible for normal training flights. As a general procedure, Tu-128 aircrews were recommended to decelerate from supersonic speed in horizontal flight with a g-loading of 1 g in order to avoid entering the high-speed buffeting regime.

An indirect cause of the Tu-128's tendency towards longitudinal pitching could probably be attributed to the very complex flight control system for that time. Longitudinal pitching occurred at maximum permitted speeds and altitudes below 10,000 m (32,800 feet) after the application of sharp deflections of the control column, giving an initial oscillation amplitude of ±0.3 g, for a horizontal stabilizer deflection of ±2°. The reason for this was light and excessively sensitive pitch control resulting from low longitudinal static stability, the increased effectiveness of the all-flying horizontal stabilizer, and the properties of the aircraft as a flexible body. Depending upon atmospheric turbulence, angle of attack and control column movements by the pilot, the aircraft could experience a cycle of 'self-oscillating' control disturbances. As a rule, this phenomenon would arise without warning, albeit detected by the pilot as g-loading of varying intensity. At altitudes above 10,000 m (32,800 feet), when performing turns, spiral turns and zoom climbs with a g-loading of 2-2.5 g at speeds greater than Mach 1.35, it was possible for auto-oscillation within the aircraft/pitch damper system to occur, as a consequence of which longitudinal pitching could follow. With auto-oscillation, the DT-128 pitch damper, independent of the pilot, would reset the horizontal stabilizer from one position to the other. With this, sharp deflections of the stabilizer could be felt as severe jolts in the control circuit. If longitudinal pitching was not eliminated by reducing g-loading and air speed, then it could lead to significant loss of speed and entry into a spin.

In order to avoid getting into these regimes, pilots were not recommended to strive for accurate holding of an assigned speed or Mach regime within the speed range Mach 0.75-Mach 0.9, to sharply counter the increase in g-loading with the control column, switch on or switch off the afterburners, or change engine rpm rapidly. It must be said, however, that pilots rarely ever got into this regime. Pilot training on the regiments and the selection of pilots in the initial stages of mastering the aircraft all had their positive effect. Co-author Nikolai Popov comments, 'I don't recall any personal experience of longitudinal pitching in the Tu-128. If everything was working normally then the aircraft would never pitch up.' The 'Fiddler' was created in that period of aviation development when large aircraft were only just beginning to enter the supersonic era, and this unusually large interceptor had inherited a 'bomber legacy' from its Tupolev stablemates in the form of a somewhat immature flight control system. A particularly problematic area of control was in the rolling plane, as a result of poor aileron effectiveness. Reduction of aileron effectiveness was attributed to:

- low dynamic pressure at speeds below 320-330 kph (173-178 kts);
- flexible 'deformation' of the wing at indicated air speeds above 800 kph (432 kts) and heights from 0 to 5,500 m (18,050 feet), leading to complete loss of lateral control;
- changes to, and migration of, shock waves over the wings and flexible 'deformation' of the wing surfaces at speeds greater than Mach 1.4.

Full loss of aileron effectiveness commenced at an indicated air speed of 1,000 kph (540 kts), aileron reversal occurring if this speed was exceeded. This had already been noted during the flight test phase and the aircraft's 'insufficiently effective lateral control' was written up in the acceptance document issued on completion of the State flight test programme. As a result, it was decided to introduce a modification to the aircraft's lateral control circuit by installing aileron-spoilers (*ehlerony-intertseptory*) on two Tu-128 test-beds, analogous in function to the so-called flap-ailerons of the Tu-22 'Blinder'. The spoilers were designed to work in conjunction with the ailerons to enhance lateral control effectiveness. Flight tests gave very promising results, and the use of aileron-spoilers would have made it possible to lift all speed restrictions imposed on the aircraft, particularly for missile launches in the supersonic regime. Without the aileron-spoilers, supersonic missile launches were only permitted up to Mach 1.35. However, for a number of reasons (the main one being financial) an in-service modification programme was not initiated and pilots had to rely instead on the recommendations of a document written by a team of senior regimental pilots. This was entitled 'Aerodynamic peculiarities and dangerous flight regimes of the aircraft Article I', and the following is an extract from the document:

In order to prevent the aircraft experiencing loss of loss of aileron effectiveness and aileron reversal it is *essential*:

- to use the rudder to initiate, or eliminate, banking at speeds where aileron effectiveness is reduced;
- to remember that aileron effectiveness is noticeably reduced at Mach numbers above Mach 1.4, particularly in connection with reverse banking reaction to deflection of the rudder pedals, so turns at these speeds should only be carried out using the ailerons;
- not to exceed the maximum permitted speed at low and medium level, since the speed margin for aileron reversal is comparatively small (100-150 kph/54-81 kts), and with the gradual reduction in the structural rigidity of the wing during operation this margin is even smaller.

As already mentioned, the phenomenon of reverse banking reaction to deflection of the rudder occurred at speeds above Mach 1.45, manifest by 'incorrect' reaction of the aircraft to sideslip created by deflection of the rudder (for example, obtaining a bank to the right after application of the left rudder). The fact is that even with a small amount of sideslip, by use of the rudder, one surface is presented to the airstream at a greater angle than the other. This led to the loss of lateral stability, which in conjunction with the greater effectiveness of the rudder at these speeds became the reason for the occurrence of the phenomenon. This significantly complicated the recovery from a descending turn at speeds greater than Mach 1.4, and pilots were recommended to use only the ailerons to carry out turns at these speeds. In the course of Tu-128 operations it had become possible to avoid these flight regimes by limiting the maximum speed to Mach 1.3, and, more broadly, by the achievement of a high level of competence, theoretical knowledge and 'psychological' preparation by pilots.[11] The latter was particularly important for Tu-128 aircrew, as this aircraft was not forgiving of a cavalier approach to handling or the slightest hint of panic in response to its behaviour. There was, however, an aspect of the aircraft's flight behaviour which the ordinary line pilots *did* have to come to terms with—namely, the deep spiral descent or spiral dive. The Tu-128 could enter this regime at any speed when putting the aircraft into a banked turn and commencing descent.

The explanation for this was that when exceeding the permitted angle of bank (60°) by 10-15° the aircraft exhibited a tendency to drop the nose, resulting in a high vertical rate of descent and forward speed. On reaching a certain speed longitudinal stability started to exceed lateral stability (the aircraft rapidly eliminated sideslip and, more slowly, the bank angle during sideslip). As a result, the angle of bank continued to increase and the nose would drop, even with the control column held in a fixed position, and the aircraft would enter a deep spiral descent. Recovery from the spiral was very difficult and did not always have a happy outcome for the crew. For the pilot it was very important to remember that:

- it was necessary to strictly observe the recommended bank angle (not more than 45°), not letting the nose drop and not allowing the aircraft to descend at high vertical rates of descent when carrying out turns;
- it was imperative not to be distracted from flying the aircraft when breaking away from the attack during an intercept.

PVO pilots first encountered this phenomenon at the beginning of 1971, when two Tu-128 crews ended up in a deep spiral during a missile firing practice at the Telemba range near Chita in Siberia. Tragically, the pilot and navigator of one of the aircraft died in the ensuing accident (described in Appendix 3). After these two incidents, the PVO Command staff decided to investigate the behaviour of the Tu-128 in this regime and appointed Col. Yevglyevskiy to head the investigative commission. The team had to go back to data collected during the flight test programme and it turned out that three deep-spiral incidents had been recorded during this period, although the parameters were not as precisely defined as the two incidents at Telemba. (Evidently the earlier events were classified in the flight test reports not as 'deep spirals' but as 'exceeding assigned speed and g-loading parameters'.) During the investigation it was established that during a deep spiral the aircraft could enter flight regimes where aileron reversal could occur, along with 'reverse reaction to application of rudder'. If the pilot could pull the aircraft out of these regimes then there was a good chance that it could be recovered safely from a deep spiral. Yevglyevskiy worked for eight months on the preparation of his report on the characteristics of deep spirals and then suggested to the C-in-C of PVO fighter aviation, Gen. Borovykh, that he should conduct a series of lectures on the topic to all Tu-128 aircrew. With Gen. Borovykh's approval he prepared lectures for all the pilots and also planned to give all senior regimental personnel first-hand experience of deep spirals by flying them in the Tu-128UT.

Col. Yevglyevskiy recalls the event:

I made flying visits to all the regiments and delivered my six-hour lecture programme at each location. In the process I was supposed to demonstrate the spiral in the Tu-128UT. Of course, I practised this procedure myself first and only then began to demonstrate it. I started with the regiment at Semipalatinsk and planned to fly the regiment commander, Colonel Yatskin, and his deputy. I gave them 6 hours of lecture study and then another 6 hours of pre-flight preparation for the demonstration. Everyone thought that it would not lead to anything, but we did actually fly the 'spiral' programme. We intentionally put the aircraft into a 'spiral' at supersonic speed, although I didn't allow the aircraft to dive with afterburners on and maximum engine rpm. We performed a banking turn and lowered the nose, allowing the angle of bank to increase to whatever value it could reach. At the same time I reduced engine rpm. The angle of bank reached 90°. I then gave the command to Colonel

Yatskin, 'Pull out!' He tried to pull out, but the aircraft did not respond. The aircraft did not respond until we'd reached an altitude of 5,000 m (16,400 feet). At 5,000 m it was necessary to apply the rudder. At the same time the g-loading started to increase. At this moment the most important thing was to push the control column forward, otherwise there was a risk of over-stressing the aircraft, possibly causing it to break up. There was nothing unusual in this procedure. It was simply necessary to know about it and be ready for such an event. I performed two 'spirals' with the CO of 356 AP at Semipalatinsk, but then the weather deteriorated and we couldn't fly again that day. The following day I received an order from PVO HQ to cease the 'spiral' demonstration flights and was told only to give theoretical lectures. Evidently, someone at HQ had complained about these 'miracles' that we were performing with the aircraft. However, I covered the theoretical aspects of the 'spiral' with all the pilots, and over the course of the next ten years there wasn't a single case of anyone getting into a 'spiral' situation.

10

Operations in Various Climatic Conditions

OPERATING IN THE CONTINENTAL ZONE

Three of the six Tu-128 regiments were located in the southern part of Siberia, which enjoyed a so-called continental climate characterised by very low sub-zero temperatures in the winter and extremely high temperatures in the summer months. The transition from winter to summer conditions in this region was accompanied by very unstable weather and strong winds. Pilots recall that at Omsk-North, for example, the wind speed could often reach more than 30 m/sec (60 kts) and severe turbulence was common, most frequently in March and April. Most turbulence occurred at high altitude as a result of jetstream activity and cumulonimbus cloud formation, both over Siberia and over the northern territories of the European part of the USSR, and had a very significant effect on 'Fiddler' operations. This was usually manifested by the phenomenon of clear air turbulence (CAT), which was not very well understood at the time.[1] On one occasion, the 'new phenomenon' forced the command staff of 445 AP at Kotlas to call upon the expertise of PVO HQ, inviting Col. Yevglyevskiy to discuss it with them. Having flown in to the base, he asked the regiment commander about the problem:

It appeared that severe airframe buffeting had been experienced by his crews at around 10,500 m [34,500 feet], in spite of otherwise VMC conditions. It was a normal flying day for the regiment, so I asked for a Tu-128UT to be prepared for me. We took off and climbed to 10,500-11,000 m [34,500-36,000 feet] and from around 10,500 m we started to experience strong buffeting. As we climbed, so the buffeting intensified. At 12,000 m (39,370 feet) the buffeting was so severe that it was impossible to read the instruments. Later, after landing, we debriefed with the weather service team about the cause of this phenomenon. They suggested that the most likely culprit was jetstream activity, albeit occurring in a completely cloudless sky.

These jetstreams created such severe turbulence that it was impossible to fly, even though the weather on the ground was definable as VMC (visual meteorological conditions)—i.e. 'simple meteorological conditions' (*prostiye meteo-usloviya* or PMU in Russian). Summer in southern Siberia arrived very suddenly, as recalled by pilots from 518 AP based at Arkhangel'sk-Talagi:

> On one occasion, during an air defence exercise, we had to land at Semipalatinsk after a particular sortie. It was still bitterly cold back at base at Talagi and we took off wearing our winter flying jackets, but when we landed at Semipalatinsk the temperature on the airfield was +35°C. [The straight line distance between the two locations was 2,774 km (1,724 miles.]

The Tu-128 regiments were equipped with mobile air-conditioning units mounted on special vehicles, but these were only used very occasionally, although they were sometimes set up for the QRA flight (*dyezhurnoye zveno*) for the benefit of crews sitting in the cockpit at Readiness 1.[2] The mobile air-conditioning units were mainly used in the summer months when checking the *Smerch* radar with HT switched on to power the transmitter. It has to be said that the Tu-128 did not like really hot weather, and when the outside air temperature on the ground was more than 25°C the wheels and brakes had to be cooled after each landing. Col. Yevglyevskiy recalls an incident relating to operating in these very hot conditions:

> I was once visiting 350 AP at Belaya during the summer period in my capacity as inspector-pilot. The outside air temperature on the ground was +36°C and there was dense cloud cover over the airfield. I took off on a weather reconnaissance sortie in a Tu-128UT with one of the regiment's pilots. The engines were still in reheat when we broke cloud, with cloud 'tops' at an altitude of around 12,500-13,000 m [41,000-42,650 feet]. There, the aircraft 'gulped in' the cold air, we chopped engine power and then plunged back into the dense broiling mass of cloud and after re-entering the airfield circuit, landed normally. However, while we were taxiing, we suffered a tyre 'blow-out' on the main gear after rolling over the protruding edge of one of the taxiway's concrete slabs. The 'blow-out' was caused by the tyres having overheated during braking on the landing roll. I stopped the aircraft and all three of us climbed out. I noticed that my pilot was drenched in perspiration from head to toe, looking almost as if someone had thrown a bucket of water over him. I'd been sitting in the instructor's seat up front, which was cooler than the main cockpit. We were driven off in one of the ground support vehicles to the KDP [air traffic control] where the regiment commander [*Kompol—Komandir polka*] asked us if the weather was suitable for flying. In reply I asked him, 'How many people do you have here to fly in this weather?' It turned out that there were around ten crews ready to fly. But apart from keeping the crews cool, it was also essential to organise cooling of the aircraft's

wheels and brakes before taxiing out to the runway, otherwise there could have been another incident like the one we'd just experienced.

The air-conditioning system of the Tu-128 was designed to cope with the demanding Arctic environment and did not adapt well to operating in the higher ambient temperatures of the south. In the aircraft's test certification documents it was even noted that with an outside air temperature of between 20° and 25°C the conditioning system did not provide a comfortable working environment for the crew. As far as the undercarriage was concerned, the tyres on the Tu-128 were not yet equipped with thermal 'witness plugs', so in the summer period the brakes often had to be cooled after landing, with one of the aircraft technicians checking by hand to determine whether the brakes were overheated or not (!). Brake cooling was carried out by the simple expedient of spraying water onto them from a KPM-4 (*Kombinirovannaya Polivochno-moyechnaya Mashina*) combined aircraft washing truck.

In the opinion of the majority of Tu-128 crews, the best weather conditions were to be enjoyed at Zhana-Semey, which was located in the Russian steppes, where it was widely considered that there were really 'only two seasons of the year—summer and winter'! Winter arrived in the steppes quite suddenly—the temperature would fall, but it was quite dry, and then one day snow would fall, heralding the onset of winter proper, which continued until the month of April. In this region Mother Nature 'assigned' only one week for the seasons to change from winter to spring and then from summer to autumn, hence the belief that there were only two seasons here. It was quite rare to have very bad weather at Semipalatinsk, although it did sometimes rain and it could be windy, causing dust storms in the normally dry conditions. In the winter and brief autumn period, some airfields were affected by industrial haze, which would remain at ground level and creep along the surface, reducing pilot visibility when landing. Nevertheless, highly trained Tu-128 crews used to land without difficulty with a horizontal visibility of 1,000 m (3,280 feet) and even 800 m (2,600 feet).

Naturally, climate dictated that all Russian aircraft required particular treatment when operating in both winter and summer conditions, but in the case of the Tu-128 special care was required in winter not only in the handling of fuel containing additive Liquid 'I' but also when handling engine lubricants. Whereas winter fuel additives were handled by a separate battalion of airfield technical support personnel, lubricants were the direct responsibility of the aircraft technicians. Each engine of the Tu-128 used 11 litres (2.42 imp. gals) of MK-8P oil, which at temperatures of between −35° and −40°C became extremely viscous and could lead to damage of auxiliary drive shafts and engine control rods. In order to prevent this happening, the ground crews were instructed to dilute the oil at the end of every day's flying in severe winter weather by adding up to 25 per cent by

026. A very clean-looking Tu-128M taxies out at Zhana-Semey for a range firing sortie, with a standard complement of training rounds. The flaps are set for take-off and the tailplane has been set to the normal take-off angle of –9°. (*Nikolai Popov*)

volume of B-70 aviation benzene, which was also used in the engine turbo-starters. After adding the B-70 to the oil tanks the engine was rotated 'cold' to allow the oil and benzene to mix, which was sufficiently effective to guarantee a normal engine start the following day, particularly in the event of an early-morning scramble. In addition to this procedure, Tu-128 squadrons could also use truck-mounted hot air blowers and, if time permitted, the engine bay doors could be opened so that the compartment could be heated directly, warming not only the oil but also the hydraulic system and pipes. If an aircraft flew four sorties in a given flying 'shift' the total flying time could be around 3.5-4 hours, and if it was an 8-hour programme the accumulated flying time could be even higher. Initially such long flying days were organised on an experimental basis, but later they became the rule. The accumulated flying time during an 8-hour programme meant that the benzene added to the oil supply would evaporate by the end of the 'shift' (*smyena*) and the oil would revert to its original consistency. Consequently, at the end of a long winter flying programme the oil dilution process had to be repeated in order to protect the engine from damage.

Even on the bleak airfields of the High Arctic, personnel tried to beautify their surroundings as much as possible. Here, the pathway leading from the dispersal area to the squadron buildings has been marked out and decorated with old aircraft tyres. (*S. Shchelokov*)

OPERATING IN THE HIGH ARCTIC (*ZAPOLYAR'YE*)³ REGION

Amderma was the only airfield beyond the Arctic Circle where the Tu-128 was permanently based, although there was one other 'Fiddler' base lying close to the Arctic Circle at Talagi (Arkhangel'sk), with Savvatiya (Kotlas) situated a little further south. Apart from operating out of these three airfields, the Siberian-based Tu-128 regiments also had to practise regular deployments (*manyovry*)⁴ to other polar region bases within the framework of a wartime reinforcement plan for the PVO fighter force. Training of crews for these deployment exercises was carried out in accordance with requirements set out in a document entitled 'Aircrew Training Programmes for Flights in Polar Conditions' ('*Programmy podgotovki lyotnovo sostava k polyotam v usloviyakh Zapolyar'ya*'). Training was carried out in two stages: ground training (Stage 1) and flight training (Stage 2).

Ground training concentrated on familiarising aircrew with the particular difficulties of operating in the northern polar region, with training taking the form of lectures and seminars on the following topics:

- The special demands of flying in the northern latitudes, the effects on the aircraft's aerodynamic performance, and the need to take this into account

233

when flying in the polar region.

- Flying during the period of the aurora borealis and carrying out landing approaches in the presence of atmospheric refraction.
- The demands placed upon visual orientation in polar conditions, and how visual orientation should be maintained.
- Effects on the performance of ground-based and aircraft radio equipment in the polar region.
- Meteorological phenomena and dangerous conditions intrinsic to the region, and their effect on flight operations;
- Survival training.

The ground training programme for Tu-128 aircrew deployed to the polar region for the first time comprised 38 hours of instruction, of which 24 hours was in the form of lectures plus 14 hours of seminar-based study. At the end of the training programme students were required to pass a test on the material studied. Aircrew who were re-qualifying for operations in the polar region followed an abbreviated programme of 16 hours' study on the same topics, mainly using the seminar-based approach. Flight training was carried out with the aim of providing practical familiarisation with actual flight conditions and obtaining authorisation for solo operations in the High Arctic. The flying element of the programme was designed for pilots who had successfully completed all of the requirements of the KBP combat training manual, possessing day and night qualifications in specified weather minima and holding a pilot category of not less than Military Pilot Second Class, plus successful completion of relevant ground training. Flight training included familiarisation with the airfield operating areas, general aircraft handling on cross-country sorties, and aircraft handling on the approach. Before undertaking pre-deployment training, aircrew carried out flights at their home airfield (*aehrodrom postoyannovo bazirovaniya*), planned to correspond as closely as possible to the type of flying they would encounter in the High Arctic, mainly involving:

- two or three approaches 'under the hood' to the BPRS (middle marker) without PRMG (mobile Ground-Controlled Approach or GCA);
- landing on runways of limited length, with the actual dimensions of the deployment airfield runway marked out on the 'home' runway';
- special training for the aircrew in turning the aircraft round at a deployment or diversion airfield.

The pilots and navigators were also given special training on the aircraft and its systems to qualify them to undertake independent post- and pre-flight checks at the deployment airfield with minimal ground support. Pre-deployment flying training was preceded by ground training in the KTS-128 flight simulator, where cross-country flights and operational training procedures could be practised which corresponded to Arctic conditions, including approaches in visibility of around 1-2 km (0.6-1.25 miles), typical of the conditions likely to be encountered at the deployment airfields. The total planned simulator time on the KTS-128 for pilots experiencing polar flight conditions for the first time was 6 hours, whilst those who were re-qualifying for the region were required to complete only 3 hours in the simulator. Such training enabled the pilots to adapt fairly rapidly to the difficult conditions of the High Arctic and in particular to 'polar darkness'. In night conditions it was possible to encounter the phenomenon of optical distortion, producing the unpleasant sensation for the pilot of suddenly seeing not one but possibly two or three runways. The aurora borealis and irregular cloud formations also created optical illusions in flight, often resulting in a false sensation of the aircraft's position in terms of angle of bank and pitch. These sensations were exacerbated when the edge of the cloud was below the level of the horizon. In order to make it easier for the pilots to become accustomed to the unique conditions of polar region flying, the PVO tried to ensure that crew changes took place in summer, to allow sufficient time for them to adapt gradually to the area. Since the High Arctic was in darkness (and subject to frequent snowstorms) for almost half the year, some training flights had to be undertaken at more southerly located airfields.

Two 72 AP crew members walk out to their aircraft, already pre-flighted by the ground crew and awaiting their arrival with canopies open. (*S. Shchelokov*)

The High Arctic also held surprises in the operation of ground-based radios and radar as well as aircraft electronic equipment, with radio interference being extremely powerful during the period of the aurora borealis, leading to problems with radar 'fixing' and maintaining reliable communications. Additionally, the aircrews experienced noise in their headphones, and magnetic instruments, such as the main compass, would give false indications. However, the pilot could also expect to encounter other, more dangerous, surprises in the harsh conditions of a polar winter, as recalled by Maj. Nikolai Popov:

> We'd landed at Yakutsk after a particular sortie—the temperature was around –45°C. After start-up for the return flight the hydraulic actuators on my aircraft did not respond. I tried to switch them on, but I couldn't even move the handles to the half-way point. I didn't have the strength to move them any further. I tried dozens of times; one engine had already flamed out and the engineers came up to the aircraft to assist, but only after my 'hundredth attempt' was I able to switch the actuators on.

There were several occasions in these temperatures (and even lower) when the aneroid-membrane instruments would begin to work only after take-off.

After many years of Tu-128 operations in the High Arctic, another rather unpleasant aspect of the far north manifested itself: corrosion was detected in various components made from aluminium, magnesium and steel alloys, particularly in the fuselage. The jet pipes and nozzle control mechanisms were especially susceptible to corrosion damage. Magnesium corrosion often led to the jamming of the aircraft's control rods, and in late 1985 one of 72 AP's pilots, Nikolai Balyuk, found himself getting airborne from Amderma with a jammed control wheel. Fortunately, in this instance the flight ended safely after he managed to free the controls. After landing, the aircraft was parked in the dispersal area and later underwent non-scheduled maintenance. It was not flown again for several months. Then, in the summer of 1986, while carrying out the post-maintenance test flight of this aircraft, Maj. Kazachenko and his navigator had to eject after the control wheel once again jammed. On this occasion the pilot was unable to rectify the situation, and the resulting accident is described in Appendix 3. Co-author Maj. Nikolai Popov had an identical experience in 1987, when he was ferrying a Tu-128 from Lyetnozerskii to the storage base at Rzhev:

> I was descending into Rzhev when the control column suddenly jammed. It was a night-time ferry flight, which made matters worse. I told my navigator that we might have to eject, but fortunately, within a minute or so, I was able to move the column again and we managed to carry out a safe landing.

(Although described here in the somewhat laconic and self-effacing manner typical

of fighter pilots, it takes little imagination to realise just how serious this situation could have been for Major Popov and his navigator—A.D.)

The complex weather conditions of the region also forced crews to do things which at first glance might seem to be rather contradictory. A typical example was to eschew the use of the high-intensity strobe lights installed at some of the northern military air bases, designed to define the approach to the airfield, with pulses of light virtually 'cutting a path' to the runway in poor visibility. However, in certain conditions these high-intensity lights could blind the pilots, who would often ask for them to be switched off. Moreover, pilots were sometimes forced to dispense with the use of landing lights and switch off the flashing anti-collision beacons because they too destroyed their night vision when descending in cloud at night. The flashing beacons were so powerful that the aircraft could be seen from a distance of several kilometres.

The weather conditions of the High Arctic also made life difficult for ground maintenance personnel, with snowstorms and blizzards being quite common in winter. There were also snowstorms with hurricane-force winds, when the wind speed could reach around 30 m/sec (60 kts) in temperatures down to –30°C and visibility almost at zero. This type of snowstorm was known by personnel based in the region as a '*Variant*', a borrowed word widely used in Russian military circles, often describing much more than a simple 'variant' of some thing or procedure. In

Even after a comparatively light snowstorm, aircraft still had to be dug out of deep snow on Arctic airfields. Here 72 AP ground crew manhandle a MiG-15UTI 'Midget' trainer in the snow-clearing operation known as *poslyepurgovaya podgotovka* – literally 'after-snowstorm preparation'. Note also the civilian An-12 'Cub' in the background, which appears to have slid off the runway. (*Vladimir Yenyutin*)

this context the term refers to the working regime of the garrison[5] declared during the onset of severe weather—a procedure known as '*Variant No. 1*'. This required that non-essential users of electrical power (i.e. equipment) should be isolated from the main supply and that working or simply *being* outside was prohibited. Everyone had to remain wherever they were at the onset of the declaration of '*Variant*'—no matter whether this was at work, in the garrison schools or nurseries, etc. These conditions could last for around three or four days, and the aircraft would end up almost completed covered with snow. At Amderma this led to the introduction of an additional category of aircraft maintenance—'after-snowstorm preparation' (*poslyepurgovaya podgotovka*). When performing this operation, the ground engineers would open up the access hatches on all the aircraft and blow air through the compartments in order to clear away any build-up of snow inside. Weather conditions were particularly bad at Amderma in the years from 1973 to 1976.

At airfields that were close to the sea, like Amderma and Talagi, ice would sometimes crystallise quite suddenly and finger-sized crystals of hoar frost would build up on the main runway. From a distance this looked like snow and seriously affected aircraft braking on landing. During the transition from winter to summer a variety of meteorological phenomena could be encountered, a typical example being recalled here by Maj. Ivan Rodyukov, a squadron navigator on 518 AP at Talagi:

Snow clearance required all hands on deck since the only mechanical tool that could be used safely in the vicinity of the aircraft was a shovel! Here, the area around Tu-128 Bort No. 45 is cleared by 72 AP ground crew at Amderma. Note the word ОТЛИЧНЫЙ (*Otlichnyi*) in front of the Bort number – the original style of designating an 'Excellent Aircraft', replaced in 1972 by an all-red stylised aircraft inside a pentagon emblem. (*Vladimir Yenyutin*)

Much effort was required to clear the snow from this Tu-128 of 72 AP after a heavy overnight downfall and the nose-wheel is still covered. Unlike snow clearance procedures on Western military airfields, the volume of snow accumulating on Arctic airfields made preventive measures virtually impossible and clearance could only begin when snowfall had ceased. (*Alexander Nikolaev*)

Weather conditions for us [at Talagi] were generally very complex. On one particular occasion, at the beginning of spring, we flew into a thunderstorm in the vicinity of Nar'yan-Mar […] We were heading north and suddenly discovered a huge cumulonimbus front ahead of us, with thunder clouds extending from ground level up to 12,000 m [39,370 feet]. There were lightning flashes all around us in the clouds. It was impossible to make a detour around the front, either to the left or right of the main cloud formation because of its broad extent, so we just selected the burners, went supersonic and 'leapt over' the top of the clouds. Flying further north towards Novaya Zemlya, where it was colder, there were no cumulonimbus build-ups at all.

In summer the weather was more stable, with close to normal visual meteorological conditions (*prostiye meteo-usloviya*) over almost all of the territory of the USSR, with the exception of the High Arctic. Here, the movement of a cold air mass coming off the Arctic Ocean into the continental area of the country could lead very rapidly to a worsening of the weather situation. Consequently, flight planning in these northern regions required very accurate analysis of local weather conditions, even in the summer period, although this notwithstanding, the airfield weather forecasters would sometimes get it wrong.

In May 1982, the duty forecaster at Alykyel' (Noril'sk) airfield carried out a rather perfunctory analysis of the prevailing conditions for the area and prepared a bulletin which did not foresee a deterioration in the weather for that day. However, almost immediately after the start of the day's flying programme, the airfield was enveloped in ten-tenths cloud at around 200 m (650 feet) and below.[6] The flight controller, noting the worsening weather situation, had to cancel all flying, and those aircraft that were already airborne were sent to the designated diversion airfield at Khatanga. It should be noted that at this particular time in the history of Soviet military air operations a weather diversion to a reserve airfield was deemed to be a 'precursor to a flying accident' (*predposylka k lyotnomu proisshestviyu* or PLP) and was not undertaken lightly. A similar PLP occurred at this airfield in June of that year when the duty forecaster's prognosis gave stable weather conditions for the entire period of the day's flying but 3 hours after the start of the programme the airfield was shrouded in fog, with horizontal visibility down to 150 m (500 feet). The controller cancelled all flights and diverted aircraft already airborne to the reserve airfield at Igarka. (Clearly, these are only fragmentary examples of the type of weather situations that could arise in the northern regions of the USSR, but are illustrative of the conditions affecting military flight operations there.)

Weather minima (*meteominimumy*) for the air forces of the USSR were established by appropriate standing orders for all pilots, aircraft types and operational airfields, and were defined as the minimum values of cloud-base and horizontal visibility in which it was safe to perform take-offs and landings. More specifically,

A 72 AP Tu-128 taxiing out from the QRA dispersal at Amderma is seen off by squadron ground crew and an airfield duty security guard, armed with a Simonov SKS self-loading carbine. Note that the photograph appears to have been retouched, creating the impression that there is no glazing for the navigator's cockpit. (*S. Shchelokov*)

individual minima were determined by the experience level of the pilot, aircraft performance, and its on-board radar and electronic equipment (avionics). Weather minima for a given airfield were determined by the electronic landing aids installed, its geographical location, and the nature of the surrounding terrain etc. Minima for the Tu-128 and associated heavy aircraft of the PVO were last promulgated by the Commander-in-Chief of the Soviet Air Forces (*Glavkom VVS*) on 10 November 1980 in the form of a document entitled 'On the establishment of the weather minimum' and are set out in the following table:

'First Weather Minimum' (*Pyervyi Minimum Pogody*)						
			DAY		NIGHT	
Aircraft type	Type of landing aids at airfield	Stage of flight	Cloud-base (metres)	Visibility (kilometres)	Cloud-base (metres)	Visibility (kilometres)
Tu-128, Tu-128UT, Tu-126	OSP, RSP, PRMG-4 (RMS)	Landing	200-250	2.5-3.0	250-300	3-3.5
		Take-off	50-100	1-1.5	50-100	1-1.5
Tu-128, Tu-128UT	OSP, RSP (without RMS)	Landing	250-300	3-3.5	200-250	3-3.5
	RMS	Landing	150-200	2-2.5	200-250	3-3.5
Tu-124	OSP, RSP, PRMG-4 (RMS)	Landing	100	1.0	100	1.5

Abbreviations used in the table:

OSP—(*Oborudovaniye Slepoi Posadki*): Blind Landing Equipment (Instrument Landing System—ILS), consisting of a system of airfield lead-in lights located on the approach to the main runway, plus outer and inner radio beacons defining the runway centreline

RSP—(*Radiolokatsionnaya Sistyema Posadki*): precision approach radar system, comprising heading (course), glideslope and panoramic scanning radars

RMS—Literal translation is Radio Beacon System (from *Radiomayachnaya Sistyema*): refers specifically to the glideslope beacon, installed to the left or right of the main runway. The RMS system on Soviet military airfields generated a glideslope with a gradient of 2°40'.

PRMG-4—Literal translation is Landing Radio Beacon Group (*Posadochnaya Radiomayachnaya Gruppa*): one of the components of the glideslope generator.

The 'Second Weather Minimum' was less stringent in its requirements, and to 'First Minimum' values the following should be added—150 m (490 feet) for the cloud-base figures and 1 km (0.6 miles) for the visibility figures.

11

Operational Aspects

BASES AND TASKS OF THE TU-128 REGIMENTS

As mentioned elsewhere, the Tupolev Tu-128 'Fiddler', armed with its four unique-to-type AA-5 'Ash' air-to-air missiles, started to enter service with the PVO in the mid-1960s. By this time, the Soviet air defence force was just undertaking its seventh post-war structural reorganisation, the sixth such event having been completed within the period 1957-60. Both of these periods of reorganisation had been managed under the tutelage of the then C-in-C of the PVO, Marshal of the Soviet Union Sergey Biryuzov, and were considered to have introduced significant improvements to the air defence of the Soviet Union. Those changes introduced at the end of the 1950s involved a reduction in the overall area and extent of the boundaries of responsibility of the Homeland Air Defence Troops (*Voyska PVO Strany*). The new organisational structure more fittingly reflected these changes and eased the task of controlling air combat against aerial intruders in Soviet airspace, rather than being aligned with the boundaries of the military districts (*voyenniye okrugy*), as was the case previously. Instead of twenty major formations and units of Homeland Air Defence linked to the number of military districts, only thirteen formations were retained: two PVO districts (*Okrugy PVO*), five PVO armies (*Armii PVO*) and six PVO corps (*Korpusa PVO*). For the first time, the zones of responsibility of the restructured formations and units embraced the entire territory of the USSR and the vulnerable access points to the country.

The seventh structural reorganisation was directed mainly at regularising control within the units of the Homeland Air Defence Troops, with changes affecting control at the operational/tactical level (*opyerativnyi urovyen'*). PVO formations were reduced in number, albeit with an increased number of assigned personnel, and the ranking of formations was raised, while a programme of automation of the command and control process was set in train. Significant changes also affected the tactical level of control of the Homeland Air Defence Troops, and instead of individual air defence artillery and fighter air corps and divisions, mixed air defence units (*smeshannyie aviatsionno-zenitniye korpusa i divizii*) were created, with a regimental structure for all branches of PVO troops. Thus, two or three aviation regiments and one to three air defence missile regiments (or brigades), dependent upon equipment and personnel establishment levels, began to form part of a standard air defence division. The unified control of air and AAA resources which had been well tried in the Great Patriotic War at the operational level was now also being achieved at the tactical level. All the wartime established VNOS posts (*Posty Vozdushnovo Nablyudyeniya, Opovyeshcheniya i Svyazi*) were replaced by PVO radio-technical troops, operating a network of early warning and missile guidance radars, whereas the monitoring posts only provided visual air observation (*vozdushnoye nablyudyeniye*), air-raid warning (*opovyeshcheniye*) and communications (*svyaz'*).

It was within this new organisational structure of Homeland Air Defence that the first Tu-128s were delivered to the Moscow District of the PVO, the 14th Independent Army of the PVO, and the 10th Independent Army of the PVO. It was decided to equip 445 IAP with the Tu-128, then based at Khotilovo, this regiment forming part of the 2nd Corps of the PVO (*2 Korpus PVO*), with its HQ in the garrison at Rzhev. As mentioned in Chapter 5, the adjective 'fighter' ('*istrebityel'nyi*') was dropped from the title of regiments that operated the Tu-128 after the adoption of a different level of equipment and personnel establishment (*shtat*) for this aircraft. So after receiving its first Tu-128s, it was the newly abbreviated 445 AP (*445 Aviatsionnyi Polk*) which relocated to its purpose-built base at Savvatiya to form part of the 3rd Corps of the PVO (*3 Korpus PVO*), headquartered in the town of Yaroslavl'. In southern Siberia the Tu-128 began to equip units of the 14th Independent Army of the PVO, the Army's HQ being in the city of Novosibirsk. In spite of the fact that the Army's HQ was located so far south, its zone of responsibility also embraced the vast territory of eastern and western Siberia, right up to the islands of the Arctic Ocean. The new interceptor equipped two air defence divisions: 33 Division of the PVO (*33 Diviziya PVO*), with its HQ in Semipalatinsk, and 39 Division of the PVO (*39 Diviziya PVO*), headquartered in Irkutsk. The first formation, 33 Division, had two regiments equipped with the Tu-128—64 AP at Omsk-North and 356 AP at Zhana-Semey. The third regiment, 350 AP, based at Belaya, formed part of the 39th 'Irkutsk' Division.

The most northerly situated major formation of Homeland Air Defence Troops was the 10th Independent Army of the PVO, with its HQ in Arkhangel'sk. The head of the 10th Army in the mid-1970s, Col. Gen. Dmitriev, described his subordinate units as comprising up to 100 AAA missile divisions, equipped with S-75 (SA-2 'Guideline'), S-125 (SA-3 'Goa') and later S-200 (SA-5 'Gammon') missile complexes, at the time the most modern systems in Soviet service. His fighter units consisted of 280 interceptors, including Su-9 'Fishpots', Su-15 'Flagons', Yak-28 'Firebars' and, of course, Tu-128 'Fiddlers', plus a squadron of Tu-126 'Moss' long-range radar picket and fighter guidance aircraft (for airborne controlled intercept—ACI).[1] The individual command posts of the fighter regiments and GCI stations were equipped with so-called 'instrument guidance' equipment (*apparatura pribornovo navyedyeniya*), a broadly generalised Russian term for what was, effectively, data-link control. Around 100 sub-units of radio-technical troops were equipped with several hundred radar systems of various types, operating in a variety of different frequency ranges. The 10th Army comprised around 56,000 personnel, including generals, senior, middle ranking and junior officers, warrant officers, sergeants and ordinary enlisted soldiers and airmen. Units of PVO radio-technical troops were deployed along the coast of the Barents, White and Kara Seas, on the island of Novaya Zemlya and the Franz Josef Land archipelago to conduct reconnaissance and provide early warning of flights by potential intruders into Soviet airspace.

The 10th Army's zone of responsibility embraced a huge territorial expanse, from the borders of the USSR with Finland and Norway and along the entire northern coastline of Soviet High Arctic to the open surface of the Kara Sea and the North Pole. Falling under 10th Army control were the 4th, 5th and 23rd Divisions of the PVO, plus the PVO's 21st Corps, with the Tu-128s of 518 AP at

Flights to operational deployment airfields of the High Arctic were very often made carrying a full complement of weapons. This was done in order to swap missiles that had been in storage for some time at the deployment base with ones that had been serviced more recently. (*Nikolai Popov*)

Talagi coming under the control of 23 Division, headquartered in the garrison at Vas'kovo (near Arkhangel'sk). The other northern Tu-128 regiment, 72 AP at Amderma, was subordinate to 4 Division of the PVO, with its HQ at Rogachyovo (aka Belushya Guba) on the island of Novaya Zemlya. The choice of base locations for the Tu-128 was not accidental but was determined by the importance of the task facing the Homeland Air Defence units. The main task of the 'Fiddler' during hostilities was to intercept missile-carrying bombers of the USAF, specifically the Boeing B-52 'Stratofortress', before they were able to launch their weapons. Destruction of an intruding bomber was planned to take place at a distance of around 1,500 km (810 nm) from the coastline of the Kola Peninsula, i.e. over the open sea area of the Arctic Ocean.

A minimum of a pair of Tu-128s was required to achieve a 92 per cent kill probability against a single B-52. The number of interceptors could be increased depending upon the actual variant of bomber identified and its anticipated use of ECM. The kill probability for a single R-4 (AA-5 'Ash') missile against the B-52 in the forward hemisphere was only 27 per cent. This seems extremely low by today's standards, although it should be remembered that this would have been achieved at a significant distance from the launch boundary of the B-52's cruise missiles. It must also be borne in mind that none of the interceptors of the 1960s and 1970s was capable of bettering or even achieving this performance.

In peacetime, the Tu-128 was also tasked with the interception and destruction of foreign reconnaissance balloons, known in Russian as 'automatic drifting aerostats' (*Avtomaticheskie Dreyfuyushchiye Aerostaty* or ADA), as well as escorting foreign reconnaissance aircraft in the 100 km (54 nm) exclusion zone off the coastline of the USSR. Additionally, they could be tasked with escorting and offering assistance to aircraft that had unintentionally violated Soviet airspace. Another supplementary task, during actual or simulated combat activity, involved the use of Tu-128s to clear (sanitise) the airspace and then escort Soviet LRAF medium and strategic bombers and provide top cover in their air-to-air refuelling zones. There was also an attempt to task the Tu-128 with the interception of the B-52's North American AGM-28 'Hound Dog' cruise missiles in flight. A research programme was set up by 518 AP at Talagi in the late 1960s with the objective of determining the possibility of intercepting and destroying 'Hound Dog' missiles after their release from the B-52. Maj.-Gen. Nikolai Skok took part in these trials as a junior officer and recalls the events:

> A group of the most highly qualified and trained crews on our regiment was assembled, which also included myself, and was led by Colonel A. M. Megyera. The commission charged with undertaking the special trials was headed by the First Deputy Commander of the 10th Independent Army of the PVO, Twice Hero of the Soviet Union, Major General N. D. Gulaev.

The results of our intercepts of a Su-9, simulating the flight profile of a 'Hound Dog' missile, were not very encouraging: the radar cross-section of the Su-9 at closing speeds greater than 3,000 kph (1,620 kts) was less than the lock-on capability of the *Smerch* radar during a forward hemisphere attack. Lock-on was achieved too late and the range to the target was less than the minimum permitted for missile launch. After this disappointing result the order was given to study the possibility of intercepting the 'Hound Dog' using a rear hemisphere lag pursuit profile, since the missile's speed exceeded that of the interceptor. The results were the same as before, although the crews who participated in the trials did obtain very useful practical experience of intercepting high-altitude, high-speed targets.

Following these trials, the plans to use the Tu-128 to intercept cruise missiles had to be shelved.

As already noted, the most vulnerable aerial approach direction over Soviet territory, which unquestionably called for obligatory and constant fighter protection, was from the north, representing the shortest distance between the USSR and the USA—the two superpowers of the Cold War period. However, in the mid-1960s, relations between the Soviet Union and the People's Republic of China had also deteriorated quite significantly, leading to the urgent need to establish another defensive sector focused on central China. Thus the fighter interceptor regiments of the 14th PVO Army would have to undertake combat air patrols in two separate sectors in the event of hostilities—in the north and along a central Chinese axis. The key installations which had to be protected by the 14th Army's 'Fiddler' regiments were located in the vicinity of, *inter alia*, Novyi Urengoy, Surgut, Omsk, Novosibirsk, Tomsk, Novokuznetsk, Kemerovo, Barnaul, Alyeisk and Biisk. Between the end of the 1970s and beginning of the 1980s it was believed that in the event of nuclear war, the potential enemy (at that time considered to be the United States of America and its allies) would carry out a strike in two waves:

- an initial wave of B-52s with thirty ALCMs (Air Launched Cruise Missiles) and fifteen SRAMs (Short-range Attack Missiles)
- a second wave of up to sixty-five B-52s with twenty ALCMs and 185 SRAMs.

It was expected that a strike deep into Siberian territory would be initiated some 7-9 hours after the launch of intercontinental ballistic missiles (ICBMs), the likely launch boundary of American ALCMs being Cape Chelyuskin (Taymyr Peninsula), Kirov Island and Cape Sporyi Navolok (on Novaya Zemlya). The PVO's fighter response would be based on these assumptions, and by way of example we list here the wartime tasks which would be carried out by the 1st and 2nd squadrons of 356 AP based at Zhana-Semey:

Wartime tasks of the 1st squadron of the 356th Aviation Regiment

The 1st squadron, comprising nine Tu-128Ms, in co-operation with the 2nd squadron of 356 AP and augmented by fighters from 849 IAP at Kupino in Novosibirsk Oblast, operating from an airfield QRA posture (*dezhurstvo na aehrodromye*)[2] at Readiness 1, was tasked with the following missions:

- prevention of enemy strikes on key installations in the Omsk and Novosibirsk industrial region and overflights by enemy aircraft towards key installations of the Kuzbass (Kuznetsk Basin) coal, iron and steel production area;
- destruction of enemy aircraft along Defence Line No. 6, Bystriy to Ishim, and Defence Line No. 7, Zarya to Narym, at medium and high altitudes;

Additionally, to be prepared for deployment to the reserve airfield at Khatanga in order to:

- reinforce PVO defensive capability using the regiment's 3rd squadron and fighter squadrons of 849 IAP at Kupino, to neutralise enemy air power along the central Chinese axis from specific defence lines;
- attack at medium and high altitude along Defence Line No. 12, Zharma to Gornaya Teli, from an airfield QRA posture at Readiness 1 and from airborne QRA (*dezhurstvo v vozdukhye*) in Zone Nos 3 and 4—see below;*
- attack at medium altitude along the Defence Line No. 11 Kaskabulak– Nizhnyaya Tayinta–Novaya Shul'ba, from an airfield QRA posture at Readiness 1;
- provide top cover for groups of forces of the Siberian Military District (Siberian Front) on their 'route of advance' between Biisk and Tashanta. In peacetime, the squadrons would be tasked with the destruction of military aircraft and drifting reconnaissance balloons of capitalist states if they violated Soviet airspace.

Wartime tasks of the 2nd squadron of the 356th Aviation Regiment

The 2nd squadron, comprising nine Tu-128s operating from an airfield QRA posture (*dezhurstvo na aehrodromye*) at Readiness 1, in co-operation with the 1st squadron of 356 AP, was tasked with the following missions:

- prevention of enemy strikes on key installations in the Omsk and Novosibirsk industrial region and overflights towards the Kuzbass coal, iron and steel production area;

In the early 1980s, one of 356 AP's aircraft technicians, Jr Sgt Igor' Marchuk, an extended service (*svyerkhsrochnaya sluzhba*) regular serviceman, poses alongside 'his' aircraft, giving scale to the large size of the 'Ash' missile. The low suspension height on the pylon meant that it was possible to load the missiles without using the inbuilt or external lifting equipment. (*Igor' Marchuk*)

- destruction of enemy aircraft at maximum possible range, before they could launch their air-to-ground missiles, operating either individually within a pairs formation or as two pairs using a forward hemisphere intercept profile at medium and high altitude along Defence Line No. 6, Bystriy to Ishim, and Defence Line No. 7, Zarya to Narym.

Additionally, to be prepared for deployment to the reserve airfield at Khatanga in order to:

- reinforce PVO defensive capability using the regiment's 3rd squadron and fighter squadrons of 849 IAP at Kupino, from an airfield QRA posture and from airborne QRA in Zone Nos 3 and 4;*
- destroy enemy aircraft approaching from the central China direction along Defence Line No. 12, Novosibirsk to Gornaya Teli, and Defence Line No. 11, Ishim–Kaskabulak–Nizhnyaya Tayinta–Novaya Shul'ba.

The regiment's airborne QRA Zone Nos 3 and 4 were set up in designated airspace within the region of the towns of Yerofeevka and Aktokai respectively.

Organisation and mounting of QRAs

Quick reaction alert (QRA), described in Russian as 'combat duty' (*boyevoye dezhurstvo*) or more correctly 'the state of being on combat duty', was defined by a series of standing orders issued by the Soviet Ministry of Defence. In the mid-twentieth century, considerable attention was focused on the protection of the USSR's borders which was embodied in a special order issued in 1960 entitled 'On the reinforcement of the state borders of the USSR'. In this period, another order was promulgated by the Defence Ministry entitled 'On the introduction of the state of operational readiness in troop formations of the PVO and the air defence units of the Ground Forces, Air Force and Navy' and some time later, a directive of the Main Command of the PVO Troops and the Soviet Air Force was issued, with the title 'On the introduction of instructions for the organisation and conduct of combat operations in fighter aviation units of the PVO and the Soviet Air Force'. These documents defined operational readiness as being the execution of given combat tasks, to be organised around the following objectives:

- permanent maintenance of part of the fighter resources of the PVO and the Soviet Air Force in a state of heightened readiness for immediate combat activity;
- timely interception and destruction of enemy combat aircraft, and escort to the nearest airfield of all passenger and transport aircraft of capitalist states observed to have violated the sovereign airspace of the USSR, or member states of the Warsaw Pact and the Mongolian People's Republic, on the territories of which units of the Soviet Air Force were deployed;
- to provide assistance to aircraft of member states of the Warsaw Pact and Mongolian People's Republic in the event of their accidental violation of Soviet airspace;
- to undertake appropriate measures to assist Soviet aircraft observed to have violated normal ATC regulations within Soviet sovereign airspace, and to offer assistance to aircraft in distress;
- to escort foreign aircraft observed to be within the 100 km (54 nm) exclusion zone off the Soviet coastline, over international waters.

A so-called operational readiness flight (*dezhurnoye zveno*) was established on all fighter bases for exclusive control of the operational readiness forces (*dezhurniye sily*), which included provision of personnel accommodation (*dezhurnyi domik*)[3] and a dispersal area for duty aircraft and supporting ground equipment. The area around the operational readiness flight was protected by guards. Operational readiness was mounted day and night by crews who had completed the obligatory exercises in the KBP combat training manual. The KBP was a series of exercises

A 'Fiddler' of the 3rd squadron of 350 AP in the QRA dispersal at Bratsk. The APA-5 auxiliary power unit mounted on a Ural-375 chassis, seen on the far right of the picture, could provide AC and DC power to two aircraft at a time. (*Nikolai Popov*)

established for each aircraft type which pilots had to master in order to be considered 'combat-ready'. Additionally, in order to stand operational readiness duty, pilots had to have an appropriate weather rating and to have valid currency 'on type', without any breaks in flying. Crews taking up QRA duty operated within specified readiness states, which for the aviation units of PVO *Strany* (Air Defence of the Country or Homeland) were designated as:

- Readiness 1 (*Gotovnost' Odin*)—Crews in high-altitude flight suits and helmets, sitting in their aircraft, in radio contact with the regimental command post while the aircraft technician was in external intercom contact with the crew; aircraft fully armed and fuelled and accepted for flight by the crew; flight controller (*rukovodityel' polyotov* or RP) in the ATC tower; crew ready for take-off within 4 minutes;
- Readiness 2 (*Gotovnost' Dva*)—Crews in high-altitude flight suits in the duty flight accommodation; aircraft technician in the duty flight accommodation, flight controller in the ATC tower or in the duty flight building; aircraft fully armed, fully fuelled and accepted for flight by the crew; aircraft ready for take-off within 7 minutes (9 minutes at night);

- Readiness 3 (*Gotovnost' Tri*)—Pilot and navigator not wearing high-altitude equipment assemblies, relaxing in the duty flight building; aircraft fully armed, fuelled and accepted for flight by the crew; aircraft technician in duty flight building; flight controller in the ATC tower or in the duty flight building; aircraft ready for take-off within 9 minutes (11 minutes for a night-time scramble);
- Readiness State (*Baikal*)—Two crews at the disposal of the regiment within their squadron crew-room or offices, or, during non-working periods (non-flying periods), 'stood down' at home; available to be driven out to their aircraft and strapping in within 30 minutes of declaration of '*Baikal*' alert. (This latter readiness state was employed only within the 14th Independent Army.)

Operational readiness on the Tu-128 regiments was mounted in accordance with regulations established for PVO air units and did not differ in any way from the procedures used by regiments equipped with the Su-9, MiG-17 or MiG-19. (Following conversion onto a new aircraft type, regiments would not be expected to mount operational readiness sorties immediately; usually a period of around six to twelve months was required before this could be achieved.) A regiment taking up operational readiness duty would receive the relevant orders from command HQ, which would be read out during a parade involving all the regiment's personnel to mark the occasion. As a rule, aircraft and technical support personnel were drawn from one squadron for one week's operational readiness duty in accordance with the flight planning roster, during which time they would not be available for normal training flights. The pilots and navigators were drawn from all three squadrons in accordance with the regiment's aircrew planning roster, authorised at divisional and higher echelon level. However, not only the aircrew but often also the aircraft themselves would be drawn from the entire regimental inventory for operational readiness duty, particularly in the latter years of the aircraft's operation. Operational readiness usually commenced on a Friday (more rarely on a Saturday) and on the morning of taking up duty the ground engineering support team would perform pre-flight checks on the aircraft declared for readiness. In the 1964 edition of the engineering service manual NIAS-64 (*Nastavlyeniye po inzhenyernoy aviatsionnoy sluzhbye*) it was decreed that 'preliminary preparation' of aircraft would be valid for five days, and for aircraft declared for operational readiness duty, three days.

So, on the day of taking up operational readiness duty, pre-flight checks of three days' validity would be carried out by the assigned ground crews. The aircraft would remain in the duty flight dispersal, but the ground crew would be rotated every 24 hours. Servicing was provided for two aircraft by a single ground crew team, which was deemed sufficient to launch a fully prepared aircraft in the event

042. A Tu-128 on QRA duty in a duty flight dispersal, plugged in to an APA-5 mobile ground power supply. The weapon on the outer pylon is an R-4RM variant of the semi-active radar guided 'Ash' with serial number 1PBP0050507041 (1RVR0050507041). Of interest is the fact that the third element of the factory serial number appears to have been changed in regimental service from a letter 'Б' ('B') to 'В' ('V'). Note also that the chocks in the foreground are marked with the letters 'БД' ('BD') meaning *boyevoye dezhurstvo*, the Russian term for QRA. (*Nikolai Popov*)

of a scramble being declared in response to an unidentified intruder; as soon as one aircraft had taken off, the ground crew would immediately pre-flight the second. The aircraft senior technician would be from one aircraft while the aircraft technician would be from the other, so that each aircraft was looked after by its own 'handler'. As mentioned, all the aircraft on the operational readiness flight were maintained in fully prepared flight-ready condition, connected to the APA truck-based power supply for engine start. If the temperature fell below freezing level the servicing crew would switch on the heating units of the AA-5 'Ash' missiles' internal batteries.

Col. Yevglyevskiy recalls his involvement in drawing up an abbreviated check-list for operational readiness sorties:

The pilots and navigators of the Tu-128, as on all other heavy Soviet combat aircraft of the time, had an obligatory pre-flight check-list which they had to follow during engine start-up. However, we had to write a separate pre-flight check-list for operational readiness sorties. After all, on taking up operational readiness duty, all aircraft systems and the engines had been checked anyway, and to reduce pre-take-off preparation time some of the systems would be switched on beforehand. That is, the crew would be sitting in the cockpit when the order to scramble was given, with electrical power switched on and some of the equipment already powering up. In this case, the check-list required a lesser number of obligatory actions than on a normal sortie.

For operational readiness duty, the Tu-128, in distinction to other PVO interceptors, was always armed with the type's unvarying weapons 'fit', namely two IR-guided AA-5 'Ash' missiles and two semi-active homing variants of the AA-5. In the second half of the 1970s, Tu-128s began to stand operational readiness armed with the upgraded R-4M variant of the AA-5, which offered some capability against low-flying targets. Around 600 missiles were held in the armouries of each of the Tu-128 bases, while a further 100 missiles were stored at the relevant deployment airfields. The number of aircraft in the operational readiness flight varied as a function of local conditions and the specific tasks assigned to the regiment and could be greater than the four machines that were standard for an ordinary flight on a PVO squadron.

In the 1970s, the following QRA readiness states were employed by 518 AP at Talagi:

- Main readiness (*Osnovnaya Gotovnost'*)—two crews on the readiness flight (Readiness 1, 2 or 3 being determined by the duty operations officer (*opyerativnyi dezhurnyi*) in the regimental command post);
- 30-minute readiness (*30-i minutnaya Gotovnost'*)—two crews at regiment HQ or on the airfield, at the disposal of the regiment and able to get to the operational readiness hut within 30 minutes;
- 40-minute readiness (*40-ka minutnaya Gotovnost'*)—one crew at regiment HQ or on the airfield, at the disposal of the regiment and able to get to the operational readiness hut within 40 minutes. This crew was dedicated to the interception of 'drifting aerostats' (reconnaissance balloons).

Dispatch riders plus vehicles and drivers were provided to deliver urgent messages and pick up crews who were accommodated outside the duty flight area. Later, the number of aircraft on operational readiness on 518 AP was increased to eight as a result of adding a further two crews at Readiness 2 to the duty roster. By contrast with 518 AP at Talagi, 72 AP at Amderma only carried out QRA duty at Readiness 3 until it received its full complement of aircraft in the early 1970s. Once this had occurred, two crews could be placed at Readiness 2 and a further two crews at Readiness 3. If the status of the first pair was raised to Readiness 1, then they had to don their VMSK immersion suits within 2 minutes and climb into their cockpits to await the command to take off. This would then require another two crews to be assigned to reinforce the operational readiness flight for that day.

A very clean-looking Tu-128 in the 72 AP QRA dispersal at Amderma in the early 1980s in a view that emphasises the considerable length of the air intake ducts. (*Valeriy Yalyaev*)

The situation for Tu-128 regiments subordinate to the PVO's 14th Independent Army, with less demanding responsibilities, was much calmer. Thus, in the 1960s and 1970s, each of the three regiments of the 14th Army provided only two aircraft for operational readiness, as on the majority of other PVO regiments, with a third 'reserve' aircraft on standby on the relevant squadron dispersal area. Gradually, however, the Tu-128 units of the 14th Army began to assign two aircraft for operational readiness, plus a further two as reserves. These aircraft were parked in the operational readiness dispersal alongside the QRA hut. Two duty crews on 30-minute readiness either occupied themselves with 'combat preparation' on the squadron or relaxed at home until required to fly. This readiness state was given the codeword '*Baikal*', and on hearing this broadcast the crews had to report to the operational readiness flight for further briefing.

Whereas aircraft assigned to the operational readiness flight were prohibited from normal training flights, the situation was slightly different for back-up aircraft (*samolyot usilyeniya*). Sometimes a situation would arise where back-up aircraft supporting the operational readiness flight could be used to enable a squadron to fly a full complement of aircraft in a routine training programme. Tasks for these aircraft were planned in such a way that their crews would be able to return to base after the training flight and then have the aircraft 'turned round' ready to fly an operational readiness mission if required. Missiles removed from the aircraft for training flights in such cases were simply left on handling trolleys on the operational readiness flight until required for reloading onto the QRA aircraft.

Crew change-over occurred during the week-long operational readiness duty, for which two different methods were adopted. The first method, the most common, required the aircrew to carry out 'day readiness' and 'night readiness' duty; in the morning the oncoming crew would take over from the night crew, and the crew being relieved would be stood down to rest at home. Using this method, operational readiness 'authorisers' counted day- and night-time duty hours from sunrise and sunset respectively, whereby one crew would be 'on call' for 14 hours

Missiles were delivered to the aircraft on special trolleys, although these had one major deficiency in that they were not equipped with lifting gear. In spite of the fact that the aircraft's pylons did have a built-in winch, this was rarely used and missiles were usually loaded by hand. This aircraft belonged to the 3rd squadron of 356 AP at Zhana-Semey and is seen here at Khatanga airfield in the summer of 1987. (*Nikolai Popov*)

(i.e. throughout the long summer day or the long winter night as appropriate) and the other crew for only 10 hours. The second procedure was used in the extreme north, i.e. in the High Arctic, and was sometimes referred to as the 'Amderma method' ('*amderminskaya metodika*'), whereby the day was divided equally into two 12-hour shifts, running from 09.00 hours and from 21.00 hours. This was to take account of the long polar day during the summer and the long polar night in winter. Crews coming off operational readiness duty were able to go home, to be replaced by oncoming crews.

The number of hours spent on operational readiness duty had a bearing on the amount of flying pay supplement for Tu-128 aircrew, with night duty attracting a higher rate than for daytime operations. Crew planning also had to take account of the aero-medical regulations in force at the time, which specified the frequency with which aircrew could carry out readiness duty, although these were not always strictly observed. The paucity of crews meant that QRA duty came round more frequently than defined by the medically specified norms. Former section navigator on 72 AP at Amderma, Lt Col. Oleg Fedoseyenko recalls:

Operational readiness in the 1980s occurred fifteen times a month [i.e. virtually every other day], particularly in the summer months. However, we were only paid for three night and two daytime duties. This was because it was forbidden to produce any documentation which would effectively legalise exceeding the medical norms (*prevysheniye sanitarnykh norm*) for operational readiness.

Apart from the aircrew, the operational readiness flight also included a duty maintenance crew and a duty pilot responsible for acceptance and dispatch of aircraft (*dezhurnyi lyotchik po priyomu i vypusku*). Depending upon individual regimental procedures, the latter either remained in the QRA hut or in the ATC tower. The two aircraft on operational readiness would be changed over every 24 hours, with the duty aircraft then going into the 'back-up' pool. In turn, the original 'back-up' aircraft would become the 'duty pair'. This change-over took place every morning, with maintenance personnel preparing the aircraft for flight and the pilots performing engine checks in the QRA dispersal before shutting down and assuming the normal alert posture. Aircrew were allowed to go onto operational readiness duty only after specific periods of rest, which were:

- not less than 8 hours after a night-flying sortie;
- not less than 4 hours after a daytime sortie;
- apart from this, a period of 2 hours was specified to prepare for operational readiness duty.

Before taking up the duty, crews received an operational readiness briefing and signed out their personal weapons (the Makarov PM pistol—*Pistolet Makarova*). The briefing was given on a parade for all those taking part in the QRA duty, i.e. officers, warrant officers and airmen (the latter group of personnel always being referred to as soldiers (*soldaty*) in the Soviet and Russian air forces). After the briefing had been read out, everyone present was given the command 'For the protection of the state borders, quick march!' (*'Na okhranu gosudarstvyennoy granitsy, shagom marsh!'*). After marching off and being dismissed, everyone would get into their respective vehicles and drive to the duty flight dispersal. This procedure varied a little between the different regiments, but always included this type of parade and the briefing.

All QRA personnel were accommodated in the building provided for operational readiness crews during their period of duty. At Zhana-Semey the '*domik*' included a room for the aircrew (with flight clothing lockers), a lounge, a room for the ground crew technicians, a room for the ordinary soldiers (airmen), a 'Lenin room' (*Leninskaya komnata*)[4] and a dining room. This was a typical layout, but could differ from regiment to regiment depending upon the extent to which the regiment commander looked after his subordinates. Pilots and navigators spoke very highly of the operational readiness facilities at Talagi, where the QRA hut was quite spacious and located in picturesque surroundings on the edge of a lake.

1. A Tu-128M, formerly on the strength of 72 AP at Amderma, displayed in the outdoor museum area of PVO Corps HQ on Rzhev airfield. Note that this aircraft is carrying R-98 (AA-3 'Anab') missiles on both inboard pylons, although the 'Anab' was never actually associated with the Tu-128 in operational service. (*Alexander Melihov*)

2. The first prototype of the Tu-128, on display at Monino, (sometimes referred to as the 'zero' prototype, since it was given the test series number '0') was the first of five aircraft used in the certification programme. The other four were numbered '1' (c/n 0201), '2' (c/n 0202), '3' (c/n 0301) and '4' (c/n 0401). The aircraft underwent remarkably few external changes between prototype stage and production, these mainly involving the navigator's canopy glazing, the addition of supplementary air intake doors on the fuselage sides above the wing, and direct alignment of the outboard missile pylons with the wing fence. (*Vladimir Pushkaryev*)

3. The Tu-128M displayed in the outdoor museum area of the PVO's 148 Combat Training and Aircrew Conversion Centre at Savasleika. The aircraft shows signs of minor damage to the starboard air intake, sustained when it was being prepared for display. (*Sergey Burdin*)

4. As mentioned in the text, the original 1RSB-70-US-8 HF transceiver was replaced on some Tu-128s by the R-846OE *Prizma* system, with its associated antenna installed in a new more conventionally shaped fin tip. (*Vladimir Pushkaryev*)

5. This Tu-128UT 'Fiddler-C' trainer (Blue 15), seen at Rzhev, was operated by 350 AP at Bratsk before its withdrawal from service and was, in fact, the last Tu-128 to fly out of Bratsk on 15 September 1988. It was also the penultimate Tu-128 to land at Rzhev. (*Vladimir Pushkaryev*)

6. An interesting overhead view of the upper glazing of the navigator's canopy, which also shows the small fixed periscope installed on late-series Tu-128s. Although offering only a narrow field of view, it did compensate in small measure for the generally poor rearward visibility from this large interceptor. (*Vladimir Pushkaryev*)

7. A rare colour photograph of four Tu-128s parked ready to scramble from 72 AP's bleak QRA dispersal at Amderma. In spite of the extreme northern location of the 10th PVO Army airfields, the Tu-128 was too large to be provided with environmental shelters, either for QRA or normal operations. (*S. Shchelokov*)

8. This slightly less desolate view of 72 AP's QRA dispersal at Amderma in 1985 also shows an An-26 'Curl' transport taxiing out and a Yak-40 'Codling' and two Mi-8 'Hip' helicopters parked further down the broad taxiway. Note the proximity of the open sea to this very low lying airfield. (*Alexander Zhabkin*)

9. Instructors prepare their aircraft for a practical 'hands-on' lesson for students at the Military Aviation School for Mechanics at Nikulino (near Moscow). The school was also known by its 'internal' designation of *Voyskovaya Chast' N⁰ 03139* (Military Unit No. 03139). (*Viktor Kudryavtsev*)

10. In a scene that could be replicated the world over wherever teamwork is performed outside, *five* Soviet ground crew of 64 AP look on as *one* of their colleagues removes the tyre from the wheel of a Tu-128 at Omsk in 1983! (*S. Shchelokov*)

11. A pair of fully armed 64 AP Tu-128s is seen on the taxiway at Omsk in 1983. Although clearly ready for flight, with missile covers and engine blanks removed, it is not known what the objects are that can be seen suspended on the fuselage in the cockpit area. (*S. Shchelokov*)

12. The five crew members of one of 64 AP's 'big trainer', the Tu-124Sh 'Cookpot', pose in front of their aircraft at Omsk-North. Although transport aircraft have been used by other air forces for jet pilot and navigator training (notably the Vickers 'Varsity' in RAF service), the elegant 'Cookpot' was probably one of the few types to be used to train fighter pilots. (*S. Shchelokov*)

13. The fin was bolted to the fuselage by means of a four-point attachment between Frame Nos 51 and 55, the leading edge incorporating an air intake to cool the afterburner section and some rear-mounted generators. (*Alexander Melihov*)

14. The main undercarriage bogies of the Tu-128 were the largest and heaviest ever likely to be fitted to a fighter aircraft. The wheels retracted rearwards into Tupolev's 'signature' nacelles, with the rear doors opening only during retraction and extension. (*Alexander Melihov*)

15. The horizontal tail comprised two all-moving slab stabilizer sections, equipped with mass-balanced elevators. Each stabilizer half was carried on a supporting beam creating the axis of rotation, the beams being attached to the fuselage at Frame No. 55. (*Alexander Melihov*)

16. The flaps occupied the inboard and mid-section of the wing, from the wing root to the ailerons. Between the wing and the flaps there was a special structure known as the 'pre-flap curtain' (*predzakrylochnaya shtorka*), designed to fill the gap between the two surfaces. An aerodynamic 'fence' was mounted on the upper surface of the wing ahead of, but close to, the inboard section of the aileron, designed to reduce spanwise migration of the airflow along the wing. (*Alexander Melihov*)

17. An unusual view of the cockpit area of the Tu-128, showing the three upper windows in the navigator's canopy, the centrally mounted periscope and the original trapezoidal window on the fixed inter-canopy frame separating the two cockpits. Without the periscope, rearward vision was extremely limited. (*Alexander Melihov*)

18. The AA-5 'Ash' missiles were mounted on four APU-128 pylons which incorporated twin lateral rails designed to be used with the built-in winch installed in the forward section of the pylon. The winch was rarely if ever used, since the pylons were low enough for the armourers to manhandle the missiles into position without the use of mechanical aids. (*Alexander Melihov*)

19. The cockpits of the 'Fiddler' were typical of a 1960s-era radar-equipped interceptor which was never expected to be involved in visual engagements, providing mainly lateral and only limited forward and rearward views outside the aircraft. (*Alexander Melihov*)

20. Many Tupolev aircraft used bolts of different lengths depending on their application on the airframe and in order to simplify identification they were painted in different colours. Consequently, a 'colour key' was painted on a separate panel near the point of attachment for the benefit of maintenance personnel during disassembly and reassembly. (*Alexander Melihov*)

21. The last of the Tu-128UT 'Pelicans' displayed in the museum area on Rzhev airfield alongside a MiG-25 'Foxbat', facing another Tu-128 and a pair of Su-15 'Flagons'. Note that the rear doors of the undercarriage bogies on this aircraft are open. (*Vladimir Pushkaryev*)

22. Another view of the Tu-128UT at Rzhev, illustrating the rather dramatic design compromise accepted by Tupolev engineers when they added a third cockpit to produce a trainer variant of the 'Fiddler'. The new cockpit had to be mounted low in order to retain adequate forward visibility for the 'pilot under instruction' in the normal cockpit, but this afforded the instructor pilot very poor forward visibility. This was further compromised by distortion in the acutely angled glazing panels, as described in the text. (*Vladimir Pushkaryev*)

23. A close-up of the unusual nose extension of the Tu-128UT, which further emphasises the limited forward visibility for the instructor in this cockpit. The starboard nose panel has sustained damage when moving the aircraft for display. (*Vladimir Pushkaryev*)

24. Beginning with aircraft from c/n 1401, the shape of the window in the inter-canopy frame was changed from trapezoidal to circular, as seen on this aircraft displayed at Rzhev. This view further emphasises the fact that the Tu-128's heavy-framed canopies were never designed to facilitate visual interceptions. (*Vladimir Pushkaryev*)

25. Russian aircraft designers were not afraid of adopting complicated solutions to create training variants of their combat designs, the grafted-on drooped nose of the Tu-128UT being one of the most innovative and challenging. (*Alexander Arkhipov*)

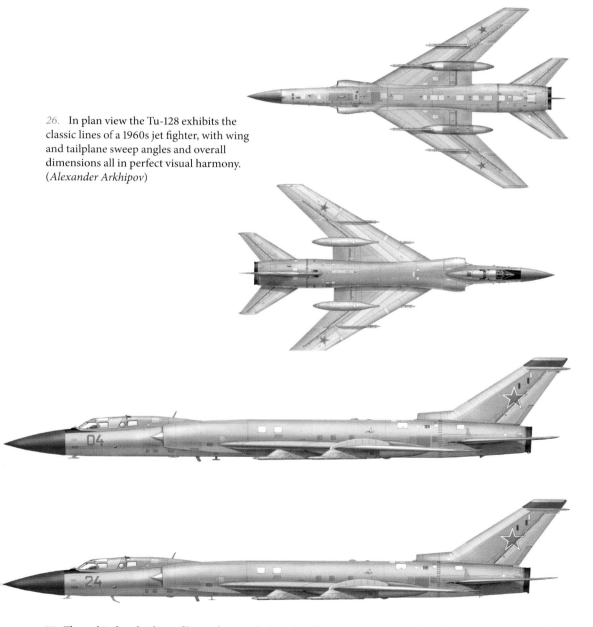

26. In plan view the Tu-128 exhibits the classic lines of a 1960s jet fighter, with wing and tailplane sweep angles and overall dimensions all in perfect visual harmony. (*Alexander Arkhipov*)

27. The unhindered side profile emphasises the length of the air intake ducts of the Tu-128. (*Alexander Arkhipov*)

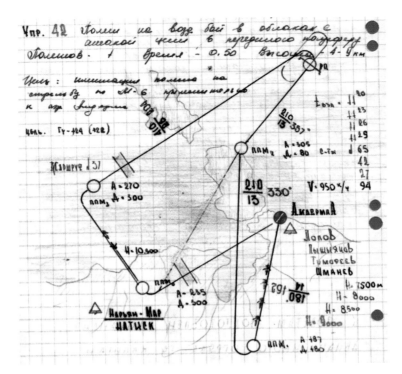

28. Exercise 42 from the KBP combat training manual, flown from Amderma airfield. This was a 30-minute forward hemisphere GCI engagement in cloud between 4,000 m and 9,000 m against M-6 heat-source targets and, here, a Tu-124 transport. Relevant colour-coded timings in red, blue, green and black plus related aircraft side numbers 65, 42, 27 and 94 and pilots' names and flight altitudes are shown on the right of the chart. Flight speed is 950 kph and the pilots' names are Popov, Pyshyanov, Timofyeyev and Shmanyev. All Soviet military aircrew of the period prepared these essential flight planning aids by hand, in the absence of the computer-based electronic facilities widely available to today's pilots and navigators. (*Nikolai Popov*)

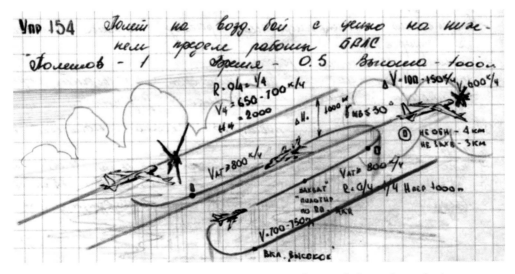

29. KBP Exercise 154 was a 30-minute, low-level GCI sortie flown at the lowest limit of radar performance (1,000 m), with target height and speed of 2,000 m and 650-700 kph and an attack speed of 800 kph. Height differential is 1,000 m, speed differential is 100-150 kph and the target is drawn as a notional B-52. (*Nikolai Popov*)

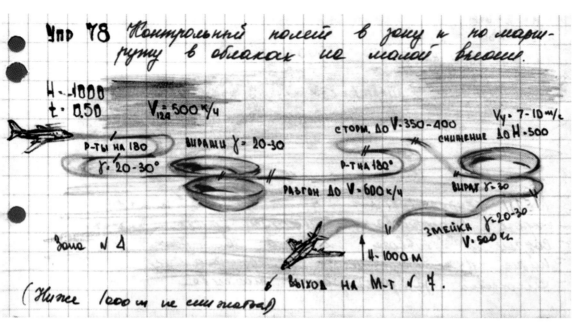

30. Handling Exercise 78 was flown in cloud and on a cross-country route at low level in the Tu-124 trainer, involving orbits at 20-30⁰ angle of bank down to 500 m and speed to 350-400 kph, acceleration to 600 kph and exit onto Route No. 7 at 1,000 m into Zone 4, with the command not to descend below 1,000 m. (*Nikolai Popov*)

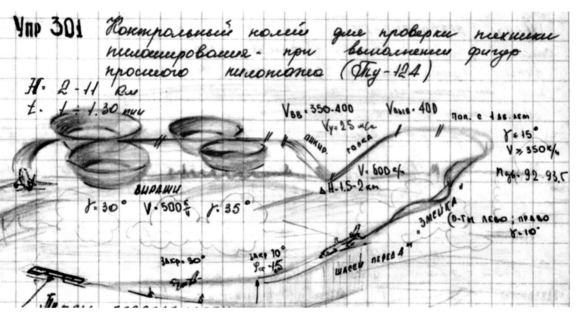

31. KBP Exercise 301 was a general handling exercise flown in the Tu-124 between 2,000 m and 11,000 m with a flight duration of an hour to 1 hour 30 minutes, involving two different orbit radii, asymmetric power, descents and steep climbs with a final 'snaking' descent to lose speed before settling onto the approach path. (*Nikolai Popov*)

32. This artistic study of the Tu-128 confirms the aptness of the NATO code-name 'Big Nose' for the aircraft's AI radar. (*Alexander Arkhipov*)

On some regiments the QRA hut was in the same building as the control tower, as at Amderma and Bratsk, with the ATC facilities eventually being shared with Aeroflot flight controllers and dispatchers at these joint-user airfields. Additionally, at Amderma, there was also separate accommodation for the duty pilot responsible for dispatching aircraft on QRA (*dezhurnyi lyotchik po vypusku samolyotov*). Capt. Vinokurov, a former section navigator on 518 AP at Talagi, describes the process of taking up QRA duty:

> It was obligatory to be given a briefing based on the latest military intelligence reports when we took up the QRA duty 'ritual'—(we always referred to this duty as a 'ritual'). These reports included intelligence on the composition and type of aircraft standing alert [QRA] at NATO bases in the northern sector. In the main we were briefed on the latest situation at Bodø in Norway and the current patrol area of the Norwegian Navy's intelligence-collection vessel *Marjata* in the Barents Sea. The 'ritual' took place on the airfield, alongside the operational readiness hut, on a specially assigned 'parade ground', with the senior officer always being one of the regiment commander's deputies.

In those areas with the highest potential risk of intrusion by foreign military aircraft, operational readiness was maintained even when regiments were converting onto a new type. For example, in 1985, a supplementary operational readiness flight was established on 72 AP at Amderma when 518 AP was converting onto

In the absence of sufficient hangars large enough to protect the Tu-128 fleet from the elements on their operating bases, aircraft were usually protected with profiled covers for the most vulnerable parts of the airframe. Here, a weather-protected Tu-128 of 518 AP is seen parked on the TEhCh dispersal at Talagi in the late 1970s. (*Ivan Rodyukov*)

the MiG-31 'Foxhound' at Talagi and had not yet been declared combat-ready. This lasted for several months until the 'Foxhound' crews had carried out their first missile firing practice against airborne targets over the Northern Fleet range and were authorised to perform QRA duty. In the summer period, when the permanent bases would usually undergo runway repairs if required, a Tu-128 regiment could relocate (in partial or full regimental strength) to a designated deployment airfield, known in PVO slang as a *podskok* (literally a 'hop' in gymnastics). If the runway repairs required a complete replacement of all the concrete surface slabs, then operational readiness would be organised at the deployment airfield (*aehrodrom 'podskoka'*). If they were of a minor nature, then the duty could be shared between the two airfields in turn, either on the basis of a 'day-night' roster or by a given number of days of operational readiness.

Aircraft at Readiness 1 on QRA were scrambled against airborne intruders quite frequently, with crews in the cockpit awaiting the order to launch. Not surprisingly, the northern Tu-128 regiments were scrambled from QRA most often, with some of the sorties being in response to Soviet aircraft that had violated ATC regulations (usually with malfunctioning IFF systems). However, most of the 'scrambles' were to escort foreign aircraft that had penetrated the 100 km (54 nm) exclusion zone off the coast of the USSR. On detection of a foreign aircraft approaching this zone over neutral waters, fighters from the operational readiness flight would be launched by the regiment responsible for the air defence of the zone in which the violating aircraft was detected. GCI controllers would then vector the fighter onto a heading parallel with the violator, in such a way that the Soviet aircraft would approach its target in the rear hemisphere with an aspect angle (*rakurs*) of not less than 2/4.[5] The intruder would be escorted with the interceptor maintaining lateral separation (*interval*) and distance (*distantsiya*) behind the target of 5-6 km (3-3.75 miles). If the intruding aircraft changed direction over neutral waters *before* actually entering the 100 km strip and took up a heading parallel to the edge of the exclusion zone, the interceptor had to fly parallel to it some 5-10 km (3-6.25 miles) from the zone boundary. In this situation the interceptor had to place itself between the intruder and the maritime border (coastline) of the USSR. Depending upon the time of day, visibility, type of interceptor, direction of flight and the intruder's distance from the state border, the following intervals and distances were maintained:

- in VMC conditions, an interval and distance of 3-4 km (1.75-2.5 miles) with a *rakurs* greater than 2/4;
- under data-link control, an interval and distance of no more than 3-5 km (1.75-3 miles) with a *rakurs* greater than 2/4.

When escorting an intruder, the radar was always kept in non-radiating (standby) mode.

In all cases whenever a foreign intruder entered the 100 km zone, the interceptor was vectored into such a position that it could, in the minimum possible time, set up for an attack if the intruding aircraft should actually attempt to violate the border. If an intruding aircraft got to within 20-30 km (12.5-18.75 miles) of the coastline the GCI controller was required to command the interceptor to set up the initial position for an attack. In all cases, the commands to switch on 'Warm-up' ('*Nakal*') and 'Radiation' ('*Izlucheniye*') modes of the *Smerch* radar were transmitted from the command post. Sometimes two fighters would be launched to escort an intruder, often from two neighbouring airfields. Interceptors were launched in such a way as to enable them to reach the state boundary line (maritime border) before an intruder could penetrate Soviet airspace. The first interceptor would be vectored onto the target to carry out an attack, or to force it to land at the nearest airfield, while the second would be directed to the initial position for an attack. During night-time intercepts against suspected foreign combat aircraft and intercepts in cloud, Soviet interceptors had to keep their navigation lights switched off. If the intercept was against a practice target (i.e. another Soviet aircraft), Soviet aircraft in violation of ATC regulations or foreign passenger and transport aircraft, the navigation lights remained on.

In the late 1960s, intelligence-gathering flights by NATO aircraft increased significantly over the northern waters of the USSR, the chief protagonist being the ubiquitous Boeing RC-135 series, operating close to or within the 100 km-wide exclusion zone over the Barents Sea and Kara Sea. The intensity of such flights increased whenever Soviet forces were carrying out live firing exercises on the Northern Fleet ranges. This period is recalled by one of the squadron navigators on 518 AP, Maj. Rodyukov:

American RC-135s, plus Norwegian and British reconnaissance aircraft [namely Royal Norwegian Air Force Grumman HU-16 'Albatross' and RAF De Havilland 'Comet 2CR' respectively], used to fly almost every day. [Because of their close proximity to the USSR, the Norwegians could have flown an Albatross almost every day, but the British Comets operated in the area very infrequently.] Sometimes, three reconnaissance aircraft at a time would fly [in our area]. This often happened when we were changing our IFF codes. Fighters from several airfields were held in readiness to intercept these targets, specifically from Rogachyovo, Amderma, Talagi, Kilp-Yavr, Afrikanda and Monchegorsk. There was a particular incident in the early 1980s when we were launched from QRA to intercept an American reconnaissance aircraft that had entered the 100-km exclusion zone. In the event, we weren't actually vectored onto the target but placed instead on airborne alert in the vicinity of Gremikha. There were some 'tiddlers'[6] already 'working' alongside the foreign aircraft. We were around 80 km [50 miles] from the intruder and would have been ordered to 'work' the target if it had been necessary to shoot it down.[7]

The PVO 10th Army's reconnaissance service had the responsibility of reporting foreign intelligence-gathering flights, with a special regiment devoted to 'radio-technical reconnaissance', i.e. signals intelligence, on behalf of the PVO fighter units. Continuous interception (*radioperekhvaty*) of NATO radio communications gave the PVO operators 1.5-2 hours' advance warning of possible reconnaissance flights over the Barents Sea and Kara Sea, as well as flight plans for operations out of Norwegian airfields for the following day. This information allowed PVO commanders to obtain timely warning of possible NATO air activity in the 10th Army's zone of responsibility. One of 350 AP's squadron navigators, Maj. Aleksandr Mamet, recalls a particular incident involving NATO air activity in the far north of the USSR:

> We had deployed [from our base at Bratsk] to Tiksi airfield to carry out a planned flying programme involving test flights and training of GCI controllers. About 30 minutes before the start of our flying programme an RC-135 suddenly turned up in the 100-km zone. The flight programme was changed, missiles were loaded onto our aircraft and one pair of Tu-128s was launched to conduct a combat air patrol [CAP] mission, with a second pair planned to take over from the first after an hour. After about 3 hours the RC-135 left the area, but [by then] we couldn't carry out our planned flights. On this occasion the situation continued for three days and although we'd changed the starting time of our flights, the RC-135 still appeared 30 minutes before. The normal procedure when escorting an intruder was to set up a rear echelon formation, with the target at a distance of around 5 km [3 miles], maintaining position between the target and the coastline. We were strictly forbidden from taking any provocative action during an interception. Of course, sometimes we would go in closer and even wave to each other. Each of us had our own jobs to do.

It was during one such close approach that the best known photograph of a Tu-128 was obtained, from a USAF 55SRW Boeing RC-135U on 29 June 1972, and subsequently published in aviation magazines around the world, albeit without explanation of the circumstances. (See the separate account of this incident in Appendix 1.)

The waters of the Barents Sea and the airspace above it came into the zone of responsibility of 518 AP at Talagi, while the Kara Sea and its associated airspace was the responsibility of 72 AP at Amderma. The deputy commander of 72 AP, Lt Col. Moiseyev, (in the 1970s a captain and section commander) remembers many interceptions made by the regiment's aircraft:

> The flight region and zone of responsibility for 72 AP was the 'Kara Pocket' ('*Karskiy meshok*'). The RC-135 used to pop up there quite frequently. In one three-year period I was involved in escorting foreign reconnaissance aircraft on nine separate

occasions. During these interceptions the *Lazur'* data-link guidance system proved itself to be particularly reliable and we used it from take-off to the landing approach (right down to the outer marker)!

The RC-135s would enter the 'Kara Pocket', a confined sea area between Novaya Zemlya, the Yamal Peninsula and the Russian mainland, approaching Soviet territory from over the North Pole, to undertake communications intelligence collection in the 'pocket' for periods of up to 6 hours. After carrying out their reconnaissance programme, the RC-135s would head off towards Arkhangel'sk and then 'round the corner' (*za ugol*) to Norway where they would refuel. After this, the aircraft would return for a second phase of intelligence collection, hanging around in the 'pocket' for several more hours. After detecting the presence of an intruding reconnaissance aircraft, PVO 'radio-technical troops' would broadcast the codewords '*polyarnaya sova*' (snowy owl) to initiate immediate shutdown of all radar stations in the area. This was done to prevent the network structure of the sites being identified by the potential adversary. The codeword was later changed to '*styena*' (wall).

Vyacheslav Gorshkov,[8] a former lieutenant in charge of a P-35 (NATO 'Bar Lock') search and acquisition radar unit supporting an S-200 (NATO SA-5 'Gammon') missile battalion based near Amderma in 1972, recalls his time in this northern outpost:

A routine 72 AP winter scene at Amderma with two aircraft taxiing onto the runway in take-off configuration. The aircraft in the foreground is a late-series Tu-128 modified to Tu-128M standard. Note the variation in flap angle between the inner and outer sections. (*Valeriy Yalyaev Archive*)

On hearing the codeword 'snowy owl' [or later 'wall'] only those radars that were tracking the intruder were kept switched on. My particular P-35 complex was part of a radio-technical [radar] battalion subordinate to the 11th Polar Radio-technical Regiment of the PVO's 4th Division, located at Amderma. The complex consisted of a radar operating in the centimetric waveband [3-30 GHz], transmitting via two parabolic antennas, with a horizontal span of around 10 m [33 feet], plus associated ground equipment including generators and support vehicles. Apart from me, the personnel strength of the unit consisted of several conscripts. There were four remote PPI displays fed from my radar in the air regiment command post. There was a camera mounted on one of them, with the state border and coastline precisely marked out on the radar screen. This was done so as to be able to produce subsequent evidence in the event that a foreign aircraft violated the state border. The three other displays were used by the regiment GCI controllers. The P-35 was used for a number of different tasks, including duty radar on a roster basis, flight watch support for 72 AP and tracking of foreign reconnaissance aircraft. In the summer months a reconnaissance aircraft would appear on an almost daily basis. On each occasion the duty QRA crew would be launched to escort the 'guest' away from Soviet territory. Two tracks would describe their intricate trajectories on the radar screen, although usually the Tu-128 would be positioned between the target and the border or coastline of the USSR. Only occasionally did the foreign intruder manage to set up a cunning feint and place 'our' [Tu-128] crew behind it, then make a dash for the border. This used to cause some consternation in the regiment command post, which was co-located with the Amderma radio-technical battalion. However, the 'rules of propriety' were observed and before reaching the coastline the intruder would make a sharp turn and head off back into the 'neutral zone'.

During exercises and when escorting LRAF bombers on routine training flights, the Tu-128s from 518 AP at Talagi and 72 AP from Amderma also flew sorties taking them over the North Atlantic and the Barents Sea north of the Kola Peninsula. On these occasions the 'Fiddlers' themselves were sometimes escorted by NATO fighters.

Coincident with the introduction of the Tu-128 into PVO service, and in consequence of the considerable range capability of the aircraft, it became necessary to clarify the boundary limits for early warning of airborne targets. It was now particularly important to detect targets as soon as possible and then to inform Tu-128 operational readiness forces in order to maximise exploitation of the aircraft's long-range interception performance. The required early warning boundary was calculated from the time of initial detection of an intruder to take-off and flight out to the intercept point. For the Tu-128 it was accepted that:

- the time taken to go from Readiness 1 to take-off was 6 minutes;
- the time lapse in providing information about the target was 5.5 minutes;
- the 'decision time' and transmission of command to take-off was 1.5 minutes.

Different flight modes were used to intercept targets, depending upon the speed and altitude of the intruder, GCI radar detection range, or the designated intercept boundary, and were based on the use or non-use of afterburner. The following programmes for reaching the assigned interception altitude and speed were used:

- the Afterburner Programme (*Forsazhnaya Programma*) for short-range interceptions;
- the Cruise Programme (*Kreiserskaya Programma*);
- the Combined Programme (*Kombinirovannaya Programma*).

The 'cruise' and 'combined' programmes were used for long-range interceptions. The selected flight programme was transmitted from the command post (GCI station) and shown on the pilot's TS-7 and navigator's TS-8 instrument panel display in the following form:

- indicator lights (K) and (F) *not* illuminated—meant that the entire flight was to be carried out in 'cruise' mode;
- indicator light (K) illuminated (denoting 'combined' mode)—after take-off and before receiving the command to select afterburner, the flight was to be conducted in 'cruise' mode until receiving the visual command (F) meaning *Forsazh* (afterburner) or (S) meaning *Snizheniye* (descent);
- indicator light (F) *alone* indicated *Forsazhnyi rezhim* ('afterburner' mode).

The Pilots' Notes for the Tu-128 included the following instructions:

The Afterburner Programme, when attacking high-altitude targets, is flown with the engines in full reheat mode from take-off to the end of intercept (break-off from attack) in the following sequence:

- take-off and climb to 11,000 m (36,090 feet) in afterburner (engine rpm 100 per cent or 96 per cent) at 950 kph (510 kts) true air speed (TAS);
- acceleration at constant altitude to TAS 1,300 kph (700 kts) or 1,400 kph (755 kts);
- climb at a constant TAS of 1,300 kph or 1,400 kph to the assigned altitude for the attack, or until receiving the command '*gorka*' (zoom climb).

A speed of 1,400 kph is only recommended in ISA conditions when performing a rear hemisphere attack against targets flying at altitudes up to 17,000 m (55,775 feet) and at speeds between 1,100 and 1,250 kph (595-675 kts).

Flight using the Combined Programme is carried out in the following sequence:

- take-off in afterburner, switching off afterburner at a height of not less than 200 m (656 feet) at an indicated air speed of not less than 450 kph (245 kts);
- climb to 9,500 m (31,170 feet) in maximum dry thrust and 870 kph (470 kts) TAS;
- cruise at 9,500 m and 920 kph (497 kts) TAS;
- when commanded by GCI, select afterburner and climb to 11,000 m (36,090 feet) at 950 kph (512 kts) TAS, carrying out remainder of flight as per the Afterburner Programme.

Flight using the Cruise Programme is carried out in the following sequence:

- take-off in afterburner, switching off afterburner at a height of not less than 200 m (656 feet) at an indicated air speed of not less than 450 kph (245 kts);
- climb to 9,500 m (31,170 feet) in maximum dry thrust and 870 kph (470 kts) TAS;
- cruise at 9,500 m and 920 kph (497 kts) TAS;
- after switching on the *Smerch* radar HT power supply, remainder of flight flown at 950 kph (512 kts) TAS until break-off from the attack.

Interception of targets flying below 10,000 m (32,800 feet), within an unlimited control and reporting zone (i.e. the long-range interception option), is flown in accordance with the following programme:

- take-off in afterburner, switching off afterburner at a height of not less than 200 m (656 feet) at an indicated air speed of not less than 450 kph (245 kts);
- climb to 9,500 m (31,170 feet) in maximum dry thrust and 870 kph (470 kts) TAS;
- cruise at 9500 m and 920 kph (497 kts) TAS;
- when commanded by GCI, descend to attack altitude with engines at 'Flight Idle' and an indicated air speed of 800 kph (432 kts) (without exceeding Mach 0.95).

The following fuel remainder figures for the Tu-128, at an altitude of 11,000 m (36,090 feet) and 80 km (44 nm) from a designated landing airfield, were used to calculate the limits of the intercept boundaries:

- descent to the airfield from 11,000 m (36,090 feet) to 5,000 m (16,400 feet) required 200 kg (440 lb);

- circuit entry to the third turn and approach for landing required 650 kg (1,430 lb);
- overshoot and second landing approach required 1,000 kg (2,200 lb);
- second overshoot and climb to 2,000 m (6,560 feet) required 350 kg (770 lb).

It can therefore be seen that the minimum fuel remainder required for over-shoots and landing in IFR or 'complex meteorological conditions' (*Slozhniye Meteorolgicheskie Usloviya* or SMU) was 2,200 kg (4,850 lb).

When planning to land at an airfield within a radius of 250 km (135 nm) of the point of intercept, the interception boundaries, based on required fuel remainder, were as follows:

- in 'cruise' mode with a forward hemisphere engagement—1,965 km (1,060 nm);
- in 'combined' mode with a forward hemisphere engagement—1,580 km (853 nm);
- in 'afterburner' mode with a forward hemisphere engagement—685 km (370 nm);
- in 'afterburner' mode with a rear hemisphere engagement—490 km (265 nm).

A fuel remainder of 2,800 kg (6,170 lb) was sufficient to facilitate landing from an altitude of 11,000 m (36,090 feet) in IFR (SMU) conditions at an airfield within 250 km (135 nm) of the point of intercept. At first glance, it might appear that 250 km was too arbitrary to factor into a dynamically changing scenario and that an airfield located so conveniently close to the point of intercept was more a matter of serendipity than precise planning. However, it must be remembered that PVO Aviation had at its disposal a number of 'ice airfields' (*lyedoviye aehrodromy*) in the far north that could be used in case of necessity when recovering a Tu-128 from a 'live' intercept sortie.

12

Ground-controlled Interception using the Lazur' *Data-link System*

Air defence and military aviation operations in the USSR at the end of the 1950s were marked by a rush to automate the control functions for ground and air forces, and Soviet industry developed a number of automatic control systems (*avtomatizirovanniye sistyemy upravlyeniya*) for this purpose. The first of these was the *Luch-1* (Beam-1) system for the air defence missile force and the *Vozdukh-1S* (Air-1S) system for Soviet Air Force fighters, as well as *Vozdukh-1P* and later *Vozdukh-1M* equipment for PVO interceptors, and by the mid-1960s, the first automated systems had been fielded by operational units. Initially, the units responsible for servicing the equipment were subordinate to the communications directorate of the PVO troops. However, the complexity of the tasks handled by these automated systems, the need to resolve design problems, plus issues with their assembly and operation, led to the creation in 1965 of a department for automated systems for the PVO's Central Command under the Head of Radio-technical (Radar) Troops. The department included groups responsible for the operational application of automated systems, as well as a repair and maintenance group. It was only in 1975 that a specialised directorate attached to PVO HQ was established, with the title of Directorate of Automation of PVO Troops (*Upravlyenie Avtomatizatsii Voysk PVO*). However, in the 1960s, Soviet military higher command authorities and staff officers at various levels had viewed the new disciplines of cybernetics and computing rather sceptically and did not understand the need for their use.

It was in this climate of increasing technological sophistication, encouraged by science and industry but accepted less enthusiastically by the Soviet military hierarchy, that the Tu-128 began to enter service. Initially, this did not bode well for the new aircraft, since the principal intercept guidance method for the aircraft was to be a newfangled 'instrument guidance' (*pribornoye navyedyenie*) procedure using the *Vozdukh-1* data-link system (the components of which were described in Chapter 3). Command posts and GCI stations were equipped with vehicle-mounted *Kaskad-M* ('Cascade-M') computer systems that calculated the appropriate intercept geometry using the raw target and interceptor tracks from GCI radars. This data was then converted into encoded guidance commands transmitted to the interceptor by the associated *Lazur'-M* data-link. The 'Cascade-M' system possessed one particularly important feature, in that the programmes for climb and acceleration to the assigned interception speed were not firmly linked to the guidance stages in the horizontal plane. This allowed the GCI controller to participate actively in the selection and forming of the interceptor's optimal flight mode in the guidance process. This in turn made it possible to have a more creative approach to the ground control of the interceptor and react more flexibly to the changing air situation. However, 'instrument guidance' using the *Lazur'* data-link was introduced into PVO fighter operations only rather slowly and over a very long period of time. This is recalled by Col. Komyagin:

> At first *Lazur'* worked rather poorly because of problems with equipment reliability and poor training of maintenance personnel. The ideal situation was supposed to be an interception during which you would be vectored onto the target without speaking on the radio (*molcha*), carry out an attack without speaking, return to base without speaking, and only [resort to the radio to] report that your undercarriage was down. Such flights *did* occasionally happen, but it was quite a rare event when they did.

Sometimes GCI controllers who were present in a command post or GCI station to check that the *Lazur'* equipment was working normally would ask Tu-128 crews to confirm by voice communications (*golosom*) that they were receiving the commands. The ground component of the system not only allowed the guidance commands to be generated automatically but also allowed the GCI controller to insert manually generated commands if necessary. In this case the guidance calculations were carried out separately, then inserted into the data transmission unit (*apparatura pyeredachi dannykh*) and transmitted to the aircraft. To the outside observer it might seem that the system was working automatically, but with manually inserted data it was not possible to achieve smooth continuous control of the aircraft and GCI stations were never able to deceive experienced pilots using this 'subterfuge'. (It should be noted here that this would only apply in the case where the *Lazur'* data-link commands were being fed through the aircraft's autopilot—this aspect of *Lazur'* operation is dealt with later in this chapter.)

In the mid-1960s, PVO Aviation units already fielded a small range of types equipped with the *Lazur'* 'instrument guidance' GCI system, namely the comparatively old Su-9 'Fishpot-A' and 'Fishpot-B', as well as the newer Su-11 'Fishpot-C' and Yak-28P 'Firebar-A' interceptors. However, GCI guidance of the Tu-128 compared with these other aircraft exhibited substantial differences in consequence of increased endurance and a better weapons system, although it had slightly worse climb and acceleration performance compared with other PVO fighters. The differences included:

- forward hemisphere intercept capability;
- large aspect angle (angle off) intercept capability;
- capability of intercepting targets with a significant height differential (targets above the interceptor);
- AI radar with long detection and lock-on ranges;
- significantly increased intercept boundaries, making it necessary to hand over control of the Tu-128 from one command post or GCI station to another. In this case the guidance process was divided into two stages:

  * launch of interceptors from QRA Readiness 1 using normal air defence warning data, vectoring them into the 'system coverage area' (*zona dyeistviya*) of the neighbouring command post or GCI station and hand-over of control;
  * data-link (instrument) guidance using *Kaskad-M* in the 'system coverage area' of the neighbouring command post or GCI station.

The main characteristic of a forward hemisphere engagement was the high closing speed and the consequent limited time for detection, lock-on and destruction of the target, and it was essential to have sufficient time to correct any GCI guidance errors. The minimum time for the interceptor to close with the target before reaching missile launch range had to be, as a rule, not less than one minute. In order to achieve this, the GCI controller had to vector the interceptor to a distance (i.e. a spatial point) no greater than the maximum target detection range, regardless of the aspect angle for the attack. The capability for carrying out forward hemisphere intercepts substantially increased the overall effectiveness of the Tu-128 weapons system since this made possible both an extension of the intercept boundaries and an interception of targets flying at speeds greater than the interceptor itself. In the opinion of Col. Yevglyevskiy, the Tu-128 was:

… in fact, the first aircraft which allowed us to launch missiles in the forward hemisphere. The Su-9 could not do this at all. The Yak-28P, which had started to enter service, was 'officially' capable of forward hemisphere engagements, but the effectiveness of the aircraft in this regime was very low. Although we trained pilots in the technique, the Yak-28P's radar [*known as* Oryol *(Eagle), or NATO 'Skip Spin'—A.D.*] with which the aircraft was equipped and the high closing speeds made this a rather fictitious claim. The forward hemisphere attack was the main intercept procedure for the Tu-128. A rear hemisphere engagement was a back-up procedure, a second attack, planned to be used in case of missing the target on the first attack.

Another noteworthy feature of a Tu-128 interception compared with that of other PVO fighters was the operation of the *Smerch* AI radar, as recalled by squadron navigator Maj. Aleksandr Mamet:

> The AI radar of the Tu-128 was a very capable piece of equipment. When searching for a target the first thing that appeared on the radar screen was a 'halo' from the target and only after this did the actual target 'blip' appear. The detection range depended to a large extent upon the radar cross section (RCS) of the target and the Tu-16 bomber could be detected at around 40-50 km [25-30 miles] and a MiG-23 fighter at 30-40 km [20-25 miles]. Of course, the Tu-128 could not detect a target against a terrain background [i.e. it did not have a 'look-down' mode], but on the other hand it did have an all-aspect capability of 'seeing' the target.

However, in the early years of operating the aircraft, target aspect angles in both forward and rear hemisphere engagements were limited to between 0/4 (i.e. directly ahead or behind the target) and 1/4 (i.e. a position one quarter to the left or right of the nose or tail of the target). These restrictions were set by the performance limitations of the early RV-80 radar fuses on the R-4 (AA-5 'Ash') missiles but were lifted on later batches.

During GCI guidance, the interceptor had to be vectored to a specific altitude depending upon the altitude and speed of the target. Additionally, the azimuth angles within which it was possible to vector the Tu-128 during GCI also depended upon target altitude and speed and were defined by the following criteria:

- for a target flying at up to 21,000 m (68,900 feet) and up to 2,000 kph (1,080 kts), the target azimuth angle for forward hemisphere engagement was not to exceed 30°;
- for a target flying at up to 21,000 m and at 1,600 kph (864 kts), the target azimuth angle for a forward hemisphere engagement was not to exceed 45°;
- for a target flying at up to 21,000 m and at 1,100 kph (594 kts) there were no target azimuth angle limitations.

High-speed targets were intercepted by the Tu-128 only in forward hemisphere engagements, a consequence of the comparatively limited speed and manoeuvrability capabilities of the aircraft. In order to execute a successful rear hemisphere attack a comparatively high closing speed was required, such as was possible with the Su-9, for example, but not achievable with the 'Fiddler'. As a result, the Tu-128's weapons system could not generate the 'Launch Permitted' (PR) command in a rear hemisphere engagement, so the forward hemisphere engagement, in concert with the long-range detection capability of the *Smerch* radar, compensated for the aircraft's relatively poor speed performance. However, the aircraft did exhibit a more positive feature, as described by Col. Yevglyevskiy:

> With the Tu-128 it wasn't necessary to get right onto the tail of a target as was case with the Su-9. Whereas on the Su-9 missile launch took place at a distance of 2 km [1.25 miles] from the target, on the Tu-128 it was possible to launch a missile from around 18-20 km [11-12.5 miles] and, moreover, the target could be significantly higher than the interceptor. Absolute precision guidance wasn't required—the radar was capable of reliable target detection over a wide spectrum of ranges and azimuth values, whereas the Su-9 had to be guided very precisely onto the target and if there was the slightest deviation then you'd have to break off the attack.

As already mentioned, the main GCI guidance method adopted for the Tu-128 was an automated 'instrument guidance' procedure, which for a typical interception could be divided into two stages or phases:

- ground-controlled guidance (*nazyemnoye navyedyeniye*);
- on-board (aircraft) controlled guidance (*bortovoye navyedyeniye*).

During the ground-controlled guidance phase, the aircraft was controlled via commands from the *Vozdukh-1M* data-link system and in preparation for this, immediately after take-off, at a height of 300-500 m (985-1,640 feet) the navigator would switch the radar to standby mode (*predvarityel'noye vklyucheniye*). After being vectored to the initial guidance point (*iskhodnaya tochka navyedyeniya*), defined as the moment when the aircraft was 'locked on to' by the *Lazur'* data-link, the pilot would start to fly the aircraft using commands passed by the ARL-S data-link. (The abbreviation ARL-S stands for *Avtomaticheskaya Radiokomandnaya Liniya-Samolyotnaya*, meaning literally 'Automatic Radio-command-Link-Aircraft', the generic term for the *Lazur'* equipment mounted in the aircraft. The name *Lazur'* applies to the entire system, i.e. the ground component *and* the airborne component, the suffix 'M' being added when a limited low-altitude capability was introduced on the upgraded Tu-128M; the suffix 'M' in ARL-SM stands for '*malaya vysota*', or 'low-altitude'.)

Maj. Rodyukov describes the actions taken by the crew:

> As soon as the aircraft was on the runway it would be captured by *Lazur'*. The heading which the aircraft had to maintain after take-off was immediately set on the course selector and after lifting off the runway, *Lazur'* would start to pass continuous

guidance commands to be flown by the pilot. On aircraft of the first series, the following parameters were displayed on the 'Put'-4P' integrated flight and navigation system indicators in both cockpits:

- differences between the assigned and current heights of the interceptor [shown on the NKP-4K indicators and the PP-1PMK flight instruments];
- assigned heading [on the NKP-4K indicator, using the assigned course marker ZK (*Zadannyi Kurs*)];
- differences between the assigned and current headings;
- lateral motion commands [using the command indicator bars of the PP-1PMK, which was also used on landing to show heading];
- vertical motion commands.

The assigned interception height (altitude) was set on the ZVS height selector by the navigator, using information on the assigned flight regime shown on his TS-8 display, the final speed of the interceptor and target altitude. When the regiments were converting onto the Tu-128 a number of difficulties arose with pilots trying to master the 'instrument guidance' method of GCI. Maj. Rodyukov remembers these problems:

Many of the older pilots did not fly the Tu-128 using the ILS system, so they had a poor understanding of the use of the command bar indications on the PP-1PMK flight director. After all, it was with the help of these indications that GCI guidance was performed using the *Vozdukh-1M* system. 'Instrument guidance' was flown without using any voice commands, but the majority of pilots had become very accustomed to GCI guidance relying solely on the GCI controller's voice commands. Before the introduction of *Vozdukh-1M* and *Lazur'*, a GCI controller would give a typical call over the radio, such as, for example, '515 [the pilot's individual callsign]— right 30 [degrees], altitude 8 [thousand metres]'. With 'instrument guidance' no one spoke—only an illuminated sign would light up with the relevant legend—ПП (PP) for *Peryednyaya Polusfyera* [a forward hemisphere] engagement, Ф (F) for *Forsazh* [afterburner], etc. During exercises, pilots would fly the entire sortie from take-off to landing without using voice calls …

After reaching cruising altitude (for a long-range interception) or the acceleration altitude (for an interception in 'afterburner' mode) the navigator would set the altitude on the ZVS stabilized height selector, depending upon the target's flight parameters and the aspect angle of the attack. When intercepting targets flying at altitudes below 10,000 m (32,800 feet), the vertical separation of the Tu-128 relative to the target had to be not less than:

- 1,000 m (3,280 feet) when attacking in the forward hemisphere;
- 500 m (1,640 feet) in a rear hemisphere attack; vertical separation had to be 200-300 m (660-985 feet) against targets flying at heights of 500-600 m (1,640-1,970 feet).

After carrying out the task, on the return to the airfield, the navigator would set an altitude of 11,000 m (36,090 feet) and would report all altitude changes on the ZVS height selector to the pilot.

The ZK assigned course signal came from the *Lazur'-M* data-link, and the current heading and altitude from the KS-6B course system and TsSV-1M-1V central air data computer. In the event of there being a difference of more than 500 m (1,640 feet) between the assigned and current altitudes, a vertical 'command to fly' signal was generated. On later-series Tu-128s, the pilot's workload during data-link (instrument) guidance was eased and he was then able to fly the aircraft by reference to steering commands on the PP-1PMK indicator alone. This meant he could focus all his attention on one indicator, rather than the two required previously (i.e. the NKP-4K and the PP-1PMK). The heading was flown by keeping the vertical director needle of the PP-1PMK indicator in the centre of the dial, without allowing it to move outside the central white ring, while the climb was performed according to the assigned flight profile. The pilot monitored the flight profile by periodically checking the position of the 'glideslope' command bar on the PP-1PMK and the horizontal bar of the NKP-4K indicator. This guaranteed that the heading and assigned altitude would be maintained correctly. The required flight speed was shown on the KUSI-2500 combined speed indicator, with an additional speed indicator, or *indeks*, used by the pilot to maintain the assigned speed produced by the '*Lazur'-M*' data-link. Later aircraft had the UISMI (*Ukazatyel' Istinnoy Skorosti i chisla M s Indeksom*) combined true air speed indicator and Machmeter, with the *indeks* needle, which was like the needle of an analogue alarm clock, commanded by the *Lazur'* data-link to align with the speed that the pilot had to maintain during an intercept.

An important feature of the Tu-128 was that it was designed from the outset to be capable of being flown automatically from the ground with the aid of the *Lazur'-M* data-link when commands from the latter were fed to the autopilot. However, this capability was only fully implemented some considerable time after its entry into service with the PVO, as Col. Yevglyevskiy recalls:

When *Lazur'* was linked to the autopilot it became obvious that it was quite unpleasant [for the pilot] to have the aircraft flown under automatic control from the ground. It has to be said, however, that in normal flight the autopilot itself operated very smoothly. There were, of course, occasional slight jolts and juddering [in the control circuit], albeit fairly insignificant, but when the autopilot was linked to the *Lazur'* system the jolts became very severe. The control column would vibrate severely or the aircraft would drop a wing etc. Altogether, it was rather unpleasant and quite similar to the action of the autopilot in the 'Return to level flight mode', where two very sharp movements in pitch and roll would restore control after exceeding the limiting angle of attack or angle of bank. [This mode was selected using a special button on the control column.] The movements were so sharp that it felt like some kind of knocking in the control circuit. It was very unpleasant.

Consequently, the automatic control option linking AP-7P autopilot operation with the *Lazur'* data-link was not used by the Tu-128 regiments.

When performing a data-link assisted intercept, the pilot was presented with a series of 'on/off' commands shown on his TS-7 display, the same commands also being shown on the navigator's TS-8 display. (These are known in Russian as *razoviye komandy* or 'one-time' commands.) Illumination of the symbol (П) (English P) on the displays meant that the intercept was to be a forward hemisphere engagement, so the pilot would have to disengage the IR-guided missiles Nos 1 and 2 using the appropriate 'Switch off missiles' selector. The two IR-guided 'Ash' missiles would also be disengaged when the attack was to be into the sun (or towards the moon in bright moonlight conditions) if the target and the sun or moon were within an angle of 25° of each other. When transferring data-link guidance of the Tu-128 from one GCI station to another, an exclamation mark (!) symbol indicated hand-over of control, accompanied by an audio signal. This control transfer procedure was known as *vzaimodyeystviye* (meaning 'interaction' or 'co-operation') or transfer to new data (i.e. control by another GCI station) and simply required the pilot to depress the (ABT) (transliterated abbreviation of *AV Tomaticheski* or auto) button on the LAS-23M (*Liniya Avtomaticheskoy Svyazi*) data-link control panel. Termination of the audio signal and extinguishing of the red ABT light indicated automatic transfer to the new data-link settings. It was also possible to manually select data-link control by a new GCI station.

Illumination of the symbols (<) or (>) on the displays alerted the crew to the fact that they were to make a left or right turn, the actual heading being shown on the dial of the PP-1PMK flight indicator. The pilot then had to keep the heading pointer within the limits of the central white ring. The NKP-4K indicator served in this case as a source of supplementary information if required. On reaching a distance to target of approximately 100 km (62 miles) the command symbol (H) [English N], standing for НАКАЛ ('*Nakal*') and meaning warm-up of electronic equipment, would appear on the navigator's TS-8 display, while (100) would illuminate on the pilot's TS-7 display. The navigator would inform the pilot that he had received the commands and had checked that the warm-up command had been passed to the missile control unit. On reaching a distance to target of 60 km (37 miles), the command (60) was passed by data-link and HT for the *Smerch* radar was switched on automatically. This coincided with automatic control of the *Smerch* antenna dish in azimuth and elevation. On illumination of the (60)-kilometre warning light on his TS-7 display, the pilot would check the position of the switches on the weapons control panel, awaiting the navigator's confirmation of target identification and its azimuth and elevation.

In a data-link assisted GCI intercept, using the *Vozdukh-1M* system and its associated *Kaskad-M* and *Lazur'-M* ground and airborne components, the main spatial parameters passed to the *Smerch* radar were:

- interceptor and target azimuth;
- interceptor and target elevation;
- interceptor and target range;
- closing speed of the Tu-128 with the target.

The first two commands were used to set up automatic control from the ground of the radar's scan pattern in azimuth and elevation to facilitate timely target detection, tracking and lock-on. Slewing the scan axis to the right or left by an angle of 40° was performed when the difference between target azimuth and current heading of the Tu-128, as an absolute value, was greater than 20°. Automatic control of scan elevation provided vertical coverage within the range −3.5° to +52.5°. The last two commands, concerning range and closing speed, were used by the weapons system computer to generate a guidance solution in the event that the radar was jammed. Using this data, the computer generated the commands necessary for the prosecution of a successful attack, synthesizing the following parameters:

- distance for the commencement of a zoom climb;
- maximum permitted missile launch range;
- minimum permitted missile launch range;
- range of end of target illumination;
- minimum safe distance to commence 'break-off' from attack;
- horizontal and vertical components of targeting error;
- horizontal and vertical components of permitted targeting error.

From these values, *Lazur'-M* generated the spatial target designation 'picture' required to control the *Smerch* radar automatically, in the form of discrete data.

			Increments	Range of values
Limits of displayed data and incremental values of *Lazur'-M* transmissions				
Command	Unit of measurement	Indication limits	of displayed values	used by *Smerch* AI radar
Azimuth from interceptor to target	degrees	0-360	2.8	0-360
Elevation of interceptor to target	degrees	±42	2.8	0-42
Range from interceptor to target	kilometres	0-100	0.8	0-45.6
Closing speed with target	kph	0-7,200	72	0-4,800

When operating the *Smerch* radar in manual mode, the navigator switched on the HT power supply and slewed the antenna in the following manner:

- in azimuth, by determining the difference between the direction of the target (angular heading of target) and the present heading of his own aircraft. With a difference of more than 20° between the two headings he would slew the antenna so as to equalise this value. Information regarding this difference was passed to the navigator from the GCI station over the radio. Shifting of the scan zone in azimuth was shown by illumination of lights around the edge of the radar screen.
- in elevation, by tilting the *Smerch* antenna dish according to pre-established data on a special graph.

Situations often arose in data-link assisted intercepts where it was necessary to vector the aircraft onto a new target, the pilot receiving this information by illumination of the exclamation mark (!) command, indicating 'Re-targeting'. On receipt of that command, all other lights on the pilot's TS-7 display would go out, apart from the one indicating 'Re-targeting'. Commencement of guidance using new data was indicated when the exclamation mark signal was extinguished, followed by illumination of one or other of the indicator lights: (<) for 'Left', (!) for 'Straight Ahead' or (>) for 'Right'.

With the radar fully powered up (i.e. with HT switched on), the navigator would then look for a target blip on the screen and identify it as friend or foe as appropriate (the former indicated by an identification marker under the blip). If the blip was stable, the navigator would gate the target using the antenna control joystick and then squeeze the 'Lock-on' (*Zakhvat*) trigger on the joystick. It was essential to achieve lock-on after the appearance of three or four stable target blips, with the marker inside the 'gate' (not less than one-third in from the edge), since a premature attempt could result in breaking lock-on. A second attempt could only be made around 8-12 seconds after loss of lock-on, albeit usually leading to the attack being aborted if it was a forward hemisphere engagement, since there would be insufficient time to repeat the procedure. Lock-on was indicated by illumination of the *Zakhvat* light on the framework of the radar screen, with the radar automatically switching to automatic tracking mode and the following symbols appearing on the screen:

- two parallel horizontal markers—the targeting zone;
- a bright-up—target error marker;
- a marker to the right of the range scale—current range marker.

The on-board guidance stage (*bortovoye navyedyenie*) effectively commenced from the moment when the radar locked on to the target, during which the pilot would correct any targeting errors in the horizontal plane and maintain altitude and speed in accordance with the assigned flight regime. This involved the pilot keeping the vertical director needle of the PP-1PMK within the central white circle. A vertical 'gorka' (zoom climb) manoeuvre was used to set up the best conditions for missile launch against a high-flying target by reducing targeting errors, minimising the height differential between interceptor and target and reducing the radar's required auto-tracking angle. The targeting errors processed by the guidance computer were converted by the *Put'-4P* system into piloting commands and displayed on the PP-1PMK flight indicator. The pilot then had to attempt to nullify these piloting errors by keeping the vertical and horizontal needles of the PP-1PMK indicator in the centre of the white circle on the dial. On illumination of the (↑) 'gorka' light on the TS-7 display, the pilot had to put the aircraft into a 'gentle' zoom climb, pulling no more than 2.3-2.5 g, but only when flying supersonically above 10,000 m (32,800 feet), with the target 3,000-4,000 m (9,840-13,125 feet) higher than the interceptor.

If, at the start of the zoom climb, the pilot pulled more than 2.5 g, then he would have to reduce the loading to 2-2.3 g by gently pushing the control column forward and maintain this until reaching a pitch angle of 17-20°. However, the 'Fiddler' was not permitted to exceed a pitch angle of 25° when performing a zoom climb. Equally, if the angle of bank was greater than 30° before commencing a zoom climb, then the pilot had to reduce this to 20-30° and only then commence the climb manoeuvre. Moreover, any heading errors had to be corrected during the zoom climb, keeping the vertical director needle in the central white ring of the PP-1PMK indicator. During the climb the pilot kept an eye on the AUASP combined angle of attack and g-meter, the KUSI-2500 combined speed indicator and the PP-1PMK flight indicator, without allowing the aircraft to exceed any dangerous flight parameters. Exit from a zoom climb had to begin when the indicated air speed had dropped to 500 kph (270 kts). In the early years of Tu-128 operations, pilots were briefed to maintain a g-loading of 0.3-0.5 on exit from a zoom climb at an indicated

During training exercises, interception results were registered by the KZA on-board data-recording system. This photograph, showing part of the pilot's instrument panel, was taken by that system's PAU-476 camera. The small white placard above the PP-1PMK flight director carries handwritten details of the KBP exercise number (324), the pilot's callsign (23373), aircraft Bort number (21) and the date. Although not particularly clear, the three-bladed propeller-shaped 'Ready to Fire' light is illuminated for the No. 2 infrared (starboard inboard) missile, immediately to the right of the placard. At top centre, the 'Ready to Fire' light is illuminated for the No. 3 (port outboard) semi-active missile. This combination indicates that the aircraft was performing a rear hemisphere attack. The PP-1PMK indicator shows that the pilot is performing a gentle climbing right turn with around 25° angle of bank. The g-meter at bottom right shows that he is pulling just over 1 g. (*Alexander Nikolayev*)

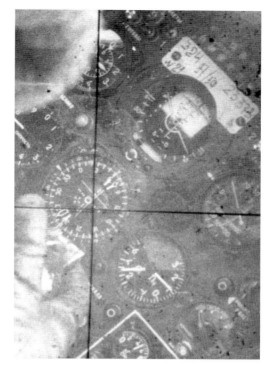

air speed not exceeding 450 kph (245 kts) and not to allow the speed to drop below 380 kph (205 kts) at exit. However, these parameters were later amended to 0.5 g, 500 kph (270 kts) and 400 kph (216 kts) respectively. Switching off the afterburners, closing the throttles and increasing the g-loading beyond 0.5 were permitted only in the descent phase of the zoom climb at a speed of less than 500 kph.

However, it must be said that Tu-128 pilots made every endeavour not to perform the zoom climb manoeuvre, as explained here by Col. Komyagin:

> Was it really possible to describe this manoeuvre by the Tu-128 as a *zoom* climb?! You only had to pull the stick back a little way and the warning lights and alarm bells of the AUASP [angle of attack indicator] would come on. The navigator would then come up on the intercom, saying, 'Gently, commander!' He, of course, also had his own AUASP indicator and alarm bells in his cockpit. [In effect, rather than performing a zoom climb,] we just raised the aircraft's nose and fired. The closer we were to the target and the greater the altitude difference between ourselves and the target, the steeper we pulled up the nose.

It has to be admitted, however, that there was no special requirement to perform the zoom climb, since the Tu-128 had the ability to launch its missiles at a target flying 8,000 m (26,250 feet) above the interceptor, and with good GCI guidance it was quite easy to eliminate targeting errors.

Approximately 13 seconds before reaching the maximum missile launch range, the weapons system computer would begin to generate the commands necessary for missile lock-on and launch. Missile lock-on was indicated by illumination of white 'Lock-on' lights on a separate control panel in the navigator's cockpit, while launch readiness of each missile was indicated by illumination of red 'Ready for Launch' lights on the pilot's instrument panel. The number of missiles capable of being launched simultaneously with a single depression of the 'Launch' (*Pusk*) button was determined by the position of the 'Launch variant' (*variant puska*) switch on a separate panel in the pilot's cockpit. Setting this switch in position '1' and depressing the 'Launch' button resulted in one missile leaving the launch rail, setting it in position '2' would launch two missiles and in position '4', four missiles. If only one launch-ready light illuminated, the pilot would launch that missile by depressing the 'Launch' button for 2-3 seconds. When performing a forward hemisphere attack, the pilot was permitted to depress the 'Launch' button before the 'Ready' lights illuminated, and in this case the button had to be held down until the missile left the rail. Maj. Popov adds:

> During missile firing practice, when the 'Lock-on' light appeared on the radar you'd press and hold the 'Launch' button. The computer would continue to perform its calculations and when the range to target came into the permitted launch bracket, the missile would leave the rail.

For a second missile launch in the same attack (with the 'Launch variant' switch in either position '1' or '2') it was essential to release the button and then depress it again. When all four missiles were ready for launch and with the 'Launch variant' switch in position '4', the firing sequence after depressing the 'Launch' button was:

- Missile 1—port inner with IR seeker;
- Missile 2—starboard inner with IR seeker;
- Missile 3—port outer with semi-active radar seeker;
- Missile 4—starboard outer with semi-active radar seeker.

The weapons system 'automatics' (*avtomatika*) provided for the launch of the next available missile if the normal sequence was interrupted by unserviceability.

As a missile left the launch rail and after automatic disconnection of the frangible power cable and plug, the following control panel lights were extinguished in the navigator's and pilot's cockpits: 'Missile suspended', 'Lock-on' and 'Ready for Launch'. When launching a salvo of four missiles, the pilot had to avoid allowing the aircraft to sideslip. With a single launch, or when launching two missiles from each wing, the sideslip value was not to exceed 3°, and it was permitted to launch missiles only when the angle of bank was no greater than 30°, at speeds no higher than Mach 1.3. In the Pilots' Notes for the Tu-128 (Tu-128M) particular attention was paid to the aircraft's behaviour with asymmetric missile release, summarised as follows:

> In the event of asymmetric release of a single missile at subsonic speed, the banking moment is insignificant and does not affect aircraft handling, even down to the landing phase. At supersonic speed, asymmetric missile release produces a significant banking moment, intensifying in effect as speed is increased. When flying with a single inner missile attached, at a speed of Mach 1.3 and an altitude of 10,000-12,000 m [32,800-39,370 feet], it is necessary to counter the bank with a one-third deflection of the control column and a one-fifth deflection of the rudder pedals respectively. In the event of asymmetric release of two missiles, a noticeable heading 'twitch' is felt and a banking moment develops in the direction of the remaining missiles at a rate of around 2-3° per second at subsonic speed and around 11-12° per second supersonically. At subsonic speed the banking is countered by deflection of the control column by a quarter of its full travel. Trimming removes the additional forces on the control column and rudder pedals. At supersonic speed the banking moment is significantly greater, increasing as a function of increasing speed. At Mach 1.3 it is necessary to deflect the control column and rudder pedals by a half and a quarter of their full travel respectively, making heading changes very difficult. With asymmetric release of two missiles (and with the BOP launch limit unit not switched on), immediately counter the developing banking moment and sideslip using the control column and rudder pedals and then reduce speed to less than Mach 1.23.

These lines in the Pilots' Notes were 'written in blood', as the crew tasked with investigating the Tu-128's asymmetric handling at supersonic speed, Maj. Mayorov and his navigator, were killed during one of the trials. They were checking the aircraft's behaviour after simultaneous asymmetric release of two missiles at the Air Force Flight Test Centre at Akhtubinsk. As a result of this accident (described in Appendix 3), it was decided to equip all Tu-128s with the BOP launch limit unit, in order to prevent such asymmetric missile releases in future.

The launch of the IR-guided variant of the AA-5 'Ash' missile did not require any further targeting action after release, or tracking by the *Smerch* radar. The aircraft could break off from the attack immediately, once the inboard green 'Missile suspended' and the red 'Ready for Launch' lights were extinguished. However, in some cases it was necessary to track the target if the first missile had missed its objective and it was still possible to launch a second. In the absence of suitable conditions for a second missile launch it was essential to break off from the attack. By contrast, after launching a semi-active radar-homing variant of the missile, the interceptor had to continue to illuminate the target until the pilot received the visual signal of an asterisk (*) on his TS-7 display, indicating 'End of (target) Illumination' (*konyets oblucheniya*). After missile launch and break-off, the navigator would clear 'Lock-on' when the pilot told him to switch off the radar ('*Vyklyuchi stantsiyu*') if this had not occurred automatically during break-off from the attack, and then switch off the radar's HT supply. On receiving the visual command (O) (*Otvorot*) on the TS-7 display and the triggering of an associated audio signal warning that the aircraft was getting dangerously close to the target, the pilot had to commence break-off immediately. A closer approach to the target to determine the effects of the attack was prohibited, in order to avoid striking target debris or striking the target itself if it was to manoeuvre suddenly. If on depressing the 'Launch' button the selected missile did not leave the pylon, the missile's power supply was totally de-energised after 2 seconds and the control surfaces were set to the 'dive' position and locked, accompanied by extinguishing of the 'Lock-on' and 'Ready for Launch' lights.

Recording ('fixing') of the parameters of an attack during missile firing practice was performed with the help of the KZA flight data recorder. Tu-128 crews made their own plastic placards, to be placed above the pilot's TS-7 data-link display, which included, *inter alia*, the PR 'Launch Permitted' warning light, and the pilot's callsign was then written on the label. During flight, one of the cameras from the KZA system would photograph the pilot's instrument panel and the afore-mentioned placard. Thus, after flight, the pilot would receive a photograph of the placard with his personal callsign and the 'Launch Permitted' light illuminated or not, as appropriate, as well as targeting errors shown by the director needles of the PP-1PMK flight indicator. If the PR lights were illuminated in the photograph this would count as an 'Excellent' (*Otlichno*) score, since the pilot would have needed to press only the 'Launch' button to achieve a successful missile release in real combat conditions. The camera used to photograph the instrument panel was located on the right-hand rear section of the cockpit canopy frame and could be operated by the crew at any time during flight using the 'Event' (*Sobytiye*) button in the navigator's cockpit. This button and the 'Event' marker allowed the navigator to override the normal flight data recorder function of the camera. After breaking off from the attack, the pilot would report this to his regimental command post, along with the number of missiles remaining, and if the command post did not have another task for him the pilot would carry out the following actions:

- switch off afterburner;
- descend to the best altitude for maximum range, having asked the navigator for the necessary information;
- set true air speed of 900 kph (486 kts).

Return to the airfield to pick up the standard airfield approach aids could be carried out in two ways: either using commands passed by the *Vozdukh-1M* system, or autonomously, with the aid of the *Put'-4P*, NVU-B, RSBN-2S and ARK-10 navigation systems.

Return to base using the *Vozdukh-1M* system was confirmed by transmission of the command '*Privod*' ('Beacon' or 'Homing') and illumination of lights on the TS-7 and TS-8 displays in the pilot's and navigator's cockpits showing the letter (T). The pilot would then return to the airfield using guidance information provided by the *Lazur'-M* system and pick up the airfield approach and landing aids when in range. This stage could also be flown autonomously, with the navigator setting up the NVU-B navigation computer to guide the aircraft to an assigned waypoint, this data then being passed to the *Put'-4P* flight navigation system and converted into steering commands. The pilot would then fly the aircraft according to the command bars of the PP-1PMK flight indicator. At a distance of 150 km (93 miles) from the airfield the pilot would request permission to descend, and after coming within range of the RSBN-2 short-range navigation beacon he would switch the *Put'-4P* to the SVOD mode. SVOD, meaning a 'collection', 'arch' or 'vault', was the generic term for the RSBN short-range radio-technical navigation

The front page of the 'Interpretation Sheet' (*Kartochka Deshifrirovaniya*') documenting interceptions by Tu-128 (*Izdeliye I*) and MiG-25P (*Izdeliye 84*) aircraft. Although only partially completed, the sheet contains the following information: Pilot – Nirodyenko; date of flight – 16 July 1975; Bort No. 75; First sortie of the flying programme; target lock-on range – 38 km; distance of transmission of 'Ready for Launch' command to missile No. 2 – 12 km; break-off distance – 10 km; launch range – 12 km; closing speed – 480 kph; start of break-off from attack – 11 km. Shared use of this document by Tu-128 and the MiG-25P aircrew arose from the commonality of radar and missile performance of these two air defence interceptors. (*Irina Sadova Archive*)

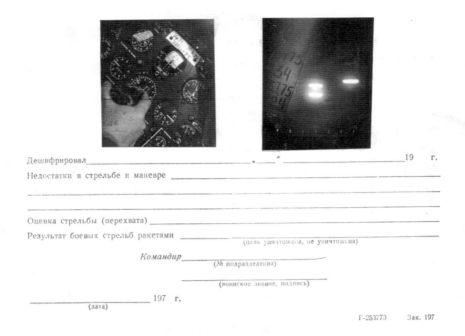

Дешифрировал_____ "___" _____ 19___ г.

Недостатки в стрельбе и маневре _____

_____

_____

Оценка стрельбы (перехвата) _____

Результат боевых стрельб ракетами _____
　　　　　　　　　　　　　　　　　(цель уничтожена, не уничтожена)

　　　　　　　*Командир*_____
　　　　　　　　　　　　　　　(№ подразделения)

　　　　　　　　　　　_____
　　　　　　　　　　　(воинское звание, подпись)

_____ 197 г.
　　(дата)

　　　　　　　　　　　　　　　　　　Г-253773　　Зак. 197

The reverse of the 'Interpretation Sheet', with attached photographs of the pilot's instrument panel and the navigator's radar screen, taken by the PAU-476 camera of the KZA flight data-recorder at the moment of completion of the attack. Small handwritten placards can be seen above the pilot's flight director and to the left of the radar screen; the pilot's data-card shows that the sortie was Exercise 34 (Упр 34) of the Combat Training Course (KBP); date – 16.7.75; Aircraft (с-т [i.e. самолёт]) No. 75. The digits 7-24 confirm the time (07.24) of this interception, since the aircraft clock itself is outside the viewing area of the camera. (*Irina Sadova Archive*)

system, analogous to TACAN. The *Put'-4P* would then receive its guidance signals from RSBN and not the NVU-B navigation computer, to generate vectors to allow the aircraft to be flown down to approach and landing.

Although not touched upon so far in this book, the Tu-128 regiments had to deal with the ever-increasing problem in the 1960s of the use of ECM by their potential adversaries during operational training intercepts. When passive jamming was encountered during the scan phase, the target was observed on the screen either as a separate return or merging with the plume of a chaff cloud. The radar's ECCM capabilities allowed the navigator to reduce the effect of jamming on the targeting process, and he could, with 'deft manipulation of the switches', still gate the target and achieve lock-on. If the target (as jamming source) released chaff behind it, then when the 'Fiddler' was attacking in pursuit mode (*dogon*) the target blip would be at the end of the chaff plume, and when attacking head-on (*vstrecha*) the blip would be at the head of the plume.

In the event of the Tu-128 being subjected to active jamming, the radar would switch automatically to anti-jamming mode. *Smerch* had two transmitters, operating on two separate frequency channels (*chastotniye kanaly*); jamming could affect the first or the second frequency channel, or both channels simultaneously. When active jamming was detected in scan mode on the first frequency channel, retuning the frequency of the first transmitter was automatic. When active jamming of the second frequency channel occurred, it was not retuned; the channel subjected to jamming shut down automatically and the radar switched to single-channel operation. When jamming was detected in scan mode on *both* frequency channels simultaneously, retuning the frequency of the first transmitter did not take place and the radar continued to operate in two-channel mode. Intensive active jamming would be seen on the screen as all-aspect interference within the scan zone. In this case, the navigator, using his skill and experience plus the radar's own capabilities, would determine the direction of the source of the interference and then lock on to it, albeit only by angle and not by range. When the radar was affected by jamming, there were two visual missile launch modes available—one using *Fi-nol'* (Φ_0) and the second using the *Fi L* (Φ_L) procedure. In a rear hemisphere intercept, in the absence of radar 'lock-on' on reaching a point 15-20 km (9-11 nm) from the target, in good visual conditions, an attack could be carried out using *Fi-nol'* and IR-guided R-4T missiles.

For this intercept variant, a number of essential actions to be performed by the pilot were described in the Pilots' Notes:

- Switch off Missile Nos 3 and 4 [i.e. the semi-active radar homing variants];
- Set the 'Target Option' ('*Vybor Tseli*') selector switch in the position corresponding to the size of target [i.e. bomber or fighter];
- Set the mode selector switch marked 'Without Radar Φ_0—With Radar—Without Radar Computer ΦL' to the 'Without Radar Φ_0' position and confirm with the navigator that the '*Nakal I*' and '*Nakal II*' lights were illuminated [i.e. system warm-up for the two IR-guided missiles had been achieved];
- After visual detection of the target, but at a distance of no greater than 8-10 km [5-6.25 miles], as reported by the command post, set the 'Guidance' switch to the 'ZP' ('Rear Hemisphere') position and take aim using the mechanical sight. [The 'Guidance' switch could not be set to the 'ZP' position earlier than 2 minutes after the 'Warm-up' signal had been passed to the missiles].
- At a distance of no greater than 8 km [5 miles] from the target, even with only one missile 'Ready' illuminated [Missile Nos 1 or 2], carry out missile launch;
- After missile launch, no closer than 2 km [1.25 miles] to the target, break off the attack, set the 'Guidance' switch to the neutral position and after

> 1.5 minutes set the mode selector 'Without Radar Φ_0—With Radar—
> Without Radar Computer Φ_L' to the central 'With Radar' position;

- De-select the 'System' switch and after a few seconds switch it back on again [in order to clear the 'Warm-up' command from the remaining missiles].

Nikolai Popov recalls an occasion when he had to use the *Fi-nol'* procedure following a radar malfunction during live missile firing practice:

> Once, I experienced a weapons system failure resulting in loss of guidance for the semi-active radar homing [SARH] missiles, so I had to switch over to *Fi-nol'* mode. After selecting this option I pressed the 'Launch' button and held it down. After this, I raised the nose of the aircraft and checked the guidance errors. As soon as the errors were 'removed' [equalized], the missile left the launch rail without any further intervention by me.

In spite of the fact that the heat-seeking variant locked on to the target itself (autonomously), target designation parameters were also passed by the *Smerch* radar to both the SARH and heat-seeking missiles. Target designation for both types of missile made it possible to employ yet another launch mode—*Fi L*. (This was used when *both* frequency channels of the radar were affected by ECM, *only* lock-on 'by angle' was possible, there were no *Lazur'-M* data transmissions from the ground *and* the weapons system computer was unserviceable.) The *Fi L* mode made it possible to launch missiles in a rear hemisphere engagement (using SARH and IR-guided variants) and in the forward hemisphere (only SARH variants). Depending on closing speed, missile launch was carried out at altitudes up to 11,000 m (36,090 feet) at ranges no greater than 12-15 km (7.5-9.33 miles) and at altitudes of 11,000 m and above at ranges of not more than 15-22 km (9.33-13.67 miles). Break-off from the attack had to be carried out at a distance of 7-9 km (4.33-5.67 miles) from the target. However, a missile launch using the *Fi L* procedure against a target in the forward hemisphere and flying below 10,000 m (32,800 feet) was not considered expedient in view of the limited time available for aiming.

A rear hemisphere missile launch in *Fi-nol'* and *Fi L* modes against targets flying below 10,000 m, plus the requisite break-off distances, are shown in the following table:

Altitude of Tu-128	Launch range	Break-off distance
10,000-5,000 m	4 to 5 km	2 to 3 km
5,000 to 300 m	3 to 4 km	2 to 3 km

By the early 1980s, commanders of all the Tu-128 regiments had made great efforts to get the most out of the automated GCI procedures described in this chapter. With certain reservations, particularly using *Lazur'-M* linked to the autopilot and the concomitant aircraft handling problems described earlier, most pilots liked using the 'instrument guidance' procedures. After almost twenty years of operational use, the ground maintenance personnel responsible for the upkeep of these automated control systems had amassed a significant amount of experience and *Lazur'-M* was by then working quite reliably. In the later years of Tu-128 operations some regiments even tried to conduct GCI training using only voice commands when training younger crews, but to be fair, it must be admitted that the quality of automated procedures depended very much on the dedication of commanders and the conscientiousness of maintenance specialists. Not all regiments were active users of the *Kaskad*, *Vozdukh* and *Lazur'-M* 'instrument guidance' system. In the latter case, they relied on the more traditional method of voice commands for GCI missions. Fighter control was conducted through regimental command posts, with guidance being taken up by contiguous GCI stations when the interception point was some distance from the aircraft's base. The GCI stations were located in such a way that the radar coverage of neighbouring sites overlapped, with no 'dead zones' during the transition from one zone to the next.

Fighter control at GCI sites was provided by officers known in Russian as 'guidance navigators' (*shturmany navyedyeniya*) or 'combat control officers' (*ofitsery boyevovo upravlyeniya*). In the 1960s, these were usually former pilots who had been taken off flying duties on health grounds. However, with the increasing sophistication of modern aircraft, greater demands were placed upon these officers, and the expansion of the network of GCI sites also led to the need for more fighter controllers. Consequently, the PVO set up dedicated training courses for specialist fighter controllers at Saratov Higher Military Aviation College for Pilots and Navigators, who, on graduation, were usually assigned to one of the fighter regiments. Here, they would generally serve for around two to three years, gaining experience before moving on to one of the individual GCI stations. A posting to one of these isolated sites was particularly tough since they were inevitably located in rather wild and remote regions of the Soviet Union. Some four to five officers and warrant officers, along with a number of conscripts, would man each GCI site, and after a further three to five years of service the fighter controllers would be transferred once again to one of the regiments. Such rotations were a permanent feature in the career progression of the 'combat control officer'. However, in the more remote GCI sites it was not always possible to provide meaningful continuous training for fighter controllers, so once every three or four months personnel would be detached to a regiment for 'hands-on' intercept training in realistic scenarios.

Interceptor crews were assigned a dedicated frequency on which to maintain contact with the GCI station, and they would switch over to this frequency as soon as required after take-off to request or be given tasking details. Soviet military pilot call-signs consisted of a five-figure numerical sequence, changed every month, although the first two digits of the callsign were not generally used in normal day-to-day operations. For example, Col. Komyagin's callsign had '66' as the last two numbers, but the full monthly changing five-figure sequence, (if, for example, it was '78266' in a given month) was only very occasionally used. The last two digits, however, remained fixed throughout a pilot's flying career. After the defection of Lt Viktor Belenko to Japan in his MiG-25 in September 1976, the system was changed. Thereafter, an interceptor pilot had to have a callsign valid for a ten-day period (*dekadnyi parol'*)—a set of numbers permitting ATC and fighter controllers to confirm that the aircraft was 'friendly'—as well as a daily changing callsign (*sutochnyi parol'*). Additionally, at the end of March 1984, a directive was issued by the Soviet General Staff which introduced a table of special codes to be used for transmitting information by voice from GCI stations to fighters and vice versa. Before the introduction of this system, a GCI fighter controller would give, for example, a typical command to a pilot, such as, '726, the target is on your left, bearing 30°, range 70 kilometres', '726' being the pilot's individual callsign. Using the new code table, the GCI controller would replace the words with the following sequence of numbers '726 51 030 070' where the number '51' indicated that the target was on his left, bearing and range being expressed in simple three-figure form. All standard commands used for GCI control were encoded in this way, i.e. switching on 'emitter radiation', 'zoom climb', 'break-off' etc., so, for example, instead of hearing the command 'Switch on Radiation' (*Vklyuchi izlucheniye*) the pilot would hear and respond to the phrase 'Command 525' (*Vam komanda 525*).

Situations would often arise when it was not possible to intercept targets from an airfield QRA posture if the distance between the fighter base and the desired point of intercept was too great. This was particularly true in the northern maritime and littoral regions of the USSR, where ground radar coverage was poor, and it was, of course, for this reason that the Tu-128 was developed in the first place. An airborne QRA procedure described in the previous chapter was developed in order to compensate for the effects of this limited GCI coverage. Airborne QRA made it possible to extend intercept boundaries without having to go to the expense of building a large number of GCI sites on the remote islands of northern Russia. Instead, the Tu-128 could set up barrier patrols (*barrazhirovaniya*) at an altitude of around 9,500-10,500 m (31,170-34,450 feet), cruising at 920 kph (497 kts) and using both its own AI radar and advisory information from ground sites to determine the presence of potential intruders. If the airborne patrol zone was located at a distance of no more than 176 km (95 nm) from the interceptor's base airfield (this being the distance required for the 'Fiddler' to climb to 9,500 m) then the intercept boundary depended only on the aircraft's loiter time. The maximum loiter time of the Tu-128 in the area of the airfield of departure was 120-125 minutes for an intercept in 'cruise regime' and 60-69 minutes for an intercept using 'combined regime'.

OPERATING THE TU-128M AT LOW ALTITUDE

After the commencement of the upgrade programme to bring aircraft up to the Tu-128M (*Modifitsirovannyi*) standard, a number of changes were introduced on the regiments concerning operational training to exploit the new capabilities of the aircraft. These are recalled by Maj. Rodyukov:

> When we were 'sent down' to low altitude we had to start to learn how to carry out intercepts at 1,000 m [3,280 feet]. Initially, we sometimes even behaved like hooligans on these flights. I remember that there was a lake alongside Talagi airfield and we would sometimes fly over the heads of fishermen at a height of about 20 m [65 feet]! This was while the aircraft were gradually being modified to '128M' standard, after which we introduced a proper programme of low-level intercept training. Then the serious work really began. Naturally, the detection range was significantly reduced at low level and intercepts were more difficult than at medium and high altitude. You had to work much quicker and concentrate more.

With the introduction of a fully developed training programme, regiments were assigned dedicated handling zones and flight routes, where low-altitude intercepts could be set up. Flights were carried out with due regard to minimum safe operating height, taking account of local topography and height above sea level. Flights below 1,000 m (3,280 feet) were undertaken only in VMC: the minimum operating height for the Tu-128M was usually around 500 m (1,640 feet). Low-level intercepts were characterised by an increased need for vigilance in maintaining spatial awareness, short detection ranges, reduction in radio communication range, rapid evolution of the attack and carrying out intercepts with small height differentials (target below interceptor) of around 300-500 m (985-1,640 feet). The navigator-operator also had to take account of ground proximity, and 'tilt' the *Smerch* radar antenna upwards further than usual to minimise terrain interference affects. However, this also had the effect of reducing detection range.

As mentioned above, certain difficulties were encountered when practising intercepts at low altitude, the most serious of which was the fact that at the time when the Tu-128M was introduced, no PVO pilot had ever practised low-level flying, whether at flying school or on a squadron. Low-level flying was difficult enough in itself, but particularly so at night, when the ground could not be seen but was only 300-500 m below the aircraft. It only required the pilot to be slightly distracted for there to be tragic consequences. Therefore, before starting to develop a low-level intercept programme for the Tu-128M, crews had to be trained to carry out 'normal' flights at low level and only after this could they begin to practise the intercept procedures. Training on this programme lasted around three months.

There was, however, another difficulty in that the aircraft had to be accelerated to its maximum permitted speed in order to carry out a missile launch at low level, since the minimum indicated launch speed of the missile at such heights was 850 kph (460 kts). However, the maximum permitted indicated air speed for the aircraft at low level was only 900 kph (485 kts) or Mach 0.95, giving a speed reserve of only 50 kph (27 kts). The aircraft had to be dived to 300 m (985 feet) to pursue the target, which at those speeds—in close proximity to the ground—was very difficult, but without attaining that speed it was impossible to launch a missile. If the GCI stations were late in detecting a target, the Tu-128M would have to climb to its assigned altitude and establish a speed close to the limits for that height. Information would be passed to the aircrew by simultaneous illumination of the 'afterburner' and 'descent' lights on the pilot's and navigator's instrument panels or by plain voice over the radio. During a low-level intercept, Tu-128M crews were recommended to fly at no lower than 2,000-3,000 m (6,560-9,840 feet) before commencing the intercept, in order to allow GCI sites to see the interceptor on radar, maintain radio contact with it and transmit the relevant guidance commands. When performing a long-range intercept against a low-flying target, the Tu-128M would climb initially to 9,500 m (31,170 feet), at which altitude the pilot would establish 'cruise' mode at a true air speed of 920 kph (496 kts). Descent to attack height would be commanded by the GCI controller, with the pilot setting the engines to 'Flight Idle' and an indicated air speed of 800 kph (432 kts), without exceeding Mach 0.95.

In mid-July 1979, an exercise was held by the 14th Independent Army of the PVO, in which 350 AP's Tu-128Ms participated for the first time, with activity centred on the firing range at Telemba in the Transbaikal region. One of the participants in this exercise, Maj. Mamet, a squadron navigator on 350 AP, remembers the events:

> My pilot was Yevgyenniy Osheiko and we were flying as wingman to our squadron commander, with another two pairs of aircraft behind, covering us. On the approach to the range, GCI spread us out to a ten-minute separation. Our target, a Lavochkin La-17, had already been launched earlier and was loitering over the range at high altitude, but of course we had to perform the intercept at low altitude. No one had ever done this before in a Tu-128 against such a small target at low level. When the leader entered the range, the target hadn't managed to descend to the assigned engagement height and he flew underneath it. I saw the target on radar at a range of around 20 km [12.5 miles]—'lock-on' was steady and we calmly shot it down.

Aircrew mastered the new intercept techniques very well and in due course all regiments which had upgraded to the Tu-128M gradually began to carry out live missile firing on the ranges, not only against high-flying targets but also against low-level targets.

OPERATIONS WITH THE TU-126 'MOSS'

As previously mentioned, the Tu-128 had been designed to operate over the High Arctic region, with sparse GCI radar coverage, and it was always intended that ground-based fighter control would be supported by shipborne and airborne guidance radars. It was calculated that the use of Soviet Navy radar picket ships (*Korabli Dal'nyevo Radiolokatsionnovo Dozora i Navyedyeniya* or KDRLDN) and Tu-126 'Moss' airborne radar pickets (*Samolyoty Dal'nyevo Radiolokatsionnovo Obzora* or DRLO) would permit extension of the intercept boundary to 1,000 km (620 miles) from the Soviet coastline for a target flying at 900 kph (486 kts). The main potential targets for detection by the (seaborne and airborne) radar pickets were expected to be USAF Boeing B-52 'Stratofortress' and B-47 'Stratojet' strategic bombers, plus RAF 'Vulcan', 'Victor' and 'Valiant' medium-range bombers, approaching the Soviet Union via polar routes. Using the Tu-126, it was possible within a comparatively short timeframe to set up an effective radar detection zone in the high northern latitudes, monitoring either airborne or surface targets approaching from any direction. An airborne picket also made it possible to provide radar coverage in the northern maritime regions when weather conditions on the surface precluded the use of naval vessels for this task. For these reasons, all of the Tu-126s assigned to the 67th Independent Aviation Squadron (*67 Otdyel'naya Aviatsionnaya Ehskadril'ya* or OAE) were subordinate to the 10th Independent Army of the PVO and based near the Lithuanian town of Shiauliai. (The airfield was sometimes referred to as Zokniai because of the proximity of this district of the town to the base. Today, Zokniai air base is an important airfield hosting regular deployments by NATO fighters which provide air defence cover for the now independent Baltic states of Lithuania, Latvia and Estonia.) The 67th Independent Aviation Squadron comprised three sections (*otryady*) of three aircraft each, a 'section' perhaps being best translated into English as 'flight', in line with the structure of medium bomber squadrons. (The Russian word '*zveno*' is generally used for a 'flight' of two or three *fighters*.)

The crew of the Tu-126 were effectively divided into two 'unequal parts' (both literally and figuratively), namely the flight-deck crew (*lyotnyi ehkipazh*) and the radio crew (*radio ehkipazh*). The flight-deck crew comprised the aircraft commander (*komandir korablya*), assistant aircraft commander (*pomoshchnik komandira korablya*), two navigators, a flight engineer (*bortovoy inzhenyer*) and a radio operator (*radist*). The flight-deck area was referred to as the first cockpit or cabin (*pyervaya kabina*). The radio crew were accommodated in the second cockpit or cabin (*vtoraya kabina*) and comprised the 'chief of the radar complex' (*nachal'nik radiotekhnicheskovo kompleksa* or RTK), an airborne radar technician (*bortovoy tekhnik RTK*), three radar operators (*operator RTK*) and a 'communications chief' (*nachal'nik svyazi*). It is believed that the latter was probably also

An elegant study of the Tu-126 'Moss' airborne radar picket (for airborne early warning of potentially hostile targets), developed in the same timeframe as the Tu-128 and designed to work in co-operation with the latter. (*Oleg Fedoseenko*)

responsible for both the signals intelligence suite (*sistyema radiotekhnicheskoy razvyedki*) and 'telecoded' (encrypted) data transmissions (described later). Occupying a position between the flight-deck crew and the back-end crew was the 'guidance navigator', an airborne fighter controller also known as a 'combat control officer'. Thus, depending upon the exact series of Tu-126 in question, the radio crew could consist of between seven and twelve individuals. Often, two or three conscripts were added to the radio crew to work as radar plotters (*planshetisty*), but since there was no established post for 'airborne plotters' they were included in the crew as 'radar operators'. Sometimes two radio crews would be carried if an extended-duration flight had been planned, involving air-to-air refuelling (AAR). There were around seven AAR-qualified flight-deck crews on 67 OAE from early 1969, and AAR training continued on the squadron until 1979. However, even without AAR, the average endurance of the Tu-126 operating over the Arctic Ocean was around 9 hours. The experienced maintenance teams who serviced the *Liana* (NATO 'Flat Jack') radar and its peripheral equipment often had to carry out repairs in flight, as recalled by former guidance navigator Maj. Oleg Makhar:

> We referred to the radio crew amongst ourselves as 'solderers' or 'soldering irons'. The reliability of the *Liana* radar left a lot to be desired, so they would often be soldering this or that and repairing things during flight. Before joining a Tu-126 radio crew, officers served as part of the ground maintenance group supporting the radar, where there was a fairly strict hierarchy. The officer had to study the radar in great depth on the ground, serving around one or two years in the maintenance area. If during

this time the officer acquitted himself well, he could be recommended to attend an aircrew medical board and if passed as fit for flying duties he could then be sent 'on board' (*na bort*).

In the 1960s and 1970s these officers were engineers taken from the PVO's radio-technical troops (*radiotekhnicheskiye voyska*), but in the 1980s graduates of the Moscow Aviation Institute (*Moskovskii Aviatsionnyi Institut*) began to appear in Tu-126 radio crews. Later, the Khar'kov Aviation Institute (*Khar'kovskii Aviatsionnyi Institut*) also began to provide graduates for these crews. (Both of these institutes have a prestigious reputation in the field of Russian aeronautical engineering.)

Guidance navigators in the 1970s and 1980s were usually graduates of Saratov flight training college, whilst the radio-technical crew comprised officers and warrant officers seconded from the PVO's radio-technical troops. The navigator service (*shturmanskaya sluzhba*) of the 10th PVO Army HQ conducted the specialist training of GCI controllers for the regimental command posts, its forty-six subordinate GCI stations and fighter controllers for the Tu-126. This work was overseen by the senior inspector navigator-pilot (*starshii inspektor shturman-ly-otchik*) of the 10th PVO Army. The fighter control techniques required in Tu-126 operations were developed by the airborne controllers and then tried out in the combat readiness zones over the open water areas of the Barents Sea and Kara Sea. An operations manual (*Kurs Boyevoy Podgotovki—KBP-L-69*) was written for the Tu-126, designed to cover execution of radar and signals intelligence (SIGINT) collection over the Kara, Barents and Baltic Seas, vectoring fighters onto airborne targets at very long range (north-west of the Novaya Zemlya archipelago) and tracking of naval targets. However, in practice, the aircraft was capable of performing only two of the required tasks: the detection and tracking of airborne targets, and joint operations with the Northern Fleet. During joint operations, the Tu-126 performed two specific tasks: searching for enemy shipping on the surface, and assisting fleet command posts in the tracking of Soviet naval aircraft on flights 'round the corner' (i.e. round the Kola Peninsula).

When searching for foreign ships in the area, the Tu-126 would determine their range and bearing and pass the data to the fleet command post. The need to assist the fleet command posts arose because ground-based radars were unable to monitor and track the flights by naval Tu-95RT 'Bear-D' and Tu-142 'Bear-F' reconnaissance aircraft as they went 'round the corner' and out of radar range. In support of these flights, the Tu-126 would operate in the designated loitering area, search for the 'Bears' and then transmit the relevant data to the command posts on board Soviet naval vessels. Flight routes for the Tu-126 passed through Arkhangel'sk to the area of Novaya Zemlya and through the Kola Peninsula to the area of Franz Josef Land. Flight time to the loiter zone was around 3 hours, and immediately after take-off the *Liana* early warning radar was switched to 'warm-up' mode (*progrev*) and then to 'radiating' mode (*izlucheniye*) once the aircraft reached an altitude of 7,200-8,000 m (23,620-26,250 feet). However, an airborne controlled intercept (ACI) was very difficult when the aircraft was on a normal flight route, the main problem being the establishment of precise coordinates for the 'guidance navigator'. Therefore, ACI was carried out only when the aircraft was established in a 'racetrack' pattern in the loitering zone (*zona barrazhirovaniya*). Loiter time 'on task' was around 2-2.5 hours, depending upon fuel state, with work on board only being interrupted in the event of an equipment malfunction requiring replacement or repair, for which a kit of spares was carried.

Target data was transmitted via the aforementioned 'telecoded' communications system on HF to the command posts of 10th PVO Army at Vas'kovo and the HQ of the Northern Fleet at Severomorsk. The encrypted 'telecode' system facilitated transmission of the following data:

- simultaneous identity of four airborne or surface targets (i.e. as friend or foe);
- simultaneous provision of coordinates of fourteen targets in a conventional coordinate system;
- altitude of targets above sea level.

When patrolling in its loiter zone at an altitude of 9,500 m (31,170 feet), the *Liana* radar could detect aircraft the size of the Tupolev Tu-95 'Bear' and Myasishchev 3M 'Bison' at a range of 400 km (216 nm), Tu-16 'Badger' and Tu-128 'Fiddler' at 350 km (189 nm), and Yak-28 'Firebar' and Su-9 'Fishpot' at a distance of 220 km (119 nm). During the Tu-126's 'troop trials' it became clear that it would not be possible to perfect a fighter control system to enable it work in automated mode (i.e. using *Kaskad*, *Lazur'* and *Vozdukh*-type processes), so the airborne fighter controllers had to rely on manual plotting and voice commands to guide the Tu-128 onto its targets. One Tu-126 and its crew could provide guidance for ten interceptors onto ten individual targets. The first Tu-128 unit to work with the Tu-126 was 518 AP at Talagi, followed a little later by 72 AP at Amderma, and over the years both regiments accumulated considerable experience of operating with the 'Moss'. Although 67 OAE's Tu-126s participated in a number of major exercises, it operated mainly on behalf of 10th PVO Army and the Soviet Navy's Northern Fleet but was not held on constant alert (*postoyannoye dezhurstvo*).

Maj. Rodyukov recalls operating with the Tu-126:

We had to work with the Tu-126 quite often. Approximately 400 km [250 miles] north of Murmansk there were four zones where these aircraft carried out their patrols. When the Tu-126 was working with fighters it used the callsign '*Sigara*' [Cigar] and fighter control was always performed using plain voice commands. In a

single sortie the radio crew would be able to perform two to three successful airborne
controlled intercepts by the Tu-128s onto their training targets

The most intensive period of co-operation between the Tu-126 and Tu-128 began
in the summer months. Each year at this time two Tu-126s would deploy from
Shiauliai to the operational reserve airfields at Olyenyegorsk or Severomorsk and
remain there for six to eight weeks. An extended programme of runway repairs
at Shiauliai airfield began in 1984, so every summer for the next four years all
of 67 OAE's aircraft deployed to the northern airfields, remaining there until
November each year. (From 1985, 67 OAE was renamed the 144th Independent
Aviation Regiment.) However, the Tu-126 still had to operate in the High Arctic
region in the winter months, as recalled in this account by Maj. Oleg Makhar:

> In winter the Kara Sea would freeze over completely, resulting in significant dis-
> tortion of surface radar reflections in the 'Kara Pocket' that was exploited by the
> American RC-135 reconnaissance aircraft, which descended to an altitude where
> they could not be picked up by our ground radars. In this situation the Tu-126
> proved to be an irreplaceable asset—we would enter the search zone, locate the 'foe'
> and guide our interceptors onto it, from Amderma or Rogachyovo.

In the extreme north, both the Tu-128 and the Tu-126 usually operated from an
airborne QRA posture at an altitude of 9,000-9,500 m (29,530-31,170 feet), with
the Tu-128s flying as a pair in a rectangular holding pattern. The Tu-126 flew a
figure of eight pattern, with around 100 km (54 nm) between the centres of each
half of the figure, the large radius at each end of the pattern allowing flat turns that
avoided degradation of radar antenna directivity and subsequent loss of guidance
of the fighters. Developing workable procedures for the Tu-126 to provide effective fighter control of the Tu-128 was very complex and at first was not always
successful. Maj.-Gen. Skok (then a more junior officer) was one of those involved
in the early trials:

> In 1972, the Ministry of Defence's *inspektsiya* [operational inspection service],
> led by Marshal K. S. Moskalenko carried out an operational evaluation check of
> the Northern Fleet and PVO 10th Army. The '*opeval*' exercise plan called for the
> Long-range Air Force to simulate an attack as a notional enemy force of strategic
> bombers approaching the Soviet Union over the North Pole. The Tu-128s of 72 AP at
> Amderma were tasked with the interception of this 'enemy' force under the control of
> a Tu-126 before the bombers reached the calculated launch boundary of the 'Hound
> Dog' missile, somewhere between Franz Josef Land and the northern tip of Novaya
> Zemlya. Our 518 AP was tasked with the 'destruction of the enemy strategic bomber
> force' before it reached the launch boundary for their SRAM [Short-range Attack

Missiles] weapons. The Tu-126 crew mistook the Amderma fighters for the notional enemy targets and directed our group [518 AP] onto our own force [72 AP]. While everyone was trying to work out exactly what was going on, the 'enemy' managed to press home its attack [as a result of which] we didn't even get an 'unsatisfactory score' [….] Regrettably, these events had a long-lasting negative impact on joint Tu-128/126 operations and largely predetermined our future involvement in inter-operative working with the Tu-126.

Flight test personnel who had flown both the Tu-114 'Cleat', from which the Tu-126 was developed, and the Tu-126 itself, noted the high noise levels in the crew working area of the 'Moss' compared with the relatively luxurious cabin of its civil progenitor. Although the rear-end crew of the Tu-126 had been provided with a rest area, with upholstered yellow (!) leatherette seats, it was located just behind the trailing edge of the wings in close proximity to noisy pressure-regulating valves and it was impossible to sleep or rest there. So it was decided to try to improve the comfort of the Tu-126 in the first instance by providing better thermal and acoustic insulation in the cabin, which included, among other things, laying a sound-deadening carpet on the floor. However, this only partially alleviated the intrinsic internal noise problem of the Tu-126, which was a cacophony generated by the large contra-rotating propellers, certain modules of the *Liana* radar, plus the metal access ladder leading up into the antenna pylon, which vibrated constantly. To add to the crew's misery, the build-up of static electricity in the cabin about 3 hours after take-off was such that it was impossible to touch any metal component with bare hands. Worse still, considering the aircraft had been designed to operate in the harsh northern climate of the Soviet Union, the working area of the cabin was not heated unless the engines were operating, so in winter crews had to strap into ice-cold seats on first entering the aircraft. Once airborne, the situation on board was still far from ideal, and if the sortie was to be flown over the Arctic Ocean the crew had to wear the MSK-3 sea survival suit for that part of the flight which was over water. The MSK-3 protected the wearer for up to 64 hours in water without risk of hypothermia, but the rubber neck seal caused severe irritation in normal wear, which in some cases persisted for a considerable time after flight. If the entire sortie was to be flown over the Baltic Sea, as some were, then this 'torture' lasted from take-off to touchdown!

However, the main concern of personnel who flew in the Tu-126 or serviced it on the ground was the intense radiation from the *Liana* radar, against which there was no effective protection. It must be noted, however, that the radiation was directional and the zone of greatest intensity was above the level of the manned section of the fuselage. Nevertheless, some of the harmful flow of radiation was reflected off parts of the airframe (e.g. the fin and wing panels) and was able to penetrate the fuselage. Apart from this direct radiation, the numerous very high frequency modules installed in cabinets inside the working compartments themselves created an additional electro-magnetic 'background'. The absence of adequate biological protection from electro-magnetic radiation led not only to a lowering of radio crew working efficiency but also to more serious consequences, with some crew members complaining of significant hair loss and, in certain cases, of total baldness. Even among Tu-126 ground crew personnel there were reported cases of damage to the cerebellum, causing balance problems, in spite of the fact that the *Liana* radar could only be tested (i.e. radiate) on the ground within a specified area of the airfield. Normal safety procedures were always rigidly observed, and the technicians should not have been exposed to this radiation, but they were perhaps vulnerable to side-lobe radiation. Local suslik (ground squirrel) and hare populations were not so lucky, and many of these small mammals fell victim to directed radiation during ground checks of the radar.

In co-operation with the aviation department of the 10th Army, the Tu-128 regiments went on to develop new tactical air combat techniques for working with the Tu-126 'radar platform'. As already mentioned, the Tu-128 was also able to work with any suitably equipped naval surface vessel performing the role of radar picket ship. In August 1977, Omsk-based 64 AP deployed to the High Arctic region to provide top cover for Northern Fleet vessels over the Kara Sea, under the control of radar picket ships. This was the first time ever in the history of the 14th PVO Army that its continental-based Tu-128s had worked co-operatively with Soviet naval vessels.

In 1984, the 67th Independent Aviation Squadron received its first Ilyushin-Beriev A-50 'Mainstay' airborne early warning and control (AEW&C) aircraft, commencing experimental operations with this advanced successor to the Tu-126 in the same year. Although the A-50 was gradually introduced to service before the Tu-128 was withdrawn, the two aircraft never actually operated together. Instead, the 'Mainstay' was to become an integral component of a vastly improved airborne radar system, employing both its own advanced radar capabilities, as well as those of the Tu-128's successor, the MiG-31 'Foxhound'. Nevertheless, the Soviet-era Tu-128 and Tu-126 provided valuable operational experience in co-operative air defence of Russia's vulnerable northern regions, experience which was 'designed' into the MiG-31 and A-50 to provide a superior level of air defence for the 'new Russia'.

13

Mastering the Airfields of the Soviet High Arctic

It will be recalled that in the 1960s the Commander-in-Chief of the PVO Air Force, Marshal Savitskiy, and his deputy, Lt Gen. Kadomtsyev, had planned to use the Tu-128 to defend the airspace of the entire Soviet north. However, it would have been very difficult to maintain the necessary number of regiments to achieve this in the High Arctic region on a permanent basis because of the huge financial outlay required. Apart from this, it was necessary to take into consideration the extreme conditions of the region and that organisation of relevant combat training was also extremely difficult. Col. Komyagin recalls the problems:

> We had Tu-128s at Arkhangel'sk, Amderma and Kotlas. We had planned to position a section (*otryad*) of Tu-128s at Pechora, but the airfield was not ready to accept them. In Siberia we had examined the possibility of basing a regiment near Surgut, but we were not allocated any space for building [an airfield] and, of course, building there would have been very expensive, with permafrost all around.

Consequently, it was decided to resolve the problem in a somewhat original manner after the military leadership calculated that a number of forward operating bases (FOBs) spread across the whole of the High Arctic would meet the requirement. These airfields were to be supplied with a stockpile of R-4 (AA-5 'Ash') missiles and essential ground servicing equipment, enabling deployed Tu-128 regiments to mount combat operations from them comparatively quickly in times of increased tension. Timely deployment of the Tu-128 to these forward bases was designed to facilitate the PVO's main task—destruction of the enemy's bomber force before it could launch its cruise missiles. The use of a forward echelon of Tu-128s was planned, providing defensive cover against cruise missile attacks in the Murmansk, Arkhangel'sk, Kotlas and Vorkuta regions, using FOBs on the Kola Peninsula, plus the main bases at Amderma and Rogachyovo and the 'ice airfield' (*lyedovoy aehrodrom*) on Graham Bell Island.[1]

Maj. Rodyukov adds:

> In times of threat, the combat task of the regiment included relocating some of our air assets to Amderma, Severomorsk, Kilp-Yavr, Olyenyegorsk and Umbozero. And we also had to master the procedure of operating out of the airfield on Graham Bell Island in the Franz Josef Land archipelago.

The airfields of the Kola Peninsula were widely used as forward bases by 518 AP, which was particularly necessary when escorting LRAF bombers on flights 'round the corner' into their North Atlantic operating area. For these flights, some of the regiment's aircraft were deployed to Kilp-Yavr and Severomorsk. Another of 518 AP's tasks was to provide top cover for vessels of the Northern Fleet, working out of the operational reserve airfield at Umbozero (airfield callsign '*Karachan*'). Umbozero was the principal dedicated deployment airfield for 518 AP, but was also used by other units as required. Located on the Kola Peninsula, it was situated 40-50 km (25-31 miles) south of the town of Kirovsk on the southern shore of Lake Umbozero, with the Apatity Hills to the north. The concrete runway (047°/227°) was 2,500 m (8,200 feet) long and 50 m (165 feet) wide, although the effective working width was only 40 m (130 feet), but it was still capable of handling heavy aircraft such as the Tu-16 'Badger' bomber. As the airfield was not used by any unit on a permanent basis, it was manned by only a small contingent of around 15-20 personnel supplied by 518 AP. This group (officially known as a *komendatura*, i.e. commandant's staff) comprised an officer, several warrant officers and a number of conscripts. In the periods between the fairly infrequent deployments of aircraft the *komendatura* guarded the airfield and looked after equipment such as refuelling bowsers, APA mobile generators and other vehicles essential for the support and maintenance of deployed aircraft. The airfield radar and radio aids were also minimal, or to be more truthful, virtually non-existent. If such basic technical support for the operation of the Tu-128 or Tu-16 is difficult to imagine, consider the fact that deployed personnel were housed in single-story wooden-planked huts that allowed the wind to whistle through the gaps! Apart from harsh conditions for ground personnel, flights from Umbozero in the rapidly changing weather conditions at the base were also quite demanding.

Capt. Vinokurov, former navigator on 518 AP, recalls the problems:

> It was no secret that every major exercise was accompanied by a very tense 'air situation'. After all, aircraft from several regiments would be operating in the same block of airspace at the same time. Consequently, even with a slight deterioration in weather conditions, you can imagine the difficulty of controlling flights at this airfield, with its meagre technical aids. In 1981, our regiment took part in a major exercise which, apart from ourselves, involved aircraft of the Northern Fleet. Our

squadron was given the task of deploying to Umbozero and operating from there during the exercise. The 2nd squadron deployed to the naval airfield at Olen'ya, near the town of Olenegorsk. After receiving the order to deploy, the squadron commander had to fly to the deployment airfield, assess the situation there and receive the squadron's aircraft, carrying out the duties of 'controller of flying' [i.e. as the ATC officer]. Two hours after reporting the airfield's readiness to receive our aircraft, the entire squadron of eight aircraft and crews was supposed to fly to Umbozero. When the squadron commander arrived, everything was normal—the airfield had VMC conditions, so he gave the order for the squadron to deploy. However, for a number of reasons, we departed around 3 hours after his call, by which time the weather had started to deteriorate. When we actually arrived in the Umbozero air traffic control zone, the weather had deteriorated significantly and was no longer VMC. It was starting to spit with light rain and there was the threat of a thunderstorm looming.

The outer beacon transmitter was quite weak and the radio compass needle was spinning around like a 'whirling dervish', so everyone was relying on the DF [direction finding] controller, but the operator wasn't particularly well trained. The RBZ controller [*Rukovodityel' Blizhnyei Zony*] for the 'near-airfield' zone also clearly could not help in any way as his radar screen was obliterated with interference. In the end it turned out that we would in fact have to find the runway ourselves, virtually blind. Two of the first three aircraft arriving at the airfield managed to land without too much difficulty, but the others had to make three or four approaches without getting in. Taking stock of the airfield's 'aids' and the weather (cloud-base 300 m and visibility of 3-4 km) the RP [flight controller] decided to divert the other six Tu-128s to the nearest reserve airfield [Olen'ya]. Olen'ya was around 100 km (62 miles) from Umbozero and it was good thing that they had taken off with a full fuel load and their remaining fuel allowed them to do this. However, when they arrived at Olenegorsk [Olen'ya], the airfield was experiencing the same weather, perhaps even worse, and darkness was descending. Lightning was flashing all around the airfield, but the airfield's approach and landing aids were all working perfectly and it also had an ILS (instrument landing) system. Since we had all turned up at this airfield at the same time, some of the crews had to make two approaches each to slot into the pattern. Of course, we had all landed at Talagi in much worse conditions and all the crews assigned to the exercise were well trained [half of the pilots and navigators had come from Amderma]. On this occasion one of the crews had made four approaches at Umbozero and another two at Olenegorsk, diverting to the latter airfield to clear the approach for another aircraft with a more critical fuel state. When he was finally cleared to land, nothing could be seen anywhere because of the rain. The pilot asked ATC, 'Where's the runway?!' Receiving the reply from the RP, who could see him visually, 'The runway is beneath you,' the pilot chopped power and literally flopped down onto the runway.

Even during the early 'troop trials' stage it was clear that the Tu-128 was not suitable for operating from packed earth airfields, but it could operate from 'winter airfields' (*zimniye aehrodromy*). The need for this arose when the concentration of aircraft on the regular bases during exercise periods exceeded their normal handling capacity. The main runway on the 'winter airfields' consisted of a smoothly rolled layer of hard-packed snow over graded earth—a comparatively cheap solution to the problem. There were, however, certain difficulties in using these 'winter airfields', as explained by Maj.-Gen. Skok, a former commander of 518 AP:

> During a routine exercise, one of our Tu-128 squadrons had to land on a packed snow runway at a 'winter airfield' in the vicinity of Severomorsk. The outside air temperature on landing was around –15°C, but some 90 minutes to 2 hours later the temperature started to rise rapidly under the influence of a warm cyclone coming in off the sea. I was 'duty controller flying' at the time, but hadn't attached much significance to the rise in temperature. Six hours later we received the command 'Squadron, scramble! Heading after take-off 360°'. As the first aircraft was taking off, a sudden snowstorm blew up and the aircraft disappeared in clouds of snow thrown up by the jet efflux. I was only able to relax when I could see in the distance two pinpoints of flame from the afterburners as the aircraft gained height. When I asked the crew on the radio how the take-off had been, they just said, 'Normal; only a bit longer than usual.' The remaining aircraft took off with a slightly shorter take-off run. When all of the aircraft were safely airborne, I drove down the runway and was confronted by a rather alarming sight—the depth of the tracks made by the departing aircraft was about half a metre [around 1.75 feet]! It turned out that the length of the take-off run of the first aircraft had been twice the calculated distance.

The operational reserve airfields on the Kola Peninsula were used mainly by 518 AP from Talagi, whereas 72 AP at Amderma generally used Nar'yan-Mar and Rogachyovo. Nar'yan-Mar was a small town located between Arkhangel'sk and Amderma, with its own airport, which was the regiment's operational reserve airfield and was sometimes used for routine flying as it was also 72 AP's designated diversion airfield. The other operational reserve airfield used by 72 AP, Rogachyovo, was located on the southern coast of Novaya Zemlya, both it and Nar'yan-Mar being subordinate to 4 Division of the PVO 10th Army.

There was one other extremely remote operational reserve airfield of the 10th PVO Army in the High Arctic, located on Graham Bell Island in the Franz Josef Land archipelago and lying between latitudes 81° and 84°N. This polar archipelago, situated 1,000 km (621 miles) south of the North Pole, comprises 196 mainly small uninhabited islands, although two provided bases for PVO radio-technical companies, with a large 'ice airfield' built on the third largest and westernmost, Graham Bell Island. These were the most northerly situated PVO bases in the

'Snow roads' had to be cut through deep drifts after winter blizzards on the airfields of the High Arctic region. Here a crew bus, mounted on a ZIL-157 chassis, makes its way along one such road to carry out a shift change of 72 AP duty personnel at Amderma airfield. (*Irina Sadova Archive*)

Soviet Union and possibly the most northerly regularly staffed military outposts in the world. A deployment support group maintained the 'ice airfield' in a condition ready to accept a detachment of Tu-128s whenever required, while a radar company and GCI station provided the associated fighter control facilities, as well as round-the-clock surveillance of the approaches to the archipelago. The population of the garrison of Graham Bell airfield comprised around twenty ordinary 'soldiers' (*soldaty*) and seven to ten officers of various specialisations, accommodated in a prefabricated wooden barracks complex.[2] Living conditions in these distant outposts of the Soviet Union were very severe, exacerbated by isolation from families and the absence of normal day-to-day 'luxuries'. There was no television and because of the magnetic influence of the North Pole, radios did not always work normally, but once every two months an Aeroflot Polar Aviation aircraft did a 'mail run' to the airfield, dropping the post bag onto the runway. Conditions were particularly harsh during the long polar nights, with frequent snowstorms, heavy frosts and low oxygen content in the atmosphere. A considerable amount of time was spent on keeping the runway clear of snow—not an easy task when it is considered that the runway length of 'ice airfields' was not less than 3,000 m (9,840 feet).

Pilots and ground crew of 72 AP pose beside (and on) a GTS personnel transporter on Graham Bell Island during a deployment to this 'ice airfield' in 1978. The GTS (*Gusyenichnoye Transportnoye Sredstvo*) – literally 'caterpillar-tracked transport means (of conveyance)' – was the principal form of off-road and airfield transport on Arctic airfields. (*Irina Sadova Archive*)

The remote garrisons of the High Arctic were usually resupplied by sea once a year during the brief summer navigation period (a procedure known as *navigatsionnyi zavoz*—meaning 'navigation delivery', where the word 'navigation' is used in its original sense of 'communication by vessel'), when everything necessary was brought in, including aviation fuel, live pigs and cattle. Delivery of supplies to the more remote radio-technical companies was particularly difficult, because the ship could not get closer than 500-600 m (550-660 yards) from the shore and there were no properly equipped moorings. Flat-bottomed motor boats had to be used for unloading, with the vessel anchored offshore, and all hands (officers, warrant officers and soldiers) were needed to transfer the cargo to the shore. Sometimes unloading would take around two or three days, working non-stop. Of the hundred or so radar units of the 10th PVO Army, the majority worked in such conditions throughout their period of active service. However, in the 1980s, the High Command of the 10th Army started to charter civilian Mi-8MT 'Hip' transport helicopters from an aviation enterprise (i.e. a sub-department of Aeroflot) in the town of Vorkuta in order to improve the frequency of delivery of goods and matériel to remote bases, including the 'ice airfield' on Graham Bell Island. Even visits by various deputations to these far-flung outposts were used for additional deliveries of supplies, the aircraft being loaded with spares for ground equipment, vegetables, fruit, books and magazines, films and mail.

Any flight in Arctic conditions was associated with considerable risk, and in order to minimise this when flying in to the 'ice airfield' on Graham Bell Island a minimum of two or three bases were always designated as diversion airfields. The need for a choice of diversion airfields was particularly important if a '*Variant*' snowstorm was to develop suddenly; it will be recalled from Chapter 11 that '*Variant*' storms were particularly severe, rendering all outside activities virtually impossible. Transit flights to Graham Bell were planned to stage through Amderma or Rogachyovo on Novaya Zemlya, flying along the western coastline of the island. A 'section' of four Tu-128s from 72 AP at Amderma was deployed to Graham Bell 'ice airfield' during a major exercise in 1978. The flight was planned meticulously, using only the most able crews with long experience of flying together as pilot and navigator and all holding First Class ratings. Having selected the crews, the next most important task was to prepare the aircraft. It was decided that in order not to put the crews at risk it was essential to use aircraft from the most recent production batches (i.e. from the 42nd series onwards),[3] with the best radio equipment. However, 72 AP did not operate the latest model of Tu-128, and indeed nor did any other regiment in the 10th Army, so the PVO High Command decided to exchange four of 72 AP's older aircraft for four late-series Tu-128s from the 14th Army's 350 AP at Belaya. The deputy commander of 72 AP, Lt Col. Mikhail Grechishkin, was designated the senior officer charged with receiving the aircraft and ferrying them to Amderma, all four aircraft being flown from Belaya to Amderma in one day, with a fuel stop at Omsk-North. After the four 'new' aircraft had been delivered to Amderma, the pilots chosen to deploy to Graham Bell were then shown a typical snow-covered 'ice airfield', flying to the winter reserve airfield at Vorkuta in a Mi-8 helicopter. This airfield had a 4,000 m (13,125 feet) packed snow runway, which was 100 m (330 feet) wide, capable of taking the heavy bombers of the LRAF. The Tu-128 pilots were able to see first the layout of the airfield from the air and then inspect the hard packed snow surface on the main runway and the taxiways after the helicopter had landed.

Lt Col. Grechishkin was also appointed controller of flying at Graham Bell and recalls the occasion well:

There was no special briefing for the controller of flying and the duty air traffic controller on Graham Bell. We studied sketch maps of the airfield in the usual way, including approach patterns etc., in fact everything required by standard operating procedures. The airfield on Graham Bell Island and the airfield at Vorkuta were both used as reserve [diversion] airfields by the Long-range Air Force. The duty ATC navigator V. Khorunzhyi and I flew over Graham Bell airfield in an An-12 transport and being on the flight-deck during the approach I was struck by the unrelieved whiteness all around, with no dark patches and nothing for the eye to focus on. Only the inner and outer marker beacon masts and the GCA radar antennas stood out on the airfield, if indeed you could call it an airfield. A senior lieutenant was responsible for the landing aids and GCA 'talk-downs', but unfortunately, after two years on the island [with no visiting aircraft], he had 'lost the knack' of handling incoming aircraft.

With this being such a rare event we had quite an audience when we landed and were met by most of the residents of the small garrison—four officers and around twenty conscripts. After we'd disembarked from the An-12, I asked if some kind of marking, however primitive, could be used to define the main runway, otherwise landing the Tu-128 in such featureless terrain would be very risky. Initially it seemed as if marking the snow-covered runway would be quite a difficult task, but eventually we decided that dissolving smoke charges in barrels of kerosene would work, to produce an *ad hoc* black liquid that could be 'painted' onto the snow. The barrel was mounted on a sledge, towed behind an APA truck, and one of the soldiers used a bucket to pour the liquid onto the 'ice runway'. During this 'operation' I sat with the driver and made sure that we were driving down the 'centreline'. Using this procedure, we also marked out the start of the round-out and over-run areas. On the following day we went up again in the An-12 to do a weather reconnaissance flight, provide some training for the GCA controller and his assistants, and check the landing aids. I also saw what the newly 'painted' runway looked like from the air.

Everything was ready to receive our aircraft and I gave the go-ahead for the Tu-128s to take off from Amderma. They took off at ten-minute intervals, the first aircraft to land at Graham Bell being a Tu-128UT carrying the Head of Aviation of the PVO 10th Army, Col. Boris Popov, followed by the other three Tu-128s. Col. Popov liked the runway markings very much, even though the centreline marking wasn't particularly straight. Nevertheless, it greatly helped the pilots on landing and they were able to taxi to the parking area without assistance. All four aircraft parked in a straight line [one behind the other], sufficiently far apart so as not to get in each other's way. We didn't take an advance engineering party with us and the aircrew themselves carried out post- and pre-flight checks—we'd all been trained to do this. The most difficult task was packing the brake parachute into its special container, which in winter conditions presented a few problems, and we had to jump up and down on the chute to ram it in and close the container. We were accommodated in the garrison's 'Lenin room' for the duration of the exercise—there was no other accommodation available. The garrison chef prepared some very tasty meals for us and I particularly liked his bread.

Unfortunately, we didn't manage to participate in the exercise in the end. We weren't authorised to fly because of the fact that the entire Arctic region was covered by dense cloud, with cloud-base of around 50-100 m [165-330 feet] and there were no suitable diversion airfields in the vicinity. Since it was only an exercise and not actual combat flying, the PVO High Command decided not to risk the aircraft and aircrew. After the exercise had ended and the weather had returned to normal we received permission to return to base at Amderma. However, during departure there were a few problems. After the first aircraft had taken off, I drove out to check the 'runway' surface and made an unpleasant discovery. The aircraft had melted a section of the surface around 150-200 m [500-650 feet] long with the flames from the afterburners. The other aircraft were able to taxi round this 'obstacle' and perform rolling take-offs. The 4,000 m [13,125 feet] length of the runway of this 'ice airfield' meant that all four aircraft were able to take off safely using full afterburner.

An even more difficult task faced the operational air group for the regiments of the PVO's 14th Independent Army which had to operate out of the reserve airfields at Alykyel' (Noril'sk), Khatanga, Tiksi, Yakutsk, Novyi Urengoy and Ostrov Srednii. This involved deploying a large number of aircraft over a considerable distance, from the south to the extreme north of Siberia. The civil airport at Alykyel', serving the mining town of Noril'sk, was designated as the wartime reserve airfield for 64 AP from Omsk-North, as recalled here by former aircraft technician Maj. Plyuta:

> We would relocate to Alykyel' in single squadron strength. The airport buildings were on one side of the main runway and our dispersal area was on the other side. 64 AP had its own deployment support group on this airfield, including fuel bowsers and ground support equipment. Squadron personnel lived in the military barracks which in winter were covered with snow up to the eaves. Food was prepared by military personnel in the airport employees' dining facility.

The Tu-128s of 356 AP used Khatanga as a deployment base, transiting from Zhana-Semey via Kansk. Khatanga was also a civil airfield, although in much poorer condition than Alykyel', with permafrost damage to the substrate of the main runway and taxiways, resulting in water oozing from the concrete slabs in summer. There was an unusable section of taxiway about 200 m (660 feet) long where, because of sub-surface water action, the edges of the slabs sometimes stood proud of the adjacent slab by several centimetres. For this reason the Tu-128s did not use the long taxiway, using two smaller taxiways instead and entering the main runway to make a 180° turn.

The airports at Yakutsk and Tiksi were used by 350 AP at Bratsk as their operational deployment fields, Yakutsk having in addition to its own civil airport a separate winter (tundra) airfield which was also sometimes used by the Tu-128. However, permanent use of the tundra airfield was not feasible because of the haze that developed over the area when the temperature dropped below −30°C, which happened quite frequently. The airfield at Tiksi was used by the 'Fiddler' only until 1980, chiefly as a result of the poor condition of its main runway; there was always the risk of small stones being thrown up into the air intakes, putting one or both engines out of action. So, after the closure of Tiksi for runway repairs, one squadron of 350 AP alternated with one squadron of 356 AP to use the airport at

With the arrival of spring, the 14th Air Army Tu-128 regiments started to practise deployments to their designated wartime 'operational' airfields beyond the Arctic Circle. Here, a 14 AA Tu-128 is parked in dispersal at Khatanga airfield, with the last vestiges of snow still visible on the edge of the pan. (*Nikolai Popov*)

Khatanga as an operational reserve airfield. Khatanga, Tiksi, Yakutsk and Alykyel' (Noril'sk) were also used in peacetime for the training of GCI station personnel deployed to these northern regions and sometimes also for combat alert duty.

The civil airport of Mirnyi (literally meaning 'peaceful'), built in the area where diamond mining had been established in Yakutia, could also be used by the Tu-128, and acted once or twice as a diversion airfield for 350 AP when Yakutsk was closed due to bad weather. In the latter years of Tu-128 operations, the new airfield of Polyarnyi (meaning 'polar') was constructed some 400 km (250 miles) north of Mirnyi to service a new diamond-mining development. Although primarily a civil facility, it too could take the Tu-128 if necessary. Since this area was surrounded by extensive boggy marshland, the delivery of supplies, including aviation fuel and gasoline, was performed in winter using temporary roads known as '*zimniki*' (from the word for winter—'*zima*'). Because of the limited stocks of fuel held at Polyarnyi airport, Tu-128 crews had to fly to Mirnyi to refuel if they were conducting operations from that airfield.

Another Arctic 'ice airfield' constructed on an island and used by the Tu-128 was situated in the Sedov Archipelago,[4] incorporating a number of smaller islands around Severnaya Zemlya (literally 'North Land'), including Golomyannyi and

A Tu-128M (c/n 502902) of the 3rd squadron of 350 AP at Bratsk, seen at Khatanga in the summer of 1987 on the type's last visit to this designated Arctic deployment airfield. Note that not all Tu-128Ms had the extended fin tip for the R-846 radio antenna. (*Nikolai Popov*)

Srednii Islands. A polar maritime hydrometeorological station had been established on the north-west tip of Golomyannyi Island in 1954, and in the 1960s a PVO radio-technical battalion set up a surveillance and GCI radar station there. This comprised a P-14 'Tall King' early warning radar, a P-35 'Bar Lock' GCI radar and PRV-13 and PRV-14 ('Side Net' family) height-finders (one of each), manned by a team of 125 officers, technicians and conscripts. Approximately 15 km (9.5 miles) to the east, on Srednii Island, there was an active frontier post (*zastava*) and an airfield, which was regarded by the 14th Army Tu-128 regiments as their forward operating base. The island of Golomyannyi was linked to Srednii Island by a narrow sand and pebble spit about a kilometre long, and the close proximity of the two large man-made structures and the two islands sometimes led to confusion regarding the actual location of the airfield. When flying to the airfield on Srednii Island, navigators would orientate themselves with reference to the 'Golomyannyi' radio-technical battalion facilities, situated close to the airfield, and in conversations it was common to hear the mistaken belief that the airfield was actually on Golomyannyi Island. In spite of the fact that the airfields on Graham Bell Island and Srednii Island were 'ice airfields' (i.e. 'winter airfields') the severe climate permitted their use for a large part of the year. Even on the most southerly of the two islands, Srednii, the average annual outside air temperature was

306

–14.7°C, while the average in the warmest month of July was +0.7°C. Therefore, the stable blanket of snow from which the runway surface was rolled flat generally formed in the middle of September and remained firm until the following June.

It was the responsibility of deployment airfield support groups set up at the main operational reserve airfields to oversee storage of the Tu-128's 'Ash' missiles, aviation fuel and ground support equipment. Such groups were formed at Alykyel' (Noril'sk), Khatanga, Tiksi and Yakutsk. Col. Yevglyevskiy was involved in the creation of the support group at Yakutsk:

> I flew up to Yakutsk with the regiment commander to look at the airfield and its layout and agreed on how we would set things up there. We also discussed the need for mutual co-operation with the civilian management of the airport in the event that our aircraft were to be deployed there.

The deployment support groups at the northern operational reserve airfields were subordinate to the 14th PVO Independent Army regimental commanders. The need to resolve the problem of providing adequate equipment for these groups, plus provision of 'combat control' (command control and communications—'C3' in today's parlance) at these airfields, was an essential element of mastering flight operations in the High Arctic. The PVO High Command understood very well that the most effective use of the Tu-128 in that region demanded a more advanced system of 'combat control', to which end they had proposed the following measures:

- Increasing the early warning distance by deploying new surveillance units on the islands of Zemlya Sannikova, Russkii and Uyedinyeniya, and also on Cape Pronchishchevoy and Peschanyi;
- Further extension of the zone of control, particularly at low level, by locating transportable GCI facilities with forward radar companies, along with the use of mobile command posts mounted in helicopters[5] and An-12 transports equipped with automatic radio-relay facilities;
- Developing mutual co-operation in terms of command, control and communications between ground stations, Tu-126 airborne early warning aircraft and shipborne command and fighter control posts (*korabyel'niye punkty upravlyeniya i navyedyeniya istrebityel'noy aviatsii*) of the Soviet Navy, with the aim of extending the zone of control;
- More extensive use of automated control systems.

Deployment to the operational reserve airfields of the High Arctic was preceded by very careful briefing of the aircrews involved. Young pilots and navigators coming to the region for the first time were taken up in a transport aircraft for a 'round-trip' of the area to view the terrain from the air in order to familiarise them with:

- the overall appearance of the 'northern' airfields;
- particular features of the approach to the airfields and the landing approach;
- individual airfield layouts;
- airfield radio and radar facilities.

Simultaneous with familiarisation training for the aircrew, an air traffic control group (*gruppa rukovodstva polyotami* or GRP) was also given a circular tour of the High Arctic airfields and briefings on the Czech-built 'Tesla' landing aids with which the civil airports were equipped. The GRP personnel had to get used to controlling the Tu-128 using civil air traffic control facilities at the airports, with particular emphasis on fighter control from command posts equipped for GCI or from radio-technical battalion command posts. GCI controllers from all sites subordinate to 22 Division PVO (HQ at Noril'sk) undertook probationary training in the relevant regimental command posts of the Independent PVO Army. Reduced complement teams in deployed regimental command posts in the High Arctic were subordinate to the regiment's chief of staff or his deputy, with the advanced party always including the senior navigator of the regiment or the regimental navigator responsible for air traffic control. When carrying out tactical or operational-tactical exercises involving deployment to airfields in the High Arctic, up to eighteen transportable GCI stations would be set up by PVO radio-technical battalions to provide fighter control. The main GCI control teams and those from 22 Division at the 'mobile' sites, performing the most challenging and important tasks, were augmented by controllers from the regimental command posts or from other PVO divisions. Radio-relay aircraft were usually sent up to provide reliable line-of-sight communication between the Tu-128 and its control authorities in those areas where ground-based communication facilities did not exist. Radio-relay aircraft were also used to tell crews to divert to their designated reserve airfield in the event of worsening weather conditions.

Deployment to operational reserve airfields took place once or twice a year and was conducted within the context of planned exercises between March and August when the weather in the north was more stable. Exercise scenarios involving deployment to an operational reserve airfield changed constantly in order to prevent crews becoming too familiar with 'scripted' situations, although the broad outlines, of course, remained essentially unchanged. Groups of aircraft would depart from base, as a rule on Monday or Tuesday, and spend between four and seven days at their deployment base. The Tu-128s would set off singly at two-minute intervals, in a column, usually comprising eight or nine aircraft drawn from the regiment's three squadrons. (A 'section', i.e. a flight, of deployed aircraft [*otryad manyevrirovaniya*] consisted of four aircraft.) Maj. Nikolai Popov remembers such deployments:

To go on detachment [deployment] in the Tu-128 was simply super. The aircraft had lots of space where you could put a suitcase and personal effects. Sometimes we would even carry vegetables if we were going to a northern airfield. Apart from that, the aircrew could replace the brake parachute without using a special press to pack it into its container. All you had to do was to gather up the canopy, put it into the container and you could go flying.

During major operational evaluations by the PVO's higher command authorities, an entire regiment could be tasked to deploy to its forward operating base. On one occasion during such an evaluation exercise, 64 AP deployed in regimental strength to its designated base at Alykyel' (Noril'sk). While the group taking part in the deployment was preparing for the transit flight, the supporting advance party flew in to the deployment airfield to prepare to accept the Tu-128s when they arrived at the new location. The advance party included an air traffic control group (GRP) from 64 AP and a 'technical party' from the regiment's engineering section, these personnel being transported in one of the unit's Tu-124Sh 'Cookpot' navigation trainers. Essential ground support equipment (aircraft tugs, spares and tools, etc.) was flown in to the deployment base by An-12 'Cub' or An-26 'Curl' transports allocated for this task by 14th PVO Independent Army HQ. On the day that the transit flight to the deployment airfield took place, routine flying there was suspended. After the fighters' arrival they were 'turned round' as if for another sortie, with missiles being mounted to simulate preparation for combat operations, and then once this procedure was completed the missiles were removed. Training flights and practice GCI flights against training targets (usually other Tu-128s of the regiment) were organised for the following day. The intensity of flight activity was less than at their home base—around three to four sorties, instead of the more usual six flights.

Almost all of the deployed aircraft took part in the flying programme, sometimes using four to six aircraft per 'shift'. Control of the group was carried out from the airport control tower, where the military controller was usually the deputy commander of one of the deployed squadrons. On deployment airfields, a Tu-128 group was subordinate to the senior military aviation authority or a representative of the PVO High Command at that airfield. Often, combat training flights and cross-country sorties during a deployment to the High Arctic were combined as integrated training exercises for the PVO missile troops and the GCI controllers of the PVO's 22 Division, with the Tu-128s acting as targets. In this case, two sorties would be carried out in a given flying 'shift', usually of 2 hours' duration, although since not all crews had VMSK immersion suits,[6] training flights involving over-water excursions in the North Arctic Ocean area were prohibited.

In the course of numerous exercises conducted by the 14th Independent Army, the operations determining the handling capacity of the Arctic deployment airfields were subjected to 'time and motion' analysis. The data obtained revealed that the most time-consuming activities affecting the ability to 'turn round' and prepare the 'Fiddler' for flight at Alykyel', Khatanga, Tiksi and Yakutsk were re-fuelling and re-arming. Groups of aircraft could be standing idle for up to 2 hours between flights at these airfields because of insufficient numbers of fuel bowsers, the limited handling capacity of the centralised refuelling system, and the distance between the POL[7] storage facilities and the airfield, this being 7 km (just over 4 miles) at Alykyel'. The distance from the Tu-128's operational bases to an Arctic deployment airfield (up to 2,100 km or 1,300 miles) and the prevailing rapidly changing en-route weather conditions made it necessary to limit weapons carriage to only two missiles on transit flights. On arrival at the deployment base, the aircraft would be armed with the standard 'fit' of four R-4 missiles, using regiment or squadron armourers, who could usually load four missiles per hour. Delivery of flight-ready missiles to the aircraft was a more lengthy process at Yakutsk than at other airfields because there was a distance of around 5 km (3 miles) between the weapons storage area and the airfield and road access was poor. Apart from this, a number of special conditions had to be observed in the interests of flight safety when preparing aircraft for flight in Arctic conditions.

Before making the transit to the Arctic, the aircraft were subjected to additional checks by the head of the second-line servicing team, and aircraft with few hours of time-between-overhauls remaining would undergo repair if necessary and then be given a test flight. The other aircraft would be withdrawn from the flying programme and the engineers would run through the check-list of vital equipment and units to ensure that they were all serviceable. The second-line engineering personnel would also check that they had the requisite amount of spares and tools, as well as establishing the type and number of transport aircraft allocated by the VTA (*Voyenno-Transportnaya Aviatsiya*) to carry the advance party. Particular attention was focused on pre-flight preparation of aircraft in winter conditions and the avoidance of exposure of ground crew when working outside. Low temperatures also resulted in loss of sealing of hydraulic systems and made engine starting more difficult, leading to further loss of time when preparing aircraft for combat operations, the special preparation after a severe snowstorm (*poslyepurgovaya podgotovka*)[8] requiring an air blower to purge snow from the wheel brakes, air intakes, fuel fillers and control surfaces, etc. The overall time required to pre-flight a squadron of Tu-128s for a combat training sortie, including missile preparation, fluctuated between 1 and 2 hours, depending on specific weather conditions.

The organisation and control of flights at the airfields in the High Arctic had their own specific problems owing to the fact that they were mainly Ministry of Civil Aviation airfields, with a very poor infrastructure of ground radar and radio installations, or meteorological stations. Additionally, when planning and controlling flights it was always essential to bear in mind that blizzards could blow up without warning in winter, or thick fog could develop equally rapidly in summer. Then there was always the presence of ground inversions to contend with, as well as icicles, deteriorating visibility, distortion of the appearance of runways and other structures, not to mention the other dangerous atmospheric phenomena of turbulence and icing. In such conditions the ATC controllers had to monitor take-offs and landings constantly in order to be able to provide pilots with timely assistance if and when needed.

In the 1980s it was decided to introduce the following measures to improve air traffic control:

- Installation of landing beacons (*Posadochniye Radiomayachniye Gruppy* or PRG—the collective term for ILS installation) at Alykyel', Khatanga and Tiksi;
- The equipping of deployment airfield support groups with a standard complement of ground radio and radar aids.

Transport crews flying advance parties to deployment airfields were given the additional task of providing search and rescue support for flights in the Arctic. At those airfields not provided with detachments of search and rescue teams from the USSR's Unified State Aviation Search and Rescue Service (*Yedinaya Gosudarstvyennaya Aviatsionnaya Poiskovo-spasatyel'naya Sluzhba—YeGAPSS SSSR*) parachutist-rescue groups were assigned from personnel serving with the deployed Tu-128 regiments. In addition to role-specific equipment, the aircraft designated to mount search and rescue missions carried a large multi-man tent (*palatka lagyernaya*— literally a 'camp tent') and one cubic metre of baled dry firewood, packaged so that it could be dropped safely from the aircraft. The firewood was an essential survival aid for aircrew awaiting the arrival of a rescue team after ejecting from their aircraft.

Tactical flight exercises (*lyotno-takticheskiye ucheniya* or LTUs) involving deployment into the High Arctic were written into the PVO's combat training plans, and one of the first regiments to participate in these operations was 64 AP from Omsk-North. Maj. Plyuta recalls this period:

We used to participate in LTUs every year. Our operational deployment airfield was Alykyel', to which we would fly, as a rule, in April. When Colonel Starovyerov was our regiment commander he would do a round flight in the winter of all the deployment airfields in *Zapolyar'ye*. He took a Tu-124Sh with him, carrying advance party personnel and he himself would fly the Tu-128. They flew from airfield to airfield [checking the equipment and conditions].

During an LTU exercise, eight or nine aircraft of 64 AP would set off from Omsk on a flight route taking them via Noril'sk, Tiksi, Yakutsk, Belaya and back to Omsk. On the final leg of the return transit crews would carry out live missile practice at the Telemba range complex. The length of an LTU exercise varied; for example, in 1970, 64 AP was based at Alykyel' for two weeks, although most were shorter than this. Enthused by his mastery of the High Arctic airfields and having been appointed Head of Aviation of 33 Division in the early 1970s, Col. Starovyerov introduced this practice to the entire division. Lt Col. Moiseyev remembers him well:

> Among the pilots Starovyerov was known as 'Baba Yaga'.[9] It didn't matter to him what aircraft he flew, or where to fly to—it only mattered that he flew! And although transit flights [to the Arctic] were also part of the combat training plans in the early days, Starovyerov did a great deal to make them more effective.

Thus, from 1973 and over the course of the next few years, LTU exercises conducted by 64 AP and 356 AP were completed in several stages:

1. Deployment to Alykyel' and Tiksi;
2. Subsequent transit to Yakutsk and Belaya;
3. Carrying out live missile firing at the Telemba range.

Gradually the circle of airfields mastered by the Tu-128 community widened and, in 1974, 64 AP started operating from Khatanga. A notable episode in the mastery of the northern airfields came at the end of 1979, when a pair of Tu-128s from 356 AP at Zhana-Semey led by squadron commander Lt Col. Zayats, with section (flight) commander Maj. Pustovalov as wingman, took off from Tiksi and landed on Srednii Island. During exercises held in the late 1970s a group of Tu-128s from 72 AP at Amderma, led by Lt Col. Boris Popov, carried out practice intercepts in the vicinity of the North Pole, after which the aircraft landed at the airfield on Graham Bell Island. It had been planned to base a squadron of Tu-128s from 518 AP on Graham Bell Island and the crews had undergone the appropriate training, but the deployment was cancelled as a result of a fatal accident involving a Tu-16 trying to land at this 'ice airfield'.

Periodically, the Tu-128 regiments of the 14th Independent Army practised combat control co-operation with the command posts and GCI stations of the 10th Independent Army, and crews from 356 AP were deployed to Amderma for this purpose in February 1980. Later, in 1983, 356 AP spent two months at their operational deployment airfield at Khatanga, carrying out QRA duty with two crews at '30-minute readiness' and others performing routine flight training. Altogether, ten flight 'shifts' were flown, a total of 140 hours being flown during the deployment. In the following year, 356 AP spent the entire summer at Khatanga while runway repairs were carried out at Zhana-Semey. Extremely useful experience of operating the Tu-128 away from home base was accumulated during these

In 1982, towards the end of the Tu-128's service life, 72 AP, under the command of Lt Col. Valeriy Yalyaev, was awarded the title of 'Excellent Regiment'. Here, a mix of Tu-128s, Tu-124s and a Mi-8 provide a backdrop for the parade at which the 'Excellent Regiment' banner was handed over. (*Valeriy Yalyaev Archive*)

deployments, which was summarised for all support services and passed on to other regiments in the form of 'methodological developments' (i.e. recommended procedures) for deployed operations. Deployments to mainland bases took place once or twice a year and were a normal occurrence, but the more demanding transit flights to island bases were, in the opinion of Lt Col. Moiseyev, '… unique, demonstrative actions, intended more to frighten a potential adversary [than operationally viable procedures]'. The last time that a Tu-128 visited the High Arctic was in 1987, when aircraft of 350 AP made a deployment transit to Khatanga from their base at Bratsk.

Exercises, Ranges and Drifting Aerostats

PARTICIPATION IN EXERCISES

The combat readiness of a regiment was established by tactical flight exercises (LTUs) held with differing levels of control authority (i.e. squadron, regiment, division, army, etc.). The most significant and regularly conducted exercises were LTUs held at the regimental level (*LTU polka*), which commenced with a combat readiness evaluation. In this case, the regiment was brought to a higher readiness state, previously known as raising the 'Alarm' signal ('*Trevoga*'). Combat readiness checks usually commenced late at night or early in the morning, in order to provide maximum tactical realism. This effect was reinforced by all personnel collecting their NBC[1] respirators and OZK (*Obshchevoyskoviye Zashchitniye Komplekty*) combined arms protective suits and assembling on the airfield. The main task of the regiment at this point was to prepare and maintain all aircraft at Readiness 1, and if no other orders were given by the higher command authorities all aircraft would be armed with a full complement of missiles. Since the loading of missiles onto the Tu-128 took up the greatest amount of time, this was the first task undertaken by the ground crews. The missiles were taken from the armoury and delivered to the 'preliminary preparation position' located in one of the hangars, where they were taken out of their transit crates and loaded onto ground handling trolleys. Here the wings would be attached and the missiles prepared for loading onto the aircraft, after which they would be delivered on the trolleys to the flight line.

In the aircraft's ground equipment set there was a special support beam for loading the missiles onto the pylons, which was attached to the nose section of the APU-128 launch rail, and a hand-operated winch was attached to this beam. The trolleys were then manoeuvred under the pylon and each missile would be winched into position in turn. Sgt Korolyov, a weapons mechanic in the second-line servicing section of 445 AP at Kotlas in 1967/68, recalls working on the Tu-128:

In normal weapons configuration (i.e. for standard combat alerts) only R-4T IR-guided variants of the 'Ash' missile were carried on the inboard pylons, with semi-active radar guided versions outboard. The variant could be further identified from the serial number carried on the port side of the missile body – in this case 1РТИ0050707048 (1RTI0050707048), RT indicating *Rakieta Tyeplovaya* – infrared missile. The additional letter 'I' (Russian 'И') in the designation indicates that the missile is equipped with an optical fuse. (*Nikolai Popov*)

The missiles were attached to the pylons with the aid of winches. The winch was attached to the forward part of the pylon and a support truss was placed under the missile. The missile was then brought up to the pylon by turning the handle of the winch and locked on to the rail. It was quite a lengthy process and [to save time] we started loading the missiles by hand—a team of around ten men would all lift together, raising the missile up to the launch rail. This greatly reduced the loading time, but deputations from High Command started to drop in on us and put a stop to our initiative.

However, manual loading of the missiles *did* gradually become the norm on all the regiments; the pylons were quite close to the ground and the contemporary military work norms allowed for manual loading if each man took only a 50 kg (110 lb) share of the weight of a weapon. The decision to load the missiles using a team of six, eight or ten men was therefore fully in accord with these norms. Maj. Plyuta adds:

If the regiment was called to readiness on the 'Alarm' signal, the first operation to be carried out was missile loading. The size of the handling team required for missile loading was determined by earlier decree and comprised officers, warrant officers and tradesmen from the airframe [AO], avionics [REO] and armament [AV] specialisations. Sometimes a reduced complement missile loading team would be used, made up of four tradesmen from the aircraft servicing crew and two armourers from the AV group. The teams were trained [by practice] to be able to load the missile directly onto the pylon in one single action.

Sometimes, after missile loading, the engines would be started and the aircraft taxied around the airfield, simulating preparation for take-off. Then, after appropriate checks and procedures, the missiles would be removed, leaving only the QRA aircraft fully armed and ready to launch if required. Thus, assembling all of the regiment's personnel on the airfield, practice missile loading, taxiing around the airfield and then towing the aircraft to their revetments after simulated post-flight checks, occupied virtually all of the first working day of an exercise.

Usually, however, exercise-related measures were considered complete only after the crews had been declared to be at 'Readiness 1' and the time taken to reach this had been recorded for subsequent assessment as part of the exercise evaluation. Maj. Rodyukov recalls his involvement in early exercises:

In the early days of operating the Tu-128, the regiment (518 AP at Talagi) achieved exercise operational readiness in 4 hours 20 minutes. In this time, four missiles were mounted on each of the regiment's 36 aircraft. By the end of Tu-128 operations, this figure had been reduced to 35-40 minutes! During an operational evaluation check by the Chief Inspectorate of the Ministry of Defence, headed by Marshal Moskalenko, the regiment, with 15 crews at Readiness 1, got airborne within 24 minutes. Outside of normal exercises we also used to hold practice 'Alarms' and on one occasion we actually launched against a real threat during one of these simulations. The whole airfield was covered with a 30 cm [12 inch] layer of snow. After achieving Readiness 1 we were given the commands 'Start-up' ('*Zapusk*'), 'On to the runway' ('*Na vzly-otnuyu*') and 'Scramble' ('*Vozdukh*'). The afterburners were lit and nothing could be seen for the clouds of snow behind the aircraft. Then the first aircraft took off, dispersing the snow a little, and all the others took off without incident.

During exercises, all personnel were initially confined to base, routine training flights were suspended, and all exercise-related sorties were controlled from the base command post (*Komandnyi Punkt*). Depending upon the task assigned to the regiment during an exercise, some of its personnel could be authorised to go home for the night (to wash and shave etc.), with the less fortunate having to stay on the base. In this period, the QRA flight was doubled in strength by reinforcing it with reserve crews, who were usually accommodated in the ATC tower. During the course of the day the aircraft would sometimes undergo NBC decontamination (*dezaktivatsiya* or *degazatsiya*) procedures, simulating the conditions expected after use of weapons of mass destruction by the enemy. As previously mentioned, some aircraft could also be launched during an exercise to undertake practice intercepts against targets flying on non-standard flight routes, attempting to attack objectives under the protective air cover of the Tu-128. The targets would use active and passive jamming for added realism during these sorties, complicating the interception process.

In the 1980s, when performing routine training interceptions drawn up in the KBP combat training manual for the 'Fiddler', training missiles were often not mounted on the aircraft, saving fatigue life on both missile and aircraft. In order to simulate the electrical connection of missile to pylon, a special device was mounted in place of the missile itself, known on the regiments as the 'beetle' (*zhuk*). The 'beetle' provided the necessary electrical link between the pylon and the circuitry of the weapons system controls in the cockpit, just as if a missile was actually attached. However, during major exercises (*krupniye ucheniya*) training missiles *would* be used, as was also the case before live missile firing practice since the 'beetle' did not simulate an interception 'right up to the terminal phase of the engagement', being unable to simulate the response of the missile seeker heads.

Tu-128 regiments participated in all the major exercises that were undertaken in the northern part of the former USSR. In 1968, 23 Division of the PVO took part

A close-up of an R-4TI variant of the 'Ash' missile (serial number 1РТИ0050702005 (1RTI0050702005) on a Tu-128 of 356 AP. Note that the windows of the NOV-80N optical (infrared) fuse are protected with covers in their three locations around the body of the missile, on the top and sides, just ahead of the leading edge of the missile's delta wing. (*Igor' Marchuk*)

317

in Exercise *'Niebiesnyi Shchit'* ('Celestial Shield') when, for the first time in PVO history, 518 AP pilots carried out practice interceptions over the Arctic Ocean. The interceptions were performed at a distance of 800-850 km (500-530 miles) from base at Talagi, using several intermediary radio-relay links for the transmission of operative commands, a landing at their operational reserve airfield and live missile firing over the sea. Another serious test for Tu-128 crews was the exercise code-named *'Sevyer-70'* ('North-70'), under the operational control of the C-in-C of the PVO. In addition to units of the 10th Independent PVO Army, the exercise plan included the participation of 64 AP from the 14th Army. The regiment was programmed into the exercise scenario directly from an en-route transit, without intermediate landing or refuelling, taking account of three specific operational elements. Considering first the 'air situation', the need for increased 'peacetime' fuel stocks and the fact that the 'enemy' (*protivnik*) strike was to be conducted in a sector strongly defended by an anti-aircraft missile group from the PVO 21st Corps, 10th Army HQ decided that 64 AP should land at Talagi, refuel the aircraft there and use them as part of 23 Division to repulse any follow-on strikes.

Maj. Plyuta was one of the participants in these exercises:

On June 22nd 1970, our regiment, 64 AP, was placed on exercise alert. We arrived at the airfield in the usual way, loaded the missiles and 'pre-flighted' the aircraft. By this time the An-12 transports had arrived, so we loaded our spares packs and equipment onto them, got on board ourselves and took off. We all thought that we'd do a circuit of the airfield and then land, but it all turned out differently. We weren't told where or why we were flying. We made an intermediate landing at Kol'tsovo [Sverdlovsk] where the An-12 navigator went off to ATC. When he returned we discovered that we were flying to Savvatiya [Kotlas]. After landing at Kotlas the situation became clear and we learned that we were going on to Arkhangel'sk. We had a meal at Kotlas and then headed off north. That day, June 22nd, was the height of the 'white nights' of the north. By the time we got to Talagi we knew how many of our Tu-128s should have already arrived before us. As we taxied past the parking area for our aircraft we noticed that one was missing. It turned out that when it was landing the nose-wheel leg went into a pot-hole on the runway, bursting one of the tyres, with pieces of rubber being ingested into an intake and putting one of the engines out of action. The engineering ground staff on 518 AP, not expecting our arrival, towed the aircraft to the second-line servicing hangar [TEhCh] and started to replace the engine. The aircraft was ready to be test flown within 23 hours of the incident, something of a record for an engine change. The nights were short, so the engineers were able to work through without a break. It was during this exercise that we discovered the actual capacity of the Tu-128's fuel tanks. Returning from an intercept detail over the Barents Sea our aircraft were landing with fuel remainders of only 200 litres each [44 imp. gals] and I had personally put 19,200 litres [4,224 imp. gals] in 'my own' aircraft during the post-flight checks.

Lt Col. Vladimir Yenyutin, former senior navigator of 64 AP, adds:

In June 1970 we took part in the major exercise 'Sevyer-70', in which one squadron of
64 AP was deployed to Talagi.[2] The exercise operational plan called for Talagi-based
518 AP to deploy to Lyetnyeozyorsk, while 72 AP and 445 AP would 'fight' from their
home bases. The transit flight from Omsk-North to Talagi involved an intermediate
landing at Savvatiya. There, we were topped up with 1,000 litres [220 imp. gals] in
the integral wing tanks. While taking off from Savvatiya on the second leg of the
transit, one of the Tu-128s, flown by Lt Col. Nikolayev and Captain Bel'skii suffered
an afterburner malfunction in the starboard engine [this incident is described in
detail in Chapter 9]. On landing at Talagi, another of the Tu-128s, flown by Captain
Fishchenko, suffered a 'blow-out' of the right-hand nose-wheel tyre, fragments of
which struck the HF 'towel rail' antenna and were sucked into the starboard engine.
Although the engine did not flame out, a post-flight inspection revealed that the
compressor blades had been damaged and the engine had to be changed [see above].

With so many aircraft in the exercise, the din ('*galdyozh*') on the radio was so
intense that it was difficult to make oneself heard. Not only that, but it was also a bit
daunting for us 'landlubber Siberians' to go out over the Barents Sea and 'round the
corner' of the Kola Peninsula. However, we felt happier on one flight when we were
intercepted by a pair of Su-9s around 300-400 km [185-250 miles] off the coast. After
all, the two engines on our 'one' aircraft were so much better than the 'two' engines
of the two Su-9s! We indulged in simulated combat activities for a week and then
flew home directly, without an intermediate landing, a distance of 2,300 km [1,430
miles]. If memory serves correctly, we were not permitted to make such transits
again. On the return flight, the senior officer of our group, Colonel Starovyerov,
the Head of Aviation of 33 Division of the PVO, flew directly to Zhana-Semey [his
HQ airfield] from abeam Perm', having captured the RSBN navigation beacon from
around 300 km [185 miles] from the airfield. At that time, such 'freedom of action'
was permitted. There were still no zonal or regional ATC centres—military aircraft
flew 'off route' and without altitude limits (*vnie trass i vnie eshelonov*). Today, this
seems quite 'wild', but in those days it was the norm. Flights to maximum altitude,
and selection of the most appropriate altitudes, were carried out based on [outside
air] temperature and this was done not just 'somewhere' over the Kara Sea but also
directly over the mainland USSR.

The C-in-C of the Soviet Navy, Admiral Gorshkov, also organised a large-scale
exercise in 1970 under his direct control, with the code-name '*Okean*', involving
not only vessels and units of the Northern Fleet but also air and ground units of
the PVO 10th Independent Army. The exercise was planned to include live firing
against RUM (*Radio-Upravlyaemaya Mishen'*) radio-controlled targets. Exercise
'*Okean*' was observed by a military delegation headed by the Minister of Defence

Marshal A. A. Grechko and his senior officers. The live firings were designed to confirm the reliability of the air cover provided not only for Soviet Naval bases and vessels but also for the protection of industrial and political centres of the country from air strikes. Shipborne anti-aircraft gun and missile units also conducted live firing against the RUM targets, which provided an element of competition between PVO and Soviet Navy anti-aircraft defensive systems. During the course of the exercise, the C-in-C of the Navy was also shown round the Tu-128 on Severomorsk airfield in order to familiarise him with its performance and capabilities.

Both 518 AP and 72 AP continued to participate in the large-scale exercises code-named '*Sevyer*' and '*Arktika*' conducted under the auspices of the General Staff of the PVO, with a particularly complex scenario being devised for the '*Arktika*' exercise in 1971. This included mass raids by 'enemy' formations flying at various altitudes, employing ECM and anti-missile manoeuvring. The PVO radio-technical troops manning the radar surveillance and GCI sites maintained round-the-clock combat alerts, and Tu-126 'Moss' airborne early warning aircraft were brought in to extend the area of radar cover over the Barents Sea. In addition to the aforementioned exercises, the Tu-128 was also involved in other large-scale exercises, such as '*Arktika-74*', '*Vesna-77*', '*Zapolyar'ye-78*', '*Arktika-81*' and '*Arktika-84*', with scenarios broadly similar to those already outlined.

Apart from involvement in the larger exercises, all PVO air regiments had to undergo periodic inspection and evaluation by the Soviet Ministry of Defence Main Inspectorate (*Glavnaya Inspektsiya Ministerstva Oborony* or GIMO). These inspections used to last around three to five days and were comparable in their aims and execution to NATO tactical evaluations (TACEVAL). Following a GIMO inspection in May 1970, 64 AP received an assessment of '*Otlichnyi*' (Excellent), which was quite a rare event for such a serious and demanding evaluation of operational readiness. In 1972, the 10th Army underwent a GIMO inspection, with 518 AP flying two of its squadrons from its main base at Talagi and one squadron from its forward operating location. After carrying out interceptions on practice targets for evaluation purposes, twenty-six crews landed back at Talagi safely in spite of their low fuel remainders. Regimental tactical flight exercises (LTUs) were carried out at least twice a year, mainly involving deployment to a forward operating location, although they were sometimes carried out from the main base. The 'Fiddler' did not emerge as victor in all exercises, since much depended on the quality of command post and GCI control, but any failings were always studied positively in order to prevent the occurrence of future mistakes.

As the Tu-128's flight endurance was very high for a fighter, it was often employed in exercises as a simulated aggressor aircraft, which was an important attribute during regimental training flights and for training GCI controllers, particularly those stationed at the more remote northern sites. In the capacity of simulated aggressors, the pilots would switch off their IFF and descend to low level, trying to mimic the actions of a real aggressor attempting to penetrate the nation's air defence cordon. In 1978, Tu-128s also took part in one of the final test phases in the 'troop trials' of the Almaz S-300 (SA-10a 'Grumble') anti-aircraft missile system, prior to its operational deployment, as recalled by Lt Col. Yenyutin:

Twelve aircraft each were involved in the trials, from 356 AP, 350 AP and 64 AP, plus a number of MiG-25 fighters as high-altitude targets and L-29 'Delfin' jet trainers acting as low-level aggressors. The exercise task was to simultaneously insert a specific number of 'targets' into the S-300's operating zone over a wide altitude range and from different directions in order to create as challenging a scenario as possible for the new missile's tracking and control systems. After the simulated 'raid', the Tu-128s from 350 AP and 356 AP were programmed to land at Zhana-Semey, while 64 AP was scheduled to land at Chagan [alternative name Dolon]. Complications arose in co-ordinating the activities of all the participants, with particular difficulties being encountered on completion of the exercise when the 36 Tu-128s started to return and were told that Zhana-Semey was closed due to 'out-of-limits' crosswinds. As a result, it was going to be necessary for *all* the Tu-128s to land at Chagan. I was the senior officer in the command post at Chagan, where the entire control group only had local experience and hadn't even seen our aircraft on television! The main problem, however, was that there was only a distance of 80 km [50 miles] between the two airfields, and the crosswind conditions at both were identical—14 to 17 m/sec [27-33 kts] straight across the runway. Even the runway headings were similar—260° magnetic at one and 256° at the other! It took a long time to shout all this down the telephone before we reached an agreement and everyone landed back at their departure airfields.

Other important tasks for the Tu-128 were acting as escorts for LRAF bombers, 'sanitisation' of the airspace for bomber operations, and provision of top cover for their in-flight refuelling zones. Sometimes, during escort sorties, Tu-128 crews would meet NATO fighters waiting to intercept the Soviet bombers. This is how Lt Col. Oleg Fedoseyenko remembers such an incident:

In September 1983, a joint exercise involving the Air Force and the PVO was being conducted over the Barents Sea. It was said that a total of 400 aircraft from both services were taking part. The aircraft of 72 AP were deployed to Kilp-Yavr for the duration of the exercise. The exercise plan involved us in providing an escort for the bombers as they went 'round the corner' [round the Kola Peninsula]. The flight routes went as far as Bear Island (*Ostrov Myedvyezhii*).[3] The whole squadron worked day and night and we were accommodated in barracks at Kilp-Yavr. Each crew had its own exercise task. On one of the flights NATO launched some F-16s from one of the Norwegian bases when we flew abeam the coastline at a distance of 100 km

[62 miles]. We were flying without missiles. The F-16s came in close, [obviously] interested in our weapons fit. It was a daytime sortie and at an altitude of 11,000 m [36,100 feet] an F-16 approached from somewhere below us. We always maintained radio contact with the command post at Severomorsk-3 and they warned us that 'strangers' ('*chuzhiye*') were coming up to us. A pair. The pilot came in close. He gestured to us as if to ask, 'Where are your weapons?'—I showed him my pistol and he showed me [the F-16's] cannon and four missiles (!). This was just after the incident in the Far East when a Boeing 707 [*sic*] had been shot down.[4] We didn't switch our radar on. Our task was to follow the planned flight route and not to take any kind of action. We reported the presence of the foreign fighter to the command post. The F-16 stayed behind us on our port side for a few more minutes and then departed.

On successful conclusion of such exercises, a large amount of operational data had been accumulated and a number of practical proposals were put forward regarding operational use of the Tu-128 in the extreme north of the USSR and in the Arctic.

MISSILE FIRING RANGES

As was the case for all combat units of the Soviet Air Force and aviation regiments of the PVO, Tu-128 crews periodically conducted missile firing practice at a number of ranges across the USSR. Ranges used by the PVO were set up within unpopulated or sparsely populated areas of the country, or over the open sea, where spent missiles and missile debris (including surface-to-air missiles) could fall without risk to people below. Missile firing zones had to provide a distance of least two and a half times the missiles' flight range from the usual point of release, and at Sary-Shagan, for example, the firing zone was around 650 km (400 miles) square. In official documentation this range was known as the 10th State Scientific Research Test Range (*10-yi Gosudarstvyennyi Nauchno-issledovatyel'skii Ispytatyel'nyi Poligon*). It was situated in the Betpak-Dala Desert in Kazakhstan, west of Lake Balkhash and not far from the town of Sary-Shagan, from where it derived its popular name. Tu-128 crews used a number of other ranges for live missile firing practice, and regiments of the 10th Independent Army often used the Northern Fleet missile range located in the Barents Sea. The northern Tu-128 regiments also used the range at Krasnovodsk in the Caspian Sea jointly with 445 AP from Kotlas, although the Caspian Sea ranges were closed down on environmental grounds towards the middle of the 1970s. As a result, most live missile firing practice for the 'Fiddler' was transferred to Sary-Shagan (Balkhash), while the Ashuluk Range was also used occasionally, the aircraft operating out of the nearby airfield at Astrakhan-Privolzhsky. The Tu-128 regiments of the 14th Independent Army generally used the ranges at Telemba in the Transbaikal region, as well as Sary-Shagan.

Up to 1980, missile firing was conducted at Telemba and, depending upon the scenario, the aircraft staged out of the civil airport at Kadala serving the city of Chita. Thereafter, all missile firing by the 14th Army's Tu-128s was transferred to Sary-Shagan, the aircraft operating out of Zhana-Semey. The flight endurance of the Tu-128 allowed it to carry out missile firing at medium altitude, return to the operating airfield and then land with a normal fuel remainder. If the aircraft was operating against manoeuvring Lavochkin La-17 targets flying at low level, then the interceptors would use Sary-Shagan's civil airport at Balkhash as an emergency diversion field, since the flight profile against the La-17 was quite variable, using a great deal of fuel and reducing endurance. If they did divert into Balkhash, they would refuel there and then return to Zhana-Semey. All three regiments of the 14th Army carried out their live missile firing in this way, staging out of Zhana-Semey.

In contradistinction to missile firing at the southern ranges, the two main northern Tu-128 regiments, 518 AP at Talagi and 72 AP at Amderma, carried out their firings on the Northern Fleet range in the Barents Sea from their own bases. However, 72 AP would, as a rule, take off from base, carry out firing practice over the range and then land at Talagi, Monchegorsk or Kilp-Yavr. The regiment would then conduct a tactical flight exercise incorporating a number of operational 'Variants', since combat readiness assessment was based not only on live missile firing but also on unit organisation, management procedures and the work of ground servicing personnel etc. Range work was, of course, a serious test of crew ability, and they had to perform live firings at least once every two years. Col. Yevglyevskiy adds:

> Live firings were often combined with a deployment to an operational reserve airfield. We used to deploy to the north every year, as I used to say, 'by the great circle' (*'po bol'shomu krugu'*).[5] The regiments from Semipalatinsk, Omsk and Belaya would go via Noril'sk, Tiksi and Yakutsk and then on to the range at Telemba. They would arrive in the range area and carry out missile firing directly from the approach route. Targets had already been released over the range. After missile firing the aircraft would depart to their base airfields.

THE TARGETS

In this period (the 1980s) the targets used on the firing ranges included the VRPM, PM-6 (M-6) parachute-based systems and the La-17 radio-controlled aircraft.

The VRPM (*Vysotnaya Rakietnaya Parashutnaya Mishen'*), literally meaning 'High-altitude Rocket Parachute Target', was similar in design to the PM-6 described below. The VRPM was fired from the ground by a long-range artillery piece and the parachute would deploy automatically at an altitude of 25,000 m

(82,000 feet), the whole ensemble then descending to earth at a calculated rate. The PM-6 consisted of an assembly of weighted corner reflectors and a heat-source container suspended beneath a parachute. The heat-source ignited after the canopy opened, burning for several minutes during the descent. Combining corner reflectors and a heat-source in the same structure allowed the target to be used for both semi-active radar and infrared-guided missiles. After leaving the APU-128 pylon, the 'Ash' missile would initially drop below the launch aircraft (i.e. 'settle') before motor ignition and acceleration towards the target. The semi-active radar-guided R-4R missile continued to be illuminated by the *Smerch* radar for a short time after launch and then switched to autonomous flight mode. Dependent upon the target dimensions (i.e. fighter or bomber) selected by the crew before launch, there was a set delay for the fuse to activate designed to ensure that the warhead detonated as close to the centre of the target as possible.

Performance data for PM-6 target
Release height—up to 17,000 m (55,775 feet)
Burn time—5-6 minutes
Vertical descent speed—3-4 m/sec (590-790 ft/min)
Radar cross section (RCS)—equivalent to that of a MiG-17-sized target
Detection range—34-36 km (about 22 miles)
Lock-on range—20-22 km (about 12 miles)

As a rule, the PM-6 target was released from a Tu-16 'Badger' bomber at an altitude of 11,000 m (36,100 feet) and after release the Tu-16 crew monitored its descent. The aircraft would leave the zone if the parachute opened normally, but in the event of a malfunction the bomber crew would release another target. Apart from this, there was a modification of the PM-6 that could also be fired from an artillery piece and set to release at various altitudes between 15,000-17,000 m (49,200-55,775 feet), but this was used only up until 1979/80. The most complex and expensive aerial target in use at this time was the jet-powered Lavochkin La-17, the basic performance details of which are given below.

Performance data for La-17 target
Operating altitude—up to 17,500 m (57,400 feet)
Maximum speed—850-870 kph (460-470 kts)
Endurance—90 minutes
Time to climb to 16,000 m (52,500 feet) –4 minutes
Time to complete 360° turn—3.3 seconds
Radar cross section (RCS)—equivalent to that of an Il-28-sized target

Live missile firing was always preceded by careful preparation, and only a certain percentage of crews were selected for this phase of training at any given time. The number of crews was dependent upon the number of targets available for a given firing detail and the level of training of the personnel involved. Everyone taking part in live firing had his own specific task. Young pilots firing missiles for the first time took part in a daytime programme against parachute targets; those crews who were improving their missile firing skills had to work with parachute targets at night; the most experienced pilots were able to work with the radio-controlled La-17 target. Since all live missile firing tasks differed slightly from each other for the above-mentioned reasons, crews were briefed separately according to their specific qualification profile, with a full week being assigned to the preparation phase. Usually only two missiles per aircraft were loaded for live missile firing, one semi-active radar-guided R-4R and one infrared-guided R-4T variant, although there was an option to use two semi-active missiles. Four missiles were mounted only in cases where it was absolutely essential to destroy the target, namely when using the La-17 target which could potentially fly outside of the limits of the range if not hit during the first pass.

When releasing the PM-6 parachute target, the Tu-16 flew a course taking it directly above that flown by the interceptors, and in one overflight of the range

In spite of the fact that a pair of Tu-128s are shown together on the runway with engines running, witnessed by the open supplementary air intake doors on the side of the fuselage, paired take-offs were never performed by these aircraft. Both aircraft are armed for live missile firing practice, each with only two missiles. (*Ivan Rodyukov*)

the aircraft would drop two targets. An attack would be carried out by one or two Tu-128s on each PM-6 target and if flying as a pair they would be in column formation, with an interval of 3-10 minutes between each aircraft. After the attack, one aircraft would break right and the other to the left, with the distance between the axes of the turns being around 20-30 km (around 12-19 miles). The order to switch the *Smerch* radar to radiate and lock-on to the target during the attack was given from the command post only when the target-dropping aircraft was clear of the area. In the majority of cases, if an interceptor crew were working a PM-6, only one missile was sufficient to destroy the target, the first missile to lock on (usually an IR-guided R-4T version) being the first missile to leave the launch rail. While the target was descending, two or three interceptors could fire their missiles at it, the third aircraft usually destroying the target at the extremely low altitude (for the R-4 missile) of 10,000 m (32,800 feet). Although a salvo firing of all four missiles was not standard procedure, there were occasions when such a firing was performed, as recalled by Col. Komyagin:

> A salvo firing was very impressive and at night it was blinding. You couldn't tell when the missiles left the rails, just like on the Su-9, only there was more flame and smoke from the more powerful rocket motors of the R-4. When the missiles were flying out towards the target they would 'wander' with respect to the line of flight—one going 'high', the other 'low' and then changing place, but going straight for the target.

The aircraft itself handled well during missile firing and was very stable. In the case where the last missile to be fired was from one of the outer rails it would experience a slight sideslip motion, but this was quite easy for the pilot to correct.

In the interests of economising on the use of live missiles, not only was the upgraded R-4M version of the AA-5 used but also the older R-4. If the R-4M was being used, then all missiles would leave the launch rail (pylon) when selected. However, in the case of the earlier R-4 variant, the probability of launch was only 50 per cent if a second crew were firing at a PM-6 target that had managed to descend below 10,000 m (32,800 feet), as the R-4 had a lower limit for target destruction of 8,000 m (26,250 feet). Thus, if the first crew had damaged the PM-6 parachute and target assembly, it would start to descend rapidly and the second aircraft in sequence would be sent round again. After the navigator signalled the 'Launch' command to the missile, its built-in pneumatic system would release the aerodynamic control surfaces from their locked position and place them in the neutral position. However, if the command was passed to the R-4 at an altitude of less than 8,000 m, the pressure in the pneumatic system was insufficient to set the controls to the required position (so-called 'Zero controls'—'*Nol' rulyey*' position), the rocket motor would not ignite and the missile would remain on the pylon. However, on the upgraded R-4M variant the pressure in the pneumatic system was twice that of the older missile and it did not therefore suffer from this shortcoming. When an aircraft returned from the range with an unlaunched R-4M missile, the ground crew would immediately check the missile control surfaces. If they could be moved by hand freely (like a weather vane), this meant that the pilot had tried to launch the missile at an altitude of less than 8,000 m—they could be fired from 2,000 m (6,560 feet) and 3,000 m (9,840 feet)—and the 'firing' was counted as valid. (The logic for this was that once the command to launch had been passed to the missile via the weapons computer, the target was obviously 'locked-on'; if it was an R-4M missile then it would have reached the target!)

The Northern Fleet range used for live missile firing by the Tu-128 had a number of peculiarities compared with the 'continental' ranges of the USSR. The main range was located over the Barents Sea a little north of Murmansk, the closest point to the coastline being some 200 km (125 miles) offshore. Because of its accessible location over international waters, any range activity always attracted the interest of NATO reconnaissance aircraft and warships, as recalled by Maj.-Gen. Skok from his days as a junior officer:

> I remember an occasion when none of the eight crews assigned to fire semi-active radar guided missiles were able to work at the range because the area was saturated with electro-magnetic interference from the NATO 'intruders'. It was evident that the

A 350 AP 'Fiddler' in the QRA dispersal at Bratsk, with electrical power cables already plugged in. The missiles, cockpit area and air intakes were usually protected from the elements when on QRA duty, but the covers have been removed here at the request of the photographer. (*Nikolai Popov*)

'enemy' had studied the peacetime frequencies of our radars and they were 'experimenting' with their equipment during our firing practice. On this occasion we were only able to use our infrared-guided missiles.

The 10th Independent Army also used to conduct combat alert checks involving live missile firing, as recalled by Maj. Rodyukov:

Crews would be sitting in the QRA quarters, playing chess or just relaxing, and then suddenly there'd be the call, 'Start engines, take-off, heading, combat heading, variant so-and-so …' On these occasions the practice target would be destroyed. On routine firings the missiles were not fitted with live warheads. Only the last aircraft to fire would be carrying live warheads. So the last aircraft had to destroy the target.

The targeting and missile launch process was 'fixed' by the KZA recording system, which used cameras installed in the cockpit of the pilot and navigator. One camera photographed the pilot's instrument panel and the 'PR' combined button switch/warning lights permitting missile launch, while the second photographed the navigator's radar screen. The KZA system also included oscillographs which recorded missile parameters.[6]

This early-1980s view shows a Tu-128M of the 3rd squadron of 356 AP carrying a row of five red stars on the fuselage below the pilot's cockpit, indicating the number of successful missile launches during live missile firing practices. (*Nikolai Popov*)

OPERATIONS AGAINST AUTOMATIC DRIFTING AEROSTATS (RECON-NAISSANCE BALLOONS)

From the 1950s, automatic drifting aerostats (ADA) were used by a number of NATO countries, albeit principally by the United States, to conduct reconnaissance flights over the territory of the USSR. A significant number of these were launched from military bases in Scandinavia (mainly Norway). Reconnaissance balloons flew (drifted) at altitudes from 10,000 m (32,800 feet) to 25,000 m (82,000 feet), usually in the direction of Yakutsk and beyond, towards Japan. The reconnaissance equipment, weighing up to 1,000 kg (2,200 lb), was carried in a container suspended beneath the gas envelope, although in the early years of operation the containers often carried propaganda material. Starting from the 1950s, the USSR took action against the balloons, using a variety of interceptors to shoot them down, including the MiG-17F 'Fresco-C' and Su-9 'Fishpot-B', and a programme of scientific research work was carried out in order to determine the possibility of destroying a balloon with a fighter aircraft. Col. Yevglyevskiy recalls this programme:

> We acquired some Soviet reconnaissance balloons, selected various types of interceptor and tried to shoot the ADA down using a number of different methods. We examined the possibility of using semi-active radar guided missiles against them, but it was obvious that their effectiveness was very low. The small dimensions of the container provided a very low level of reflectivity for an AI radar and it could not 'see' the synthetic material of the balloon envelope. In addition, the closing speed of the interceptor with the balloon was very high and the probability of destroying it was correspondingly low.

In 1972, the C-in-C of the PVO ordered the publication of a document to inform crews of the reconnaissance balloon threat and how to deal with it, entitled 'Instructions on how to destroy ADAs' (*Instruktsiya po unichtozheniyu ADA*'). Over time, the document was amended slightly, but for the 'Fiddler' it remained largely unchanged until the end of the aircraft's service life. According to the instructions, the most effective intercept profile against an ADA with a radar cross section of 1 m² (10.75 sq. ft) was a forward hemisphere attack using the AI radar. However, it was assumed that on detection of the interceptor's radar emissions, the balloon could release ballast and ascend to an altitude unattainable by an aircraft. Thus, it was decided to use infrared-guided missiles to shoot down drifting reconnaissance balloons. The most propitious time for shooting down an ADA was in daylight, about 1.5-2 hours after sunrise, when the balloon exhibited the highest optical contrast because of heat and light reflection off the envelope. Guidance to the ADA was given by voice commands from the GCI station from an initial range to target of around 40-50 km (25-31 miles), with subsequent commands regarding range and target height differential being passed until the balloon was in visual range.

It was essential to conduct a visual search in azimuth within the following sectors, depending upon the distance to the target:

- ±30° at a range of up to 30 km (19 miles) and greater;
- ±40° at a range of up to 20 km (12 miles);
- ±50° at a range of up to 10 km (6 miles);
- ±60° at a range of up to 5 km (3 miles) and an elevation above the horizon of 10-15°.

The visual detection range of a drifting reconnaissance balloon with a diameter of around 8-10 m (26-33 feet), depending upon its height differential above the interceptor, was:

- 30-40 km (19-25 miles) with a height differential of 1,500-2,000 m (4,920-6,560 feet);
- 20-25 km (12.5-15.5 miles) with a height differential of 800-1,000 m (2,625-3,280 feet);
- 15-17 km (9.3-10.5 miles) with a height differential of 300-500 m (985-1,640 feet);
- 8-10 km (5-6 miles) with a zero height differential.

If the diameter of the balloon was around 40-50 m (130-165 feet) then the detection range was of the order of 70-90 km (44-56 miles). The optimum height differential for the Tu-128 when attacking an ADA was 500-1,000 m (1,640-3,280 feet) and at a distance of around 5-7 km (3-4 miles) details of the target structure could be made out.

In spite of the foregoing, the Tu-128 was only rarely used against drifting reconnaissance balloons, as confirmed by Maj. Rodyukov:

> Su-15s from Bessovets and Poduzhem'ye were scrambled against ADAs. We were practically never scrambled against them. The R-4 missiles were expensive and it would have been like 'using a cannon to kill sparrows' to use them against a balloon.

Nevertheless, there *were* occasions when the Tu-128 was scrambled to intercept an ADA. In June 1972, a crew from 72 AP at Amderma, with Col. Zdatchenko as pilot and Maj. Karabanov as navigator, shot down an ADA over the Kara Sea. This event is recalled by Vyacheslav Gorshkov, at the time a lieutenant in charge of a P-35 'Bar Lock' radar unit in the radio technical battalion at Amderma:[7]

In the summer of 1972 we were given a holiday in connection with the visit of President Richard Nixon to the USSR. For two weeks before the visit and two weeks afterwards there was absolute silence on the airwaves, with no 'uninvited guests' [i.e. NATO reconnaissance aircraft] coming into our airspace. In this 'rest period', the Americans compensated for having to suspend their reconnaissance flights by sending up an ADA. We noticed its strange 'blip' on our radar screens when we were supporting flight operations by 72 AP during their routine training programme. This balloon ruined the careers of quite a number of personnel! The small target was not detected by those units who ought to have been the first to locate and fix its position. My radar unit had been declared the best on technical performance in the 11th Radio-technical Regiment during evaluation checks in May of that year and showed itself well on this task. A MiG-19 which was sent up to intercept it from Rogachyovo was unsuccessful. So a 72 AP Tu-128 was scrambled from QRA at Amderma. The aircraft had to make two sorties. The damage inflicted by the first missile did little to change the situation, although the crew had reported that the ADA had split into three sections and dropped into the sea. However, within half an hour, a blip from the target reappeared on the screens. [Evidently, the balloon must have simply released its ballast and continued its flight.] It was only possible to destroy it on the second flight.

In August 1973, a crew from 64 AP at Omsk, with Maj. Maslennikov as pilot and Lt Col. Parshin as navigator, destroyed an American reconnaissance balloon at a distance of more than 900 km (560 miles) from their base. Since information on the overflight of a reconnaissance balloon was always generated in a timely fashion, it was unnecessary to scramble an aircraft from QRA, but a dedicated crew were usually selected to deal with these targets. In 1974, a group of Tu-128s from 356 AP at Zhana-Semey shot down a Soviet ADA that had drifted from its intended course and for a number of reasons it was decided to destroy it. (These reasons would have included the desire to prevent sensitive monitoring equipment falling into the wrong hands.) At the end of the 1970s, two foreign ADAs were shot down by crews from 518 AP at Talagi, but probably the last Tu-128 to destroy a drifting reconnaissance balloon was flown by Maj. Savotyeyev and his navigator Maj. Shirochenko from 350 AP at Belaya on 19 July 1985. Maj. Savotyeyev was flying as wingman in a pair which had been launched to intercept and destroy the ADA. Maj. Mamet, a squadron navigator with 350 AP, remembers this incident:

It was always recommended to shoot down an ADA with a heat-seeking missile, because of the low radar reflectivity of the envelope surface. There was still the widely held theory that an ADA could jettison its reconnaissance container if it detected that it was being 'painted' by the AI radar of an intercepting aircraft. The lead aircraft of the pair had been forbidden to use its radar because of the fear that the balloon would jettison its ballast [and container] and gain altitude. So the pilot used his [back-up] collimating gun-sight to try to fire off an infrared-guided R-4T missile, but the target was a little higher than originally calculated and the aircraft could not get into a successful firing position. As a result, the second crew switched on their radar independently, locked on to the target and shot the ADA down with a semi-active R-4R missile.

Readers might consider the use of jet fighters to deal with the threat represented by drifting reconnaissance balloons to be an 'asymmetric' response, but in the 1950s pre-satellite era, aerostat-based reconnaissance was a significant threat to the territorial integrity of the Soviet Union. The USAF reconnaissance balloon programme was authorised by President Dwight D. Eisenhower in December 1955, operating under the code-name 'Project Genetrix', which exploited technology developed for earlier balloon projects. (Cover-names for some of these, and later, programmes were, *inter alia*, 'Project Skyhook', 'Project Mogul', 'Project Moby Dick', 'Project Grandson' and 'Project Grayback'.) Two types of balloon envelope were developed for operational 'Genetrix' missions (which were flown under another [secret] code-name, 'Project Gopher'); these could be filled with hydrogen or helium, depending on the required flight altitude and duration. The larger envelope was designated 128TT and the smaller 66TT; at high altitude the 128TT inflated to a height of around 54 m (177 feet) and a diameter of around 39 m (128 feet—hence the 128TT designation), while the 66TT inflated to a cylindrical shape of around 20 m (65 feet) diameter. The 'Gopher' balloon payload, designated AN/DMQ-1, was carried in a gondola and comprised a reconnaissance camera system and an automatic ballast adjustment system for altitude control. In 1953, 'Gopher' was developed into a fully operational reconnaissance balloon system, designated WS-119L (WS standing for 'weapon system'!), but by presidential decree the ballast-controlled flight altitude was limited to 16,800 m (55,120 feet). This was done, evidently, so that the Russians would not be inspired to develop a higher-reaching defensive weapon system that would have been capable of destroying the Lockheed U-2 which was then under development. The code-name 'Genetrix' was created to apply specifically to the WS-119L reconnaissance flights, launched from locations in Scotland, Norway, Germany and Turkey which were planned to exploit the winter jetstream system, taking them over the Soviet Union from west to east. The later WS-461L system, designed to drift for almost a month at around 30,000 m (98,400 feet) and equipped with an Itek Corporation HYAC-1 high-resolution panoramic camera, exploited the higher summer jetstream which flows from east to west. Although the WS-461L programme was formally terminated in 1961, it remained classified for many years after that, but continuing Soviet air defence activity against reconnaissance balloons well into the 1980s suggests that this type of activity was ongoing throughout that period.

Regular Frontal Aviation and PVO fighter units had borne the brunt of the balloon interception effort from the beginning of the American reconnaissance programme, but the Soviet Union had also initiated a specific response in the form of dedicated anti-balloon interception systems. Perhaps the most innovative of these was a development of the An-2 'Colt' biplane, equipped with a turbo-charger and propeller reduction gearing to enable it to reach a record-breaking altitude (for a single [piston]-engined aircraft) of more than 11,000 m (36,000 feet). With a powerful searchlight for target acquisition and tracking, and a turret-mounted remotely-controlled 23-mm cannon, the An-2A 'fighter' was a unique response to the balloon threat. However, the emerging threat from Western high-altitude reconnaissance aircraft within the same 1950/60s time-frame meant that the Soviet Union had to develop a weapons system capable of dealing with both aircraft and balloons.

Yakovlev had already produced the Yak-25RV (*Razvedchik Vysotnyi*) Mandrake, for both high-altitude tactical reconnaissance and as a target aircraft for its own forces, and this formed the basis for a specialised anti-balloon interceptor variant, the Yak-25PA (*Pyerekhvatchik Aerostatov*). However, the performance of the aircraft's two Tumansky R11V-300 engines proved inadequate for the task and the project was cancelled. Nevertheless, the need for a specialised high-altitude interceptor remained, and the Myasishchev design bureau was next to take up the challenge. Myasishchev had previously developed the M-series 'Bison' heavy jet bombers and in-flight refuelling tankers, but for this new task they offered an elegant twin-boom design with a high-aspect ratio straight wing. Under an in-house project named 'Subject 34' ('*Tyema 34*') this was to evolve into the M-17 'Mystic' and beyond that, into the M-55 *Geofizika* ('Mystic-B') high-altitude research platform. Although not known to have ever operated as a high-altitude interceptor (of balloons or aircraft), the significance of the development of the M-17 and its hurried and tragic first flight in 1978 is that the balloon threat was still considered to be substantial at that time. Designed in the 1970s specifically for 'the interception and destruction of automatic drifting aerostats, both as singletons and in mass raids', the M-17 reaffirmed the Soviet Union's profound concern about drifting reconnaissance balloons overflying its territory. This also explains why so much effort was expended in trying to stop them, and in this context the use of the Tu-128 in this role is fully understandable.

At the other end of the threat spectrum, a method of intercepting the tri-sonic Lockheed SR-71 reconnaissance aircraft had also been studied and developed for use by Tu-128 crews, but as the operating speeds of the two aircraft were vastly different, the latter's forward hemisphere attack was impossible. For this reason the method adopted to attempt to intercept an SR-71 envisaged the use of a rear hemisphere 'lag pursuit' profile. One of 72 AP's navigators, Maj. Oleg Fedosyeyev, remembers the problems thrown up by this task:

We were lectured on the intercept method, but I don't remember whether anyone actually carried it out successfully. The problem was getting into a [predicted] accurate position for a rear hemisphere engagement, with the SR-71 actually 'approaching' from behind. The angle of tilt of the radar antenna was very large. In these conditions it was essential to detect the aircraft flying above you at an altitude of 20,000-21,000 m [65,600-68,900 feet]. In all of this, your manoeuvring capability was limited, since the Tu-128 was flying supersonically.

Pilots did not take this intercept method very seriously, and the authors know of no cases where an attempt was made by a Tu-128 to intercept the SR-71.

SEMI-AUTONOMOUS OPERATIONS

Lt Gen. Kadomtsyev was a firm adherent to the idea of using the Tu-128 for semi-autonomous operations in the Soviet High Arctic. The idea was not new, since three scholarly dissertations had been written on this theme at the end of the 1960s. The two more serious of the three studies were written by a lecturer at the Air Force Academy by the name of Govorukhin and a student at the academy named Shub. The former head of the First Department of Combat Training of PVO Aviation, Col. Elektron Yevglyevskiy, remembers his involvement with these academic studies:

> Kadomtsyev set me the task of proving the theoretical conclusions put forward in these dissertations. I proposed that Govorukhin and Shub should take part in the research effort, but they declined because they were preoccupied with their main work. As a result, I had to get involved in the organisation of this trial myself.

The concept of semi-autonomous combat operations focused on the fact that a group of interceptors could create a broad collective 'radar formation', with each aircraft conducting a simultaneous search for enemy aircraft, enabling the group to monitor a huge expanse of airspace. Such a formation would not need guidance from ground radar sites; it would simply suffice to have early warning of the expected time and direction in which an enemy group might appear. A pair of Tu-128s could cover a sector with a front of around 105 km (65 miles), while two pairs could cover an arc of around 250 km (155 miles).

In order to set up such search procedures, however, it would be necessary to develop optimum formation groupings, group manoeuvring tactics and subsequent attacks on targets on opposing and pursuit headings. Col. Yevglyevskiy had to work out the scientific basis of this approach, which soon revealed complications.[8] Interceptors flying in formation had to be able to see each other in flight, requiring them to fly alongside each other, but if they were in close formation the area of scanned airspace ahead would be quite limited. Yevglyevskiy designed a formation in which the Tu-128s flew in broad echelon with a distance (the along-track distance between each aircraft) of 36 km (22.37 miles) and an interval (wing-tip to wing-tip distance) of 17 km (10.5 miles), eventually becoming known as the '36 x 17' formation. In this formation structure the aircraft were in constant radar contact and did not allow a target to get past them, while maintaining this 'interval' and 'distance' enabled them to avoid mutual interference of their AI radars.

There was another feature of this formation in that the group commander was at the end of the echelon since it was necessary for him to monitor the group and control all the aircraft in it. Such a formation placed a huge burden of responsibility on the flight leader's navigator-operator; in a normal intercept, all he had to do was to approach the target, lock on, fire a missile and after breaking away from the attack, vector his pilot back to base. However, in semi-autonomous operations, in addition to this, he had to monitor his own position in the formation from take-off to landing and check that the other aircraft maintained their position with respect to each other. The 'distances' and 'intervals' were considerable in terms of station-keeping, and even in the best case it was only possible to see the closest neighbouring aircraft visually, so formation was maintained by monitoring the AI radar screen. For this, the navigator could turn the antenna slightly to see the aircraft ahead of him and check the position and range relative to his own aircraft.

Col. Yevglyevskiy recalls the initial trials of this procedure:

I discussed the situation with the PVO aviation commander in 1971-72 and I was told that 356 AP from Zhana-Semey would participate in the research flights. Quite recently, several young navigators had been posted into the regiment, having completed their training. I took ten officers from this group and started training them. I gave them some graph paper and got them to draw the combat formations, associated manoeuvres and attack profiles etc. Over the course of one month they used up 2 km [1.25 miles] of graph paper. When I turned up they were complaining about the fact that they had to sit in the classroom and not fly. I said to the most boisterous of the navigators, 'Be patient! We'll start flying when you've all finished here; I'll take you as my navigator. You'll fly with me, but don't whine afterwards.' He agreed to this and, true to my word, I took this officer to fly with me as my crewman.

We flew 'research' flights for three hours during the day, and then when night flying started I would sometimes fly with the entire regiment simply 'for myself'. On one of the days it was planned that we should do two daytime flights in cloud as part of our research 'theme'. With this lieutenant navigator I had to lead the group in cloud. Following these two flights we were also programmed to carry out a supersonic intercept at altitude. This was planned to take place after dark, since I had to build up my night hours to retain my flying category. We did the two daylight flights, which were of fairly long duration, and the navigator (not to mention myself) sweated over the task. To fly for two and a half hours in cloud *and* command the group was hard going. We completed the two flights and I was so exhausted that I didn't feel like doing any more flying that day. After the second landing, we taxied onto the parking area and I said to the technician as I climbed down from the aircraft, 'Close everything down, we're not flying any more today.' I then went for a walk with the navigator and had a smoke. He was quiet for a while and then said, 'Comrade Colonel, there was really no need to decline doing the third flight. Even doing one normal flight you'd fly and then rest afterwards.'

A Tu-126 'Moss' airborne early warning aircraft was made available to support Col. Yevglyevskiy's research group and was co-located with the group at Semipalatinsk for the duration of the trials. During the training flights, the fighter controller on the Tu-126 only had to provide the interceptor crews with early warning of the presence of targets and nothing more. Moreover, according to the trials criteria, the fighter controller could not report coordinates for the same target more than three times in a single 'event'. Using this information, the lead Tu-128 naviga- tor-operator then had to draw up the anticipated heading of the target on his navigation chart and inform his pilot and the other crews in the group where to fly in order to execute a successful interception. During this early phase of the trials another problem manifested itself. The Tu-126 was designed to operate over the icy wastes of the Soviet High Arctic, but when operating over land the *Liana* ('Flat Jack') early warning radar was severely affected by ground reflections (clutter), which worsened as the aircraft gained height. This forced the design bureau to incorporate a 'quick-fix' modification to enable the Tu-126 to operate over varia- ble topography inland and determine target altitude when flying at no more than 1,000 m (3,280 feet) itself. In this case, the returns from ground interference were minimal. Two exercises were carried out, based on the results of the research flights. Col. Yevglyevskiy remembers these events:

The first exercise was carried out in the vicinity of Surgut. Here, we intercepted Tu-128s from another regiment—we intercepted them all. Everything was actually done in realistic conditions. The fact was that our targets had made a mistake with their sortie times and we met up with them not quite as it was envisaged in the exercise plan. During these exercises, the interceptors took off from Zhana-Semey and landed at Omsk-North after completing their intercepts.

The first exercise was, effectively, the concluding phase of the research flights, enabling fighter control methods to be defined for semi-autonomous operations with the Tu-128, based on the results obtained. Now, to prove their efficacy, tactical flight exercises (LTUs) would have to be carried out in the proposed theatre of military activity—in the harsh conditions of the High Arctic—and the airfield at Tiksi was selected to be the forward operating location for the exercise. Two enlarged sections of interceptors (eight Tu-128s in all) took part in the LTU, supported by an An-8 'Camp' twin-turboprop transport. It was arranged for the An-8 to fly the 356 AP ground engineering personnel from Zhana-Semey to Tiksi, and then to use it during the exercise itself as an airborne communications relay platform to extend the air-to-ground range of the Tu-128's radios. The targets for the exercise were LRAF bombers which were to penetrate the Soviet Far East region from the North Pole but whose crews had not been informed of the real purpose of the LTU. Col. Yevglyevskiy continues the story:

We arrived three days before the proposed start of the exercise in order to carry out some additional training. However, immediately after landing at Tiksi we were informed that the targets would be arriving in the area in three hours' time. We could either commence the task immediately or wait a further three days. We decided not to wait. We could grab an hour's sleep and the aircraft could be refuelled and pre-flighted for the sortie. Along with the exercise controllers we'd also agreed to operate over the Arctic Ocean until we were down to a fuel remainder of 8 tonnes [17,640 lb].

As soon as the fuel was down to 8 tonnes, irrespective of whether we had the targets in sight or not, we would turn round and return to the airfield. So we found ourselves airborne over the icy wastes with the needles on the fuel gauges approaching the 8 tonnes mark. There were no targets to be seen anywhere. I was thinking that the crews would begin reporting that their fuel remainder was down to 8 any time now and, sure enough, this was the case. First one reported 'Fuel remainder 8' ('*Ostatok 8*'), then the second and finally all of them. I gave the order to my navigator to send a WT9 message that we were down to 8 tonnes of fuel and there were still no targets in sight. At that particular moment Colonel Tolokin, the regiment commander, was controlling our flight from the ATC tower at Tiksi and Major General Starovyerov, Head of Aviation of the 14th Independent Army, was in the exercise command post controlling the LTU itself. After I'd reported our collective fuel remainder of 8 tonnes, Colonel Tolokin telephoned Major-General Starovyerov and asked him what to do. The senior officer took the decision to continue down to a fuel remainder of 7 tonnes [15,430 lb]. As we discovered later, Colonel Tolokin had called Major-General Starovyerov one more time and told him, 'Boris Ivanovich, when you decide that they can go down to a fuel remainder of 6 tonnes [13,225 lb], don't forget to call me.' Major-General Starovyerov couldn't understand why he had to call him at that stage, so Tolokin replied, 'I'll be going to bed then, because there won't be anyone at the airfield to see the aircraft in.' This is how they joked about it […] But we only learned this later, and having received the instruction to continue down to 7 tonnes remaining we carried on with the sortie. According to our calculations it would be possible to do this safely. Soon we were getting close to 7 tonnes, but still with no sign of the targets, and I was ready to order the group to turn round and return to base [Tiksi]. Then, suddenly, one of the group (*lyevyi krainii*—i.e. on the outer left of our starboard echelon formation) shouted, 'I can see the target!' Then there was a second and third call, and eventually everyone reported having their target in sight.

I gave the command 'Everyone carry out one attack, make a left turn and then head home.' We had intercepted the targets at a distance of 1,200 km [745 miles] from the airfield and 800 km [500 miles] from the Russian coastline, over the Arctic Ocean. Each Tu-128 had attacked its own target, and even though it was in daylight this was quite impressive. At first the bomber crews thought that they were being attacked by a real enemy. The distance from the Soviet coast was so great that they simply did not expect to see 'our' ('*nashi*') fighters there and raised the alarm on their radios that they were being attacked over the ocean. However, when we broke off from the attack and flew past them they could see the 'red stars' and were reassured that we were 'friendlies'. Each of the Tu-128s set course for home at its own assigned flight level and no longer in combat formation, all of which had been planned and rehearsed beforehand, and in the end everything was completed normally.

Col. Yevglyevskiy was able to present the results of this work to the General Staff of the PVO, although they were unable to implement them fully, as it seemed to too many senior officers that these fighter control methods were extremely 'scientific'. Here again, the Russian understanding of 'scientific' has more to do with the application of special procedures than laboratory-based practices. Apart from this, the reorganisation of the PVO that commenced in 1980 enabled some aspects of it to be implemented and, nevertheless, methods of semi-autonomous combat operations continued to be developed on fighter squadrons as an integral part of the military pilots' KBP flight training manual.

15

The Final Years

The winding down of Tu-128 operations began in the second half of the 1980s, although the first regiment to relinquish its aircraft did so almost a decade earlier, in 1975. This was the 445 AP based at Savvatiya (Kotlas) in the south of the Arkhangel'sk Oblast, which exchanged its Tu-128s for the MiG-25P 'Foxbat-A' in that year. It is difficult to say what led to this decision, after only eight years of operating the Tu-128, although it is possible that PVO commanders did not consider the undisputed long-range capability of the 'Fiddler' to be so vital to the air defence of the Soviet Arctic with the aircraft operating out of a base located in the far south of the region. This task fell to the two other Tu-128 regiments of the 10th Independent Army of the PVO actually based in the Arctic region—72 AP at Amderma and 518 AP at Talagi. Backed up by the Tu-128 regiments of the 14th Independent Army, these units were dedicated to the air defence of the Soviet Union's vulnerable northern periphery. The aircraft relinquished by 445 AP were distributed among the remaining Tu-128 regiments, which enabled them to make up for losses due to accidents and write-offs suffered within the first ten years of the aircraft's operation. Apart from this it was now also possible to retire several Tu-128s from the early production batches (up to and including the 7th series), which had proved to be rather capricious in service. Some of these early-model Tu-128s had been transferred to PVO maintenance training units, including the PVO School for Young Aviation Specialists (ShMAS) in Moscow and the Higher Military Aviation College for Pilots and Navigators at Stavropol.

The decade up to the end of the 1970s also virtually coincided with the end of the so-called 'golden age' of air defence of the USSR, marked by the beginning of the eighth post-war reorganisation of the PVO. This reorganisation was undertaken with the objective of creating a 'Unified System of Air Defence and Armed Forces' and, in June 1978, the Chief of the General Staff, Marshal of the Soviet Union Nikolai Vasil'yevich Ogarkov, spoke on this topic at a session of the

Defence Council of the USSR. Then, on 27 December 1979, a resolution was issued by the Defence Council, entitled 'On the Increased Effectiveness of Control of the Armed Forces of the USSR and Further Improvements in their Organisational Structure' and based on the results of a paper exercise conducted in the Baltic Military District. This led to a reorganisation of the armed forces, later acknowledged to be seriously flawed, with the acting C-in-C of the PVO Troops (*Voyska PVO*), Marshal of the Soviet Union Pavel Fyodorovich Batitskiy, refusing to implement the 'pernicious' reforms and asking the Defence Minister to relieve him of his responsibilities.

However, on 5 January 1980, an order was issued by the Minister of Defence, commanding that reorganisation should begin immediately. Under this, the High Command of the PVO Troops retained considerably less authority than before, and instead of the word '*Strany*' (Country) in the title of the service (i.e. *PVO Strany*), this became *PVO Strany i Vooruzhonnykh Sil* (Air Defence of the Country and Armed Forces). For the fourth time in the post-war period, the territory of the Soviet Union was divided into border (*prigranichniye*) and interior (*vnutrenniye*) regions. Three new command formations were created and given the title of 'Strategic Echelons'. The 'First Strategic Echelon of the PVO System of the Country and the Armed Forces' had centres (HQs) in Arkhangel'sk, Baku and Khabarovsk, while the 'Second Strategic Echelon' had centres (HQs) in Leningrad, Minsk and Kiev. The 'Third Strategic Echelon' was formed by the air defence systems of the member states of the Warsaw Pact and the Groups of Soviet Forces on their territory. The latter comprised the Group of Soviet Forces in Germany (GSFG), Northern Group of Forces (NGF) in Poland, Central Group of Forces (CGF) in Czechoslovakia, and the Southern Group of Forces (SGF) in Hungary. In this shake-up, a considerable number of fighter units were transferred from the PVO and handed over to units of the Soviet Air Force in the military districts. Only surface-to-air (SAM) and supporting radio-technical troops of the PVO retained their previous titles and function, within a Corps and Divisional structure, described more generally as an *Ob'yedinyeniye* (a large strategic formation) and a *Soyedinyeniye* (a tactical formation) respectively.

Even the Armavir Higher Aviation School for Pilots, previously an exclusively air defence training establishment, was transferred to the Soviet Air Force in this period. Centralised control was only retained by the C-in-C of the PVO Troops in the interior of the country, i.e. in the Moscow Region of the PVO, the 4th Independent Army and the 14th Independent Army. However, even here some fighter regiments were handed over to the Soviet Air Force, but it must be emphasised that no Tu-128 regiment was ever assigned to the air force, although they did not escape the reorganisation process. The 14th Independent Army in particular was subjected to a fairly rigorous shake-up; in 1982, 33 Division of the PVO was disbanded at Semipalatinsk, with 356 AP based at Zhana-Semey and

64 AP at Omsk North being re-subordinated under a new divisional structure, with HQ at Novosibirsk (Tolmachevo). Reorganisation also affected 350 AP at Belaya, which had been part of 39 Division, but as a result of reorganisation this division was given the status of a corps, becoming the 39th Corps of the PVO, with its HQ remaining in Irkutsk. Restructuring did not end here, and within a short time 350 AP was re-subordinated to a corps with its HQ at Chita, followed soon after, in July-August 1984, by permanent relocation to Bratsk. The 'experiment' in controlling the nation's armed forces continued until January 1986, when the largely unsuccessful reform programme was rescinded by a decree of the Central Committee of the Communist Party of the Soviet Union (CPSU) and the Council of Ministers of the USSR.

A year earlier, in 1985, with the era of the Tu-128 drawing to a close, 518 AP at Talagi became the first of the five remaining 'Fiddler' regiments to re-equip with the more modern MiG-31 'Foxhound-A', simultaneously reverting to its original status as 518 IAP, i.e. 518 *Fighter* Aviation Regiment. Some of the regiment's Tu-128s were passed on to 72 AP at Amderma and others were ferried to Rzhev airfield, the home of the PVO's 514 Aviation Repair Plant (*514 Aviaremontnyi Zavod* or ARZ), for storage and subsequent scrapping. Apart from 514 ARZ, the airfield also housed 1082 Aviation Repair Base (*1082 Aviatsionnaya Remontnaya Baza* or ARB) and 4884 Reserve Aircraft Base (*4884 Baza Rezerva Samolyotov* or BRS).[1] It is likely that all of the Tu-128s withdrawn from service at this time were destined for handling by 4884 Reserve Base, whose task was the storage of any aircraft with some airframe life remaining and disposal of those which were no longer airworthy. However, not all Tu-128s ended up at Rzhev—at least one example remained at Talagi for a while, but this aircraft was eventually broken up for scrap *in situ*. Meanwhile, the Sokol plant at Gorky continued to roll out MiG-31s at a brisk pace, enabling 356 AP to convert onto the new fighter at Zhana-Semey in 1986 and, as with 518 AP, to revert to its original status as a fighter aviation regiment. (The Tu-124s which had played such an important part as proficiency trainers on the Tu-128 regiments but were superfluous as training aids for the MiG-31 were passed on to various Soviet Air Force transport regiments.) After re-equipping with the MiG-31 in 1986, 356 IAP was removed from the 14th Independent Army inventory and re-subordinated to the 37th Corps of the PVO with its HQ at Alma-Ata.

An interesting story surrounds the fate of around six to eight ex-356 AP Tu-128s left to rust away at Zhana-Semey in 1989 and declared incapable of being flown out to Rzhev for disposal because of their condition. These aircraft had been parked on a separate hardstanding about 500 m (1,640 feet) from one of the regiment's buildings and it was decided that they should be employed 'in the service of the state' for one final time. This is recalled by Col. Vasiliy Popov, commanding officer of 356 AP from 1989 to 1991, who states:

An early-series Tu-128 parked in the open at Rzhev. Special water-repellent tape and sealant was applied to those areas of the airframe susceptible to water ingress during long-term external storage, such as access hatches, cockpit canopies and air intakes. (*Nikolai Popov*)

> Evidently the military leadership considered that 'potential enemies' ought to be persuaded [i.e. deceived] into thinking that there was a *4th* Aviation Squadron sub-ordinated to 356 Regiment. We were given this task and had to carry it out. So we set up a false location on the base for the regiment's '4th Squadron', using the remaining Tu-128s as decoys and we even had to create protective embankments ('*obvalovaniya*') around the hardstandings for added authenticity. The old Tu-128s were then towed into position and left there.

These aircraft were broken up and scrapped in the 1990s. Although coming rather late in the day to be completely convincing to NATO photo-interpreters, the belief seemed to be that the deception might have caused analysts to reconsider their assessment of the strength of a Tu-128 regiment. In essence, of course, it was more a mischievous than a useful deception, since the actual numbers of aircraft held by each service had to be declared officially at the signing of the Treaty on Conventional Forces in Europe (CFE).

With regard to conversion from the Tu-128 onto the MiG-31, 1987 could be considered as something of a record year, with 64 AP at Omsk-North and 72 AP at Amderma both re-equipping with the new interceptor in that year and reverting to their original *fighter* aviation regiment status. Tu-128s with sufficient airframe life were ferried to the storage airfield at Rzhev, although some remained on their original bases, and six 'Fiddlers' operated by 72 AP at Amderma remained for a time on the operational reserve airfield at Obozerska (Letnyeozersk). These were eventually ferried to Rzhev in August and September of 1987 by crews from 350 AP. A somewhat oblique reminder of 72 AP's relationship with the Tu-128 was the continued presence at Nar'yan-Mar of one of the regiment's Tu-124Sh 'Cookpot' trainers long after the 'Fiddlers' had departed. The '*big sparka*' remained at 72 AP's operational deployment airfield for another four years following the retirement of the Tu-128, parked in the central refuelling area (*tsentral'naya zapravochnaya*), serving variously as a control point for the airfield engineering service personnel, a pre-flight briefing facility, and a flight clothing locker room! After re-equipping with the MiG-31, 72 IAP operated the new interceptor for only six years before disbanding in 1993, whilst 64 IAP, which converted onto the 'Foxhound' at the same time, operated for a further five years before it too disbanded, on 1 May 1998. The last Tu-128 regiment to re-equip with the MiG-31 was 350 AP at Bratsk, which received the first of its new aircraft in 1988.

Some non-airworthy examples of the 'Fiddler' remained at Bratsk before being broken up for scrap in the late 1980s/early 1990s, and 350 AP veterans recall a curious incident that occurred during the scrapping process:

> This started when our CO complained to the commander of a locally based army tank unit about the problem of scrapping his time-expired Tu-128s. The commander of the tank unit promised him that one of his tanks could crush and pack our aircraft into briquette-sized blocks [!]. One of the Tu-128s was towed out from dispersal and we all sat around the edge of the revetment, like spectators in an open-air theatre. A newish-looking tank was then driven in to the revetment, all freshly painted and looking very threatening. At first the driver decided to break off one of the main undercarriage legs, which he managed to do, but the aircraft and the tank became entangled and had to be separated by a crane. The tank lost one of its radio antennas and suffered damage to its electro-optical viewing system, but the driver made several more attempts to 'storm' the Tu-128's fuselage, with the result that the tank suffered extensive damage. In the end, it had to be placed on a tank-transporter and hauled back to the depot to be repaired, with the soldiers' concern for their damaged tank being assuaged with the promise of a supply of alcohol!

After this incident, army sappers were employed to break up the aircraft, and the resulting scrap metal was sent to the Bratsk aluminium plant for reprocessing. However, one ex-350 AP Tu-128 was reprieved and served as a memorial (*pamyatnik*) at Bratsk until the end of the 1990s, before it too was scrapped.

The last recorded flights by Tu-128s occurred in the autumn of 1988, when the remaining aircraft of 350 AP were ferried to Rzhev, as recalled by regiment navigator Maj. Mamet:

I converted onto the MiG-31 when the rest of the regiment was already flying this aircraft. Until then, I'd been involved in ferrying Tu-128s to Rzhev; overall, I ferried 17 aircraft. Apart from my own regiment's aircraft, I also collected aircraft from Semipalatinsk, Novosibirsk and Letnyeozersk. The scene at Rzhev at this particular time was awful; before we got there, the dispersal area had been packed with Su-9s and they had to find space for us rather urgently. This was done quite simply. They removed the wings from the Su-9s and bulldozed the fuselages into the boggy ground surrounding the parking area. Those Tu-128s which for a variety of reasons were unlikely ever to fly again were broken up *in situ*.

As far as can be ascertained, the last 'Fiddler' to be scrapped was a Tu-128M, Bort No. 83, which was being ferried to Rzhev on 10 October 1988 by Maj. Kvasnitsyn and Capt. Vtyurina. The aircraft suffered a malfunction en route and diverted into Bol'shoye Savino airfield near Perm' where it remained for some time before being scrapped on site. That ferry flight effectively signalled the end of the Tu-128 era in the PVO, virtually coincident with the demise of its associated Tu-126 'Moss' airborne early-warning radar picket. In 1985, the 67th Independent Aviation Squadron, which had operated the Tu-126, was re-formed as the 144th Independent Aviation Regiment to operate the new Ilyushin-Beriev A-50 'Mainstay' AEW&C system. Although never operating alongside the A-50, the Tu-126 remained in PVO service until 1988, when the single R&D airframe and the eight 67th Squadron aircraft were scrapped with almost indecent haste at Shiauliai.

'Fiddlers' flown to Rzhev for disposal were dismantled by 4044 Disposal, Conversion and Weapons Dismantling Base for PVO Aviation (*4044 Aviabaza po Likvidatsii, Pyereoborudovaniyu i Demontazhu Vooruzheniya Aviatsii PVO*), the successor to 4884 BRS and 1082 ARB mentioned earlier. This unit functioned for two and a half years, from 1 November 1993 to 1 July 1996, and was responsible for the scrapping of virtually all the remaining Tu-128s. (According to our information, however, it is still possible to see four Tu-128s on display in Russia: namely, the first prototype at the Central Museum of the Air Forces at Monino; a Tu-128M in the museum of the 148 Combat Training and Aircrew Conversion Centre at Savasleika; plus a Tu-128M and a Tu-128UT in the 'garrison' museum on Rzhev airfield.) As the aforementioned events were taking place, the Soviet-era PVO organisation had begun a gradual metamorphosis in preparation for its reincarnation as the air defence 'umbrella' of the armed forces of the Russian Federation. The PVO Troops continued to operate all homeland early warning radars, surface-to-air missile systems and GCI sites, while PVO Aviation continued to be responsible for the operation and control of all manned interceptors.

However, a new era was now dawning for Russia's long-range air defence fighter force, represented in the first instance by the introduction (in 1982) of the angular,

The fate of the majority of Tu-128s after their long years of service with the PVO was to be packed into a dispersal area on the territory of 4884 Reserve Aircraft Base at Rzhev airfield, before being broken up. (*Vladimir Pushkaryev*)

'brutish' and quintessentially 'Soviet' MiG-31 'Foxhound', offering significantly better all-round performance than the Tu-128. Then, in 1984, the Sukhoi Su-27 'Flanker' entered service as the second of the PVO's new long-range interceptors—an elegant, 'cosmopolitan' and technologically refined design at least equal to and in many respects superior to the best Western fighters of its class. Nevertheless, the air and ground crews who had operated the comparatively unsophisticated Tu-128 'Fiddler' throughout almost twenty-five years of service in the defence of Soviet Russia can be justifiably proud of the legacy they have passed on to the defenders of twenty-first-century democratic Russia.

Appendix 1

That Tu-128 photo!

Anyone reading this book because they have a particular interest in the Tu-128 will already be familiar with a remarkable photograph of the aircraft that first appeared in the 1970s in a number of Western aviation journals and in *Jane's All the World's Aircraft*. For many years this was the only clear photograph of an operational Tu-128 available to Western defence analysts and Russian aircraft enthusiasts, but the circumstances of how, where and by whom it was obtained have remained unpublished until now. Remarkably, while researching material for this book, we have been able to establish the exact provenance of the photograph, as well as the name of the pilot and navigator of the Tu-128 and the regiment which operated it. It is very rare for an event such as a Cold War interception of a Western reconnaissance aircraft by a Soviet fighter to be written up so as to bring together details relating to both participants. However, in this case we can provide an account of the incident given by former USAF Boeing RC-135U 'Combat Sent' co-pilot Capt. Richard 'Zot' Barazzotto, who took the photograph, and brief details of the Russian crew of the Tu-128 and their actions on the day of the interception. The circumstances are described below in a recent letter from 'Zot' (now a lieutenant colonel in the USAF Reserve) to the 55th Strategic Reconnaissance Wing Association historian Robb Hoover in reply to the latter's request for confirmation that he was the pilot who took the picture. Responding to Robb Hoover's request, 'Zot' provided the following declassified narrative account of events leading up to and following the interception. The flight log extract given below covers the period of the interception by the Tu-128 in June 1972:

Dear Robb,

Guilty as charged: I took the 'Fiddler' picture. Checking my Form 5 [flight log] it was flown in 792 [Boeing RC-135U tail number 63-9792] on 28th June 1972 (out of

```
PREPARED 72 JUL 17                              PCS INDIVIDUAL FLIGHT RECORD              AS OF 72 JUL 16

BARAZZOTTO RICHARD A          CPT  ▇▇▇▇▇▇            PILOT              0055        SAC  1V

DATE    M/D/S   TAIL  MSN  DUTY  TOTAL     DAY        NIGHT      SIML      LANDINGS       PENT  APPR     NR OF
MO DY           NMBR  SYM  POSN        VFR  INST   VFR  INST    INST    TYPE AND NMBR     S  W  P  N     SORTIE

06 11   RC135U  792   09   FP    6.0     6.0                                                                1
06 11   RC135U  792   09   CP    6.0     6.0
06 11   RC135U  792   09   AC    5.9     5.9
06 11   RC135U  792   09   FP    6.0     6.0                                                                1
06 11   RC135U  792   09   CP    6.0     6.0
06 11   RC135U  792   09   AC    5.9     5.9
06 16   RC135U  792   T3   FP    2.8     2.5                         .3         LL  1     1     1           1
06 16   RC135U  792   T3   CP    2.8     2.5     .3
06 25   RC135U  792   T3   FP    1.4     1.4
06 25   RC135U  792   T3   CP    1.4     1.4                                                                1
06 26   RC135U  792   09   FP    6.8     6.5                         .3         RL  1     1     1
06 26   RC135U  792   09   CP    6.7     6.7                                                                1
06 28   RC135U  792   09   FP    7.0     7.0
06 28   RC135U  792   09   CP    9.9     6.8     .1                                                         1
07 01   RC135U  792   T3   FP    2.7     2.5                         .2         RL  1     1     1           1
07 01   RC135U  792   T3   CP    3.0     3.0
07 06   KC135A  302   T3   AC     .3      .3
07 06   KC135A  302   T3   FP    4.4     2.9                        1.5         TG  3     1     2  1        1
07 06   KC135A  302   T3   CP    1.1     1.1
07 12   RC135C  844   T3   FP    2.7      .6    1.0   .6     .5                                             1
07 12   RC135C  844   T3   CP    2.7      .6    1.0   .7     .4
07 12   RC135C  844   T3   AC    2.7     2.7
07 13   RC135C  844   T3   AC    3.5     3.5
07 13   RC135C  844   T3   FP    3.5     3.2          .3                                                    1
07 13   RC135C  844   T3   CP    3.7     3.3          .4
                                101.9   94.3   2.4   2.0    .9    2.3          6          4     4  2       10

PILOT                 TOTAL    T/PILOT     PILOT    COPILOT    CMD PILOT    AUX PLT    OTHER    COMBAT  CMBT-SPT
THIS MONTH            101.0               43.3     40.3                    18.3
TO DATE             1238.9      3.9      891.5    284.6                    58.9               681.0
   STUDENT           248.7
   CIV(OVER 450)
   OTHER US MIL
   FOREIGN MIL
   TOTAL TIME       1487.6
```

Eielson AFB, Alaska, but over the international dateline, so it was the 29th in Zulu time, i.e. Greenwich Mean Time). The sortie duration was 13.9 hours. I have both FP [first pilot] & CP [co-pilot] time on my Form 5. I remember that there were only two 'drivers' [pilots] on all the flights except June 11th. Now let me see if I can write the rest of the story to set the stage for the picture:

That entire month was the 'trip from hell'. It was a Combat Sent mission and I remember that Larry Staringer was one of the guys who appeared, grabbed a load of tapes [and disappeared] to take them back to Offutt. It was the 'trip from hell' because the inertial navigation system kept breaking. The INS was recycled from the 'Hound Dog' missile and when it broke it really broke. The failure item was the nav equipment air-conditioner and it was usually accompanied by a loud bang and clouds of smoke billowing up from under the cockpit floor. That caused many interesting problems, especially the first time it happened after we hooked up with the tanker.

This was what happened according to my Form 5 (the official AF record of where I was and what I was doing.). A good memory refresher given that this event happened 34+ years ago!

Date	Mission Symbol	Duration (hours)	Comments
June 01	T3	5.6	Ferry flight to Eielson AFB
June 04	09	12.7	Operational sortie
June 07	T3	3.2	Aircraft broken before tanking
June 08	T3	5.7	Home to Offutt AFB
June 11	09	17.9	Operational sortie with AAC

June 13	09	10.6	Air File* to Offutt AFB
June 16	T3	5.6	Back to Eielson AFB
June 21	Baseball played at midnight without lights		
June 25	T3	2.8	Broken plane—Eielson-Eielson
June 26	09	13.5	Operational sortie
June 28	09	13.9	LOX problems. (Intercepted by the Tu-128 on this mission)
July 01	T3	5.7	Home to Offutt AFB (with tree!)

*i.e. filed an airborne flight plan

Being SAC 'trained killers' we were supposed to fly with nothing personal other than ID cards. It was June, we were supposed to be gone 30 days and our families had gone on vacations. The first time we went unserviceable (June 07) we hadn't yet hit the tankers so we landed at Eielson, where it was determined that they couldn't fix the plane. Next day we headed home for repairs. Because we were now 6 hours further away from our target we needed a third pilot [i.e. an Alternate Aircraft Commander or AAC] to make it a sortie from Offutt. They found an AAC, set up the tankers and we headed north on June 11th. That sortie was uneventful and we landed at Eielson after a scenic tour through the Kara Sea. SAC [Strategic Air Command] was too mean to pay for a ticket for the AAC to get home, so he was sent south on a tanker heading for California.

On June 13th we had just hit the tanker, all tanks were full and we were headed north when the now familiar loud bang and cloud of smoke rose from the cockpit floor. We immediately knew that the air-conditioner's cooling unit had again bitten the dust. Since we would have to dump gas to land, the command post at Eielson 'air filed' us to Omaha [i.e. filed an airborne flight plan] and home again we went. I know that we beat the AAC back to Omaha [Offutt AFB]. They fixed the plane and we 'dead headed' [i.e. made a direct non-working transit] back to Eielson. Most of the sorties were 'Round Robins' from Eielson and ran around 14 hours. This broken nav system plagued us throughout the month. We had other incidents that generated a theme song for the trip—'When You're Hot, You're Hot' by Jerry Reed. It was on the juke box at the club and we played it often. That went right along with the other line, 'I've Got Good News and Bad News'.

The flight on June 28th [the day the photo was taken] went smoothly until we were in 'the area'. We were flying between Novaya Zemlya and the mainland looking for signals from a new Soviet radar. We were supposed to be all alone in international airspace, just boring holes in the sky. I looked out the right cockpit window and much to my surprise there was the Tu-128. He was flying a nice fighter-style wing tip formation, maybe 10-15 feet off our starboard wing. Since he wasn't supposed to be there, it was a shock to say the least, and I have no idea how long he had been alongside. I think I poked the Aircraft Commander [Capt. Robert 'Bob' Line] and pointed to the Tu-128. He leaned around so he could see the right wing tip, and then I remember that he slapped my shoulder and said, 'Take a picture!' The picture was taken over the Kara Sea at 71 20N 60 55E.

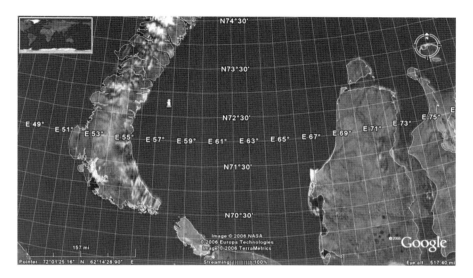

I had two cameras. A government issued Pentax with B&W film and an 80-200 mm lens, and my own Minolta with colour slide film and also with an 80-200 mm lens. The focusing glass had been installed backwards in the Pentax so I wasn't sure that it was working right. That is why there is only the B&W picture. I grabbed the Pentax from the floor by my left foot and shot the now famous picture. Once he [the Tu-128 pilot] saw me duck for the camera he decided that flying formation with an RC-135 may be fun but he didn't want it caught on film for all the world to see. So he made a turn to depart. I snapped the first picture and by the time I picked up the Minolta and shot what was left of the scene, he was history. Never saw any results from the colour film. It was all over in a few seconds. I don't recall telling anyone in the plane except Bob [the Aircraft Commander] that the Tu-128 was there. By the time that would have been useful information, he was gone. On that sortie I understand that a good signal [i.e. ELINT signal] was collected, but the picture was the most important 'take' from the month. When we got back to Eielson and debriefed, the 'intel' folks processed the B&W film. They had an 8x10 before we left and everyone was talking about it.

We had a few other incidents that caused consternation and got us a lot of attention in places like SAC HQ. We were scheduled to fly about every three days, so a few of us decided to go to Denali National Park and tour Mt McKinley. It was all cleared with the 'powers that be' and since we weren't scheduled to fly for a few days some

For many years this was the best photograph available of an operational Tu-128, taken by former USAF captain 'Zot' Barazzotto in June 1972. (*'Zot' Barazzotto*)

of us made plans to 'overnight' in the Park and catch the sightseeing trip early the next morning. When those who had just made it a day trip got back off the train they were met with the question—'Where's Zot?' Turns out we were actually scheduled to fly the next day and I was AWOL, looking at the sights in Denali! After a bunch of tries to make the mission happen (like finding a co-pilot from the Eielson crews but none was qualified on the 'U') and scheming ways to get me back from the Park (including sending a rescue helicopter or a Piper 'Cub'), they finally gave up and told SAC HQ that we would fly in two days' time.

We had two other incidents that come to mind with our theme song. On one occasion the nav cooling system blew up while we were still on the ground. It went with its usual big bang and a cloud of smoke. Since we were just starting engines I called the tower to tell them that we had a fire on board, were shutting down and would be abandoning the plane. By the time that message got to the Base Commander he heard that we were on fire in one of his hangars. For some reason that really upset him (!).

The other incident I think was on the June 28th flight and it had to do with the oxygen system. Monitoring the quantity of LOX on board was my job as co-pilot. As I noticed the unusual loss of oxygen I had all the regulators turned off. When that stopped the loss I had them turned on again in stages. Cycling the regulators did the job and the loss stopped. However, the nav system was up to its usual tricks, and about 2 hours north of Eielson it decided to die with the usual bang and a cloud of smoke. Since the mission was essentially over, the guys in the back had cleaned everything up and were taking naps. With the bang I went to the emergency position on the intercom (which overrode whatever else they were listening to) and made the following announcement. 'Crew, this is the co-pilot—I have some good news and some bad news. The good news is that we have plenty of oxygen left. The bad news is that we are going to have to use it because we are on fire.' That got the attention of everyone still on a headset and the whole back end was awake and back in their boots in short order. The good news was that there was no real fire and we safely got back to Eielson. But our reputation continued to grow in the wrong direction.

With the plane broken and the mission nearing its scheduled end a decision was made to cease flying operational sorties. So we had a day to get packed and ready to return home. Alaska is a wonderful place with all kinds of things that aircrews like to bring home. Frozen crab legs and salmon ranked high on the prize list. There were places in the plane where a block of frozen fish would stay frozen and they were usually well filled. For some reason I decided that I wanted a birch tree. Fairbanks is in the permafrost zone, so even though it was June the ground was only thawed about 8 inches deep. I enlisted the help of some guys and we dug up a rather large birch tree and dragged it back to the plane. We put the roots by the over-wing hatch on the right side and it went almost all the way across the plane. The problem arose when it warmed up and all the mosquitoes hatched. We had to 'fog' the plane before we could take off to kill all the little blighters looking for lunch! Back home, I took the right seat out of my wife's VW Bug and we moved the tree home looking like a Keystone Cop car.

All in all it was a very interesting trip. The flying was good, we 'cheated death' several times and not only did we get a prime picture but we also got a lot of good 'war stories'. There is one more aspect to this tale that almost no one knows [and is the lead-up to how Dick Barazzotto ended up flying the RC-135]. My first operational assignment as a pilot was in Viet Nam flying Rockwell OV-10s as a Forward Air Controller. I was stationed in Da Nang and Bien Hoa and flew in Laos and Cambodia as a 'traffic cop' on the Ho Chi Minh Trail. My job was to stop stuff coming from North Viet Nam and help the Cambodians fend off the 'bad guys'. When my tour in South East Asia was almost over I received orders to go to B-52s. I called MPC [Air Force Military Personnel Center] and tried to explain that I was the only rated pilot in the USAF with a Photographic Science degree (from Rochester Institute of Technology and they only graduated about 20 of us a year.) I'd also been a flight test engineer at Wright-Patterson AFB before entering the USAF and [thought that] I should probably go to some 'recce' outfit. However, I didn't 'make a sale' on getting new orders and I was bummed [i.e. very disappointed].

One evening I was crying in my beer about the situation and Arch Battista, another Covey FAC, offered to write a letter on my behalf to the commander of MPC explaining why they had made a mistake [in assigning him to B-52s]. Having considerable mastery of the written word (later put to good use when he went to law school, eventually serving thirty years on active duty and in the reserves), Arch wrote the letter; I signed it and we dumped it in the mail box, no stamp required. About two weeks later I received new orders to go to the 55th SRW. Military Personnel Center couldn't get me out of Strategic Air Command, but they *did* get me moved out of B-52s, which was a blessing. And that completes the story of how a few years later a guy with a broken camera got a lucky shot of one of Russia's most elusive interceptors.

Zot Barazzotto

INTERCEPTION OVER THE KARA SEA

The Tu-128, subordinate to 72 AP of the PVO based at Amderma airfield, had been launched from QRA in routine reaction to the then unidentified intruder. Its approach to the RC-135U had not been detected by the 'Combat Sent' crew, suggesting that the interception was under data-link guidance, since the Soviet-wide GCI VHF voice frequency would have almost certainly been monitored constantly 'in area'. Consequently, any approaching Russian fighter would have been detected if it had been a voice-controlled intercept. Moreover, in accordance with standard operating procedure, the Tu-128 crew (pilot Maj. Vladimir Nirodyenko and navigator Capt. Mikhail Drozhzhin) would not have used their *Smerch* radar during the interception and the two procedures would have thus combined to enable them to make a 'silent' interception. The entry in Maj. Nirodyenko's log book for 29 June 1972 is very succinct, the flight being described simply as 'Sortie from duty force (i.e. QRA) to escort foreign reconnaissance aircraft' ('*Vylyet iz DS [Dezhurnykh Sil] na soprovozh[dyeniye] inostran[novo] s-ta[samolyota]-razvyedchika*')—flight duration was 2 hours 30 minutes and maximum altitude of the sortie was 8,000 m (26,250 feet). The interception was 'time-stamped' on Dick Barazzotto's camera at 0529Z at 71°20'N 60°55'E while flying at an altitude of 8,840 m (29,000 feet), giving the local time for the event as 08.29 hours. This gives a discrepancy of 840 m (2,756 feet) between the maximum flight altitude entered by Maj. Nirodyenko in his log book (see page extract) and that registered on Dick Barazzotto's film.

This could be explained by the understandable absence of synchrony between the altimeters of the two aircraft and/or the fact that Maj. Nirodyenko climbed above 8,000 m to close with the RC-135 and did not enter this fact in his log. (Technically, he was in breach of PVO standard operating procedures by getting that close to his target and probably chose not to incriminate himself in writing.)

Maj. Vladimir Nirodyenko poses for the regiment photographer with his navigator, in the cockpit of their Tu-128, although the nature of this occasion was not recorded. (*Irina Sadova Archive*)

Sadly, he is now deceased, but we were able to obtain a copy of the relevant page from his log book via his daughter, Irina Sadova, which gives brief details of the interception of the RC-135. Maj. Nirodyenko was known by everyone in the 10th Army as an excellent pilot who was never happier than when he was flying, and his superiors rewarded his enthusiasm and flying skill by appointing him to the position of divisional inspector-pilot in December 1969. However, he felt that the job was more of a 'paper duty' (*bumazhnaya dolzhnost'*) than one requiring flying ability, relinquishing the position a year later and flying as a regular (albeit senior) squadron pilot at the time of the intercept.

Vladimir Nikolayevich Nirodyenko was born in Ukraine on 1 January 1934. His mother was a student at the Mironovsk Agricultural Institute, his father was a teacher who died when Vladimir was only 3 years old, and he was subsequently brought up by his grandmother. The family moved to Kiev in 1945, and three years later, when he was 14 years old, he enrolled in the Kiev Special Air Force School after completion of 7th grade education. In 1951, he graduated and entered the 10th Military Aviation College at Kremenchug to undergo basic flight training, continuing his training in the following year at the Kachinsk Military Pilots College at Stalingrad (now Volgograd). He graduated from the college in 1955 as a fully fledged pilot and was posted to the 518th Fighter Aviation Regiment

(518 IAP), located at that time at Vas'kovo and equipped with the MiG-15 'Fagot'. After serving for four years at Vas'kovo he was posted to 174 IAP at Kilp-Yavr in 1959, after which he then served on the following units:

- 1961-1965—57 IAP at Bessovets.
- 1965-1966—265 IAP at Poduzhem'ye.
- from 1966—518 AP at Talagi, having converted onto the Tu-128.

Maj. Nirodyenko was appointed to the post of divisional inspector-pilot at Talagi in December 1969, relinquishing this duty in 1970 and transferring to 72 AP at Amderma, voluntarily accepting 'demotion' to senior pilot in the rank of major. He continued to fly the Tu-128 until his retirement from military service, on 1 December 1976, having served for twenty-three years and eleven months as a military pilot in the Soviet Air Defence Forces.

The extract from Maj. Nirodyenko's log book for the day of the interception is given opposite.

Entry to and exit from the cockpit of the Tu-128 required agility and care to avoid striking the heavy canopy frame, which did not open very wide. Here, Maj. Vladimir Nirodyenko climbs out of his aircraft at the end of a routine sortie, still wearing his flying helmet for protection from the canopy edge. (*Irina Sadova Archive*)

ARCTIC

Date	Aircraft type	Day (D)	Seat from which flown	No. of Exercise in Combat Training Manual (Kurs Boyevovo Primyenyeniya—Kbp) and Brief Description of Task	Number of flights	Sortie duration Hr	Sortie duration M	Under blind-flying hood Hr	Under blind-flying hood M	In cloud Hr	In cloud M	Above cloud Hr	Above cloud M	In limited viz and on cloud-base Hr	In limited viz and on cloud-base M	In stratosphere Hr	In stratosphere M	Max altitude (Km)	Weather conditions during flight	Name of system	Apps	Landings	T/off	Ldg	Sortie evaluation
26	Tu-128UT	D	3	Exercise 13—Zonal flight in cloud	1	0	32	–	–	0	18	–	–	0	14	–	–	8	9/10 cloud along route between 8500/7000	ILS	1	1	–	–	–
26	Tu-128UT	D	P	Exercise 12—Flight on duplicated instruments	1	0	31	0	27	–	–	–	–	0	04	–	–	6/09	Cloudless sky	ILS	1	1	–	–	–
26	Tu-128	D	P	Exercise 14—Zonal flight in cloud	1	0	32	–	–	0	18	–	–	0	14	–	–	8	9/10 cloud along route between 8500/7000	ILS	1	1	–	–	–
26	Tu-128	D	P	Exercise 28—Subsonic intercept	1	2	04	–	–	0	06	1	37	0	21	–	–	9/11	Cloudless sky, then 9/10 cloud along route between 8500/7000	ILS	1	1	–	–	4
28	Tu-128	D	P	Exercise 33—Intercept in cloud	1	1	34	–	–	0	44	0	30	0	20	0	25	13/8	9/10 cloud along route between 8500/7500	ILS	1	1	–	–	5
29	Tu-128	D	P	Sortie from QRA to escort foreign reconnaissance aircraft	1	2	30	–	–	–	–	–	–	2	30	–	–	8	8/10 cloud between 8000/7000	ILS	1	1	–	–	5
30	Tu-128	D	P	Sortie from QRA to escort foreign reconnaissance aircraft	1	2	31	–	–	1	00	–	–	1	31	–	–	9	8/10 cloud between 8500/7000	ILS	1	1	–	–	5
				Tu-128 Day	5	9	11	–	–	2	08	2	07	4	56	0	25	–	–	ILS	5	5	–	–	–
				Tu-128UT Day	2	1	03	0	27	0	18	–	–	0	18	–	–	–	–	ILS	2	2	–	–	–
				Total	7	10	14	0	27	2	08	2	07	5	14	0	25	–	–	ILS	7	7	–	–	–

Signed by Chief of Staff of Military Unit (Voyskovaya Chast—v/ch) 42135—Guards Lt Col. Romanika

Appendix 2

Performance

PERFORMANCE DATA FOR THE TUPOLEV TU-128 'FIDDLER'

The data provided in the following tables are taken from the Soviet Air Force 'Tu-128 Operating Instructions' manual written by the engineering and design teams of OKB-156, (the Tupolev Design Bureau). The data derive from aerodynamic calculations and stability and control results obtained from tests of models of the Tu-128 in the TsAGI wind tunnels at Zhukovskiy. These were carried out in wind tunnel T-102 (for take-off and landing performance calculations), T-106 (for investigation of subsonic and transonic performance) and T-108 and T-109 (for the study of supersonic performance) plus, of course, flight tests of the actual aircraft.

Flight performance	
Type and number of engines	Two Lyul'ka AL-7F-2 turbojets
Crew	Two—pilot and navigator (WSO) seated in separate tandem cockpits on KT-1 ejection seats
Armament	Four AA-5 'Ash' air-to-air missiles
Maximum speed with four missiles, in full reheat, at altitude: 11,000 m (and at 32,000 kg AUW) Without missiles at 12,000 m	1,665 kph (Mach 1.57) 1,910 kph (Mach 1.8)
Service ceiling (at flight weight of 32,000 kg): In maximum reheat In maximum dry thrust	15,400 m 12,800 m
Reference* altitude: For acceleration to Mach 1.22 For acceleration to Mach 1.38	13,000 m 11,000 m

Optimal supersonic speed to guarantee a successful intercept of a high-altitude target from the maximum intercept boundary	1,300 kph
Patrol speed and maximum range speed (cruising speed)	910 kph (Mach 0.855)
Maximum permitted manoeuvring g-load at the centre-of-gravity when performing an intercept: at altitudes below 10,000 m at altitudes above 10,000 m at all altitudes and weights greater than 37,000 kg with asymmetric missile load (i.e. missiles on one wing only) at weights greater than 37,000 kg at weights from 35,000 kg to 37,000 kg at weights less than 37,000 kg	2 g 2.5 g 2 g 1.8 g 2 g 2.2 g
Achievable range at 910 kph (Mach 0.855) calculated for a weight of 43,400 kg (loaded weight of aircraft before start-up and taxiing), with missile launch at mid-route point and leaving a fuel remainder of 1,800 kg for landing	2,510 km
Achievable flight duration at 910 kph (down to complete fuel exhaustion and with launch of all four missiles after consumption of 50 per cent fuel)	3 hours 20 minutes
Maximum intercept boundaries (with relevant fuel load) in IMC conditions: Rear hemisphere attack in full reheat in combined mode in cruise mode Rear hemisphere attack with *rakurs* 0/4 (i.e. from directly behind target) with the target flying at 1,100 kph at altitude of 21,000 m: in reheat in combined mode	580 km 930 km 1,230 km 420 km 770 km

Reference altitude (opornaya vysota in Russian) is the optimal altitude at which the aircraft could accelerate to the given Mach number, Mach 1.22 being the speed at which the Tu-128 still exhibited good handling qualities, established during flight testing. Mach 1.38 was the maximum speed at which a missile launch could be safely carried out, from the point of view of aircraft handling. These figures are somewhat theoretical, albeit broadly characterising the aerodynamics of the Tu-128, whose operating ceiling at supersonic speed was less than that when flying subsonically.

Dynamic pressure limits: maximum speeds							
H (km)	0	2	4	6	8	10	>10
Vind max (kph)	870	844	810	770	734	725/960	960
q_{max} (kg/m^2)	3650	3440	3160	2850	2600	2540/4450	4450

Dynamic pressure limits: limiting speeds							
H (km)	0	2	4	6	8	9	>9
Vind max max (kph)	870	870	860	820	784	767/1000	1000
q max max (kg/m^2)	3650	3650	3560	3240	2950	2840/4800	4800

Dynamic pressure is the pressure q felt by an aircraft due to the velocity v of onrushing air molecules with density ρ.

$q = \frac{1}{2}\rho v^2$

Take-off and landing performance	
Take-off run at weight 43,000 kg in maximum reheat (with overspill doors open) • With outer and inner flaps set to 30° (C_L 0.8) • With inner flaps set to 30° and outer sections to 15° (C_L 0.92)	1,600 m 1,350 m
Landing run at landing weight of 31,000 kg, with inner and outer flaps set at 30°, using brake chute, spoilers and wheel brakes	830 m
Landing speed	290 kph
Maximum permitted equivalent air speed for the retraction and extension of flaps and for flight with flaps set at: • 20° • 30°	550 kph 500 kph
Maximum permitted equivalent air speed: • with undercarriage extended • for extension and retraction of undercarriage	550 kph 500 kph
Minimum indicated air speed while manoeuvring vertically in reheat mode, pulling not more than 0.3 g	380 kph
Time to climb to 10,000 m at take-off weight 43,000 kg: • In maximum reheat • In maximum dry thrust	3.5 minutes 14 minutes

Dimensions	
Length	30.06 m
Wingspan	17.53 m
Wing area	96.94 m^2
Height	7.15 m
Tailplane (horizontal stabilizer) span	8.00 m
Horizontal stabilizer area (including elevators)	25.86 m^2
Wheel track	6.20 m
Wheelbase	10.543 m

Mean aerodynamic chord (MAC)	6.138 m
Area of fuselage mid-section including intake ducts	5.00 m^2
Aspect ratio	3.17
Wing taper in plan view	3.7
Wing sweep at 25 per cent chord line	56°22' 24"
Tailplane sweep angle at 25 per cent chord line	54°59' 37"
Vertical fin sweep angle at 25 per cent chord line	54°02' 23"
Anhedral	-2°30'
Wing angle of incidence	+1°

Deflection of control surfaces	
Horizontal stabilizer settings: • Down • Neutral • Up	−22° −1° +2°
Ailerons: • Up • Neutral • Down	24±1° +1°30' 24±1°
Elevators: *With horizontal stabilizer set at −22°:* • Up • Down With horizontal stabilizer set at −1°: • Up • Down With horizontal stabilizer set at +2°: • Up • Down	 0° +21°30' +22°30' +3° −25° 0°
Spoilers: • Inner • Outer	50° 60°
Inner flaps: • In direction of flight • Relative to axis of rotation	30° 30°
Outer flaps: • In direction of flight • Relative to axis of rotation (with differential* extension of flaps, the deflection angle of the outer sections is reduced from 30° to 15°)	30° 41°52'
Airfoil section at wing/fuselage junction and thickness/chord ratio	P-60 t/c = 7 per cent

Airfoil section at 79 per cent span, perpendicular to the secondary wing spar and thickness/chord ratio	P-57M t/c = 9 per cent
Airfoil section at wing tip and thickness/chord ratio	P-57M t/c = 4 per cent

*Differential deflection here refers to the two different deflection angles applied equally *and simultaneously to the inner and outer flap sections of each wing,* not *totally different flap settings for each wing*

Weights		
Parameter	Weight with standard flight recorder set (KZA)	Weight with full flight recorder set (KZA)
Weight of aircraft loaded, before engine start and taxiing	43,400 kg	43,400 kg
of which fuel load:	15,250 kg (full fuel uplift, without counting non-usable fuel)	14,900 kg
Take-off weight, made up by:	43,000 kg	43,000 kg
Weight of aircraft empty	25,960 kg	26,310 kg
Crew (pilot and WSO)	200 kg	200 kg
Oxygen	14 kg	14 kg
Crew ration pack (two sets)	24 kg	24 kg
Oil	52 kg	52 kg
Four AA-5 'Ash' missiles	1,900 kg	1,900 kg
Fuel (specific density 0.79)	14,850 kg	14,500 kg
distributed in tanks:		
1 and 1a	1,510 kg	
2, 3, 4	3,800 kg	
5, 6, 7	3,540 kg	
8	300 kg	
Integral fuel tank	5,700 kg	
Normal landing weight	31,000 kg	31,000 kg
Permitted landing weight for touch and go (roller) landings:		
with four missiles	34,000 kg	34,000 kg
with two missiles	34,000 kg	34,000 kg
without missiles	34,000 kg	34,000 kg
Weight empty including:	25,960 kg	26,310 kg
Monitoring and recording equipment (KZA)	25 kg	500 kg
Balance weight	200 kg	50 kg
Unusable fuel	250 kg	250 kg

Appendix 3

Accidents

THE ACCIDENT RECORD OF THE TU-128 AND BRIEF OVERVIEW OF OPERATIONAL RELIABILITY

The Tu-128 was, broadly speaking, a robust and reliable design, although at various times during the course of its operation a number of serious problems were encountered. For example, aircraft from the first series-production batch were susceptible to fatigue fractures of the fuel pipes where they were connected to the engine, causing fuel to leak onto the hot engine casing and invariably resulting in a fire. The problem had been more or less dealt with by the time large-scale series production of the 'Fiddler' had got under way, but nevertheless, in the early period of operation, at least three aircraft were lost as a result of engine fires. Additionally, false warnings were occasionally generated by the fire detection system, as recalled here by Col. Komyagin:

> I myself landed a Tu-128 with the fire warning lamps illuminated. I asked the navigator whether there were flames or smoke coming from the rear of the fuselage. There was nothing. So we landed at our home airfield in spite of the fire warning lights being on. When I climbed down from the aircraft the technicians opened the inspection panels and everything appeared to be covered with a sooty deposit; they told me that this often formed in certain areas of the engine compartments, leading to the triggering of false fire warnings.

In other respects the engines themselves proved to be quite reliable; the air intakes were mounted very high on the fuselage, so stones and debris from the taxiways were not usually a threat to safe operation of the engines. However, during operation there *were* cases where engines had been damaged as a result of foreign object damage (FOD) following ingestion of small stones and 'crumbs' of concrete thrown up by the nose-wheels. This usually happened when the joints between the concrete panels of the taxiways and main runway had been sealed with sub-standard mastic. When taxiing, pebble-sized 'crumbs' of concrete embedded in the mastic would stick to the tyres and during the take-off run would be thrown up into the intakes by centrifugal force. The engines continued to operate normally, but during post-flight checks slight indentations and fractures could be detected on the first stage compressor blades. The damaged engine would be removed and sent off to the re-fit base for repair. Engine overhaul life was only 300 hours, which was sufficient for around two years of fairly intensive operation, and they retained their full performance characteristics after overhaul. Airframe life was 500 hours, with major overhauls being carried out at the maintenance unit at Novosibirsk-Tolmachevo airfield.

Among early teething problems suffered by the Tu-128 was the poor reliability of the hydraulic actuators of the horizontal stabilizer. Like those on the Tu-22 'Blinder' bomber, they had a naval provenance and at first were not particularly well adapted to the demanding environment of supersonic flight. Large temperature fluctuations (particularly in the summer months—i.e. very hot on the ground and very cold at altitude), the high rate of directional changes in the travel of the actuator rods during flight, and a wide variation in production tolerances unexpectedly began to impact on the reliability of the actuators.

A very serious 'near accident' involving a failure of the horizontal stabilizer actuator occurred on one of 64 AP's Tu-128s just after take-off from Omsk-North. This caused the stabilizer to jam in the take-off setting and the aircraft commander, Maj. Zimin, was unable to reset it to neutral. With the stabilizer set for the climb, the aircraft's pitch angle continued to increase as the speed dropped off and it would have inevitably stalled and crashed had it not been for the skill of the pilot—an 'old and experienced Tu-128 hand'. He put the aircraft into a steep banked turn after which the nose began to drop, reducing the pitch angle, and after returning the aircraft to horizontal flight he unlocked the elevators and continued to fly the aircraft with manual elevator inputs. Using the MUS-7A (*Mekhanizm Upravlyeniya Stabilizatorom*) tailplane control mechanism, Maj. Zimin set the stabilizer to a position as near as possible to neutral, after which he carried out his landing approach and made a successful emergency landing. Former aircraft technician, Maj. Plyuta, was a witness to the event and commented, 'The aircraft taxied into dispersal and the crew climbed out. Major Zimin placed his bone-dome on one of the nose-wheels and said, "That's it! I'm not flying this aircraft ever again …".' His handling of the situation was a real achievement, and was the only known case of a Tu-128 being flown, and carrying out a landing, solely using the elevators for pitch control. The skilful action of the pilot not only saved the aircraft but also allowed engineers to examine the control system and reveal the cause of the failure. This was particularly important, as there had already been one accident

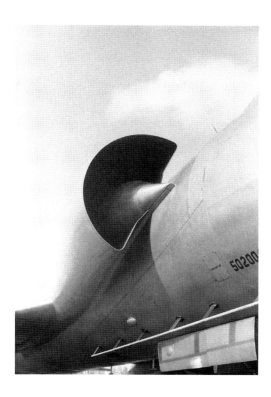

This view of the intake area and wing root of the Tu-128 illustrates the application of the 'area rule' to the design of the aircraft and emphasises the noticeable 'waisting' of the fuselage in this region. The small panel behind the construction number is stencilled with the Russian word for 'Control' (i.e. mechanical or electrical) – управление. (*Nikolai Popov*)

as a result of an actuator failure, although the precise reason for that failure had never been established.

Following the incident involving Maj. Zimin, a delegation of representatives from industry and the 'military equipment acceptance group' (*voyennaya priyomka*) was sent to Omsk to investigate the cause of the actuator failure. The group started by checking the RM-2 (*Rulyevaya Mashina*) actuators from the aircraft and discovered that they were defective and in specific conditions could lead to failure of the control system (as indeed was the case!). At first the industry representatives tried to put the blame on the regiment's ground engineers for the poor quality of their maintenance, suggesting that they had damaged the actuators when checking them on the EGU (*Elektro-Gidro Ustanovka*) hydraulic-electrical test unit, although the EGU had a working pressure of 150 kg/m^2 (31 lb/sq. ft) for ground test purposes, significantly less than the 220 kg/m^2 (45 lb/sq. ft) in the aircraft's own hydraulic lines in flight. They then started to check the RM-2 actuators on other aircraft on the regiment. The technicians removed the actuators from the aircraft and sent them to the regimental TEhCh, where the investigative commission checked them on a test-bench. Several of the removed actuators revealed the same defect as on Maj. Zimin's aircraft. The defective items were then sent off to the component re-fit base (similar to an RAF maintenance unit—MU) and were replaced with new stock from the technical stores. Former Tu-128 aircraft senior technician Maj. Plyuta recalls the event:

> It was my aircraft's turn for the check. I replaced the RM-2s and it turned out that one of them was defective. I was told to get another new one from the technical stores. Then one of the military representatives suddenly had a bright idea. 'Why are we clearing all the new actuators for operation without first *testing* them? Let's check *all* the new ones!' When we checked the new actuator [i.e. one straight from the factory], it was also defective. Following an additional check of all the newly re-installed RM-2s we managed to find several which were defective. Thus, we were able to prove that the defect was caused during the manufacturing process and so eliminate the problem.

By the end of the 1970s, 518 AP at Talagi and 72 AP at Amderma, charged with the defence of the most vulnerable northern approaches to the Soviet Union, were, paradoxically, equipped with the oldest versions of the Tu-128. So, in 1978, in an attempt to equilibrate the average age of the 'Fiddler' inventory, it was decided to swap the older Tu-128s of 518 AP and 72 AP with the newer variants operated by 350 AP at Belaya. In this way it was hoped to obviate any further age-related fatigue problems on the aircraft. However, towards the end of Tu-128 operations another fairly serious problem surfaced, this time regarding the reliability of the PTS (*Parashutno-Tormoznaya Sistyema*) brake chute system. In design terms, the PTS had been very successful during the entire period of the Tu-128's service, and pilots used to say:

> You could fold the parachute any old way. You'd remove the container, turn it upside down, stuff the parachute inside, close the container, put it back into its housing and you'd be ready for the next sortie. There was no need to pack or compact it like on modern aircraft types, which was very useful when landing away from base, where there were no supporting personnel qualified on the aircraft and the aircrew had to do their own post- and pre-flight turnaround checks. The only inconvenience was that the heavy container required two men to install it in the rear fuselage housing.

However, by the end of its service life the Tu-128 began to exhibit a number of brake chute related failures as a result of wear and tear (literally) in the canopies, including failure to open. By way of example, the following data from 1984 reveal the extent of the problem with regard to the brake chute's contribution to the statistics of 'events leading to the potential for flying accidents' (*predposylki k lyotnym proisshestviyam*).

PTS brake chute failure

Tu-128—50 per cent

MiG-25 and Su-15—both 15 per cent

MiG-23 and Yak-28—both 10 per cent

As the above data reveal, half of the 'near accidents' involving the 'Fiddler' were attributed to brake parachute failure.

Towards the end of the Tu-128's service life, it was already felt that it was an old aircraft, and crews noted that in its final years the cockpit had become very noisy, due, *inter alia*, to chafing cables and deteriorating wiring. There was also a problem with strange smells in the cockpit and the breakdown of soldered joints in the electrical wiring of avionics and other electrical components. On several aircraft the wing-mounted fuel tanks had started to leak, intensive operation over the years having led to the breakdown of hermetic seals and the appearance of microscopic cracks. As it was imperative that fuel did not drip onto the missiles, the technicians used to attach absorbent 'wicks' to the aircraft to 'encourage' the fuel to drip into collector tanks away from the aircraft. On aircraft which had leaking wing tanks, the ground crew would put fuel only into the fuselage tanks.

Throughout its service, the aircraft had exhibited a tendency for the pilot's or navigator's cockpit canopies to fly open without warning. This could occur at any height from ground level up to an altitude of 10,000 m (32,800 feet). If the navigator's canopy flew off, the crew could generally land at the nearest airfield without further incident, but it was obviously more difficult if the pilot's canopy came off. In this case, the pilot would have to lower his seat as far and as quickly as possible in order to protect himself from the blast of air in the open cockpit. Such an incident occurred in 1986/87, involving a Tu-128 from 72 AP at Amderma flown by aircraft commander Reshetnik and navigator Prus. They were performing a transit flight from Komsomol'skii to the Novosibirsk (Tolmachevo) re-fit base when the pilot's canopy flew off, breaking his collar bone as it left the aircraft. Thanks to the cool-headedness of the pilot and his heroic actions at the controls he was able to return to the departure airfield and make a successful landing, using virtually one hand to fly the aircraft. There was also at least one case of a navigator flying a Tu-128 back to base using the autopilot joystick controller, with the pilot taking control on reaching the airfield and landing the aircraft while squatting low in the open cockpit. These incidents could arise both as a result of aircrew error when selecting switches etc. in the cockpit, or because of manufacturing defects in the canopy locking mechanism.

In the 1970s, the Tu-128 was considered to have been fairly well 'mastered' (*osvoyennyi*), leading to complacency on the part of air and ground crews alike and a reduction in attention to flight safety when operating what was still a fairly complex aircraft. By 1979, there had been a total of twenty-six accidents and pre-cursors to accidents. Half of this total was attributed to aircrew error. The most difficult phase of flight, right up to the end of its service, was the take-off and landing, accounting for 34 per cent of accidents and precursors to accidents. The remaining accident-prone phases of flight were circuit flying in the vicinity of the airfield, i.e. flying the box pattern (8 per cent) and navigational route flying (23 per cent). Aircrew error involving Pilots First Class was cited in 66 per cent of cases, Pilots Second Class in 14 per cent of cases, Pilots Third Class in 17 per cent of cases and unclassified pilots in 3 per cent of cases. The following tables provide a 'snapshot' statistical review of accident precursors (*predposylki k lyotnym proisshestviyu*) by aircraft type for the third and fourth quarters of 1982. They are included to show that in that year the Tupolev interceptor exhibited a smaller number of such precursors in terms of manufacturing design defects compared with MiG, Sukhoi and Yakovlev fighters, and that the Tu-128 had become, by that stage, a very reliable aircraft.

Third quarter of 1982

Reason for potential accident			Su-15, TM, UM, UT	MiG-25P, PD, PDS, PU	MiG-31	MiG-23M, ML, P, UB	Yak-28P, U	Tu-128, Tu-128M, Tu-128UT, Tu-16, Tu-126	MiG-21, L-29, L-39	VTA—Military Transport Aviation	Total	By percentage
Personnel error		Aircrew error	13	5	–	10	3	6	3	–	40	13
	Error on part of engineering service (IAS)	Result of poor preliminary preparation	3	4	–	2	1	1	–	–	11	3
		Result of poor pre-flight preparation	3	3	–	–	5	3	–	2	16	5
		Result of unsatisfactory execution of repair and modification work	1	–	1	1	3	3	–	–	9	3
		Total	20	12	1	13	12	13	3	2	76	24
		Servicing error at repair base	18	5	–	3	17	4	2	–	49	15
		Manufacturing design defect	31	42	11	69	14	7	16	6	196	61
		In sum	69	59	12	85	43	24	21	8	321	100
		By percentage	21	18	4	26	13	8	7	3	100	

Fourth quarter of 1982		Su-15, TM, UM, UT	MiG-25P, PD, PDS, PU	MiG-31	MiG-23M, ML, P, UB	Yak-28P, U	Tu-128, Tu-128M, Tu-128UT, Tu-16, Tu-126	MiG-21, L-29, L-39	VTA—Military Transport Aviation	Total	By percentage
Reason for potential accident											
Error on part of engineering service (IAS)	SD	7	5	1	1	4	4	–	2	24	9
	AO	–	2	–	2	3	2	–	–	9	3
	REO	–	–	–	–	2	1	–	–	3	1
Servicing error at repair base	SD	6	1	–	2	–	3	2	–	14	5
	AO	8	4	–	1	6	1	–	–	20	7
	REO	4	–	–	–	11	–	–	–	15	5
Manufacturing design defect	SD	9	19	1	20	6	2	7	1	65	23
	AO	11	12	9	33	–	1	5	2	73	26
	REO	11	11	1	16	8	4	4	3	58	21
	Total	56	54	12	75	40	18	18	8	281	100
By percentage		20	19	4	27	15	6	6	3	100	

Key to abbreviations:

SD (*Samolyot i Dvigatyel'*)—Aircraft and engines maintenance group
AO (*Aviatsionnoye Oborudovaniye*)—Aircraft equipment maintenance group
REO (*Radio-elektronnoye Oborudovaniye*)—Avionics maintenance group

Unlike its accident-prone stablemate, the Tu-22, the Tu-128 was never actually regarded by its crews as a 'widow-maker', although more than forty aircraft were involved in accidents and write-offs during its service with the PVO. The objective of this appendix is to provide as complete a picture as possible of its accident record based on existing data, in order to allow readers themselves to assess the accident susceptibility of this unique 'fighter'. (Unfortunately, not all incidents have been written up as a formal report; nor has it been possible to provide specific dates for every incident.)

As part of standard release-to-service procedures, Tupolev Design Bureau engineers and officers from the Soviet Air Force and PVO were jointly required to draw up a list of circumstances in which aircrew would be justified in abandoning the aircraft. For the Tu-128 these were:

1. failure of the flight control system;
2. uncontained fire on board the aircraft;
3. flame-out, or other engine failure preventing relight before reaching a height of 2,000 m (6,560 feet);
4. structural failure of the aircraft;
5. inability to recover from a spin or deep spiral before reaching an altitude of 4,000 m (13,125 feet);
6. inability to lower the main undercarriage bogies or the nose-wheel;
7. loss of orientation and impossibility of re-establishing control;
8. loss of spatial awareness and impossibility of regaining control before reaching an altitude of 4,000 m (13,125 feet);
9. complete failure of the flight instruments at night or in IFR conditions, when other flight guidance methods were not available;
10. inability to stop the aircraft within the limits of the main runway in the event of engine failure on take-off at speeds of 140-600 kph (76-324 kts);
11. deterioration of the pilot's well-being (*samochuvstvie*) and inability to continue the flight;
12. running out of fuel;
13. failure of DC generators, with accumulator voltages less than 22 volts;
14. speed falling below 300 kph (162 kts) at heights below 600 m (1,970 feet).

The table below shows the sequence followed by the pilot and navigator in the event of having to eject.

Pilot	Verbally issue the command to the navigator 'Abandon aircraft' (*Pokin' samolyot*) and follow it up by raising the safety guard and selecting the 'Override Ejection' switch (*Prinudityel'noye Katapul'tirovaniye*). Assume the pre-ejection posture and, having checked that the canopy has been jettisoned and the navigator has already ejected, grasp the ejection seat hand grips and raise them up to the stops. Confirm that the control column (wheel) and rudder pedals have been disconnected. Lower the ejection seat hand grips and squeeze.
Navigator/WSO	Having received the command 'Abandon aircraft', immediately assume the pre-ejection posture, raise the ejection seat hand grips up to the stops and lower them only after the canopy has been safely jettisoned.

After abandoning the aircraft it was essential to 'follow through' (*dublirovat'*) the operation of the seat's automatic systems. For autonomous separation from the seat, this required the following actions to be performed:

1. On ejecting above 3,000 m (9,840 feet), descend in the seat to an altitude of 3,000 m. At this altitude, but no lower than 1,000 m (3,280 feet) above *ground* level, pull out the release handle between the legs to its fullest travel. Push away firmly from the seat and after 2 seconds deploy the

parachute canopy manually.

2. On abandoning the aircraft below 3,000 m, the above actions had to be carried out 3 seconds after ejection.

3. If the seat adopted an erratic and unstable descent profile on ejecting above 3,000 m, it was essential to separate from the seat and deploy the parachute canopy manually at an altitude no higher than 5,000 m (16,400 feet).

Special training was provided on the regiments to prepare crews both physically and psychologically for the rigours of ejection, and once a year they were required to undergo training on a static inclined simulator rig to familiarise them with the seat and its life-support attachments. Additionally, they were given annual training on a full ejection simulator with the seat being fired by a special pyrotechnic charge, subjecting the occupant to an acceleration force of 10 g as the seat travelled up the rails before being slowed by a special braking mechanism. This training was recorded in the pilots' and navigators' log books.

REVIEW OF TU-128 ACCIDENTS AND WRITE-OFFS DURING OPERATION WITH THE PVO

Non-fatal write-off—Tu-128—1966

Weather conditions: VMC
Circumstances: A crew from 518 AP at Talagi, comprising aircraft commander Pilot First Class Maj. 'B' and navigator Maj. 'K', were landing at base, but the pilot failed to set up the aircraft correctly on the landing approach. As a result, the aircraft ran off the edge of the runway after touchdown and suffered extensive damage. Although the aircraft was beyond repair, the two crew members escaped uninjured.
Cause: Lack of training on the part of the pilot and a poor level of training on the part of the air traffic control officer.

Non-fatal write-off—Tu-128—Summer 1967

Weather conditions: Night
Circumstances: A crew from 518 AP, comprising regiment commander Pilot First Class Col. Korotyeev and his navigator, were carrying out a flight in accordance with the KBP combat training manual from their base at Talagi. During the flight, the aircraft suffered a total failure of the electrical system. The pilot and navigator were unable to restore electrical power to the various user systems, as a result of

which the fuel pumps ceased to function. This led to the subsequent flame-out of both engines. The crew ejected safely in the vicinity of the historical township of Kholmogory.

Cause: The accident investigation commission concluded that engine flame-out was due to fuel starvation caused by the failure of the electrical supply to the fuse-lage tank fuel pumps, preventing fuel delivery from both groups of fuselage tanks.

Col. Nyefyedov recalls this incident:

> The crew were carrying out an evening flying detail to build up their night-flying hours. They were scheduled to take off in twilight so that they could perform a night landing. They took off and just disappeared [...] No one knew where they'd gone and everyone was concerned for their safety. It was two in the morning before a call was received saying that they were safe and sound. They'd taken off, departed the airfield and then all electrical power was lost. They couldn't see any of the instruments, but the engines were still functioning. Where could they fly to? They could only perform an approach on instruments, but how could they do that at night, unable to see the instrument panel? They orbited for a while, but in the end they had to eject.

Clearly, this brief account differs from that of the accident commission, in that the engines appeared to continue operating after the loss of electrical power.

Fatal write-off—Tu-128—4 October 1967

Weather conditions: Daylight VMC

Circumstances: A crew, comprising senior inspector-pilot Col. Elektron Yevglyevskiy from PVO Headquarters and navigator Ryzhenkov, were performing a test flight of a Tu-128 from 615 UIAP based at Savasleika. Whilst carrying out the flight, one of the engines flamed out and, responding to instructions from the flight controller (RP), Col. Yevglyevskiy began to set up for the landing approach. However, whilst carrying out the third turn of a standard box-pattern approach at normal circuit height, the number two engine flamed out. The crew ejected on the command of the RP, but as a result of a malfunction of his ejection seat the navigator was killed.

Cause: The accident commission concluded that the reason for the engine flame-out was a manufacturing defect in the fuel system. The death of the navigator was attributed to the failure of the seat separation mechanism, preventing his parachute from being withdrawn from its housing.

An outline description of the Tu-128's fuel system is given in the following account by the pilot involved—Honoured Military Pilot Col. Elektron Mironovich Yevglyevskiy:

Before this incident, we were already aware of the ejection [in similar circumstances] from a Tu-128, by the regiment commander at Talagi. Then there were another two incidents after this. The accident commission concluded that [in all three cases] the fuel booster pumps had not been working [prior to engine flame-out]. As a general rule, the fuel system of fighters incorporated a service tank, fed from all the aircraft's tanks, from where fuel was supplied to the engine(s). However, the Tu-128 had a fuel system similar to that of the Tu-22 bomber and did not have a service tank—fuel was fed straight from the tanks into the port and starboard main fuel lines and then directly to the engines. Since the aircraft had a very long fuselage, the main fuel lines were commensurately lengthy and, in order to guarantee normal uninterrupted engine operation while manoeuvring in flight, booster pumps were employed in the fuel delivery circuit, designed to provide the necessary pressure in the fuel lines. The three pilots involved in the aforementioned incidents were held responsible [for the loss of the aircraft], for failing to switch on the booster pumps, as a result of which the engines shut down in flight. I had conducted extensive correspondence on this matter and even visited the Tupolev Design Bureau, where we discussed the problem at some length.

The reason for carrying out the test flight and a description of the accident is given in Col. Yevglyevskiy's narrative account:

At the time, I was due to take part in a routine flying programme with 615 UIAP at Savasleika. However, General Kadomtsyev suddenly approached me and said, 'I'd like you to test fly a Tu-128 for me! I want to perform a flight in this aircraft to the Far East.[1] Select a good navigator and get him to check the navigational equipment and all the other systems etc.' So we selected an aircraft from the training regiment at Savasleika and I went to perform the test flight with my chosen navigator, Ryzhenkov, telling him that he had to check all the equipment as instructed by General Kadomtsyev. After a short flight we duly arrived in the general handling zone and almost immediately the starboard engine flamed out. My first reaction was to check the fuel pumps—they were all switched on [there was a whole line of switches on the side panel]. The lamps indicated that everything was normal. At the same time I told the RP on the radio what had happened. He then asked, 'How's the port engine? Is it normal?' I replied that it was operating normally. He then ordered us to carry out a single-engined approach, so we set up for the landing and descended to 3,000 m [9,840 feet]. The RP once again asked us how the second engine was behaving. I reported that everything was normal. Then the RP suddenly called again. 'Make another circuit of the airfield. We have a squadron of Su-9s approaching to land and they are running short of fuel—their low-fuel warning lamps are on.' I acknowledged the call and went round again. The RP then asked me to do yet another circuit as there were still some aircraft on the approach, so I started to set up a second single-engined holding pattern. While all this was going on, I'd been constantly reporting to the RP how the pumps were working and how the port engine was behaving, passing him the engine parameters etc., but I could not get the starboard engine to re-light.

Finally the RP told me to commence my approach, so I descended to 500 m [1,640 feet] and lowered the undercarriage. I was already approaching the third turn when the RP once again asked me to hold off and then suddenly the remaining engine flamed out. Our height was only 500 m—not very high at all. The RP was Viktor Kotsyubinskiy, a friend, and he immediately told me to eject. I acknowledged his call and then shouted to my navigator Ryzhenkov on the intercom, yelling, 'Ryzhenkov, eject, eject!' I shouted to him about six times until the canopies were jettisoned. The system worked in such a way that by operating either jettison lever on either seat the first canopy to go was the navigator's, followed by the pilot's canopy. Once the navigator's canopy had gone it was pointless trying to talk and, in addition, smoke from his ejection seat filled the cockpit. So I concluded that he'd already gone and therefore gripped the ejection levers on my seat to start the ejection sequence. There was an interlock in the system—if the navigator hadn't ejected then the pilot's seat-operating levers were interlocked and would have to be unlocked before the pilot could eject. However, the interlock on my seat had been released, so the navigator *must* have definitely ejected. An enormous force propelled me from the cockpit—'10 g straight up the arse' (10 g *v odnu zhopu* …) as we used to say at the time! When the parachute canopy opened I could see the aircraft below me—it had pitched up into a nose-high attitude. The shroud lines of my parachute had become entangled and I was preoccupied with untangling them, so the next time I looked for the aircraft it had disappeared from sight. However, below me there was already a cloud of smoke and flames from the wreckage.

I turned into wind as we had been taught in survival training and saw that there was a wood below me. I could see that I was being carried towards a tall pine tree and I tucked my legs in so that I wouldn't end up sitting on top of it. I passed through the tree in a flash—I didn't even notice it. (However, three days later my left leg was black and blue from the ankle to the groin, so it seems that I *had* struck the tree quite hard.) The most unpleasant aspect of the landing was that I struck my back on some tree roots. (The KT-1 seat design was such that the back panel of the seat was integral with the parachute harness and provided spinal protection for the occupant after ejection. The seat back panel came down to just above the waist and so the force of striking the tree roots was passed directly to my waist. I've been aware of this pain throughout my life, ever since the ejection. My vertebrae had 'shifted' in that area and I didn't fly for seven months after the accident.) After landing, I crawled into a clearing in the trees, so that it would be easier to find me. The search party didn't exactly find me very quickly—it took them about 40 minutes. During the search for the navigator, some children came up to us (i.e. the search party and myself) and told us where he was. He was lying in his ejection seat. He'd flown into the ground still in the seat. When the accident investigation team started to consider the possible reasons for his death it was obvious that the seat separation mechanism had failed to operate [*sic*]. The normal procedure was for a special triggering mechanism in the seat to automatically release all the straps connecting the occupant to the seat, including leg and arm restraints, and release him from it within a specific time following ejection.

There was a large drive-spring in this mechanism, inside a circular box assembly, designed to pull out the cable which started the release process. However, in this tragic incident the spring had rotated about 30° and then jammed inside the box. When the accident commission checked the hinge moments along the entire length of the cable they were around two to twenty times greater than the permitted values and the mechanism was incapable of operating correctly. There was provision for a manual override, in the form of a rubber-sheathed cable ring which had to be pulled in the event of failure of the automatic system in order to initiate separation from the seat, but the navigator was unable to pull this ring. He was, however, holding the pear-shaped toggle of the NAZ emergency survival pack in his right hand.[2] The pilot and navigator of the Tu-128 did not sit directly on their parachutes, but on the NAZ pack, the parachute being packed into a pouch behind them. In order to reduce the force of impact with the ground, the NAZ was suspended on a halyard that hung 15 m [50 feet] below the survivor and was released during the descent by a special toggle. As the NAZ was, therefore, the first assembly to hit the ground and also quite a heavy item, the crew member's rate of descent was suddenly reduced and resulted in a slightly softer landing.

It was a tragic accident—Ryzhenkov was a very good guy and had come to PVO Aviation from the 'transport world'. Perhaps if he had carried out ejection seat training on a simulator rig [which existed at that time] he might well have survived. Instead of pulling the NAZ release toggle he might well have pulled the manual separation release handle, the seat would have separated and the main parachute would have deployed in the normal way. However, as we calculated later, Ryzhenkov had only 13.5 seconds in which to do all that, and we had, after all, ejected at only 500 m.

After the ejection I was taken to HQ, where I asked for a telephone so that I could let General Kadomtsyev know what had happened. Having listened to my 'report', he asked, 'Have you spoken to your wife yet?' He was considered to be a very severe character, but here he showed a more caring side to his personality. I told him that I hadn't yet spoken to her, so with his intervention I was put through to my wife immediately and told her that I'd had to eject but that I was OK. The following day General Kadomtsyev flew in to Savasleika from Moscow and assembled an accident investigation team in the office of the head of 148 Combat Training and Aircrew Conversion Centre. The first question that Kadomtsyev put to me was, 'Yevglyevskiy, are you sure that you'd switched on all the booster pumps?' I replied, 'Comrade Commander, I'm not only sure—I reported all my actions over the radio. They can be analysed—everything was recorded. What was switched on, what was switched off, when it was done.' General Kadomtsyev put another question to me. 'Are you sure that there was still fuel in the tanks when the second engine flamed out?' I replied that there was around 2,800 kg [6,170 lb] of fuel left. This amount was entirely sufficient for the approach and landing. The General accepted this information.

Next, I was taken to the local hospital and everyone was forbidden from visiting me. General Kadomtsyev appointed an engineer and a pilot from the accident investigation group who he authorised to visit me in hospital, adding that he would bring others if he thought it necessary. The following day, every bone in my body ached; I could neither walk nor sit normally. The day after that, General Kadomtsyev came back to see me with some industry representatives. I got up from the bed, but Kadomtsyev said, 'No, no, don't get up. We'll do the interview with you lying down.' It turned out that the representatives had already decided with the General what questions they would put to me and I dutifully replied to each one. At the end of the session, the General escorted the delegation out of the ward and brought in a group of ejection seat specialists. There were a number of observations relating to the seat; firstly, on the Tu-128 it was possible to initiate ejection of the navigator from the front seat, independent of the navigator himself, using a special toggle switch. However, this toggle switch was mounted high on the cockpit coaming and with the canopy jettisoned it was impossible to reach it due to the severe turbulence inside the cockpit. It was impossible to see anything, and the force of the airflow prevented the arm being raised to the necessary height to grasp the toggle. I told them about this and suggested that the switch should be moved down, accessible to the right hand. Then I suggested that it should be removed altogether. Instead, I proposed that ejection of both crew members should be initiated via the handles on the pilot's seat, with simultaneous jettisoning of the two canopies, followed by sequenced ejection of first the navigator and then the pilot. Afterwards, they did move the toggle switch down, although not exactly where I'd suggested.

The KT-1 was, of course, a good ejection seat and it had, after all, saved my life, but it did have a number of shortcomings. One of these was the absence of an automatic leg restraint system, the pilot himself having to place his feet in the footrests before ejection. During my ejection I didn't put my feet on the footrests and didn't give much thought to it at the time. However, after the incident, I was taken to a hotel. A colleague took my flying boots off and said, 'Why are you still wearing these socks? Look at the heels—they're full of holes.' He took the other boot off and there were holes in the heel of that sock too. He then said, 'Ah-ha—you didn't put your feet on the footrest!' When the seat shot upwards, my feet had obviously struck the seat frame, and because the initial acceleration rate wasn't too great it was only my socks that were torn and my feet weren't injured. As a consequence of this accident I was even nominated for the award of the title Hero of the Soviet Union because from my debriefing it had been possible to gain a better understanding of the problem concerning the fuel system. In the end I was given a more modest award, but this wasn't really important.

The reason for the engines flaming out in flight was attributed to a manufacturing defect in the fuel system. Tank No. 8 was an important element of the system, located under the engines in the rear fuselage, of comparatively small capacity, designed to be consumed during the taxiing phase, and should have been empty on take-off. The fuel had been totally consumed from the tank but the pumps had not shut down and had continued to operate, pumping air into the fuel system. As a result, in certain conditions, this produced a cavitation effect and instead of kerosene the pumps would pump a mixture of air and kerosene. Consequently, the amount of fuel going to the engines was reduced and in specific circumstances they would flame out. The problem was discovered during the investigation into this particular accident, leading to modification of all the Tu-128s in service at that time. A further twelve aircraft which were awaiting delivery at the factory at Voronezh were also modified. These aircraft were ready for handing over to the military acceptance team, but General Kadomtsyev forbade this until they had all been modified. Because of this, factory personnel did not receive a salary for around eight months and the whole affair proved to be something of an epic, but the problem was finally resolved to everyone's satisfaction.

Non-fatal write-off—Tu-128—7 March 1968

Weather conditions: Daylight IMC

Circumstances: A crew from 518 AP at Talagi under the command of Maj. 'K' as pilot, with Capt. 'K' as navigator, were carrying out a routine flight in accordance with the regiment's training plan. During the landing approach, the weather deteriorated sharply in the vicinity of the airfield, although the regiment commander, Col. Korotyeev, did not authorise a diversion to the designated airfield at Petrozavodsk. While carrying out the final phase of the landing, the aircraft entered a powerful snowstorm and because of the reduced visibility the touchdown was made at an angle to the runway centreline, and after a short distance it ran off the edge of the runway. After hitting a large snowdrift, the aircraft's undercarriage was torn away and, having slid for around a further 800 m (2,625 feet), it came to a halt. At this point, a fire broke out. The navigator climbed out of the cockpit without assistance, but the pilot got one of his legs tangled up in the seat harness straps and ended up hanging upside down on the side of the fuselage. He was freed with the aid of the search and rescue party (*poiskovo-spasatyel'naya komanda*) when they arrived on the scene and both crew members emerged from the incident unharmed. The aircraft, however, could not be repaired and was scrapped.

Cause: The accident was attributed to the error of setting up the landing in weather which was below the specified minima. The accident investigation commission placed the blame for this on the regiment commander for failing to cancel the flying programme at the airfield and not sending those aircraft that were already airborne to the designated diversion airfield.

Non-fatal write-off—Tu-128—10 July 1968

Weather conditions: Daylight VMC

Circumstances: A crew from 356 AP at Zhana-Semey comprising aircraft commander Pilot First Class Capt. 'O' and navigator Lt 'O' were scheduled to perform a local flying detail, carrying out their first joint 'solo' flight in the Tu-128. The pilot taxied out to the holding point for the main runway. As a result of the high ambient temperature (around +40°C in the shade) the mastic used to seal the concrete slabs of the runway had started to melt. On increasing engine rpm and selecting reheat, the aircraft began to slide forward on the melted mastic. (The pilot took the aircraft's forward movement as indicating release of the parking brake.) The aircraft continued to slide on the melted mastic with the brakes on, but on the left-hand side of the runway the slabs suddenly cleared of the substance, facilitating normal braking action on the left bogie. However, the braked starboard bogie continued to skid over the surface, rotating around the braked port bogie. Then, as a result of the considerable heat loading due to skidding on the hot surface, the tyres on the left bogie burst, leading to the aircraft swinging 30° to the left and ultimately rolling off the edge of the runway surface onto the surrounding earth. The crew did not react to advisory commands transmitted by ATC. While moving over the ground, the starboard undercarriage bogie collapsed, followed by the left-hand unit, with the aircraft then bursting into flames. After the aircraft had stopped moving, the crew exited the aircraft without assistance. The aircraft was subsequently burnt out.

Cause: The major contributory factor was the presence of a large quantity of RBV binding mastic on the main runway, which in the high ambient temperature on that day had melted and spread over the runway surface. (RBV is a Russian proprietary crushed rubber, bitumen and polymer binding mastic used to seal ferro-concrete slabs on runways.) This in turn led to deterioration in traction of the main undercarriage bogies, causing the braked starboard bogie to 'skid' around the braked port bogie, taking the aircraft 30° to the left of the centreline. The other significant factor was the insufficient level of professional training of the pilot, evident in his failure to line up the aircraft correctly on the runway after being displaced from the centreline.

Non-fatal write-off—4 August 1968

Weather conditions: Daylight VMC

Circumstances: A crew from 518 AP at Talagi, comprising aircraft commander Pilot First Class Capt. Davidovskiy and navigator 'U', were carrying out a routine navigation exercise from base. During the flight, at an altitude of 12,000 m (39,370 feet), both engines flamed out simultaneously. The crew were able to eject from the stricken aircraft.

Cause: The accident investigation commission concluded that both engines flamed out due to the 'failure of the automatic systems of the fuel delivery system'.

The following is an account (given later) by Pilot First Class Maj. Aleksandr Grigor'yevitch Davidovskiy:

The temperature was around 30°C. We had taken off without having had a meal. We flew a route taking us out to the Kanin Peninsula and were actually on the return leg. Suddenly one engine flamed out, then the second. We were flying at 12,000 m [39,370 feet]. I worked out a plan of action, overflew the airfield and when we were in the 'ejection zone' we both ejected, the navigator going out first, followed by me. Luckily, my parachute opened normally, although the main canopy had had to pass through a reduced aperture, about the size of two fists; it turned out that one of the pins in the parachute pack had not released. The parachute had been incorrectly packed. The navigator and I landed in a swamp, although because of the recent very high temperatures in the area, it had dried out. The aircraft itself penetrated the swampy edge of a lake, sinking to a depth of 32 m [105 feet]. There were two fishermen on the lake, fishing off a raft. When they saw that an aircraft was crashing down towards them, they both jumped into the lake. As I was descending on my parachute I could see them swimming away. Then, when they saw that the aircraft would not crash onto them, they scrambled back onto the raft. They sailed to the bank and came towards us. The distance was about one kilometre. At that moment a Li-2 flew overhead. It was actually looking for us. We indicated that we were both alive and everything was normal. The aircraft flew off.

We then went over to the fishermen's campfire. They greeted us and decided to share some of their fish soup. We opened our NAZ survival packs to use some of the rations. Within about half an hour a helicopter turned up, hovering about one metre above the ground. We jumped onto it. Once again we'd failed to have a meal! We gave the NAZ survival packs to the fishermen. We only took one of the parachutes: I couldn't carry anything because my diaphragm had been ruptured after landing awkwardly in a large depression in the ground. In one of the pockets in the right leg of my flying suit I had three bars of chocolate in a duralumin sheath, which had struck me under the ribs when I landed and damaged my diaphragm. I left my parachute behind, but the navigator took his with him. That's how we were taken back to the airfield. Then we had to explain why we'd ejected. The 10th Army Head of Aviation 'asked' me everything. 'Did you switch over to the first emergency channel [121.5MHz] or not?' I told him that I had. But he kept on asking, 'Do you remember switching over, or not?' I again replied that I *had* (using the standard Soviet terminology—'*Tochno!—Pereshyol!*' meaning 'Exactly!—I switched over!'). The Head of Aviation actually insisted on a diver going down into the wreckage of the aircraft to retrieve the control panel for the radio from the cockpit. It was easy to get out and the diver brought it back to the surface. It turned out that I was (of course) telling the truth. The Head of Aviation then said to me, 'Good lad! You remembered everything that you did!'

Fatal write-off—Tu-128—28 May 1969 (1968?)

Weather conditions: Night
Circumstances: A crew from 445 AP at Savvatiya, comprising deputy regiment commander for political affairs Lt Col. 'P' as pilot and Sr Lt 'P' as navigator, were carrying out an air combat (GCI) sortie as one of a pair of Tu-128s. While carrying out the task, one of the fire warning (*Pozhar dvigatyelya*) lights illuminated, indicating an engine fire. The crew were unable to examine the rear fuselage area to establish whether there really was a fire since the aircraft, an early-series example, was not fitted with a periscope for this purpose. The second Tu-128, which was acting as the target in the GCI sortie, formated on Lt Col. 'P's aircraft and took up a position behind it to check for signs of fire. Lt Col. 'P' spoke at length on the radio with the crew of the other aircraft, as well as the ATC controller at Savvatiya airfield, although the conversation was not made available for this report. When Lt Col. 'P's Tu-128 reached a point to the north of Syktyvkar, at an altitude of 9,000 m (29,530 feet), the aircraft exploded, killing both him and his navigator. (No mention is made in the somewhat abbreviated account of this incident as to whether the second 'Fiddler' was flying in close proximity at the time of the explosion.)
Cause: The precise reason for the engine fire could not be established, since the wreckage from the aircraft was spread over a wide area, in marshland and the dense taiga forestation of the region.[3] The largest piece of wreckage found was a turbine disc from one of the engines. The most probable cause of the engine fire was thought to have been a leak in the fuel pipe at the point where it was attached to the engine.

Fatal write-off—Tu-128—14 September 1969

Weather conditions: XXX
Circumstances: A crew from 72 AP at Amderma, comprising Maj. 'F' as pilot and navigator (Capt.) 'F', were landing at their base airfield. During the landing, the port main undercarriage bogie started to collapse immediately after touchdown. The aircraft struck the ground with the port mainplane and then skidded off the runway to the right. The ATC controller ordered the crew to eject and the navigator ejected at a ground speed of 140 kph (75 kts), while the pilot left the aircraft at a speed calculated to have been only 80 kph (43 kts). However, for the escape system to function properly and for the parachute to deploy completely, the speed had to be not less than 120 kph (65 kts) and because of the low ejection speed, the pilot was killed. During its travel across the airfield, the aircraft struck an An-12 transport which was awaiting its turn for take-off, standing with engines running on the second taxiway. Both aircraft were engulfed by fire and destroyed in the collision. The crew of the An-12 and all the passengers on board were killed. The navigator of the Tu-128 received burns to his back on ejection but survived the ordeal, albeit requiring a long period of convalescence.
Cause: The collapse of the port main undercarriage leg was determined later by the accident board to have been due to a manufacturing defect in the down-lock mechanism of the port bogie.

Non-fatal write-off—Tu-128—24 December 1970

Weather conditions: VMC, outside air temperature –40°C
Circumstances: A crew from 356 AP at Zhana-Semey, comprising Pilot First Class Maj. 'G' and section navigator Lt 'T', were performing a transit flight from base to Omsk-North, combined with Exercises 63 and 64 of the 1969 edition of the combat training manual 'KBP Tu-128-69'. During the descent the horizontal stabilizer actuator failed, leading to jamming of the control column (wheel) and control rods. The crew ejected safely from the aircraft.
Cause: Failure of the stabilizer actuator was attributed to a manufacturing defect.

Fatal write-off—Tu-128—6 April 1971

Weather conditions: Daylight IMC, severe snowstorm
Circumstances: A crew from 64 AP at Omsk-North, comprising squadron commander Lt Col. 'K' as pilot and senior regiment navigator Lt Col. 'K', were carrying out a live missile firing detail at the Telemba range. The task was slightly modified

because of poor weather conditions at the transit operating base at Kadala (near Chita), resulting in the take-off being conducted from Kadala, followed by live missile firing over the range and a landing at Belaya. The crew successfully completed the take-off in extremely poor weather conditions, but the pilot deselected afterburner prematurely during the climb-out. This resulted in a marked reduction in the rate of climb, the loss of thrust making it impossible to climb above the mountains in the immediate vicinity of the airfield. The aircraft struck sloping ground and was destroyed, killing the pilot and navigator.

Cause: In spite of the wreckage being strewn over a wide area following impact with the ground at comparatively high speed, the accident commission came to a unanimous decision. The regiment executives were held responsible, having allowed the take-off to take place in conditions which were 'on weather minima' for the crew at an unfamiliar airfield. Apart from this, flights in such meteorological conditions should have been preceded by very careful pre-flight planning and familiarisation with the specific geographical features of the given airfield.

Fatal write-off—Tu-128—14 (25?) May 1971

Weather conditions: Daylight IMC

Circumstances: A crew from 350 AP at Belaya, comprising section commander Maj. 'T' as pilot and section navigator Capt. 'P', were detailed to carry out practice missile firing at Telemba range (Exercise 86 in the 1969 edition of the KBP combat training manual—'Training flight for daylight missile firing against a VRPM target'). It will be recalled that the VRPM target is a parachute target fired from the ground by a large artillery piece to an altitude of 25,000 m (82,000 feet). The crew took off from the airfield—callsign '*Trek*' (Track)—at 13.28 hours local time, carrying two R-4R semi-active radar homing missiles. In the forty-seventh minute of flight, the pilot launched both missiles at the slowly descending target. After the launch, in response to instruction from the command post, the pilot reported, 'I've broken off left, 884' (884 being his callsign). After this, all communication with the crew ceased and radar tracking of the flight was lost. It seems that after launching his missiles the pilot made a fatal handling error that resulted in the aircraft entering a deep-spiral descent. According to the flight data recorder, an increase in speed was registered 10 seconds after missile launch. Indicated air speed went from 544 kph (294 kts) to 1,120 kph (605 kts) in 43 seconds. Attempting to pull out of the spiral descent, the pilot applied 2.5 g back pressure on the control column at an altitude of 5,000 m (16,400 feet), this being the maximum permitted g-loading for the Tu-128, but he was unable to bring the aircraft back to level flight. He continued to attempt to pull out of the dive, but in doing so the aircraft was subjected to a vertical load of 7 g (the ultimate failure loading being 5.8-6 g).

The aircraft subsequently broke up at an altitude somewhere between 3,000 and 5,000 m (9,840-16,400 feet), the crew apparently making no attempt to eject and perishing in the accident. The impact point of the 'Fiddler' was located by the crew of a Mi-4 'Hound' helicopter at a distance of 78 km (48 miles) and bearing of 33° from the town of Telemba. The wreckage was scattered over an area of land about 4-6 km (2.5-3.75 miles) long and 0.8-1 km (0.5-0.6 miles) in width.

Cause: The probable cause of the accident was the pilot's handling error when attempting to pull out of the deep spiral. This error was, in turn, a consequence of there being no specific instruction in the Tu-128's Pilots' Notes concerning the actions required to deal with unintentional entry into the deep-spiral regime. Unintentional entry into a spiral descent when firing missiles can result in partial damage to the aircraft or the flight controls by missile fragments as a result of flying into their detonation zone, or temporary (short-period) failure of the aileron or rudder actuators, or be the consequence of the pilot's attention being distracted at the moment of breaking off from the attack.

Aircraft history

Tu-128 c/n 504302 rolled out of the factory with an airframe life of 500 hours; had not yet undergone periodic servicing.

Total time since entering service—170 hours.

Port engine AL-7F-2-300 No. V0126031 'T', delivered from the Salyut plant on 11 April 1970 with an operating life of 300 hours; had not yet undergone periodic servicing. Total time on airframe—130 hours.

Starboard engine AL-7F-2-300 No. V0126007 'T', delivered from the Salyut plant on 11 April 1970 with an operating life of 300 hours; had not yet undergone periodic servicing. Total time on airframe—130 hours.

Col. Elektron Yevglyevskiy, at the time deputy head of the Department of Combat Training for PVO Aviation, was a member of the investigation team set up to examine the cause of this accident and provides the following narrative account:

> I'd been told that an aircraft had exploded in mid-air over the range at Telemba during missile firing practice. I flew to the range with the Commander of PVO Aviation, General Borovykh and from the helicopter started to examine the area where the wreckage of the aircraft had fallen. The aircraft had broken up at around 3,000 m [9,840 feet] at high speed, so the wreckage was distributed over an area with a radius of around 5,000 m [16,400 feet]. During the search we found part of the fuselage from the cockpit area and wing centre-section junction. Evidently, the fuselage had descended without the wings, which had both been torn off simultaneously by the excessive g-loading, only the heavy attachment points remaining. Later, on close

examination, we noticed an unusual smear of paint along the fuselage, unusual in that it resembled the colours of a rainbow. The smear consisted of strips of green, blue, red and white paint. Everyone was convinced that there must have been some kind of 'foreign object' in the area that had collided with the aircraft. [The term used was 'unidentified flying object' (*nyeopoznannyi lyetayushchiy ob'yekt* or NLO, the Russian term for UFO, although in this context it was not thought to have been used to describe an 'alien craft'. In fact, the feeling was that it might have been a reconnaissance balloon.] When we returned to Kadala airfield, I began to check the types of paint used on weather balloons, but nowhere was there any reference to the combination of colours that we had seen on the crashed aircraft. The theory regarding a collision with a 'foreign object' gained more support because that combination of paint colours could not be found anywhere. The paint smear was around 5 m [16.5 feet] long down the right-hand side of the fuselage. General Borovykh put forward another idea—perhaps the pilot of the second aircraft had shot down the aircraft flying in front of it, having mistaken it for the target? The Tu-128s were flying in a pair, with a large horizontal separation between the aircraft. The crew of the first aircraft had carried out their missile firing and after breaking off from the attack it suddenly dropped out of the sky.

The missiles were being fired against parachute flare targets, with first one aircraft releasing a missile, then the second. It was quite possible that this is what had happened here. The second aircraft had been flying behind the leader and could, theoretically, have shot him down. We began to assemble all the data from the KZA flight data recorder of the crashed aircraft. There was a 'Lock-on' recorded, then 'Clear Lock-on', followed by another 'Lock-on'. We examined the film carefully and noted that during the first 'Lock-on' by the *Smerch* radar, the target did not move relative to the Tu-128. In this case, the target was definitely the aircraft flying ahead of this interceptor. The information on the second 'Lock-on' showed that the interceptor was closing on the target at high speed; in other words, this was the parachute target, which was effectively stationary with respect to the intercepting aircraft. Thus, the hypothesis that the second aircraft had shot down the leader was erroneous; in this scenario the catastrophe could not have happened. It was decided to use the logs, which were written up in the command post (GCI station) to record each intercept event, in order to check the GCI guidance chronology. From the GCI controllers' logs, the commands passed to the interceptor and the radar plot of the interceptor's flight were also checked. We tried for some time to try to understand what had happened in the air over the range, but we couldn't find the answer. At the time, the accident investigation team were working at Belaya airfield and General Grishin called me from there; General Grishin was the Deputy Chief Engineer of PVO Aviation. He called me and said, 'Elektron Mironovich, come down to Belaya. I've got something interesting to show you here.'

So we flew down the following day and General Grishin led us over to one of the Tu-128s and said, 'Climb onto the wing and go down to the wing root. Look at the fuselage.' I did as I was told. I looked at the fuselage and it was all crooked. I climbed down from the aircraft and looked at it from underneath and it was crumpled all along the underside of the fuselage. I looked at the aircraft from the side and there on the fuselage, above the wing, was a dent about the size of a man's hand made by the flaps. The dent wasn't opposite the flap, but above it by about 10 cm [4 inches]. Clearly, the aircraft had been subjected to a huge g-loading in flight. As a result of this g-loading, the wing and the flaps had been so bent that they had left an imprint on the fuselage. I asked what had happened and was told that this Tu-128 had flown over the range just before the aircraft which had broken up during missile firing. I told General Grishin about the puzzling paint smear which we'd noticed on the damaged aircraft; he thought for a moment and then asked about the combination of colours in the paint smear. He continued to mull it over and then led us back to the crumpled aircraft. A small ladder was dragged over to the aircraft for us and we climbed up onto the wing. General Grishin showed us the junction between the wing and the fuselage, which was covered with a fairing, attached by bolts. The heads of the bolts were painted in the same colours that we'd found on the fuselage of the crashed aircraft. It turned out that these bolts were of different lengths and the Tupolev engineers had painted them correspondingly in different colours, to ease the task of matching them to the appropriate aperture following disassembly and reassembly during maintenance. Thus, when the wing was torn off, it was these bolts that had scraped along the fuselage and left the 'rainbow' trace of paint.

So the puzzle of the 'unidentified flying object' had been solved, but we still hadn't advanced an explanation for the cause of the break-up of the crashed Tu-128. Next, we began to examine the film from the KZA flight data recorder, which had been removed from the damaged [second] aircraft. It turned out that this aircraft had made a left turn after breaking off from the attack, still in afterburner and flying supersonically, but the pilot had not deselected reheat. During this manoeuvre he had lowered the nose, since he had to break off in the descent. The pilot was apparently still watching the target and passed it by. At this point, the aircraft's nose was lowered quite considerably and the vertical rate of descent increased significantly. The afterburners were still lit and the aircraft was in a steep descent, and at this point the pilot attempted to pull the aircraft out of the dive, albeit without shutting down the afterburners. Instead of pulling out of the dive, the aircraft entered the deep-spiral regime. While pulling out of this regime, the pilot exceeded the permitted g-loading for the aircraft. A camera was installed in the cockpit of the Tu-128, designed to photograph the pilot's instrument panel during combat training. The camera was retrieved from the damaged aircraft and from the photographs we could clearly check the flight parameters when the missiles were released. When I checked these for myself, my hair practically stood on end! The pilot had exceeded the g-loading and limiting speed for the aircraft. The angle of bank was 90°, the nose of the aircraft was pointing down, and it had flown towards the ground in this attitude. It also turned out that the pilot had already warned the navigator to prepare to eject.

However, at the speed in question, an ejection would have proved fatal anyway.

At this point, the aircraft was flying below 5,000 m [16,400 feet] and had entered a denser layer of the atmosphere, where its aerodynamic behaviour changed; indicated air speed increased, but true air speed and Mach number decreased. Handling of the aircraft began to improve slightly and the pilot attempted to reduce the angle of bank, turning the control wheel through 180° and gripping the right-hand 'horn' with his left hand [his hands were clearly visible on the photograph of the instrument panel]. He was also pushing the rudder pedals hard against the stops. The combined force of the ailerons and the rudder was sufficient to bring the aircraft out of the steep banked turn and the pilot was finally able to regain horizontal flight. The aircraft had dropped from 12,500 m [41,000 feet] to 2,500 m [8,200 feet] and the command post and GCI stations had simply lost contact with it. We compared the KZA film from this aircraft with the film from the other Tu-128 and found them to be identical except for one factor. If you took the flight parameters of the first aircraft as being an arbitrary factor of 1.0, then the parameters for the destroyed aircraft were an arbitrary 1.2, so the surviving crew were extremely lucky not to have exceeded the critical g-loading. This aircraft had been so over-stressed that it had to be scrapped.

After the loss of the Tu-128, a programme was introduced on the regiments for objective control (i.e. monitoring) of all flight parameters using the K9-51 oscillograph print-out from the KZA *between* flights. Before this, there had been no objective control checks between flights and KZA results were checked only at the end of the flying programme, once in every 'flying shift'. Following the accident investigation, a number of deficiencies were uncovered in the organisation of practice missile launch flights over the range. Evidently, there was no photo-recording of the P-35 'Bar Lock' radar screen in the GCI post at Chita for aircraft carrying out missile firing against VRPM parachute targets. Moreover, the display of radar data in the 158 RTP (*Radiotekhnicheskiy Polk*) radar regimental command post and in the Chita GCI station was slipshod and inaccurate. All of this served to inculcate the view among many pilots that the aircraft which had been lost had been shot down by a missile from the aircraft flying behind it. The commission that investigated the cause of the accident made the following proposals:

- Insertion of a section in the Pilots' Notes detailing the actions of the pilot in bringing the aircraft out of a 'deep descending spiral' in the event of entering this regime unintentionally.
- Use of specialists from State research institutes and the Tupolev Design Bureau to conduct exercises with Tu-128 regiment flight crews, focused on the aircraft's aerodynamic characteristics and the actions required of the pilot to bring it out of a 'deep descending spiral' in the event of entering this regime unintentionally.

- Determine the fitness for purpose of the aircraft's aileron and rudder circuits by sending the GU-100 and GU-102 hydraulic actuators and NP-43 hydraulic pumps for testing at the State Scientific Research Institute of the Air Force for Aircraft Operation and Repair (GosNII ERAT).

Non-fatal write-off—Tu-128—1972

Weather conditions: No data
Circumstances: A crew from 72 AP at Amderma, comprising aircraft commander Pilot First Class 'E' and navigator 'I', were landing at base. During the landing, the pilot did not correctly monitor his position and height on the glideslope, as a result of which the aircraft touched down 45 m (150 feet) from the runway threshold on rough earth. The aircraft was badly damaged, but the crew escaped injury.
Cause: The accident was attributed to the pilot's lack of discipline in setting up a correct approach.

Fatal write-off—Tu-128—12 May 1972

Weather conditions: Daylight VMC
Circumstances: A crew from 356 AP at Zhana-Semey, comprising Pilot Third Class Lt 'A' and navigator Lt 'D', were taking off from their base airfield. During the take-off run the afterburner of one of the engines shut down spontaneously. The aircraft became airborne briefly but settled back on the runway before running off the end and striking a roadside embankment some 1,300 m (4,265 feet) from the threshold, sustaining severe damage and catching fire. The crew did not use their ejection seats and perished in the fire.
Cause: The afterburner failure on take-off was attributed to a manufacturing defect in the engine. The relatively inexperienced pilot had graduated from the Grozny training centre of DOSAAF in 1969, and it was considered that his indecisive actions in handling the emergency were also a contributory factor.

Non-fatal write-off—Tu-128—9 June 1972

Weather conditions: Not recorded
Circumstances: A Tu-128 from 350 AP at Belaya, flown by aircraft commander Pilot Third Class Capt. 'C' and navigator Capt. 'C', was scrambled from QRA status, but during the take-off roll the pilot was unable to get airborne. After being ordered to do so by the ATC controller, the pilot shut down both afterburners,

resulting in momentary nose-up pitching which allowed the aircraft to become airborne. However, continuation of the take-off was impossible because of insufficient thrust from the engines, which were now in non-reheat mode. The ATC controller (RP) ordered the crew to abandon the aircraft, and both the pilot and the navigator ejected safely and were unhurt. The aircraft struck the ground a short distance from the far end of the runway and was destroyed.

Cause: Pilot error. The pilot was held responsible for the loss of the aircraft, having failed to switch on the tailplane hydraulic actuators.

The accident is recalled by one of the members of the accident investigation commission, Col. Yevglyevskiy, who has provided this narrative account of events:

> The crew had been scrambled from the operational readiness flight; such exercises were included in the KBP combat training manual. They had started engines and begun to move along the taxiway. However, before reaching the line-up point, they were told to hold by ATC since there was another aircraft on the approach. After the aircraft had landed, they were finally cleared for take-off. In accordance with standard pre-flight procedures, the pilot had selected the –9° setting for the horizontal stabilizer. [At this setting, the aircraft would leave the ground in a properly trimmed condition immediately after unstick.] The pilot selected afterburner and the aircraft commenced its take-off run, but the ATC controller noted that the ground roll was rather protracted and the nose was not lifting. The pilot had pulled back on the control column as normal, but the nose was still not lifting. In this situation the RP ordered the pilot to take the only action possible—to abort the take-off. Hearing the command, he shut down the afterburners and chopped the power. [The engines on the Tu-128 were mounted above the fuselage waterline, providing a high thrust axis and creating a slight nose-down pitching moment. If engine power was suddenly reduced, this created a corresponding nose-up pitching moment.] The aircraft's speed was already higher than the normal take-off speed and it should have been capable of getting airborne, but it was still on the runway. Thus, as soon as the pilot chopped the power the aircraft's nose lifted and it became airborne. However, the engines were throttled back and reheat had been shut down, which the ATC controller had observed from the tower, so when he saw the aircraft lift off the runway he ordered the crew to eject. The crew ejected immediately, one crew member landing alongside the main runway and the other alongside the taxiway; the aircraft crashed just beyond the end of the runway and caught fire.
>
> An accident board was convened and we began to investigate the cause. We all assembled in a classroom on the base and initially sat around discussing the incident, albeit still without hearing inputs from either the pilot or the flight controller. We were discussing everything in broad terms, then suddenly the pilot appeared in the room and asked me to go outside with him. All the pilots knew who I was. I went outside with the pilot and he said to me, 'Comrade Colonel, I am to blame for this

accident.' I was rather surprised and replied, 'And how do you know that it was your fault? Where is the evidence that it was your fault?' He replied, 'I don't have any evidence, but it must be found. I am to blame!' I asked him again to explain why he thought that. He then said, 'I didn't switch on the stabilizer hydraulic actuator.' I was now very surprised. 'How could you take off without the stabilizer actuator switched on? How *did* you get airborne?' He then explained to me how the aircraft ended up getting into the air. The speed was quite high and as soon as he reduced power the nose lifted and the aircraft leapt off the runway, although he had been unable to raise the nose using the control column. He didn't have the strength, as [on his own admission] the actuators were switched off. I heard him out and then said, 'OK, We'll have to sort this out, but you'll have to keep quiet about it for the time being. We need to find the evidence. This should be quite simple. First of all, we'll check the position of the levers in the cockpit. Then, we'll look at the position of the levers on the actuators themselves at the time of impact. If your statement can be confirmed, then I can say that you have already reported this to me.' So I ordered the engineers to look for the actuators.

Obviously, for the above-mentioned reasons, it was important to know the position of the flying controls at the time of the accident, and by the end of the day we had the answer. The engineers brought the items to us from the crash site and they reported that the actuators had not been switched on, placing them on the table in front of us so that we could see for ourselves. The pilot had switched on two sectors, but not the third—having been distracted by the other aircraft when preparing to take off. It should be remembered that he'd been scrambled from the QRA dispersal and everything was usually switched on when the aircraft was taxiing out to the runway, in order to save time. So, being distracted at a crucial time, he continued taxiing without having switched on the actuators. Later, when we began to discuss the incident in more detail, a babble of opinion and comment started flying around the room, so I suddenly shouted, 'Stop! The pilot himself has already reported everything to me about the crash this morning. Didn't you see him come into the classroom and ask me to go outside with him?! He described the circumstances of the crash to me. You can now draw up the charge and prosecute him—that's the correct thing to do, but I'm going to report the circumstances to the C-in-C.' So I flew to Novosibirsk to speak to the C-in-C of the 14th Army, General Abramov. I reported how it had all happened and he asked me for my opinion. I told him that not only should the pilot not be punished for what he did but he should be given an award. After all, he'd admitted his mistake quite honestly. The General was quite indignant and said, 'What on earth are you saying?! The aircraft crashed and was destroyed and you are suggesting that the pilot should be decorated!' However, we decided that the Army HQ would issue a directive on the matter and we on the PVO General Staff would also do the same. In the end, the High Command authorities did not take any action against the pilot and indeed he went on to become a regiment commander some time later.

Lt Col. Kaplun, 350 AP deputy regiment commander for engineering, adds:

On that unfortunate day all the regiment's personnel were on the base, taking part in an exercise conducted by the Ministry of Defence. We all knew that this was to involve the interception of targets which could appear from any direction at any time. However, time went on and 'the enemy' had not appeared and it was getting dark. Everyone was suffering from the enforced idleness and we were beginning to look forward to hearing the signal to stand down ('*signal otboya*'). Still no information was forthcoming. I was strolling along the line of parked aircraft when I suddenly heard the whine of engines starting up. Within a few minutes one of the aircraft taxied out from the dispersal. By habit I observed its movement along the taxiway, saw the ignition of the afterburners and watched the take-off run. Almost immediately after the aircraft took off I noted the unusually steep climbing angle. Then I was suddenly aware that I could see the entire upper surface of the fuselage and wings. After that I saw the flames from the ejection seat motors and a huge fireball rose up from the point of impact as it crashed back to the ground. The duty engineer initiated the relevant calls on the radio in the event of a crash. At that moment I was standing very close to one of the fire engines and having jumped aboard I told the driver to go directly to the crash site and within a few minutes we were there.

I can say without exaggeration that the fire was contained within a radius of not less than 20 m [65 feet], but the height of the flames rose up to the height of a ten-storey building. This didn't surprise me too much since the aircraft had taken off with full tanks—about 15 tonnes [33,070 lb] of aviation kerosene. We approached so close that we were unable to stand the heat. Moving back a little, the firefighters turned on their foam dispensers to extinguish the blaze. Having established quite quickly that this was a hopeless task, we stopped firefighting and occupied ourselves with searching for the two crew members whom we'd seen ejecting. Fortunately, they turned out to be safe and well and were already explaining events to the regiment commander in the command post—their well-being was the most important thing. I remained on the airfield with other engineering personnel and specialists. By morning, the fire was out and we started looking for components and parts which might have been defective and the cause of the accident. Apart from this, we also had to find the 'black box' containing vital information for the accident investigators. We discovered what we were looking for quite quickly—the tailplane actuator selector was found in the 'Off' position. The condition of other parts and units also indicated that the pilot for some reason had not selected the tailplane actuators 'On' after starting engines.

Fatal write-off—Tu-128—18 July 1972

Weather conditions: Not recorded

Circumstances: A crew from the State Scientific Research Institute of the Air Force (GNII VVS), comprising Lt Col. V. V. Mayorov as pilot and Col. G. A. Mitrofanov as navigator, were carrying out a test flight to investigate the longitudinal control effectiveness of the Tu-128 when performing an asymmetric launch of two of the aircraft's four missiles at high altitude. The task was to launch two missiles from one wing at an altitude of 10,000 m (32,800 feet) at an indicated air speed of 1,010 kph (545 kts) or Mach 1.6 and then determine the effectiveness of the ailerons in countering the bank angle arising from the asymmetric launch. Since the Tu-128 exhibited poor acceleration performance at speeds above Mach 1.4, the pilot accelerated to the required speed for the trial in a shallow dive. This led to the aircraft descending to 9,800 m (32,150 feet) and reaching a speed of 1,020 kph (550 kts), slightly higher than planned for the task. However, the slight deviations in altitude, speed and Mach number were not detected by the crew. Carrying out the missile launch, the pilot, as required by the task, did not make any control inputs for 4 seconds, simulating the potential error of an 'ordinary' line pilot. Within this time, the situation for the crew had become critical and continued to worsen rapidly. The left-hand bank began to increase and the nose dropped. When the pilot tried to counter the bank angle with full deflection of the control wheel, the angle of bank had already reached 45° and was continuing to increase. The aircraft then entered the critical deep-spiral regime at supersonic speed and the pilot was unable to pull the aircraft out of the ensuing descent. Aileron control in this regime at these speeds (i.e. supersonic) was impossible, either because of their almost zero effectiveness or the phenomenon of aileron reversal. When the aircraft had reached the inverted position, the crew ejected. On ejection, the pilot's seat back-plate did not separate from the seat frame correctly and one of the arm-rests struck his pelvis. The parachute had opened automatically, but Mayorov was already dead in his harness. For some unknown reason, the navigator Mitrofanov did not attempt to use his ejection seat and he too was killed.

Cause: In the opinion of Hero of the Soviet Union and Honoured Test Pilot Stepan A. Mikoyan:

> Mayorov, while monitoring the Machmeter and altimeter, had not noticed that the indicated air speed had exceeded 1,020 kph [550 kts]. Perhaps when preparing for the flight, it had not been emphasised to the pilot that the main flight parameter influencing the effectiveness of the ailerons was indicated air speed, and that it was forbidden to exceed the limiting value (1,010 kph) [545 kts]. Mayorov could, perhaps, have neutralised the bank angle if he had thought to use the rudder, like Kuznetsov, but he literally had only seconds to make this decision.[4]

Fatal write-off—Tu-128UT—14 December 1972

Weather conditions: Daylight, sleet, crew weather minima
Circumstances: A crew from 356 AP at Zhana-Semey, comprising squadron commander Capt. Mikhailov as instructor pilot, regiment commander Lt Col. Yatskii as 'second pilot' and Sr Lt 'B' as navigator, were landing at base after a weather reconnaissance sortie over the local area. During the box-pattern landing approach, part of the main runway became obscured by dense ground fog and smoke from a local brick factory. Eyewitnesses said, 'The airport buildings had ceased to be visible from the domestic site about 300-400 m [985-1,300 feet] away.' ATC gave the command to divert to the alternate airfield. However, the crew reported that they could see the approach end of the runway and the airfield buildings from circuit height. Those on the ground could also see a clear sunny sky above them. The crew took the decision to land, and the flight controller did not insist on diverting and gave them permission to land. After passing over the inner beacon, the aircraft entered fog, after which it deviated to the right of the runway centreline. Evidently, the crew, having taken the edge of the taxiway to be the beginning of the main runway, then landed. According to eyewitnesses, 'Even if they hadn't landed, it was all the same; they would not have been able to go around.' The aircraft struck the searchlight vehicle with its starboard wing,[5] causing fatal injury to the two occupants, Sr Lt A. I. Byezrukov and Pte V. N. Ivanov of the airfield OBATO Field Post Office 54984. It then struck other obstacles on the airfield and was destroyed. The regiment commander and the navigator were killed on impact with the vehicle. The squadron commander, Capt. Mikhailov, suffered multiple injuries and died six weeks later in hospital.
Cause:
1. Failures in flight planning organisation, leading to the launch of a crew that were unprepared for flight in the given weather conditions.
2. Unsatisfactory assessment of the weather situation by regiment executives and specialists from the regiment meteorological service when planning the flight.
3. The crew's decision to descend below their authorised minima without establishing visual contact with airfield reference markers.
4. ATC—the flight controller was culpable in authorising the crew to descend further when they had already reached their minimum authorised height.
5. Action by the crew—the crew did not take action to stop their descent and go around again on reaching their minimum authorised approach height or establish visual contact with the ground.

Deputy regiment commander Lt Col. Nikolyaev, an eyewitness to the events, provides the following account:

At the time of the accident I was in the POL dispersal area so everything happened before my own eyes. They were carrying out a flight in the Tu-128U following the regiment commander's two-month break in flying due to being on leave. They'd been doing box-pattern circuits and during the final approach between the inner beacon and the runway threshold the aircraft entered a bank of fog, caused by smoke from the local brickworks. This caused the crew to deviate to the right of the runway centreline and line up on the taxiway. Before touchdown, the aircraft struck the landing searchlight with its starboard wing. Because of the increased rate of descent the pilot was unable to establish the correct landing profile and struck the concrete surface of the taxiway with the nose-wheel, which collapsed on impact. The nose section of the fuselage was damaged right up to the navigator's cockpit and the aircraft continued to bounce further over the snow, which was around 40 cm [about 16 inches] deep. The aircraft's track over the ground was around 500 m [1,640 feet] long, with parts of the airframe being scattered in all directions. After it had ceased moving forward, the centre section of the aircraft rose up and then rolled over on its side. Then, when parts of the aircraft were no longer flying around, I ran along the aircraft's path towards the runway.

When the aircraft was breaking up, the first person to be ejected from the cockpit was the regiment commander, followed by the instructor and then the navigator. About 100 m [330 feet] from the runway threshold I found the navigator, who had been killed instantly, having suffered severe facial and head injuries. I ran on further about another 20 m [65 feet] and found Captain Mikhailov, lying motionless on his back, and then about the same distance further on I found the regiment commander. He had also been killed instantly and was severely cut and bruised, and one of his arms was broken. All three pilots were drenched in kerosene and covered in soot. Next, I went back along the path of the aircraft and I noticed that the fingers on Captain Mikhailov's right hand were twitching. I started to shout for help and the doctor quickly arrived on the scene in an ambulance; we carefully placed him into it and he was taken off to the base hospital. After examination he was sent to hospital in the nearby town of Kemerovo, since it was impossible to treat his severe internal injuries *in situ* in the base hospital, particularly his kidney damage. After being attached to a kidney dialysis machine he regained consciousness and remained in that hospital for about a month, but two weeks later his condition worsened and he died.

Accident—Tu-128—24 January 1973

Weather conditions: Not recorded
Circumstances: A crew from 518 AP at Talagi, with aircraft commander 'K' as pilot, failed to correct the aircraft's deviation from the landing heading when landing at base, as a result of which the aircraft ran off the edge of the main runway after touchdown.
Cause: Pilot error.

Tupolev Tu-128 'Fiddler'

Non-fatal write-off—Tu-128—30 March 1973

Weather conditions: Daylight IMC
Circumstances: During the approach, the aircraft flown by Pilot First Class Maj. 'B' and navigator 'C' of 72 AP at Amderma dropped below the recommended glideslope. While executing an overshoot for a second approach the pilot selected afterburner, resulting in a momentary loss of thrust, as was typical for this aircraft. The aircraft failed to remain airborne, struck the ground, rolled onto the parking area in front of the airport buildings and caught fire. The pilot and navigator were able to escape from the aircraft, although the pilot suffered multiple fractures and had to be assisted from the aircraft by the navigator.
Cause: The poorly executed approach and landing was attributed to pilot error.
  Col. Yevglyevskiy comments:

> When the accident occurred, four aircraft had been returning from training sorties and the airfield was about to close because of an approaching snowstorm. The first three crews landed without incident, although they were rather 'bunched up' on the landing approach. The fourth aircraft deviated a little to the right and the pilot then decided to go round again. He increased power and selected reheat. If he had only increased engine rpm, then perhaps nothing untoward would have happened, but on selection of reheat the engine nozzles open fully and afterburner ignition takes a finite time to kick in, resulting in momentary reduction of thrust. The aircraft lost flying speed, 'settled' and struck the snow-covered surface. There was a lot of snow cover on the airfield and the aircraft dug into it with the starboard undercarriage bogie, which broke off, spinning the aircraft round tail-first, causing it to shoot backwards. At this moment, the afterburner finally cut in. So, with two tongues of flame from the afterburners, the aircraft slid tail-first towards the airport buildings. It went past one civilian aircraft, which had braked to a halt, fortuitously 'allowing' the Tu-128 to miss it, and then continued on to the parking area in front of the main building. Here it finally came to rest, burst into flames and burned out only a few metres from the passenger terminal. The navigator suffered only minor injuries and jumped out of the aircraft to assist the pilot in climbing out of his cockpit. The pilot had suffered about four or five fractures, including two broken arms and two broken legs. Although he recovered from the accident, he was later taken off flying duties.

Non-fatal write-off—Tu-128—21 May 1973

Weather conditions: Daylight VMC
Circumstances: The aircraft, flown by 356 AP's deputy regiment commander for flight training at Zhana-Semey, Pilot First Class Lt Col. A. P. Nikolayev and

navigator Capt. Yu. R. Taras'yants, was taking off from base on a test flight after a 100-hour maintenance check. During the take-off run a fire broke out in the port engine bay, which the crew were unable to extinguish. Both crew members ejected from the aircraft safely, the aircraft continuing to descend in a flat trajectory and landing in a field, where it burst into flames and was destroyed.

Cause: The precise reason for the triggering of the fire warning light(s) could not be established, because of the total destruction of the airframe.

The incident is recalled here by Lt Col. Aleksandr Nikolayev:

I'd been planned to do one flight during the day flying shift—a test flight of the aircraft after a long period of maintenance. After that I'd then been planned into the night-flying programme as controller of flying. I performed a normal take-off run, and after unsticking I retracted the flaps and undercarriage in the normal way. At that moment I noticed that a warning lamp had illuminated, indicating 'Fire in the starboard engine'. I reported this to ATC, shut down the starboard afterburner and then selected manual operation of the fire extinguisher for the starboard engine and continued to climb towards the third turning point in the circuit. I shut down the port afterburner at a height of 4,000 m [13,125 feet]. Then when I was abeam the inner beacon I became aware of severe lateral vibrations and decided that we should eject. I ordered the navigator to eject and he quickly abandoned the aircraft, followed immediately by myself. It would have been possible to eject when we were abeam the runway caravan, but the main railway line between Semipalatinsk and Alma-Ata was coming up ahead of us and there was a passenger train on the line. So I decided to eject only after we'd passed over the railway line. After I'd ejected, during the descent, I could see the aircraft descending below me with two huge tongues of bright yellow flame (about 10 m [33 feet] long) from the engines, but no smoke. Having lost speed, the aircraft went into a left turn and began to descend, rocking from wing tip to wing tip, in a falling leaf motion. I got the impression that forward speed had dropped to zero, and the aircraft landed comparatively softly in a field.

There was a slight thump followed by a cloud of black smoke and the aircraft was not badly damaged in the landing, although it did start to burn quite severely before the rescue team got to the scene. Because the impact had been slight and the aircraft had not broken up on landing, the flight data recorder [in the shape of an orange sphere] had not been ejected automatically and the recorded data was destroyed in the fire. When I was landing, the oxygen bottle which was part of the parachute harness struck my coccyx rather painfully. The navigator landed without injury. Eyewitnesses reported that from the second to the third turn of the circuit pattern there had been a long black trail of smoke behind the aircraft. The accident commission concluded, 'The fire was caused by a crack in the afterburner section of the engine.' After a month of medical checks and tests followed by convalescence, I was cleared to go back onto flying duties. This ejection had been the third during

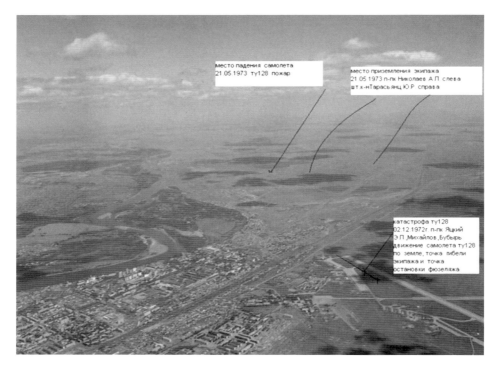

A panoramic view of the accident sites at Zhana-Semey in 1972 and 1973. The highlighted area in the lower right of the picture shows the impact point of the Tu-128UT flown by Lt Col. Yatskii on 2 December 1972 and the extent of its travel over the ground after impact. The highlighted upper part shows where the Tu-128 flown by Lt Col. Nikolayev crashed on 21 May 1973 and the locations where he and his navigator Capt. Taras'yants landed. (*Montage by D. Nikolaev*)

my flying career; before this I'd twice had to eject from the Su-9, as detailed here in extracts from my log-book:

'14-03-1963—ejection from Su-9; engine flame-out due to ingestion of parts of disintegrated oil pump drive shaft; over Omsk, on third turn of the airfield circuit pattern (landing course, 225°), altitude 8,000 m [26,250 feet], daylight, VMC.

'17-03-1966—ejection from Su-9; engine flame-out due to ingestion of parts of disintegrated fuel pump; 150 km [93 miles] west of Semipalatinsk, altitude 18,000 m [59,055 feet], night, IMC.'

Non-fatal write-off —Tu-128—Winter 1974

Weather conditions: Not recorded
Circumstances: The aircraft flown by Maj. 'E' of 72 AP at Amderma was approaching base, but touched down in the clearway ahead of the runway threshold, sustaining

some damage as a result. Repairs to the aircraft took longer than anticipated and because of a severe shortage of space in the dispersal area, the regiment commanders decided to park the unserviceable Tu-128 on the ice on the nearby lagoon until work could be completed. However, during an unanticipated early spring thaw the aircraft sank beneath the melting ice and slid to the bottom of the lagoon. Attempts to recover the aircraft proved to be unsuccessful and the aircraft had to be scrapped. *Cause*: Landing in the undershoot was attributed to pilot error in flying a poorly executed approach.

Fatal write-off— Tu-128—21 May 1974

Weather conditions: Night

Circumstances: A crew from 518 AP at Talagi, comprising Maj. 'C' as pilot and Capt. 'C' as navigator, had been performing a 2-hour-plus night combat air patrol sortie, with other Tu-128s of the regiment, in the patrol area over the Barents Sea. Upon completion of the task, when they were on the landing approach, a strong crosswind began to blow across the airfield. The crew were using the standard radio navigation aids for the runway in use, approaching over the town of Arkhangel'sk on a heading of 82°. After passing over the inner marker beacon it was obvious that the aircraft was lined up to the right of the main runway and passed over the runway caravan with a very large angle of bank. The pilot had been trying to turn the aircraft so as to line up on the runway, then level out and land. However, the control response of the Tu-128 at landing speed was insufficient to carry out such a manoeuvre. As a result, the aircraft hit the ground beyond the edge of the runway, struck a reinforced concrete building and exploded. Before striking the ground, the navigator ejected and survived, but the pilot remained in the aircraft and was killed.

Cause: Aircraft handling error (pilot error) during the approach in severe crosswind conditions.

The accident is recalled by Oleg Vydryenok:

The aircraft was approaching from the direction of the River Kuznechikh. There was an early-morning haze. They had lined up *not* on the main runway but on the taxiway. When the pilot noticed his error, he started to turn in towards the runway, but it was too late. The pilot did not react to the navigator's call to overshoot or to instructions from ATC. Contact with the runway was made at an angle of 30-35° to the centreline and about 3-4 m [10-13 feet] to the left of it. The navigator saw the runway from his right-hand cockpit window and did not wait for any instructions— he just 'banged' out. Seconds later, the aircraft struck the reserve runway caravan and the pilot was killed on impact.

The Tu-128 was a very unresponsive aircraft in landing configuration. This was the tragic result of a pilot attempting to realign his aircraft with the runway in severe cross-wind conditions, instead of overshooting and going around for another approach. (*Oleg Vydryenok*)

Fatal write-off— Tu-128UT—25 March 1975

Weather conditions: Daylight

Circumstances: A crew from 518 AP, comprising deputy regiment commander Lt Col. Safronov as 'second pilot', Capt. Pilipyenko as navigator and Honoured Military Pilot Col. Pyotr Komyagin, a PVO Aviation inspector-pilot, occupying the instructor's seat, were detailed to perform a weather reconnaissance flight out of Talagi. During the climb-out, the fire warning lights triggered, signalling the presence of a fire in one of the engines. Convinced that there *was* an actual fire, the crew abandoned the aircraft. During the ejection process for the navigator and the 'second pilot', the latter's seat suffered some kind of malfunction, leading to both seats travelling up the rails virtually simultaneously. After the seats had passed the edges of the cockpit framework, the force of the first stage of the 'combined firing mechanism' of the pilot's seat struck the navigator's ejection seat, propelling it against the fuselage. The navigator was killed.

Cause: The death of the navigator was attributed to a manufacturing defect in the pilot's interlock system, leading to practically simultaneous ejection of both seats. The accident board concluded that the most probable cause of the engine fire was a fracture in the main fuel line at the point where it was connected to the engine (*The report does not specify whether it was the port or starboard engine –A.D.*)

The following narrative account of the events leading up to the accident and the ejection has been provided by Col. Komyagin:

A couple of days before the accident I'd been involved in missile firing training with aircrew of the 6th (Leningrad) Independent Army of the PVO (*6 OA PVO*) and I'd flown up to Talagi (*10 OA PVO*) from the 6th Army on March 23rd, 1975. When I arrived, the regiment commander came up to me and said, 'Great to see you, there's work for you.' At this particular time, the deputy regiment commander Yuri Safronov and senior navigator Pyotr Pilipyenko had just returned to their 'home regiment' ('*rodnoy polk*') on completion of their studies at the Air Force Academy in Monino, just outside Moscow. They'd been programmed into a series of refresher flights at Talagi and I took them up for a night 'check ride' in a Tu-128UT, but I had to do a further check flight with them. For the second flight, the regiment engineer asked us to take the other '*sparka*' as the aircraft we'd just flown had to undergo unspecified maintenance before flying the next day, which was the beginning of a 10th Army exercise. So I agreed and I flew the second sortie with the deputy commander and his navigator as requested. The following day I went to the regiment HQ (518 AP) to sign the log books of the pilot and navigator I'd just flown with and then decided to take a walk around the town for the rest of the day, before flying to Moscow that evening.

Then the regiment commander phoned me. 'Pyotr Ivanovich, can you help me out?! We need to do a weather reconnaissance flight, but my own crews are already up on the Kola Peninsula and an aircraft [*i.e. a transport aircraft—A.D.*] still has to go up there with the engineers.' I told him that I didn't have anything with me; I didn't have my flight suit or anything. The regiment commander was getting desperate. 'We'll find everything for you. We're not expecting the weather to worsen immediately, but the synopsis is not too good and we need to have a weather reconnaissance flight. There's a trainer available and it's ready to fly. Take it and the pilot and navigator [Safronov and Pilipyenko] from yesterday. Fly out over the sound towards the White Sea, then up to the north. You can then land at Severomorsk.' I was trying to tell the regiment commander that I had a ticket for a flight to Moscow that evening, but he was very persuasive. 'We won't hold you up. You'll catch your plane.' So I arrived at the airfield and the navigator and pilot met me. 'We're ready and our aircraft, Bort No. 16, is ready.' They gave me a 'bone-dome' which had the name 'Smertin'[6] on it—evidently, there was a pilot on the regiment by that name. I somehow managed to get myself changed into the assorted flying kit that I'd been given and we went out to our Tu-128UT. After running through the checks we taxied out for take-off and got airborne.

The sun was shining right into my eyes so I told the pilot that he should fly the aircraft, while I would observe the weather. The sun was bright, but over to the right of us there was a dark build-up. Then the pilot called me on the intercom and said, 'Comrade Colonel, the fire warning lights are on.' Because of the sun it was difficult to see them, but I looked again and saw that the fire warning lights were definitely on. In fact, four sectors of the warning panel were illuminated. The navigator had a periscope in his cockpit, so I said to him, 'Petya, have a look and see what's happening.' He reported that there were yellowish clouds of smoke trailing behind us. I reported this to ATC and they asked me if we'd shut down the afterburners and then told us that we had flames shooting out behind the aircraft which were visible from the ground. The navigator was pressing me to eject, but I told him to wait—I was thinking of turning back and landing downwind at Talagi. We were passing overhead Arkhangel'sk at the time, in a turn, with the settlement of Solombala directly below. The navigator was still very anxious about our situation, but the pilot was very quiet, not saying anything; I'd resumed control by this time. I said to them both, 'Stay calm, but get ready to eject anyway. I have control and I'll carry on flying.' The pilot said, 'I'm ready,' followed by the navigator saying that he too was ready.

I looked down but we couldn't eject there—there were houses below us. As it turned out, it was actually a timber-yard with logs piled up so that they looked like small houses, covered with snow.[7] Between the piles there were pathways which looked like streets, with tractors driving along them, so from above it looked very much like a village. I decided to turn away. Then the navigator was getting even more agitated and I could see that the situation was now pretty bad. We were on fire. So I gave the command 'Prepare to eject!' and then '*Nu davai!*' [a standard military preparatory command which perhaps best equates to 'OK, let's go!']. The navigator jettisoned the canopies and everything immediately started swirling around in my cockpit—the front cockpit of the Tu-128UT did not protect the occupant particularly well from the incoming blast of air. My oxygen mask was battering my face, but I could see from the warning panel lights that the pilot and navigator had already ejected. My own green light was on, meaning that I could eject too. However, before that, I had one last look for the airfield—was it still possible to land?! After all, Voblikov [the Voronezh factory test pilot] had landed safely without a canopy, but Talagi airfield was not really that close, so I chose to eject. I went out quite smoothly; it was OK. I was actually a sport parachutist, with 112 jumps to my credit, but a survival parachute is difficult to control and I looked around to see where it was carrying me.

There, below me, was a warehouse—with cable drums, metal items and pipes lying all around. I thought if I landed there I'd break every bone in my body, so I turned away from the warehouse as best I could. Then it turned out that I was being carried towards high-voltage power lines! I obviously wouldn't have got under the wires and if I'd actually hit them there would only have been a cloud of ash floating to the ground. I pulled myself up in the harness, raised my legs as much as I could and managed to drift over the top of them. Then I felt a blow as I hit the ground and lost consciousness. When I came to, some children were standing round me, with two men. It appeared that I'd landed on the icy slope of a reservoir and struck the back of my head very hard, causing me to black out. While I'd been manoeuvring around the pipes in the warehouse yard, I wasn't able to adopt the correct position for a good landing. One of the men told me that the 'first' pilot had landed by parachute, but the second person was still in his seat when he hit the ground. I tried to find out more and the man said, 'His parachute didn't open. I'm a former aircraft mechanic. I know about these things.' It turned out the other two crew members had landed some distance away from me. I opened up my portable emergency pack [NAZ], took out the hand-held radio and made contact with the search and rescue party. I started to feel quite unwell and my head and chest were aching from the hard landing. The rescue party took me back to the airfield, where it was confirmed that the other pilot had ejected safely but the navigator had been killed. The aircraft had crashed into the Northern Dvina River, broken through the ice and sunk to the bottom.

The accident is recalled by Col. Yevglyevskiy, a senior member of the accident investigation commission, who has provided these additional comments:

I was deputy president of the board of inquiry convened to investigate the circumstances of this accident. The president was the C-in-C of the 10th Independent Army of the PVO, but since he was not an aviator he was only there as the most senior authorising officer to sign any of the resulting documentation. In fact, the entire investigation was essentially my responsibility. The main focus of the investigation was on the faulty operation of the crew escape system, since the ejection seats of both the pilot and navigator fired almost simultaneously due to a malfunction of the pilot's ejection seat interlock system. The malfunction was itself due to a technical defect in the mechanism, and we established that the navigator was killed by the jet blast from the pilot's ejection seat propelling him into the fuselage. However, the pilot swore that he hadn't deselected the interlock; he was an honest man and said that we should call in criminal investigators. 'I wasn't wearing gloves and if I'd touched the seat interlock lever, then my fingerprints would be on it.' So I called in the police and they confirmed that the pilot's fingerprints were not on the lever. We then began the process of trying to determine how the seat interlock had been 'unlocked'. First of all, we began by considering the time normally required for the pilot and navigator to eject. The pilot had to perform up to nine separate actions which, although simple, nevertheless required a finite time to complete. The navigator, on the other hand, had only one single action to take after jettisoning the canopy—to pull the ejection levers.

The pilot could not physically do this from his seat. I asked for an ejection seat to be brought into the classroom that we were using, so that we could carefully examine the interlock system and how the failure could have occurred. A seat was brought in and placed on a stand in the classroom and we all gathered round it. The interlock system consisted of two substantial plates—one on the interlock mechanism and one on the seat itself, with an aligning aperture. If the safety pin was pushed through the apertures of these plates the ejection system could not work. If the pin was removed, then the firing mechanism could move freely and begin the ejection sequence for the seat. An 'override' lever was provided for the situation where, in an emergency, the pin could be withdrawn manually to release the plates. This lever was situated on the right-hand side of the seat, readily accessible to the pilot. A cable was attached to the handle, which via a system of mechanical linkages released the safety pin. If the handle was pulled even just a small amount its locking wire would remain intact, but the safety pin could be withdrawn from one of the plates, effectively unlocking the system. If the lever was now returned to its original position the cable would be slightly kinked. This could be seen in the cockpit, when looking at the seat from above. Because of the kink in the cable, the safety pin could not return to its proper position and the seat would remain in the *unlocked* condition, although the 'override' lever would remain (or appear to remain) wire-*locked*.

An ejection seat technician-specialist should have known about this peculiarity of the system. As soon as we'd hit upon this fact ourselves, I ordered the entire investigation team to get onto a bus and we all went out to the flight line. One of the team was head of the 'emergency egress systems' group, i.e. an armourer specialising in the ejection system of the Tu-128. We also took several conscripts to remove the protective covers from the canopies, and when we arrived in dispersal I said to the assembled group, 'Now we'll find other aircraft with unlocked seats.' On the second aircraft we examined we found a small ring from this cable. I said, 'Stop! Did everyone see? Let's get down! Close the canopy! Let's look further!' I asked for the special hoist used to remove the seats to be brought out to us, so that we could examine the underside of the seat and the interlock mechanism itself, as well as check what position it was in. While we were waiting for the hoist to arrive, we went further along the line of parked aircraft and examined them all, but didn't find any more seats like that. We returned to the second aircraft, by which time the hoist had arrived; the head of the SAPS [emergency egress systems] group opened the canopy and attached the hoist to the pilot's seat. The hoist was manually operated and his mechanics started to wind the handle to slowly lift the seat from the cockpit. All 35 members of the investigation team waited alongside the aircraft for the seat to be lowered to the ground.

That same day I decided that I *had* to go in to the garrison, since there were still rumours circulating around the base that the pilot had 'fired' his navigator from the aircraft and killed him by ejecting too early. The rumours were not only circulating among the officers but also among their wives, and I ordered all the officers to assemble in the garrison officers' mess (*garnizonnyi dom ofitsyerov*) so that I could explain to them in detail exactly what had happened. At the end of my address I told them, 'Your deputy regiment commander is in no way to blame for this accident, so please desist from spreading these rumours and also tell your wives to refrain from discussing the matter.' Instead of going straight to PVO HQ on my return from Arkhangel'sk, I went to visit the pilot, Yuri Safronov, in the PVO hospital at Funiki outside Moscow. He was very upset about the tragedy of his navigator's death, and it was probably some small comfort to him when I went in to see him and was able to say, 'Yura! We found a defect in the seat interlock mechanism, so it wasn't your fault!'

Who pulled the override handle, and *when*, was difficult to say. Mechanics were in and out of the cockpits all the time, and when the seats were removed for maintenance it could have happened quite by accident. It's possible that the lever had snagged something when the seat was being pulled out of the cockpit and then replaced in the cockpit without anyone realising. Such a scenario was possible during the aircraft's lifetime and it would have been very easy to have done this. You'd touch the lever and then …

Non-fatal write-off—Tu-128UT—2 September 1975

Weather conditions: No data

Circumstances: A crew from 72 AP at Amderma, comprising deputy regiment commander Lt Col. 'T', deputy regiment commander Lt Col. 'S' and senior regiment navigator Lt Col. 'F', were landing at base after a training sortie. The aircraft touched down fast, at around 350 kph (189 kts), higher than normal for the type, and the brake parachute was torn off. Attempts by the crew to reduce speed were unsuccessful, even using emergency braking (which was commanded by the navigator). The aircraft continued to career down the runway and ran off the end. It then hit a snow bank, causing the nose-wheel leg to break off. Apart from this, a significant crack developed in the fuselage behind the cockpit as a result of the severe impact. The three crew members were unhurt, but the aircraft was written off.

Cause: The cause of the accident was determined to have been inadequate pre-flight preparation by the crew, which did not include clear instructions for individual responsibilities at various stages of flight. The accident once again drew attention to the inappropriateness of planning a crew comprising an instructor and a 'pilot under supervision' who were of the same rank and level of experience.

Non-fatal write-off—Tu-128UT—September 1975

Weather conditions: IMC

Circumstances: A crew from 356 AP at Zhana-Semey, comprising instructor and deputy regiment commander Lt Col. 'M' and aircraft commander Maj. 'N', were carrying out a check flight on a newly arrived pilot.* After completion of the task, the crew landed back at base. The landing was made at higher than normal speed, but the pilot did not select the brake chute and this was not double-checked by the instructor. As a result, the aircraft rolled off the end of the runway, breaking off the nose-wheel leg, and the fuselage cracked just behind the navigator's cockpit, although fortunately fire did not break out. The crew were able to exit the aircraft without assistance, but the aircraft was damaged beyond repair.

Cause: Aircrew error.

Tupolev Tu-128 'Fiddler'

(*Although not stated, it seems likely that the newly arrived pilot was occupying the navigator's station for this flight, since the other two crew members on the Tu-128UT were also pilots.)

Non-fatal write-off—Tu-128—21 June 1976

Weather conditions: No data

Circumstances: A crew from 350 AP at Belaya, comprising aircraft commander Pilot First Class Maj. 'A' and navigator Maj. 'B', were taking off from base when, immediately after unstick, longitudinal control became impossible. The crew successfully ejected from the aircraft at a height of 50 m (165 feet).

Cause: Loss of control was attributed to failure of the RM-2 hydraulic actuator.

The incident is recalled by Col. Yevglyevskiy, a member of the accident investigation commission:

> We investigated this accident but could find no specific cause. So I then suggested that we should all assemble in one of the training rooms. (That is, all the specialists.) Then, each would write under his name on the blackboard his version of what he thought might have happened. We would call each individual up to the front of the classroom to defend his 'thesis', like at university. If he could not defend it, then his name was wiped off the board. So after 2 hours of this procedure, only one version remained—failure of the tailplane hydraulic actuator [booster]. We thought that some part of the component must have disintegrated inside the actuator. However, the 'industry representative' on the base said that it was necessary to send the actuator away to be examined. 'We can't just *say* that the actuator is at fault.' So I said, 'Fine, let's send it off now to the factory in Irkutsk. They'll dismantle it and we'll see whether it was serviceable or not!' We sent the actuator back to the factory and then went off to HQ. There, the Tupolev OKB representative asked me to help him set up a telephone link with Moscow. I gave the order and he was offered a telephone in the regiment commander's office. He stayed in the office while we went into another office and listened in to what he was saying on the other line. The Tupolev OKB people were asking, 'Who is to blame?' The representative replied, Someone … You are to blame!' It was clear that we had correctly determined the cause of the accident. We waited until the following day, when the dismantled actuator was sent back from the factory, showing quite clearly that it *had* disintegrated. We had established the cause of the failure correctly.

Non-fatal write-off—Tu-128—1 December 1976

Weather conditions: No data
Circumstances: A crew from 356 AP at Zhana-Semey, comprising aircraft commander Pilot First Class 'P' and navigator 'N', were performing a routine training flight when fire broke out in the port engine. The crew were unable to extinguish the fire and ejected safely at an altitude of 5,500 m (18,045 feet).
Cause: Engine failure.

Non-fatal write-off—Tu-128—4 May 1977

Weather conditions: Daylight VMC
Circumstances: A crew from 350 AP at Belaya, comprising aircraft commander Pilot Third Class Sr Lt 'K' and navigator Third Class Sr Lt 'O', were performing a routine training flight (Exercise 34 from the combat training manual 'KBP Tu-128-69'—'Interception of a manoeuvring target in cloud'). Nine minutes into the flight, at an altitude of 9,000 m (29,530 feet) and flying at 900 kph (486 kts), the pilot heard a buzzing sound from the port engine area and reported this to the navigator. Engine rpm at the time was 88-90 per cent. The navigator confirmed the buzzing sound. Fifteen minutes into the flight, the pilot reported to the GCI station at Ust'-Boleya that the rpm reading of the port engine was 'hunting'. The variation (creeping) was of the order of ±3 per cent, with an oil pressure drop of 1.5 kg/cm² (21.3 lb/sq. in.). Then the creeping in the port engine rpm setting increased rapidly to ±7 per cent and on prompting by the navigator, the pilot reduced the rpm of the port engine until the buzzing disappeared. Turning in towards Belaya airfield, the pilot increased the port engine rpm to 75 per cent, after which the 'Look at Warning Panel' illuminated. The 'Fire' and 'Fire in Left Engine' warning lights were illuminated on the central warning panel. The pilot then brought the throttle lever back to the 'Flight Idle' stop and checked the operation of the first stage of fire extinguishing, switched off the engine and reported to the GCI station that they had a fire on board. The navigator reported that he could see a trail of smoke behind the aircraft through his periscope. The pilot then selected the second shot of the fire extinguisher, but when the warning light did not go out he reported to the airfield ATC that they were on fire, and on his command, at an altitude of 8,700 m (28,550 feet) and at 700 kph (378 kts) the crew ejected safely from the burning aircraft.
Cause: Unspecified failure of the port engine, leading to severe vibration, disintegration of internal components and fire. The precise nature of the failure could not be established because of the almost total destruction of the aircraft.

Aircraft history

Tu-128 c/n 504102 rolled out of the factory with an airframe life of 1,200 hours; had not yet undergone periodic servicing.

Total time since entering service—918 hours.

Port engine AL-7F-2-300 No. V8126021 'T', delivered from the Salyut plant on 12 September 1969 with an operating life of 300 hours.

Underwent first major overhaul on 30 September 1976; life after overhaul—300 hours.

Total time since start of operations –347 hours; time since last overhaul—47 hours.

Starboard engine AL-7F-2-300 No. V8126043 'T', delivered from the Salyut plant on 20 July 1969 with an operating life of 300 hours.

Underwent first major overhaul on 24 November 1976; life after overhaul—300 hours.

Total time since start of operations—347 hours; time since last overhaul—47 hours.

The following suggestions were put forward by the accident investigation commission on the basis of the evidence examined:

- State Enterprise V-2877 to adopt measures to protect the K9-51 data-recorder storage unit (or derivatives) from damage by high temperatures, with the aim of preserving vital data in the event of major accidents.
- Install a cockpit voice data recorder (tape-recorder) for post-flight analysis of the crew's actions in the event of in-flight emergencies.
- The AL-7F-2 engine No. V8126021 'T', ancillary units and jet pipe to be sent off for examination by the 13th State Scientific Research Institute for Aircraft Operation and Repair (13 GosNII ERAT).

Fatal write-off—Tu-128—24 May 1977

Weather conditions: Not given

Circumstances: A crew from 356 AP at Zhana-Semey, comprising aircraft commander Unclassified Pilot Lt 'M' and navigator Sr Lt 'Sh', were landing at base with four AA-5 'Ash' missiles loaded. On the glideslope the crew failed to monitor the aircraft's speed, as a result of which it dropped significantly below the required glidepath trajectory. Struggling to combat the loss of speed the crew carried out an emergency jettison of all four missiles (although this was forbidden when the undercarriage was down). However, it was still not possible to increase speed, so they decided to eject. Unfortunately, because of a malfunction in the ejection sequencing system, the first to go out was the pilot and the flames and blast from his ejection-seat gun were directed at the navigator when he left the aircraft seconds later, resulting in his death.

Cause: Lack of attention in monitoring the speed during the landing approach, the pilot and navigator having allowed it to drop below the minimum permitted for the aircraft. Additionally, there was a manufacturing design defect in the ejection sequencing system, leading to both crew members ejecting virtually simultaneously.

Non-fatal write-off—Tu-128—March/April 1978

Weather conditions: Daylight IMC

Circumstances: A crew from 518 AP at Talagi, comprising aircraft commander Pilot Third Class Sr Lt 'A' and section navigator Capt. 'S', were landing at base. They failed to monitor the landing heading on the approach, as a result of which the aircraft touched down at an angle to the runway centreline. After touchdown, the aircraft ran off the edge of the runway onto the surrounding rough earth, sustaining major damage, but the crew were unhurt. The aircraft was declared a 'write off'.

Cause: Aircrew error—poor handling of the aircraft on the approach.

In-flight collision between two Tu-128s—17 July 1978

Weather conditions: Daylight, no cloud, visibility more than 10 km (6.25 miles)

Circumstances: Two Tu-128s from 72 AP at Amderma were performing a special task, operating out of Nar'yan-Mar, which involved escorting a MiG-25 'Foxbat' conducting a test flight over the Arctic Ocean in connection with the MiG-31 'Foxhound' development programme. While flying at an altitude of 10,000 m (32,800 feet) and some 300 km (186 miles) from Nar'yan-Mar, the wingman of the pair of Tu-128s allowed himself to get into a position directly underneath his leader, through a lapse in concentration. At about the same time, the leader reported switching on his autopilot, which always led to the aircraft's flight trajectory 'settling' before it became fully engaged, and he collided with the wingman directly below him. The leader's aircraft suffered damage to the starboard air intake after being hit by the lower aircraft's fin and the nose cone was bent upwards, but the lower aircraft started to disintegrate and the crew were forced to eject over the sea 60 km (37 miles) north-east of Kolguyev Island. Both crew members were wearing VMSK-4 immersion suits and landed uninjured in the sea, almost immediately below the point of impact.

They had ditched in an area covered in fairly large ice floes consisting mainly of a type of slushy ice known as '*shuga*'. The pilot managed to scramble onto an ice floe about 6 m (20 feet) long, placed his dinghy under his back and sheltered from the wind, but the navigator landed on the water some distance away and was unable to get onto an ice floe. They both then had a long wait of several hours before the rescue party reached them, after they were spotted on the surface by the deputy regiment commander Lt Col. Bramnik, searching for them in a Tu-128UT. In all, the two crew members waited for around 5 hours before being rescued and evacuated from the scene by helicopter. As a result of long-term ill health resulting from his long immersion in the freezing water, the navigator was taken off the 'supersonic aircrew list' by an aero-medical board but continued flying for several years as a second navigator on the Tu-126 'Moss' airborne early warning aircraft. Eventually, after returning to the full medical category required to fly the Tu-128, he rejoined 72 AP at Amderma. The crew of the second Tu-128, which had been damaged in the collision, were forced to shut down the starboard engine but were able to return to Nar'yan-Mar where they made a safe landing, although the aircraft did run off the end of the runway on completion of roll-out. The pilot and navigator were not injured in the incident.

Cause: The accident was attributed to the wingman's lack of flight discipline and awareness when flying close to his flight leader.

Non-fatal accident—Tu-128M—February 1981

Weather conditions: Night IMC, fog, cloud-base 25 m (82 feet)

Circumstances: A crew from 518 AP at Talagi, comprising aircraft commander Capt. Yakovlev and squadron navigator Maj. Rodyukov, had carried out a night landing at base, right on weather minima limits. The aircraft had touched down in fog with a visibility of less than 300-400 m (985-1,300 feet), cloud-base of around 25-30 m (80-100 feet) and at an angle to the centreline. Immediately after touch-down, and after a short landing run, the main undercarriage bogies broke off and the aircraft slid on its belly before coming to a full stop after about 900 m (3,000 feet). The two crew members were unhurt.

Cause: The accident was attributed to the severe weather conditions, with dense fog almost down to the surface, compounded by the erroneous action of the flight controller (RP) and the regiment commander, who was in the command post at the time, neither officer giving the order to divert to the designated alternate airfield.

This incident is recalled by Maj. Rodyukov:

> We had been launched at night [in Bort No. 07] in response to an exercise alert (*po uchebnoy trevogye*) and departed the airfield to our combat patrol zone as part of a group of several Tu-128s. Returning to base after completion of our task, at a distance

Capt. Yakovlev and his navigator Maj. Rodyukov stand beside Bort No. 07 only a few hours after their very lucky escape from this potentially tragic crash in February 1981. (*Ivan Rodyukov*)

Using makeshift support equipment, aided by the lubrication effect of the deep snow, the aircraft was removed to the regiment's TEhCh facility the day after the crash. (*Ivan Rodyukov*)

of around 120 km [75 miles] from the airfield, the runway lights started to come into sight. When we descended to 3,000 m [9,840 feet] we encountered a small amount of mist and then at a distance of about 5 km [3 miles] from base the lights disappeared. We descended to the outer beacon on instruments and then continued on to the inner beacon. For safety reasons, the cloud-base at night was not to be less than 350 m [1,150 feet], but there we were, passing the inner beacon with nothing visible ahead of us. An inspector-pilot from Army HQ [Col. Bramnik] had landed ahead of us; he'd landed the aircraft, but as became clear afterwards, the visibility was such that he could not see the taxiway in order to turn off the main runway. There was already dense fog over the airfield by that time, but we began our approach descent.

Behind us there were another three Tu-128s on the approach. In such weather conditions we ought to have diverted to another airfield, but in those times a landing at a diversion airfield was considered to be a 'precursor to an accident'. The RP did not give us the command to divert and we continued with the approach, penetrating the thick cloud. Cloud-base appeared to be around 25 m [82 feet], but visibility below this was very bad [!] because of shrouds of mist and fog. In fact, alongside the airfield there was a cellulose-paper plant, which used to dump 'technical water' [i.e.

Bort No. 07's severe impact with the ground in the February 1981 crash caused the main undercarriage legs to collapse and the starboard nacelle fairing to detach from the wing. (*Ivan Rodyukov*)

This photograph, taken minutes after Bort No. 07 came to rest, shows the thick carpet of snow which prevented the outbreak of fire. The aircraft is illuminated by a vehicle whose headlights have scarcely penetrated the thick fog on the airfield. (*Ivan Rodyukov*)

industrial effluent] into the tributary of the North Dvina River. Consequently, this tributary never froze over because of the high temperature of the technical effluent and in winter there was always fog over the surface. If the wind was blowing from the west then this fog stretched as far as the airfield. When we emerged from the cloud, we were told to go round gain, but it was already too late. During this attempt, the aircraft went into the 'second regime' [explained briefly in Chapter 9], from which it was practically impossible to escape at low level.

We landed rather hard on the fourth or fifth taxiway section, some 5-10 m [16-33 feet] to the left of the main runway, and the aircraft started to travel at an angle to it. During its passage, the aircraft struck the corner of a small weather station building. But the biggest impact was felt when the aircraft 'jumped' onto the main taxiway, along which were snow banks piled up about 1.5-2 m [5-6.5 feet] high on either side. Our aircraft was carrying two missiles, which were torn off by the impact, along with the pylons. The undercarriage was also torn off. When the aircraft struck the snow bank a lot of snow was ingested into the engines. The snow actually saved us. First of all, the piled up snow softened the blow. Secondly, it prevented an outbreak of fire in the engines. In the meantime, the aircraft continued to slide along on its belly.

During its progress, the aircraft not only sliced the branches of some bushes but also tree trunks of around 25-30 cm [10-11 inches] in diameter and continued on for another 600 m [2,000 feet]. It was, of course, severely battered and bashed, but the

Tu-128 was a very strong aircraft and did not break up. At the end of its travels across the airfield the aircraft ended up nose-first in a small lake, having broken through a 1.5 m [5 feet] sheet of ice. At the same time, it had also turned through 180°, some 180-200 m [590-660 feet] from a two-storey building. At the start of the emergency we could have considered ejecting, but the likelihood of a safe outcome in this case was not too good. When the aircraft turned round and stopped, smoke started to fill the cockpit and it was impossible to see anything. Around us there was also dense fog, which it was only possible to penetrate with searchlights. We were debriefed and then hidden in a 'prophylactorium' from the inquisitive 'big-wigs'.

Fatal write-off—Tu-128—11 March 1980

Weather conditions: Night IMC
Circumstances: A crew from 518 AP based at Talagi, comprising aircraft commander (pilot) Capt. Valyeyev and section navigator Capt. Matyukin, were performing an inter-airfield flight from Talagi to Amderma during an exercise programme. On approach to land at Amderma the aircraft commander failed to comply with an instruction to make a second approach given by ATC. On his own initiative he also shut down one engine. The navigator ejected at almost ground level, but survived. The pilot ejected after the aircraft struck the ground, but with insufficient forward speed his ejection trajectory did not allow the parachute to deploy fully and he was killed.
Cause: Pilot error in setting up the landing approach.

This account of the accident is given by Capt. Matyukin:

At the beginning of March 1980, our regiment was ordered by the command authorities of the 10th Independent Army of the national Air Defence Forces to allocate a number of trained crews to participate in a tactical flying exercise named '*Niebiesnyi Shchit-80*' ['Celestial Shield-80']. The exercise would involve a large number of personnel and equipment (air assets, anti-aircraft missile forces and supporting radar units of the PVO). At the time, our regiment's manning situation in terms of combat-ready crews was a little 'tight'—some were on leave, others were attending an aero-medical board, and the regiment commander, Colonel Pavel Pavlovich Sapozhnikov, was himself absent for some unspecified reason. For the period of his absence he had appointed his deputy Lt Col. Viktor Sergeyevich Fishchenko to take over the running of the regiment. Fishchenko was an exceptional character—a fine pilot and a good companion who allowed nothing to get in his way, (including progress up the 'promotion ladder'). However, having shown myself to have the best organisational skills, I was the one detailed to carry out the order from 'on high' to select suitably qualified crews. There was only one question: 'Where to find them, with the required level of training?!' In the end, we somehow managed to scrape together eight crews. Seven of these crews were suitable in terms of the level of training and experience, but one of them quite clearly 'dropped off the bottom' of this list. This was the crew comprising aircraft commander Captain Valyeyev and myself, section navigator Captain Matyukin. Sasha Valyeyev had just got married on March 1st and the regiment command staff had allocated him ten 'happy honeymoon days', but he had not been authorised to travel too far from the base. Then, in the early morning of March 10th he was dragged back from this cosy 'honeymoon situation' and told to prepare for the exercise and a brief deployment to Amderma. This news did not exactly fill him with joy. The exercise was to start on March 11th, signalled by the standard 'trevoga' alarm call, although we didn't know the precise time. March 11th was also my birthday, an event which always meant a lot to aircrew and wherever possible it was a day on which you were generally not programmed to fly. It was really a day to be celebrated in the company of friends and family with a glass of 'tea' ['*chai*'—probably a euphemism for something a little stronger!].

Aircrew involved in the exercise were sent off to the training room to be given their specific flight briefings, fill in the planning board, plot the deployment route from Talagi to Amderma and select crews. Captain Valyeyev was in our 'section', comprising section commander Captain Vydryenok and myself as section navigator. A section navigator could fly with any pilot of that section, so I was placed with Captain Valyeyev. Sasha Valyeyev was a sporting type, who loved to follow football in his spare time, but it was a different thing where his flight training was concerned and this did not please me much. It was no secret on the squadron that Lt Col. Fishchenko knew perfectly well his [limited] level of training and ability. I knew Fishchenko from our service together on 72 AP at Amderma and we got on well, so I approached him and we had a chat on the subject. 'Sergeyevich! You can't plan him into the exercise! He's only got two landings in his log book at the deployment airfield and even these were in daylight VMC conditions. Also, it's my birthday tomorrow. Can't you swap us with another crew?' Fishchenko replied, 'What are you saying, Valera! They'd have my head on a plate!' It's essential to allocate ten crews and I've only found eight. We'll celebrate your birthday when you get back. Keep an eye on Valyeyev. You flew at Amderma for six years—you know the airfield well. Everything will be OK.' So that's how we discussed the situation. There was nothing else we could do—we were military people. Exercise preparation and planning took up all our time well into the evening. As usual, this involved route planning, plotting the headings to fly on navigation charts, performing 'engineer-navigation calculations' [*Inzhenyerno-Shturmanskie Raschyoty* or IShR][8] and studying the airfield data for Amderma and the designated alternate airfields. Everything was checked and then we were stood down to our quarters. On the following day, March 11th, after morning parade we had our pre-flight medical checks and then relaxed until lunchtime. After lunch we were driven out to the airfield and sat around waiting for the '*trevoga*' exercise alarm signal. We did some 'simulation' training in the cockpit and received our pre-flight briefings. The alarm was sounded some time around 16.30 hours [local time] and the airfield suddenly burst into life, like a disturbed ants' nest.

Technicians started to rush around the aircraft, crews strapped into the cockpits, and APA self-propelled generator vehicles were plugged in to provide power for engine start-up. Now the howl of jet turbines disturbed the silence and the last vestiges of daylight signalled the end of the day. Our Tu-128s began to taxi out to the holding point to take off in accordance with the sequence written in the exercise plan. Our crew took off as last but one, the last aircraft being flown by section commander Oleg Vydryenok. We taxied out and took off. The time was 17.10 hours. We retracted the undercarriage and flaps, climbed to the designated height and set off on a route taking us from Talagi, via Cape Mikulkin, Kanin Nos Peninsula, overhead Rogachyovo airfield and then into Amderma airfield. The planned flight time was 2 hours 15 minutes and everything was normal during the transit. Overhead Rogachyovo we set course to the calculated top of descent point (40 km) [25 miles] for Amderma airfield and established top of descent at a height of 2,000 m [6,560 feet]. The runway headings at Amderma are 254°/074° and we approached on 254°, calling ATC to request landing conditions. While we were en route the weather in the vicinity of Amderma had worsened significantly, the wind close to the ground had strengthened to around 8-10 m/sec [15-19 kts], gusting to 12 m/sec [23 kts]. Wind direction was from 90° left of the landing heading and eight-tenths low cloud was blowing in off the tundra, with the ground and coastline visible through the gaps. We commenced the descent and selected Amderma's ILS channel—the pointers began to quiver as we entered the glideslope. When we were 24 km [15 miles] out we lowered the undercarriage—our fuel remainder was 2 tonnes [4,400 lb]. Through gaps in the cloud the ground was visible. I asked Valyeyev, 'Sasha, can you see the runway?' He replied in a slightly strained voice, 'I don't see it.' We descended further. We were maintaining the crosshairs of the ILS indicator on zero [i.e. centralised]. We were approaching on a normal heading. At a distance of 18 km [11 miles] Sasha suddenly reported, 'I can see the runway.' Now I felt a lot happier. There was dense cloud at a distance of 12 km [7.5 miles], with cloud-base at 180 m [590 feet]. We entered cloud and selected landing flap. At 10 km [6 miles] the heading needle moved to the left of the centre of the dial, indicating that we needed to go a little to the left. I gave the command, 'Go left six degrees' but Sasha remained silent.

Even at a distance of 8 km [5 miles] from touchdown we'd barely corrected our heading. The glideslope needle had deflected down. We were flying to the right and above the recommended approach trajectory. The heading needle was moving further to the left. I shouted, 'Sanya—go left 15 degrees! We're drifting right.' He remained silent. And everyone else was silent. The ATC tower, the RP [ATC controller] and the GCA controller—all remained silent. At 6 km [3.75 miles] from the runway our speed was 480 kph (260 kts) and our height was 350 m [1,150 feet].

The scene at Amderma after the crash on 11 March 1980. Visible on the left of the picture is the pilot's ejection seat and, in the mid-foreground, the starboard R-4R missile. The forward section of the missile can be seen in the right foreground, minus its nose cone, revealing the receiving antenna of the semi-active guidance unit. (*Valeriy Matyukin*)

Something must be blocking out my pilot and I was thinking that it was vital to somehow get him out of this situation. I said to him calmly, 'Sanya, look; where are the needles? Turn. You're not in the simulator.' The needle of the automatic radio compass had deflected left and we were passing over the outer beacon. Then the GCA controller sprang to life: 'Turn left onto the landing course.' [Capt. Matyukin does not explain why the GCA controller played such a limited part in these difficult approach conditions.] Valyeyev remained silent, but he started to turn left. We emerged from the cloud over the right-hand side of the town of Amderma. There was another characteristic visual orientation point here—the POL storage facility, with its large circular storage tanks. If the landing approach was set up normally in terms of heading and glideslope then the tanks would be visible about 45° to the left of the aircraft, but I could see that they were about 70° to the left. At this moment the aircraft was banking 45° to the left. Valyeyev had seen the runway. As soon as I'd taken all of this in, I gave the command, 'Increase rpm [power]! We're going round again! We're not going to get in!' but Sasha remained silent and continued to turn [towards the runway]. Then the air traffic controller in the visual control tower became aware of the situation. The RP for that day was Lt Col. G. N. Sadovnikov, who gave the command 'Go round again!'

We were now only 2 km [1.25 miles] from the runway, approaching the landing heading, with Valyeyev trying to align the aircraft with the runway centreline by turning right over the inner beacon, but he failed to correct. I relayed the RP's command to him, 'Go round again!' at which point Valyeyev reported to the RP, 'I see the runway. Permission to land.' The RP replied, 'You should have got the approach sorted out earlier, but land now.' (!!) We were flying to the left of and over the inner beacon at 450 kph [245 kts] and a height of 70 m [230 feet]. Valyeyev realised that he was high on the approach and the speed was high. He shut down one engine so that the aircraft would not accelerate in the descent. We went further to the right towards the runway. This was it! From this moment on it was 'each to his own'. Everyone went silent. Valyeyev tried to put the aircraft down. He made a left turn just before reaching the runway—the control column was fully back, but it was too late. The nose-wheel leg struck the runway first, followed by the main bogies. I felt a dull pain in the small of my back. We bounced high from the first impact and the nose leg must have broken off. We departed the main runway, rising about 15 m [50 feet] above the beams of the landing searchlights and hurtled forwards. To the left, the lights of the airport buildings were twinkling; the nose began to drop. We dropped below the searchlight beams. Here, I thought again, 'This is it!' However, the self-preservation instinct is powerfully embedded in all of us, to be triggered at the appropriate moment, and my specific training also played its part. I'd always loved parachuting and jumped whenever the opportunity arose and my commanders authorised it. I was actually a parachute jumping instructor with 150 jumps in my log book. On all my previous regiments (Kotlas, Amderma, Arkhangel'sk [i.e. Talagi]) I had acted as head of the PDS (*Parashutno-desantnaya Sluzhba*) service where there was no one else established in post. [The Parachute Landing Service (PDS) provided an airborne rescue service for aircrew who had ejected in inhospitable territory, possibly equating to Combat Survival and Rescue (CSAR) teams in the West.] All this helped in my present situation, although I didn't manage to adopt the recommended pre-ejection posture in the seat—I put my right foot on the footrest of the ejection seat, but not the left. I pulled the operating lever of the KT-1 seat upwards until it hit the stop [triggering canopy jettison] and then down to operate the seat to eject myself.

Thank you Tupolev designers! The seat worked like clockwork. I ejected practically from ground level and according to the findings of the accident investigation commission, I had ejected 0.5 seconds before the second impact with the runway. The powder charge of the ejection gun carried the seat to a height of 80 m [262 feet]. The main canopy pack was extracted and the parachute cracked open under the force of the onrushing air; I'd ejected at a speed of 280 kph [150 kts]. The main canopy reduced the speed of descent and the seat itself dropped away beneath me. At that moment the landing searchlights, runway lights and the floodlights of the central refuelling area went out and it suddenly became very dark. I tumbled around for about 5 seconds under the canopy and then I was on the ground. The wind blowing in off the tundra had taken me to the right of the main runway by about 20 m [65 feet]. While I was releasing myself from the harness assembly the chute dragged me about another 10 m [33 feet] over the snow. I managed to stand up and

The *Smerch* radar was removed soon after the crash in order to protect its sensitive electronics from prying eyes, although it is unlikely that the satellite-borne cameras of the day could have produced exploitable imagery from an overhead aspect. (*Valeriy Matyukin*)

I discovered that I had a boot on my right foot but only a sock on my left foot. I realised that when I ejected I hadn't placed my left leg on the footrest, which allowed the boot to be ripped off when I entered the airstream. My back was aching. My eyes were gradually getting used to the darkness and I noticed that my NAZ emergency survival pack was lying close to the runway. [On ejection, as soon as seat and occupant separate, the NAZ drops away and descends on a 15-m long (50-foot) halyard attached to the survivor to hit the ground first, reducing the crew member's speed of descent.] I slowly edged my way towards it and wrapped the empty NAZ haversack around my foot over my sock. I stood up and waited for help—it was dark and the cold wind continued to blow in off the tundra. The time was 19.20 hours.

After I ejected, events unfolded in the following sequence [according to the report of the accident investigation commission and eyewitnesses]: There was a second impact with the runway. Valyeyev pulled the control column fully back into his chest, which struck his rib-cage, breaking several ribs. The impact was so powerful that the stock of his Makarov PM personal weapon was twisted, the magazine had sprung off and the cartridges had spilled out into the pockets of his flying jacket from the holster and he lost consciousness. (I'm certain that if that were not the case he would have ejected at the same time as I did.) The impact load had cracked the wing torsion box in the middle. The nose section, minus the nose leg and the rear fuselage struck the runway surface. The aircraft slid off to the right of the main runway into a snow bank, raising a swathe of snow into the air and surrounding it in a cloud of snow and

415

steam. The nose radome had broken off and a missile and pylon had been ripped off the starboard wing. Leaving a trail of debris behind it, the aircraft continued to slide forwards, tearing up an electrical power supply cable, extinguishing the floodlights of the TsZT central fuelling area. The aircraft gradually began to slow down, ploughing a furrow in the frozen snow crust with the now 'radome-less' nose at the front and the tailplane surfaces at the rear. This caused the aircraft to begin to turn to the right, and then finally it came to a stop at an angle of 120° to the runway, 30 m [100 feet] from the GCA installation. Evidently, a few moments earlier Valyeyev must have regained consciousness and saw that he was heading towards the GCA and ejected. Unfortunately, he did not have the necessary speed; the KT-1 was capable of saving the pilot from zero height, but only with a forward speed of more than 130 kph [70 kts]. Valyeyev landed alongside the aircraft, still in his seat. The main canopy pack had been extracted, but the canopy itself was still folded and packed and lying in the snow. The post mortem on Valyeyev revealed that all his vital organs had been damaged by fragments of his ribs. At what point did all this happen? Was it during the second impact with the runway, when his chest cavity was crushed by the control column, or was it when he ejected from a height of only 80-100 m [260-330 feet], falling to the ground still in the seat? No one could tell.

I was picked up by a rescue team after about 10 minutes and taken by fire tender to a classroom used by the meteorology service on the base. They brought me my left boot which they'd found near where I landed and told me that Valyeyev had lost his life in the accident. Then I was taken by ambulance to the local hospital, where I was diagnosed with a compression fracture of two vertebrae in my spine and severe bruising of the soft tissue of my left leg. Later, the inner part of my leg came up in bruises of all the colours of the rainbow, but mainly black, blue and yellow. I was kept in hospital overnight. On the following day a commission headed by PVO air force commander Col. Gen. Nikolai Ivanovich Moskivityelev came from Moscow to see me. They came into my ward in a large group. The General posed the first question: 'Now, my lad, tell us the whole truth. What happened?' I told them the whole story as I had recalled from the events of the day before. They questioned me for about 40 minutes. The final question was the inevitable age-old Russian question, 'Who was to blame?' I told him, 'We were to blame. I, because I wasn't able to persuade Valyeyev to go round again, and Valyeyev, because he didn't carry out the orders given to him by ATC. It was an inadequate level of training.' Moskivityelev replied, 'Fine, we'll look into it,' and just as he was leaving said, 'You've nothing to worry about. Just remember that you did everything correctly. Get well. Tomorrow, I'll take you with me to Moscow, to hospital.' They didn't take me to Moscow, but instead we flew to Arkhangel'sk where I was placed in the local military hospital and remained there for almost three months. I must say a big 'thank you' to the doctor who treated me there. She was a lovely woman—a post-doctoral researcher. She operated on me using a procedure developed by her, and even to this day my spine does not give me any pain. So that birthday was a sad event for me, being both my last (*krainii*) flight and last parachute jump, but for Sasha Valyeyev it was his final (*poslednii*) flight. [The Russian word *'krainii'* means, *inter alia*, the last in a continuing sequence, whereas *'poslednii'* is absolutely final. Russian aircrew avoid the word *'poslednii'* if what is meant is the last in a continuing sequence.] This was our fate. For me, life and military service continued, but that is another story ...

This is an account of the incident, as described by former section commander Maj. Oleg Vydryenok:

We had been briefed to carry out Exercise 100 from the KBP [combat training manual] for the Tu-128. The task required us to perform a night take-off from Talagi and then fly a route taking us to Cape Mikulkin on Kanin Peninsula, then on to Rogachyovo (Belushya Guba) airfield on Novaya Zemlya, intercepting Yak-28Ps based there, before landing at Amderma. The approach to the airfield was carried out in severe weather minima, with a powerful crosswind blowing in off the tundra. Valyeyev knew that if he flew along the coastline then he would come to the airfield. The wind had broken up the ice, and the whiteness of the tundra contrasted sharply with the dark surface of the sea at a distance of 18-20 km [11-12.5 miles]. From there the ground was still visible, but at a distance of 10-12 km [6-7.5 miles] from Amderma airfield there was a bank of dense low cloud and a strong drift to port. Just before Amderma the coastline followed a line to the right, and the sea was

With the radar removed, the front cockpit and the forward 'technical compartment' were then covered with tarpaulin. The aircraft's final impact with the ground resulted in the front and rear sections of the fuselage separating in the vicinity of the wing centre-section. (*Valeriy Matyukin*)

visible through gaps in the cloud. Valyeyev flew along the coast and did not react to calls from ATC; there was now strong drift to starboard. He passed some 250-300 m [820-985 feet] to the right of the outer beacon, heading for Amderma. He began to turn left to pick up the glideslope so that he could then make a right turn to take him towards the runway. It was frightening to descend into the unknown. He descended towards the inner beacon at a height of 70 m [230 feet] and a speed of 450 kph (245 kts); realising that his height and speed were high for that stage of the approach, he shut down one of the engines. This was to avoid accelerating in the descent. His navigator, the GCA controller and the runway controller all ordered him to go round again, but Valyeyev suddenly reported, 'I can see the runway. Permission to land.' The ATC controller, Lt Col. Sadovnikov, responded with the call, 'You should have sorted out the approach earlier, but land now.' The KZA on-board flight data recorder registered a sharp forward movement of the control column, almost to failure point, and then 2 seconds later it was pulled back to the normal [central] position. After a few more seconds, the column was once again pulled back, to –16°, then to –22°, full rearwards deflection.

However, it was too late. The aircraft struck the runway with the nose-wheel leg, followed by the main bogies. It bounced high with a high angle of pitch and the nose leg detached from the aircraft. The navigator, Valera Matyukin, saw the airport buildings through his port side window and ejected. It was like fireworks going off above the aircraft as it was picked up by the beams of the landing searchlights when it left the runway. The '*Tushka*' [an affectionate name for any Tupolev aircraft] struck the runway heavily with its nose, at the same time breaking off the starboard under-carriage bogie. A missile was released from the port wing and embedded itself in the snow between the main runway and the civil aircraft parking area. The Tu-128 slid off the runway to the right, raising a swathe of snow into the air with its starboard wing, severing the power cable for the runway lighting and landing searchlights, which were extinguished instantly, along with the floodlighting for the central fuel-ling area. In the darkness, in a cloud of snow and steam, the aircraft turned through 180° and came to a stop a few metres from the airfield GCA installation. There was another firework display above the aircraft and then … silence. I didn't know where to taxi—it was my first visit to this airfield, not to mention the fact that it was a night arrival. I used the taxi lights to guide me to the central refuelling area—every-one was rushing out to the runway. I stopped behind other parked aircraft, shut down the engines and climbed down from the aircraft over the closed canopy of my navigator onto the fuselage, then onto the wing and onto one of the missiles and then ran towards Valyeyev's aircraft. So everything happened in front of my eyes. At the time I was Valyeyev's section commander and that night I had a mountain of explanatory reports to write, but in the morning, when General Moskivityelev arrived, I became a simple aircraft commander again and the squadron commander became the deputy squadron commander. Someone *had* to be blamed. [Here Maj.

Vydryenok uses the popular Russian saying '*strelochnik vinovat*', meaning literally 'the signalman is guilty', an expression deriving from early railway practice but which has come to mean more generally 'it is always the little man who is blamed'.] What was interesting was that it was Matyukin's birthday on that day and Valyeyev had just got married on March 1. His commanders had given him only ten days off instead of the usual 'honeymoon month', although before recalling him from leave I had gone to see the 'deputy commander flying' (*zamestityel'po lyotnoi rabotye*) and told him that Valyeyev would probably *not* have flying on his mind at this particular time …

Non-fatal write-off—Tu-128—14 August 1980

Weather conditions: Daylight VMC

Circumstances: A crew from 350 AP at Belaya, comprising aircraft commander Pilot First Class 'M' and navigator and squadron chief of staff Capt. 'O', were programmed to carry out Exercise 88 of the Tu-128 combat training manual (KBP APVO-78—'Flight in the handling zone to practise flying in cloud'). The crew took off at 21.37 hours, Irkutsk time. Having been authorised to take off, the pilot selected reheat and commenced his take-off run. During the take-off run, he lifted the nose-wheel at 260 kph (140 kts) and after reaching a speed of 320 kph (173 kts) the aircraft lifted off the runway and immediately pitched up with concomitant loss of forward speed. The aircraft did not respond to the pilot's control inputs and continued to pitch up. At a height of 80-100 m (260-330 feet) and flying at 280-300 kph (150-162 kts) both crew members ejected on the pilot's command. The aircraft hit the ground to the left of the main runway, around 75 m (250 feet) from the threshold, broke up and was partially burnt out. Both crew members were unhurt.

Cause: On the basis of conclusions drawn by the 13th State Scientific Research Institute for Aircraft Operation and Repair (13 GosNII ERAT), the accident was the result of the failure of the aircraft's longitudinal control circuit. This, in turn, was caused by the release of the elevator locking lever in the pilot's cockpit before flight. Deflection of the tailplane by aerodynamic loading caused additional displacement of the input rocker arm of the RM-2 actuator and the stabilizer, independent of the position of the control column.

Aircraft history

Tu-128 c/n 503501 rolled out of the factory on 30 May 1969 with an airframe life of 1,200 hours ±200 hours.

Underwent first intermediate overhaul in December 1974.

Total time since start of operations—531 hours; time since last overhaul—379 hours.

Col. Yevglyevskiy, a member of the accident investigation commission, comments:

> In this incident, immediately after take-off the aircraft became uncontrollable
> in pitch. An accident commission was convened and even while we were still on
> the approach to Belaya airfield we learned that the cause of the accident had been
> discovered. We landed and were immediately taken to a classroom that had been
> commandeered for the occasion. Various components and technical drawings were
> laid out on a table; we took our places and the regimental engineer commenced his
> report. There was a fractured control rod on the table and this was passed round the
> group. The stabilizer had ceased to function—all fairly logical. There was only one
> thing that we couldn't understand. How did the rod fracture? I asked the question
> directly, 'Why did it fracture? It must have been damaged in the crash.' The Chief
> Engineer, General Grishin, then suggested that we should all break for lunch and
> think it over. So we all went off for lunch. By the end of the day's discussion session
> it had become clear that the elevators on the stabilizer must have unlocked, but the
> stabilizer had been working. The elevator locking lever was located on the left-hand
> side of the pilot's cockpit, and this had a specific design failing in that it was possible
> to partially release it and unlock the tailplane inadvertently. If the lever was then
> returned to its original position, no one would notice that it was still unlocked. In
> the cockpit everything would appear normal. In this case, the pilot checked it, did
> not notice anything untoward and they took off, but the unlocked elevator was able
> to move in response to air loads. The Research Institute examination revealed that
> the lever had been unlocked on the ground, although it was not possible to establish
> who was to blame.

Non-fatal write-off—Tu-128—10 (12?) March 1981

Weather conditions: Daylight VMC
Circumstances: A crew from 356 AP at Zhana-Semey, comprising aircraft commander Capt. 'B', and section navigator Capt. 'F', were carrying out a test flight.
Whilst flying at an altitude of 4,000 m (13,125 feet) and a speed of 870 kph (470 kts)
they felt a sudden jolt at the rear of the aircraft, followed by illumination of the
fire warning lights. A fire had broken out in the starboard engine, resulting in
the first sequence of fire extinguishing operating automatically. However, the fire
continued unabated. The pilot reduced power to 'Flight Idle' on the port engine but
was still unable to extinguish the fire, and smoke had started to enter the cockpit.
With no likelihood of extinguishing the fire and at an altitude of 2,000 m (6,560
feet) and a speed of 480 kph (260 kts), the pilot decided that they should eject.
Cause: Disintegration of the blades of the first stage of the compressor in the starboard engine, which resulted in damage to the compressor casing and elements

of the fuel system, leading to fire in the engine compartment. The accident investigation commission proposed that measures should be adopted by industry to protect the K9-51 accident data recorder, or its replacement, from high-temperature damage in such accidents.

Fatal write-off—Tu-128M—18 February 1982

Weather conditions: Night IMC
Circumstances: A crew from 356 AP at Zhana-Semey was taking part in an exercise at their base airfield, under the command of section leader Military Pilot First Class Capt. 'Sh' with section navigator Military Navigator First Class Capt. 'L'. They were performing a practice intercept against a 'controlled target' group comprising three Tu-16 'Badger' medium bombers operating out of Sary-Shagan. On analysis of the KZA flight data recorder it was established that in the forty-sixth minute of flight, while breaking off from the attack at an altitude of 6,000 m (19,685 feet), the Tu-128M slipped into the jet wake of one of the target aircraft. This led to an increase of the interceptor's bank angle to 70-80°, drawing it into the deep-spiral regime. The aircraft then exceeded the speed and g-load limits for the type and began to disintegrate. Unable to use their ejection seats, the pilot and navigator were killed.
Cause: Erroneous action by the pilot on breaking off from the attack, leading to unintentional entry into the deep-spiral regime as a result of hitting the jet wake of the group of three large targets. The tragedy was exacerbated by poor control of the Tu-128 crew by the regimental command post (GCI station) team. The accident investigation commission proposed that an MS-61 cockpit voice recorder should be fitted to the Tu-128 in order to obtain additional information about the crew's actions in emergency situations.

Non-fatal write-off—Tu-128M—12 August 1982

Weather conditions: Daylight VMC
Circumstances: A crew from 518 AP, comprising aircraft commander Sr Lt 'P' and navigator Lt 'I', were taking off from Talagi when the navigator's cockpit canopy blew off because it had not been locked correctly. The pilot aborted the take-off at a speed of 250 kph (135 kts) on hearing the navigator's panicked shouts. The aircraft overran the runway by 800 m (2,625 feet) and was damaged beyond repair, but the crew were unhurt.
Cause: Poor level of training exhibited by the crew in their response to a non-standard situation.

Fatal write-off—Tu-128M—18 August 1982

Weather conditions: Daylight VMC

Circumstances: A crew from 350 AP at Belaya, comprising the head of 39 Corps PVO Flight Safety Service, Military Pilot First Class Lt Col. 'K' and section navigator Military Navigator First Class Capt. 'Z', were taking off from Khatanga airfield on a transit flight to Kansk. (The flight was planned under the provisions of Exercise 40 of the combat training manual KBP APVO-80—'Navigation flight with landing at another base'.) The crew taxied out to the main runway and, on receiving permission from the flight controller, the pilot selected reheat on both engines at 18.55 hours (local time) and commenced his take-off run. After selection of reheat on the starboard engine, it ignited, albeit with reduced fuel delivery, and 12 seconds later reheat extinguished spontaneously. The crew took the loss of thrust (in the second half of the take-off run) as simply being 'slow acceleration' and so continued with the take-off. On counting off the speed at 280 kph (151 kts), the navigator reported the slow rate of acceleration to the pilot, having determined this from the long gaps between the latter's own speed read-outs. Some 2-3 seconds later the pilot replied, 'It's normal.' At a speed of 300 kph (162 kts) the navigator noticed the runway caravan to his right, but the aircraft still had all three undercarriage units on the ground as it continued its take-off roll. From his two previous flights he recalled that the aircraft had left the ground by this point.

This was also noted by another crew who were taxiing nearby, as well as the ATC controller, who both told the pilot by radio to raise the nose-wheel. The pilot eventually lifted the nose around 100 m (330 feet) from the end of the runway and at a speed of 330-340 kph (178-183 kts); 51 seconds after starting the take-off roll, the aircraft achieved unstick speed. The aircraft left the ground at the end of the runway, but because of the lack of thrust it did not gain height, remaining level at no more than 2-3 m (6.5-10 feet) above the ground. The pilot, just holding the aircraft above stalling speed, struggled to accelerate in order to put the aircraft into a climb, but at a distance of around 180-650 m (590-2,130 feet) from the end of the runway it struck two wooden radio masts with the left undercarriage bogie and the starboard flaps. Then, around 300 m (about 1,000 feet) from the runway, it hit a wooden tower, banked sharply to the right and started to descend. The navigator, assessing the seriousness of the situation, ejected just before the aircraft hit the ground and survived. At a distance of 650 m (2,130 feet) from the end of the runway, flying at 340 kph (184 kts) and 58 seconds into the flight, the aircraft hit the ground and exploded. Having no time to save himself, the pilot was unable to use his ejection seat and was killed.

Cause: The accident was attributed to technical failure. Using data from the KZA flight data recorder, it appeared that the starboard afterburner had not developed full thrust, and 12 seconds after commencing the take-off roll had shut down spontaneously. As established by the Soviet Ministry of Defence's 13th State Scientific Research

Institute for Aircraft Operation and Repair (13 GosNII ERAT), the afterburner failure was due to a fracture of a spring in the drive shaft of a pump (specifically *Agregat* [Unit] *661*) in the engine's 'automatics'. As a result, the afterburner shut down, the bleed valves of the fourth and fifth compressor stages opened, the compressor guide vanes translated from the −3° position to −15° and the jet nozzle remained open. Engine thrust dropped immediately because of the afterburner shutting down, with the opening of the exhaust nozzle further reducing thrust in non-reheat mode.

Aircraft history

Tu-128 c/n 501803 rolled out of the factory on 7 May 1967 with an airframe life of 2,300 hours.

Underwent first intermediate overhaul on 29 January 1978; airframe life after overhaul—2,000 hours.

Total time since entering service—1,556 hours.

Port engine AL-7F-2 No. V9426006 'S', delivered 12 December 1969 with an operating life of 300 hours.

Underwent first major overhaul on 28 August 1979; life after overhaul—350 hours.

Total time since start of operations—611 hours; time since last overhaul—312 hours.

Starboard engine AL-7F-2 No. V0426046 'T', delivered 22 January 1971 with an operating life of 300 hours.

Underwent first major overhaul on 27 September 1979; life after overhaul—350 hours.

Total time since start of operations—611 hours; time since last overhaul—312 hours.

Non-fatal write-off—Tu-128M—16 September 1982

Weather conditions: Not given

Circumstances: A crew from the 2nd squadron of 350 AP at Belaya, comprising Unclassified Pilot Lt 'P' and Military Navigator First Class Capt. 'K', were taking off from base. After getting airborne and retracting the undercarriage, a cloud of thick brown smoke trailed behind the aircraft. At a height of 200-250 m (650-820 feet) the flight controller ordered the crew to shut down the afterburners, dump fuel and return to land. At the same time the crew reported that the fire warning lights had come on, along with automatic firing of the first shot of fire extinguishant into the left engine. Having seen flames coming out of the engine when the afterburners were switched off, the flight controller ordered the crew to eject. Both crew members did so safely.

Cause: The incident was attributed to an engine fire due to a fatigue fracture and subsequent loss of sealing in the fuel pipe leading to the control unit for the port engine exhaust nozzle.

Tupolev Tu-128 'Fiddler'

Non-fatal write-off—Tu-128M—7 April 1983

Weather conditions: IMC, cloud-base 350-400 m (1,150-1,300 feet), occasional snow showers

Circumstances: A crew from 64 AP at Omsk-North, comprising Maj. 'C' as pilot and navigator Capt. 'N', were landing at base. After overflying the outer beacon, performing left and right corrective turns using the PP-1PMK director instrument, the crew allowed their concentration to lapse in checking their height and speed. The pilot did not react to the GCA controller's command to level the wings ('*Gorizont*'—meaning literally 'horizon'). When landing at this airfield in IMC conditions, the runway threshold was not always clearly visible, and the pilot mistook the approach lights for the main runway lights and a section of the inner beacon for the beginning of the runway (!). Having realised his error, the pilot made an attempt to go round again for another approach. However, when climbing away he allowed the aircraft to bank to such an extent that the wing tip struck the ground. The aircraft touched down at a high angle of attack some 3.8 km (2.4 miles) from the runway and offset around 132 m (433 feet) from the centreline. It then turned on its back and crashed alongside a road; fortunately, the cockpit ended up directly over the top of a ditch running alongside the taxiway, which saved the crew's life. The navigator used his emergency axe to smash the canopy glazing and was able to get out of the aircraft unaided, but the pilot had suffered multiple fractures of his legs and could not abandon the aircraft without assistance. However, the airfield search and rescue party arrived fairly quickly and managed to extricate him from the cockpit.

Cause: The pilot had failed to monitor the height of the aircraft on the approach, and the navigator was negligent in failing to assist his pilot in this critical phase of flight. Additionally, the crew did not react in a timely fashion to commands given by the flight controller.

Non-fatal write-off—Tu-128M—1 February 1984

Weather conditions: Daylight VMC

Circumstances: A crew from 72 AP at Amderma, comprising squadron commander Military Pilot First Class Lt Col. 'V' and Military Navigator First Class Maj. 'D', had taken off from base on a test flight following replacement of a stabilizer actuator. Having climbed to 5,000 m (16,400 feet), the pilot checked the aircraft trim with the hydraulic actuators switched on. Then he climbed to 10,000 m (32,800 feet), turned onto the airfield beacon and commenced his checks in accordance with test schedule. After checking the operation of the flying controls at supersonic speed, they then descended back to 5,000 m, set speed to 550 kph (297 kts), trimmed the aircraft using the standard trim controls, switched off the rudder hydraulic actuator and selected the cross-feed valve. Next, the pilot again trimmed the aircraft using the normal trim controls and accelerated to an indicated air speed of 650 kph (350 kts).

After around 20-30 seconds of flight at this speed, the aircraft suddenly banked sharply to the left. The pilot started to counter the bank with control inputs to the right, but the aircraft then went into a right-hand bank. He switched on the rudder hydraulic actuator without having selected cross-feed. The aircraft then started to rotate rapidly about the longitudinal axis and, having rapidly assessed the situation, the pilot ordered the navigator to eject and then abandoned the aircraft himself. They both ditched in the Kara Sea about 100 km (62 miles) from Amderma airfield. The pilot landed on an ice floe, but the navigator dropped into the water and then managed to scramble onto the same ice floe. The water temperature at the time was minus –20°C, with a wind speed of 4 m/sec (about 8 kts), giving a wind-chill effect of around –29°C, and the flight controller at Amderma used all of his available resources to try to rescue them as quickly as possible. An Mi-8 'Hip' rescue helicopter was scrambled, taking off 12 minutes after the incident was first reported. The two crew members were spotted on the ice floe 22 minutes after ejection and evacuated from the scene after a further 20 minutes. *Cause*: The precise reason for the accident was never established, but the most likely cause was a failure in the stabilizer gearing mechanism during acceleration, with the rudder actuator engaged, leading to the aircraft's rapid rotation about the longitudinal axis.

Non-fatal write-off—Tu-128M—Winter 1984/85

Weather conditions: Snowstorm developing into a blizzard
Circumstances: A crew from 72 AP at Amderma, comprising aircraft commander Maj. 'K' and navigator Capt. 'O', were landing at base after completing a routine task. During the approach, the weather conditions deteriorated significantly, leading to the development of a '*pozyomka*'—a type of blizzard accompanied by a ground wind. Affected by the worsening visibility, the pilot flared the aircraft higher than normal, and after touchdown and the subsequent short ground roll it ran off the end of the runway, sustaining serious damage which could not be repaired. The crew were unhurt in the accident, but because the pilot's cockpit canopy frame became distorted in the accident it could not be opened and the pilot had to squeeze through the opening side-window to climb out of the aircraft. *Cause*: The accident was attributed to pilot error on final approach.

Tupolev Tu-128 'Fiddler'

Fatal write-off—Tu-128M—6 June 1985

Weather conditions: Daylight IMC
Circumstances: A crew from 64 AP at Omsk-North, comprising deputy squadron commander for political affairs Sniper Pilot Lt Col. 'K' and squadron Military Navigator First Class Maj. 'K', were conducting a test flight from their base airfield. At an altitude of 5,000 m (16,400 feet), while checking the aircraft's balance (trim) with the hydraulic boosters switched off, the aircraft suddenly entered an 'energetic' left-hand turn, accompanied by rapid loss of height and an increase in speed. At a speed of 580 kph (313 kts) and a height of 1,000 m (3,280 feet), radar contact with the aircraft was lost and communication with the crew ceased. It transpired later (from the flight data recorder) that the aircraft had struck the ground some 118 km (73 miles) from the airfield in a 60° dive at an indicated air speed of more than 1,000 kph (540 kts). The crew ejected during the descent and although their emergency egress systems worked normally, the sun visor of the pilot's ZSh-5 helmet was in the raised position on ejection, creating a powerful lift vector which broke his neck when he entered the airstream after leaving the aircraft. The navigator received a number of injuries and was taken to hospital for treatment.
Cause: The accident investigators concluded that the pilot had mistakenly deselected two hydraulic actuator channels at the same time—i.e. 'roll' and 'pitch'. This led to the loss of longitudinal control and partial loss of lateral control. However, a significant number of experienced Tu-128 pilots on the regiment considered that the tragedy was caused not by pilot error but as a result of an actual failure in the hydraulic system.

Fatal write-off—Tu-128—6 August 1985

Weather conditions: Daylight IMC
Circumstances: A crew from 350 AP at Bratsk, comprising aircraft commander and squadron commander Military Pilot First Class Maj. 'T' and deputy squadron commander for political affairs Military Navigator First Class Maj. 'Sh', were landing at base after a GCI sortie. (The actual sortie was Exercise 42 in the Tu-128 combat training manual KBP APVO-80—'Attack of target in the forward hemisphere'.) After the intercept, the crew were instructed by GCI to contact the airfield controller and carry out their approach using a standard circuit pattern. After the fourth turn, before entering the glideslope, they reported lowering the undercarriage and flaps at a distance of 16 km (10 miles). They descended on the standard glideslope, without any heading deviation. On passing over the outer beacon, the crew again reported that the undercarriage and flaps were down and received clearance to land. However, the pilot had *not* selected landing flap and touched down with an overshoot of some

500-600 m (1,640-1,970 feet) at a speed of around 330-340 kph (178-184 kts), where the accepted maximum landing speed *without* flaps was 310 kph (167 kts). The flight controller ordered the pilot to release the brake chute and shut down the port engine. However, the pilot appeared to be a little confused and shut down only the left engine after about 5 seconds and did not release the brake parachute, nor did he use emergency braking correctly, which led to two main wheel tyres bursting. This led to further deterioration in braking. The crew did not react to the commands of the flight controller to eject, or follow standard operating instructions for emergency egress from the aircraft, and at a speed of 200 kph (108 kts) they struck the roof of an electrical substation 440 m (1,445 feet) from the end of the runway. Neither crew member made any attempt to eject and both were killed on impact with the building. *Cause*: The accident commission concluded that the cause of the accident was due to the pilot's failure to lower the flaps on the approach, failure to deploy the brake parachute and incorrect use of the brakes after landing 'long' from a poorly executed approach. This incident occurred on an early-series aircraft, after which an order was issued for flights by all early Tu-128s to cease and for the aircraft themselves to be withdrawn from service.

> **Aircraft history**
> Tu-128 c/n 500801 rolled out of the factory on 10 October 1965 with an airframe life of 2,300 hours.
> Underwent two overhauls, with the second 'major' overhaul carried out on 20 May 1983; airframe life after overhaul—2,000 hours.
> Total time since entering service—1,281 hours; time since last overhaul—116 hours.

The accident is recalled here by squadron navigator Maj. Mamet:

Flights had been organised as usual, with crews preparing for live firing at Sary-Shagan, flying via Semipalatinsk. By evening the visibility had worsened due to mist and haze. The crew were approaching to land in visibility of around 1,000 m [around 3,300 feet]. At a distance of 14 km [8.7 miles], the pilot reported that he had lowered the flaps and was slightly above the glidepath. He picked up the runway at a higher speed than normal and was unable to get the aircraft onto the ground; touchdown occurred midway down the runway (which was 3,150 m [10,335 feet] long at Bratsk). The pilot immediately shut down one engine [the port engine] and commenced emergency braking. He did not deploy the brake parachute. Several tyres burst and he shut down the other engine, leading to loss of pressure in the braking system.

The aircraft ran off the end of the runway at a speed of around 140 kph [about 75 kts]. At around 400 m [about 1,300 feet] from the end of the runway there was some kind of building. The aircraft literally jumped over it, but struck the roof with one of the undercarriage bogies, which became embedded in it. Immediately behind this building, the ground began to slope away from the runway, with approach lights mounted on concrete posts so that they would be level with the airfield. The aircraft hit a couple of these posts, causing a fire to break out. The pilot was found in his seat immediately beyond the small building, while the navigator was located nearby. On examination of the aircraft, it was discovered that the flaps were still retracted.

Accident—Tu-128—9 January (other sources 6 January) 1986

Weather conditions: Daylight IMC

Circumstances: A crew from 350 AP, comprising aircraft commander and deputy squadron commander Military Pilot First Class Maj. 'K' and Military Navigator First Class Sr Lt 'T', were landing at base. The crew performed their approach at an indicated air speed of 400-450 kph (216-245 kts) with power set at 78-80 per cent rpm. They passed over the outer beacon at a height of 220 m (720 feet), a speed of 400 kph and engines at 78 per cent rpm. After passing over the beacon, engine rpm was reduced to 76 per cent, while speed was reduced to 390 kph (210 kts) by the time they had reached the inner beacon. The inner beacon was overflown at a height of 100 m (330 feet), where power was reduced to 'Flight Idle'. The aircraft touched down at 315 kph (170 kts) on the right-hand side of the main runway, with an angle of drift, leading to the aircraft rolling out onto the safety strip (*bokovaya polosa bezopasnosti*) alongside the runway. At this particular moment there was a civilian Mi-8 'Hip' helicopter waiting on the packed earth runway 50 m (164 feet) from the main runway for permission to cross to the parking area. The helicopter crew, seeing the Tu-128 heading towards them, lifted off vertically and then headed for the edge of the safety strip. Ahead of him, the pilot of the Tu-128M caught sight of the tail boom of the helicopter, shrouded in a snow cloud, moving from one side of the main runway to the other, and turned his aircraft to the right, but was unable to avoid hitting it. The helicopter caught fire and was destroyed and the Tu-128 was seriously damaged, but the crews of both machines were reportedly unharmed.

Cause: Serious pilot error during landing, leading to the aircraft running off the edge of the main runway into the safety strip and subsequent collision with the helicopter.

Aircraft history

Tu-128M c/n 501805 rolled out of the factory on 20 October 1967 with an airframe life of 2,300 hours.

Underwent first major overhaul on 29 February 1984; airframe life after overhaul—616 hours.

Total time since entering service—1,843 hours; time since last overhaul—159 hours.

Non-fatal write-off—Tu-128M—July 1986

Weather conditions: Daylight VMC

Circumstances: A crew from 72 AP, comprising deputy squadron commander Maj. Kazachenko and navigator Kleinman, were performing a test flight on an aircraft after a long period of storage. (*In conformity with the 1978 edition of the engineering service manual NIAS-78, each aircraft had to be test flown at least once a year to confirm its continued airworthiness—S.B.*) During the take-off run from Amderma, as the pilot pulled the stick back to the required position for unstick, the control column jammed. After lift-off, the aircraft's angle of attack continued to increase and the crew decided to eject. Ejection occurred at a distance of 300-400 m (984-1,312 feet) from the end of the runway over land, but because of the geographical layout of Amderma airfield the crew landed in the sea about 1,000 m (3,280 feet) from the runway. The pilot managed to scramble onto an ice floe, but the navigator had to remain in the water until he was picked up by a rescue boat. Because of the ongoing exercise at Amderma, there was no search and rescue helicopter available on the base (!). The strong wind blowing in off the sea prevented rescue boats getting close to the navigator for quite some time, resulting in him suffering from exposure.

Cause: The precise cause of the accident could not be established since the aircraft sank in very deep water. However, the most likely reason for the jamming of the control column was as a consequence of severe corrosion of the magnesium alloy control rods during long-term storage.

The prelude to this incident is recalled by deputy squadron commander, navigator-operator Maj. Oleg Fyodoseev:

A year before this incident, my good friend and an outstanding pilot, Nikolai Balyuk, had managed to land this particular aircraft (if memory serves correctly, it was Bort No. 31) after suffering a control system failure. After this flight, the non-smoking Kolya [diminutive of Nikolai] took up smoking. During a year on the ground, a total of seventeen major components were replaced on the aircraft, after which it was decided to reassemble it and fly it to the re-fit base at Novosibirsk. So it was reassembled and a test flight was planned. We were sitting in the HQ building and Kolya asked me, 'Would you like to test fly it with me?' I agreed to go wherever he wanted to do the test flight, but suggested that he shouldn't try 'experimenting' with this aircraft for a second time. He knocked on the plywood partition between our room and the deputy commander of the 1st squadron, Major Kazachenko, and asked him if *he* wanted to do the test flight. Kazachenko agreed and said that he would fly with his navigator, Kleinman. The next day the weather was excellent: there was an offshore wind of around 3-4 m/sec [6-8 kts] and the air temperature was 15-20ºC. Kolya and I returned from a study session on the aircraft and Kazachenko did a short taxiing check on the runway.

Then we went off to the pre-flight briefing room and everything else happened as described above. They ejected over dry land, but the wind carried them out to sea. The sea was almost calm, with ice floes of various sizes floating on the surface. Kazachenko scrambled onto one of them without any difficulty, but Kleinman started to look around for a thicker piece of ice, during which time he cut his face and hands on the sharp edges. Later, we asked him, 'Didn't you know that the ice is eight times thicker below the surface?!' He just replied, 'I discovered that after ejecting.' The inflatable dinghy brought in by the rescue team turned out to have had an empty gas bottle, so while they waited for a second to arrive, the crew had to float around in the sea. They *were* eventually picked up and taken back to the airfield. They were each given a glass of spirits (vodka?) to warm them up and then taken off to the medical centre 'to discuss their responses' [i.e. 'their story'] for the accident commission.[9] But it would all come down to the same thing; the crew would be blamed [as usual]. I decided, with the commander of the third squadron, to dive down to retrieve the KZA flight data recorder (he and I were keen divers and we had the equipment) but permission was refused.

Non-fatal write-off—Tu-128M—15 January 1987

Weather conditions: Night, snowstorm
Circumstances: A crew from 72 AP at Amderma under the command of Maj. 'K' were landing at their operational reserve airfield at Nar'yan-Mar after a weather reconnaissance flight. The weather had deteriorated significantly during the landing approach and a powerful snowstorm had developed. Although the pilot could see well enough to continue the approach, he performed the flare too high, to the right of the centreline, and after touchdown and a short landing roll, the aircraft departed the runway and came to a halt. The aircraft was severely damaged in the incident and could not be repaired.
Cause: The accident was attributed to severe deterioration in the weather conditions during the approach.

Accident—Tu-128UT—27 January 1987?

Weather conditions: Not given
Circumstances: During the landing at Omsk-North and around 1,000 m (3,280 feet) from the point of touchdown, the left main landing gear bogie of the Tu-128UT collapsed. As a result, the aircraft left the runway, damaging the left wing and tearing off the nose undercarriage.
Cause: Not given

Accident—Tu-128M—16 March 1987?

Weather conditions: Not given

Circumstances: A crew from 64 AP at Omsk-North were performing a routine training flight during which fire broke out in the starboard engine. The crew ejected when they realised that they could not extinguish the fire.

Cause: The cause of the fire was attributed to fractures in the blades of the fourth stage of the compressor.

Appendix 4   Operational Limitations

Data as presented in the 'Instructions for Tu-128 (Tu-128M) aircrew' dated 1977	
Item No.	Limitation	Reason For Limitation
---	---	---
	By speed, g-loading and weight	
1	Maximum permitted speed and Mach number: • at altitudes from 0 to 5,500 m—850 kph; • at altitudes from 5,500 to 10,000 m—Mach 0.95; • at altitudes from 10,000 m and above—1,100 kph.	Aircraft static and dynamic structural strength (aileron reversal and flutter)
2	Maximum Mach number with failed dry friction damper—Mach 1.2	At speeds above Mach 1.2 control vibration can arise
3	Maximum speed with DT-128 pitch damper, AU-128 auto-stabilizer and aileron, rudder and stabilizer boosters switched off (not exceeding Mach 0.95)—600 kph	At high speeds with DT-128 and AU-128 switched off, the forces on the control column are small when pulling g With aileron boosters switched off, stick forces are high With stabilizer boosters switched off and control effected via the MUS-7A, pitch instability is possible
4	Maximum permitted speed: • with undercarriage extended—550 kph; • when lowering and retracting undercarriage—500 kph; • with flaps at 30°—500 kph; • with flaps at 35°—450 kph.	Structural strength of the undercarriage and flaps
5	Maximum permitted g-loading—2.5 g. A brief excursion above this limit is permitted when carrying missiles (with vertical gust action while manoeuvring, or as a result of 'over-control' during energetic handling): • to 3.1 g with a fuel load of 12,000 kg; • to 3.2 g with a fuel load of 7,000-12,000 kg; • to 3.3 g with a fuel load of 2,000-7,000 kg; • to 3.4 g with a fuel load of less than 2,000 kg. When not carrying missiles, the fuel figures can be increased by 2,000 kg	Structural strength of the airframe
6	Maximum permitted g-loading with an asymmetric missile load (two missiles on one wing)—2 g	Structural strength and controllability of the aircraft

Item No.	Limitation	Reason For Limitation
Data as presented in the 'Instructions for Tu-128 (Tu-128M) aircrew' dated 1977		
7	Maximum Mach number with an asymmetric missile load: • with two missiles on one wing—Mach 1.23; • with one missile—Mach 1.3	At high speed a large deflection of the control column is required to correct the resulting banking effect
8	Minimum flight speed is determined by the limits set for the triggering of the AUASP angle of attack and sideslip indicator. With a failed AUASP the speed should not be less than 450 kph	
9	Maximum permitted angle of bank—60°	On increasing the angle of bank to more than 60°, the aircraft can drop the nose and enter the deep-spiral regime
10	Rudder deflection angle at altitudes less than 10,000 m and a speed greater than 500 kph should not be greater than ±15° (signalled by illumination of the 'Rudder Deflection High' warning light)	Structural strength of the fin
11	In all flight regimes, with undercarriage and flaps retracted, the maximum permitted sideslip angle is 3°	Structural strength of the missile pylons and the aircraft's vertical fin
12	Maximum take-off mass—43,650 kg (fuel load with four missiles—5,000 kg; without missiles—7,000 kg)	Structural strength of the airframe
13	Maximum landing mass—34,000 kg (fuel remainder with four missiles—5,000 kg; without missiles—7,000 kg)	Structural strength of the undercarriage
14	Flights carried out from a concrete runway surface. Separate take-offs and landings on packed earth surface are permitted if the bearing strength is not less than 10 kg/cm^2. Landings outside the airfield are forbidden	Structural strength of the undercarriage
15	Maximum permitted ground speed: • at unstick point—350 kph; • at touchdown—320 kph.	Structural characteristics of the tyres
16	Brake parachute deployment speed not to exceed 320 kph	Structural strength of the parachute and attachment to fuselage

Data as presented in the 'Instructions for Tu-128 (Tu-128M) aircrew' dated 1977

Item No.	Limitation	Reason For Limitation
17	In flight an excess of fuel of not more than 500 kg in the rear (second) group of fuel tanks, relative to that in the first group, is permitted, but the centre of gravity of the aircraft should not vary from normal by more than 0.5 per cent MAC	Stability margin
18	Maximum permitted crosswind component (wind at 90° to the axis of the runway): • with symmetrical carriage of missiles, or without any missiles—not more than 12 m/sec; • landing with two missiles carried asymmetrically—not more than 8 m/sec (wind from the side without missiles). The use of the brake parachute is obligatory for crosswind landings	Because of the difficulty in taking off and landing with a large crosswind component
19	Permitted tailwind—not more than 5 m/sec; when landing, the fuel remainder should not be greater than 2,000 kg on an aircraft carrying four missiles, and not more than 4,000 kg on an aircraft with no missiles	With a tailwind of more than 5 m/sec flow separation can occur, leading to a touchdown at a speed higher than permitted by the structural strength of the tyres
	By engine parameters	
20	Increasing engine rpm in flight, from any power setting to 'maximal', by moving the throttle within 1-2 seconds (acceleration time) is permitted: • up to a height of 1,000 m without any speed limit; • at an altitude above 1,000 m and a speed not less than 450 kph. During the acceleration time it is permitted to engage reheat	In consideration of stable operation of the engines
21	Continuous flight with negative and near-zero g-values (±0.2 g) should not exceed a period of 15 seconds at any engine power setting	In consideration of normal lubricating oil flow through the engine
	By emergency egress and life support systems	
22	Safe emergency egress from the aircraft is guaranteed for the crew during the take-off and landing run at a speed of not less than 130 kph	By conditions essential for the safe operation of the parachute systems (of the ejection seats and the crew's survival parachutes)

Data as presented in the 'Instructions for Tu-128 (Tu-128M) aircrew' dated 1977		
Item No.	Limitation	Reason For Limitation
23	Safe emergency egress in horizontal flight is guaranteed without altitude limits above the ground at speeds not greater than 500 kph, and at heights not less than 60 m above the ground at speeds not greater than 970 kph	By conditions essential for the safe operation of the parachute systems (of the ejection seats and the crew's survival parachutes)
24	Safe emergency egress when descending is guaranteed at an altitude equal to the value of the aircraft's vertical rate of descent, multiplied by a factor of 7	By the time required for the parachute systems to operate
25	Safe emergency egress, dependent upon the type of aircrew equipment assembly used, is guaranteed: • in pressure helmet and VKK pressure suit, up to the maximum permitted ejection speed; • in ZSh helmet, with lowered visor, up to 900 kph; • in ZSh helmet, with raised visor and oxygen mask removed, or open faceplate of pressure helmet, up to 700 kph. Flying with canopies jettisoned is forbidden	In consideration of the action of the airflow on the body
	By aircraft systems	
26	Switching on the AP-7P autopilot to stabilise angular position, altitude and course mode is permitted in the established flight regime with an angle of bank of not more than 45° and a pitch angle from +25° to −13° at a height of not less than 1,000 m	To guarantee flight safety with an autopilot failure
27	Switching on the AP-7P autopilot in the 'return to level flight' mode is permitted at altitudes of not less than 2,500 m	Because of loss of height during the time of recovery to level flight from negative pitch angles
28	Emergency jettison of missiles is permitted in level flight without sideslip at altitudes of 9,000–10,000 m within the speed range corresponding to Mach 0.85–0.9	Emergency jettison of missiles in other conditions can result in the missiles striking the airframe on release
29	In a case of extreme emergency, jettison of missiles is permitted in level flight and when descending with a rate of descent of up to 40 m/sec at altitudes not greater than 12,000 m within the speed range from 450 kph IAS up to a TAS of 1,100 kph	Emergency jettison of missiles in other conditions can result in the missiles striking the airframe on release

Endnotes

Chapter 1

1. The first of these was a USAF Boeing RB-29 'Superfortress' (44-61810) reconnaissance aircraft of the 91st Strategic Reconnaissance Squadron operating out of Yokota, Japan, shot down over the Sea of Japan on 13 June 1952 by Soviet MiG-15 'Fagot' fighters. The second incident occurred on the same day, when a Swedish Air Force SIGINT-equipped Douglas C-47 (Tp 79 79001 'Hugin') was shot down over the Baltic Sea near Ventspils by a Soviet MiG-15, killing all on board. A second RB-29 (44-61815) was shot down on 7 October 1952 over the Kurile Islands by two Lavochkin La-11 Fang piston-engined fighters. All twenty crew members were killed in the two USAF incidents.

2. The term *Voyenno-Vozdushniye Sily*, commonly abbreviated to and universally known as VVS, literally means 'military air forces'. Since no other formation was so named, it did not require the adjective *Sovietskiye* (Soviet) to indicate that it was the *Soviet Air Force*. More generally, the word '*aviatsiya*' can mean 'aviation', 'air force', 'air component' or even 'air power' in specific contexts and is used to describe the integral air component of the Army (*Aviatsiya Sukhoputnykh Voysk*—'air component of the land forces'), the Navy (*Aviatsiya Voyenno-Morskovo Flota* or AVMF—'air component of the military naval fleet') and the PVO (*Aviatsiya PVO*—'air component of the air defence forces').

3. Pre-dating the adoption of code-names for Soviet aircraft issued by the Air Standardization Coordinating Committee, no NATO reporting name was assigned to the Lavochkin La-5.

4. See Chapter 12 for a detailed description of the data-link system.

5. Namely the Boeing AGM-28 'Hound Dog' carried by Boeing B-52G/H strategic bombers.

6. This is, of necessity, an extremely abbreviated account of Gen. Kadomtsyev's early career, which is clearly worthy of more detailed treatment, albeit beyond the scope of

the present work. It also glosses over the indiscipline of the young Kadomtsyev and why Malinovskiy was prepared to give his backing to such a maverick young officer.

7. The P-15 missile was developed by the Raduga Design Bureau as a ship- or ground-launched anti-ship missile and known as the SS-N-2 Styx in the West. Little is known about the intended use of this missile in an air-launched capacity in the 1960s.

8. Tu-28 was the original military designation of the aircraft, the appellation '80' deriving from the Bisnovat Design Bureau K-80 project number for the aircraft's missiles, assigned at the early development stage. The aircraft was formally designated Tu-128 in December 1963 (see later in this chapter).

9. Although most frequently referred to as RP-S, the radar was also known as RP-28 (*Radiolokatsionnyi Pritsel-28*), literally 'radar sight for the Tu-28', 'radar sight' being the standard term for an airborne interception (AI) radar.

10. He would later lose his life in the crash of the prototype Tu-144D Charger supersonic airliner at the 1973 Paris Air Show.

11. RTS-8 telemetry stations, designed by the Serpukhov Radio Engineering Plant (later renamed JSC RATEP), were originally used to monitor flight trajectories of Soviet intercontinental ballistic missiles.

12. *Liana* (or liane) is the universal term for any large woody vine that climbs on other plants and trees, famously used by Tarzan to swing his way through the jungle.

13. Lag pursuit is an attack profile where the nose of the interceptor is pointed slightly behind the intended target, allowing it to preserve available energy for closure and keeping it out of the opponent's visual detection envelope.

14. The Bort number is the aircraft side number.

15. '*Sparka*', plural '*sparki*', is the traditional Russian term for the training variant of (usually) a single-seat fighter.

16. In Western practice this kind of incident would have rendered the runway unusable until the aircraft had been towed clear of the runway and was no longer a danger to other traffic.

17. '*Sparochka*' is the diminutive form of '*sparka*' and means 'little *sparka*'.

18. Waterline is the Z-axis of the three-station XYZ coordinate system used in aircraft design drawings (derived from ship- and boat-building, as the name suggests) and is generally used to determine the height of an aircraft with respect to the static ground line.

19. The Russian definition is *Divizionnaya Aviatsionnaya Remontnaya Mastyerskaya*, abbreviated as DARM.

20. M for *mishen'*—a *mishen'* is (usually) an expendable practice target, as opposed to a piloted aircraft used for practice ground-controlled interception. The latter, and *actual* intruders, are described by the word *tsel'*.

21. Pokryshkin was a legendary wartime fighter pilot, three times awarded the title of Hero of the Soviet Union, with at least fifty-nine confirmed personal victories, although his post-war career was blighted by his persistent heavy drinking and low

political standing. The phrase 'cometh the hour, cometh the man' could well have been coined specifically for Pokryshkin, who shone as a Second World War commander but was never to achieve similar status in the 'jet age' Soviet Air Force.

22. This proposed re-use of the Tu-28 designation for an aircraft intended to be a *successor* to the Tu-128 clearly added to the confusion that already surrounded the true designation of the 'Fiddler' throughout its service.

23. These missiles were developed by a branch of OKB-155 and included designs such as the KSR-2 (NATO AS-5 'Kelt') and KSR-5 (AS-6 'Kingfish').

Chapter 2

1. Grivation is a contraction of 'grid variation', i.e. the angular difference between grid north and magnetic north, measured east or west from grid north.

2. There were probably two variants of RAS—the VHF transmitting and receiving station, and an HF/MF installation.

3. These four parameters provided data to monitor the timeliness of the crew's actions in switching on HT to the semi-active homing heads of the R-4R, power to the IR seeker heads of the R-4T, and the moment of lock-on of the R-4R. The data was used to analyse the cause of failure of early-series missiles to leave the launch rail on low-level interceptions.

4. The word '*liter*' (pronounced as 'lityer' in Russian) is probably a variant spelling of '*litera*', as in 'letter of the alphabet' or 'character' in typography.

5. The fuses were developed by LOMO (*Leningradskoye Optiko-Mekhanicheskoye Ob'yedinyeniye* or Leningrad Optical-Mechanical Association) known universally today as the manufacturer of a range of highly acclaimed consumer cameras and related equipment.

6. This aircraft was given the nickname *Buratino* because of its extended nose radome housing the Tu-128's *Smerch* antenna, which recalled the Pinocchio-like nose of the eponymous character in a children's story by Aleksey Tolstoy *The Adventures of Buratino*, the author of which was a distant relative of the famous Russian writer. 'Burattino' is simply the Italian word for 'wooden puppet'.

7. All Russian military aircraft undergo two stages of acceptance trials—Stage 'A' conducted at the State Flight Test Institute at Zhukovskiy to confirm the aircraft's basic flight performance, and Stage 'B' at the State Flight Test Centre at Akhtubinsk (Vladimirovka) to confirm anticipated combat performance.

8. Located in the Moscow region—not the Baltic enclave of the same name. Factory No. 455 traces its history back to 1942, undergoing a number of name and status changes before becoming the Zvezda-Strela State Scientific and Production Centre in the mid-1990s, but continuing to design and manufacture missile systems, most notably the Kh-31 (NATO AS-17 'Krypton') air-launched cruise missile.

Chapter 4

1. Although VKK high-altitude pressure suits were ostensibly part of the standard aircrew equipment assembly for Tu-128 crews, they were never worn for high-altitude protection as such. However, the associated GSh pressure helmets did form an integral part of the VMSK exposure suit, providing a protective micro-environment for the pilot and navigator both during flight and in the event of ejecting over and alighting on water.
2. The convention is to use the abbreviation 'Tu' for Tupolev aircraft, but Tupolev-designed ejection seats were often designated with the capital letters 'TU'.

Chapter 5

1. The Great Patriotic War is the preferred term used by Russians to describe the purely Soviet component of the campaigns of the Second World War.
2. At this stage the aircraft was still known by the Soviet Air Force as the Tu-28, although it was also referred to in industry circles as 'Aircraft 128'.
3. Broadly speaking, the Chief of VOTP in a Soviet air regiment combined the duties of qualified flying instructor (QFI) and qualified weapons instructor (QWI), involving the implementation and supervision of specific training exercises from the KBP combat training manual. He also assisted the regiment commander with exercise planning and preparation of reports on various aspects of the regiment's training programme for submission to higher authority.
4. The RD-45 was a modified (albeit unauthorised) and reverse-engineered copy of the Rolls-Royce Nene engine, twenty-five of which were donated to the Soviet Union by the UK as a goodwill gesture in 1947. The 'RD' of the designation stood for '*reaktivnyi dvigatyel*'—literally 'reaction or jet engine', with '45' deriving from the number of the design bureau which improved the basic design.
5. The aircraft was redesignated Tu-128 in December 1963. Contrary to the widespread misconception among the Russian aviation enthusiast fraternity, the aircraft was *never* given an interceptor 'P' suffix [for *Pyerekhvatchik*], either in its earlier guise as the Tu-28 or as the Tu-128, since it was designed unequivocally as an *interceptor* from the outset. Other proposed variants did, however, receive relevant suffix designations, although none was actually flown, apart from the Tu-128LL, flying test-bed, described in Chapter 1. The Tu-128M was, of course, an in-service modification of the standard 'Fiddler-B', the 'M' being a standard suffix for modified aircraft.
6. Although not stated specifically, the evaluation of the Tu-16 (and the Tu-104) as an interim trainer for pilots converting onto the Tu-128 *was* the purpose of this visit.
7. These would not have been defining criteria in Soviet 'command economy' terms, but the obvious efficiency of being able to train several navigators on a single training flight would probably have impressed the Communist Party 'machine'.

8. The word 'fighter' would later be dropped from the title of regiments converting onto the Tu-128.

9. Later, on 23 February 1968, the college was further upgraded in status, being awarded the title of Armavir Order of the Red Banner Higher Military Aviation College for Pilots (*Armavirskoye Vysshyeye Voyennoye Aviatsionnoye Ordyena Krasnovo Znamyeni Uchilishche Lyotchikov* or AVVAKUL).

10. DOSAAF, the Voluntary Society for the Support of the Army, Air Force and Navy, was the Soviet-era paramilitary training organisation that prepared young volunteers for careers in the armed forces. (See also endnote 1 to Chapter 8.)

11. The 'company' structure approximates to a 'course' or 'entry' in a British or US military training organisation.

12. In the Soviet era the rouble was not convertible against Western currencies; it is therefore difficult to calculate this value in pounds sterling or US dollars.

13. A *voyennyi gorodok* (literally a small military township) is essentially a closed garrison town, supporting the domestic needs of an adjoining military base. It was probably more self-contained than the 'married quarters' area of a UK-based RAF station, but not unlike those on bases in RAF Germany in the same period.

14. This play on words only works in Russian, where '*sukhoi*' and '*mokryi*' mean 'dry' and 'wet' respectively, but entirely loses impact in translation.

Chapter 6

1. A bandura is a Ukrainian stringed instrument similar to a large mandolin, and here presumably refers to the shape of the bomb-sight and its mounting in the glazed nose of the Tu-124Sh.

2. This Russian term is a contraction of *zamestityel' politicheskovo otdyela*, meaning literally 'deputy of the political department'. The office of *zampolit* was a uniquely Soviet creation dating back to the revolutionary period, and in the Soviet Air Force was an organic part of the staff system. Although operating within a separate chain of command and communication, the *zampolit* was specifically answerable to the regiment commander for the organisation and content of party-political work on the regiment.

Chapter 7

1. The Soviet Air Force had an overseeing role in the acquisition and signing-off of all aviation-related equipment for the flying services of the other branches of the military.

2. See Chapter 6 on the structure of a PVO regiment.

3. Bort No. 15 was unofficially named *Lyusya* (Lucy) and Bort No. 25 *Matilda* when operated by 356 AP.

Chapter 8

1. The stated goal of DOSAAF, founded in August 1951, was 'the patriotic upbringing of the population and preparation for the defence of the Motherland', achieving this by means of paramilitary training relevant to the three main branches of service, including flying training for the air force branch.
2. A rouble at that time was worth around 90 US cents but was not truly convertible.
3. The word '*shtorka*' derives from the word for a Venetian blind or curtain. For obvious reasons, the instructor's cockpit did not have a blind-flying screen or hood.
4. All calls were logged in the control tower for possible use as evidence, if required for a board of inquiry etc., as well as for this more prosaic reason!
5. Here, the implication is that things would only get done if you knew 'the right people'.

Chapter 9

1. Reheat could only be selected three times at altitude.
2. 'Snow-blower' vehicles were known by air and ground crews as '*Zmei Gorynych*' (literally 'The Dragon Gorynych') because their appearance was loosely reminiscent of the mountain-dwelling, three-headed, fire-breathing dragon of that name from traditional Russian mythology.
3. This exercise is recalled by other participants as Exercise '*Sevyer-70*'—see the incident involving Lt Col. Nikolayev in Chapter 14.
4. Military pilots in the USSR were instructed in the science of practical aerodynamics using two simplified terms describing airflow over the wing, a so-called 'first regime' (or 'working regime') describing normal flow within permissible limits. 'Second regime' described disturbed airflow over the wing, such as would occur, for example, when the angle of attack was greater than permitted, leading ultimately to a complete stall.
5. On initial selection of reheat, the nozzles open fully in anticipation of the greater flow of exhaust gases and burning fuel at this setting, but if ignition does not occur, a lesser quantity of air flows through a larger aperture, resulting in a reduction in thrust. Shutting down an inoperative afterburner would allow the nozzle to close and maximum military power (*maksimal*) to be selected instead, producing more thrust through a smaller opening.
6. The word 'chandelle' derives from the French for 'candle', embracing the figurative notion that the manoeuvre is akin to 'climbing around a candle', i.e. an upward climbing minimum radius turn, usually with a change of heading of 180°.
7. This is typical communist-era jargon, not directly translatable, although conveying the combined notions of 'morale' and 'psychology', often used when describing the superior 'mindset' of the Soviet serviceman in his approach to military duty. However, in this context, it is none other than the need for increased spatial awareness from the pilot in low-level, high-speed flight.

8. Note, however, that this contradicts point 2 of the Pilots' Notes above, which required the pilot to lower the flaps and undercarriage at 230 m (755 feet).
9. Clearly, this would depend upon the spin entry height, although since the spin was not demonstrated during the flight test phase there was no empirical data from which to establish spin recovery procedures.
10. During the Tu-128 flight test programme in the early 1960s, whilst conducting a high-level pitch stability check at around 10,000 m (32,800 feet), test pilot Yuri Rogachyov and test navigator Mozgovoy exceeded the critical angle of attack and the aircraft inadvertently went into a spin, from which Rogachyov recovered less than 5,000 m (16,400 feet) above the ground. It can therefore be assumed that 5,000 m would have been the *minimum* height lost during spin recovery.
11. 'Psychology' seemed to play a more prominent part in Soviet pilot training than it did in Western air forces.

Chapter 10

1. Although clear air turbulence was first noted in the 1940s, it only became widely recognised as an aircraft safety hazard in the 1960s.
2. For a detailed explanation of QRA operations and readiness states see
3. *Zapolyar'ye* is the term for the region lying between the Arctic Circle and the North Pole. It literally means 'beyond the Pole' and although used as an everyday geographical and regional term in Russian, it does not translate readily into English on a word-for-word basis. For convenience, the term 'High Arctic' has mostly been used in this book.
4. Apart from its literal meaning of 'manoeuvre', the Russian word *manyovr* has a meaning identical with that of the Western military term 'manoeuvre', as in 'going on manoeuvres' and in a military aviation context best translated as 'deployment' (American TDY—Temporary Duty).
5. The word 'garrison' in Russian does not have the exclusive association with an *army* base that it has in a British or American context.
6. Russian weather reporting uses a procedure for describing cloud cover in 'balls', equivalent to the Western okta system. Ten 'balls' refers to total cloud cover and is analogous to eight oktas in Western forecasting.

Chapter 11

1. See the paragraph on Tu-126 operations in Chapter 12.
2. There is no exact equivalent in Russian of the Western term 'QRA', but the term *boyevoye dezhurstvo* or 'the state of being on combat duty' describes a military procedure which is analogous in organisation and function to QRA.

3. Diminutives are used extensively in Russian, '*domik*' being the diminutive form of '*dom*' (house) and meaning literally 'little house', although the term can be applied to any small building, such as a hut or a shed.

4. The 'Lenin room' contained propaganda displays, such as pictures of social unrest in Western countries and 'uplifting' Soviet political literature. The Soviet soldier was instilled with a sense of dedication to the communist cause, a readiness to defend the motherland and a xenophobic dread of foreign subversion.

5. '*Rakurs*' in aviation terms means 'aspect angle'.

6. The Russian word used here was '*myelkiye*', meaning literally 'very small', 'minute' things etc. and used in the Tu-128 community to refer to all other Soviet fighters which were considerably smaller than the big Tupolev interceptor (i.e. the Su-9, Su-15 and MiG-23).

7. It is not clear why the other Soviet fighters would not have done this.

8. In later years, Vyacheslav Gorshkov held a higher doctorate in mathematics and became a university professor in Kiev in Ukraine.

Chapter 13

1. Named after Alexander Graham Bell, the Scots-born scientist, inventor and innovator who created the first practical telephone.

2. These were known as '*Sborno-shchitoviye kazarmy*' in Russian—literally 'assembled-panel barracks', i.e. barrack buildings assembled from prefabricated panels consisting of heat-retaining insulation sandwiched between thin outer and inner plywood sheets. The panels were of unified sizes, optimised for ease of manufacture, with some incorporating apertures for doors and windows. First introduced after the Great Patriotic War to provide cheap, simple-to-assemble housing in remote areas, they were often referred to in the USSR as 'Finnish houses', although similar prefabrication technology had been developed in Russia in the early 1900s.

3. In other words, from the last twenty-five Tu-128s built—see Chapter 1 for details of manufacturing batches.

4. Named in memory of noted Russian Arctic explorer Georgiy Yakovlevich Sedov.

5. At the time of proposing these measures there were two helicopter-borne mobile command posts, one based on the versatile Mi-8 'Hip', known as the Mi-9 and given the code-name 'Hip-D' by NATO, and the other based on the huge Mi-6 'Hook', designated Mi-22 and known as 'Hook-C'. Neither of these helicopters was an '*airborne* command post' in any sense—the standard operating procedure for both was to deploy to a pre-surveyed helicopter alighting area (HAA) with good line-of-sight communication and, after landing, the communications crew would deploy the antenna array and start up the ground power unit. Thereafter, they operated like a normal ground station.

6. See Chapter 4.
7. POL—Petrol, Oil and Lubricants.
8. See Chapter 10.
9. In Russian folklore, Baba Yaga is a complex witch-like character who, in some interpretations, was sought out for her wisdom to guide young men into adulthood. This interpretation would seem appropriate here, since there is no indication that the nickname was used pejoratively.

Chapter 14

1. NBC—Nuclear, Biological and Chemical warfare; i.e. protection from the effects of the use of these weapons by wearing special masks and overalls.
2. This is recalled by other participants as Exercise '*Okean-70*'. See the incident involving Lt Col. Nikolayev in Chapter 9.
3. Bear Island (Bjørnøya) is a Norwegian possession lying midway between Svalbard and the north Norwegian coast and between the Barents Sea and Norwegian Sea.
4. This is an erroneous reference to the infamous shooting down of Korean Airlines KAL 007 by a PVO Su-15 'Flagon' on the night of 1/2 September 1983, the aircraft being a Boeing 747, *not* a 707.
5. 'We' here means the PVO as a whole, and the 'great circle' is probably a light-hearted reference to the circuitous route taken by the regiments to deploy from their base to the northern reserve airfields and then round to Telemba range. The normal geographical term for a 'great circle' navigation route is '*ortodromiya*'.
6. See Chapter 2 for a detailed explanation of the Tu-128's KZA system.
7. See also Chapter 12—GCI using the *Lazur'* data-link system.
8. The Soviet and Russian concept of 'science' (*nauka*) in a military context emphasises the *application* of knowledge, whereas the Western view of science stresses the *discovery* of knowledge. Here, the 'scientific basis' is simply the 'application of knowledge' of intercept techniques.
9. WT—wireless telegraphy, i.e. a Morse code message. At long range the radio would only work in WT (telegraph) mode.

Chapter 15

1. The Russian convention is for military unit abbreviations to be written in lower case letters, although capital letters are often used for major enterprises such as a repair plants. However, for ease of reading by English speakers, capital letters have been used throughout this book for all numbered formations.

Appendix 3

1. The Russian Far East at this time was a heavily defended region of the Soviet Union, organised to retaliate to both the military potential of China and Japan as well as the United States Navy's Pacific Fleet. Although the Tu-128 would have provided effective air defence for the region, there is no evidence that there were plans to deploy the aircraft to Soviet Far East bases.
2. *Nosimyi Avariinyi Zapas* (NAZ) literally means 'portable emergency reserve', equivalent to an emergency survival pack in Western air forces.
3. Taiga, a word of Siberian origin, is the zone of forest vegetation encircling the Northern Hemisphere, characterised by the prevalence of spruce, pine, fir and larch trees, among others.
4. Clearly, Kuznetsov was a pilot known to Mikoyan, but the context of this reference is not explained here.
5. Mobile searchlights were used extensively on Soviet airfields to provide artificial illumination of the touchdown area of runways at night, angled so as not to blind pilots in the circuit and on the approach.
6. This name was almost too close for comfort to the Russian word for 'death' (*smert*), but it was, in fact, a genuine surname.
7. The Arkhangel'sk region was and still is a major centre of the forestry industry.
8. Essentially these were calculations performed by a ground engineer, working with the aircraft's navigator, to determine the amount of fuel required for a particular mission, taking account of the speeds and altitudes to fly and the missile load for that mission. Also taken into account would be the amount of fuel required for diversion; on a single-engined aircraft IShR calculations were carried out by the pilot.
9. This is probably intended to be a somewhat sardonic comment, since the first concern would be for the health and safety of the crew after the ordeal of ejecting over, landing in and being rescued from the icy cold waters of the Pechora Sea. However, the culture of blame that prevailed in Soviet times meant that someone *had* to be held accountable, and with military air accidents this was invariably the pilot or crew.